In Marx's Laboratory

Historical Materialism Book Series

The Historical Materialism Book Series is a major publishing initiative of the radical left. The capitalist crisis of the twenty-first century has been met by a resurgence of interest in critical Marxist theory. At the same time, the publishing institutions committed to Marxism have contracted markedly since the high point of the 1970s. The Historical Materialism Book Series is dedicated to addressing this situation by making available important works of Marxist theory. The aim of the series is to publish important theoretical contributions as the basis for vigorous intellectual debate and exchange on the left.

The peer-reviewed series publishes original monographs, translated texts, and reprints of classics across the bounds of academic disciplinary agendas and across the divisions of the left. The series is particularly concerned to encourage the internationalization of Marxist debate and aims to translate significant studies from beyond the English-speaking world.

For a full list of titles in the Historical Materialism Book Series available in paperback from Haymarket Books, visit:
www.haymarketbooks.org/category/hm-series

In Marx's Laboratory

Critical Interpretations of the *Grundrisse*

Edited by
Riccardo Bellofiore, Guido Starosta,
and Peter D. Thomas

Haymarket Books
Chicago, IL

First published in 2013 by Brill Academic Publishers, The Netherlands
© 2013 Koninklijke Brill NV, Leiden, The Netherlands

Published in paperback in 2014 by
Haymarket Books
P.O. Box 180165
Chicago, IL 60618
773-583-7884
www.haymarketbooks.org

ISBN: 978-1-60846-374-9

Trade distribution:
In the US, Consortium Book Sales, www.cbsd.com
In Canada, Publishers Group Canada, www.pgcbooks.ca
In the UK, Turnaround Publisher Services, www.turnaround-psl.com
In Australia, Palgrave Macmillan, www.palgravemacmillan.com.au
In all other countries, Publishers Group Worldwide, www.pgw.com

Cover design by Ragina Johnson.

This book was published with the generous support of
Lannan Foundation and the Wallace Global Fund.

10 9 8 7 6 5 4 3 2 1

Library of Congress Cataloging-in-Publication data is available.

Contents

Part Four: Technology, Domination, Emancipation

Part Five: Competition, Cycles and Crisis

Part Six: Society and History in the *Grundrisse*

Introduction: In Marx's Laboratory
Riccardo Bellofiore, Guido Starosta and Peter D. Thomas

The initial idea for this book dates back to the *Reading the Grundrisse* conference which took place at the University of Bergamo (Italy) on 15–18 July 2008.[1] This initiative was a part of the activities of the 'International Symposium on Marxian Economic Theory' (ISMT) and aimed at an in-depth critical reconsideration of Marx's 1857–8 manuscripts in the context of their 150th anniversary. The conference highlighted a variety of important issues and themes for future research, some of which were not directly addressed in the twelve papers originally presented at the event. In light of the scholarly importance of that early version of the Marxian critique of political economy and the various controversies to which it gave rise, we came to the conclusion that a wider volume, which expanded the scope of the themes covered at the conference, would be a very valuable addition to contemporary Marx studies. We thus decided to invite more contributions from diverse perspectives, intellectual traditions and 'geographies', which either engage with some of the fundamental issues that were not covered extensively by the papers originally presented at the conference, or provide a different view of the topics that have generated such heated debates among Marx scholars (particularly, for example, the connection between abstract labour and

1. The conference was organised under the direction of Riccardo Bellofiore in the Dipartimento di Scienze Economiche 'Hyman P. Minsky'. It was part of the Bergamo Unit activities for the Inter-University Research Program *Issues of German Classical Philosophy: Edition of Text and Critical Studies* 2006 PRIN (funded by The Italian Ministry of Universities), of which Mario Cingoli was the National Coordinator and Riccardo Bellofiore was the Local Coordinator in Bergamo.

value, or the so-called 'Fragment on machines'). Despite the great variety of approaches included in the volume, they all share a common ground in representing methodologically-minded readings of Marx's critique of political economy, understood as a critical investigation of the historically-specific reified forms of social mediation of capitalist society. Such perspectives coincide with the 'spirit' that motivated the initial constitution and subsequent development of the ISMT. A few more words on this long-standing intellectual forum and its scholarly purpose are in order, therefore.

The ISMT is an original forum gathering together philosophers and economists in the Marxian tradition. It was constituted in 1991 thanks to the efforts of Fred Moseley. The members have changed over the years. Along with Moseley, since the beginning there were Chris Arthur, Martha Campbell, Patrick Murray, Geert Reuten and Tony Smith; the group now also includes Riccardo Bellofiore, Andrew Brown, Roberto Fineschi and Guido Starosta. Over the years, Guglielmo Carchedi and Paul Mattick Jr. (both part of the original group) and Nicola Taylor have also been members. A distinctive feature of the ISMT is that the debating scholars are united by shared problems, rather than by common answers. The problematics that particularly interest the participants are the Hegelian roots of Marx's method and the close interaction between value and money, conceived not as separated topics, but as integrated ones. Members treat these themes in very different ways, sometimes radically so. In preparing this volume, we intended to stay true to, and further enrich, this non-dogmatic, pluralist spirit of critical research in Marxist theory which has defined the ISMT since its inception more than twenty years ago.

The ISMT organises regular conferences and has produced many edited collections, in addition to the individual scholars' monographs and articles.[2] A prominent place in these publications has been occupied by the reappraisal of Marx's main economic works. Hence, three conferences and edited volumes were devoted to careful inquiry into the three volumes of Marx's *Capital*.[3] A natural development was another conference, involving many other participants, in Bergamo in 2006, dedicated to re-reading Marx after the critical edition.[4] This conference included the participation of MEGA[2] editors (Rolf Hecker for Volume II and Regina Roth for Volume III), and other German and Italian scholars (Michael Heinrich, Roberto Finelli and Massimiliano Tomba). Against this background, it

---

2. A full list of the ISMT meetings and their proceedings can be found at <http://chrisarthur.net/ismt>.

3. See Bellofiore and Taylor 2004 on Volume I; Arthur and Reuten 1998 on Volume II; and Campbell and Reuten 2002 on Volume III.

4. The proceedings from this conference were published as Bellofiore and Fineschi 2009.

seemed obvious that a critical inquiry into such a crucial work as the *Grundrisse* was in order. The 150th anniversary of their composition was the perfect occasion for such an engagement.

However, there were many other important reasons for editing a book on the 1857–8 manuscripts. The *Grundrisse* are a founding text, the first that really gives evidence in a written form of the writing of *Capital*. At the same time, it is a text of transition, in the long journey that begins with the *Economic and Philosophical Manuscripts of 1844*. The enormous manuscript should be taken for what it is: a frenetic, and genial, intellectual note-taking. Marx tried, in these pages, to 'fix' some problems and some categories. He did this, for the first time, in an embryonically systematic and dialectical presentation of the theory of value and of capital. It is in this movement that he clarifies for himself the terms of his own problematic. In this sense, the *Grundrisse* can be seen as a veritable 'laboratory' in which we can observe Marx in the very process of unfolding his dialectical investigation of the movement of capitalist social and economic forms. It is thus an ideal text for stimulating a discussion about the articulation and development of the Marxian critique of political economy. Nevertheless, one could argue that the fate of that book in the English-speaking world in particular has so far been quite disappointing in comparison to its many potential riches.

The *Grundrisse* were made widely available in the West only in the late 1960s and early 1970s.[5] While it was extensively discussed not only in Germany (editions were published in 1953 in the East and 1967 in the West), but also in France and Italy as early as 1967–8, during a period when Marxian theory was on the rise and often very militant, it was only fully translated into English in 1973. It was, of course, absorbed into wider debates much later, in years when Marxism began to undergo a series of crises, frequently becoming, in the process, somewhat academic and specialist (a similar if not worse fate plagued the reception of the 'Results of the Direct Production Process').[6] This fact may, indeed, explain why the secondary literature in English is not comparable to that available in many other languages.

This volume aims to contribute to redressing this unsatisfactory situation, through an extensive and in-depth critical engagement with the *Grundrisse* from a variety of different perspectives. It aims to assess both the achievements and limitations of this preliminary version of the Marxian critique of political economy. Moreover, many of the chapters in this volume attempt to do this by

---

5. For accounts of the international dissemination and reception of the 1857–8 manuscripts, see the third part of Musto 2008.

6. The publication of a translation of Rosdolsky's *The Making of Marx's Capital* in 1977 played a crucial role in the dissemination of the *Grundrisse* in the Anglophone world.

means of a shared 'retrospective' reading strategy. They seek, that is, to throw light on the different dimensions of the 1857–8 manuscripts from the perspective of the most developed version of Marx's dialectical presentation of capitalist forms contained in *Capital*.

Re-reading the *Grundrisse* after *Capital* in this way is a worthwhile effort. On the one hand, we may find in the earlier work suggestions for unexpected tentative solutions to many problematic points in the later work. On the other hand, obscure formulations in the younger work may be enlightened, and thus at the same time revealed as hidden treasures, when read from the perspective of Marx's 'mature' work. Indeed, the *Grundrisse* can and must be valorised – without giving rise to unacceptable drifts towards objectivist or subjectivist readings, fundamentally not very faithful not only to the letter but also, and above all, to the spirit of Marx's theory – to the extent to which they are read against the background of *Capital*.

Some preliminary examples can illustrate the fertility of this approach, which is extensively demonstrated in the chapters of this volume. In the section on the pre-capitalist forms of production, the divide between the 'natural' and the 'historical' gives us a bridge between the *1844 Manuscripts* and *Capital*: the 'universality' of labour is recognised as a peculiarly historical and contradictory potentiality that begins with capitalist production, a theme which will be deepened in *Capital* Volume I's inquiry into cooperation, the division of labour and machines. In another way, the uncertainties in the 1857–8 manuscripts about money open the way to a 'symbolic' view, which does not quite easily fit with the understanding of the genesis of the money-form later developed in *Capital*, where the latter is unambiguously posited as a commodity. Something similar can be said about the deduction of 'abstract labour', whose meaning in the *Grundrisse* remains less unequivocal than in 1867. While some scholars actually welcome those tensions in Marx's early arguments on abstract labour (since they contain some insightful formulations that were abandoned in later drafts, for instance, regarding the explicit connection between abstract labour and capitalist exploitation), others see them as a sign of the preliminary status of Marx's investigation, which would undergo further necessary 'improvements', or at least, developments.

The text is also intriguing in terms of aspects of its 'crisis-theory': in 1857–8, in the section on 'circulation', Marx links absolute and relative surplus-value extraction, disproportionalities, credit, and overproduction of commodities. This organic unity is either absent or implicit in later works. At the same time, for the Marx of the *Grundrisse*, capitalist development and crises lead secularly to a tendential fall in the rate of profit which looks rather mechanical, in opposition to what we can now understand from the original development of the argument in the manuscripts for *Capital* Volume III, in a certain sense distorted by Engels's editing work. Again, however, the *Grundrisse* help us to understand the later Marxian logic. The so-called 'Fragment on machines' is a particularly controversial section, especially in terms of its interpretation by the Italian workerist and post-workerist traditions,[7] and a section that should, similarly, be interpreted against this background.

These were some of the questions that motivated the gathering in Bergamo in 2008 and the subsequent commissioning of additional papers to compose the present volume. The book is organised into six broad thematic sections, each of which aims to explore the development of central perspectives and concepts of the Marxian critique of political economy in and beyond the *Grundrisse*. The first section, 'Achievements and Limits of the *Grundrisse*', opens with Riccardo Bellofiore's attempt to re-read Marx 'backwards'; namely, the attempt to read the *Grundrisse* after *Capital*, which, in turn, allows us to see a continuity of themes from the *1844 Manuscripts* onwards. The *Grundrisse* are argued to represent a watershed in Marx's thought because of the divide between 'natural' and 'historical' situations as defined in the 'precapitalist forms of production'. At the same time, it is in the *Grundrisse* that the 'universality' of labour is recognised as a peculiar potentiality starting with capitalist production. At this stage, Marx uses the term 'labour' ambiguously: it is used both for 'labour-capacity' (labour-power) and also 'living labour', as well as the bearers of labour-power, that is, workers. These ambiguities are argued to disappear in *Capital*. Another rich and ambiguous theme stressed by Bellofiore is 'money': here, Marx begins with a symbolic view, stressing money as 'command'; a second deduction is convergent to subsequent Marxian deductions of money as a commodity, leading to the first section of *Capital* Volume I. Bellofiore argues that these ambiguities have allowed for serious interpretative distortions, which have, however, also been instrumental in revealing new aspects of Marx's argument in *Capital*. Two intriguing arguments of the *Grundrisse* are the presentation of 'abstract labour' (this time linked to the capitalist social situation as well as generalised commodity-exchange) and 'crisis-theory'. Another positive ambiguity is that the *Grundrisse* are open to a quite different accent on struggles over living labour as the source of new value. Bellofiore concludes by arguing for an 'actualisation' of the conceptual acquisitions present in the *Grundrisse*, in part achieved by reading the *Grundrisse* not 'against', but 'together' with, *Capital*.

---

7. Although workerist interest in the 'Fragment on Machines' can be traced back to its publication in Italian in the fourth issue of *Quaderni Rossi* in 1964 and Panzieri's early studies, it was undoubtedly Negri's *Marx Beyond Marx* (Negri 1991), published in French and Italian in 1979, that has constituted the most influential view of those controversial passages of the *Grundrisse* coming from that that tradition, particularly in light of the international reception of Negri's work.

Juan Iñigo Carrera's chapter, 'Method: from the *Grundrisse* to *Capital*', explores the development of Marx's method, from the 1840s onwards. Iñigo Carrera argues that the *Grundrisse* constitute a step in the development of an original method: the reproduction of the concrete by means of thought, as opposed to its representation – a method which, however, is only fully discovered and developed in the writing of *Capital*. Thus, an engagement with the latter text can help us to throw light upon both the methodological innovations and limitations of the former. From this perspective, we can see that the discovery of the determinations of value in the *Grundrisse* still follows an essentially analytic course. *Capital*, on the other hand, overcomes these limitations in the flow of synthetic reproduction from its point of departure, allowing Marx to develop the substance of value into its necessary concrete forms. Iñigo Carrera thus argues that the transition from the *Grundrisse* to *Capital* involves not simply a change in the method of presentation, but also in the method of inquiry itself.

Roberto Fineschi's chapter, 'The Four Levels of Abstraction of Marx's Concept of "Capital". Or, Can We Consider the *Grundrisse* the Most Advanced Version of Marx's Concept of Capital?', analyses Marx's different plans for his critique of political economy. Fineschi argues that Marx successfully improved his theory after the *Grundrisse*, in the subsequent drafts leading to *Capital*, in order to overcome some difficulties that arose from the insufficient dialectical development of categories in his project in 1857–8. Engaging with both the German debate (the so-called *neue Lektüre*) and Italian workerist perspectives, and drawing upon new philological findings of the MEGA,[2] Fineschi argues that Marx's initial attempt to derive a conceptual structure for *Capital* from Hegel was later replaced by the project of developing a theory of capital by following its own inner dialectical logic. The concept of capital is divided into four levels of abstraction: a sort of level zero of 'simple circulation'; a first level, called 'generality'; a second level, or 'particularity'; and a final level of abstraction, or 'singularity'. The progressive transformation of the outline of the *Grundrisse*, however, does not imply any rupture or radical discontinuity. Rather, Marx further developed a general outline in order to arrive at a more consistent dialectical presentation of categories.

The second section, 'Abstract Labour, Value and Money', opens with Chris Arthur's chapter on 'The Practical Truth of Abstract Labour'. Arthur argues that there are two important determinations of abstract labour in the *Grundrisse* that are absent from *Capital*: first, the 'practical truth' of abstract labour is a feature only of the most modern society (industrial capitalism); and second, this form of labour is thematised in the framework of the capital-relation (not of simple commodity-circulation). The chapter argues that the latter determination, in particular, can be read in the light of the proposition that the form-determinations of labour should be thematised only subsequent to the derivation of the general formula for capital. Moreover, this implies a 'negative labour theory of value' in which productive labour is cognised in value only in sublated form. Immediately value positing is a function of 'the time of capital'; nonetheless, because this pure motion in time is borne by labour, socially-necessary labour-time is, in a sense, a determinant of its magnitude.

Patrick Murray's chapter, 'Unavoidable Crises: Reflections on Backhaus and the Development of Marx's Value-Form Theory in the *Grundrisse*', re-examines Marx's criticisms of the banking reforms proposed by the Proudhonist Alfred Darimon, which were intended to ward off financial crises. Prodded by the first world economic crisis, which started in the autumn of 1857, Marx began the *Grundrisse* with a critique of Darimon. Marx discovered the root of economic crisis in the value-form, that is, in the need for value to appear as money. This necessity meant that the difference between value and price is not a nominal one, which confutes Say's Law, discloses the role of supply and demand in Marx's value theory, reveals the illusion of the 'labour-money' or 'time-chit' proposals of the Proudhonists, and opens the door to crises. Crises come with the commodity-form. Murray argues that, by exposing the inner connection between value and money, Marx moves beyond classical political economy. The *Grundrisse*'s critique of Darimon brings out a fundamental feature of his later analysis of the value-form, namely, the *polarity* of the value-form: the commodity form (the relative value-form) and the money form (the equivalent value-form) are opposed yet inseparable. In assessing the place of the *Grundrisse* in the development of Marx's account of the value-form, Murray turns to consider the proposals of those recent currents in Marxian theory and the interpretation of Marx that have been labelled 'the new dialectics' and 'value-form theory', particularly Hans-Georg Backhaus's 1969 essay 'On the Dialectics of the Value-Form [*Zur Dialektik der Wertform*]'. Considering the extent to which Marx's exploration of the value-form in the *Grundrisse* counts as an early version of the dialectic of the value-form, the chapter offers a reassessment of key claims in Backhaus's influential study.

In the third section, 'The Concept of Capital', Martha Campbell's chapter, 'The Transformation of Money into Capital', compares the transition from simple circulation to capital in the *Grundrisse* to the two other versions in the *Original Text* of the *Contribution* and *Capital* Volume I. Campbell argues that the comparison of the three texts clarifies Marx's terminology. In particular, in the transition section of the two earlier texts, Marx uses the term 'value' to refer to capital. Drawing on this textual evidence, the chapter posits that the basis for the transition between simple circulation and capital is logical in all three versions. That is, Marx turns from simple circulation to capital, on the grounds that commodity-exchange cannot exist as an ongoing and continuous or established process except as one phase of the circulation of capital. In other words, according to Campbell's reading, simple circulation necessarily presupposes capital. A first implication of this is that simple circulation was conceived by Marx as an abstract aspect of the capitalist mode of production and unique to it. This conclusion challenges those readings that see Part One of *Capital* as referring either to simple commodity-production, conceived as an historical antecedent of capitalism; or to 'the commodity form of production in general', conceived as an abstract moment of capitalism, 'at which all that exists are individuals who are taken to be producers for exchange', but which is, nonetheless, not specific to capitalism. A further implication of Campbell's argument is that capital is implicit in, and so derived from, results established in Part One. In this sense, there is no break between the introduction of capital in Part Two and what has come before.

Howard Engelskirchen, in the chapter 'The Concept of Capital in the *Grundrisse*', argues that Marx's efforts to develop the concept of capital, on the basis of his life-long study of Aristotle, are similar to what contemporary philosophers of science call the 'real definition' of a natural or social kind. Marx's analyses can thus be seen as contributing significantly to efforts to extend thinking about natural kinds from natural to social science. He used the concept of capital in order to identify decisive causal structures of social life, and to specify those few properties of capital that are constitutive of it. Building upon Charles Bettelheim's work, Engelskirchen explores the double separation that is the central characteristic of the capitalist mode of production: the separation of enterprises from one another and the separation of direct producers from their conditions of production. This double separation, Engelskirchen argues, aptly captures the *Grundrisse*'s concept of 'capital in general', in the movement from circulation to production and valorisation, and to the unity of production and circulation. However, the real definition of the resulting structure consists not only in labour's separation from the means of production, but also in its subordination to these as values; its fundamental determination is argued to consist in the appropriation of living labour by objectified labour for the sake of increasing objectified labour. Thus, clarity on this dimension points towards capital's transformation: to associated labour's self-determined unfolding of human needs and abilities.

The fourth section, 'Technology, Domination, Emancipation', considers themes related in particular to the so-called 'Fragment on machines' and the concept of 'General Intellect', which have been widely debated so-called years. Michael Heinrich's chapter, 'The "Fragment on Machines": a Marxian Misconception in the *Grundrisse* and its Overcoming in *Capital*', begins by noting that some authors have conceived the so-called 'Fragment on machines' as a central document for a Marxian 'break-down theory' of capitalism, or at least as a description of a process in which capitalism clashes with a new mode of production inaugurated by capitalism itself. In such considerations, the results of the 'Fragment' are taken for granted. Heinrich argues that these results derive, on the one hand, from a one-sided conception of crisis in Marx's thinking since the early 1850s; and, on the other hand, from some shortcomings in the conception of basic categories in the *Grundrisse*. In the years after *Grundrisse*, Marx overcame both misconceptions. The chapter concludes by suggesting that *Capital* Volume I, particularly in the sections dealing with the production of relative surplus-value, contains an implicit critique of the 'Fragment on machines' – a critique that is often neglected by interpreters who want to rely on this early text for a reformulation of the critique of political economy.

In 'The General Intellect in Marx's *Grundrisse* and Beyond', Tony Smith engages with recent debates regarding the role of the 'General Intellect', a term that is used only in the *Grundrisse*. In particular, Smith questions the extent to which this text from the *Grundrisse* presents an account of capitalist development that diverges in significant respects from the views Marx presented elsewhere. Engaging with studies by Paolo Virno and Carlo Vercellone, Smith questions the claims as to the unprecedented role the diffusion of the General Intellect plays in contemporary capitalism. According to Virno, the flourishing of the General Intellect, which Marx thought could only take place in communism, characterises post-Fordist capitalism. Vercellone adds that Marx's account of the real subsumption of living labour under capital is obsolete in contemporary cognitive capitalism. Against these arguments that Marx's value theory has been historically superannuated, Smith argues that these views rest on a confusion of value and wealth, a neglect of Marx's account of the role of 'free gifts' to capital, an underestimation of the role of the General Intellect in the period prior to the rise of post-Fordism/cognitive capitalism, and an underestimation of the restrictions on the diffusion of the General Intellect in contemporary capitalism.

Guido Starosta's chapter, 'The System of Machinery and Determinations of Revolutionary Subjectivity in the *Grundrisse* and *Capital*', argues that Marx's exposition of the forms of the real subsumption of labour to capital – in particular, the system of machinery of large-scale industry – constitutes the dialectical presentation of the determinations of revolutionary subjectivity. Starosta argues that the development of the emancipatory subject is, for Marx, the immanent result of the unfolding of the reified forms of social mediation of capitalist society. More specifically, it is the outcome of transformations of the materiality of human productive subjectivity that they bring about. The essence of this capitalist transformation of the production process of human life lies in the mutation of the productive attributes of the collective labourer according to a determinate tendency: the individual organs of the latter eventually become universal productive subjects. This is the inner material content underlying the political revolutionary subjectivity of the proletariat. However, Starosta argues that Marx's dialectical exposition of those transformations in *Capital* is truncated and does not unfold the plenitude of the material determinations underlying the revolutionary being of the working class, which is presented as no more than an abstract possibility. A gap thus remains between the 'dialectic of human labour' unfolded in the chapters on relative surplus-value in *Capital*, and the revolutionary conclusions at the end of Volume I in the chapter on 'The Historical Tendency of Capital Accumulation'. Starosta argues that it is possible to find the elements for the completion of the systematic exposition of determinations of revolutionary subjectivity on the basis of a careful reading of the relevant passages of the so-called 'Fragment on machines' from the *Grundrisse*.

In 'From the *Grundrisse* to *Capital* and Beyond: Then and Now', George Caffentzis explores the relationship between the two main revolution-producing 'tendencies' or 'laws' in the development of capitalism that Marx identifies in the *Grundrisse*: namely, the falling rate of profit and the 'breakdown' of the creation and measurement of wealth by labour and labour-time. Caffentzis argues that the increasing incommensurability of wealth and labour-time, initially in tension with the thesis of the falling rate of profit, was transformed in Marx's work following the *Grundrisse* into an essential preliminary for the 'law' of the rate of profit to fall. Caffentzis further traces the impact of the reading of the *Grundrisse* on the project of the journal *Zerowork I*, and the reconceptualisation of the workday initiated by socialist feminists, particularly in the Wages for Housework campaign, revealing the manifold forms of work in capitalist society. His chapter concludes by traces some politically significant parallels in Marx's thought between 1857 and 1882 and the succession of some themes in the anti-capitalist movement between the 1960s and the present. He compares the increasing 'techno-scepticism' of the anti-capitalist movements over the last forty years to a similar development in Marx's thought, which shifted from an emphasis on the superhuman machines of the *Grundrisse* and the General Intellect to the political forms of the Paris Commune and the Russian *obschina*.

The fifth section, 'Competition, Cycles and Crisis', opens with Fred Moseley's chapter, 'The Whole and the Parts. The Beginning of Marx's Theory of the Distribution of Surplus-Value in the *Grundrisse*'. Moseley argues that the *Grundrisse* are mainly about the production of surplus-value, that is, the determination of the total surplus-value produced in the sphere of production in the capitalist economy as a whole. However, he notes that Marx makes several brief comments on the distribution of surplus-value, that is, the division of the total surplus-value into individual parts, especially the equalisation of rates of profit across industries. This chapter reviews the initial discussions of Marx's theory of the distribution of surplus-value in the *Grundrisse*, arguing that in this early work, Marx clearly stated the key logical premise of his theory that the total surplus-value is determined prior to its distribution, and that this total amount is not affected by the distribution of surplus-value. Moseley further argues that this relation between the production of surplus-value and the distribution of surplus-value is the quantitative dimension Marx's logical structure of capital in general and many capitals (or competition).

Jan Toporowski's chapter, 'Marx's *Grundrisse* and the Monetary Business-Cycle', argues that, although Marx explicitly rejected the monetary business-cycle in the *Grundrisse*, he 'smuggled' it back again into his theory of crisis in *Capital* Volume III, where crises arises because 'interest-bearing capital' circulates in production (and exchange) and therefore is not available for the repayment of financial liabilities on demand (an element at the core of Minsky's theory of financial crisis). Toporowski argues that Marx's initial rejection of a monetary business-cycle, and the reappearance of that cycle in his later crisis theory, reflects Marx's dialectical approach to finance. More specifically, the financing needs of capitalist production induce financial innovation ('interest-bearing capital'), which comes to have a dominant, rather than a subordinate, role in relation to production. According to Toporowski, it follows from this that the dominance of finance allows credit-cycles to determine the nature and dynamics of capitalism. In other words, having emerged to serve industrial capitalism, financial markets can become a much more liquid source of profit; they can depress capital accumulation or stimulate it with credit-cycles. These arguments lead Toporowski to reject functionalist readings of the role of finance in the capitalist mode of production.

The chapter by Geert Reuten and Peter D. Thomas, 'Crisis and the Rate of Profit in Marx's Laboratory', examines the role of 'the tendency of the rate of profit to fall' in Marx's successive drafts of the critique of political economy. On the basis of a philological analysis of the *Grundrisse* and the drafts for *Capital* Volume III, they argue that Marx's views on the 'law' or 'tendency' of the rate of profit to fall developed from a law about the historical destination of the capitalist system as tending towards breakdown, to a theory about the functioning of the capitalist mode of production as a (potentially) reproductive system. They argue that Marx's analysis of the tendency of the rate of profit to fall in the *Grundrisse*, as in his earlier economic writings from the 1840s, remains indebted, in many key respects, to the conceptual matrix in which this theme had been previously developed in classical political economy, particularly in Smith and Ricardo. As his research-project develops, Marx's texts begin to display a development away from a notion of an 'empirical' trend for the rate of profit to fall, and towards a notion of tendency as operative power, which results in a notion of the cyclical variation of the rate of profit. On the basis of this textual analysis, Reuten and Thomas attempt to indicate some of the theoretical and political reasons that may have encouraged Marx to undertake this development. In conclusion, they outline some themes for future research that arise from this understanding of Marx's intellectual development, including a reassessment of the relative weight of Marx's debts to classical political economy, on the one hand, and Hegel's thought, on the other; the relationship between politics and economics in Marx's mature critique of political economy; and the implications of this analysis for contemporary debates regarding both the tendency of the rate of profit to fall and the status of Marxian research as social theory.

The sixth section, 'Society and History in the *Grundrisse*', confronts the problem of social theory in Marx's work from the late 1850s to the successive drafts of *Capital*. Luca Basso's chapter, 'Between Pre-Capitalist Forms and Capitalism: The Problem of Society in the *Grundrisse* (*Outlines of the Critique of Political Economy*)', focuses on the concept of society in the *Grundrisse*, and particularly its distinction between the various modes of production. However, Basso argues that, rather than writing a general history of humanity, Marx wanted to analyse the distinctive signs of capitalism. The pre-capitalist forms were characterised by the unity of man with the land and the community to which he belonged. The capitalist system broke down these communities [*Gemeinwesen*], which had been based on traditional hierarchical structures, thus representing a 'new beginning', a radical change from the past. Only with the birth of capitalism did it become possible to truly speak of the individual as such, autonomous but also subjected to the objective power of money, and of society, paradoxically isolating individuals from each other but also characterised by subjective insurgences, which constantly threaten its to rupture its totality.

Amy Wendling's chapter, 'Second Nature: Gender in Marx's *Grundrisse*', analyses the role of gender in the 1857–8 manuscripts, in a 'deliberately anachronistic' reading. Noting the relative absence of reflections on gender-related themes in the *Grundrisse*, particularly in relation to their presence in Marx's early works and the return to the topic in *Capital* and other later works, Wendling reconstructs Marx's continuing research on these themes in the 1850s, drawing in particular on one of Marx's excerpt-notebooks from 1852, soon to be made available in the MEGA[2]. Wendling argues that Marx's inquiries into what is today called gender are the product of the intersection, and then the supersession, of both the *querelle des femmes* and the political economy of Marx's time. Without downplaying the obvious limitations of Marx's treatment of gender in the *Grundrisse*, the chapter argues that it provides some powerful conceptual tools for working on the issue of gender. This is especially true of Marx's critical revival and reworking of the Aristotelian idea of a 'second nature' produced via social and historical shaping. Marx's ultimate conception of gender as an enormously complex, socially imbedded, yet transhistorical political structure, exceeds the discourses that Marx inherited. The *Grundrisse* are thus depicted as a developmental stage in Marx's thinking. Wendling argues that the treatment of gender in Marx foreshadows twentieth-century debates in Marxist feminism and in feminist theory more generally, particularly regarding debates about labour, technology, and class-divisions among gendered subjects.

Joel Wainwright, in the chapter 'Uneven Developments: from the *Grundrisse* to *Capital*', compares the way in which the two texts frame the problematic of uneven development, that is, the way that capitalism's inherently uneven development is thematised as a problem for explanation. In the *Grundrisse*, the uneven nature of capitalism as development is examined principally through the emergence of capitalism from precapitalist relations. While this analysis is not entirely absent from *Capital* (for example, the discussion of primitive accumulation), precapitalist formations are not treated as systematically in *Capital*. By contrast, Wainwright argues, uneven development enters *Capital* in the final section, particularly where Marx criticises Wakefield. Reading these texts together, he argues that the problematic of uneven development shifts from the *Grundrisse* to *Capital* in a way that underscores Marx's growing stress on capital's imperialist character. This shift is argued to have its roots in political events of the period when Marx developed the research of the *Grundrisse* into the drafts of *Capital*.

The final chapter in the volume, Massimiliano Tomba's 'Pre-Capitalistic Forms of Production and Primitive Accumulation. Marx's Historiography from the *Grundrisse* to *Capital*', focuses on the pre-capitalist forms of production in the *Grundrisse*. Tomba argues that in these notebooks, Marx studied the precapitalist forms through a twofold interpretive schema: he joined a kind of evolutionary history to a repetitive history, a history of invariants. He did this in order to understand the nature of the historical break that the capitalist mode of production represents, the new form of social relation and the anthropological transformation of the human being, producing in this way a novel historical and historiographical perspective. However, Tomba argues that Marx's attempt to sketch the dynamics of the capitalist mode of production through the scheme of genesis, development, and crisis also resulted in a typical sequence of a philosophy of history. Only in his late works, in his rethinking of 'primitive accumulation', did Marx think the historical contemporaneity of different forms of productions, and the synchronism of different historical temporalities.

We hope that the chapters published in this volume provide a sense of the diversity of contemporary approaches to critical Marxist research generally, and to the reading of the *Grundrisse* in particular. They attest to a common intent to examine critically the foundations and development of Marx's thought. Albeit in different ways and with different emphases, each chapter proposes to re-read Marx's project today both in the light of recent philological advances and also in terms of the capacity of such a philologically-informed reading to contribute to our understanding of the contemporary capitalist mode of production. Taken in their totality, these contributions will help us to re-read the 1857–8 manuscripts as an intense 'laboratory', in which we can observe a crucial stage in the development of Marx's critique of political economy.

Part One

Achievements and Limits of the *Grundrisse*

The *Grundrisse* after *Capital,* or How to Re-read Marx Backwards
Riccardo Bellofiore

The *Grundrisse* are a founding text, the first that really gives evidence in a written form of the genesis of *Capital*; they are, at the same time, a text of transition, in the long journey that begins with the *Economic and Philosophical Manuscripts of 1844.* The enormous manuscript should be taken for what it is: frenetic, and genial, intellectual note-taking. Marx tried to 'fix' some problems and categories in these pages. He did this, for the first time, in an embryonically systematic presentation of the theory of value and of capital. It is in this movement that he clarifies for himself the terms of his own problematic.

Due to this, it is also, inevitably, a text full of ambiguities. These ambiguities have allowed counterposed readings to be derived from it, characterised by extreme subjectivism, on the one hand, and extreme objectivism, on the other. Furthermore, they were readings by authors, we should note, who saw themselves in not only a positive relation, but also in a relation of strict continuity with the *Grundrisse*.

What I propose, here, is the result of a sustained and complete re-reading of the entire work, from which I have emerged with a series of intuitions that I will try to verify in successive works. Here, I want to sketch out a sort of agenda, articulated on a central thesis that is, essentially, the following: Marx should be read 'backwards'. Stated in other words, the *Grundrisse* can and must be valorised – without giving rise to unacceptable drifts, fundamentally not very faithful not only to the letter but also, and above all, to the spirit of Marx's theory – to the extent to which they are read against the background of *Capital*. It should not be read in the inverse sequence, which has somehow been imposed and historically affirmed: namely, the *Grundrisse* 'before' *Capital*, which then sooner or later slides into the contraposition of the *Grundrisse* 'against' *Capital*. Such a reading gained currency soon after the diffusion of this work in the West, at the end of the 1960s and start of the 1970s, a period that has been followed by a certain oblivion.

Given the limits of space, and as I have to cover a seemingly unending argumentative terrain, I will be forced to proceed apodictically. I will not quote the numerous citations that would expand and support my case. My point of departure are the pages dedicated to the 'forms that precede capitalist production'. From here I will try to give an account, if not of all, then at least of many of the themes that run through the *Grundrisse* and that, in a continuous and complete reading of the text, bring out, underneath the apparent disorder, a guiding thread of unitary reasoning.

The aim of my rereading is to contribute to clarifying the origins of the alternative stereotypes of the *Grundrisse* that I have already mentioned, of extreme subjectivism and extreme objectivism. It is within these conventional readings of the *Grundrisse* that we can also locate that genuine 'philosophy of history' that was constructed by early workerism [*operaismo*], roundly criticised by Massimiliano Tomba in a number of texts.[1] Here I refer, in particular, to 'theoretical' workerism, with idealistic, 'actualist' and irrationalist traits, as in Tronti and Negri, more than to early workerism in its totality, which is an experience much richer that the current vulgate recognises.[2] However, it is certain that this 'ideological' and 'irrational' workerism ended up seeing in the *Grundrisse* the privileged, if not exclusive, point of access to Marx. It was a mistaken reading, though not without its reasons and insights. My aim will, therefore, be to highlight the aspects to which this reading can appeal for justification. In conclusion, I will try to say something about a possible 'actuality' and a potential 'good use' of the *Grundrisse* today.

The *Grundrisse*: a rapid re-reading

I begin with the theme of the relation between the individual and universality. It is a point that is also present in Marx's concept of labour. It thus imme-

---

1. Cf. Tomba 2007 and 2009.
2. On workerism, cf. Wright 2002 and Bellofiore and Tomba 2008. See also Bellofiore 1982.

diately concerns the disputed relation between the *Economic and Philosophical Manuscripts of 1844*, the *Grundrisse* and *Capital*.

There is no doubt that the category of labour as it is configured in the *1844 Manuscripts* has many Feuerbachian accents. Nor can we doubt the reference to a still undefined 'human being', marked by metahistorical traits. For the Marx of the *Manuscripts*, the human being as such is 'natural', because it is always a part of nature. At the same time, it is a 'generic' being, because the genus is its object, not only theoretically, but also practically. In so doing, Marx says, the human being relates to herself or himself as a 'universal' and free being. Practical production of an objective world is the confirmation of the human being as a generic conscious being, and thus universal.

The question is posed, and has been repeatedly posed by interpreters, of whether this theoretical horizon is reduced or abandoned by the mature Marx. Here, we have an all too easy dichotomy between 'continuists' and 'discontinuists'. The authors who read Marx on the basis of *Capital* tend to locate themselves on the latter side. They maintain, stated briefly, that there is a pure and simple rupture of the 'mature' Marx with the 'young' Marx. It seems to me that there exists, instead, a continuity that can be established by reading the texts backwards; in this journey backwards, the *Grundrisse* are the fundamental connecting point. We need to resist the temptation of reading the notion of the 'human being' as a 'natural and generic being' as if it were a notion that Marx fixed once and for all in the *Manuscripts*, and which he would then apply just as it is, or, alternatively, reject completely, in *Capital*. On the contrary, we are dealing, here, with a perspective that Marx never abandons, but which he certainly redefines in a radical way in his mature work, beginning from the *Grundrisse* and from the meaning he assigns to notions to naturalness and historicity.[3]

For the Marx of the *Grundrisse*, the 'natural' connection is the spontaneous connection of individuals within determinate and limited relations of production. The 'universally developed' individuals – those individuals whose social relations, as their own, communal relations, are subjected to their communal control – are not a product of nature, but a product of history. Marx continues: the degree and the universality of development of capacities due to which this kind of individuality becomes possible presupposes the production of (exchange-) values. It is the universalisation of exchange, which occurs only with the generalisation of capitalist production, that generates, for the first time, universality together with estrangement: that is, both the estrangement of the individuals from themselves and from others, as well as the universality and versatility of their relations and abilities.[4]

---

3. This interpretation is developed further in Bellofiore 1998.
4. Marx 1975–2005a, p. 99.

According to the Marx of the *Grundrisse*, capitalism breaks with 'natural' pre-capitalist forms of production – 'natural' in the sense that within those forms the reproduction of relations of the individual with its own community, given by the past, is the foundation of a limited development. The confrontation is established beginning from bourgeois society, therefore, beginning from the scientific comprehension of modern relations of production. It is only by beginning with capitalism that Marx can formulate a vision according to which a social form shows development superior to another, without however being its necessary product. Outside of any philosophy of history, it is by beginning from bourgeois society that we can reveal a perspective that simultaneously illuminates both the past as well as the possibilities of the future.

To me, these pages seem to provide a representation of the problematic of the 'universality' of the human being, as an entity that is not only 'natural' but also 'generic': the theme of the *Manuscripts*, in short. It returns, however, in new clothes, and in an argumentative context that is radically changed. The 'universality' and the 'genericity' of the human being are now historically determined. A human 'nature' constituted in this way can be properly 'thought' only at a certain point in history, when it is given concretely as a hidden and latent possibility in capitalist reality, which realises it in the distorted form of estrangement. What is wealth, asks Marx, when it throws off the limited bourgeois form, if not the universality of needs, of capacities, of enjoyment of the productive forces of individuals generated in universal exchange? It is in history that the universal individual, as concrete possibility, is constituted. This possibility is linked to the circumstances that, according to the reasoning of the *Grundrisse*, only capitalism signals the birth of 'society' in the strict sense. Also due to this, the 'precapitalist forms of production' are 'natural': they are 'social' only in a very limited sense.

These are points well grasped by a long line of interpreters, from Lukàcs to Schmidt.[5] Does all of that disappear in *Capital*? This does not seem to me to be the case. For reasons of space, I will limit myself to a few significant lines, drawn from Chapter Fifteen of Volume I.[6] Towards the end of that long chapter, Marx emphasises strongly how modern industry does not consider, and does not ever treat as definitive, the existing form of a process of production. Due to this, he writes with unconstrained enthusiasm, its technical basis is revolutionary, while the basis of all the other modes of production was substantially conservative. With machines, capital is not limited to subverting constantly the technical aspect of production. According to Marx, it revolutionises from top to bottom the functions of the workers, the social combinations of the labour-process. It therefore revolutionises the division of labour in society, which means that it

---

5. Cf. Lukács 1923 and Schmidt 1971a.
6. Marx 1975–2005b, pp. 489–91.

overturns from top to bottom the world of exchange, insofar as the technical and social revolution is linked to the birth, death and continuous transformation of branches of production. All of that brings with it the 'variation' of labour, the 'fluency' of functions and the universal 'mobility' of the worker in every sense.

After having described the 'negative' side of these processes, Marx insists on their potentially 'positive' side. If, today, the variation of labour is imposed only as a dominating natural law, and with the blindly destructive effect of a natural law that encounters obstacles everywhere, large-scale modern industry, with its catastrophes, works in such a way that the recognition of the variations of labour and therefore the greatest possible versatility of the worker as the general social law of production becomes a question of life and death. This question of life and death is the substitution of the partial individual – the detail-worker, a mere fragment of a human being – by 'the totally developed individual', for which the different social functions are modes of activity that interchange the one with the other, as is (potentially) constituted by the 'collective' and 'combined' worker of the fully developed, specifically capitalist mode of production.

Here re-emerges, once again, a problematic that goes back to the *1844 Manuscripts* and the *German Ideology*, but which is now completely rethought. In the evident continuity there abides the maximum discontinuity, and the first can be valorised only by means of the second – only, that is, if the discourse on labour and on the human being is re-read backwards, from *Capital* to the *1844 Manuscripts*, going by way of the *Grundrisse* of the '*Formen*' and the '*Weltmarkt*'.

Allow us to leave this line of argumentation for a moment and turn to the analysis of some of the other themes treated in the *Grundrisse*. I will make a selection, which, more or less, follows the argumentation of the *1857–8 Manuscripts*. Obviously, I will have to proceed rapidly. And, initially at least, I will leave aside the consideration of the first very interesting part on money.[7]

General exchange on the market establishes the social connection between reciprocally indifferent individuals. This connection is expressed in exchange-value. In the universal exchange of commodities – but therefore in capitalism itself, given that the exchange of commodities becomes general only with capital – labour is not 'immediately social'; rather, on the contrary, it is immediately private. It must become social, via the exchange of 'things'. The producer has to give life to a universal production, to an '(exchange-) value' that, isolated and individualised, is money. Here we refer to the sequence according to which exchange is first given in ideal money, and then in real money. In this way of reasoning, there is evidently an implicit definition of 'abstract labour', the labour whose sociality is only mediated.[8] In *Capital*, Marx will write with more clarity than there is in

---

7. Cf. 'II. Chapter on Money', in Marx 1975–2005a, pp. 51–170.
8. Marx 1975–2005a, pp. 93–4.

the *Grundrisse* – but by deepening a line of thought that starts here, albeit tentatively, to be delineated – that the only labour that is really 'immediately social' is the labour that produces money as commodity.[9] We will put aside these two interconnected points – the theory of money, the definition of abstract labour – for a moment, and return to them later. For the discourse on abstract labour in the *Grundrisse* certainly doesn't finish here, and the complexity of its analysis remains one of the central interesting themes of the *1857–8 Manuscripts*.

Once Marx arrives at money in its third determination in his categorial deduction, to money as money, how does it happen that money begins to produce more money, to 'transform itself' into capital? In *Capital* – though the same thing happens at a point in the *Grundrisse* – Marx systematically uses the metaphor of the 'chrysalis' that, wrapping itself up in the cocoon, manages to transform itself into a 'butterfly'.[10] How is it possible that value gives life to more value, that is, a self-valorisation of value? The answer naturally lies, in the last instance, in the reference to the category of 'living labour', which is crystallised in more value than the capital-value that is advanced. The point is that in the *Grundrisse*, Marx, who has very clearly seen the distinction between 'living labour capacity' and labour as such, as 'activity', expresses himself with great ambiguity. The expression 'living labour', or even simply 'labour', is often and easily used generically in order to indicate the two dimensions: an ambiguity that will disappear altogether in *Capital*.

Marx sometimes even speaks, somewhat dismissively, of an exchange of 'labour' with capital, an exchange in which labour is ceded to capital, and capital obtains in this very exchange more labour. The worker obtains in return nothing other than the 'value' of this 'labour', which in reality is the labour-capacity 'stuck onto' living human beings. If we read these phrases 'backwards' from *Capital*, the confusion disappears and the ambiguity is resolved. We are dealing with the twofold nature of the social relation between the capitalists and the working class: a social relation marked, on the one hand, by the 'sale' on the labour-market of labour-power acquired by wages; on the other hand, by the 'use' or exploitation of labour-power in the immediate process of production. We are thus speaking about how the first moment, in circulation, opens to the second moment, in production: that is, how it opens to the extraction (potentially conflictual) of the labour 'in movement' of the labourer; an 'activity' that in its nature is 'fluid', in becoming. This process can be defined as 'exchange' only figuratively, as Marx himself does not stop reiterating in his subsequent reflections.

In my opinion, this is the direction in which Marx is already moving in 1857–8: that of a conceptual articulation in which, when we speak of 'labour', it is

---

9. Cf. the first chapter of Marx 1996.
10. Marx 1975–2005a, p. 472.

necessary always to distinguish carefully between the 'labour-capacity', which is the potential of labour as 'activity', and the performance of labour as such. Both the first (labour-power) and the second (living labour) are inseparable from the 'free' labourer, qua socially determined human being. The ambiguity of the writing may be due to the fact that we are dealing with notes for personal use, but also perhaps to the circumstance that Marx has not completely clarified this crucial point. But certainly that ambiguity opens the way to the vision of living labour 'as subjectivity',[11] where living labour can be identified with 'labour-capacity' or with the labourer. This ambiguity opens the way to those who now refer the notion of living labour to non-activity rather than activity: thus a 'living labour' that in the end is everything, except 'labour'; right up to the oxymoron that is today the proposal of an 'exodus' of living labour from labour.

It is beginning from this distinction of 'labour-capacity' and 'living labour', and it is from this vision of the second as a capitalist 'use' of the first, that Marx gives an account of the origin of surplus-value, referring it to the extraction of surplus-labour. This genetic explanation of capitalist valorisation, already in the *1857–8 Manuscripts*, is based on what may be called the 'method of comparison' which we will find many times in the successive versions of the critique of political economy, and which is given its final and classical version in the seventh chapter of *Capital* Volume I.[12] Beginning from a certain level of productivity of labour, surplus-value is born from the 'lengthening' of the working day: from a prolongation of the socially necessary (living) labour-time expended by the totality of workers in excess of the time of 'necessary labour', which is defined as the labour-time required for the production of the subsistence-wage expressed in money.

The impulse to the extraction of surplus-value is in agreement with the impulse to produce 'more' abstract wealth, in a spiral without end. In the *Grundrisse*, it is already clear that capital is identified with the universal tendency to maximal and unlimited extraction of surplus-labour, well beyond necessary labour. Here is the seed of the universality of capital, of a world of needs evermore developed, of a general laboriousness – in short, of the world-market. In order to understand in which sense this is the case, we cannot stop here at immediate production. We must go further, and consider the circulation of commodities, as these manuscripts do extensively.

---

11. For a reconstruction of this notion in workerism from a sympathetic perspective, see Zanini 2007.

12. An instance in the *Grundrisse* of Marx's 'method of the comparison' is Marx 1975–2005a, pp. 268–70. The expression 'method of comparison' is Rubin's (cf. Rubin 1972); my use, however, is different. On this, a summary of my views and a survey of the debate can be found in Bellofiore 2007. The point is developed in Bellofiore 2002 and 2004.

Marx is crystal clear, here just as in *Capital*, in maintaining that value does not exist outside of exchange. The 'latent' value and 'ideal' money must be actualised truly on the final market of the commodities. This leads him immediately to the treatment of what is later defined as the problem of the 'realisation' of (surplus-) value. The *Grundrisse* follow, in this perspective, an original line of reasoning, which here I must unfortunately synthesise to an extreme degree.

Capital, in the drive to maximise surplus-value, but therefore also in the drive to push surplus-labour to an extreme beyond necessary labour, ends up squeezing wages in relative terms. In its 'pure' form, this tendency is actualised by means of methods aiming at the extraction of relative surplus-value, which leads to the reduction of the quota of wages on the new value added, even if the real wage is augmented (as long as this rise does not exceed the increase of the productive power of labour). Certainly, Marx reminds us in these pages that the workers employed by the 'other' capitalists are part of the market. The single capitalist, if she or he resists the rise of the wages of her or his own workers, is not in fact unhappy that the wages of workers employed elsewhere are increased. This reasoning cannot, however, be valid if we consider 'capital in general'.[13]

If this is the case and if valorisation is pulled by demand, how can the problem of the realisation of values in commodities be overcome, if the latter must include surplus-value, without falling into the 'harmonism' of a Ricardo or a Say, or into the 'underconsumption' of a Malthus or a Sismondi? In the *Grundrisse*, Marx clarifies how already with the extraction of absolute surplus-value, but even more systematically with that of relative surplus-value, the expansion of one capital without the contemporaneous constitution of other capitals in unthinkable. This means, evidently, the simultaneous presence of other points of labour and other points of exchange. The creation of value and surplus-value, the extraction of labour and surplus-labour, proceed, and must proceed, side by side with the multiplication of branches of production, and consequently with the realisation of the tendency towards the world-market.

It is on this basis that the question of the relation between immediate production and the 'actualisation' of exchange-value on the final market of commodities is redefined. To the 'quantitative' extension and to the 'qualitative' deepening of the division of labour on the market. There must correspond, in order for supply to find somewhere a corresponding and adequate demand, the effective emergence of definite and precise quantitative relations between branches of production in exchange. Now, the *Grundrisse* tells us, these genuine conditions of 'equilibrium' are linked in a necessary way to a determinate relation between surplus-labour and necessary labour: therefore, they are linked to

---

13. Marx 1975–2005a, pp. 345–50.

the rate of surplus-value that is fixed in immediate production. They depend, furthermore, on how this surplus-value is divided into consumption (spending of surplus-value as income) and investment (spending of surplus-value as capital). There must correspond, to the relations in terms of '(exchange-) value', particular relations in terms of 'use-value' (raw materials, machines, workers, and so on), which must be available in adequate quantities and qualities. If the conditions of equilibrium express an 'internal necessity' in order for the accumulation of capital to occur without being upset, the fact that this internal necessity is really affirmed in reality is completely casual.[14]

Already in the *Grundrisse*, Marx goes beyond this point, and tells us that the possible contradiction between the immediate production of value and its 'actualisation' in the circulation of commodities can be overcome, not only thanks to the continuous extension of points of exchange (and of labour) that have been mentioned, but also due to the intervention of credit. Credit allows one to be paid before another who must cede money for the acquisition of a commodity is paid in a final way.[15] The expansion of production is emancipated from the given limits of the market in a certain moment and in a certain place. In some other passages of notable interest, Marx notes another way of pushing forward the contradiction: the extension of 'unproductive' areas. There are passages in which, exceptionally, there is more than one positive reference to Malthus.[16]

For Marx, the problem is not so much, or fundamentally, the 'casuality' of exchange-relations, the 'erraticity of conditions of equilibrium' in and of themselves. It is much more the fact that, precisely because capital is the impulse to the continuous growth of surplus-value, the rate of surplus-value cannot but continuously change. At the same time, therefore, the relations of equilibrium between industries must change, both in material terms and in terms of value. If intersectoral relations of equilibrium continuously vary, a 'balanced' reproduction, in equilibrium, cannot but be broken at a certain point. The crisis of 'overproduction of commodities' then occurs, not due to the mere 'anarchy' of the market, but for reasons 'internal' to capital, related to the distinctive features of the production of surplus-value and the establishment of a 'specifically' capitalist mode of production. The crisis, from being merely 'possible', becomes ever more 'probable': and it is precisely its dilation thanks to credit that renders it more devastating at the moment when it occurs.

In truth, the more you go into reading the *Grundrisse*, the more another deeper reason for the crisis that is internal to capital becomes evident: a limit that is a genuine 'limit', not simply an 'obstacle' or 'barrier'. Capital, Marx says,

---

14. Marx 1975–2005a, pp. 341–3, pp. 371–3.
15. Marx 1975–2005a, p. 472.
16. For instance, Marx 1975–2005a, p. 328.

is 'contradiction in movement', the embodiment of contradiction.[17] On the one hand, the exigency of valorisation impels it to maximise the quantity of labour 'sucked up' or absorbed. On the other hand, however, the methods that must be used in order to obtain surplus-value on a growing scale, and in particular the extraction of relative surplus-value, leads ineluctably to an expulsion, explicit or implicit, of workers from immediate production. They therefore lead to the exclusion from the 'hidden abode of production' of those human subjects that, alone, can deliver living labour, which is the exclusive source of the new value produced in the course of each period.

Initially, capital can resolve the difficulty by 'extending' or 'intensifying' labour-time in the individual labour-process. Another solution is to multiply the 'simultaneous' working days. This, seen properly, is precisely the other side of the coin of the multiplication of points of exchange and of points of production that we have said to be connected to the extraction of relative surplus-value: a multiplication that, in itself, signifies inclusion of new workers in the spiral of valorisation and extraction of new labour. Nonetheless, it seems to me to be relatively evident that Marx in the *Grundrisse* thinks that these processes will lead, sooner or later, to a fall of the rate of profit due to a purely economic dynamic. The reason lies, substantially, in the fact that the progressive augmentation of dead labour, of labour 'objectified' in the material elements of constant capital, does not have limits. The 'social working day' that can be extracted from a given working population, on the other hand, does have a limit. 'Living labour' that must be supplied by 'living workers', bearers of the 'labour-capacity', is, for Marx, a 'fluid'. Their labour-expenditure 'in actuality' is therefore elastic and able to be extended. But that is true within a determinate limit or ceiling.

Proceeding a little roughly, this capitalist drive opens up to a possible reading of the tendency of the fall of the profit-rate, whose residues are able to be found in Marx's subsequent reflections. The reasoning is as follows: at the level of the system, the numerator for the profit-rate is total gross profit. Let us imagine that the latter is identical to the total surplus-value, that is, that surplus-value is distributed entirely to 'industrial' capital. We can even add the hypothesis, which Marx tries out elsewhere, that the workers can live on air: a situation in which, seen properly, nobody would turn up on the labour-market to sell their labour-power to capital. If things were really so, variable capital would be zero, and surplus-value would absorb the entire social working day. Surplus-value would therefore be the most elevated possible, and the rate of profit would be at a 'maximum' (being the inverse of the composition of capital). It would be so because, even if the human beings, beyond living on air, lived only in order

---

17. Marx 1975–2005a, p. 350.

to work, so that the time of life would be dissolved entirely into labour-time, it would remain true that, with a defined working population, the social working day cannot exceed a certain upper limit.

Now we turn to the denominator of the rate of profit. The progressive augmentation of the elements of constant capital derives from the general tendency of the dynamic of capital that links the maximum possible extraction of labour and surplus-labour to the institution of a specifically capitalist mode of production. The 'material' growth of the means of production with respect to the workers is translated, by Marx, into a rise of constant capital relative to variable capital in terms of 'value'. In the case in which variable capital is zero, we must consider only the increase, tendentially without end, of constant capital: as a consequence, the escalation of the denominator proceeds without interruption. As constant capital progressively grows, the maximum rate of profit continually falls, which leads to the fact that sooner or later the actual rate of profit must also decline.[18]

The introduction of machines is a significant part of Marx's theorisation of the specifically capitalist mode of production, in its turn at the basis of the extraction of relative surplus-value and the tendential fall of the profit-rate. Another couple of points that are treated in the *Grundrisse* should be briefly mentioned in this perspective.

The machines are the 'body' of capital in its material constitution, which includes within itself 'labour'.[19] The means of production are no longer instrument of labour: on the contrary, it is labour that becomes an instrument of its instruments. This is an evident case of 'real hypostasis', of inversion of subject and predicate. Also in this case, an element of Marx's youthful critique of Hegel returns, transfigured, and becomes an essential and ineliminable part of the critique of capital. This inversion is essential in order to produce that increment of the productive power of social labour that is mystified as 'productivity of capital'. The property of producing surplus-product and surplus-value seems to be a 'natural' property of means of production and gold themselves, as 'things'. This 'fetishism', *Capital* will say in a better way, derives from the 'fetish-character' of capital: those 'things', when they are within the capitalist social relation, really have those 'supersensible' properties; not as a 'natural' character of 'things', but

---

18. Marx 1975–2005c, pp. 129 ff. What is proposed here is a 'reconstruction' of the spirit of Marx's argument, rather than a literal 'interpretation'.

19. Marx's notion of embodiment as 'inclusion' of labour within capital will be maintained and expanded in *Capital*. In that more mature work, there will be a crucial second meaning of 'embodiment', which does not seem equally present in the *Grundrisse*: namely, the 'incarnation' of the 'ghost' of value in the 'body' of gold as money. The point is further developed in Bellofiore 2008a and 2009a.

due to the social nature of capital. The same 'social' dimension of the cooperation within labour is imposed on the workers by capital.

It is not in fact an illusion. Science and its capitalist use enter into the machines, into the 'body' of the productive process. 'Wealth', that is, use-value, quantitatively and qualitatively, depends increasingly on the employment of the 'General Intellect'. For this, labour-time must at a certain point cease to be the measure. According to the *Grundrisse*, there would be here another reason for the 'breakdown' of production based on exchange-value:[20] an idea that has been taken up and valorised very greatly by an extensive literature, especially in Italy. But how these visionary pages are to be connected to the rest of the discourse contained in this manuscript is anything but given. We will return to this later.

The 'world-market' expresses the universalisation of capital: surpassing time and again its given limits, but reproducing and deepening its internal contradiction. Within production, there is constructed this 'material body' in which 'labour' is alienated, which now necessarily produces in a way that is internally 'socialised', and to which corresponds externally, in general exchange, an intensive network of universal relations. This occurs without there being a systematic law that guarantees the required proportionality of growth of this 'inner' and this 'outer'. The relation cannot but be imposed by the traumatic means of crisis.

An 'enormous consciousness'[21] is needed, the *Grundrisse* says, to recognise that in all this there is nothing but estranged labour. But it is capital itself, Marx maintains, that creates the conditions for this enormous consciousness. It is capital itself that renders possible a re-appropriation of the social power transferred into capital by the workers as a class: a re-appropriation that sometimes assumes a too easy character, almost automatic. Marx, in the thirty-second chapter of *Capital* on the historical tendency of capitalist accumulation – perhaps the true conclusion of the book – even uses the expression: 'The knell of capitalist private property sounds. The expropriators are expropriated'.[22] Both Luca Basso and Roberto Finelli are correct:[23] here, we are evidently dealing with clear traces of a philosophy of history. However, these failings are immersed in a more general reasoning that cannot be thrown away in haste, because it alludes – even if in a 'rude' form, and, as has been said, ambiguously – to the integration in a unitary line of reasoning of the theory of development and the theory of crisis, grafted onto a centrality of class-conflict in production. I will return also to this theme in the next two sections.

---

20. Marx 1975–2005c, pp. 90–2.
21. Marx 1975–2005a, pp. 390–1.
22. Marx 1975–2005d, p. 750.
23. Cf. Basso 2008b and Finelli 2008.

Limits and acquisitions of the *Grundrisse*

In order to render more transparent my judgement on the 'ambiguity' of the *Grundrisse*, I will now try to undertake an operation that is admittedly a little risky: namely, that of drawing up a kind of 'balance-sheet' with a list of points that can be placed in the 'assets' of the *Grundrisse*, of conquests that can be individuated in that text, on the one hand, and of points that are instead in the 'liabilities', of approximative formulations, which Marx must overcome in his subsequent theoretical journey, on the other.

We begin from the theory of money. In the *Grundrisse*, Marx deals with money in two great sections: for the first time at the beginning, for the second time towards the end of the manuscript.[24] He is evidently clarifying his ideas. I advance, here, a first hypothesis. In the first pages of a text that is recognised by almost everybody as being very Hegelian – more so than *Capital*, where this aspect becomes ever-lesser in the successive editions[25] – money, more than 'expounding' or 'exhibiting' the value and labour crystallised in it, 'represents' it in the sense of 'acting in its place' or 'standing in for it'. It is the second section on money, later on in the text, that takes a decisive step towards the later formulations. Whether this is true or not, the uncertainties of an analysis not definitively finished are certainly among the 'liabilities'. It is precisely this incompletion, however, that gives rise to two paths of research that should be ranked among the 'assets'.

The first is that of treating money, including its aspect as commodity-money, as a 'symbol': this is evidently linked to the fact that the expositive dialectic does not begin from the commodity and value, as in *Capital*. In these pages, precisely because of their nature as notes written for himself, Marx can allow himself to leap from one level of abstraction to another. Thus, once he has introduced capital, money is immediately defined essentially as a 'draft on new labour', a 'command over new labour'.[26] This characterisation necessarily has nothing to do with the existing quantity of labour already supplied. But it also necessarily has nothing to do with the quantities of labour that have produced money as a commodity.

This point is important because, conversely, in the first section of *Capital* Volume I, money as a commodity is an unavoidable category for founding the referral of value to labour by means of its 'monetary expression'. In the journey from the *Grundrisse* to *Capital*, Marx evidently realised the crucial nature of this point, which, furthermore, has often escaped most interpreters, both new and old.

---

24. Cf. Marx 1975–2005a, pp. 51–170 and Marx 1975c, pp. 171–98.
25. For a dissenting opinion, see Fineschi in this volume, and also Fineschi 2009c.
26. Marx 1975–2005a, p. 292.

Labour that produces individual commodities is a 'determinate' labour. Insofar as it is abstract labour, immediately private and only mediately social 'activity', an activity expended according to socially necessary labour-time, it corresponds to a 'value' still only 'imagined', that is, expressed in an 'ideal' money. When does this value really come concretely into existence? When, that is, is the abstraction of labour still only latent in immediate production eventually accomplished and perfected? When, in other terms, is living labour conceivable not only as useful activity, but doubled into 'concrete' labour (producer of use-value) and 'abstract' labour (producer of exchange-value, money)?

In *Capital*, Marx responds that the invisible abstract labour of the commodity becomes visible in the exchange quantitatively determined with gold, insofar as 'money as a commodity' is produced by concrete labour. The esoteric world of value makes itself exoteric thanks to the fact that the use-value gold – money as 'excluded' commodity – 'exposes' the exchange-value of any other commodity. In this same movement, not only is the use-value of gold as money that of being the universal purchasing power, but the concrete labour that produced that gold is demonstrated as the only 'immediately social' labour that 'exhibits' the abstract labour of any other commodity (insofar as spent according to the socially necessary labour-time). This vision moves from the point of view of the totality. It is complemented and animated by a dialectical exposition moving from the 'inner' towards the 'outer', and from the 'substance' towards the 'form': because that 'exhibition' of money corresponds also to a movement of 'expression' going from value to money, from the abstract labour that produces the commodities to the concrete labour that produces money. The totality, which includes production and final circulation of commodities as distinct moments, has a 'centre' in the social relation of production that includes the buying and selling of labour-power and the (capitalist) processes of labour.

The reasoning is crystal clear. Value in the single commodity, considered in its 'ideal' existence, is still nothing other than a pure 'ghost'. Marx says this, explicitly, in *Capital*. That spectre must 'take possession' of a body: in this sense, it must 'incorporate' or 'incarnate' itself. The body of which value takes possession is that of commodity-money: this is truly an 'embodiment' of value. If this is the case, 'money as a commodity' is in these pages essential not so much for the aspects of monetary theory (where the commodity-nature of money will be very much qualified subsequently within the categorial deduction of the three volumes) than for its function as guarantee of the very existence of a nexus between value and labour. Here is the pillar on which is essentially based that which, inappropriately but not nonsensically, has been defined as Marx's 'labour theory of value', but which is, rather, a 'value theory of labour'.[27]

---

27. For an extension, see Bellofiore 1989, and Bellofiore and Finelli 1998.

This connection between value and labour by means of money as a commodity is however not a little problematic. The 'interpretation' must at this point give way to a 'reconstruction', if we want to maintain a role for labour in Marxian value-theory. It cannot but be so, at least for those who are convinced that Marx's theory of value is above all a theory of exploitation. In the *Grundrisse*, in comparison to *Capital*, there seems to be a greater independence of money from its 'incarnation' in the commodity produced by labour. In the *1857–8 Manuscripts*, the vision of money as a 'symbol' that is at the same time a 'command of future labour' refers precisely to that path that elsewhere has appeared to me to be the most promising. This path establishes a connection between value and labour that is adequate to the capitalist mode of production: not, therefore, by means of money as 'universal equivalent', but rather by means of the 'bank financing of production'. The banks advance to the firms the nominal money wage-bill that allows the purchase of labour-power on the labour-market. The financing of production plays, here, the role of a monetary ante-validation of labour performance in capitalist production-processes. The underlining of the symbolic nature of money is related to a shift in the emphasis in Marxian value-theory. Now the monetary foundation of the identity between the new value added and the living labour of the wage-workers (which is, we recall, the activity spent in the period) takes centre-stage, instead of the identity between the 'objectified' labour in the commodity-product, labour only putatively social, against money, the only immediately social labour.

Let us move on from money to labour. I have already argued that 'labour' is a term that in the *Grundrisse* is used to cover too many different conceptual determinations. This will be progressively corrected in the successive expositions, until the clarity of the drafting of *Capital*, where the few exceptions will be accurately justified and qualified. In the *Grundrisse*, when Marx has to speak of 'living labour capacity', he uses the term 'labour-power', whose use is 'living labour'; that labour-power is an attribute of the workers insofar as they are human beings, and that labour is expended therefore by themselves. In *Capital*, when Marx speaks of 'labour', without any other qualification, he refers always with clarity to 'activity', to living labour, which is at the same time both concrete labour and abstract labour. In this confusion of the writing of the *Grundrisse* there is therefore another 'liability'. What can we count on the side of the 'assets'? The answer refers us back to the definition of 'abstract' labour that we can read in some sections of the *1857–8 Manuscripts*, where abstract labour is sometimes characterised by Marx as nothing other than the labour 'in movement' of the wage-worker.[28]

---

28. Marx 1975–2005a, pp. 221–4. The dual deduction of abstract labour from exchange as such and from the capital-relation is stressed by Napoleoni 1975.

Abstract labour is not, simply, the labour of a generic producer in a society of general commodity-exchange understood as a 'simple commodity society'. It is, instead, the labour of the separate producers of a capitalist society, of the many capitals in competition, where the workers are subjected to the capital-relation. This activity is 'abstract' insofar as the performance of the wage-worker tends to lose 'all craft-like character'. This is the side of Marx's reflection that Roberto Finelli has emphasised.[29] But there is more. The labour of the wage-workers 'lacks an object'. This 'lacking of an object' invests all dimensions of 'labour'; and it is perhaps only this that justifies in some way the terminological ambiguity in the use of this term by Marx. This lack invests 'living labouring capacity'; for the workers do not have property or possession of the means of production, and therefore cannot even procure for themselves the means of subsistence and are constrained to alienate their labour-power to the capitalist. It invests, consequently, also labour *qua* 'activity', insofar as the use of such capacity is now 'of the others'. Insofar as it is a product of an activity now itself 'estranged', the product itself also does not belong to them; it is the property of others. The worker, as human being, is 'naked subjectivity'. She exits from the process just as she entered it. She is 'absolute poverty', a 'pauper',[30] whatever her retribution might be.

It is in this ambiguity that we find the source of the totality of errors on which the first workerism was constructed in its 'ideological' and 'irrational' aspects: a current that flattens out labour as 'activity' onto labour as 'labour-capacity' and that refers 'living labour' back to the mere subjectivity of the living being.[31] The attribution of 'cooperation' as property of 'social' labour to living workers, and finally to any subject, before and independently of 'incorporation' in capital, also leads to this result.[32]

When Marx comes to the description of the introduction of machines – to the stages that later in the *1861–3 Manuscripts* and in the *Results of the Capitalist Process of Production* will give life to the 'specifically' capitalist mode of production and to the 'real subsumption of labour to capital' – it will be more clear that the concrete 'properties' of labour, just like the productive power of social labour, are in reality dictated and in some ways produced, by capital itself, which has, precisely, 'taken on a body'. A 'material body', a 'mechanical body', of monstrous traits, that renders the alterity of 'living' labour, labour 'in becoming', internal to objectified and dead labour, because it brings into itself the 'labour-capacity' and

---

29. Marx 1975–2005a, p. 223. Cf. Finelli 1987 and Finelli 2007, which is a comment on Arthur (cf. Arthur's effective reply in Arthur 2009a).
30. Marx 1975–2005a, p. 222. But also pp. 381–2 and pp. 522–3.
31. I refer, here, especially to Tronti and Negri. Cf. Tronti 1971 and Negri 1991.
32. Within this tradition, cf. the post–workerist writings of Virno 2007, Vercellone 2007, and Fumagalli 2008.

therefore the workers in flesh and bone. This monster now begins to work 'as if its body were by love possessed':[33] a citation from Goethe's *Faust*, which also appears once in the *Grundrisse*.

We should be very careful as we travel around this analytical hairpin-bend. Already in the *Grundrisse*, Marx maintains – without any nostalgia whatsoever, we should emphasise – that with production on a large scale, with properly capitalist production, labour as immediately concrete activity of the single individual is 'dissolved'. In *Capital*, he will be even sharper: the single worker is no longer able to produce commodities, because she is no longer able, alone, to produce any use-value. Thus she does not supply concrete labour. But the single worker is inserted within the working body of the 'factory'. It is this working body, combined and collective, that gives life to the commodity-product. This collective worker of the capitalist firm must always produce use-value for others on the market: otherwise, it would not produce the commodity, which is characterised by this duality of use-value and value, which is exposed and expressed in exchange-value. The 'collective' worker – constructed by, and subject to, capital – cannot not perform a certain activity with useful properties, and thus it remains true that this labour necessarily must have a concrete side alongside an abstract side. The 'concrete' labour for the collective worker does not ever disappear at all, in fact. The point here is not the deskilling, or degradation, or 'deconcretisation' of labour: different accents of the same incomprehension of Marx. The point is rather that the concrete 'qualities' are now attributed to the collective worker, but therefore to the firm in its unitary whole of 'objective' and 'subjective' factors, by an 'external' will and conscience, as Marx writes in the *Grundrisse*.

If, already in these pages, we encounter 'combined' labour, in *Capital* Marx will even speak, in terms of the capitalist 'factory', of 'immediately socialised' labour. 'Immediately socialised' labour is, for example, the productive activity as it occurs in the Indian community, or the labour-performance in future communism. In those social formations, 'total' or 'common' labour, which is always the 'social' foundation for production, is not employed within production, in activity, according to particular ways that could, in the firms within the various branches of production, not correspond to the 'technical average' or to 'social need'. In those societies, labour in production is rather 'immediately social'; that is, labour without need of passing through the mediation of money. Nonetheless, with the specifically capitalist mode of production, with the real subsumption of labour to capital, that activity is spent in the 'factory', in the workplaces, in a way now 'immediately socialised' whatever those 'things' are, material or immaterial, that assume the form of commodities. It becomes 'practically true' that labour,

---

33. Marx 1975–2005c, p. 90 (translated here as 'as though it had love in its bosom'). But see also Marx 1975a, pp. 398–9.

activity, within these capitalist *atelier*, is 'immediately socialised', because the technical division within production demands that there is a social connection *ex ante* within the productive unity. From the point of view of the division of labour within society, that is, of general exchange, labour thus 'combined' nevertheless remains an 'immediately private' labour: social labour only 'mediately', which must be given a sanction of sociality *ex post*. As much as it may appear paradoxical, the 'immediately socialised' labour of the capitalist producers is not an 'immediately social' labour; it is rather a labour that still has to 'become' social. This means, as we have seen, a continual enlargement and deepening of the sphere of exchanges.

Capital grows quantitatively on itself only if in the actual reality of the labour-processes it increasingly cancels the individual worker; if, therefore, in production the collective worker is substituted for the individual worker; if, finally, in exchange, capital itself is articulated in ever richer qualitative ways. For Marx, it is precisely in this internal and necessary dynamic that we can see the 'civilising side of capital', its 'historic role'. It is in this same dynamic that the irresistible march of capital in the constitution of the global market sets down its roots, as that which corresponds to relative surplus-value extraction.[34]

At this point we can discuss the 'theory of crisis', though very briefly. Here, once again, on the side of the inevitable 'liabilities', there is the fact that the theory of crisis in the *Grundrisse* is no more than a summary sketch. The point of arrival of the discourse on the crisis seems to me to be the formulation of a theory of the 'collapse' of capitalism: the 'tendential fall of the rate of profit'. It is a breakdown-rhetoric that not by chance joins up with the enthusiasm on the expansive and dynamic potentialities of capital that here and there makes even the *Manifesto of the Communist Party* itself seem a little pale. Marx will modify not a little this perspective in *Capital*, where he will be much more sober. Furthermore, he will develop the theme of the fall of the rate of profit differently, as a theory of the movements of profitability that is within the capitalist cycle. The traces of a 'secular', long-run reading of the fall in the rate of profit will however remain present in the background. I suspend the judgement on a cyclical reading of the fall of the rate of profit. But in its aspect as a secular fall, or even in its aspect as a reason for collapse, the 'tendential' fall of the rate of profit seems to me to be unsustainable. The reasons of this judgement can be clarified by recalling the successive developments of Marx's critical political economy. It is precisely the incessant innovative dynamic of capital, on which these same *1857–8 Manuscripts* insist, that lead to the continuous 'devaluation' of individual commodities, namely the cheapening of their value. The phenomenon affects

---

34. Marx 1975–2005a, pp. 334–7.

also, if not above all, the value of the 'elements' that constitute constant capital. If therefore the numerator of the maximum rate of profit has a ceiling, even if 'elastic', it is not in any way given that the denominator grows. On the contrary, it could even be reduced over time.

This is what is a 'liability' in the theory of crisis as it is presented in the pages of the *Grundrisse*. Among the 'assets' is a compact and coherent discourse about the crisis of realisation: compact because it comprehends in a unitary totality tendencies that in the more mature work are not ever found thus explicitly connected with each other; coherent because they do it in a way that perhaps will never again be so convincing. The line of reasoning to which I refer can be reconstructed in the following way. The definition of 'socially necessary' labour-time does not regard simply the technical average of the producers, but refers also to the correspondence of the production to social need, that which in *Capital* Volume III will be the dimension of 'ordinary' demand. For the first (and perhaps the only) time, with great clarity, Marx proposes in the *Grundrisse* a synthesis of the so-called disproportionality-crisis and of the crisis due to the so-called 'restricted consumption of the masses': these tendencies to crisis that in the *Manuscripts* of *Capital* Volume II and Volume III will be dislocated in different points in the categorical exposition.

Let us examine the matter more closely.[35] The extraction of relative surplus-value imposes, but also establishes, a multiplication of labours and of needs. The drive to the maximum increase of the rate of surplus-value, however, modifies without pause the equilibrium-ratios between different branches of production. 'Disproportions' are then more likely, and they may give way to an insufficiency of demand in significant spheres of production, compensated by excesses of supply in others. The consequent reduction of levels of production and employment in branches where there is excess supply generalises the glut of commodities to the economic system: this means that the disproportions turn into an excess of supply over demand for the whole system. This synthesis between disproportions and general overproduction gives us a suggestion that is in the spirit of the *Grundrisse*: to proceed to an integration in the theory of crisis that also includes, as immanent tendency, the tendential fall of the rate of profit itself.[36] This tendency is in fact contrasted even more efficaciously, and therefore not realised in a pure form, the more capital is able to increase the rate of surplus-value by means of a greater exploitation of labour. This means that the tendential fall of the rate of profit is overcome only if precisely the dynamic is reinforced that

---

35. Marx 1975–2005a, pp. 341–75.
36. Something along these lines has been hinted at, though only tentatively, by Napoleoni, in his lectures on crisis-theory at the University of Turin, 1971–2 and 1972–3, still unpublished. Cf. Bellofiore 2009b.

leads sooner or later to those disproportions that degenerate into the general overproduction of commodities. This, however, in its turn, and in determinate historical circumstances, can give way to struggles in the immediate production-process because the pressure on living labour is intensified. We have here the ultimate reason for the crisis of capital. It is a crisis that this time invests directly, in the capitalist processes of labour, the social relation of production, and that leads back to 'class-struggle in production'.

Is the controversial 'Fragment on machines' an 'asset' or a 'liability' in this first summary balance sheet?[37] Also here, I believe, we should see the 'Fragment' both as an asset and a liability. This text seems to me, in many respects, very confused: at the least, too cryptic. It appears to be grounded in a vision according to which the reduction of the labour-time contained in the single commodity would be equivalent to a fall of the extraction of labour that is the very foundation of capitalism.[38] It does not seem to me that this perspective can be maintained, at least from the point of view of Marx in his more mature work: but, fundamentally, also from the point of view that the *Grundrisse* itself presents.

The reduction of the labour-time crystallised in the single commodity means only that the labour-time (paid by capital) that is necessary for the reproduction of the working class according to a certain subsistence level is reduced, directly or indirectly. By means of the continual augmentation of the productivity of labour to which capital gives life, 'superfluous' labour-time is liberated, as time rendered 'disposable'. In other, more advanced modes of production, this greater disposable time could be dedicated to other activities, rather than obsessively to labour.[39] A partial liberation 'from' labour – that is the condition that renders possible the liberation 'of' labour itself, on which Marx insists in these same pages (for example, the sections on the vision of labour of Smith)[40] – could then be implemented. Only then can labour really become the first need. This is an essential dimension of the human being, according to Marx's most authentic perspective, that runs through all of his thought, from 1844 up to the *Critique of the Gotha Programme*. The original sin of capitalism, for Marx, is fundamentally, precisely this: that the totalisation, absorbing and exclusive, of labour ends up killing the active dimension of the human being.

But the Marx of *Capital* – but also, it seems to me, the Marx of some sections of the *Grundrisse* – tells us that capital does not ever realise a reduction of labour-time in this sense, that is, a shortening of the working day. The immanent

---

37. Marx 1975–2005c, pp. 90–2.
38. This mistake seems to lay behind the very different reading of the 'Fragment' offered by Negri 1978. For a critique, see Bellofiore and Tomba 2009.
39. On disposable time, cf. Marx 1975–2005c, pp. 92–4.
40. Marx 1975–2005a, pp. 529–33.

dynamic of capitalism means that the disposable time remains constrained in the cage of surplus labour-time, living labour 'sucked up' and 'appropriated' by capital. The very machines that 'incorporate' the 'General Intellect', those machines in which the extraction of relative surplus-value is realised, carry with them a turn of the screw in the extraction of absolute surplus-value. Furthermore, the extension of labour-time is accompanied by a greater intensity. The use of feminine and child-labour, and often the deskilling of large masses of labour-power, gives rise to a further saving on the cost of labour. There is a 'simultaneity' of times of exploitation.[41] Any sequential vision is fundamentally negated, in favour of a circular vision (or better, a 'spiral') of the relation between absolute surplus-value and relative surplus-value. More generallly, we have here an incredibly close imbrication of what the Marx of the *1861–3 Economic Manuscripts* and of the *Results of the Capitalist Process of Production* will call the 'formal subsumption' and the 'real subsumption' of labour to capital. From a certain point of view, there is, here, a deepening of the unavoidable 'negative side' of the tendency of expansion towards the world-market.

If this critical reference to *Capital* justifies the location of the 'Fragment on the Machines' among the 'liabilities', there are arguments that tend in the other direction. Fundamentally, Marx is fairly clear in these pages on the fact that, when he speaks of the 'productivity of capital', he is referring to productivity in terms of real 'wealth'; therefore, he refers to the productivity in terms of use-values. In the commodity, as we know, there is always 'use-value' and (exchange-) 'value'. Capital, which produces commodities in order to produce money and more money, organises and commands a 'collective' worker. This 'combined' worker is also a technical body on which capital sets its stamp. The material, quantitative, side of this process cannot be unfastened from its 'formal determination', which marks the qualitative side of the commodity-product that is always to be realised on the market, in final circulation. It follows immediately that the passage on the 'General Intellect' and on the 'collapse' of production based on exchange-value cannot be read separately from the tendency to general overproduction of commodities, induced in its turn by the combination of the 'disproportions' and of the 'restricted consumption of the masses'.[42] That tendency places radically in doubt the possibility that the greater use-value is able to be produced and is confirmed as such on the final market.

The reason for this is soon given. The potential shortening of the working day that the 'specifically' capitalist mode of production carries with it cannot be actually realised, due to capital's inexhaustible hunger for 'living' labour and

---

41. This point is rightly stressed by Tomba 2007.
42. A very rich reading of the 'Fragment' along these lines is proposed by Napoleoni 1976.

surplus-labour of capital. However, it is precisely this tendency to the maximisation of surplus-labour that leads to the concretisation, sooner or later, of a limit to capital posed by capital itself: because this means the general crisis from the side of demand. We could thus, following the logical path of the *Grundrisse*, propose the following argument: capital, expanding, needs more market. An extension of the market requires a development of needs, which in its turn leads to the constitution of 'universally developed individuals'. But there are universally developed individuals only if a shortening of the working day is enacted at a certain point; only if, in other words, the disposable labour-time is not translated integrally into surplus labour-time, but also into time dedicated to something other than production. This, however, is exactly what capital, given its very nature, cannot allow, if not forced by social conflict and within determinate limits. The 'self-valorisation' of capital depends on the fact that money and means of production and means of subsistence, *qua* capital, are dead labour that must transform itself into a 'vampire', an 'undead' that incessantly 'sucks up' evermore labour and surplus-labour as activity 'in becoming'.

It is due to this that the 'theft of alien labour-time' becomes a 'miserable foundation' for the development of the productive forces. In other words, it is due to a broader reasoning that integrates the 'Fragment on machines' within the discourse on the crisis of overproduction. It is in this larger context that we can comprehend in what sense the 'General Intellect' and the 'collapse' of production based on (exchange-) value go together – without placing in discussion in any way the validity of the Marxian value-theory as a theory of the exploitation of 'labour'.

An actualisation

This unitary reading of different theories of crisis, which includes in its logical line the 'Fragment on machines', opens up to a 'actualisation' of the conceptual acquisitions present in the *Grundrisse*. This reading is possible only beginning from the result achieved by Marx's theoretical journey: only by reading the *Grundrisse* after *Capital*. At the same time, and inversely, it allows the reciprocal movement: to re-read *Capital* in the light of the *Grundrisse*; this time, however, not reading the *Grundrisse* 'against' *Capital*, but 'together' with *Capital*.

In effect, on the basis of the reasoning that I have presented here, we can suggest that Marx's theory of value, as theory of exploitation and of crisis at the same time, has been revealed and continues to be revealed today as valuable as ever in the reconstruction of the capitalist dynamic. This judgement can be better understood if we have in mind an extremely synthetic historical sketch of the great phases of the accumulation of capital, from the end of the nineteenth century to today. The end of the nineteenth century and the beginning of the twentieth century can be contextualised without great difficulty by using the lens of the 'tendential' fall of the rate of profit in its relatively 'traditional' reading, which I have argued can be found more in the *Grundrisse* than in *Capital*. The composition of capital increased in value-terms, and at a certain point it increased more than the rate of surplus-value could counter. The consequence was the crisis that went by the name of the Great Depression in the late nineteenth century.

Capital reacted with an attack on the class-composition of the then prevalent 'craft-workers'. Fordism – understood as technical-productive innovation, and not in the meaning attached to this term by the regulation-school – is the emblematic point of this response, which ends with modifying radically the technical/social body of the factory, incorporating elements of Taylorism and of other organisational innovations that were diffused before WWI. The 'assembly-line', increasing intensity as well as the productive power of labour (because it modified, at the same time, the techniques of production) was able to succeed where instead Taylorism had encountered a barrier (because the impulse towards high intensity took place on a non-modified technical basis). In this context, the rate of surplus-value began to grow more than the value-composition of capital.

At a certain point, however, that made capitalism fall into a crisis from overproduction due to the insufficiency of effective demand in the entire economic system. Contributing to this was the overlapping of the speculative and financial dynamics that in the 1920s first produced euphoria, and then led the financial instability to degenerate into panic and debt-deflation. The Great Crash that followed the stock-market crisis of 1929 and then extended throughout the 1930s can thus be read, again without great difficulty, using the lenses of the crisis of generalised overproduction of commodities for the intersecting of 'disproportions' and 'restricted consumption of the masses', as in the *Grundrisse*.

The consequence was not, once again, the 'final collapse', the breakdown of capitalism. If anything, it meant the drastic redefinition of the constitution of capital, one of the many structural turning points that periodically reshape capitalism. It gave way to the affirmation of the 'mass-worker' and of Keynesianism, and before that to the Second World War, as the way out from depression and permanent stagnation. Warfare and welfare: a pair that characterised, indissolubly, the Keynesian era that many unilaterally recall as a 'Golden Age'. Intertwined with the increasingly more important role that the state began to assume within the economy is the considerable expansion of forms of labour and of strata not directly productive of surplus-value. If that favoured capital from the point of view of the realisation of commodities on the market, it imposed at the same time an ever-greater pressure on the extraction of surplus-value from the workers directly producing value, who had to sustain the entire class-structure. For this reason, once again, the mechanism depended on the continuous increase of the rate of exploitation in immediate production: such dependence, indeed, increased.

Here, between the 1960s and 1970s, a further form of crisis emerged, one that can be described as an authentic, directly 'social crisis' rooted in class-struggle at the point of production and in the capital-relation. The accent on the dialectic of dead labour and living labour, which runs through all of Marx, renders it perfectly comprehensible, and is in someway its code. 'Labour as subjectivity', to use the words of the *Grundrisse* (that is, the workers) is included within capital, thanks to the fact that capital has acquired their labour-power on the labour-market. This labour-power, this 'labour-capacity', has to become ever-more 'liquid' living labour until capital attains, for itself and for immediately unproductive strata, surplus-value in an absolutely and relatively growing quantity. But the 'fluid' of living labour has to be extracted from bearers of labour-power, and the bearers of labour-power are the workers themselves, a determinate social subject that can 'resist' or must be induced or forced to cooperate.

Marx is very clear. Capital is characterised by a 'real hypostasis', by an inversion in which the predicate dominates the subject. In what sense? For capital, what counts is labour-power, and the workers are simply bearers of this potential 'labour-capacity'. The same is the case for living labour: the worker must be dragged into the hidden abode of production, because labour-power is stuck to the worker, and only she supplies 'labour' as such. It is not possible 'to use' labour-power without making the worker labour as a socially determined human being. As we have seen, she is a worker who produces ever less in an 'isolated' way, and who is increasingly a part of a 'combined' and 'collective' worker. Capital is not interested in the worker as such, it is interested in labour, which is the source of value; but in order to have labour, it must acquire labour-power. It must, therefore, include and subordinate workers in immediate production. In the *Grundrisse*, Marx argues that capital's preference would be to obtain labour without workers. It is true that, once acquired by capital, labour-power is 'capital's' labour-power; and thus also its use, the performance of labour, is capital's. Nonetheless, it is equally true that living labour cannot but remain always, and simultaneously, an activity of the worker. This is the basis for the unavoidable 'class-struggle in production'.

This refers to a problem in which we find the essence of Marx's theory of value. This is a problem that is already posited in the *Grundrisse*, but in a still preliminary and confused way, at least in the sense of exposition. It is a problem that would, rather, be made clear in *Capital*, until it constitutes its true hidden 'centre' and moves its dialectic, beginning from Volume I: the problem of the contradictory internal unity, in capital, of labour-power and living labour in the figure of the worker, or, better, of the workers as a social subject, as a class. Paradoxically, however, precisely the confusion of the *Grundrisse* gives the possibility of thematising this internal unity between the various determinations of 'labour' and their possible contradiction, because in the *Grundrisse*, 'labour as subjectivity' synthesises in an extreme form, on the one hand, labour as 'potency', and, on the other hand, labour as 'activity', within 'subjectivity'. There is a unity of 'living labour-capacity' and 'living labour' in the 'living worker'. The point is then that the real inversion of capital cannot ever be realised all the way down. Labour must forever be extracted from workers in flesh and blood. That labour, though in alienation, in its being 'alien' and 'estranged', inevitably remains the activity of the workers: it remains always 'their' labour, as well as capital's. Here is the key to capital as a 'contradiction in movement'.

The 'social' crisis of the relations of production between the end of the 1960s and the beginning of the 1970s to which I referred – in extreme synthesis: the capacity that the 'mass worker' then had to contribute in an essential way to the rupture of the process of valorisation in that historically defined figure of capital – can be read relatively easily within an optic of this kind. The reverse is also true. Those struggles opened to dimensions of Marx's work that had remained latent and little understood before. At the same time, this reading also allows us to understand the reaction of capital to those struggles, which has determined our present. The new emerging configuration of the labour-capital relation, permanent and still always changing within capitalism, helps us to re-read Marx once again: the Marx of *Capital*, just as the Marx of the *Grundrisse*.

Indeed, what is the globalisation and the financancialisation of our days?[43] Let us take up again the theory of money as 'symbol' in the *Grundrisse*. The manipulation of the symbolic nature of money is an essential part of the new forms of economic policies, which are nothing but a mediated 'command' over labour. It is by these means that the 'casualisation' of labour becomes universal. Casualisation is, in its turn, the other side of an unprecedented 'centralisation without concentration'. The merging of capitals, the 'centralisation', no longer proceeds along with technical 'concentration'. At least in this sense: that the 'large scale' of production, the use of science within it, the design and the capitalist use of machines and knowledge – in short, the mode of production that is 'specific' to capital, and with it that extraction of relative surplus-value that brings along with it greater extension and intensity of labour – do not necessarily anymore require an increase in the technical dimension of the units of production, the continuous broadening of the 'factory', the amassing of workers in the same site,

---

43. The reader is referred to Bellofiore 1999 and 2001, and Bellofiore and Halevi 2009a and 2009b.

their juridical and qualitative homogenisation. The accumulation of capital does not necessarily mean anymore, as Marx correctly maintained for his time and as was the case for at least the century after him, the augmentation of the workers commanded by single capitals in the same place of production, under the same roof. From being a 'tendency', both the concentration of capital as well as the homogenisation of the workers appear to become a 'counter-tendency'. The fragmentation and dispersion of labour is now the 'tendency'.

It is exactly in this overturning of 'tendency' and 'counter-tendency' that we find the ultimate response of capital to the 'social' crisis of the 1960s/1970s: the cause, in the last instance, of that dramatic 'deconstruction' of 'labour' that is the condition of current valorisation, and which, however, creates the seeds of new crises and new conflicts. To be sure, in this reading that sets in tension the *Grundrisse* and *Capital* there emerges, so to speak, a Marx 'against' Marx. But the unprecedented character of the 'new' capitalism that cannot be found in the letter of the texts – except if we reduce Marx to the dubious status of a prophet or engage in idiosyncratic readings – cannot ever be comprehended if not by 'beginning' anew from Marx. We must begin from a Marx that is, above all, his value-theory, with the centrality of the living labour of the wage-worker and of money as capital; while purging it, however, of those excesses of optimism on the historical role of capital and of those seeds of the philosophy of history that the *Grundrisse* contains in ample proportions.

Translated by Peter D. Thomas

Method: From the *Grundrisse* to *Capital*
Juan Iñigo Carrera

Questions of method: concerning the point of departure

In August 1857, Marx began writing the drafts of what was eventually to become *Capital*, now published as the *Grundrisse*. In the opening lines of the manuscript, he states: 'Individuals producing in society – hence socially determined individual production – is, of course, the point of departure'.[1]

In the same notebooks, he laid out the sequence that the development of his ideas was to take: '(1) the general, abstract determinants which obtain in more or less all forms of society, but in the above-explained sense. (2) The categories which make up the inner structure of bourgeois society . . .'.[2]

Marx had earlier established the need for the same point of departure together with Engels.[3] However, barely a year after penning that first draft, and as a direct consequence of it, he started working on the *Contribution to the Critique of Political Economy*, making the commodity his new starting point.[4] From then onwards, Marx not only re-vindicated this latter beginning of the critique of political economy but, when presenting it in the opening paragraph of *Capital*, also stated its necessity: 'The wealth of those societies in which the capitalist mode of production prevails,

1. Marx 1993, p. 83.
2. Marx 1993, p. 108.
3. Marx and Engels 2004, p. 42.
4. Marx 1911, p. 19.

presents itself as "an immense accumulation of commodities", its unit being a single commodity. Our investigation must, therefore, begin with the analysis of a commodity'.[5]

Towards the end of his life, Marx once again emphasised the necessity of this starting point: 'In the first place, I do not start out from "concepts", hence I do not start from the "concept of value", and do not have "to divide" these in any way. What I start out from is the simplest social form in which the labour-product is presented in contemporary society, and this is "the commodity"'.[6]

Only the actual argument unfolded in the text of the *Grundrisse* mediates in the shift from the starting point laid out in its first paragraph cited above to the one in the *Contribution*. The text of the *Grundrisse* itself must, therefore, be the place in which to seek the traces left by that transition.

Several Marxist theorists have considered that the change in the point of departure reflects the passage from the process of inquiry to that of presentation, whose different modalities Marx alluded to in *Capital*.[7] Thus, some scholars have asserted that the development leading from the *Grundrisse* to *Capital* essentially pertains to the presentation.[8] Furthermore, others have claimed that the dialectical development only belongs to the method of presentation.[9] Finally, some authors have argued that Marx deliberately tried to conceal the method of inquiry in the published versions of his critique of political economy.[10] The implication of this line of argument is that any attempt to find the key to the method of inquiry would have to focus on the *Grundrisse*, rather than on *Capital*. However, one cannot but wonder whether the change in the point of departure is not, rather, a development of the method of inquiry itself, which only reaches its plenitude in *Capital*. In this case, the key to the question lies in recognising the actual concrete content of that development.

This question of the redefinition of the point of departure places us squarely before another problem. In the *Grundrisse*, Marx begins his study of capitalist economic forms by firstly taking as his object the categories established by political economy. He thus faces the determinations of value by engaging in a critique of the theory of the 'time-chit': 'The point to be examined here is the convertibility of the time-chit. . . . [A] few observations can be made about the delusions on which the time-chit rests, which allow us an insight into the depths of the

---

5. Marx 1965, p. 35.
6. Marx 2002, p. 241.
7. Marx 1965, p. 19.
8. Rosdolsky 1977, p. 189.
9. Fraser 1997, pp. 97–8; Carchedi 1993, pp. 195–7; Arthur 1993, p. 68.
10. Nicolaus 1993, p. 60; Reichelt 1995, p. 41.

secret which links Proudhon's theory of circulation with his general theory – his theory of the determination of value'.[11]

One can recognise a similar approach to the real subject matter in his 1844 Paris manuscripts:

> We have started out from the premises of political economy. We have accepted its language and its laws.... It is true that we took the concept of *alienated labour* (*alienated life*) from political economy as a result of the movement of *private property*.[12]

In contrast, Marx opens the *Contribution* with his own positive unfolding of the determinations of the commodity. It is precisely this latter development that culminates with the *raison d'être* of the categories of political economy, including the theory of the time-chit. In other words, the critique of political economy no longer proceeds by accompanying the development of the theories of political economy up to the point in which the critical discussion puts it before the need to address the real determination. On the contrary, the critique starts by confronting the real determination itself and follows it in its development to the point where the categories of political economy are revealed as necessary ideological forms of existence of that real determination. This new course of the argument only reaches maturity in *Capital*, especially in the definitive version of the first chapter in the second edition. Marx begins there by unfolding the determinations of the commodity, and concludes the dialectical development contained in that chapter by showing how both classical and vulgar political economy are two necessary forms taken by consciousness held captive by commodity-fetishism.[13] Once again, we face the question of the nature of the methodological change entailed by the modification in the form of Marx's argument. Just as the result of this change materialises for the first time in the *Contribution*, we are only able to track down the path of its development in the text of the *Grundrisse*.

Representation or reproduction of the concrete

The second way in which the point of departure is transformed puts us before a third methodological issue that is far more intriguing and complex. No reader, much less one well versed in current scientific research-methods, could have failed to notice a peculiar aspect of the aforementioned quotation from the *Notes on Adolph Wagner*: 'In the first place, I do not start out from "concepts"...'

---

11. Marx 1993, p. 136.
12. Marx 1992a, p. 322, 332.
13. Marx 1965, pp. 80–3.

How so? Is not the representation of reality that arises of necessity from the definition of concepts or theoretical categories the only method of developing scientific knowledge? Nowadays, two main forms of human knowledge can be distinguished: intuition, namely immediate non-rational knowledge, and rational conception, namely the representation that starts from concepts and establishes relations among them according to a constructive necessity, that is, a *logic* (more on this below). However, in the *Grundrisse*, Marx opposes a third form of knowledge to those two, which he defines not only as having a rational character, but also as a way of overcoming representation as such: 'The concrete is concrete because it is the concentration of many determinations, hence unity of the diverse. It appears in the process of thinking, therefore, as a process of concentration, as a result, not as a point of departure, even though it is the point of departure in reality and hence also the point of departure for observation [*Anschauung*] and conception [*Vorstellung*].[14] Along the first path the full conception was evaporated to yield an abstract determination; along the second, the abstract determinations lead towards a reproduction of the concrete by way of thought'.[15]

The name of each method itself indicates the specific differences between them. To *represent* the concrete means taking its manifestations as they are presented to us at face-value, in order to present them once again as if they were subject to relationships of necessity dictated by the constructive logic of representation itself. Those manifestations can be either those that appear immediately to our eyes, or those that can only be apprehended through the mediation of an analytic process that has managed to abstract the manifestations themselves based on the (more or less) universal features of the concrete in question. However, regardless of the degree of detail achieved by the analysis, the necessity represented always corresponds to the externality of the manifestations that it has put in relation to each other. Penetrating this externality to extract the true necessity at stake is, by definition, alien to its aim.

By contrast, *reproducing* the concrete by means of thought implies that the course taken by the progression of ideas must be the same as that followed by the development of the necessity of the concrete, namely by its determination, in its real actuality. The movement of thought cannot introduce any necessity

---

14. Nicolaus translates *Vorstellung* as 'conception'. Hegel uses the term *Vorstellung* to refer to thought that stops at the apparent exteriority of its object, precisely in opposition to conceptual thought, which, always via an idealist inversion, engenders the object as a concrete form of realising its concept (see Inwood 1992, pp. 257–9). Putting the question of the forms of knowledge back on its feet, although a conception is the result of the process of representing something, the actual term *representation* expresses directly the very form of the method utilised.

15. Marx 1993, p. 101.

not found in its real object. Thus, it cannot resort to any constructive necessity that establishes a certain point of departure. Consequently, this form of knowledge cannot start out from concepts, but only from the actual concrete.

The existence of two methods of rational thought that are essentially at odds may appear strange. However, this could not have been the case for Marx, who was very familiar with Hegel's work and who had 'skimmed' once more through *The Science of Logic* while writing the *Grundrisse*.[16] In his texts, Hegel persistently contrasts dialectics – which he terms 'speculative thought' in his idealistic inversion – and the method of representation that bases its constructions on formal foundations, that is, on the formal externality of its object.[17] However, his idealistic inversion made him stop at the appearance that the unfolding of logical necessity itself engenders the real. His own theory was thus condemned to being a representation of reality.

Now, beyond principally formal references, the contrast between *representation* and *reproduction* has received scant attention from Marxist theorists working on the issue of method in the *Grundrisse* and its relationship with Hegel's method. In general terms, the specificity of the method developed by Marx is presented as if this were an issue bearing on the form of the constructive necessity, hence of the logic used, and thus as if it were about the difference between two kinds of representation. In some cases, *representation* and *reproduction* are employed as interchangeable terms.[18] On the other hand, even those who recognise that Marx opposes his method to representation tend to replace the term *reproduction* [*Reproduktion*] with that of *reconstruction*.[19] The etymology of this word refers to the joining of elements that are mutually external to each other. In that condition of mutual exteriority, they therefore lack any immanent necessity to establish a relation. The latter can only be established through a necessity stemming from the constructive process itself rather than from its object. As Hegel pointed out – precisely in order to show the limits of representation – maybe this is a case in which 'that which is known in general terms, precisely for being *known*, is not acknowledged'.[20]

Now, it is clear that since its foundation political economy has known no other method than that of logical representation. Yet, the paragraph quoted above where Marx presents the method of the *reproduction* of the concrete flows directly from this one:

---

16. Marx and Engels 1983, p. 248.

17. See Hegel 1999, pp. 458–61, pp. 496–8, pp. 624–5; Hegel 1977, pp. 8–9, 18–20, 34–43.

18. Musto 2008, p. 15.

19. Dussel 1985, p. 33, p. 48, p. 52; Smith 1990, p. 20, pp. 34–5, p. 60; Psychopedis 1992, p. 33; Meaney 2002, p. 3; Ilyenkov 1982, p. 136.

20. Hegel 1977, p. 18; translation modified.

> The economists of the seventeenth century, e.g., always begin with the living whole, with population, nation, state, several states, etc.; but they always conclude by discovering through analysis a small number of determinant, abstract, general relations such as division of labour, money, value, etc. As soon as these individual moments had been more or less firmly established and abstracted, there began the economic systems, which ascended from the simple relations, such as labour, division of labour, need, exchange value, to the level of the state, exchange between nations and the world market. The latter is obviously the scientifically correct method.[21]

How is it possible for Marx to say that the method used by political economy is the right one, while at the same time defining the outcome of its deployment as *reproduction*, in opposition even to political economy's own self-understanding of the nature of its theories as *representations* of reality?

Furthermore, in the afterword to the second edition of *Capital*, as in the *Theories of Surplus Value*, Marx indicates how the method used by classical political economy leaves room for the element of vulgar political economy to emerge. He also highlights how, on the basis of such a methodological approach, the historical development of political economy reveals it as a form of consciousness doomed to lose all scientific content in order to become the pure apology for the capitalist mode of production as the latter progresses towards its own supersession:

> For the development of political economy and of the opposition to which it gives rise keeps pace with the *real* development of the social contradictions and class conflicts inherent in capitalist production. Only when political economy has reached a certain stage of development and has assumed well-established forms ... does the separation of the element whose notion of the phenomena consists of a mere reflection of them take place, i.e., its vulgar element becomes a special aspect of political economy. ... Since such works only appear when political economy has reached the end of its scope as a science, they are at the same time the *graveyard* of this science.[22]

In utter contrast to this destiny of political economy inherent in its method, Marx defines the historical role of the method of the critique of political economy, 'my dialectical method', by stating: 'In its rational form it is a scandal and abomination to bourgeoisdom and its doctrinaire professors, because it includes in its comprehension and affirmative recognition of the existing state of things, at the same time also, the recognition of the negation of that state, of its inevitable breaking up; because it regards every historically developed social form as in fluid movement, and therefore takes into account its transient nature not less

---

21. Marx 1993, pp. 100–1.
22. Marx 1971, pp. 921–2.

than its momentary existence; because it lets nothing impose upon it, and is in its essence critical and revolutionary'.[23]

On the other hand, the same point made by Marx about the two historical stages followed by classical political economy – from its seventeenth-century beginnings to its maturity with the works of Smith and Ricardo – makes it clear that its naturalisation of capitalist relations does not derive, *pace* Rosdolsky,[24] from the fact that it confines its procedure to the analytical stage without subsequently returning to the more concrete forms.

Once we disregard any possibility of incoherence on Marx's part, the only possible answer is that, while both methods (logical representation and the ideal reproduction of the concrete) go through the two-fold path of analysis and synthesis, each form of scientific knowledge undertakes each of these two steps in different concrete forms. These concrete forms need to be so different from each other that their respective outcomes are, in one case, the *representation* of the concrete in thought and, in the other, the *reproduction* of the concrete in thought. What is more, their difference must be so profound that while the historical development of the former turns it into 'the graveyard of science' and the apologetic for capitalist social relations, the other becomes the scientific form of consciousness which buries those social relations. The divergence in historical trajectories does not arise from taking a different real content as an object of inquiry, but from the very form in which the same content is appropriated in thought.

It is thus clear that Marx's methodological remarks at the start of the *Grundrisse* do not constitute an unproblematic synthesis that could straightforwardly resolve the issue of the specificity of the method of the critique of political economy. On the contrary, they raise more questions than answers. The 1857 introduction provides no more than a concise rendition of certain aspects of the dialectical method whose content must be further developed in a critical fashion. In this chapter, we shall therefore firstly elaborate on the question of the difference in form between the representation and the reproduction of the concrete in thought. On this basis, we shall subsequently discuss the other two methodological evolutions on which we commented above that lead from the *Grundrisse* to the *Contribution* and *Capital*.

---

23. Marx 1973, p. 20.
24. Rosdolsky 1977, p. 567.

The methods of scientific knowledge[25]

Both the representation and the reproduction of the concrete are constructions of an ideal nature, in other words, constructions of thought. As Marx points out, both start by facing a real concrete. Moreover, both aim to appropriate in thought the determinations of the concrete in question with a view to intervene in its development, that is, to act upon it. Both intend to give such an action the character of an action that is objectively aware of its own cause. In this sense, they depart from the premise of not accepting any necessary content other than that found in its object, nor forcing on its object any necessity springing from the subjectivity of the researcher. In turn, this means that they begin by facing the real concrete in order to go beyond the appearance that it presents to immediate cognition in search of its true determination. In other words, both methodological approaches begin with the *analysis* of the real concrete. In the following sections, we explore in more detail each form of the process of cognition in order to bring out the fundamental differences that set the two scientific methods apart.

Logical representation

Let us start by examining the way in which the analysis characteristic of logical representation conceives the foundations of its own objectivity. The latter is seen as ruling out all possibility that an existing concrete may carry within itself a causal necessity other than the immediate manifestation of its very form. On this basis, there is no other possible expression of the general nature of causality other than the greater or lesser regularity of its manifestations. It follows that the analysis that leads from the immediate concrete to the discovery of the most simple and general determination must consist in the identification of recurring attributes.[26] Therefore, the necessity of its simplest concepts and categories is founded on the repeated presence of an attribute in the original concrete. The qualitative development that determines the general, specific and singular is represented indistinctly from, if not confused with, the merely quantitative development of the universal, particular and individual. This also implies that those simpler concepts are obtained by assuming a *purely ideal* concrete bereft of non-recurring real attributes. They therefore cannot correspond to any *actually existing* concrete simpler than that with which the analysis began.

---

25. I have originally presented the fundamental aspects of the following discussion on method in Iñigo Carrera 1992 and Iñigo Carrera 2008, pp. 235–368.

26. Hempel 1965, pp. 231, pp. 253–4.

Once the degree of repetition considered sufficient for the abstraction of those general concepts from the original concrete has been achieved, the process must reverse its direction. In this second phase, the representation of the concrete arises as a unity in which the more and less general concepts obtained in the analytical phase are placed in a necessary relation to each other. Thus, on the basis of the simplest necessary element identified in the first phase, progress is subsequently made by re-incorporating the attributes formerly excluded as accidental, or, in other words, by removing 'simplifying assumptions'. However, given that the analysis began by conceiving each concrete as devoid of any causal necessity that transcends the objectivity of its immediate affirmation, the concepts arising from it cannot but preserve this condition. As a result, they must be placed in relation to each other by recourse to a *constructive necessity* that is inevitably external to them and that simultaneously preserves the mutual externality of those concepts in the represented unity. *Logic* is thus this constructive necessity which represents all objective connection as if it were an external relationship between concepts. It gives coherence to the reciprocal externality of all concepts and relationships involved in representation based on its own necessarily tautological nature. Hence the tautological nature of the synthesis itself.[27]

True, most Marxist authors referred to earlier do not necessarily subscribe to this manner of proceeding.[28] They oppose to it what they define as a dialectical approach. However, they rarely explicitly state the specific form that the analysis should take within the dialectical investigation. Thus, it is stated that the key resides in distinguishing between necessary and contingent moments,[29] between empirical and substantive abstractions,[30] or between general and determinate abstractions.[31] These contributions recognise that abstract forms must be sought within more concrete ones. However, they usually do not explain either the way in which this search should be made, or the basis on which those differences could be established. In the cases in which the form of analysis is made explicit, this is sometimes seen as entailing the repetition of common attributes (thus not differing from representational analysis).[32] Alternatively, other scholars have characterised the analytical process in a Cartesian fashion, namely, as the decomposition of the complex totality into mutually external simple elements.[33] Finally, some authors have argued that elemental concepts should be defined in terms of the aim or finality of the theoretical construction, in other words, that

---

27. Carnap 1959, p. 143, p. 145.
28. An obvious exception is that of analytical Marxists. See Burns 2000, pp. 86–98.
29. Reuten 1988, p. 143.
30. Bonefeld 1992, pp. 104–5.
31. Fraser 1997, p. 93.
32. Dussel 1985, p. 33.
33. Murray 1988, pp. 121–9; Dussel 1985, p. 51.

they should be posited by the criterion of the researcher *prior to* the scientific development itself.[34]

Given that the concepts arising from these modes of analysis are bereft of a necessity which would drive them to self-transcendence, the relationship between them is represented by a constructive necessity defined as a *dialectical logic*. In some cases, it is stated that a concept should be logically derived from another until a system is structured, although the concrete form in which this process is to take place is not actually explained.[35] In other cases, the derivation is founded in a parallel with the development of Hegel's *Logic*,[36] or in the doubling of abstract notions,[37] or in the unfolding of determined categories as the condition of existence of determinant ones.[38] Other approaches see dialectical logic as involving the attempt to place the parts in a relationship to the whole, which implies relapsing into a process of synthesis in which the general and specific are reduced to the mutually external nature of the universal and particular.[39] In all cases, the inevitable result is a concrete in thought whose nature as the outcome of a purely ideal intertwining of concepts is beyond question, hence its condition as a systematic conceptual representation in opposition to a reproduction.[40]

Other Marxist conceptions posit that the dialectical-logical development should be driven forward by the tendencies for determinate actions of social agents that are intrinsic to the social form referred to by each theoretical category,[41] or by the practical insufficiency of each form achieved.[42] However, these approaches do not explain how to solve the rift that these procedures generate in the actual consistency of the conceptual development. On the one hand, this implies following a sequence that responds to a constructive necessity, and on the other, a sequence that follows the movement of the real concrete itself.[43]

These ideas have provided the grounds for the claim that developments based on dialectical logic are not tautological in nature.[44] However, the very same developments undertaken with the purpose of structuring a dialectical logic capable of bringing coherence to the representation of the concrete as a unity of opposites have concluded that such logic necessarily requires each of them to

---

34. Mattick 1993, p. 122; Smith 1990, pp. 34, 68; Psychopedis 1992, p. 34.
35. Foley 1986, pp. 3–11.
36. Uchida 1988; Arthur 1993, p. 73; Smith 1990; Murray 1988, pp. 161, 184, 231.
37. Reuten 1988, p. 52.
38. Arthur 1993, p. 67; Carchedi 1987, p. 75.
39. Dussel 1985, p. 52.
40. Marx 2002, p. 244.
41. Smith 1993, pp. 19–20.
42. Mattick 1993, p. 128.
43. Marx 2005, pp. 120–4.
44. Arthur 1993, p. 67.

be defined as simple immediate affirmations.[45] This is not a circumstantial fact. If each pole were accorded the capacity to affirm through self-negation, it would then have to be recognised as the bearer of a necessity whose realisation would set it into *self*-movement independently of its opposite. In this case, one would have to accept that the introduction of a constructive necessity representing all movement as a relationship between opposites would be redundant. What is more, inasmuch as this logical movement would collide with the real one of affirmation through self-negation, it would lead the process of cognition towards incoherence. Hence the external and tautological nature underlying, in the last instance, all conceptual relationships representing the real movement by means of a dialectical logic.[46]

Let us now see how the application of this method appears in the very point of departure of political economy. For example, Adam Smith uses it to ground the simplest determination on which to develop his theory of the organisation of social life. 'The principle which gives occasion to the division of labour', he argues, stems from 'a certain propensity in human nature ... to truck, barter, and exchange one thing for another' whose discovery lies in observing that 'it is common to all men, and to be found in no other race of animals'.[47]

This same form of analysis appears when Smith has to ground the general determination which dictates that the labour-content of exchange-value is not directly expressed as such, but rather as quantities of another commodity, and, more concretely, as price. The entire foundation is reduced to the assertion that the first expression is 'more frequently' observed and 'is more natural, therefore' than the comparison 'with labour', while at the same time, 'every particular commodity is more frequently exchanged for money than for any other commodity'.[48]

Let us note, in passing, how the recurrence of the most immediate appearance allows this mode of analysis to present it in an inverted form as the true general determination. This is what Hegel had in mind when he said that:

> [S]ince in this procedure the ground is derived from the phenomenon and
> its determinations are based on it, the phenomenon certainly flows quite

---

45. Joja 1969, pp. 111–13, 157; Lefebvre 1984, p. 154.
46. In his defence of dialectical logic, Ilyenkov (1982) falls into circular reasoning by arguing that the identification of the relevant aspect to be abstracted by analysis 'presupposes the comprehension' of its specific role and place in the whole (Ilyenkov 1982, p. 103). In turn, he conceives the process of synthesis as the 'combination' (p. 37) of a pair of the abstracted concepts, which are complementary as each of them presents an aspect lacking in the other (pp. 88–92). Consequently, he can only ground the capacity to identify which pair of opposed aspects is determining in each case by asserting that it 'is an axiom of dialectics' (p. 138).
47. Smith 1852, p. 6.
48. Smith 1852, p. 13.

> smoothly and with a favourable wind from its ground.... The exposition
> begins with grounds which are placed in mid-air as principles and primary
> concepts;... Therefore he who aims to penetrate such sciences must begin
> by instilling his mind with these grounds, a distasteful business for reason
> because it is asked to treat what is groundless as a valid foundation.[49]

It is precisely by virtue of the way in which logical representation opens the door
to the inversion of immediate appearances into the content of the determination
that political economy exhausts its role as science to engender its apologetic
form as vulgar economics.

As for the return to the concrete by lifting simplifying assumptions, both
Adam Smith and David Ricardo offer a particularly illustrative example in the
aesthetically-naturalising form taken by their depiction of the transition from
the 'early and rude state of society' to 'the accumulation of stock'. This transition is reduced to the substitution of the assumption that 'capital' belongs to the
labourer for the more realistic one that 'all the implements necessary to kill the
beaver and deer might belong to one class of men, and the labour employed in
their destruction might be furnished by another class'.[50]

Dialectical reproduction: from 'Capital' to the 'Grundrisse'

Already before the *Grundrisse*, Marx had exposed the ultimate result of the analysis based on the construction of an abstract representation of the concrete by
forcefully stripping it of its attributes: 'In consequence of thus abstracting all the
so-called accidents, animate or inanimate, men or things, we are right in saying
that in the final abstraction we have as substance the logical categories'.[51]

Even earlier, Marx had exposed the inversion inherent in all representation
by which logic appears as the necessity that sets the concrete into motion, with
the latter in turn conceived of under the appearance of being inert and therefore
incapable of self-movement. Initially, he had limited himself to making a case
for replacing a constructive necessity of a general nature with one that corre-
sponded to the specificity of its concrete object: 'the proper logic of the proper
object'.[52] However, later he advanced in the development of a scientific method
capable of overcoming the externality of the constructive necessity *vis-à-vis* the
real necessity of its object, making it clear that this externality was inherent in
logic itself, no matter how concrete one might wish to make it: 'Logic is the

---

49. Hegel 1999, pp. 459–60.
50. Ricardo 1821, p. 17.
51. Marx 2005, p. 115.
52. Marx 1982, p. 92.

currency of the mind, the speculative *thought-value* of man and of nature, their essence which has become completely indifferent to all real determinateness and hence unreal, *alienated thought*, and therefore thought which abstracts from nature and from real man: *abstract* thought'.[53]

It might seem that, in the same text on the method in the *Grundrisse*, Marx is leaving room for a form of analysis guided by the search for a recurring attribute: 'As a rule, the most general abstractions arise only in the midst of the richest possible concrete development, where one thing appears as common to many, to all. Then it ceases to be thinkable in a particular form alone'.[54]

However, at stake in this passage is the condition of universal existence of the concrete that allows its abstraction to be thought up. In turn, the representation that starts out from an analysis based on repetition is the most immediate form of thought. Yet, precisely because of this it is unable to transcend the appearances of repetition itself. For example, freedom and equality can only be conceived of as abstract categories when they have become universal forms of the general social relation. However, despite this recurring presence, the latter says nothing about their content or, in other words, of their necessity: '[T]he stale argumentation of the degenerate economics of most recent times . . . *which demonstrates* that economic relations everywhere express *the same* simple determinants, and hence that they everywhere express the equality and freedom of the simple exchange of exchange values; this point entirely reduces itself to an infantile abstraction'.[55]

Now, the specific aim of this paper is to address the issue of method in the *Grundrisse*. However, let us recall the methodological observation made by Marx in the latter book itself: 'Human anatomy contains a key to the anatomy of the ape. The intimations of higher development among the subordinate animal species, however, can be understood only after the higher development is already known'.[56]

Thus, *pace* Mepham, let us thus begin by taking as the concrete object of our study of the dialectical method in the *Grundrisse* the fully-developed shape that it would acquire in *Capital*.[57]

The analysis pertaining to the dialectical method begins by confronting a determinate concrete. However, far from seeking out others alike to see what

---

53. Marx 1992a, p. 383.
54. Marx 1993, p. 104.
55. Marx 1993, p. 249.
56. Marx 1993, p. 105.
57. Mepham also resorts to this same analogy to discuss the evolution of Marx's method from the *Grundrisse* to *Capital*, but to argue against its use as an appropriate way of approaching the question. In an Althusserian fashion, he thus postulates a 'radical discontinuity' between those two texts. See Mepham 1989, pp. 232–3.

recurs in their manifestations, it attempts to uncover the necessity whose immediate self-realisation has taken the form of (hence determined) the original concrete. In other words, dialectical analysis penetrates the real concrete in search
of the necessity that makes it what it is. It does so by separating the necessity in
question in what it has as a pure potentiality, from its already realised result. The
analysis thus separates the content of necessity (and hence, abstract existence)
from its realised form (hence, concrete existence).[58] Once this first step has been
made, the process must advance step-by-step towards the discovery of an ever
simpler potential necessity. This is done by taking the content of the recently-
discovered necessity as a concrete form in which its own necessity-content has
in turn self-realised. In other words, the analysis moves forward by taking the
abstract form uncovered in its determination as a concrete form itself.

In *Capital*, Marx makes evident how the analysis begins by facing the specific determination of the commodity as a social relation under the concrete
form in which this determination presents itself, that is to say, under the form
of exchange-value. He points out how, at first glance, it seems impossible that
this concrete form is able to carry within itself a different content from its outward appearance.[59] However, this immediate appearance of exchange-value as
an abstract quantitative relation dissolves as soon as it is analysed. In asking
about the necessity for the existence of the quantitative relationship of equality
between different use-values, it becomes clear that the latter immediately entails
the existence of a common content. Let us note that what is at stake, here, is not
the search for a recurring attribute, but the discovery of the source that allows
each one of these two qualitatively different use-values indifferently to take the
place of the other. Thus, such content cannot arise from the exchange-relation
but, instead, must find expression within it.[60] The analysis continues by facing
that common substance crystallised in the commodity in order to separate its
realised form from its necessity as pure potentiality yet to be realised, that is to
say, as the very action capable of engendering this common substance. At this
point, the analysis faces the potentiality of human productive action, in other
words, of labour, as the source of the commodity's exchangeability. Still, it discovers this potentiality only when taking a further step that abstracts labour
from its concrete forms of realisation. This means it discovers that the necessity of value so far has the following as its simplest content: '[H]uman labour in
the abstract. . . . [T]he same unsubstantial reality in each, a mere congelation of

---

58. '. . . all science would be superfluous if the outward appearance and the essence of
things directly coincided' (Marx 1966a, p. 817).
59. Marx 1965, p. 36.
60. Marx 1965, p. 37.

homogeneous human labour, of labour-power expended without regard to the mode of its expenditure'.[61]

Now, the analysis cannot stop there. It has discovered abstract labour as the realised action that endows the commodity with value. However, inasmuch as abstract labour is itself a potentiality that has been realised, it appears to be devoid of all qualities except, precisely, its qualitative indifference. Thus, the analysis must search for the content of the necessity of abstract labour that produces commodities, which it finds in the material nature of abstract labour: 'Productive activity, if we leave out of sight its special form, viz., the useful character of the labour, is nothing but the expenditure of human labour-power.... [A] productive expenditure of human brains, nerves, and muscles...'.[62]

The analysis must now answer the following question: how can this material expenditure of human body, a condition of human life in general, be the determinant for the social specificity of the commodity? It thus continues by separating this materiality as an individual expenditure of labour-power from its necessity as an active organ of the process of social metabolism. Accordingly, the analysis discovers that this material expenditure has as its specific qualitative content the way in which the individual carrying it out rules his/her participation in the organisation of social labour. It is a productive expenditure of a human corporeality in general, which is made for others, whose concrete realisation is fully controlled by the will of the individual performing it. The commodity-producer controls by means of his or her own individual will how and what to produce for other members of society. Thus he or she consciously controls, free from personal dependence, the exercise of his or her individual capacity to perform social labour. At the same time, however, his or her consciousness is excluded from the organisation of the labour carried out by any other individual commodity-producer. There is no alien individual will, nor any collective will, organising the expenditure of the individual labour-power applied to the production of commodities. The labour that produces commodities is thus social labour privately undertaken by mutually independent producers: 'Only such products can become commodities with regard to each other, as result from different kinds of labour, each kind being carried on independently and for the account of private individuals'.[63]

---

61. Marx 1965, p. 38.
62. Marx 1965, p. 44.
63. Marx 1965, p. 42. This translation obscures Marx's direct reference to 'mutually independent private labours' [*voneinander unabhängiger Privatarbeiten*] as the determinant of commodities. Nevertheless, the translations by E. and C. Paul and the one by Fowkes directly omit the word 'private'. Such an omission at this crucial point has prevented us from using them for our quotations. It is noteworthy how Marxist political economy has displaced the private form with which social labour is performed in capitalism as the specific determinant of the commodity-form. From this perspective, two main

The analysis that gives way to the reproduction of the concrete by means of thought does not end because the researcher arbitrarily decides to cease identifying recurring features in order to produce an even more abstract concept. Instead, it concludes, because when searching for the necessity of the recently-discovered content, it becomes plain that it can only be found by accompanying the self-realisation of that content in its necessary concrete form. Let us return to the case of the value-content of the commodity. Analysis has allowed us to discover that the commodity has value, that is to say, the attribute of exchangeability, because privately and independently performed socially necessary abstract labour has been materialised in it. This places us squarely in front of another question: why is it that this private and independent realisation of the material expenditure of human labour-power in general endows its product with the social attribute of value? The analysis, however, is unable to answer this question.[64]

In fact, if we examine the manner in which Marx presents how this point has been reached, the limit of the analysis appears as emerging from a change in its modality. Up to this point, it involved the search of the necessity of the content. Conversely, in its latest step, Marx presents it as if it were unable to penetrate through the exteriority of a recurring attribute, namely, that of being the product of private and independent labour. In other words, the analysis appears as having to assume the modality characteristic of the method of representation.

The question about the necessity of value now faces us in such a way that it can only be answered by accompanying the realisation of the specific potentiality that the analysis has discovered as an immanent actuality in the commodity. The commodity's exchangeability, posited by the materialisation of abstract socially necessary labour carried out in a private and independent manner, confronts us in the manner of a content that must account for its own necessity by realising it. Hence, the development must follow the movement of value in its necessary concrete form of expression as exchange-value.[65]

Marx thus successively unfolds the forms of the exchange-relation, asking each one in turn which content it progressively reveals. Let us note that this development does not imply a simpler form engendering a more concrete one. Instead, the unfolding of the former's necessity evidences the necessity of the

---

strands can be identified. The first one, principally based on the work of Sraffa, maintains that value is determined by the immediate material unity between social production and consumption, thus replacing private labour with one that is directly social as the foundation of the commodity-form. The second, which stems mainly from Rubin, holds that the specificity of commodity-producing labour is its 'abstract' character, which is defined in opposition to the materiality of abstract labour pointed out by Marx as a simple productive expenditure of the human body. On this issue, see Iñigo Carrera 2007, pp. 107–80.

64. Marx 1965, p. 47.
65. Marx 1965, pp. 47–8.

existence of the latter. The starting point from which to follow the development of the necessity of value to manifest in the concrete form of exchange-value is the simplest expression of the latter, namely, the exchange-relation between two different commodities: 'The whole mystery of the form of value lies hidden in this elementary form. Its analysis, therefore, is our real difficulty'.[66]

Already in this simplest form, it is clear that the value of a commodity, i.e. the socially-necessary abstract labour materialised in it in a private and independent form, does not only manifest itself in a purely relative manner. In addition, it does so necessarily through the use-value of another commodity that acts as its equivalent.[67] Above all, this first step in the process of unfolding of the value-content of the commodity in its necessary form as an exchange-value makes evident the same determinations already uncovered by the analysis:

> We see, then, all that our analysis of the value of commodities has already told us, is told us by the linen itself, so soon as it comes into communication with another commodity, the coat. Only it betrays its thoughts in that language with which alone it is familiar, the language of commodities. In order to tell us that its own value is created by labour in its abstract character of human labour, it says that the coat, in so far as it is worth as much as the linen, and therefore is value, consists of the same labour as the linen.[68]

Thus it might appear as if all that is at stake, now, is to present what the analysis has already discovered. Yet, we immediately discover that, in appropriating the 'language of commodities', that is, in reproducing in thought the commodity's immanent movement, certain determinations that the analysis was unable to discover now come to the fore. In first instance, the commodity affirms itself as the real subject whose development must be followed in thought: 'It therefore follows that the simple form of value of the commodity is at the same time the simple form of value of the product of labour, and also that the development of the commodity-form coincides with the development of the value-form'.[69]

The analysis could not account for the necessity of the commodity as its starting point. Matters are different as soon as thought begins to reproduce the

---

66. Marx 1965, p. 48. With this statement, Marx brings out the specific difference between the representation and reproduction of the concrete. In the former, the key to the discovery of the law of determination lies in formal generalisation. By contrast, in the latter the key resides in the simplest expression of the content. See also Hegel 1999, p. 280.

67. Marx 1965, p. 19.

68. Marx 1965, p. 52.

69. Marx 1990a, p. 67. We were forced to resort to this edition of *Capital* for this particular quotation because the edition we are normally using introduces here an alleged reference to the historical development of commodities that is completely absent from the German original.

movement of a commodity in its social relationship with another. In this second phase, the commodity shows itself as the necessary point of departure for the discovery of the concrete determinations of the specific form in which the materiality of the process of social metabolism in the capitalist mode of production is organised. The exposition here reflects the actual course of the research, which moves along a path alien to that of any analysis.

In this ideal reproduction of the concrete, the research moves forward and uncovers the necessity according to which the general materiality of the labour represented in the value of the commodity appears in the very form of the exchange-relation.[70] At the same time, it reveals that the apparent absence of all unity in the materiality of the labour represented by value is the indirect form in which the general unity of the material process of social labour is realised.[71] Subsequently, it makes evident that this unity needs to acquire an expression that can synthesise it in the very movement of its own organisation, in other words, in the very movement of commodities.[72] In effect, in the exchange-relation, the corporeal materiality of any concrete form of the product of social labour mutates into that of the general equivalent as a synthetic expression of the indirect unity of social labour. This reveals that the unity of social labour is specifically established in capitalism on the basis of the general materiality of human labour, namely of the simple productive expenditure of the human body:

> The substance linen becomes the visible incarnation, the social chrysalis state of every kind of human labour.... In this manner the labour realised in the values of commodities is presented not only under its negative aspect, under which abstraction is made from every concrete form and useful property of actual work, but its own positive nature is made to reveal itself expressly. The general value form is the reduction of all kinds of actual labour to their common character of being human labour generally, of being the expenditure of human labour-power.[73]

We can now see that the reproduction of the necessity of the commodity in its realisation not only progresses by discovering determinations that the analysis was impotent to bring out. At the same time, it exposes the actual appearances to which it would have stuck had the research been interrupted at that stage. In the process of analysis, the unity of social labour expressed in the exchangeability of the commodity may appear, at first, as something determined by the absence of all material content in abstract labour. Only in a second step does the

---

70. Marx 1965, p. 63.
71. Ibid.
72. Marx 1965, p. 66.
73. Marx 1965, p. 67.

analysis inevitably face this materiality. By contrast, in the development of the value-form taken by the determination of the indirect unity of social labour, it becomes clear that such unity is predicated on the real material quality of abstract labour as a productive expenditure of human corporeality. This evidence comes up already in the simplest expression of value. In effect, the concrete labour that produced the equivalent can express the abstract labour that produced the commodity occupying the relative pole, only because its materiality as a simple expenditure of human labour-power is identical to that of the latter. As Marx points out, inasmuch as the analysis is the necessary first step in the scientific cognition of an actual concrete, it appears as easier to deal with, and even as sufficient, *vis-à-vis* the difficulty inherent in the second phase comprising the reproduction of the concrete in thought. Yet, it is only this second phase that has the power to account for the possible apparent abstractions that could have emerged in the course of the first, analytic phase: 'It is, in reality, much easier to discover by analysis the earthly core of the misty creations of religion, than, conversely, it is, to develop from the actual relations of life the corresponding celestialised forms of those relations. The latter method is the only materialistic, and therefore the only scientific one'.[74]

The development of the value-form taken by the product of social labour performed privately and independently has shown us that, in the capitalist mode of production, the organisation of social production and consumption is not realised directly by consciously ruling the concrete material form taken by each individual labour. On the contrary, social labour achieves its unity indirectly, premised on the material identity of labour as human productive activity in general, that is, as labour whose materiality as the expenditure of human labour-power has not yet assumed a specific concrete form.[75] Thus, the unfolding of this form of organisation of the social labour-process cannot come to a halt without accounting for the necessary form in which it is borne in the consciousness of its subjects. Having arrived at this point, that which in the analytical stage could only be uncovered in a rather external fashion on the basis of mere repetition, is now exposed as emerging from the reproduction in thought of its own movement:

> [A]rticles of utility become commodities, only because they are products of the labour of private individuals or groups of individuals who carry on their work independently of each other. The sum total of the labour of all these private individuals forms the aggregate labour of society. Since the producers do not come into social contact with each other until they exchange their

---

74. Marx 1965, pp. 372–3, n. 4.
75. Marx 1965, p. 67.

products, the specific social character of each producer's labour does not show itself except in the act of exchange. In other words, the labour of the individual asserts itself as a part of the labour of society, only by means of the relations which the act of exchange establishes directly between the products, and indirectly, through them, between the producers.[76]

In sum, the development of the form of value does not simply consist in the exposition of the determinations of value that were already discovered through analysis. On the contrary, only such a development is able to reveal that, when organising their social labour, the mutually-independent producers cannot rely on any social relation other than their general condition as individual bearers of the capacity to expend their bodies productively, in other words, to carry out labour in general. It is incumbent on each private producer to expend this generic capacity in a determined concrete form. In other words, each of them privately exerts his or her abstract labour in the form of a determined concrete labour. If this expenditure of labour-power has materialised under a socially-useful concrete form, the corresponding abstract labour will be represented as the social attribute of its product to establish an exchange-relation with another bearer of an identical objectification of abstract labour. The materiality of socially-necessary abstract labour is represented as the value of its product, which thus acquires the specific social determination of a commodity. The material unity of privately and independently undertaken social production is established in this indirect form. The value-form taken by commodities is the general social relation indirectly established by the mutually-free producers. This is the reason why the product of their own labour confronts them as the bearer of an alien social power that dominates them.

The scope of the dialectical method in the *Grundrisse*

Let us return to the *Grundrisse*. Already in these manuscripts, Marx reveals the historical specificity of the commodity as the general social relation in a society where social labour is organised privately and independently, which determines its producers as mutually-free persons:

> The dissolution of all products and activities into exchange-values presupposes the dissolution of all fixed personal (historic) relations of dependence in production, as well as the all-sided dependence of the producers on one another. Each individual's production is dependent on the production of all others; and the transformation of his product into the necessaries of his own life is

---

76. Marx 1965, pp. 72–3. Again, Marx's direct attribution of the private character to labour, *Privatarbeiten*, becomes an attribute of the individuals in the translation.

[similarly] dependent on the consumption of all others. . . . The reciprocal and all-sided dependence of individuals who are indifferent to one another forms their social connection. This social bond is expressed in *exchange-value*, by means of which alone each individual's own activity or his product becomes an activity and a product for him; he must produce a general product – *exchange-value*, . . . The individual carries his social power, as well as his bond with society, in his pocket. . . . Each individual possesses social power in the form of a thing. Rob the thing of this social power and you must give it to persons to exercise over persons.[77]

It might seem, then, that the difference in the development of the dialectical method mediating between the *Grundrisse* and *Capital* is limited to the greater wealth of detail with which the latter presents the same essential question already uncovered in the former (namely, the simplest form of the general social relation in a society of mutually-free individuals). However, as soon as we examine the path taken by Marx in the *Grundrisse*, we can see that the discovery of the determinations of value still follows an essentially analytical course. In fact, from a methodological viewpoint, the specific richness of this part of the *Grundrisse* among Marx's works lies in the fact that it gives transparency to the limits weighing on progress during the analytical phase. The argument in *Capital* overcomes these limitations in the flow of synthetic reproduction. As we shall see below, the primacy of the analytical course is reflected in the limits on the cognition of the substance of value and, hence, in the development of this substance into its necessary concrete forms.

In progressing analytically, Marx discovers in the *Grundrisse* that at stake in the determination of use-values as commodities is the organisation of the materiality of social labour. He also discovers that the unity of this materiality manifests itself indirectly through the circulation of commodities. Yet, he only comes to face the materiality of abstract labour under the external appearance of its opposite, as the total absence of all materiality:

> In becoming an exchange value, a product (or activity) is not only transformed into a definite quantitative relation, a relative number . . . but it must also at the same time be transformed qualitatively, be transposed into another element, so that both commodities become magnitudes of the same kind, of the same unit, i.e., commensurable. The commodity first has to be transposed into labour time, into something qualitatively different from itself (qualitatively different (1) because it is not labour time as labour time, but materialised labour time; labour time not in the form of motion, but at rest; not in the form of the process, but of the result; (2) because it is not the objectification of labour time

---

77. Marx 1993, pp. 156–8.

in general, which exists only as a conception (it is only a conception of labour separated from its quality, subject merely to quantitative variations), but rather the specific result of a specific, of a naturally specified, kind of labour which differs qualitatively from other kinds), in order then to be compared as a specific amount of labour time, as a certain magnitude of labour, with other amounts of labour time, other magnitudes of labour.[78]

The general social relation thus appears bereft of the simplest material content bestowed by its historical specificity. This means that Marx has not yet discovered that its movement originates in the unity of society's material capacity to undertake labour in general, in order to impose itself indirectly through the concrete material forms in which this capacity has been privately and independently exerted. Thus, its movement is presented as if it emerged from the abstractly-ideal nature assigned to its simplest specific content. With such content reduced to the condition of a mere representation, namely to an abstractly ideal construction, the development of its concrete forms by means of thought appears correspondingly inverted. Instead of responding to the fact that thought follows the real movement, it appears as if the movement of thought itself were conceptually engendering those concrete forms: 'The product becomes a commodity; the commodity becomes exchange-value; the exchange-value of the commodity is its immanent money-property; this, its money-property, separates itself from it in the form of money . . . '.[79]

Marx himself subjects his development to criticism, exposing its upside-down nature: 'It will be necessary later, before this question is dropped, to correct the idealist manner of the presentation, which makes it seem as if it were merely a matter of conceptual determinations and of the dialectic of these concepts. Above all in the case of the phrase: product (or activity) becomes commodity; commodity, exchange-value; exchange-value, money.'[80]

Let us leave aside any improvements in the exposition of what has already been uncovered in the *Grundrisse* to focus on the key to the qualitative leap in the dialectical development that mediates between its point of departure and that of the *Contribution*, and which would be fully completed later in *Capital*. This key lies in the discovery of the material quality of abstract labour as a generic productive expenditure of human labour-power, of the human body,

---

78. Marx 1993, p. 143. The difficult path taken by the reproduction of the concrete by means of thought has a noticeable expression when, in the *Contribution*, Marx discovered for the first time the materiality of abstract labour as a simple productive expenditure of the human body while, at the same time, he was not yet able to fully separate this materiality from that corresponding to the material difference between simple and complex labour (Marx 1911, p. 24).

79. Marx 1993, p. 147.

80. Marx 1993, p. 151.

of muscles, brain, and so on, which, inasmuch as it is performed privately and independently, becomes represented as the social attribute of its product. Such a discovery was made possible only by Marx's development of the form of value.

In turn, this development of the progress from the simplest determination of the commodity to its concrete forms impinges on the mode in which Marx undertakes the analysis. The latter no longer progresses from the immediate concrete to arrive at 'abstract or simple categories', as Marx still put it at the beginning of the *Grundrisse*. Instead, the analysis moves with the aim of discovering the simplest specific form of the immediate concrete. Hence: '[N]either "value" nor "exchange-value" are my subjects, but the commodity . . . [T]he simplest economic concretum'.[81]

Thus, the analysis does not merely move from the concrete to the abstract. More precisely, it penetrates the concrete itself until discovering the form constituting the simplest manifestation of its specific necessity. On the other hand, neither does the analysis progress by searching for the generic necessity in the apparent universal repetition of its manifestations. Hence, it can only reach the simplest concrete in its condition as a singular existence: '[T]he reader who wishes to follow me at all, must make up his mind to pass from the special [*einzelnen*] to the general [*allgemeinen*]'.[82]

Let us now summarise the issue by returning to the way in which Nicolaus reduces the development of the dialectical method from the *Grundrisse* to *Capital* to a difference between the mode of research, in the former, and the mode of presentation, in the latter. This reading overlooks the fact that the research is in full swing, and actually in its most powerful stage (hence able to overcome all appearance), in the development of the form of value unfolded in *Capital*. Nicolaus also argues, along with Reichelt, that the research-method is clearly visible in the *Grundrisse* but deliberately concealed in *Capital*. They thus overlook the fact that Marx resorts to a mode of exposition in *Capital* that at each step reveals the unity of the two moments inherent in dialectical research. Broadly put, he starts each presentational 'node' by facing what appears to be an immediate concrete in order to proceed to analyse its necessity. Once the latter is uncovered, he follows it through in its self-realisation until the initial concrete is reproduced but now as a *known* concrete. This does not mean that no change has occurred in the dialectical presentation between the *Grundrisse* and *Capital*. Specifically, Marx removed from the exposition the explicit reflections on the direction that the development of the content in its necessary form should take. However, those reflections are, strictly speaking, external to the ideal reproduction of the

---

81. Marx 2002, pp. 230, 242.
82. Marx 1911, p. 9. In a more precise translation, *einzelnen* corresponds to the 'individual' and *allgemeinen* to the 'universal'. See Inwood 1992, p. 302.

content's self-development. In light of his interpretation, Nicolaus recommends the following reading strategy in order to 'understand' Marx's method of research: firstly, the contemporary reader should approach the *Grundrisse*, then (in line with Lenin's aphorism) Hegel's *Logic*, and finally *Capital*.[83] The approach put forward in this chapter leads to very different implications. Thanks to the fact that Marx had to produce the *original knowledge* that progressed from the *Logic* to the *Grundrisse* and from the latter to *Capital*, we can empower our process of *recognition* by firstly appropriating the 'anatomy' (the method) of the most developed subject, namely, *Capital*. This more developed form of the critique of political economy contains the key to the understanding of the method of the *Grundrisse*, and the more primitive one of the *Logic*.

Now, however inverted the sequence in search of the dialectical method may be presented, there will always be an abyss between the approaches just mentioned and Althusser's grotesque '*imperative* recommendation' (emphasis in the original) that *Capital*'s entire first section be skipped in order to avoid the 'highly damaging' 'Hegelian influence' which would prevent an understanding of 'what must be understood'.[84]

Once again concerning the point of departure ... of working-class consciousness as revolutionary subject

We have discussed the substantive difference of form and content between the *reproduction* and the *representation* of the concrete by means of thought as methods of rational cognition. We have also seen how the *Grundrisse* are a step in the original development of the former, which only reaches the plenitude of its development in *Capital*.

However, still pending is the question of the change in the point of departure from the *Grundrisse* to the *Contribution*. We stated at the outset that the change should be traced in the very text of the former. We also claimed that in those earlier manuscripts the discovery of the determinations of the commodity as the simplest form of the general social relation in the capitalist mode of production was developed through an essentially analytical process. However, we should now add that, as Marx moves forward in the unfolding of the concrete forms taken by this general social relation, the unity of the text of the *Grundrisse* becomes increasingly determined by the stage of dialectical reproduction. This fact acquires its clearest expression at a crucial juncture much later in the text. Specifically, after unfolding the determinations of the capitalist mode of

---

83. Nicolaus 1993, p. 60.
84. Althusser 1971, p. 93.

production in its concrete unity, the dialectical reproduction reaches the point at which it fully uncovers capital's necessity to supersede itself in the conscious organisation of social life. The analysis is, at this point, incapable of uncovering the necessity at stake, as all that matters in the existing concrete is its immanent potentiality to affirm through its own negation as the general social relation. In the face of this, the analysis is unable to go beyond the presentation of that potentiality as deprived of its own concrete content, conceiving it under the form of a 'recipe ... for the cook-shops of the future'.[85] In reproducing in thought the determinations of the capitalist mode of production in their unity as constituting the existing concrete, Marx makes it evident that the historical necessity of this mode of production stems from the specific form in which it radically transforms the materiality of the worker's productive activity through the socialisation of private labour:

> The exchange of living labour for objectified labour – i.e. the positing of social labour in the form of the contradiction of capital and wage labour – is the ultimate development of the *value-relation* and of production resting on value ... No longer does the worker insert a modified natural thing [*Naturgegenstand*] as middle link between the object [*Objekt*] and himself; rather, he inserts the process of nature, transformed into an industrial process, as a means between himself and inorganic nature, mastering it. He steps to the side of the production process instead of being its chief actor. In this transformation, it is neither the direct human labour he himself performs, nor the time during which he works, but rather the appropriation of his own general productive power, his understanding of nature and his mastery over it by virtue of his presence as a social body – it is, in a word, the development of the social individual which appears as the great foundation-stone of production and of wealth. .... Capital itself is the moving contradiction ... On the one side, then, it calls to life all the powers of science and of nature, as of social combination and of social intercourse, in order to make the creation of wealth independent (relatively) of the labour time employed on it. On the other side, it wants to use labour time as the measuring rod for the giant social forces thereby created, and to confine them within the limits required to maintain the already created value as value. Forces of production and social relations – two different sides of the development of the social individual – appear to capital as mere means, and are merely means for it to produce on its limited foundation. In fact, however, they are the material conditions to blow this foundation sky-high.[86]

---

85. Marx 1965, p. 17.
86. Marx 1993, pp. 704–6.

Almost immediately after thus discovering the concrete historical determination of the capitalist mode of production, Marx confronts again the commodity and its value-determinations in the *Grundrisse*. Yet, this is no longer something abstractly analytic. Following the simple note 'this section to be brought forward',[87] Marx begins to unfold the determinations of the commodity as the simplest concrete form of the general social relation in this mode of production. However, having barely begun this development, those earlier manuscripts break off. The body of their text has given way to what would be the 1859 *Contribution*. Nevertheless, it is the 1857–8 version of Marx's critique of political economy that has brought to light that the development of the reproduction of the concrete by means of thought (rather than the analysis) is what determines the necessity of the point of departure.

Now, how has the starting point concretely changed? At the outset of the *Grundrisse*, Marx posited that the point of departure was 'individuals producing in society' while in the *Contribution* and *Capital*, this becomes 'the commodity'. Let us take the 'individuals producing in society'. The first step that these individuals need to make to undertake their social production consists in organising it: that is, each of them must be assigned with a useful concrete labour to be performed for others. The mode in which they unfold this organisation is but the exercise of their general social relation at the point at which each cycle of society's life-process is set into motion. Thus, the point of departure in the study of the 'individuals producing in society' is that of the simplest specific form presented by their general social relationship in each historical period. What is this form in the capitalist mode of production? It is not a direct social relation between persons. Conversely, it is an indirect relation that they establish through the exchange of the products of their privately and independently-undertaken social labour as materialisations of equivalent quantities of abstract labour. In brief, that social relation is the commodity. The *Contribution* and *Capital* both begin from exactly the same point that Marx had been propounding as the necessary one until then. However, his progress in the reproduction of the concrete by means of thought allows him to recognise that this thing, the commodity, is the simplest concrete form bearing the capacity to organise social labour – and hence social consumption – in a society where individuals are free of personal dependence. The full conscious control over one's own individual labour corresponding to its private and independent realisation entails, at the same time, the complete lack of conscious control over its social character. Hence the subordination of the human individual to the social powers objectified in the product of his or her own labour.

---

87. Marx 1993, p. 881.

Let us look once again at the question of method. Logical representation is not the *natural* form of scientific method. As all forms of consciousness, and hence of the human capacity to organise action, scientific method is itself a historically-determined social form. Against this form of consciousness stands the reproduction of the concrete by means of thought, also as the bearer of a historically-determined social relation. Marx developed the historical necessity of this method, 'in its essence critical and revolutionary', as the necessary form of consciousness in the supersession of the capitalist mode of production. Yet it subsequently fell into oblivion, nearly to the point of being forgotten altogether, or rather erased, even by Marxist scholars themselves. The aim of this text is to put the question back at the heart of the discussion of the form of working-class consciousness with the power to organise capital-transcending practice.

The Four Levels of Abstraction of Marx's Concept of 'Capital'. Or, Can We Consider the *Grundrisse* the Most Advanced Version of Marx's Theory of Capital?

Roberto Fineschi

Marx began his economic studies in Paris in 1844. However, only in the late 1850s did he write a first organic draft of his theory of capital: the *Manuscripts of 1857–8* (generally known as the *Grundrisse*). Philological research has shown that before this time he was still linked to Ricardo's ideas,[1] or only dealt with issues of the 'surface';[2] he did not write an organic outline of his political economy. The 'research' continued in the *Manuscripts of 1857–8*, but, in this text, the 'exposition' began as well.[3]

In these manuscripts, Marx defined progressively the structure of 'capital' as a whole; it therefore represents a turning point and its relevance needs to be emphasised. Nonetheless, this process did not finish with the *Grundrisse*: relevant parts of the theory were changed or improved both in the *Manuscripts of 1861–3* (in particular with reference to the concepts of market-values

---

1. See Tuchscheerer 1980, pp. 222–45; Vygodskij 1967, pp. 10–35, and 1975a; and Jahn and Nietzold 1978, pp. 149–52; see also Jahn and Noske 1979, pp. 21–2.

2. He studied, for example, different monetarist schools at the beginning of the 1850s. The literature on this subject is mainly in German; see the contributions in Arbeitsblätter 1979a and 1979b.

3. 'Mode of research' [*Forschungsweise*] and 'mode of exposition' [*Darstellungsweise*] are the expressions used by Marx to define his own method in the afterword to the second German edition of *Capital* Volume I (in Fowkes's translation: 'method of inquiry' and 'method of presentation') (Marx 1993, p. 102). The category 'exposition' (or 'presentation') is a crucial one; in fact, the German term *'darstellen'* does not simply regard the way given results are presented, but the way the theory itself develops through its different levels of abstraction toward totality. It is in fact explicit that Marx is referring to Hegel's *Darstellung* when he uses this word. The process of exposition posits results.

and production-prices),[4] and in the *Manuscripts of 1863–5*, where we have the only extensive exposition of credit and fictitious capital. Moreover, a proper terminological and conceptual distinction between value, use-value, and value-form as part of the theory of the 'commodity' (the 'economic cell form') was worked out only in the second German edition of *Capital* Volume I (in 1872–3, even if this had been latently considered since the *Manuscripts of 1857–8*).[5]

However, despite Marx's efforts, his theory as a whole remained an unfinished business, in particular the parts for Volumes Two and Three. Philologists have shown that Engels's editing was at most a good attempt to *conclude* Marx's drafts; according to the author, those could not absolutely be published because they needed to be developed.[6] Thanks to the new critical edition, we know that one can make sense of Marx's theory of capital only if this mass of unfinished materials as a *whole* is taken into account, with a particular focus on the different phases of its development.[7]

In the traditional debate, some scholars have pointed out that the *Grundrisse* should have a predominant position in the interpretation of Marx's thought, because there he made some theoretical points that later were dropped. In Germany, the so-called *neue Lektüre* and in particular authors such as Backhaus and Reichelt claimed that one can find a proper dialectical exposition of categories only in that text, while the logical consistency was weakened in subsequent writings.[8] For other reasons and with other goals, the 'workerist' view shared the idea that the *Grundrisse* contain 'more' than *Capital*, especially with reference to class-struggle and antagonist subjects.

In this chapter, I shall try to show how Marx *successfully* improved his theory after the *Grundrisse* exactly in order to overcome some difficulties that arose from the *insufficient dialectical development* of categories in the *Manuscripts of 1857–8*. This mainly regards the German debate (with which I am sympathetic in spite of some disagreements) but I think that, for some implications, the workerist positions are affected as well (in my view, these are wrong regarding some basic definitions).[9]

---

4. Vygodskij 1967, p. 91, Jahn and Nietzold 1978, p. 158, Skambraks 1978, pp. 32–3 and Müller 1983, pp. 9–13.

5. On the development of Marx's theory in the various editions of Volume I, see: Hecker, Jungnickel and Vollgraf 1989, Hecker 1987, Jungnickel 1989, Lietz 1987a and 1987b; Schkedow 1987; Schwarz 1987; Henschel, Krause and Militz 1989; Fineschi 2001, Appendix C, and 2008, Chapter One.

6. See Hecker 2009 and Roth 2009.

7. See Bellofiore and Fineschi 2009.

8. See Reichelt 1973 and Backhaus 1997. For a summary of these debates, see Fineschi 2009b and Elbe 2008.

9. I shall not deal here with these positions. For an introduction to the historical impact and the theoretical limit of workerism, see Bellofiore and Tomba 2008.

The aforementioned *neue Lektüre* have dealt mainly with the value-form and considered the alleged 'reduction' of dialectics with reference to this point. East-German scholars in charge of the new critical edition disagreed with them and maintained that only in the second German edition of *Capital* did Marx consistently define the difference between value and value-form, thus completing the value-form development.[10] Although I agree that the 'final' version presents problems regarding the relationship of the 'logical' and the 'historical', the evidence shown by the philologists demonstrate in my view a real improvement in *Capital*.[11] I shall not go in detail into this debate here. However, I would like to point out that, from a methodological point of view, it seems to me not to be possible to limit the analysis of the reduction of dialectic only to the value-form; we have to take into account also the concept of 'capital in general' and its relationship with other parts of the theory, which in the *Grundrisse* were set aside. In the English speaking world, Rosdolky's famous inquiry into 'capital in general' was generally accepted as the last word on this issue. In his view, 'capital in general' was only a sort of methodological ladder that was useful whilst setting up the general framework to shed light on the central role of industrial capital. It could, however, be dropped when the real exposition moved forward to more concrete levels such as competition and credit. These were included in the theory to avoid a double exposition of an essential part and its repetition in the inessential one. Therefore, 'capital in general' would not be included in the final plan.

This position was contested in the German debate, especially in two important studies by Müller and Schwarz. Even if their conclusions are different in relevant points, they share the idea that 'capital in general' was not abandoned at all, but was simply redefined because its relation with competition and other more concrete parts of the theory changed. Even though a few concrete categories were included within the framework of generality, this does not imply that the concept of generality as such was abandoned. We need to understand why a few parts were included and how this can be justified. I cannot go into their analysis here.[12] Rather, this chapter is an attempt to answer those questions in a different way. My starting point is Schwarz's conclusion: 'capital in general' still works after *Manuscripts of 1861–3*, although it is almost never explicitly mentioned, and we have to explain why and how especially accumulation was included within the framework of generality.

---

10. See Footnote 5.

11. See Fineschi 2006b.

12. On the subject see Rosdolsky 1977, pp. 34 ff., pp. 76 ff., Vygodskij 1967, pp. 133 ff., Reichelt 1973, p. 90, Jahn and Nietzold 1978, pp. 166 ff.; Jahn and Marxhausen 1983, pp. 51 ff., and especially Müller 1978, pp. 62 ff., Schwarz 1974, pp. 246 ff. and 1978, pp. 102 ff., p. 157, pp. 175 ff., pp. 241 ff., pp. 273 ff. For a summary of this debate, see Fineschi 2009a.

A preliminary remark: the starting point of this debate was implicitly or explicitly the question: 'what kind of relation exists between capital in general and
competition?'[13] I think this is misleading, because there are not, in fact, only *two*
levels of abstraction. According to the most elaborated plans Marx made in the
1850s (particularly in C, E and F), the concept of capital is divided into *four* levels
of abstraction: a sort of level zero, or 'simple circulation'; a first level, called 'generality'; a second one, called 'particularity'; and a final one, called 'singularity'.
Presenting this sketch, Marx was clearly referring to the division of the Hegelian
'doctrine of concept'.[14] In order to deal with the issue of the overall consistency
of this division and the particular problems linked to 'capital in general', we have
to reconstruct how all of these categories were defined at the beginning and how
their framework changed while the theory was worked out through its various

---

13. This view is shared by other authors that later dealt with this issue, such as Heinrich 1989, Arthur 2002a and Moseley 2009.

14. Cf. Hegel 1995/6, § 163: 'Der *Begriff* als solcher enthält die Momente der *Allgemeinheit*, als freier Gleichheit mit sich selbst in ihrer Bestimmtheit, – der *Besonderheit*,
der Bestimmtheit, in welcher das Allgemeine ungetrübt sich selbst gleich bleibt, und der
Einzelheit, als der Reflexion-in-sich der Bestimmtheiten der Allgemeinheit und Besonderheit, welche negative Einheit mit sich das *an und für sich Bestimmte* und zugleich
mit sich Identische oder Allgemeine ist'. Evidently, this is not the adequate place to go
into the problems that arise from translating Hegel, but a few remarks are necessary.
First of all, both in Wallace's translation of the *Shorter Logic* § 163 ff. (Hegel 1975), and in
Miller's of *Science of Logic* §§ 1323 ff. (Hegel 1969), 'Begriff' is rendered with 'Notion'. This
can be misleading when we consider Marx's 'concept' of capital. As regards the category
of 'general', a few remarks are necessary. Hegel presents this concept within the triad
Allgemeinheit/Besonderheit/Einzelheit, which is 'Universality/Particularity/Singularity'.
'Allgemeinheit' is then correctly translated as 'Universality'. We should note that this is
the same word Marx uses when talking about 'capital in general'. Thus, in German we
have the same word, and the same category, while in English sometimes we read 'Universality', sometimes 'Generality', or 'capital in general', which is actually the 'universality
of capital'. Further and more relevant problems emerge with 'Einzelheit'. Both Wallace
and Miller translate it with 'Individuality', similar to Croce's Italian translation. In more
recent translations, particularly in Italian, scholars have preferred to use 'Singularity', in
order to avoid not misinterpretations but mistakes. In fact, in Hegel's theory there is a
proper concept called 'Individualität' that specifically regards the Philosophy of Nature,
section II: Physic (but not only there). In a second moment, this 'Individualität' corresponds – as Hegel explicitly states – to the moment of 'Particularity' (Hegel 1995/6,
§ 252). In the *Science of Logic*, the concept is connected to those of 'life' and 'living individual' (Hegel 1996b, pp. 473 ff.). This distinction disappears in English; this can cause a
misinterpretation of the concept of singularity, which is universality reflected into itself.
Universality exists as universal in the particular, while the individual is not properly
universal; it is only latently universal, not in itself and for itself. 'Note also that the "general equivalent"' is actually '"universal equivalent"' as well. This misleading translation
was introduced by Marx himself in the French edition of *Capital* Volume I and later by
Engels in the English edition. Such translations were probably due to his intention to
popularize dialectical categories' (Fineschi 2009a, p. 73). In the value-form, the universal/
general equivalent is the result of a development, which has previously passed though a
'singular' and a 'particular' form of equivalent. As a matter of fact, these categories occur
also in *Capital*.

drafts. The book on capital was supposed to be only the first book in a plan of six (see Appendix). In a letter to Lassalle [Plan D], where he presented this plan for six books, he wrote that book I on *Capital* had some 'Vorchapters', or preliminary chapters. In another letter to Lassalle [Plan E], he made explicit that these 'Vorchapters' were value and money, presuppositions to capital in general, which is still determined as we saw in the preceding plan. So, before the exposition of capital, there should be a sort of 'preliminary frame', the simple circulation that will be called a presupposition that presupposes.[15] In a letter to Engels [Plan F], Marx wrote about the further division of the book on capital, and, although he did not use the words particularity and singularity, he mentioned exactly the subjects that should be treated in these sections: respectively, competition and credit/share-capital. This same structure, although within a different general outline, can also be found in the three volumes of *Capital*.

1. Generality and particularity of capital

'Capital in general' should be the first part of the first book.[16] However, with the development of the theory the plan underwent significant though not radical changes. 'Capital in general' should in fact have been the title of the continuation of *A Contribution...*; but, while writing this part – that is, the *Manuscripts of 1861–3*, which originally bore that title – this category progressively disappeared and from that moment on was only sporadically mentioned.

When he dealt for the first time with the general concept of capital, Marx characterised it as what every capital has in common, the quintessence of it.[17] There are neither capitals nor one capital, but the concept of that which is so far not determined as plurality or unity. The question of capitals, of plurality, arises when the self-development of the theory posits the passage to particularity. The other point strictly connected with 'many' capitals is competition. This is the outline in the *Grundrisse:*

– In the most developed plan of the *Grundrisse* [Plan C], 'competition', the particularity of capital, is placed in the same framework as 'accumulation'. In *Capital*, on the other hand, 'competition' as such is not in the same framework of 'accumulation'.

---

15. I am not going here into 'level zero' because that would require a proper paper. It was only in the *Manuscripts of 1863–5* that Marx finally decided to consider this section as a part of *Capital* as such; see Boldyrew 1989, pp. 157 ff. I set aside this problem here in order to approach the question of generality/particularity/singularity.

16. The book on capital, in the sense outlined in the original plan of six books he presented in Plan D and in the Preface to *A Contribution...*

17. See Marx 1993, p. 352.

– In the outline of 1857–8, 'accumulation' occurs not only after the circulation of capital, but even after the transformation of capital into capital and profit. In *Capital*, it is before both the circulation and the transformation of capital into capital and profit.
– In the outline of 1857–8, both competition and accumulation occur not only after the transformation of capital into capital and profit, but even after the transformation of capital into capital and interest. In *Capital*, competition is between profit and interest.

These are the changes that need to be explained. Trying to follow Hegel's division of the 'Concept', the exposition begins with the most *general* categories, the quintessence of capital; at a certain point of development, however, capital's multiplication into many *particular* capitals is implied; in each of those, generality is incarnated. Once capital is posited, it distinguishes itself from itself and thus is multiplied into many capitals:

> The third form of money, as independent value in a negative relation *vis-à-vis* circulation, is capital which does not step out of the production process into exchange again to become money. Rather, it is capital which becomes a commodity and enters into circulation in the form of value that refers to itself. (*Capital and interest*). This form presupposes capital in the earlier forms and at the same time forms the transition from *capital* to the *particular capitals*, the real capitals; since now, in this last form, capital already in its very concept divides into two capitals with independent existence. Along with the duality, plurality in general is then given.[18]

Thus far, accumulation is not required for capital to be posited. According to this plan, also reproduction will come later; interest, on the other hand, can be already introduced. Moreover, interest represents the link to proceed from capital to capitals, and many capitals and competition seem to be the same. Therefore: generality coincides with capital before the plurality is posited and plurality seems to coincide with competition. Accumulation is not required to move to posited capital.

Can such a structure be consistent, that is, can capital be posited, without or before accumulation? And can we have interest before competition?[19] Accumulation seems to be the decisive passage to move to posited capital, so it is the

---

18. Marx 1993, p. 449 (translation modified); Marx 1976–81 (*MEGA*² II/1), pp. 358 f.
19. What does 'to be posited' mean? In order to be posited, capital has to produce as its own result that which at the beginning (logically) it presupposed, and was not posited by it. In order to be a 'process', capital needs to reproduce what was given as a result of its own process. We should establish if such position of presuppositions can be logically consistent without accumulation.

change of its position in the theory that determines the redefinition of the relationship of generality and particularity. I will now attempt to demonstrate how and why accumulation became part of generality.

Already in the index of 1861 [Plan H], in Chapter IV of capital in general, we find the title 'Primitive accumulation' divided into further chapters.[20] The idea of dedicating a chapter to accumulation before the positing of capital is here clearly expressed, even though still in a hybrid form where there is no definitive distinction between primitive accumulation and properly capitalistic accumulation.

A first, not planned exposition of accumulation is however already in the *Grundrisse*, just after the category of relative surplus-value. Marx goes into the effects of the reinvestment of the surplus-value produced in the previous process of production.[21] We have a second unplanned occurrence in circulation where he distinguished between primitive accumulation and the properly capitalistic one,[22] and between pluscapital I and pluscapital II.[23] This was preceded by a first draft of the law of population.[24] We are evidently dealing with categories that in *Capital* will be part of the theory of accumulation. According to the plan he was following at that moment, these should have been considered later, but evidently it was the dialectical *exposition of the thing itself* that took them to their proper place.

This new framework for accumulation, which was first attempted in the *Grundrisse*, was taken up again in the final part of the *Manuscripts of 1861–3*,[25] where, at the same time, issues such as accumulation, general reproduction, the relation between one and many capitals, and their levels of abstraction arise clearly.

In *Capital*, accumulation is in Volume I, general reproduction as a form of extended social accumulation is in Volume II (circulation of capital is between them) and the whole is before the capital/profit-relation, which is within generality.

The reason why accumulation is a prerequisite of posited capital is explained by Marx in *Capital* Volume I: if capital has to be a self-developing process, it needs to produce its presuppositions as a result. In order to do that, it incorporates living labour to get surplus-value; it exists inasmuch as it repeats again and again this process, re-implying what it had produced in the same actual process. So *reproduction*, which takes place in the form of accumulation in the capitalist mode of production, is part of the *essence* of the concept of capital. The single

---

20. In English, this is usually called 'primitive accumulation'.
21. Marx 1993, pp. 386 ff.; Marx 1976–81 (*MEGA*² II/1), pp. 294 ff.
22. Marx 1993, pp. 459 f.; Marx 1976–81 (*MEGA*² II/1), pp. 367 ff.
23. Marx 1993, pp. 456 f.; Marx 1976–81 (*MEGA*² II/1), pp. 365 f.
24. Marx 1993, pp. 398 f.; Marx 1976–81 (*MEGA*² II/1), pp. 306 f.
25. Marx 1978–82 (*MEGA*² II/3), pp. 2243 ff.

process of production is an *essential* link in a chain that presupposes – and at the same time is the presupposition – of the reproduction of itself and of others.[26]

The sentence 'of itself and of others' introduces the question of plurality inside accumulation, but it is the exposition itself that takes us there. In *Capital*, in fact, we find plurality of capitals before profit and before circulation. This means that not only accumulation but also the 'many' capitals appear before capital is posited. Let us try to understand why this is logically required.

It is logically required, first, because the 'commodity' is the 'economic cell' of the capitalist mode of production, the form assumed by 'products' in it. Commodity production presupposes independent and individual producers (a plurality of actors is thus already at stake from the very beginning, the 'level zero'). Even if we assume that originally these are not capitalists, they will become capitalists because (i) money is adequately posited only if transformed into capital, (ii) capital tends to grow and to expand to all branches of production (exactly because of its higher productivity). If commodity production is general, then everything is produced as commodity, including means of production and labour-power; the production process will be possible thus only in capitalist conditions. Those who intend to participate in social reproduction will be able to do so only according to the capitalist rules.

This trend of generalisation is suggested by Marx himself in the *Manuscripts of 1861–3*.[27] Moreover, the necessity of many capitals before profit is thematised explicitly when Marx considers the circulation of capitals as a whole.

What we were dealing with in both Part One and Part Two of Volume II, however, was always no more than an individual capital, the movement of an autonomous part of the social capital. However, the circuits of individual capitals are interlinked, they presuppose one another, and it is precisely by being interlinked in this way that they constitute the movement of the social capital. Just as a single commodity turned out to be nothing but one term in the series of metamorphoses of the commodity world as a whole, now individual capital appears as one term in the series of metamorphoses of social capital.[28]

It is logically required because, second, the fact that the whole production takes place under capitalist conditions does not mean that it is realised by a *single* capital; on the contrary, that is exactly what is impossible. We know in fact that each producer will become a capitalist in the long run, not that there

---

26. See Marx 1990a, pp. 711 ff.; Marx 1991a (*MEGA*² II/10), pp. 506 ff.; cf. *Manuscript of 1861–3*, Marx 1976–82 (*MEGA*² II/3), pp. 2243 ff.
27. Marx 1976–82 (*MEGA*² II/3), pp. 2223.
28. Marx 1992c, pp. 429 f.; Marx 2008, p. 328.

will be only *one* capitalist, because production is still commodity production (we still have the commodity-money relation, exchange, and so on).

The impossibility of a universal capital is clearly stated by Marx in the *Grundrisse*:

> Since value forms the foundation of capital, and since it therefore necessarily exists only through exchange for *counter-value*, it thus necessarily repels itself from itself. A *universal capital*, one without alien capitals confronting it, with which it exchanges – and from the present standpoint ... is therefore a nonthing. The reciprocal repulsion within capitals is already contained in capital as realized exchange value.[29]

It is logically required because, finally, a plurality of actors were present from the very beginning, because this is a presupposition implicit in the notion of commodity. Thanks to capital, we have, instead, an inner trend that changes each single producer into a capitalist.

This is why we need accumulation in order to posit capital. Moreover, in order to have accumulation in a proper way there also needs to be a first analysis of the relationship among capitals (plural) and their accumulation (so going through circulation as well). The whole process of the accumulation of the 'many' capitals (social general reproduction) must be included in its general concept before particularity and competition.[30] The social general reproduction is the last link before particularity.

Marx became aware of the preliminary character of the social general reproduction – that is, accumulation through many capitals – in the *Manuscripts of 1861–3*. There he wrote the following: 'Furthermore it is necessary to expose the circulation or reproduction process *before* dealing with the posited capital – *capital and profit* – since we have to explain, not only how capital produces, but also how capital is produced. But the actual movement comes out from the

---

29. Marx 1993, p. 421; Marx 1976–81 (*MEGA*[2] II/1), p. 334.

30. This is a clear example of how we have to consider Hegel's legacy in Marx. At the beginning Marx follows schematically Hegel's pattern and tries to derive the plurality of capitals from the generality evoking explicitly its logic. This is a very undialectical attitude, the negation of Hegel's method. While working out his own model, Marx understands finally that his theory can be consistent only if he follows and presents its own dialectical logic, not an external one applied to it. This seems to me to be one of the mistakes – a methodological one – that many scholars have been repeating for a long time: trying to apply Hegel's logic to Marx's theory of capital, instead of respecting Hegel's method itself, that is, to follow the dialectic of the thing itself – in our case, 'capital'. A schematic repetition of Hegel's patterns was Lassalle's mistake, sharply criticised by Marx himself in a letter to Engels (Letter to Engels, February 1, 1858, in Marx and Engels 1986, pp. 260 f).

available capital – i.e. on the basis of the developed capitalistic production, starting from itself and presupposing itself'.[31]

I call 'accumulation I' the process of a single capital reproducing itself. It turns out that, from the beginning, the reproduction of this single capital sets up a relationship with 'others' (we have seen that in the end these others can be only capitals). Each one is a link in a chain, and to posit properly the accumulation of a single one, we have to consider the condition of the accumulation of each of them in their reciprocal relation. What are the abstract conditions that allow a society of many single capitals to survive as a whole? The answer to this question is the general social reproduction that I call 'accumulation II'.

The main difference from the first plan is that, although we have many capitals, we do not yet have particularity or competition. In fact, we have not yet inquired into the trend of each capital acting as such, trying to oust other capitals. On the contrary, Marx's question is: what are the material conditions, which appear as value, that might allow this kind of society to survive? And to grow? We are at the point of view of the totality of capital, not yet at the point of view of the particular capital.

If we can preliminarily take into account the accumulation of a single capital to show its general laws, we cannot however properly reach profit, yet, because the single accumulation needs the accumulation of the society as a whole.

The core of the distinction in the *Grundrisse* between generality and particularity – that is, the passage from capital as a whole to particular capitals – turns out to be unacceptable. 'Many' capitals are already necessary in the generality, although this does not mean competition. On the contrary, in the *Grundrisse* many capitals and competition were in the same framework.

What, then, is the main difference between generality and particularity after this change? In generality we have, first, a general attitude to the whole and, second, the coincidence of production and consumption. Marx wants first to study how categories work in pure conditions, that is, setting aside the troubling effects of competition- and realisation problems. These are not marginal of course, but their decisive role will be considered later, in particularity.

This condition is still valid in *Capital* Volumes I and II, and for the first section of Volume III. While dealing with accumulation, Marx claims that there are at that level two clauses of abstraction: 1) all produced commodities are sold and all means of production can be purchased without problems on the market; that is: circulation- and realisation-difficulties are for the moment left out of consideration; 2) it is presupposed that surplus-value is not divided into specific

---

31. Marx 1976–82 (*MEGA*[2] II/3), p. 1134.

and more concrete forms such as profit or interest or rent, which belong to a more determined and advanced level.[32] These two clauses were already valid in simple circulation,[33] and are also still valid in circulation of capital. Note that circulation of capital has *always* been considered part of generality since the very beginning. This is also valid for social reproduction at the end of Volume II, where Marx explicitly states that, even if we have many capitals and their material replacement and reproduction, this does not imply that they are 'particular'; they are not taken into account as many self-valorising particular capitals, but inasmuch as they act as molecular parts of the whole. Therefore we can have a first study of the many capitals within generality.[34]

The framework of the *Grundrisse* was dropped because the dialectic of the thing itself implied a more consistent development, which was outlined in the new structure. However, other limits of the original structure need to be overcome.

---

32. 'On the one hand, then, we assume here that the capitalist sells the commodities he has produced at their value, and we shall not concern ourselves with their later return to the market, or the new forms that capital assumes while in the sphere of circulation, or the concrete conditions of reproduction hidden within those forms. On the other hand, we treat the capitalist producer as the owner of the entire surplus-value, or, perhaps better, as the representative of all those who will share the booty with him'. Marx 1990a, p. 710; Marx 1991a (*MEGA*² II/10), pp. 505 f.

33. 'Let us suppose... that every piece of linen on the market contains nothing but socially necessary labour-time. In spite of this, all these pieces taken as a whole may contain superfluously expended labour-time. It the market cannot stomach the whole quantity at the normal price of 2 shillings a yard, this proves that too great a portion of the total social labour-time has been expended in the form of weaving... The division of labour converts the product of labour into a commodity, and thereby makes necessary its conversion into money. At the same time, it makes a matter of chance whether this transubstantiation succeeds of not. Here, however, we have to look at the phenomenon in its pure shape, and *must therefore assume it has proceeded normally*' (my emphasis). Marx 1993, pp. 202 f.; Marx 1976–81 (*MEGA*² II/1), pp. 101 f.

34. Demand equals supply is general precondition of Volume II: 'In order to grasp these forms in their pure state, we must first of all abstract from all aspects that have nothing to do with the change and constitution of the forms as such. We shall therefore assume here, both that commodities are sold at their values, and that the circumstances in which this takes place do not change. We shall also ignore any changes of value that may occur in the course of the cyclical process' (Marx 1992c, p. 109; Marx 2008, p. 28). Furthermore, this coincidence is presupposition of the general social reproduction with capitals and material replacement of production conditions, but without competition: 'Moreover, we assume not only that products are exchanged at their values, but also that no revolution in values takes place in the components of the productive capital' (Marx 1992c, p. 469; Marx 2008, p. 365).

'Scheme of the changes to Marx's concept of capital in general between 1857–8 and 1863–5'

	Generality/Universality	Particularity
Original plan	What is produced is consumed *ex machina*	Competition
	Capital as a whole undivided	One/many capitals Accumulation
Final plan	What is produced is consumed *ex machina*	Competition
	Capital as a whole divided into one/many capitals Accumulation	One/many capitals in competition

2. Particularity

The main achievements due to the process of accumulation are:

1. What was presupposed (the capital/labour-relation, the material preconditions of production, and so on) has now been posited by capital itself; now capital can be a process;
2. We have the total social reproduction as a whole with the many capitals not yet free to act. Marx needs now to put together these two dimensions of his theory: the whole should include the dynamics of the particular capitals aiming at valorisation. Therefore, capital can no longer be considered as ideal average and must become a result of their real dynamics in order to be properly posited and proceed to another more concrete level of abstraction.

The produced surplus-value is result of the whole process of capitalist production (production + circulation) and this process is a self-developing one. The fruit of its work, surplus-value, appears as the result of the whole and so, at the surface, it seems that its rate has to be calculated with reference to all of the anticipated capital, not only to the variable part. We thus have profit and rate of profit. In the original plan this was the final step of generality that then, thanks to the further point 'interest', moved to particularity.

After the changes, Marx does not consider interest yet, but capitals' 'particular' interaction, the forms of their reciprocal fight for self-valorisation, that is, for profit. Each one realises its general laws (yielding profit) as a particular agent, among various other particular ones. So far, we already looked at these already existent various capitals as necessary, but they were regarded as subordinated moments of capital's dynamics as a whole; now we go further and consider their particular action as real actualisers of generality. At this point, Marx drops one of the crucial clauses of abstraction of Generality: supply no longer equals demand. In Particularity, Marx inquires into the interaction of capitals when these are free to move in conformity not with an average established from outside as hypothesis, but with their real movement; that is, competition.[35]

Marx considers two kinds of competition: the first is inside a branch and produces a market-value for all products realised (and sold) in that branch. This is already a social value that does not correspond to individual ones (only the commodities produced by the capitals which apply the average technical conditions have an individual value magnitude that corresponds to the social one). The second kind of competition is among different branches and produces the price of production. This is the average of the average, that is, a particular market-price, whose profit is at the same time socially average. Marx achieved this result for the first time in the *Manuscripts of 1861–3*.[36] The argument is taken up again in the *Manuscripts of 1863–5* while exposing the rules of competition that give production-prices as a result and, finally, thanks to Engels, in *Capital* Volume III. See, for instance, the following passages:

> What competition brings about, first of all in one sphere, is the establishment of a uniform market value and market price out of the various individual values of commodities. But it is only the competition of capitals in *different* spheres that brings forth the production prices that equalizes the rates of profit between those spheres.[37]
>
> It has been said that competition equalizes profit rates between the different spheres of production to produce an average rate of profit, and that this is precisely the way in which the values of products from these various spheres are transformed into prices of production ... This uninterrupted emigration and immigration of capitals that takes place between various spheres of production produces rising and falling movements in the profit-rate which more or less balance one another out and thus tend to reduce the profit-rate everywhere to the same common and general level.[38]

---

35. Only in this context and taking into account the gap – that is, the discontinuity and the continuity among the different levels of abstraction – can the transformation-problem be properly posed and resolved.

36. Marx 1976–82 (*MEGA*² II/3), p. 854.

37. Marx 1991b, p. 281; Marx 1992b (*MEGA*² II/4.2), p. 255.

38. Marx 1991b, p. 310; Marx 1992b (*MEGA*² II/4.2), pp. 278 f. I obviously cannot go into the transformation problem here, but if we consider that the value-theory of Chapter One is part of generality and that the market-values (and then the production-prices) are part of particularity, we cannot only pose the problem in different terms but also propose a different solution to it. In the second case, in order to determine value-magnitudes, what and how much is produced is as essential as what and how much is consumed. Trying to compare prices and values as two different criteria of measurement will always result in contradictions. But they do not have this relationship: they are two different levels of abstraction of the same thing (commodities/money-relation). Note *en passant* that also

A general rate of profit for the entire society is no longer an abstract concept, but a result of the real dynamics of particular capitals. A particular case incarnates the general average. This social average is obviously not unchangeable once fixed; it changes following exactly the two trends of competition toward new 'standards'.[39]

The crucial achievement we were interested in, however, is that the presupposed social average is now a result of the real process of competing capitals; the abstract magnitudes that referred to the whole are now a concrete profit gained by a particular branch of production. An average that will obviously change, but which will be replaced by another average. Particular and general are actual in a single moment. This result is the link to proceed towards singularity. We will see that interest-bearing capital is very important to achieve this, but interest is another category that changes its position from the *Manuscripts of 1857–8* to those of 1863–5.[40]

---

in simple circulation what and how much is produced/consumed would be decisive to determine value-magnitudes if *we* did not *assume* that supply equals demand. But this is only an assumption to study how the model works even if there is no obstacle, not because consumption is inessential.

39. Value-magnitudes are thus posited, at this level, by the standards of production achieved through competition. Thus it is also possible to measure value-magnitudes through labour-time once the standards are given (and for a certain period they are given). This implies that value-magnitudes are never given *ex ante* (and this is a sharp criticism of the traditional – so called – labour-theory of value, a definition never used by Marx and invented by Böhm-Bawerk!) because it is consumption that essentially co-determines them (we cannot know before the exchanges which and how many already produced commodities will be consumed); however, it is at the same time implied that these can be measured by labour-time as far as the standards last. In the long run, value-magnitudes are determined by embodied labour, but the run is caused by the mutual relation of production and consumption that are both essential to fix the resulting 'standards'. Marx refers to these standards in the manuscript of Volume III, but this disappeared in the printed version (Marx 1991b, pp. 295 f.; Marx 1992b (*MEGA*[2] II/4.2), p. 268): 'If one seller produces more cheaply and can more easily undercut the others, carving out a bigger share of the market by selling below the current market price or market value, then he does so, and the action once begun, it gradually forces the others to introduce the cheaper form or production and thereby reduces the socially necessary labour to a new and lower level'. The translation of Engels's edition is imprecise; the German text uses 'measure', not 'level': 'auf ein neues geringeres Maß reduziert'. However, Marx's original was: 'auf einen neuen standard reducirt'; 'to a new standard'.

40. Part of 'particularity' is also the tendency of the rate of profit to fall, which, in my view, can be read as a first attempt at a theory of economic cycles. See Fineschi 2001 and more recently Reuten 2004. Actually, this chapter and also the second section on the transformation of values into prices seems to be halfway between universality and particularity. I cannot deepen this point here; however, I think that this is one of main reasons why scholars have proposed so many different solutions to these issues, and why it is so difficult to find a proper one. In fact, Marx put the two levels next to each other and was not able to give a proper mediation. Chapter Nine, which does not require competition, is just next to Chapter Ten, which requires it; in the chapter on the fall of

3. Towards singularity

In the *Manuscripts of 1861–3*, after an analysis of the tendency of the profit-rate to fall, Marx deals for the first time with a few questions linked to the further development of the theory, which previously had been only sporadically indicated. We need to understand if these categories correspond to the concept of singularity sketched in 1857–8. In the cited letter to Engels [see Plan F], he spoke about the division of the book of capital into four points. In the *Grundrisse* draft, particularity (competition) was followed by singularity, which was further divided into three points [see Plan C]: credit, share-capital and money-market. The reconstruction of the inner logic of this part and its connection with the preceding one are made more difficult by the increasing reduction of the dialectical terminology.

We find here a further difference with reference to the *Grundrisse*; the logic of the argument shows that Interest-bearing capital is required to proceed to singularity. In the *Manuscripts of 1857–8* it was the step between generality, which ended with capital/profit-relation, and particularity. We have seen above how Marx defined it.[41] The end of generality was the capital/profit-relation, $M - M'$, that is, an increased quantity of money compared with the anticipated capital. The dynamics that produced it disappears in the result: we have more money as a sort of fact. The 'thing' money seems to be able to generate money, as if this should be a quality of it. This is the foundation of the category 'interest-bearing capital' and of the 'fetishism of capital' (not to be confounded with 'fetishism of commodities'). Successively, this definition is partly conserved, partly changed.

In the *Manuscripts of 1863–65* the same concept is taken up again with these words:

> With interest-bearing capital the situation is different, and this is precisely what constitutes its specific character. The owner of money who wants to valorize this as Interest-bearing capital parts with it someone else, puts it into circulation, makes it into a commodity *as capital*; as capital not only for himself but also for others. It is not simply capital for the person who alienates it,

---

the profit-rate, the growth of the organic composition, which does not need competition, is next to the draft of the cycle-theory, which needs it. These issues are connected with the change of the plan that occurred at the end of 1862 [See Plan I]; a further change occurred while Marx was writing the manuscripts of 1864–5. See a first attempt to analyse these difficult passages in Fineschi 2008, Chapter Two and Fineschi 2011. A revised version of the latter paper will be published in the proceedings of the 2011 conference of the International Symposium on Marxian Theory.

41. Marx 1993, p. 449; Marx 1976–81 (*MEGA*² II/1), pp. 358 f.

but it is made over to the other person as capital right from the start, as value that possesses the use-value of creating surplus-value or profit.[42]

The two expositions could seem similar, but the difference is essential, exactly because of the change in the general framework we previously analysed.

As we saw, generality consisted in an ideal average that had to proceed to a real posited average. This occurs thanks to the action of the 'many' capitals in competition that leads to average profit and production-prices. In order to posit 'interest-bearing capital' as moment of the real process, the mere generality is then not enough; to have capital *perceived* as a thing, the actors of the process at the surface of the society need to become aware somehow of this 'average'; the existence of an average fruit of capital must be socially perceived as a fact, 'naturally' generated by capital, disregarding the real process that put it in existence. This is possible however only *after* competition has posited the ideal average as a real fact as average social profit, something given to the social actor at the surface. This seems a fact because it appears as 'given'.[43]

Since profit-yielding appears as a quality of the thing capital/money, capital can be lent as a sort of commodity; its use-value is profit-generation, as though we could set aside the real process of valorisation. What was a general achievement in the capital/profit relation becomes now a phenomenal economic category, which really operates at the surface and also in the mind of the actors. The consequences are relevant:

> The characteristic movement of capital in general, the return of money to the capitalist, the return of capital to its point of departure, receives in the case of Interest-bearing capital a completely superficial form, separated from the real movement whose form it is...
>
> Here therefore the return does not appear as a consequence and result of a definite series of economic processes, but rather as a consequence of a special legal contract between buyer and seller. The period of the reflux depends on the course of the reproduction process; in the case of Interest-bearing capital, its return as capital *seems* to depend simply on the contract between lender and borrower. And so the reflux of the capital, in connection with this transaction, no longer appears as a result determined by the production process, but rather as if the capital lent out had never lost the form of money. Of course, there transactions are actually determined by the real refluxes. But this is not apparent in the transaction itself.[44]

---

42. Marx 1991b, p. 464; Marx 1992b (*MEGA*[2] II/4.2), p. 416.
43. Marx posits this transition for the first time in the *Manuscripts of 1861–3* dealing with 'Revenues and their sources'. This manuscript is decisive even on this point.
44. Marx 1991b, pp. 469 f.; Marx 1992b (*MEGA*[2] II/4.2), p. 421.

Two points seem to be decisive:

1. Thanks to capital's relation with itself as mere quantity of money (where its increase in quantity seems to be property of the object 'capital'), the generality of valorisation is concretely individualised in interest-bearing capital; therefore interest-bearing capital distinguishes itself from all concrete processes of capitalist production, representing, tangibly in front of them, their ideal dimension. In this way it empirically exists in front of the all the other operating capitals as their essence and these appear as one particular mode of its incarnation. General capital appears phenomenally in front of particular capitals as their immaterial form of movement, as pure M – M'. In the *Manuscripts of 1861–3*, Marx claims:

> This is the quite tangible form of self-valorising value or of money-making money, and at the same time the quite irrational form, the incomprehensible, mystified form. In the discussion of capital we started from M – C – M', of which M – M' was only a result. We now find M – M' *as the subject*...The incomprehensible form we encounter at the surface and which has therefore constituted the starting-point of our analysis, is found again as the result of the process in which the figure of capital is gradually more and more estranged and unrelated to its inner essence.
>
> We started with money as the converted form of the commodity. What we arrive at is *money as the converted form of capital*, just as we have known that the commodity is the pre-condition and the result of the production process of capital.[45]

Valorisation as intrinsic property of the thing 'money', the contradictory riddle that was the starting point of the inquiry into capital, is now a result of the process of capital as a whole.

2. This is the starting point of the 'fetishism of capital'. In simple circulation, the thing 'money' seemed to be value in itself; now it is 'capital' that seems to be a thing that generate interest in itself.[46]

---

45. Marx 1971, pp. 466 f. (translation modified); Marx 1976–82 (*MEGA²* II/3), p. 1464.
46. Marx's words are explicit: 'In Interest-bearing capital, the capital relationship reaches its most superficial and fetishized form...but for all that it exposes itself as the product of a social *relation*, not the product of a mere *thing*': Marx 1991b, p. 515 (translation modified); Marx 1992b (*MEGA²* II/4.2), p. 461. 'The *thing* money (money, commodity, value) is now already capital simply as a thing; the result of the overall reproduction process appears as a property devolving on a thing in itself; it is up to the possessor of money, i.e. of commodities in their ever-exchangeable form, whether he wants to spend this money as money or hire it out as capital. In Interest-bearing capital, therefore this automatic fetish is elaborated into its pure form, self-valorizing value, money breeding money, and its pure form, it no longer bears any marks of its origin. The social

We have thus achieved the particular existence of capital in general.[47] Interest-bearing capital appears as capital *par excellence*, existing capital as such that stays in front of the real processes of production as if it generated profit by itself, without going through them. Interest seems to be what repays its natural lucrativeness, while profit appears to be the result of the real material application of that abstract universality in a particular branch.

Several times in this manuscript, Marx focuses on the division of capital into Interest-bearing capital as '*Kapital an sich*' (Hegelian words) and its particular existing forms as operating, working capitals:

> *Interest* is definitely posited as the offspring of capital, separate, independent and outside the capitalist process itself. It is due to *capital as capital*. In enters into the production process and therefore proceeds from it. Capital is impregnated with interest. It does not derive interest from the production process, but brings it into it. The surplus of profit over interest, the amount of surplus-value which capital derives solely from the production process, i.e., the surplus value it produces as operating capital, acquires a particular figure as *industrial profit* (employer's profit, industrial or commercial, depending on whether the stress is laid on the production process or the circulation process), in contrast to interest as value creation due to *capital in itself, capital for itself, capital as capital*.[48]

Interest is a fruit of capital in itself, profit of capital in process. The abstract separation of real dimension and value-dimension in the realisation of capital, two dimensions that are immanent to each capital, has now become an actual one.

---

relation is consummated ion the relationship of a thing, money, to itself. Instead of the actual transformation of money into capital, we have here only the form of this devoid of content': Marx 1991b, p. 516; Marx 1992b (*MEGA*[2] II/4.2), pp. 461 f.

47. This was outlined already in *Manuscripts of 1861–63*: 'On the other hand, *Interest-bearing capital* is the consummated fetish. It is capital in its finished form – as such representing the unity of production process and circulation process – and therefore yields a definite profit in a definite period of time. In the form of interest-bearing capital only this determination remains, without the mediation of either production process or circulation process. Memories of the past still remain in capital and profit, although because of the divergence of profit from surplus-value and the uniform profit yielding by all capitals – that is, the general rate of profit – capital becomes very much obscured, something dark and mysterious'. 'In Interest-bearing capital, this *automatic fetish* is consummated, the self-valorising value, the money-making money, and in this form it no longer bears any trace of its origin. This social relation is consummated as a relation of things (money, commodities) to themselves...It is clear that capital, as the mysterious and automatically generating source of interest, that is, source of its [own] increase, finds its consummation in capital and interest. It is therefore especially in this form that capital exists for the representation [*Vorstellung*]. It is capital *par excellence*': Marx 1971, pp. 454 f. (translation modified); Marx 1976–82 (*MEGA*[2] II/3), p. 1454.

48. Marx 1971, p. 490 (translation modified); Marx 1976–82, p. 1490.

This implies a doubling of the figure of the capitalist: on one hand, the juridical owner of capital; on the other, the real operating capitalist:

> There are not two different kinds of capital – Interest-bearing and profit yielding – but the *selfsame* capital which operates in the process of production as capital, produces a profit which is divided between two different capitalists – one standing outside the process, and, as owner, representing capital *as such* (but it is an essential condition of this capital that it is represented by a *private owner*; without this it does not become capital as opposed to wage-labour), and the other representing operating capital, capital which takes part in the production process.[49]

At the end of particularity, we had average profit produced by a particular branch. This was a necessary step to go further. Now, that average valorisation of capital exists as universal/general form in a particular capital – but representing capital as such – in front of all other particular capitals. The universality of capital, present in each of them, is now concretely incarnated in a particular existing capital in front of them. Universal exists as particular and therefore is singular.

This is a further relevant improvement with reference to the outline in the *Grundrisse*, where profit and interest overlapped in the end. The logic of the thing itself has shown how interest and interest-bearing capital can be posited just after competition and represent a link to singularity.

4. Singularity

Now we have an 'existing capital in general'. We now need to see how the whole of capital works when we reach this final level of abstraction.

This part was developed by Marx almost exclusively in the *Manuscripts of 1863–5*. Until a few years ago we could read only Engels's edition of Marx's manuscript of Volume III. Thanks to the new critical edition of the works of Marx and Engels (*Marx-Engels Gesamtausgabe*),[50] the original manuscript appeared in 1992.[51] This was the occasion for a broad debate – mainly on the transformation-problem. That text, however, is also very useful as regards the question of the levels of abstraction, in particular regarding 'singularity'.

---

49. Marx 1971, p. 473; Marx 1976–82 (*MEGA*² II/3), p. 1471.

50. On the *MEGA* and its history, see Mazzone 2002 and the Introduction to Bellofiore and Fineschi 2009.

51. Marx 1992b. See other manuscripts for Volume III in Marx 2003. The few remaining manuscripts have appeared in 2003 in the third tome of Volume Four, second section of the *MEGA*.

If we compare Marx's outline of the manuscript with Engels's published version, we see immediately how relevant the differences are. In particular, what was indicated by Marx as the final chapter of the part on capital – Credit and fictitious capital – became *one* chapter *among* several others, a single point put *next to* various others, not the *title of the whole part*. On the contrary, Marx quite clearly intended to work out a whole divided into three chapters that are coherently signed as I, II and III. Moreover, Engels *created* several chapters, also giving them a title. Some of those were produced out of passages that Marx had eloquently entitled 'Confusion'. This part was a collage of citations that as such, evidently, did not belong to the exposition (page-numbers were also different). Engels transformed these passages into a 'text' by putting together citations and adding a few pages of his own, before, after and in the middle of Marx's quotes. If the real subject of the section became one chapter among several others (all on the same level) and if some of those were even created by Engels himself, going back to Marx's original manuscript is then evidently crucial.

As said, Marx's manuscript seems to be an exposition of a general framework entitled 'Credit and fictitious capital', divided into three steps:

1) a part with an outline of the features of properly capitalist credit: commercial and bank-credit.[52] In Engels's edition, this became Chapter Twenty-Five, with, however, a few modifications: he put many footnotes directly into the text;

2) a second part, where Marx sketched the functions of credit in the capitalist mode of production. Here he concretely dealt for the first time with share-capital.[53] In the published book this is Chapter Twenty-Seven;

3) the exposition, divided into three points, of this level of abstraction as a whole.[54] In Engels's edition, this is Chapters Twenty-Eight to Thirty-Two.

If we compare the structure of the manuscript with the hypothesis of the four levels of abstraction, we find interesting evidence. First, we have Chapter Five, where interest-bearing capital represents the link to proceed towards the exposition of credit and fictitious capital as a whole. Credit as totality constitutes then the last step of the exposition of capital as such. Moreover, interest-bearing capital clearly represents the link to it.[55] Second, the central categories of credit

---

52. Marx 1992b (*MEGA*[2] II/4.2), pp. 468–75.

53. Marx 1992b (*MEGA*[2] II/4.2), pp. 502 ff.

54. Marx 1992b (*MEGA*[2] II/4.2), pp. 506–61, 584–97.

55. Marx reasserts in several passages that credit constitutes the consummation of Interest-bearing capital and of the capital-concept as a whole: 'Interest-bearing capital receives the form peculiar and corresponding to capitalistic production in *credit*. It is a form created by capitalist production itself'. Marx 1971, p. 518 (translation modified); Marx 1976–82 (*MEGA*[2] II/3), p. 1514. See also Marx 1971, pp. 468 f.; Marx 1976–82 (*MEGA*[2] II/3), p. 1466.

and share-capital are outlined as the most concrete forms of existence of capital (it could be shown that fictitious capital corresponds to the most developed exposition of share-capital). This structure of singularity corresponds to that presented by Marx in the *Grundrisse* and in the aforementioned letter to Engels. This would confirm that he *further elaborated* a structure that was *already* outlined in the *Grundrisse*.

A detailed analysis of this level of abstraction cannot be conducted here. I will limit myself to an outline:

1. In the first part of singularity, Marx shows how the (logically) developed capitalist mode of production reshapes inherited pre-existing categories, which is here credit from the simple circulation (derived from money as means of payment), positing it in a form adequate to the new level of abstraction;[56] this becomes the new basis of the capitalist credit-system.[57] The first new category is that of bank-credit: the capitalist division of labour implies that the functions linked to the management of money as such are monopolised by an individual capitalist: the banker.[58] Since money is now an 'interest-bearing thing', by managing money the bank has the general formula of capital (M – M') under its control, as if it were a phenomenal object. Thus, the bank is the phenomenal, *empirically existing representative* of capital as such. Capital in general, which at the beginning was a mere abstraction, exists empirically as a category in interest-bearing capital and operates thanks to the universal capitalist, the bank.[59] The money-market is the further development of bank-credit.[60]

---

56. Marx 1992b (*MEGA*[2] II/4.2), pp. 469 f.; Marx 1991b, pp. 525 f.

57. Marx 1992b (*MEGA*[2] II/4.2), p. 535; Marx 1991b, p. 610.

58. Marx 1992b (*MEGA*[2] II/4.2), p. 387; Marx 1991b, p. 431.

59. Marx 1992b (*MEGA*[2] II/4.2), p. 463; Marx 1991b, p. 517. Here, we find the culmination of an idea that Marx sketched already in *Manuscripts of 1857–8*: 'Before we go any further, just one remark. *Capital in general*, as distinct from the particular capitals, does indeed appear (1) *only as an abstraction*; not an arbitrary abstraction, but an abstraction which grasps the specific characteristics which distinguish capital from all other forms of wealth – or modes in which (social) production develops. These are the determinations common to every capital as such, or which makes every determined sum of value into capital. And the distinctions within this abstraction are likewise abstract particularities which characterize every kind of capital, in that it is their position or negation (e.g. fixed capital or circulating capital); (2) however, capital in general, as *distinct* from the particular real capitals, is itself a *real* existence ... For example, capital in this *general form*, although belonging to single capitalists, in its *elemental form* as capital, forms the capital which accumulates in the banks of is distributed through them and ... distributes itself in accordance with the needs of production ... While the general is therefore on the one hand only a mental mark of distinction [*gedachte* differentia specifica], it is at the same time a *particular* real form alongside the form of the particular and singular'. Marx 1993, pp. 449 f.; Marx 1976–81 (*MEGA*[2] II/1), p. 359.

60. Marx 1992b (*MEGA*[2] II/4.2), pp. 440 f.; Marx 1991b, pp. 490 f.

2. The second step consists in showing (i) the genesis of share-capital, (ii) its fictitious nature and then (iii) the general achievement of this level of abstraction that actually can be clear only in the light of the following point.[61]

3. The third step is the explanation of how capital works as a whole, once it has achieved its most concrete level – credit and share-capital. This argument is divided into three further steps. The most important issue regards the independent but interconnected lives of fictitious and real capital.

First, to fix the general nature of monetary flow, Marx shows that capital and circulation are not independent concepts. Disputing the accounts of Tooke and Fullerton, he leads the problem back to the different functions of money, which can exist both in revenue-form and as capital.[62]

Second, he shows the conceptual origin of share-capital and its natural trend to become fictitious. Thus, the money-market is extended to speculation.[63] Each capital has a double nature, material and monetary. The two of them do not exist separately, but interest-bearing capital allows that separation to appear possible and thus these are split and act – each one on its own – respectively in the financial market and in material production. The first is of course dependent on the second one, but value-magnitudes have to correspond only at the end; insofar as the first undergoes its fictitious experiences, its value can apparently change according to demand and supply. This causes real money transfers.

Third, he tries to outline the relationship between fictitious accumulation, which seems to become autonomous, and real accumulation. He starts with (i) the analysis of commercial credit setting aside the bank credit, then of commercial and bank credit together, considering the consequence on the rate of interest;[64] he then (ii) proceeds taking into account the relation between boosted shares and real accumulation of capital;[65] finally, he considers (iii) the accomplished unity (or re-unification) of value (apparently independent thanks to share- and fictitious capital) and use-value (the real material process of reproduction), of abstract and concrete form of wealth in capitalist production: the crisis.[66]

---

61. Marx 1992b (*MEGA*² II/4.2), pp. 502 ff.
62. Marx 1992b (*MEGA*² II/4.2), pp. 506 f.; Marx 1991b, pp. 575 f.
63. Marx 1992b (*MEGA*² II/4.2), pp. 536 ff.; Marx 1991b, pp. 610 ff.
64. Ibid.
65. Marx 1992b (*MEGA*² II/4.2), p. 542; Marx 1991b, pp. 619 f.
66. Marx 1992b (*MEGA*² II/4.2), pp. 540, 543, 594 f.; Marx 1991b, pp. 609, 620, 638 f.

Conclusion

In the *Manuscripts of 1857–8*, Marx's plan for the book on capital was divided into three main sections that, following Hegel's articulation of the concept, were called Generality, Particularity and Singularity. While writing his theory according to that scheme, a few changes occurred. Some features that should have been part of particularity were included in generality (that is, the relationship between one and many capitals). Some features that should have been the link between generality and particularity became the link between particularity and singularity (namely, interest-bearing capital). However, the triad continued to constitute the core of the dialectical exposition of capital (as regards the logic of the system, even if those terms were not explicitly mentioned).

If, at the beginning, Marx tried to apply Hegel's scheme to a given matter, he later understood that the very theory of capital could be worked out only following *its own inner dialectical logic*. That is why changes occurred and the final structure is *more* dialectical and consistent than the original one.

The consequence is that the *Grundrisse* were insufficient, first, for the development of the theory as a whole, because particularity and singularity were not yet considered; second, because even generality needed corrections regarding the level of abstraction of the 'many' capitals. These changes represent improvements, because the 'final' outline is more consistent and dialectical than the original one. On the other hand, this does not imply any rupture or radical discontinuity between the first manuscript and the subsequent ones. Rather, Marx further developed a general outline (the structure of generality/particularity/singularity) that he had initially sketched out in the *Grundrisse*. We then have some changes (improvements regarding the general soundness of the theory) in the same plan. However, this was not concluded and remained a draft.[67]

---

67. The recently published manuscripts for Volumes II and III and also the materials for the revision of Volume I written after 1867 do *not* present *any* new outline of the structure either of the theory of capital as a whole or of single books. This needs to be seriously taken into account. In fact, some argue that because Marx was not satisfied with what he had written and announced that he wanted to make some changes, we are allowed to speculate on what he would have done differently if he could have finished his work. However, the evidence is that Marx did not make any substantial change to the outline of his theory. The fact that Marx's theory of capital is unfinished business does not permit us to set aside what he did and to replace Marx's writings with the interpreters' ideas about never realised hypothetical modifications. This is in my view a relevant methodological mistake.

Appendix: Marx's plans

Plan A
Introduction to *Manuscripts of 1857–8* (Marx 1986, p. 45; Marx 1976–81 (*MEGA²* II/1), p. 43).

(1) The general abstract determinations, which therefore appertain more or less to all forms of society, but in the sense set forth above. (2) The categories which constitute the internal structure of bourgeois society and on which the principal classes are based. Capital, wage-labour, landed property. Their relation to one another. Town and country. The three large social classes. Exchange between them. Circulation. Credit-system (private). (3) The State as the epitome of bourgeois society. Analysed in relation to itself. The 'unproductive' classes. Taxes. National debt. Public credit. Population. Colonies. Emigration. (4) International character of production. International division of labour. International exchange. Export and import. Rate of exchange. (5) World-market and crises.

Plan B
Manuscripts of 1857–8 (Marx 1986, pp. 194 f.; Marx 1976–81 (*MEGA²* II/1), p. 187).

I. (1) General concept of capital. – (2) Particularity of capital: circulating capital, fixed capital. (Capital as means of subsistence, as raw material, as instrument of labour.) (3) Capital as money.
II. (1) Quantity of capital. Accumulation. – (2) Capital measured in terms of itself. Profit. Interest. Value of capital, i.e. capital in distinction from itself as interest and profit. (3) The circulation of capitals: (aa) Exchange of capital with capital. Exchange of capital with revenue. Capital and prices; (bb) Competition of capitals; (cc) Concentration of capitals.
III. Capital as credit.
IV. Capital as share-capital.
V. Capital as money-market.
VI. Capital as source of wealth. The capitalist.

Plan C
Manuscripts of 1857–8, (Marx 1986, pp. 205 f.; Marx 1976–81 (*MEGA²* II/1), p. 199).

Capital. I. Generality: (1) (a) Evolution of capital from money. (b) Capital and labour (mediating itself by alien labour). (c) The elements of capital, distinguished according to their relationship to labour (product, raw material, instrument of labour). (2) Particularisation of capital: (a) Circulating capital, fixed capital. Turnover of capital. (3) Singularity of capital: Capital and profit. Capital and interest. Capital as value, distinct from itself as interest and profit.

II. Particularity: (1) Accumulation of capitals. (2) Competition of capitals. (3) Concentration of capitals (quantitative difference of capital as at the same time qualitative, as measure of its volume and effect).
III. Singularity: (1) Capital as credit. (2) Capital as share-capital. (3) Capital as money-market.

Plan D
Letter to Lassalle, 22 February 1858 (Marx and Engels 1986, p. 270; Marx and Engels 1973, pp. 550 f.).

The whole is divided into 6 books: 1. On Capital (contains a few introductory chapters [*Vorchapters*]). 2. On Landed Property. 3. On Wage-Labour. 4. On the State. 5. International Trade. 6. World-Market.

Plan E
Letter to Lassalle, 11 March 11 1858 (Marx and Engels 1986, p. 287; Marx and Engels 1973, pp. 553 f.).

It ['the first instalment', that is: the part he intended to send first to the publisher, which a line before had been defined as a 'relative whole'] contains 1. Value, 2. Money, 3. Capital in General (the process of production of capital; process of its circulation; the unity of the two, or capital and profit; interest)

Plan F
Letter to Engels, 2 April 1858 (Marx and Engels 1986, p. 298; Marx and Engels 1973, pp. 312 ff.).

1. Capital falls into four sections. a) Capital *en général*. (This is the substance of the first instalment.) b) Competition, or the interaction of many capitals. c) Credit, where capital, as against individual capitals, is shown to be a universal element. d) Share-capital as the most perfected form (turning into communism) together with all its contradictions.

Plan G
Index of the seven notebooks 1857–8 (Marx 1987, p. 423; *MEGA*² II/2, pp. 3 ff.).

III) CAPITAL IN GENERAL
Transformation of money into capital
   (1) The production-process of capital
   (a) The exchange of capital with labour-capacity
   (b) Absolute surplus-value

(c) Relative surplus-value
(d) Primitive accumulation
(Presuppositions for the relation of capital and wage-labour)
(e) Inversion of the law of appropriation (Ricardo VI, 1, 2) (VI, 37, 38).
(2) The circulation process of capital

Plan H
Plan of 1859 (or 1861) (Marx 1987, pp. 511 ff.; *MEGA²* II/2, pp. 256 ff.)

THE PROCESS OF PRODUCTION OF CAPITAL
1) Transformation of money into capital
  • Transition
  • Exchange between commodity and labour-capacity
  • The labour-process
  • The valorisation-process
General concept of surplus-value
Increase in productive power, quantity and quality.
With a given productive power and absolute labour-time, the number of simultaneous working days must be increased
Simultaneous working days ibid.
Population
Increase in productive power identical with growth of the constant part of capital as compared with its variable part
How capital must grow in order to apply the same number of workers with an increasing productive force
Disposable time
Combination of labour
McCulloch
[5] 2) Absolute surplus-value
Absolute and necessary labour-time
Surplus-labour. Surplus-population).
Surplus labour-time
Surplus-labour and necessary labour
Senior
3) Relative surplus-value
aa) Cooperation of masses
bb) Division of labour
Slave-labour more productive than free labour, if the latter is not combined.
cc) Machinery
Gain of raw material (saving) through the machinery.
Prices of commodities. Proudhon

4) Primitive accumulation
 Surplus-product. Surplus-capital
 Capital produces wage-labour
 Primitive accumulation
 Concentration of labour-capacities
 Surplus value in various forms and through various means
 Connection of relative and absolute surplus-value VII, 23, 24. Multiplication of branches of production. Population.
5) Wage-labour and capital
 Capital, COLLECTIVE FORCE, CIVILISATION.
 Capital = advances
 Reproduction of the worker through the wages
 Self-transcending limits of the capitalist production. DISPOSABLE TIME
 Labour itself transformed into social labour
 Real economy. Saving of labour-time. But not antagonistically
 Manifestation of the law of appropriation in the simple commodity-circulation. Inversion of this law.

Plan I
End of 1862 (Marx 1989, pp. 346 f.; Marx 1976–82 (*MEGA*² II/3), p. 1861)

The third section 'Capital and Profit' to be divided in the following way:

1) Conversion of surplus-value into profit. Rate of profit as distinguished from rate of surplus-value.
2) Conversion of profit into average profit. Formation of the general rate of profit. Transformation of values into prices of production.
3) Adam Smith's and Ricardo's theories on profit and prices of production.
4) Rent. (Illustration of the difference between value and price of production.)
5) History of the so-called Ricardian law of rent.
6) Law of the fall of the rate of profit. Adam Smith, Ricardo, Carey.
7) Theories of profit. Query: whether Sismondi and Malthus should also be included in the Theories of Surplus-Value.
8) Division of profit into industrial profit and interest. Mercantile capital. Money-capital.
9) Revenue AND ITS SOURCES. The question of the relation between the processes of production and distribution also to be included here.
10) REFLUX-movements of money in the process of capitalist production as a whole.
11) Vulgar economy.
12) Conclusion. 'Capital and wage-labour'.

Plan L

Letter to Kugelmann, 13 October 1866 (Marx and Engels 1987a, p. 328; Marx 1974, p. 534).

The whole work is thus divided into the following parts: Book I. The Process of Production of Capital. Book II. The Process of Circulation of Capital. Book III. Structure of the Process as a Whole. Book IV. On the History of the Theory.

Part Two

Abstract Labour, Value and Money

The Practical Truth of Abstract Labour
Christopher J. Arthur

In 1857, Marx considered a central issue in his critique of political economy, namely, the nature of the category of 'labour'. He argues that only in the most modern society is the abstract category, precisely in the *determinateness of its abstraction*, 'true in practice'. This remarkable formulation of the issue comes to us from the 'Introduction' Marx wrote to his *Grundrisse* manuscripts.[1] Moreover the *Grundrisse* contains a further discussion of 'abstract labour', written later that same year, which is unlike anything to appear ten years later in *Capital*.[2] In the first chapter of *Capital*, Marx derives the category from *simple circulation* through the chain of reasoning: exchange value – value – labour – abstract labour. This is not how it is done in the *Grundrisse*. There it is situated within *capitalist production*. The crucial passages are in 'the chapter on capital' in a section on the capital-relation.[3] Yet the insights present in the *Grundrisse* are not carried forward; in particular the notion of 'abstract labour' having practical truth, and the situation of it in the capital-relation. This last aspect has been almost entirely overlooked because in *Capital* 'abstract labour' is found only in Chapter One

---

1. Marx 1986, p. 41; the English translation of the *Grundrisse* text used here is that in the Marx-Engels *Collected Works* which I find superior to the one by Martin Nicolaus: see Arthur 2008.

2. Nonetheless, value-theory in *Capital* is more sophisticated in many respects, e.g. the distinction between value and exchange-value does not exist in the *Grundrisse* (indeed, it is not fully accomplished until Marx's note *On Wagner* – Marx 2002); nor the associated derivation of money through the dialectic of the forms of value. Below I shall advance a 'value-form' interpretation of 'abstract labour'; its absence in the *Grundrisse* accounts for the uncertainties in it remarked below.

3. Marx 1986, pp. 222–3.

and rarely thereafter.[4] (We shall see there are three different definitions of 'abstract labour' in it.)

The aim of the present chapter is to see how and where the category of 'abstract labour' becomes 'true in practice'. However, although I address the relevant passages in the *Grundrisse*, and also *Capital*, I go beyond them in developing the consequences of the practical abstraction intrinsic to the capitalist mode of production and exchange. (This is in accord with my more general project to reconstruct Marx's *Capital*.)

Marx's *Grundrisse*

In the 'Introduction', Marx draws attention to the specific character of labour under capitalist conditions. Since Smith, labour in general, not any specific kind of labour, was taken to be the source of wealth in general. But the *determinateness* of the category of 'abstract labour' is the outcome of specific historical conditions and retains its validity only within these conditions.[5] Crucially, Marx argues, this abstraction is not merely the conceptual result of a concrete totality of labours, but it is a reality when individuals pass easily from one labour to another indifferently.[6] It is not entirely clear what Marx means here by 'wealth in general'; hence it is not clear if the 'abstraction' refers to concrete labour in general or to that 'abstract labour' which pertains specifically to value, to abstract wealth. However, in the later sections of the *Grundrisse* there is less ambiguity; the discussion of abstract labour pertains to the positing of value. Labour, Marx says, 'as activity' is not itself value but is 'the *living source* of value'.[7] As such, it is 'labour pure and simple, abstract labour', regardless of its shape, but capable of taking on any shape. He goes on: 'Labour must of course correspond to the particular substance of which a particular capital consists as a particular labour; but since capital as such is indifferent to every particularity of its substance, and is both the totality of all its particularities as well as the abstraction from all of them, labour confronting capital has subjectively this same totality and abstraction in itself. That is to say, though labour is in every individual case a specific kind of labour, capital can confront any specific labour; the totality of all labour confronts it potentially and it is fortuitous which particular one confronts it at any particular time'.[8]

---

4. This is pointed out by Geert Reuten in Moseley (ed.) 2005. He surmises that 'abstract labour' as a category of unity serves as a placeholder for money until that is introduced as the real form of unity of the economy.

5. Marx 1986, p. 42.

6. Marx 1986, p. 41.

7. Marx 1986, p. 222.

8. Marx 1986, pp. 222–3.

The important thing about this passage is that it is *capitalist production* that imposes on labour its determination as abstract (not simply commodity-exchange). This is because the aim of such production is wealth in its abstract form. As a productive power capital exists in the various factories; but as a body of value capital is positioned as an abstract totality over against all its particular substances; waged labour likewise exists as an array of specific jobs, yet as a 'source' of value it confronts capital as an abstract totality, to be deployed as capital sees fit, in the creation of abstract wealth, of value.

In the next couple of paragraphs Marx pushes the theme of abstraction almost (but not quite) to the point of reducing labour simply to pure activity. In these paragraphs, Marx speaks of it as 'purely abstract activity', merely 'formal [*formelle*] activity'[9] and as 'the positing of value'.[10] Here he comes very close to abstracting altogether from the character of labour and treating it as pure movement. (Unfortunately at one point Marx plays with the notion that the actuality of abstract labour requires the empirical emptiness of all labours;[11] but it is the social abstraction itself that is real, regardless of any changes in material production).[12]

Marx goes on, in several related passages in the *Grundrisse,* to explain that labour as 'the *form-giving* activity' passes from the form of *activity,* of unrest, to that of fixity, of rest, when condensed in the material result, in the form of 'Being' [*Sein*].[13] Moreover this dialectic is inscribed within capital itself because in the production-process the productive consumption of the elements of production is at the same time the consumption of labour. Having appropriated the labour-process, capital divides into 'the objective elements... in the form of rest, labour... in the form of activity'.[14] However, Marx does not take this thought far enough because here he remains in the use-value dimension, not that of value; for the result is characterised as 'product', as a use-value. What also should have been said is that this new product is formed as *value*; this is the true 'Being' in which the *pure* form of activity is fixed.

In the *Grundrisse* (as in the chapter in *Capital* on the labour-process), Marx treats the process of production *abstractly* as a form-giving act. There is nothing wrong with such an abstraction *from* the concrete character of the various material production-processes as long as the abstraction is not hypostatised and said to be the real basis of the concrete. If one treats the abstract formula as having a

---

9. German distinguishes *'formal'* and *'formelle'*: the latter is used where it is relevant to bring out the emptiness of the form.
10. Marx 1986, pp. 223–4.
11. Marx 1986, p. 223.
12. See Arthur 2002b, pp. 43–4, Finelli 2007, Arthur 2009a.
13. Marx 1986, pp. 226–7; cf. Marx 1976a, p. 287.
14. Marx 1986, p. 228; cf. p. 238.

separate existence from the concrete as the latter's 'truth' such that the concrete is then simply a body for the logic, then this inversion is mystical. But in the process of valorisation there is indeed an autonomous existence of the ideal insofar as the concrete labour-process carries a distinct set of abstract determinations that posit value. Here the abstract formula of production, namely 'positing', is *in its very abstraction* a reality. A real inversion has occurred; value positing is the truth of the labour-process and determines the latter as the effective carrier [*Träger*] of the valorisation-process.

As such the labour-process is 'subsumed' under the valorisation-process.[15] As thus subsumed, labour is not regarded under its specific useful forms but it is reduced to an abstraction of itself. Thus, even though all real labour is particular in its action, here indifference towards the specific content of labour is not merely an abstraction made by the observer, it is also made by capital. When the process of valorisation is borne by the material production-process, this labour-process takes the abstract form of the pure activity of value positing.

The source of value

The question is frequently raised as to whether abstract labour is predicated on exchange or production. In truth the answer to this presupposes the answer to the question regarding where value is created. Following the value-form approach, pioneered by I.I. Rubin, it appears as if value is created in exchange. He therefore defined abstract labour as that part of total social labour equalised through the equation of the products of labour on the market.[16] It is clear then that it is the *form* of value that imposes such abstraction, thus linking the category of abstract labour inseparably with money.[17] However, as Rubin stressed, if production is carried on for the sake of exchange of commodities, value exists latently, so to speak, prior to its realisation in exchange. However, this verbal solution requires further concretisation. According to an orthodoxy descended from Engels, exchange is first to be studied in the context of so-called simple commodity-production (or at least in the context of consideration of production in general without regard to its specification as capitalist).[18] But this approach inevitably results in the *naturalisation* of production because social determinations seem to arise only within exchange and circulation. By contrast, if value is actual only in capitalist commodity-production then production is carried on within the circuit of capital, thus itself is value-formed; hence abstract labour is

---

15. See Arthur 2009b.
16. Rubin 1994, p. 48.
17. Rubin 1994, p. 49.
18. See my critique: Arthur 2002b, Chapter Two.

also a determination of production insofar as it is subsumed under capital. As we noted above, this is how the *Grundrisse* presents it: abstract labour is here a determination of the capital-relation, something that is not true if it is derived in the context of some vaguer notion of commodity-production as such.

However, given the unity of production and circulation, the two aspects are complementary.[19] Value as pure form is posited in developed circulation, culminating in the general formula [*die allgemeine Formel*] for capital; then this formula is shown to be the form of a *content* insofar as it sinks into production. But new value arises in production under the impulse of capital to valorise itself; in this perspective the capitalist production-process is from the start considered as value-formed insofar as all inputs including labour-power are commodities purchased with money-capital.[20] Production is form-determined when located in the circuit of capital. The objects of value entering production are not 'devalorised' when they become active as material factors. The totalisation effected by the circuit is impressed on everything constituted in it. Hence we shall find two moments of abstraction according to whether the context is production or circulation.[21]

However, first I will argue that it is capital, not labour, that posits the product of labour as a value; and then I will argue that the value-form of the product abstracts not only from concrete labour but from labour altogether.

(a) *The Positing of Value*

In the first published result of Marx's *Grundrisse* meditations, his *Contribution*... of 1859, a definition implicit in the *Grundrisse* is brought out: 'concrete labour' is 'the source of material wealth', in short it is 'labour in so far as it produces use values;' 'abstract labour' is 'the source of exchange value'.[22]

The claim that labour is the 'source' of new value should not be confused with the claim that labour 'creates' value. I shall argue that *capital* creates value, but it does so only through its appropriation of the labour that creates the bearer of value.[23] On the ground of the separation of the worker from the object of productive activity there results the subordination of the workers to capital, and therewith the expropriation of their productive powers by capital which exploits

---

19. See my comment on H. Reichelt in Arthur 2009a, pp. 178–80.
20. For a macro-monetary reconstruction of the abstract labour-theory of value see Bellofiore 2009a.
21. Compare Bellofiore and Finelli 1998, p. 53, where they similarly distinguish abstract labour objectified in commodities on the market and abstract labour as abstract activity aimed at producing a commodity.
22. Marx 1975–2005c, p. 277
23. See Arthur 2005a, p. 211.

them for its own ends; but the essentially contested nature of this exploitation requires a new understanding of the labour theory of value as a dialectic of negativity.

Adam Smith thought the labourer needs recompense for their 'toil and trouble'; this was the basis of his value-theory; but there is no process through which the individual labourers commensurate their toil and trouble with that of others. The products have a unitary form as products *of capital*. Thus capitals commensurate *their* toil and trouble, namely the time they are tied up in the production-process, the time taken to pump out labour from recalcitrant workers.

If 'socially necessary labour time' is situated in the capital-relation, it is seen to be the time required to appropriate labour-services from the immediate producer. The imposition of the value-form on the product of labour is complemented by the material reality of exploitation, which must go beyond the technical economising of time to the 'pumping out' of labour, so it is determined as forced labour as well as abstract labour. Value is the result of 'forced labour', and its magnitude is determined by the time of such exploitation. In truth, new value is not 'produced' at all because the movement of its generation is practically abstract.[24] The logical abstraction of production is *positing*. In the production-process capital posits the result as value. Concrete labours produce use-value, but the positing of the commodity as value is due to capital. While value is not *produced*, it is *created*. How do I make this distinction? Clearly in both cases something new results; however, value is created when a new *form* is acquired by *what is produced*. Productive activity transforms one configuration of matter to another. Thus 'a product' is 'made out of' such material. On the orthodox view, value is made out of congealed labour. But if value is essentially a social form, and contains 'not an atom of matter', it is not 'made out of' anything at all; rather, it gives social form to what production has made. It is an unobjectionable metaphor to speak of the product as the objectification of living labour; but this ahistorical fact should not be translated into a claim about the specific social character of the commodity.[25]

Waged-labour engages in its own objectification-process as a *mode of existence* of capital. The power of *preserving value* and creating *new value* is therefore capital's power and the process appears as one of capital's *self-valorisation*, while the workers who produce what *has* value – *value alien to them* – are, in contrast, impoverished. Thus living labour realises itself in the mode of denial, when reified in value. However this is a *determinate* negation such that its origin

---

24. Geoffrey Kay (Kay 1999 p. 256) says only concrete labour is productive.

25. Thus one should not speak of the substance *of* value as Marx does in the first chapter of *Capital*; but one can speak of value as itself *a* substance (appearing in different forms), becoming 'subject', as he does later (1976a, pp. 255–6).

in labour is preserved in sublated form. The term 'sublation' indicates that something is denied, here that the valorisation-process is a labour-process, and something preserved, here that waged labour is a precondition of value positing. In short, capital is the subject of production, producing above all itself, while labour is negatively posited as its sublated ground.[26] In this paradoxical sense waged labour may be considered the 'source' of value. (But this is an Alice-in-Wonderland sense of 'source' because it is not to be taken positively as when the sun is a source of energy, but rather in the sense of an unfortunate necessity.) The determination of labour as source of value is preserved in the negation of the negation wherewith capital negates that which opposes it (the recalcitrant worker), and presents value as a positive result. The workers labour but do not 'produce' value; capital 'produces' value but does not labour.[27]

Now if we ask in this context about the practical truth of abstract labour we reach a paradoxical conclusion. Labour is practically abstract only in its negation. Of course the specificity of every labour-process requires in each case a specific technique to impose the despotic rule of capital. But, as the abstract other of capital, its original concrete character is thoroughly sublated, preserved only in the specificity of the commodity that *has* value. Labour, considered positively as essential to production, is that concrete labour corresponding to the specificity of the product. Labour considered negatively is forced labour exploited by capital for whatever time is socially necessary to produce a commodity.

Capital *wants* its production-process to be frictionless, but, as forced labour, production retains the moment of negativity. However, this negation of its negation allows capital to posit itself as the author of value and surplus-value. In sublating the living labour that is the material ground of valorisation, capital sublates therewith the specificity of its shapes of dominance and the character of any recalcitrance overcome. This is why in exchange-value labour does not appear at all because capital represses its origin in this negativity and presents the commodity to exchange as its own product. It follows that, while what concrete labour produces *has* value, abstract labour does not 'produce' value.

(b) *An ill-formed formula*

I now question the orthodox way of distinguishing abstract from concrete labour.

---

26. See Arthur 2002b, Chapter Three. This theory of value is not merely political, in that it roots value in struggle at the point of production; at the limit it is internally related to the revolution against self-valorising value because for labour the problem is not merely that the wage-form determines it as an exploited commodity, but that its proper activity is reificatory.

27. This chiasmus I adapt from Carchedi 2009, p. 164.

In a text on 'abstract labour', there is no avoiding the canonical formula: concrete labour produces use-value; abstract labour produces value.[28] While this idea is unquestioned in all commentary on *Capital*, I believe this double formula is not well-formulated. More precisely, abstract labour does not stand to value in the way concrete labour stands to use-value.

I follow the parallel already solidly established in the case of value itself. In that case we know that value 'contains not an atom of use-value', not even use-value in the abstract. Yet we know value must exist as commodities and money, transubstantiating them such that they provide a shell or bearer of value. Marx argues not only that exchange-value cannot be reduced to any specific useful property but that it is abstracted from the *genus* 'utility'. Although use-value remains as the precondition of commodity-exchange, value has no *immediate* relation to use-value *at all*; it does not register the commodity's utility, however abstractly this is taken. When value totalises all commodities in the form of an abstract identity, even though they differ materially, use-value is *sublated*, that is, both preserved and negated. It is preserved because it remains as a precondition; it is negated because when considered as values commodities are not considered as use-values; value cannot be reduced to use-value but is *other* than it. To put the two points in the form of a condensed antithesis: value *is* not-use-value. When posited in exchange as all equally values, commodities are subject to an 'infinitely negative judgement'; they *are* what they are *not*, because nothing of their material shape survives their transformation into values; this form of negative unity is not *their own* but is an *imposed* social form. Yet the negation of use-value here stands in a determinate internal (hence dialectical) relation to the original term; this origin is hence *sublated* rather than rendered irrelevant.

So the process of *positing* the product as a value must be treated in the same way. Concrete labour is sublated in an exactly parallel manner to use-value. Just as the useful character of the commodity is completely abstracted from in the resulting value, so must the labour that produced it be completely abstracted from. What would it be to abstract entirely from labour in the same way that value is abstracted from use? The answer is that what is left is the pure activity of value positing. If value is ontologically distinct from use-value, albeit consubstantial with it in the commodity, then the process of valorisation is also distinct from the labour that carries it. The labour-process is the carrier of the valorisation-process, just as use-value is the bearer of exchange-value. Concrete

---

28. As a matter of fact, I have not found a place where Marx says abstract labour 'produces' value, even though this term appears in translations and commentaries. He speaks of 'source', as we have just seen; I do not object to this. He also speaks of 'posits' [*setzen*] and 'forms' [*bilden*]. I object to these and, *a fortiori*, to 'produce'.

labour enters into value not *as* abstract labour but as abstracted *from*, entirely sublated in the movement of positing value. The value-form is *imposed* on labours as an alien universal identifying them *against* their reality as concrete rather than elucidating explicitly a generality they already have. Living labour provides the necessary bodily counterpart to the pure activity of value positing under the rule of capital but does not 'produce' anything over and above the commodities that *have* value, these having been socially imputed therewith in the form of capitalist production for exchange.

Nevertheless, just as value is borne by material commodities, so the abstract activity of value positing is carried by living labour in general. But it is not conceptually identical with it, however abstractly 'labour' is taken, because the *genus* 'labour' is also abstracted from. While the labour-process provides material support for the valorisation-process, the movement is that of value itself rather than labour; hence it is to be considered logically as *pure* activity. In sum, labour now 'counts' not as itself but simply as the carrier of the activity of value positing.

Let us now bring together the two arguments just given, and review the various determinations assumed by labour in capitalism. a) To begin with, living labour takes concrete specific shapes, which differ according to the social form of production, of course; b) The concrete shapes may be mentally disregarded so as to generate an abstraction, 'labour in general', but this is an empty universal, although within capitalism it has practical relevance for someone 'looking for work', *any* work; c) By contrast, it is undoubtedly the case that living labour is concretely universal in being able to move fluidly between different tasks – here the universal collates the concrete not in opposition to the particular but as *self-specifying* in its particularisations; d) Marxian practically abstract labour differs from this last; like (b), it is opposed to specificity but it also establishes a real connection between labours through the mediation of the value-form; e) Finally, I have introduced a further refinement when reducing form-determined labour to a pure activity, eliminating reference to material labour altogether; this is based on two arguments: firstly, that value is not 'produced' but posited by capital over the dead body of the worker's labour; and secondly, that if (d) is taken seriously, and the real connection of labours is solely through their inscription in the form of value, the living labour is present only as negated when reduced to the mere carrier of the movement of capital, just as use-value bears value as its other. What is abstracted from is not merely the particular shapes which make labours *different* from each other, but also the characteristics of labour that are *common*, such as the fact that labour is expenditure of energy. This is because the abstract act of value-*positing* does not involve expenditure of energy, although of course *producing* commodities does so.

The process of abstraction

A number of distinctions need to be set out at this point that are central to the argument of this chapter. As does Hegel, I distinguish between two kinds of universality: i) concrete universality; ii) abstract universality. Concrete universality expresses itself in *different* particularisations of the universal and they are held within it as part of its sense. Abstract universality negates particularity and covers a set of singulars taken to be *identical* with each other in some common respect. Then there is the difference between the technical division of labour *within* the enterprise and the social division of labour *between* enterprises, in other words, between production and circulation; in the one case, mediated through a plan, in the other, by exchange. The couple concrete/abstract is determined differently in these spheres. But in both cases the potential concrete universality of a) the collective worker in the factory, b) the sociality of labour in the economy as a whole, is realised only in the mode of denial because it is not the universality established by labour itself. It is capital that a) organises the relations of the collective worker according to its purposes (real subsumption); and b) establishes the sociality of labour through subsuming the product under exchange.

It follows that there are *four moments* at which a shape of universality of labour is real: (i) The aggregation of the labours *within* an enterprise is predicated on the *technical* division of labour. However, this universal labour distributed among jobs is not abstract in the sense opposed to the concrete, it is simply *concrete labour in general* which is allocated to the individuals as particularisations of this generality; (ii) A further universality *within* an enterprise is predicated on the subordination of the labourers to capital, which exploits them for the purposes of valorisation *indifferently* as *sources* of labour in the *abstract*; (iii) There is the concrete totality of social labour disaggregated in the *social* division of labour, and yet mediated in commodity-circulation. This is to be distinguished from (iv), that *socially* abstract universality predicated on the identity of the products of labour as exchange-values. Also, it is necessary to distinguish the labour in socially equalised 'abstract labour' from the labour commensurated in 'socially necessary labour-time'. The former – a qualitative notion – is socially abstract labour pertaining to the comparability of all commodities as values. The latter reduces to pure time the concrete totality of labours that are materially necessary for production of each specific commodity (allowing for additive quantitative determination). In the production of a commodity the various concrete labours have to be homogenised so as to be *added*; and then averaged over firms to establish the time socially necessary.

The concrete labour that produces a commodity is in fact that of the *collective* worker.[29] There is also an interesting dialectic, here, if we attend to how this is

---

29. See Bellofiore and Finelli 1998, p. 61.

made up of individual labours, which, when abstracted from this whole, have no meaning. It is not a social whole made up of whole individuals; rather the singulars of which it is composed are themselves merely abstract moments of it because they have no subsistence outside it. The worker is reduced to a fraction of the concrete wholeness of the labour producing the commodity when it is the bearer of this universality. The collective worker is like a giant machine in which each motion is parcelled out to individually detailed labours. (Conversely, a welder for example does much the same work whether in a car-factory or a shipyard.) Such work is not necessarily unskilled, but its character is determined by capital, and it is unable to act outside the collectivity of labour. So here the whole is what is concrete and unifies its abstract moments. But the singulars do not in return constitute the collective as their own; rather they see it as an alien totality to which they are 'indifferent', as Marx stresses in various places.

In his chapter on the labour-process, Marx asserts that it is not changed by its social form. This is untrue. When really subsumed by capital the workers become like bees, not architects, with no necessity to understand the ultimate purpose of their activity. The only purpose of work for the labourer separated from the objectives of production is the wage; hence if this is all that counts, the workers may well be indifferent to the content of their labour. However, indifference is not the definition of abstract labour; it is the consequence of the double abstraction imposed by the value-form on the product and on labour-power.

The determination of labours as abstract flows from the fact that their unity is objectively constituted only when so conceptualised by capital. The reason for this is that it is capital that organises the collectivity in such a manner that, although really specifications of the concrete universal, the labours are alienated from their own sociality. As alienated from their bearers, the labours' own universality is supplanted by capital's universal presence.

The concrete labour producing a commodity is, then, in one sense nothing but the 'labour' *of capital*; because its production is here subordinated to the purpose of valorisation. But in a further twist this 'concrete labour of capital' is itself rendered abstract through the *social* division of labour. What is striking about the value-form is that the wealth of productive power generating an enormous range of commodities is collapsed to a single result, value, imputed to a single source, abstractly identical 'labour'. Yet the integration of concrete labours through exchange involves different determinations from those characteristic of the collective worker in the factory. The latter is organised by capital as a concrete whole of labours; but the former is predicated on an asocial sociality in which the ideal totality of capital-in-general sublates the array of concrete 'labours' organised by capital as a system. The different capitalist production-processes supporting value positing are structurally ignored for the sake of commensurating the values to be realised. While all capitals count as value creating, the specific forms of the pumping out of labour from the immediate producers are ignored in this abstract universality which registers them all as homogenous with one another.

Yet social labour is the suppressed precondition of the abstract whole because capital requires this concrete universal if it is to allocate and regulate labour as required not only in the factory but across the economy. Indeed, the social division of labour, and the possibility of its redrawing, is a precondition of capitalist production. It depends on a concretely universal form of labour able to transfer easily between different occupations and tasks, unconstrained by natural scarcity of talent, or social barriers to mobility. It may well be that the concrete universality of social labour is a necessary precondition for the positing of abstract labour but it is not to be identified with it.[30]

Now there is a paradox in that the practical truth of 'abstract labour' is realised only as a social totality of labours, but this social labour never exists immediately, because the totalisation is effected by capital, which reduces concrete labours to moments of *its* totalising drive.

Time and the concept

In the collective worker the material differences are absorbed in the whole, and this reflects back on the labour-process so as to posit it virtually as a universal production-process carried out by undifferentiated human labour. Yet the sum of labours making up the collectivity seems a false aggregate because it really exists only as a material combination of detailed labours, not just one type of labour defined by the product. While such concrete labours cannot be aggregated in any meaningful way, capital *makes* this senseless aggregation ideally; and it does so under the aspect of time only, because it needs to get the commodities out as quickly as possible. Since labour is necessary to produce what has value, capital must time it, because that is datum in its competition with other capitals; capital not only imposes the qualitative reduction of labour to motion, but its quantitative reduction to time of production as a determinant of magnitude of value. The real question is how and why it is relevant to abstract from all the features of this collective worker the one dimension of time.

Why time? Marx gives a wrong answer when he observes in the *Grundrisse* that 'all economy is ... economy of time'.[31] This is so only from our modern perspective in which 'Time is Money'. In pre-capitalist society, time was not an issue, precisely because it cost nothing (and in any case it was dictated by

30. See Arthur 1979.
31. Marx 1986, p. 109.

natural cycles). As for post-capitalist economy: it is clear now that economising on scarce resources will be prioritised over economy of time, even were that to be time for the free development of the individual.

Time cannot 'produce' anything, of course; but it counts in crystallised form as the value-substance, once the produced commodity is granted the form-determination of valorised value.[32] The only possible dimension of the valorisation-process is the time it takes. It is not at all obvious that labour has to be measured solely by duration (as the classical thinkers assumed); but it *is* necessary that pure activity exists solely in the dimension of pure time. Because of the inversion of the concrete and abstract aspects of activity here, this time is abstract time, time in its concept, the passage between two intervals.

And whose time exactly? Because it is capital that brings commodities into relation, and capital that commensurates them, it is *capital's* time that counts. Capital measures its rate of return as the generation of an increment of money between two intervals. Hence, having sunk into production, the circuit of capital determines the time of production as the time *of capital*. New value cannot be generated all at once, but takes time, because living labour takes time to produce what *has* value. So material labour is *required* of value positing, by the necessary descent into the finitude of the logic of valorisation. The time of the capital-circuit must pass from the logic of succession to the real time of duration. What really moves is always a concrete material process, yet this is determined as the carrier of the ideal logical movement; thus the time it takes is now resignified as capital's time. The magnitude of value is determined by the elapsed time *of capital*. The adding of concrete labours by time is required because this is the dimension in which the comparison of one process with another is undertaken by capital. One could even speak of production in terms of a 'socially necessary time of capital', but this has to be mapped onto the source of value measured in socially necessary labour-time.

In sum, capital is a totality of value-in-process, and when it totalises the living labours it exploits, it determines each as the carrier of its own predicate: the time it takes. This hypostatisation was already noted by Marx in his *Poverty of Philosophy* (1847) where he says the worker becomes *time's carcass*.[33] The worker is predicated of their own predicate.

Materially the worker moves in time, but ideally time moves in them. In the valorisation process it is not that *the worker takes time* to produce something; rather *time takes the worker* as its carrier. The value 'output' of such abstract motion is substantially nothing but elapsed time commensurable with other such elapsed times. The time it takes becomes fixed as the time taken. The labour

---

32. Arthur 2002b, p. 171.
33. Marx and Engels 1976, p. 127.

process is determined as the trace time leaves in the world. This socio-historically specific shape of time is 'empty time', unqualified by any natural rhythms, because the force of abstraction is a practical reality.[34]

There are not two different kinds of labour, concrete labour and abstract labour, but material labour which is the carrier of the time of capital and thus, by reflection from it, is *counted* as simple duration because that is what *capital* counts as effective in generating value. But materially only *concrete* labour is subject to reshaping. Capital cannot 'economise' on labour in the abstract. Only labour as concrete can be measured and minimised, and each industry has its specific way of pumping out such labour, even if ideal demands are presented to it abstractly and require concrete interpretation by managers. (The structure is tailor-made for institutional blindness: 'Don't tell me how you do it, just meet that order in time'). In this sense, therefore, the concrete labour-times are inputs to socially necessary labour-time.

It is usual in value-form theory to say that money is the measure of abstract labour.[35] However, this requires careful explanation. After all, money is the measure of value, not of its substance. But as we know from physics, indirect measure is common; for example heat is measured by the expansion of mercury even though the dimension of heat is not extension but vibration. In our case, however, it is not a matter of making do with an external measure because we cannot measure directly, it is that the magnitude to be measured is itself indeterminate until money makes value actual and therewith determines how far the time of production counts socially. Nonetheless it seems clear that the *dimension* of 'abstract labour' is elapsed time (what Marx called the 'immanent measure') even if its measure is money.

The naturalistic view that each hour of 'embodied labour' *is* value fails to see that value is a social form and that it is this social determination that reduces labour to an abstraction of itself, to elapsed time. For example, the time that is said to determine the magnitude of value is that which is *socially* necessary. If we understand this as the average across the competing firms then the unity established between them in a common price means that hours in the less efficient firms count for less than in the more efficient one. Such an abstraction from the real times already makes clear that abstract labour-time is socially imputed. In the case of weight, an individual weight is given regardless of the weight of other objects; but the valuation of a product of labour depends on that of all others. Their commensuration is mediated by money.[36]

---

34. For a similar view, see Bonefeld 2010.
35. Reuten 2005.
36. Other social determinants, such as the organic composition of capital, also impose themselves in such a way that an hour counts for more or less than other hours as value positing. See Arthur 2005b.

Marx's later presentations

Unfortunately Marx never makes his distinction between concrete and abstract consistent. In his work after the *Grundrisse*, we find a number of further defini-tions of 'abstract labour'. In the first chapter of *Capital*, the distinction between concrete and abstract is first presented in the following passage: 'With the disap-pearance of the useful character of the products of labour, the useful character of the kinds of labour represented in them also disappears; this in turn entails the disappearance of the different concrete forms of labour ... all together reduced to ... labour in the abstract ... There is nothing left of them in each case but the same spectral objectivity; they are merely blobs of undifferentiated human labour'.[37]

This is presented as a purely logical requirement if value is to be adequately grounded; but it raises the issue of the real meaning of 'labour in the abstract'. In order to elucidate this Marx gives a number of glosses.

(a) The most well-known of these definitions is that given in terms of *physiol-ogy*. This is already present in the 1859 *Contribution to the Critique of Political Economy*.[38] In 1867 the same idea reappears in *Capital*, where he says that, however different labours may be, it is a physiological truth that they are essentially expenditure of human brains, nerves, muscles, hands, etc.[39] In the second edition there first appears the canonical definition: 'On the one hand, all labour is an expenditure of human labour-power, in the physiologi-cal sense, and it is in this quality of being equal, or abstract, human labour, that it forms [*bildet*] the value of commodities. On the other hand, all labour is an expenditure of human labour-power in a particular form and with a definite aim, and it is in this quality of being concrete useful labour that it produces [*produziert*] use-values'.[40]

(b) A quite different point is made in *Capital* when Marx stresses the *fluidity* of labour. He supports the claim that values 'are the objective expression of homogeneous labour' by arguing that the same worker may undertake both tailoring and weaving; moreover, because of this adaptability social labour in our capitalist society may be supplied in either shape in accordance with changes in demand for labour.[41] Here labour is taken to be a universal capa-ble of specification in a wide range of different concrete labours.

---

37. Marx 1976a, p. 128, translation modified; Fowkes illegitimately inserts the word 'quantities'; but the discussion at this point is qualitative.
38. Marx 1975–2005c, pp. 272–3.
39. Marx 1976a, p. 134, p. 164.
40. Marx 1976a, p. 137.
41. Marx 1976a, p. 134.

(c) In the section on the forms of value he argues that it is the *form* of equivalent exchange that reduces concrete labours to 'abstract human labour'. For 'It is only the expression of equivalence between different sorts of commodities which brings to view the specific character of value-creating labour, by actually reducing the different kinds of labour embedded in the different kinds of commodity to their common quality of being human labour in general'.[42]

In the first edition he stressed 'In each social form of labour, the labours of different individuals are related to one another as human labours too, but in this case this *relating itself* counts as the *specifically social form* of the labours'. Conversely, this 'specifically social form of abstract human labour' is actual only in commodity-relations, he says.[43]

Let us consider these three.[44]

The definition that refers to expenditure of energy is merely a mental abstraction, a common feature of labour in that production is always hard work. This has no social significance. Therefore it does not meet the *Grundrisse's* criterion of 'practical truth' as a category of capital specifically.

The next point is that labour can *really transform its expression* from one concrete labour to another, and that such supplies of labour-power are readily available to capital. Here, the stress is not on the *reduction* of the concrete to the same featureless abstraction, but, on the contrary, on the wealth of different forms taken by labour as a universal activity. This brings out that here labour is a *concrete universal*. But this has to do with its productive power in relation to use-value. However, it is a separate point that, when concrete labours realise themselves as use-value, simultaneously capital posits their product as value. *They* do not do this themselves; they simply carry out this alien intention.

Now, only the last definition – namely (c) above – pertains to a *social abstraction* that reduces all cases to the same identity. This abstraction has actuality only on the assumption that the products concerned are products of capital. As a *result* of the social equivalence of commodities established in capitalist competition, the labours are socially related only through the value-form of the product, which results from the absenting of *all* characteristics of living labour. The labour-process, in the absence of such concrete determinations as make it labour, is simply a spectral movement, once capital has formed it as a valorisation-process. When Marx stresses that labour is not itself value but is expressed as such only

---

42. Marx 1976a, p. 142.
43. Marx 1976c, p. 32.
44. Patrick Murray's tripartite concept of labour is similar. He distinguishes a) abstract ahistorical work; b) general labour; c) practically abstract labour (Murray 2000, p. 46, p. 61). Only the last is value-producing labour.

in objective form,[45] this has to be read as a spectral objectivity. So to speak of this labour as 'materialised' is misleading.[46] Value is a spectral substance that inhabits commodities and money, but absents their materiality so as to give the ideal substance a 'body', but a spectral body since it is dematerialised.

Value-in-process is carried by the labour-process; but it is not labour *as abstract* that 'produces' value; rather labour is *abstracted from* when socially signified as pure motion in time. Yet, when the unity established in capital's time is reflected onto the labour-process as if that were its ground, it appears as if the material labour underpinning value positing is labour in the abstract, i.e., hypostatised as such. But this is an ideal imputation; and because value can only be generated along with the commodity that bears this social imputation it is easy to conflate the ideal social process with the material production-process. In his *Grundrisse*, Marx argues that 'the incorporation of labour into capital', along with the object and instruments of production, means that 'the process of production of capital is not distinct from the material process of production in general. Its determinateness of form is completely extinguished'.[47] The upshot is that the material process of production in its immediacy appears as 'the self-moving *content* of capital'.[48] Capital as absolute form of value determines everything inscribed within it as its own; but having taken possession of labour it can absent itself and make its avatar do all the work. This has important consequences for the fetish-character of commodity-production.

Labour and fetishism

I distinguish between the fetish-character of the commodity and fetishism, in the following way: (i) A thing acquires a *fetish-character* when it has socially imputed to it a power it (really) has only as a consequence of its objective positing by a social form, but where the social determinations are hidden in the objectivity of the form; (ii) *fetishism* occurs when that power is taken to be natural to it in social consciousness.[49]

---

45. Marx 1976a, p. 142.
46. Marx 1976a, p. 129.
47. Marx 1986, p. 230.
48. Marx 1986, p. 231.
49. Riccardo Bellofiore and John Clegg both drew my attention to the importance of this distinction and to the mistranslation of the section-heading *'Der Fetischcharakter der Ware und sein Geheimnis'* as 'The fetishism of commodities...' in English translations. (However, the least known, that by Eden and Cedar Paul, got it right.) But it is interesting that in the first edition of *Capital* 'Der Fetischismus der Waarenform...' is found in the subhead. Marx 1976c, p. 59.

The social positing of commodities as values leads to the fetish-character of commodities because the commodity as product *per se* appears as a value. Marx makes the important point that the fetish-character of the commodity has 'objective validity'. The gold-fetish is a very clear example. What is decisive, here, is the ideality of the form, not the particular material that is posited as the bearer of the form by the relations within which it is inscribed. Yet the role of gold as value in autonomous form is objectively posited and therewith effectively functions as such because it bears this *form-determination*. This fetish-character becomes outright fetishism when gold is taken to be uniquely valuable by nature.

In the context of capitalist production the product is what *has value* but as such it is a formless substrate. This allows the transubstantiation of the material body of the commodity into a value-'substance'. Because of this, the fetish-form has effectivity but it is a *borrowed* effectivity; the commodity is posited as 'a value' yet its apparent power (of exchangeability) registers the effectivity of the form within which the object is inscribed.

If the commodity is fetishised it is reasonable to surmise that the activity producing it may be fetishised. This is true of those who claim to have seen through the vulgar form of commodity-fetishism on the market to the *production* of commodities. So productive labour is taken as value positing in classical political economy (and especially by Ricardian socialists), yet its apparent power of creating value really registers the effectivity of the *social form* within which production is carried on.

How does this happen? Just as value inhabits the natural body of the commodity so we find value positing is carried by living labour. This makes it look as if it is *living labour itself* that 'produces' value as well as use-value. This is nonsense if taken as a natural property of labour, but this attribution of a power of producing value has a certain 'objective validity' just as in the parallel case of the commodity itself. No matter that we show how this fetish-character occurs, it is not merely an illusion. Just as the commodity provides a 'body' for value, so the appearance that 'labour produces value' has objective validity when the labours are determined as carriers of the positing of new value. This double character of the labour-process (positing value at the same time as use-value) is objectively determined. The positing of labour as a hypostatised pure activity gives material labour a fetish-character because the pure movement of value is introjected into its carrier. (Just as the value-form is internalised by the commodity.) But if this abstract labour is identified with the material labour *given* to the value-form, then we have full-blown fetishism.[50] If the social valorisation-process is conceptually

---

50. Kicillof and Starosta think that the physiological definition is the only meaningful one and characterise it as 'a purely material form, bearing no social or historical specificity'; nonetheless this labour, when performed privately, acquires the purely social form of value (Kicillof and Starosta 2007a, pp. 34–5). But in privileging the attribute of labour

collapsed to the labour-process that bears it, then productive labour in some material definition is taken to produce value. Labour – understood as a material activity – is fetishised as inherently productive of value.

This is precisely what Marx does when giving a physiological definition of abstract labour. Amy Wendling has drawn attention to the influence on Marx of the new 'science of bodily power', physiology, which was transferred from the physicists' discovery of the transformation (and conservation) of energy.[51] The consequence of the value-form is that capital treats all labour as identical in its bearing on value and surplus-value. But the further identification of this *socially abstract universal* (a hypostatisation) with the *empirical similarity* of labours as expenditure of energy is intended by Marx to bolster this imputation naturalistically. This is unfortunate because it puts social determinations aside in favour of an *abstract materialism*. The common characteristic of work as an expenditure of energy is, as a category, ahistorical, unlike the practical abstraction imposed by commodity-exchange.[52] Of course the universality of labour becomes evident only in modern capitalist society. However, the identification of this universality with expenditure of energy in the abstract is an ideological reduction of the productive potential of labour to the level of a labour-power machine. But this fits beautifully capital's reflection of its own homogeneity into an equally homogeneous ground, work in the physiological sense.[53]

Conclusion

We have argued that there are processes of abstraction pertaining to both circulation and production. In the hidden abode of *production* the hegemony of capital

---

of pure materiality they risk fetishising it. In truth it is the value-form that abstracts this pure materiality from the concrete richness of social labour. This materiality of an abstraction is precisely the social form of labour in capitalist production. They think it is right to stress the materiality of labour so as to secure the determination of value-magnitudes by labour-times; but it is the value-form that determines its measure is time. Moreover the actual times qualify the *concrete* labours; and it is systemic causality which transforms such times into socially necessary time. For a critique of Kicillof and Starosta, see Bonefeld 2010.

51. Wendling 2009, Chapter Two. It should be added that there followed the reverse effect when the physicists (such as Joule, whose work was known to Marx and Engels) took from political economy the category of 'work'.

52. See Robles 2004.

53. For a robust assertion of the physiological definition of abstract labour complete with a measure in calories, see Carchedi 2009, pp. 149–52. For any 'embodied labour' theory of value, Carchedi's instinct that calories should be the real measure is correct; for energy expended could be properly considered transferred (less waste) to the product. But Marx and Engels did not accept the reductivist thermodynamic model of physiology (still less a measure in calories) because they were aware of the bio-chemical aspects, it has been shown; see Burkett and Foster 2009, pp. 134–5.

over waged labour reduces labour to the recalcitrant source of value when subsumed under capital. Here capital confronts labour abstractly as its generalised other when it exploits it for the sake of producing what has value. Capital in its practice must concretely engage in the 'labour of the negative' and struggle to really subsume labour. But when it presents the commodity to exchange it represses this knowledge of its origin in blood and sweat as if its ideality infuses its material ground with the form of pure activity. Thus in *circulation* the actuality of production vanishes due to the logic of abstraction in exchange. Concrete labours are sublated in the alien universality of value. It follows that the category of 'labour in the abstract' is problematic; the movement of value positing is not that *of* abstract labour but a movement that *abstracts from* living labour altogether. Abstract labour is the reflection onto the labour-process of the unity of production established by capital on the ground of pure time.

So labour is posited as abstract in two senses: qualitatively as homogeneous 'source'; quantifiably as the bearer of time of production. In commensurating labour, time is what capital selects as its relevant parameter; other determinations of labour (effort, fluidity, fragmentation, indifference) are cognate to this key attribute but not to be identified with it.

Because labour *serves* as carrier of value positing it seems as if work as such is immediately 'productive' of value, and as if then value were a 'product' of labour like use-value. Since practically abstract labour has only a spectral existence, it is easily identified with more real generalities such as expenditure of energy. The result is that such a general form of labour is fetishised as if it produced value.

Marx thought the category of 'abstract labour' was one of the best things in his *Capital*. But this term is capable of many readings. I resist the identification of abstract labour with simple expenditure of energy. I prefer an interpretation rooted in the way the value-form imposes this abstraction on labour. This relies upon an insight present in the first chapter of *Capital* but extends it behind exchange to the production-process itself, as first sketched in Marx's *Grundrisse*.[54]

---

54. I thank James Furner, and Iren Levina, for their useful comments.

Unavoidable Crises: Reflections on Backhaus and the Development of Marx's Value-Form Theory in the *Grundrisse*

Patrick Murray

> But within bourgeois society, based as it is upon *exchange-value*, relationships of exchange and production are generated which are just so many mines to blow it to pieces.[1]

One hundred and fifty years after Marx stopped work on the *Grundrisse*, we find turmoil in financial markets linked to sub-prime mortgage lending practices and a remarkable real-estate bubble. What motivated Marx to write the *Grundrisse* was the first world crisis of capitalism, beginning in 1857. Then, as now, proposals for banking reform arose in answer to the financial crisis. Marx begins the *Grundrisse* with an extended criticism of the proposals advanced by the Proudhonist Alfred Darimon. Darimon soon leads Marx to one of the most revealing topics of his analysis of the capitalist mode of production, *the value-form*, or *exchange-value*. In not grasping the value-form, Darimon failed to recognise why capitalism requires money and is crisis-prone. While financial reforms may help to forestall or better manage crises, they cannot root them out. In thinking that the troubles of the capitalist mode of production could be overcome by making changes to circulation, Darimon exemplified misconceptions regarding the relationships among production, distribution, exchange and consumption that Marx addressed in the general introduction to the *Grundrisse*.

---

1. Marx 1986, p. 96.

For Marx, crises provide dramatic, recurrent evidence for the most fundamental claim of his critique of political economy, namely, that the capitalist mode of production is historically specific and transitory. Marx's stomach turned at the economists' pronouncement: 'Thus there has been history, but there is no longer any'.[2] As Marx came to see, recognition of the historically specific character of the capitalist mode of production begins with the value-form of the wealth it produces: 'The *value-form of the product of labour* is the most abstract but also most general *form* of the *bourgeois* mode of production, which hereby is characterised as a *specific* type of *social* mode of production and thereby likewise as *historical*. Therefore, if one misperceives it for the eternal natural form of social production, one, then, naturally also overlooks what is specific in the value-*form*, thus the *commodity*-form, and, further developed, the money-*form*, the capital-*form*, etc'.[3]

Notice the weight that Marx places on social form here. Marx has been widely misunderstood because the questions that preoccupy him, questions regarding the specific social form and purpose of labour and wealth, lie outside the discursive horizon shared by the mainstream of modern philosophy and the social sciences, notably economics. There, Marx's questions do not register; they gain no traction. No wonder Marx's account of the specific social form of wealth in capitalist societies, the value-form, has been overlooked, ignored, shunned, garbled and parroted, due not simply to its conceptual complexity or any shortcomings of Marx's multiple efforts to explicate it, but primarily because it aims at answering questions that few ever ask.

Over the past four decades, however, this interpretive situation has been changing. Certain currents in recent Marxian theory and Marx scholarship have been labelled 'the new dialectics' or 'value-form theory'.[4] A seminal text emphasising the mutuality of dialectics and value-form theory is Hans-Georg Backhaus's 1969 essay 'On the Dialectics of the Value-Form' [*Zur Dialektik der Wertform*].[5] Backhaus trenchantly diagnosed many deep misconceptions held by the bulk of Marx's interpreters, without sparing Marx from criticism. In Backhaus's judgment, despite multiple attempts to work out his radically new ideas, Marx's dialectic of the value-form flopped. Backhaus points out that Marx published four versions of the dialectic of the value-form: in the first chapter of the 1859 *Critique*, in the first chapter of the first edition of *Capital* Volume I, in an appendix to the first chapter of the first edition, and in the first chapter of the second and later editions. Whether the first draft of *Capital* Volume I, which is

2. Marx 1963a, p. 121.
3. Marx 1966b, p. 275. All translations from 'Ware und Geld' are my own.
4. See Arthur 2002.
5. Backhaus 1969.

almost entirely lost, stated the dialectic of the value-form in terms much different from the two versions that appeared in the first published edition, we do not know. In all likelihood, prior to the four published versions, there was a draft in the *Original Version* (*Urtext*) of the *Critique*; unfortunately, that part of the manuscript is also lost. Surely an *Urtext* version, which may or may not have differed significantly from the *Critique* itself, would have been based on relevant sections of the *Grundrisse*.[6]

The present chapter will consider to what extent Marx's exploration of the value-form in the *Grundrisse* counts as an early version of the dialectic of the value-form and lays the basis for its presentations in the *Critique* and *Capital*. First, in order to understand what we are looking for in the *Grundrisse*, I will point out the scope and main ideas involved in Marx's value-form theory, using the *Critique* and *Capital* Volume I as primary points of reference. Second, I will turn to Backhaus with several purposes in mind: (a) I begin by highlighting a number of his seminal contributions; (b) I argue that Backhaus is wrong to attribute the gross failures to understand Marx to Marx's own mistakes and omissions, even if he did make them. Misconceptions that deep must be attributed to the blind spots created by 'the bourgeois horizon', the discursive horizon that dominates modern philosophy and social science. It excludes realism about form, including social form; hence it lacks the conceptual space for paying attention to forms and the 'content of forms', which is largely the focus of Marx's inquiry; (c) I argue that Backhaus is wrong to charge Marx with failing to present a coherent theory of value and with offering no dialectic of the value-form. My criticism extends to those who have followed in Backhaus's footsteps on these counts, among them, the Konstanz/Sydney group (Eldred and Hanlon), Michael Heinrich, and Geert Reuten. By contrast, I will defend Marx's argument in *Capital* regarding 'the analysis of the commodity' and, more particularly, the dialectic of the value-form as presented in section three of Chapter One. In the third part of the paper, I will survey the extent to which Marx's dialectic of the value-form is developed in the *Grundrisse*.

The scope and main features of Marx's value-form theory

The key insight of historical materialism provides the conceptual context needed for understanding Marx's theory of the value-form. Marx, in his early collaboration with Friedrich Engels, developed historical materialism not simply to insist on the significance of wealth and its production, but to call attention to the overlooked phenomenological point that *wealth and its production always*

---

6. See Heinrich 2004, p. 2.

have historically specific social forms and purposes. Marx and Engels write in *The German Ideology*: 'This mode of production must not be considered simply as being the reproduction of the physical existence of the individuals. Rather it is a definite form of activity of these individuals, a definite form of expressing their life, a definite *mode of life* on their part'.[7]

Here, Marx and Engels oppose traditional attitudes that, precisely because they abstract from the definite social forms that belong to the production of wealth, dismissing the latter as bearing solely on the mere 'reproduction of the physical existence of human beings' rather than determining their '*mode of life*'.[8] The traditional view finds in the provisioning for human life little food for thought. Marx's complaint against traditional ways of thinking is that they ignore the fact that wealth and its production always have historically specific social forms and that those forms are pervasive and of great consequence. The idea that *specific social form reaches all the way down* and therefore must be an *element* in the fundamental concepts of a social theory is the watershed-idea of Marx's historical materialism. The value-form, or exchange-value, is a specific social form of the products of labour where the capitalist mode of production predominates. It is inseparable from value-producing labour, which is a specific social form of labour under capitalism.

With this background in mind, let us turn now to indicating the scope and main features of Marx's theory of the value-form. Marx's theory of the value-form is one aspect of his analysis of the commodity. The double character of the commodity as a use-value that has an exchange-value, that is, a valid price, leads Marx to argue that exchange-value is the expression of a 'third thing' that is common to commodities, namely value. There is a double movement to Marx's theory of value: he reasons first from exchange-value to value and then from value to exchange-value. The dialectic of the value-form, which argues that value necessarily appears as exchange-value, belongs to Marx's joint examination of value's *substance*, the determination of its *magnitude*, and its *form* of appearance. These three, value's substance, magnitude, and its form of appearance, are inseparable in Marx's account. Failure to recognise that inseparability, in particular by splitting off the form of value from its substance and magnitude, leads to interpretive blind alleys.

---

7. Marx and Engels 1976, p. 31.

8. 'The production of life, both of one's own in labour and of fresh life in procreation, now appears as a twofold relation: *on the one hand as a natural, on the other as a social relation* – social in the sense that it denotes the co-operation of several individuals, no matter under what conditions, *in what manner* and *to what end*' (Marx and Engels 1976, p. 43, my emphases).

The crux of Marx's value-form theory lies in the proposition that *money is the necessary form of appearance of value.*[9] That means that *the price-form is the value-form*, for only in money can the value of commodities be expressed. Furthermore, it means that commodities, value, exchange-value, money, and prices constitute, for Marx, a whole from which no moment can be extracted. He titles the first part of *Capital* Volume I 'Commodities and Money' for good reason. As Marx repeatedly insists, what is exchanged in barter are use-values, not commodities; commodities are use-values that have (valid) prices.[10]

The necessity of money, as distinct from commodities, to express value reveals a fundamental, if hard to discern, feature of the value-form; it is necessarily *polar*. Furthermore, the polarity of the value-form harbours an antagonism that makes capitalism irremediably prone to crises: 'It is by no means self-evident that the form of direct and universal exchangeability is an antagonistic form, as inseparable from its opposite, the form of non-direct exchangeability, as the positivity of one pole of a magnet is from the negativity of the other pole'.[11]

Recognising the necessary polarity of the value-form and the necessarily antagonistic character of that polarity are among Marx's major, if overlooked, discoveries.

Commodities and money are the two poles of the value-form, which is another way of saying that the price-form *is* the value-form. The value-form, or exchange-value, is the expression of the value of a commodity in the only thing that can express it, namely money. Marx, apparently drawing on Ricardo's phrase 'relative value', terms the pole in which the commodity whose value is being expressed finds itself, the *relative value-form*.[12] At the other pole, money, in which the value of the other commodity is being expressed, occupies the *equivalent value-form*. Marx writes of these two forms: 'The relative form of value and the equivalent form are two inseparable moments, which belong to and mutually condition each

---

9. See Murray 1993. Marx had the idea of the necessity of money at least by the time of *The German Ideology* (1845), where he and Engels write, 'money is a necessary product of definite relations of production and intercourse and remains a "truth" so long as these relations exist' (Marx and Engels 1976, p. 203). The necessity of money figures heavily into Marx's 1846 critique of Proudhon, *The Poverty of Philosophy* (Marx 2005).

10. 'Their [the products of labour] taking the form of commodities implies their differentiation into commodities [on the one hand] and the money commodity [on the other]' (Marx 1976a, p. 188, n. 1; compare also Marx 1976a, p. 179). Compare this passage from the *Critique*, 'Direct barter, the spontaneous form of exchange, signifies the beginning of the transformation of use-values into commodities rather than the transformation of commodities into money. Exchange-value does not acquire an independent form, but is still directly tied to use-value' (Marx 1970, p. 50).

11. Marx 1976a, p. 161, n. 26.

12. Regarding Ricardo, see Marx 1963a, pp. 43 and p. 47.

other; but, at the same time, they are mutually exclusive or opposed extremes, i.e. poles of the expression of value'.[13]

As a consequence, money has no price. We are, perhaps, better acquainted with the peculiarities of the equivalent form, but the relative form of value expresses in its own way three features of value that Marx uncovers in the exploration of the substance and magnitude of value in sections one and two of Chapter One. Two conclusions that Marx drew regarding the *substance* of value were (1) it is congealed abstract labour and (2) it is 'purely social'. The relative form of value expresses both of these features of the substance of value. The relative value-form also expresses Marx's conclusion that the quantity of labour a commodity contains determines the *magnitude* of its value: 'A given quantity of any commodity contains a definite quantity of human labour. Therefore the form of value must not only express value in general, but also quantitatively determined value, i.e., the magnitude of value'.[14]

The relative value-form accomplishes this by equating a definite quantity of the commodity with a definite quantity of money, where those quantities are determined by the quantities of labour each contain. (How else can the quantities of the two be fixed?) Marx then explores the consequences for the relative form of the fact that changes in productivity may decrease or increase the amount of labour contained in the commodity or money or both. He concludes: 'Thus real changes in the magnitude of value are neither unequivocally nor exhaustively reflected in their relative expression, or, in other words, in the magnitude of the relative value'.[15]

This provides Marx's answer to those who seek a fixed measure of value; there can be none.

Direct exchangeability is what characterises the *equivalent value-form*: its three peculiarities are (a) 'use-value becomes the form of appearance of its opposite, value';[16] (b) 'concrete labour becomes the form of manifestation of its opposite, abstract human labour';[17] and (c) 'private labour takes the form of its opposite, namely labour in its directly social form'.[18]

In the notorious section three of the first chapter of *Capital* Volume I, 'The Value-Form or Exchange-Value', Marx presents a dialectical argument for the necessity of money in order to express value by 'working backwards' from the price-form

---

13. Marx 1976a, p. 140.
14. Marx 1976a, p. 144.
15. Marx 1976a, p. 146.
16. Marx 1976a, p. 148.
17. Marx 1976a, p. 150.
18. Marx 1976a, p. 151.

to 'the simple, isolated, or accidental form of value'.[19] In presenting the dialectic of the value-form in section three, Marx begins with that simple value-form and works his way up to the money-form (or price-form). The dialectic proceeds by identifying the defects of the first three candidates to serve as the expression of value: the *simple form*, the *total or expanded form*, and the *general form*. Each new form, culminating in the fourth and final form, the *money-form*, represents an advance over the previous one inasmuch as it more adequately expresses value. Finding a fully adequate expression of value is what drives the dialectic in section three: defects and advances are judged against this standard. Clearly, the examination of the substance and magnitude of value in sections one and two are necessary in order to establish the standard. Until we know what value is, we cannot ascertain what can adequately express it.[20]

Marx's presentation in section three is open to misinterpretation. First, in actuality, there is only one value-form, the price-form; the three inadequate forms leading up to the money- or price-form are conceptual devices designed by Marx to instruct the reader by unpacking the price-form in order to establish that it alone can express value.[21] The movements, then, from one form to the next, are dialectical ones that should not be treated as directly historical, even if they may

---

19. See Marx 1976a, p. 163. The version of Chapter One in the first edition contains much of what is familiar from the second and later editions of *Capital*; however, it has no sections, and its exposition of the value-form ends not with the money-form but with a curious form in which every commodity is equated with a disjunction of all other commodities as the equivalent form. This form is judged to be defective because it allows for no socially valid occupant of the general equivalent form (a point made in the second edition in regard to the defectiveness of the general form). The version of the dialectic of the value-form offered as an appendix to the first edition does not have that odd fourth form; it has sections and concludes with the money-form.

20. In his translation of Volume I of *Capital*, Ben Fowkes makes a mistake in labelling the sections and subsections under (a) 'The Simple, Isolated, or Accidental Form of Value'. He has sections (1) '*The two poles of the expression of value: the relative form of value and the equivalent form*' and (2) '*The relative form*' right, as well as the two subsections of (2): '(i) The content of the relative form of value' and '(ii) The quantitative determinacy of the relative form of value' correct. But then he makes what should be sections '(3) *The equivalent form*' and '(4) *The simple form of value* considered as a whole' into subsections (iii) and (iv) of (2). This mistake does not occur in the Moore and Aveling translation of *Capital*.

21. One indication of this is that Marx insists on distinguishing the simple value-form from the similar form for the direct exchange of products (barter), 'The direct exchange of products has the form of the simple expression of value in one respect, but not as yet in another. That form was × commodity A = y commodity B. The form of the direct exchange of products is × use-value A = y use-value B. The articles [*Dinge*] A and B in this case are not as yet commodities' (Marx 1976a, p. 181). Since articles A and B are not commodities precisely for the reason that there is no universal equivalent, no money, we must conclude that the simple value-form is abstracted out of a social context in which there is money.

have implications for the genesis of money and commodities.[22] Another way that Marx indicates that this is how he understands these forms is by dedicating Chapter Two, 'The Exchange Process', to the actual genesis of money.[23]

This, then, is a further feature of how Marx investigates the value-form; he offers an account of the genesis of money in the process of exchange.[24] This historical chapter is required by the account he offers of the money-form, for only social action in the sphere of exchange can validate one commodity as the sole, socially valid 'universal equivalent'. 'Money necessarily crystallises out of the process of exchange, in which different products of labour are in fact equated with each other, and thus converted into commodities'.[25] In the chapter on the exchange-process, Marx makes explicit the conundrum latent in the joint theory of the substance, magnitude, and form of value presented in Chapter One – *value and exchange are inseparable*:

> their exchange puts them in relation with each other as values and realises them as values. Hence commodities must be realised as values before they can be realised as use-values.... On the other hand, they must stand the test as use-values before they can be realised as values.... Only the act of exchange can prove whether that labour is useful for others, and its product consequently capable of satisfying the needs of others.[26]

---

22. 'The historical broadening and deepening of the phenomenon of exchange develops the opposition between use-value and value which is latent in the nature of the commodity. The need to give an external expression to this opposition for the purposes of commercial intercourse produces the drive towards an independent form of value, which finds neither rest nor peace until an independent form has been achieved by the differentiation of commodities into commodities and money' (Marx 1976a, p. 181).

23. See the first edition of Chapter One of *Capital* Volume I for a final, transitional paragraph to the second chapter. (This paragraph was omitted from later editions.) In it, Marx stipulates that the treatment of the contradictory character of the commodity has up to that point been 'analytical' and that Chapter Two will take up the 'actual' relations of commodities to one another in the exchange-process (Marx 1966b, p. 246). See also Marx 1976a, p. 280.

24. 'It [money] is a crystallisation of the exchange-value of commodities and is formed in the exchange process' (Marx 1970, p. 48). In the *Critique* we find many of the ideas of the first three chapters of *Capital* Volume I. These include the double movement from exchange-value to value (substance and magnitude) back to exchange-value as the necessary form of appearance and a version of the dialectic of the value-form that delineates the simple form, the expanded or total form, the general form, and the money-form, along with their defects and advances. While the terminology of the polarity of the value-form and the two poles of the relative form and the equivalent form are not established in the *Critique*, the basic ideas and hints of the terminology are present. Key ideas associated with section four of *Capital* Volume I on the fetishism of the commodity are present, though the phrase 'fetishism of the commodity' is not. Points that appear in Chapter Two, 'The Exchange-Process,' in *Capital* Volume I are also present in the *Critique*. All of this material is found in the *Critique*, without any sections, in Chapter One, 'The Commodity'.

25. Marx 1976a, p. 181.

26. Marx 1976a, p. 179.

Much of the controversy within and over 'value-form theory' involves playing one aspect of this conundrum off against the other.

The fetishism of commodities, which was listed as the fourth peculiarity of the equivalent value-form in the appendix to the first edition of Chapter One, belongs to the analysis of the value-form and appears in all four versions of the value-form analysis noted by Backhaus.[27] For Marx, the value-form of the product of labour, and the commodity- and money-fetishisms that are inseparable from it, are rooted *in the peculiar social form of labour* in capitalist societies, 'As the foregoing analysis has already demonstrated, this fetishism of the world of commodities arises from the peculiar social character of the labour which produces them'.[28] This recognition illustrates the point that Marx was making in the general introduction to the *Grundrisse*, namely, that production, distribution, exchange and consumption are inseparable.

Backhaus opens the door onto the tremendous scope of Marx's theory of the value-form when he writes, 'The analysis of the logical structure of the value form is not to be separated from the analysis of its historical, social content'.[29] So the investigation of the vast 'qualitative sociological' consequences of the value-form, which, as we see now, encompasses the commodity-form and the money-form, belong to the scope of Marx's inquiry into the value-form.[30] By the same token, Marx's theory of the value-form has momentous implications for historical dialectics and the philosophy of history.

Hans-Georg Backhaus's 'On the Dialectics of the Value-Form'

Backhaus's contributions

Any reflections on Backhaus's essay 'On the Dialectics of the Value-Form' must begin with an appreciation of its contributions. Already on the first page we encounter four potent observations. (1) Marx's theory of value has been mistakenly identified with the classical, or Ricardian, labour theory of value. Marx's theory is actually cut from different cloth; it is all about the specific social form of labour. (2) Marx has been mistaken for a political economist, when, in fact, he

---

27. For example, 'it is a characteristic feature of labour which posits exchange-value that it causes the social relations of individuals to appear in the perverted [*verkehrte*] form of a social relation between things' (Marx 1970, p. 34).

28. Marx 1976a, p. 165. Compare Marx 1970, pp. 31–2.

29. Backhaus 1980, p. 107.

30. 'The basic error of the majority of Marx's critics consists of: 1) their complete failure to grasp the qualitative sociological side of Marx's theory of value' (Rubin 1972, pp. 73–4).

is a profound critic of political economy. (3) What Rubin called the 'qualitative sociological' side of Marx's theory of value has been missed. (4) Marx's theory of the value-form has been ignored, misunderstood, or parroted back. On the next page appears another agenda-setting finding. (5) The dialectical nature of Marx's presentation in *Capital* has been either ignored or grossly misunderstood. These are five of the most important broad theses taken up by the best Marx scholarship of the last four decades. To these he adds several more. (6) 'It is first to be recalled that use-values are always posited in the price-form'.[31] (7) 'Innumerable authors ignore the claim of the labour theory of value to derive money as money and thus to inaugurate a specific theory of money'.[32] (8) 'Ricardo's false theory of money is the quantity theory, whose critique is intended by the analysis of the value-form'.[33] (9) 'The analysis of the logical structure of the value form is not to be separated from the analysis of its historical, social content'.[34] All in all, Backhaus's contribution in this essay is remarkable.

'A certain blindness' is the problem

Very early in the essay, Backhaus starts to spread the blame for the disordered interpretive situation to Marx himself: 'The deficient appraisal [*Rezeption*] of the value-form analysis, however, is not to be attributed solely to *a certain blindness* to the problem on the part of interpreters. The inadequacy of its presentations can only be understood on the presupposition that Marx left behind no finished version of the labour theory of value'.[35]

So, Marx had the idea for a post-Ricardian theory of value that included a dialectical presentation of the value-form, but he botched the job. Backhaus expresses further reservations about Marx's presentation, this time emphasising Marx's faulty or absent dialectics: 'In the Foreword to the first edition of *Capital* Marx speaks explicitly of the fact that 'dialectics' characterises his presentation of the labour theory of value. If the conventional interpretations without exception ignore these dialectics, then the question must be gone into whether the 'defectiveness of the presentation' concerns not only the value form analysis [section three] but also the first two sections in the first chapter of *Capital*'.[36]

---

31. Backhaus 1980, p. 105. Compare this with Martha Campbell's observation, 'Although Marx never regards exchange value as anything but money price, he does not specify that it is until he shows what money price involves' (Campbell 1997, p. 100).
32. Backhaus 1980, pp. 102–3.
33. Backhaus 1980, p. 108. Compare to Campbell 2005, especially pp. 144–5.
34. Backhaus 1980, p. 107.
35. Backhaus 1980, pp. 99–100, my emphasis.
36. Backhaus 1980, p. 100.

For Backhaus, then, there is a reflux from the problems with Marx's dialectic of the value-form back to his account of the substance and magnitude of value.

I find Backhaus's move to spread the blame to Marx implausible, and I say that even if Backhaus is right that there are serious lapses in Marx's presentation.[37] In the next section of the paper, I will defend Marx from Backhaus's charges. But, setting that aside, I do not find it credible that shortcomings in Marx's presentation can explain how interpreters can altogether miss the topic of the value-form or fail to notice the conceptual gulf separating Marx from Ricardo, or remain unaware of the bearing of Marx's theory of value on his theory of money or overlook the dialectical nature of Marx's presentation in *Capital*. It is more plausible to attribute misinterpretations of this magnitude to 'a certain blindness' to the value-form and to dialectics. The problem is one of discursive horizons.[38]

Underlying the major failures of interpretation that Backhaus identifies is the incapacity to detect the topic of the specific social form and purpose of wealth and labour. Backhaus notes, 'the "economistic one-sidedness" chastised by Marx consists in the fact that economics operates as a separate branch of the scientific division of labour on the plane of pre-constituted economic objects'.[39]

Fine, but Backhaus does not explain *how* these 'economic objects' are 'pre-constituted' or *why* they are objectionable. What is wrong about the way that 'economic objects' are 'pre-constituted' is that they exclude specific social form and purpose. Because human needs, labour and wealth always have specific social form and purpose, by omitting them from its fundamental concepts, economics engages in bad abstraction. As a consequence, the discourse of economics, which purports to be generally applicable, is impoverished – worse, false. Marx grants that some general observations may be made about the provisioning process, but

---

37. Marx did worry about how he was presenting the analysis of the commodity and the dialectic of the value-form. In a letter to Kugelmann (13 October 1866), Marx wondered if something was 'defective' [*Mangelhaft*] in the 'analysis of the commodity' in the *Critique* (Marx 1954, pp. 131–2, my translation). Like Backhaus, Marx was troubled by the fact that so many 'good minds' ['*gute Köpfe*'] did not catch on. Here I think that Marx may have paid too little attention to how 'a certain blindness' can effect even good minds. In any case, Marx did make at least three or four attempts at improving his analysis of the commodity. To mention a few changes that may count as improvements: making explicit the distinction between value (essence) and exchange-value (appearance); the introduction of sections into the chapter on the commodity; the separation of the dialectic of the value-form into its own section; the separation of the dialectic of the value-form from the treatment of the exchange-process; and the treatment of the fetishism of the commodity in a separate section. I do not think that we should take Marx's worries and his efforts at improving his presentation as evidence of something seriously wrong with it, as Backhaus does. It seems to me that his basic line of thought is sound and remains much the same going back to the *Grundrisse*, perhaps even to the *Poverty of Philosophy*.

38. With his phrase 'the bourgeois horizon' and similar ones, Marx frames the difficulties in these terms.

39. Backhaus 1980, p. 107.

they do not constitute a science. The idea that there can be a generally applicable science of economics is a terrible misapprehension. In *Capital*, Marx's *critique* of political economy, he informs his readers from the opening sentence that his undertaking is not of the purportedly general sort. Rather, what he provides is a thorough investigation of social forms and purposes specific to the capitalist mode of production, beginning with the analysis of the commodity-form. Marx's discourse, then, is a radically different and vastly richer one, freed of the bad abstractions of economics.[40]

A defence of Marx's dialectic of the value-form

I begin with a couple more of Backhaus's criticisms of Marx on which to focus my reply:

> To me it seems that the mode of presentation in *Capital* in no way makes clear the expository (*erkenntnisleitende*) motive of Marx's value-form analysis, namely, the question 'why this content assumes that form'. The defective mediation of substance and form of value is already expressed in the fact that in the development of value a gap can be shown. The transition from the second to the third section of the first chapter is no longer sensible as a *necessary* transition.[41]

Put more bluntly, 'Marx's analysis of the commodity, then, presents itself as an unmediated "jump from . . . the substance to the form of appearance"'.[42] In that case, Marx fails to meet the standard that Backhaus spells out for dialectics: 'The dialectical method cannot be restricted to leading the form of appearance back to the essence; it must show in addition why the essence assumes precisely this or that form of appearance'.[43]

I agree with this expectation; moreover, this is the standard that Marx set for himself and thought that he met. 'Our analysis has shown that the form of value, that is, the expression of the value of a commodity, arises from the nature of commodity-value'.[44] But did Marx succeed? I believe so.

---

40. As Martha Campbell observes, 'there are no counterparts to Marx's economic concepts in either classical or utility theory' (Campbell 1993, p. 152).

41. Backhaus 1980, p. 101.

42. Ibid.

43. Backhaus 1980, 102.

44. Marx 1976a, p. 152. Even more explicit is the concluding sentence to the presentation of the dialectic of the value-form in the first edition of the first chapter, 'What was of decisive importance, however, was to uncover the inner, necessary conjuncture [*inneren notwendigen Zusammenhang*] of value-*form*, value-*substance*, and value-*magnitude*' (Marx 1966b, p. 240).

Marx repeatedly states his intention to pursue a double movement, from exchange-value to value (substance and magnitude) back to exchange-value or the value-form.[45] Put more abstractly, his strategy is to move from appearance to essence to the necessity of the appearance based on the essence. This is the course that Marx follows. To show the necessity of these appearances (exchange-values, in this case), we first have to get to the essence (value). The only justification for positing value, though, is that it appears. So the analysis of the commodity must start from the appearance of value, that is, the valid [gültige] prices of commodities. In a two-step argument, Marx reasons that the replaceability of commodities as exchange-values demonstrates that their exchange-values express something equal and so must be manifestations of a 'third thing' underlying their disparate natural characteristics that makes them commensurable.[46] This he calls value. The second step is to argue that congealed abstract labour must be that 'third thing'; it constitutes the *substance* of value, which is utterly abstract and wholly social. Marx proceeds to argue that the *magnitude* of value is determined by the amount of labour-time contained in the commodity. These, then, are the three salient points for the dialectic of the value-form that emerge from Marx's account of the *substance* and *magnitude* of value: (1) value is wholly abstract; (2) value is a purely 'social substance'; and (3) values are quantitatively definite as determined by the amount of labour-time in the commodity. These three features of value provide standards against which candidates for the value-form are to be judged. In section three Marx keeps calling our attention to this fact. This fits Backhaus's expectation of dialectics, to show why *this* essence, value, must take exactly *that* form of appearance, exchange-value (price).

Backhaus skates over the first three paragraphs of section three, which precede the introduction of the simple form of value, giving us the impression that Marx

45. After determining the *substance* of value, Marx interjects, 'The common factor in the exchange relation, or in the exchange-value of the commodity, is therefore its value. The progress of the investigation will lead us back to exchange-value as the necessary mode of expression, or form of appearance, of value. For the present [zunächst], however, we must consider the nature of value independently of its form of appearance [Erscheinungsform]' (Marx 1976a, p. 128). Problems arise in value-form theory when one mistakes treating the substance of value independently of the form value with taking the substance of value to be independent of the form of value. It is not, which is why Marx keeps reminding us that the substance, magnitude, and form of value all go together. Once Marx completes the examination of the *magnitude* of value, he gives us another reminder that the dialectic of the value-form is still to come, 'Now we know the substance of value. It is labour. We know the measure of its magnitude. It is labour-time. The form, which stamps value as exchange-value, remains to be analysed' (Marx 1976a, p. 131). Lastly, at the outset of section three, Marx flags the double movement of his analysis of the commodity, 'In fact we started from exchange-value, or the exchange relation of commodities, in order to track down the value that lay hidden within it. We must now return to this form of appearance of value' (Marx 1976a, p. 139).

46. Marx 1976a, p. 127. See Murray 2005 and Murray 2006.

has nothing to say about the transition from value's substance and magnitude to its form. In fact, Marx is not drawing a blank; he is making key arguments in those paragraphs, with more arguments to come when he identifies the defects and advances involved with the different value-forms.

As Hegel realised, *essence must appear*; what other justification can there be for positing essence in the first place? Accordingly, Marx begins section three:

> Commodities come into the world in the form of use-values or material goods [*Warenkörpern*], such as iron, linen, corn, etc. This is their plain homely, natural form. However, they are only commodities because they have a dual nature, because they are at the same time objects of utility and bearers of value. Therefore they only appear as commodities, or have the form of commodities, in so far as they possess a double form, i.e., natural form and value form.[47]

Commodities are use-values *and* values. Value is the specific social form of the commodity, but how does value present itself? The natural form of a commodity gives expression to its nature as use-value, but how can its specific social character, its value-nature, be expressed? Immediately, we face a twofold conundrum *posed by the results of the investigation into the substance of value*: how can what is wholly abstract present itself to us in the material make-up of a commodity and how can what is wholly social appear in the natural form of the commodity? Yet value must appear. I cannot express the value of linen in linen. As Marx says, 20 yards of linen = 20 yards of linen is not an expression of value.[48] How then? The solution to the twofold conundrum leads us to exchange-value, to the price-form.

Marx offers the answer, here in the first-edition version, 'But commodities are material things [*Sachen*], whatever they are they must be either materially [*sachlich*] or they must show in their own relationships with material things'.[49] Since commodities cannot show their value nature materially – value is supersensible, not material, as Marx reminds us with a coarse reference to Dame Quickly – they must show it in their relationships with other material things, with other commodities: 'Since a commodity cannot be related to itself as equivalent, and therefore cannot make its own physical shape into the expression of its own value, it must be related to another commodity as equivalent, and therefore must make the physical shape of another commodity into its own value-form'.[50]

That is the fundamental point, and, as Aristotle observed, it can be illustrated just as well by the simple value-form, for example, 20 yards of linen = one coat,

47. Marx 1976a, p. 138.
48. Marx 1976a, p. 140.
49. Marx 1966b, p. 227.
50. Marx 1976a, p. 148.

as the money-form. Marx nicely pulls together this line of dialectical reasoning in the first edition version of Chapter One:

> The commodity is by nature a twofold thing, use-value and value, the product of useful labour and congealed abstract labour. In order to present itself as what it is, it must therefore double its form. The commodity comes by the form of a use-value naturally. It is its natural form. Value-form it comes by only in commerce with other commodities. But its value-form must itself also be an objective form. The only objective forms of commodities are their useful shapes, their natural forms. Since the natural form of a commodity, linen for example, is precisely the opposite of its value-form, it must make another natural form, the natural form of another commodity into its value-form.[51]

The solution to the first part of the conundrum, how to represent the supersensible value of a commodity in a commodity, is just what is needed to solve the second part, how to represent something 'purely social' in the natural form of a commodity.[52] Marx reminds us of the second outcome of his investigation of the substance of value: 'However, let us remember that commodities possess an objective character as values only in so far as they are all expressions of an identical social substance, human labour, that their objective character as values is therefore purely social'.[53]

Marx follows this up, reasoning again from specific properties of the essence (value) to a specific form of its appearance (exchange-value): 'From this it follows self-evidently that it [value] can only appear in the social relation between commodity and commodity'.[54] Value, which is 'purely social', cannot be expressed in the natural form of a single commodity, yet what but the natural form of *another* commodity is there in which value can be expressed? Marx concludes: 'The simplest value-relation is evidently that of one commodity to another commodity of a different kind (it does not matter which one). Hence the relation between the values of two commodities supplies us with the simplest expression of the value of a single commodity'.[55]

As indicated earlier, Marx's presentation of the relative value-form divides into two sub-sections. These two are designed to track the results of Marx's investigations of the substance of value and its magnitude, respectively. The first subsection rehearses the points we have just covered. As Marx puts it, the relative

---

51. Marx 1966b, p. 229.
52. Marx later calls attention to this fact, 'in the expression of value of the linen the coat represents a supra-natural [*übernatürliche*] property; their value, which is something purely social' (Marx 1976a, p. 149).
53. Marx 1976a, pp. 138–9.
54. Marx 1976a, p. 139.
55. Ibid.

form of value expresses, 'everything our analysis of the value of commodities previously told us'.[56] In other words, Marx says he is doing just what Backhaus says a dialectical presentation should do. The relative form of value expresses the two conclusions that Marx drew regarding the *substance* of value: (1) it is congealed abstract labour and (2) it is 'purely social'.

The second sub-section addresses the conclusions Marx reached regarding the *magnitude* of value. That the quantity of labour a commodity contains determines the magnitude of its value is also expressed in the relative value-form: 'A given quantity of any commodity contains a definite quantity of human labour. Therefore the form of value must not only express value in general, but also quantitatively determined value, i.e., the magnitude of value'.[57]

Marx explicitly appeals to the results of the investigation of the magnitude of value (the essence) as a standard for the expression of value (appearance). This is accomplished by a definite quantity of the commodity in the relative value-form equating itself with a definite quantity of another commodity, where those quantities are determined by the quantities of labour each contain.[58]

The value-form gives expression to *the contradictions of the commodity-form*, the overarching topic of the analysis of the commodity. The commodity is at once a material use-value and a supersensible thing, value. Producing value, the concrete labour involved in making the commodity counts as abstract labour. Thirdly, as value producing, the privately undertaken labour employed in making the commodity counts as directly social labour. The value-form expresses these three contradictions of the commodity in the three peculiarities of the equivalent value-form. In the equivalent value-form, value, which is supersensible, is expressed in a concrete use-value; abstract labour is expressed in (the product of) concrete labour; and directly social labour is expressed in (the product of) privately undertaken labour.

Marx's dialectic of the value-form in section three is completed by identifying the defects and the advances involved in the several candidates to be the value-form, culminating in the conclusion that only the price-form adequately expresses value. The defect of the simple value-form is obvious enough: 'The expression of the value of commodity A in terms of any other commodity B merely distinguishes the value of A from its use-value, and therefore merely places A in an exchange-relation with any particular single different kind of

---

56. Marx 1976a, p. 143.
57. Marx 1976a, p. 144.
58. This point returns in Marx's insistence, in Chapter Three, that, to serve as the measure of value, money must itself be a valuable commodity.

commodity, instead of representing A's qualitative equality with all other commodities and its quantitative proportionality to them'.[59]

In other words, an adequate expression of value must present (1) the commodity's qualitative equality with all other commodities, and (2) its quantitative proportionality to all other commodities.

The expanded or total form does that, but it has its own defects:

> Firstly, the relative expression of value of the commodity is incomplete, because the series of its representations never comes to an end. . . . Secondly, it is a motley mosaic of disparate and unconnected expressions of value. And lastly, if, as must be the case, the relative value of each commodity is expressed in this expanded form, it follows that the relative form of value of each commodity is an endless series of expressions of value which are all different from the relative form of value of every other commodity.[60]

So the expanded form establishes no uniform relative value-form.

These defects are corrected by the general [*Allgemeine*] value-form: 'The commodities now present their values to us, (1) in a simple form, because in a single commodity; (2) in a unified form, because in the same commodity each time. Their form of value is simple and common to all, hence general'.[61]

Marx adds, reminding us again that it is the nature of value that guides his judgements about how value must appear, 'By this form, commodities are, for the first time, really brought into relation with each other *as values*, or permitted to appear to each other as exchange-values'.[62] One way in which this is true hearkens back to the conclusion of the investigation of the substance of value that it is 'purely social':

> The general form of value, on the other hand, can only arise as the joint contribution of the whole world of commodities. A commodity only acquires a general expression of its value if, at the same time, all other commodities express their values in the same equivalent; and every newly emergent commodity must follow suit. It thus becomes evident that because the objectivity of commodities as values is the purely 'social existence' of these things, it can only be expressed through the whole range of their social relations; consequently the form of their value must possess social validity.[63]

One defect of the general form remains, and it concerns the social validity of the commodity in the equivalent value-form:

59. Marx 1976a, p. 156.
60. Ibid.
61. Marx 1976a, p. 157.
62. Marx 1976a, p. 158, my emphasis.
63. Marx 1976a, p. 159.

> The universal equivalent form is a form of value in general. It can therefore
> be assumed by any commodity.... Only when this exclusion becomes finally
> restricted to a specific kind of commodity does the uniform relative form of
> value of the world of commodities attain objective fixedness and general social
> validity.[64]

For any commodity to attain this fixed, general social validity as the universal
equivalent is not a matter of conceptual dialectics, it requires social action in the
process of exchange. Consequently, the examination of the exchange-process,
Chapter Two of *Capital* Volume I, belongs to the complete investigation of the
value-form.

Value-form in the *Grundrisse*

The second sub-section under the treatment of the general value-form in section three provides a natural transition into the final section of this chapter, on
the value-form in the *Grundrisse*. What Marx's dialectic of the value-form shows
is that the contradictions inherent in the commodity-form require money and
register social antagonisms. Marx writes:

> It is by no means self-evident that the form of direct and universal exchange-
> ability is an antagonistic form, as inseparable from its opposite, the form of
> non-direct exchangeability, as the positivity of one pole of a magnet is from
> the negativity of the other pole. This has allowed the illusion to arise that
> all commodities can simultaneously be imprinted with the stamp of direct
> exchangeability, in the same way that it might be imagined that all Catho-
> lics can be popes. It is, of course, highly desirable in the eyes of the petty
> bourgeois, who views the production of commodities as the absolute sum-
> mit of human freedom and individual independence, that the inconveniences
> resulting from the impossibility of exchanging commodities directly, which
> are inherent in this form, should be removed. This philistine utopia is depicted
> in the socialism of Proudhon.[65]

The 'inconvenience' of world-economic crisis spurred Marx to begin the
Grundrisse with the critique of Proudhon's disciple Darimon.

It does not take Marx long to get at the underlying point of his critique of
Darimon. Marx describes the crux of Darimon's reform-proposals as follows:

> abolish this privilege of gold and silver, demote them to the level of all other
> commodities. Then you do not abolish the specific evil of gold and silver

---

64. Marx 1976a, p. 162.
65. Marx 1976a, p. 161, n. 26.

money, or of notes convertible into gold and silver. You do away with all evils. Or rather promote all commodities to the monopoly status now possessed by gold and silver. Let the Papacy remain, but make everyone Pope. Do away with money by turning every commodity into money and endowing it with the specific properties of money.[66]

Darimon's discursive horizons are the problem: the most important questions are not questions for him. Marx observes:

> The answer can often consist only in the critique of the question, can often be provided only by denying the question itself.
>
> The real question is: does not the bourgeois system of exchange itself make a specific instrument of exchange necessary. Does it not of necessity create a special equivalent of all values? ... Darimon naturally passes over this question with enthusiasm.[67]

Of course, this question is the one Marx takes up in the dialectic of the value-form in *Capital*, and, as we have seen, his answer is yes, commodity exchange requires money. Moreover, money expresses the contradictions of the commodity-form antagonistically. Marx gives the same answer in the *Grundrisse*, where, in his 'chapter on money', he works out so many of the ideas that appear in the first three chapters of *Capital* Volume I.

Darimon proposes to eliminate money and the inconveniences associated with it by replacing money with labour-time certificates.[68] Marx had already criticised the earlier 'labour money' schemes of Bray and Gray in *the Poverty of Philosophy*. Marx renews his criticism in the *Grundrisse*, observing:

> The first basic illusion of the champions of labour-time tickets consists in this: that by abolishing the nominal distinction between real value and market value, between exchange value and price, by expressing value in labour time itself instead of in a particular objectification of labour time, SAY, gold and silver, they also remove the real distinction and contradiction between price and value. On that basis it is self-evident how the simple introduction of labour-time tickets would remove all crises, all defects of bourgeois production. The money price of commodities = their real value; demand = supply; production = consumption; money simultaneously abolished and retained; the labour time whose product the commodity is, which is materialised in the commodity,

---

66. Marx 1986, pp. 64–5.

67. Marx 1986, p. 65.

68. The use of the word 'ticket' in the *Collected Works* translation of the *Grundrisse* is questionable, since Marx's point in comparing Robert Owen's 'labour money' to theatre tickets was precisely to say that they had nothing in common with the 'labour money' of Bray, Gray, Proudhon and Darimon. See Marx 1976a, pp. 188–9, n. 1.

would need merely to be stated to produce its corresponding counterpart in a token of value, in money, in labour-time tickets. Each commodity would thus be directly transformed into money, and gold and silver for their part reduced to the rank of all other commodities.[69]

The 'labour money' proposal denies the polarity of the value-form; effectively, it wants all commodities to be in the equivalent form, that is, to be directly exchangeable, directly social. In arguing that *price does not equal value*, Marx is arguing that commodities are not directly exchangeable. Due to unavoidable fluctuations in supply and demand, prices fluctuate around values; while at the same time values may change due to changes in productivity. Marx reasons that because price does not equal value, because commodities are not directly exchangeable, labour-time cannot express value; money must:

> *Because price does not equal value, the element determining value, labour time, cannot be the element in which prices are expressed. For labour time would have to express itself at once as the determining and the non-determining element, as the equivalent and the non-equivalent of itself.* Because labour time as a measure of value exists only ideally, it cannot serve as the material for the comparison of prices. (This also explains how and why the value relationship assumes a material and distinct existence in [the form of] money. This point to be developed further.) The distinction between price and value demands that values as prices be measured by a yardstick other than their own. Price as distinct from value is necessarily *money price*.[70]

As this passage shows, Marx's response to Darimon is to reject 'labour money', affirm the necessity that value be expressed in money-prices, and to set himself the task of working through the dialectic of the value-form in order to explain 'how and why the value relationship assumes a material and distinct existence in [the form of] money'.

In the pages that follow, a section called 'The Origin and Essence of Money', Marx explores the dialectics of the value-form, anticipating many of the points that are better articulated and more deliberately developed in the *Critique* and the first two editions of *Capital*. Since the form of value must express value, we must first know what value is. Marx answers that the value of the commodity is something 'different from the commodity itself' because as use-values, commodities 'are of course distinct, possess different properties, are measured in

---

69. Marx 1986, p. 76.
70. Marx 1986, pp. 77–8. As a consequence, speculative bubbles and related crises are unavoidable. The problem is that prices may not reflect values, but there is no reliable way to tell since price is the only observable measure of value.

different units, are incommensurable'.[71] Yet 'value is a commodity's quantitatively determined exchangeability'.[72] The quantitative determination of value presupposes that: 'As values, all commodities are qualitatively equal and only quantitatively different, hence they can be measured in terms of each other and are mutually replaceable (exchangeable, convertible into each other) in definite quantitative proportions'.[73]

In *Capital* Volume I, Marx appeals to this 'mutual replaceability' to prove that there is some 'third thing' that commodities have in common, which he calls 'value'.[74] Since as use-values commodities are incommensurable, the 'third thing' must be something abstract, something other than any natural property of a commodity. Marx identifies labour as this 'third thing' and the quantity of labour-time as the determinant of the magnitude of value: 'Its value ... is equal to the quantity of labour time realised in it'.[75] If value is nothing natural, what sort of thing is it? The answer anticipates *Capital* Volume I: 'value is their social relationship'.[76] In short order, we have here in the *Grundrisse* the basics of Marx's account of the substance and magnitude of value in place: the substance of value is something abstract, 'labour', which is wholly social (non-natural). The magnitude of value is determined by the amount of labour-time.

A phrase that Marx employs again and again throughout this section is 'as value, the commodity...'. Here is a revealing case:

> As value, the commodity is at the same time an equivalent for all other commodities in a particular ratio. As value, the commodity is an equivalent: as an equivalent, all its natural properties are extinguished; it no longer bears any particular qualitative relationship to other commodities, but it is the general measure, the general representative, and the general means of exchange for all other commodities. As value it is *money*.[77]

This 'as value' rubric is Marx's way here in the *Grundrisse* of working out the dialectic of the value-form. For the whole point of the value-form is to express the nature of the commodity *as value*.[78] Only money accomplishes that. We see here

---

71. Marx 1986, p. 78.
72. Ibid.
73. Ibid.
74. Marx 1976a, p. 127.
75. Marx adds the qualification, 'This proposition is based on the assumption that exchange value = market value; real value = price' (Marx 1986, p. 78), just after he has been hammering away at the point that the difference between value and price is not nominal, as it would have to be for the 'labour money' schemes to work.
76. Marx 1986, p. 78.
77. Marx 1986, p. 79.
78. Marx later calls attention to this: 'In short, all the properties that are enumerated as particular properties of money are properties of the ... product *as value* as distinct from the value as product' (Ibid., my emphasis).

the terminology of the 'equivalent value-form' in development; in the exchange-value relation, it is precisely the role of money to function 'as value', that is, to be the equivalent.

Of course, Marx does not mean that the commodity is money; rather, and here he affirms the basic point of value-form theory, 'its property as value not only can, but must, at the same time acquire an existence distinct from its natural existence'.[79] Why?

> Because, since commodities as values are only quantitatively different from each other, every commodity must be qualitatively distinct from its own value. Its value therefore must also have an existence qualitatively distinguishable from it, and in the actual exchange this separability must become an actual separation, because the natural distinctions between commodities must come into contradiction with their economic equivalence; the two can exist alongside one another only through the commodity acquiring a dual existence. A natural existence and alongside it a purely economic one.[80]

Marx follows up with an 'as value' litany of the contradictions inherent in the commodity-form that necessitate money:

> As value, every commodity is uniformly divisible; in its natural existence, it is not. As value it remains the same, no matter how many metamorphoses and forms of existence it goes through; in reality, commodities are exchanged only because they are different and correspond to different systems of needs. As value, it is general, as an actual commodity it is something particular. As value, it is always exchangeable; in actual exchange it is exchangeable only if it fulfils certain conditions. As value, the extent of its exchangeability is determined by itself... in actual exchange, it is exchangeable only in quantities related to its natural properties and corresponding to the needs of the exchangers.[81]

Among the other points found here is the idea that *direct exchangeability* defines the equivalent (money).

Though Marx does not work up the four value-forms that he employs from the *Critique* on, in effect, he calls attention to the defect of the simple value-form when he writes: 'in order to realise the commodity at a stroke as exchange value and to give it the general effect of exchange value, its exchange for a particular commodity is not sufficient. It must be exchanged for a third thing which is not itself a particular commodity but the symbol of the commodity as commodity,

---

79. Marx 1986, p. 79.
80. Ibid.
81. Ibid.

of the commodity's exchange-value itself; *which therefore represents, say, labour time as such*, say a piece of paper'.[82]

He follows this with the familiar observations that this 'symbol' 'presupposes general recognition', 'is a product of exchange itself, not the execution of a preconceived idea'.[83] Here, Marx makes two key points in value-form theory: money requires social validation that comes only through the exchange-process, and the emergence of money through the exchange-process is spontaneous. 'In fact, the commodity which serves as the mediator of exchange is only transformed into money, into a symbol, gradually. As soon as that has happened, a symbol of the mediating commodity can in turn replace the commodity itself'.[84] This claim that money as means of circulation can be replaced by a non-commodity symbol, such as a paper bill, recurs in Marx's treatment of the topic in Chapter Three of *Capital* Volume I.

Marx then brings the foregoing investigation into the value-form back to bear on his critique of Darimon's reform-proposals:

> The exchange value of a product thus produces money alongside the product. Just as it is impossible to abolish complications and contradictions arising from the existence of money alongside specific commodities by changing the form of money... it is likewise impossible to abolish money itself, so long as exchange value remains the social form of products. It is essential to understand this clearly, so as not to set oneself impossible tasks, and to know the limits within which monetary reform and changes in circulation can remodel the relations of production and the social relations based upon them.[85]

Marx briefly alludes to what we recognise as the fetishism of the commodity and of money: 'In proportion as the producers become dependent upon exchange, exchange appears to become independent of them; the rift between the product as product and the product as exchange value appears to widen. Money does not create this opposition and this contradiction; on the contrary, their development creates the apparently transcendental power of money'.[86]

As the commodity-form is generalised, producers become increasingly subject to the power of the mutual relations of their own products, that is, to the price-system. In the same process, social power concentrates in valuable commodities and money.

By way of exploring the consequences of the value-form, Marx poses a follow-up question: 'The next question which confronts us is this: does not the existence

---

82. Marx 1986, p. 82.
83. Ibid.
84. Ibid.
85. Marx 1986, p. 83.
86. Marx 1986, p. 84.

of money alongside commodities contain from the outset contradictions inherent in this very relationship?'[87] He has already prepped us for the answer, which is 'yes'. First, he observes, 'the contradiction between its [the commodity's] specific natural properties and its general social properties, contains from the outset the possibility that these two separate forms of existence of the commodity are not mutually convertible'.[88] Marx will later express this point in terms of the polarity of the value-form (of which there has been no mention through these parts of the *Grundrisse*), by which only the commodity in the equivalent value-form (that is, money) is directly exchangeable. Commodities, which are in the relative value-form, are not. The next three consequences concern topics that Marx takes up in *Capital* after the first two chapters.

Second, the necessity of money to express value splits exchange into:

> two mutually independent acts: exchange of the commodity for money, exchange of the money for a commodity, buying and selling.... their immediate identity ceases to exist. They may correspond or not.... It is possible that consonance between them may now be fully attained only by passing through the most extreme dissonances.[89]

Crises, then, are native to the generalisation of the commodity-form of wealth.

Third, the separation of buying and selling opens the door to a merchant-estate. The separation between the motives of merchants and consumers can give rise to trade-crises.[90] Moreover, the rise of a merchant-estate, whose characteristic form of circulation is M-C-M (actually, M-C-M + delta M– the first form of capital), indicates the *reversal* consequent to the emergence of the value-form (money), 'Money is originally the representative of all values; in practice it is the other way round, and all real products and all labour become representatives of money'.[91] Marx's statement that 'it is inherent in money... to turn itself from a means to an end' suggests that money presupposes capital.[92]

A fourth consequence of the value-form is that 'money also comes into contradiction with itself and its determination because it is itself a particular commodity (even if only a symbol) and thus, in its exchange with other commodities, is again subject to particular conditions of exchange which contradict its universal unconditional exchangeability'.[93]

---

87. Ibid.
88. Ibid.
89. Marx 1986, p. 85.
90. Marx 1986, p. 86.
91. Marx 1986, p. 87.
92. Marx 1986, p. 88.
93. Ibid.

These difficulties, which might include recoinage-issues, a dual monetary standard (silver and gold), and competing fiat-currencies, bring home the problems involved in establishing the social validity required by the money-form.

Marx's explorations in the *Grundrisse* of the 'qualitative sociological' and historical implications of the value-form deserve separate treatment.[94] I will conclude by selecting just a few highlights from this rich material. Marx's observations concern people's attitude toward things, toward their own productive activities, and toward other persons. Here, Marx emphasises the venality that comes with the value-form of the product of labour:

> The exchangeability of all products, activities, relationships for a third, *objective* entity, which in turn can be exchanged for everything without distinction – in other words, the development of exchange values (and of monetary relationships) is identical with general venality, with corruption. General prostitution appears as a necessary phase in the development of the social character of personal inclinations, capacities, abilities, activities. More politely expressed: the universal relationship of utility and usefulness.[95]

Regarding attitudes towards one's productive activities and toward other persons, Marx observes:

> The absolute mutual dependence of individuals, who are indifferent to one another, constitutes their social connection. The social connection is expressed in *exchange-value*, in which alone his own activity or his product becomes an activity or product for the individual himself. He must produce a general product – *exchange-value*, or exchange value isolated by itself, individualised: *money*. On the other hand, the power that each individual exercises over the activity of others or over social wealth exists in him as the owner of *exchange values*, of *money*. He carries his social power, as also his connection with society in his pocket.[96]

As indifferent to one another, participants in commerce are guided strictly by their private interest. But Marx is quick to disabuse us of the idea that this private interest is something natural which commercial society has liberated from the encumbrances of traditional societies: 'The point is rather that private interest is itself already a socially determined interest and can be attained only within the conditions laid down by society and with the means provided by society, and therefore tied to the reproduction of these conditions and means. It is the

---

94. A number of these insights turn up in section four of Chapter One on the fetishism of the commodity.
95. Marx 1986, pp. 99–100.
96. Marx 1986, p. 94.

interest of private persons; but its content, as well as the form and means of its realisation, are given by social conditions that are independent of them all'.[97]

The society in which the product of labour takes the value-form as its social form is one where purely private interests clash with one another within an alienated system of 'absolute mutual dependence', a price-regime in which people are 'ruled by *abstractions*'.[98] As such, the emergence of the value-form as the specific social form of the product of labour marks a watershed in world-history. Marx employs this observation to set out a three-stage account of world-history, whose third stage lies in the future:

> Relationships of personal dependence (which originally arise quite spontaneously) are the first forms of society, in which human productivity develops only to a limited extent and at isolated points. Personal independence based upon dependence *mediated by things* is the second great form, and only in it is a system of general social exchange of matter, a system of universal relations, universal requirements and universal capacities, formed. Free individuality, based on the universal development of the individuals and the subordination of their communal, social productivity, which is their social possession [*Vermögen*], is the third stage. The second stage creates the conditions for the third. Patriarchal conditions and those of antiquity (likewise feudal ones) therefore decline with the development of trade, luxury, *money, exchange value*, in the same measure in which modern society grows with them step by step.[99]

Marx underlines the point that the second stage creates the conditions for the third by observing: 'Universally developed individuals, whose social relationships are their own communal relations and therefore subjected to their own communal control, are not products of nature but of history. The degree and the universality of development of the capacities in which this kind of individuality becomes possible, presupposes precisely production on the basis of exchange value, which, along with the universality of the estrangement of individuals from themselves and from others, now also produces the universality and generality of all their relations and abilities'.[100]

In the recurrent crises precipitated by the value-form, Marx saw catalysts for that third historical stage.

---

97. Marx 1986, p. 95.
98. Marx 1986, p. 101.
99. Marx 1986, p. 95.
100. Marx 1986, p. 99.

Part Three
The Concept of Capital

The Transformation of Money into Capital
Martha Campbell

Besides 'The Transformation of Money into Capital' – as Part Two of *Capital* Volume I is called – there are two drafts on the same subject in the *Grundrisse* and the *Urtext*.[1] Scholars disagree over both the proper interpretation of these texts and whether Marx's argument is the same in all of them. I will focus on the version of the transformation in *Capital*, and argue that the same line of reasoning is present in the earlier drafts.[2] In this final version, Marx achieves the most tightly organised and sparest statement of his argument. Moreover, he has by then refined his economic terminology and is using it consistently. *Capital* and the two drafts are, therefore, mutually illuminating. On the one hand, the strict order and terminology of *Capital* provide a guide to understanding the drafts, first, because it reveals the argument whole, without digressions; second, because it dispels confusions arising from imperfections in Marx's language. On the other hand, the

---

1. The earlier drafts are *Grundrisse* (Marx 1993, pp. 258–75) and *Urtext* (1858b, pp. 475–507). The *Urtext* is a true intermediate version between the *Grundrisse* and *Capital*: substantial parts of it are copied directly from the *Grundrisse* and, as in *Capital*, Marx proceeds by comparing C-M-C and M-C-M. A third draft in the *Economic Manuscript of 1861–3* will not be considered here (Marx 1861–1863b, pp. 9–54). Throughout this paper, I refer to the second draft by its German name, the *Urtext*. Its title is then parallel to the title of the *Grundrisse* and its translated title, the *Original Text of A Contribution to the Critique of Political Economy*, is cumbersome. In addition, because I will refer primarily to *Capital* Volume I, I will simply call it *Capital*.

2. Reichelt maintains that there is a historical dimension (but not in the sense of the 'logical-historical' method) to Marx's argument in the *Grundrisse* that is dropped from *Capital* (see Reichelt 2007, pp. 17, 31, 43; see also Reichelt 1995). I set aside this issue. My claim is that the drafts contain the same logical argument as *Capital*.

drafts, especially the *Grundrisse*, alleviate the brevity of *Capital*; elaborations on and alternative statements of the same points clarify Marx's meaning and lend additional support for interpreting *Capital*.

How the transformation from money to capital is understood evidently depends on the interpretation of the first section of Marx's argument. His reference to 'the capitalist mode of production' in the opening sentence of *Capital* might seem to make at least this version of the starting point unambiguous. By itself, however, this reference settles nothing since it does not specify the particular way that capitalism is addressed in Part One. At least three different interpretations of *Capital*'s beginning have been proposed, all of them consistent with the opening sentence. It has been argued that Part One refers to: (1) simple commodity-production, conceived as an historical antecedent of capitalism;[3] (2) 'the commodity form of production in general', conceived an abstract moment of capitalism, 'at which all that exists are individuals who are taken to be producers for exchange';[4] and (3) simple commodity-circulation, conceived of as an abstract aspect of the capitalist mode of production and unique to it.[5]

These different interpretations of Part One of *Capital* imply different conceptions of its relation to Part Two, or in other words, of the principle underlying the transformation of money into capital. Here, there are two alternatives: either the introduction of capital in Part Two marks a break with what has come before, or capital is implicit in, and so derived from, results established in Part One. The simple-circulation interpretation of Part One is consistent with the second conception of the relation between the two parts. The transformation of money into capital can be accomplished by a logical transition because simple circulation, as one aspect of the capitalist mode of production and unique to it, implies other aspects of the same system.

---

3. Several interpretations (especially (1) and (3)) have many adherents and varied forms; citations are illustrative rather than all-inclusive. Reichelt states that the simple commodity-production interpretation was 'canonized in Marxist orthodoxy as the relation between logic and history following some unfortunate formulations by Engels' (Reichelt 2007, p. 17). Banaji identifies Meek as its principal proponent (Banaji 1979, p. 24). Heinrich reports that it 'prevailed for decades' in East Germany but notes that it was ultimately abandoned in the 1988 edition of a major textbook on political economy (Heinrich 2009, p. 75). For an account of the debates over this interpretation in German language scholarship, see Fineschi 2009b, pp. 50–7, 61–6.

4. Bidet 2005, p. 139. Bidet maintains that this abstraction is not specific to capitalism, since he states that the transition to capital is 'to the specifically capitalist form' (Ibid.). Elsewhere he states that Part One is 'commodity production/circulation in general'; he specifically rejects the 'simple circulation' interpretation of Part One because it excludes production, which he takes to be the main topic (as he states, Marx deploys 'the concept of commodity *production* in general': Bidet 2005, p. 134).

5. For example, Arthur 2002b, especially Chapters One and Two; Banaji, 1979, and Reichelt, 2007.

In this chapter, I proceed on the assumption that the simple-circulation interpretation of Part One is correct, and focus on the argument of Part Two, to make the case that capital is derived as the presupposition for commodity-circulation. More specifically, I argue that Chapter Four of *Capital* demonstrates that commodity-exchange cannot exist as an ongoing and continuous or established process except as one phase of the circulation of capital. Because circulation is a permanently existing process but is unable to recreate itself, it presupposes capital. With this, our conception of circulation is transformed: what was formerly conceived as simple circulation is revealed to be the sphere of circulation, a phase of the circulation of capital, and 'simple circulation' – the conception of commodity-exchange independent of capital – is recognised as the appearance form of the capitalist mode of production.

Preliminary evidence for capital as the presupposition of simple circulation

In the most general terms, the case that capital is derived as the presupposition of simple circulation rests on the principle Marx attributes to the 'completed bourgeois system' as an 'organic system': that 'every economic relation presupposes every other in its bourgeois economic form'.[6] Second, applying this principle specifically to the relation between simple circulation and capital, he says: 'The consideration of simple circulation shows us the general concept of capital, because within the bourgeois mode of production simple circulation itself exists only as the presupposition of capital and as presupposing' capital.[7] In a third passage, Marx claims that simple circulation presupposes the capitalist system in its entirety. Disclosing the presuppositions of simple circulation, he maintains, will demonstrate the inversion of the 'law of appropriation' as it appears in simple circulation. Evidently referring to the analysis that he will present, he says that: 'An analysis of the specific form of the division of labour, of the conditions of production on which it rests and of the economic relationships of the members of the society to which these conditions of production are reduced, would show that the whole system of bourgeois production is presupposed by exchange value appearing on its surface as a simple point of departure, and [by] the exchange process, as it unfolds in simple circulation.... It would thus follow [from this complete analysis, MC] that already *other*, further developed relations of production, more or less conflicting with the freedom and independence of individuals ... are presupposed so that, as *free private producers in simple relations of*

---

6. Marx 1858b,, p. 278.
7. Marx 1858b, p. 945 (my translation). See also Marx 1993, p. 505.

purchase and sale, they could confront each other in the circulation process and figure as its independent subjects'.[8]

I will come back to this third passage later and focus, for the moment, on the second. As it indicates, Marx conceives the interdependence of simple circulation and capital to run in both directions: each is the premise of the other. The line of argument in one of these directions is nearly self-evident in *Capital*. Given Marx's thesis that capital is value in process, or, in other words, value preserved and expanded as it alternates between the money- and commodity-forms, it is obvious that capital presupposes money and commodities and so simple circulation. While dependence in this direction is clear, it is not clear what drives the transition from simple circulation to capital or makes the transition in that direction necessary (or, in other words, why simple circulation presupposes capital).[9]

To make the point in different terms, the argument of *Capital* from the commodity to wage-labour exhibits the principle of increasing independence of value.[10] Briefly stated, just to describe the sequence: value, first identified as one aspect of the commodity, is shown to acquire an independent embodiment in money. Value's increasing independence then appears in the increasing prominence of money in Marx's account of its functions in Chapter Three. Money is first ideal as measure, then real, but transient, as means of circulation, and,

---

8. Marx 1858a, p. 907 (my translation); see also Marx 858b, pp. 466–7, underlining added as emphasis (this repeats sections of Marx 1859, p. 160 and p. 179).

9. It is the account given of this transition by the scholars who are called value-form theorists that their opponents find so problematic. For example, Saad-Filho (Saad-Filho 2002, p. 13) rejects Murray's presentation of the transition as 'purely logical', claiming that Murray 'presumes that the concepts of money and capital are self-acting subjects which somehow actualize themselves historically because of purely logical imperatives'. Murray's account (Murray 1988, pp. 177–9) may be informed by Hegel, as Saad-Filho claims, but it is also clearly based on the *Grundrisse*. Bidet makes essentially the same criticism of Arthur 2002; see especially Bidet 2005, p. 136, pp. 140–2. Bidet argues that in *Capital*, Marx abandoned the strategy of the *Grundrisse* because 'there is, in reality no conceivable dialectical transition [from what Bidet calls "the market form" to the "capital-form"', MC]. And it is for this reason that Marx finally had to abandon any such enterprise in *Capital*. He had to recognize that he could not proceed by *transition*, but only by *rupture*' (Bidet 2005, pp. 141–2). Both criticisms relate to the appeal by Murray and by Arthur to the argument in the *Grundrisse* that hoarding involves a contradiction between money's character as universal wealth and the limited size of any given sum of money and the transition from money to capital on the grounds that capital mediates this contradiction (see for example Marx 1993, p. 271). In what follows, I argue that Marx does present this argument in *Capital*, although not so straightforwardly as in the *Grundrisse*. Preliminary evidence for this is that Marx calls Part Two of *Capital* 'The Transformation of Money into Capital'.

10. Marx's term for the increasing independence of value is *Verselbständigung*. In English translations of Reichelt's work, it is translated as the 'autonomisation' of value (see Reichelt 2007, pp. 31–40).

finally, the goal of exchange in its third set of functions.[11] In Part Two, value as capital is independent in the sense that it has the capacity to reproduce itself and so is truly able to stand on its own. Then, because value as capital requires that value increase continually and this cannot be accomplished entirely within the sphere of commodity-exchange, the existence of capital is shown to require the purchase, within circulation, of labour-capacity as the commodity wage-labour and the consumption of that commodity outside the sphere of commodity-exchange (but within the circulation of capital). Last in this sequence, the existence of wage-labour in turn requires the two conditions that make the worker doubly free. This second way of describing the argument-sequence in *Capital* raises the same question as before: why must value move from being free in the sense of having its own form (money) to being free in the sense of being self-reproducing (capital)?

To answer this question, the sequence may be considered in reverse (as noted earlier, Marx claims that the presupposition-relation runs in that direction as well). The last step in the sequence, from wage-labour to the conditions that make the worker doubly free, makes clear what the presupposition-relation entails. The first condition, that workers own themselves, makes the form of labour-power consistent with the social relations considered up to that point, the relation of capitalist and wage-labourer is (to begin with, at least) one instance of an exchange-relation. Exchange exists historically along with relations that are immediately recognisable as relations of unequal power ('relations of dependence' as Marx calls them), such as slavery or the social hierarchy of feudalism. As I will argue later (in connection with Chapter Four of *Capital*), exchange is incidental to these other relationships and to the modes of production they constitute (if commodities are products with value, strictly speaking, exchange in these instances is not commodity-exchange). By contrast, exchange is necessary to capitalism and its character as necessary is distinctive of capitalism. Marx excludes these 'other relations of dependence' and confines our attention to the implications of 'the exchange of commodities' to disclose the *necessary* connection between commodity-exchange and the capital/wage-labour relation (in other words, he is establishing that the capital/wage-labour relation of dependence is implicit in the 'nature' of commodity-exchange).[12] The second condition,

---

11. Reichelt presents an exceptionally clear demonstration that, in the *Grundrisse*, the sequence of money's functions is based on the increasing autonomy of value, but he maintains that the principle cannot be detected in *Capital* (Reichelt 1995, p. 58, p. 71). Other scholars, however, have explained Chapter Three of *Capital* precisely along these lines (see for example Ong 1983, Campbell 2005).

12. Marx 1990a, p. 271. In the same way, Marx disregards divergences between value and price a few pages earlier. There he says that 'the transformation of money into capital has to be developed on the basis of the immanent laws of the exchange of commodities' (p. 268). Like the 'other relations of dependence,' divergences between value and price

the worker's propertylessness, forces the worker to sell labour-power. Because it makes the sale of labour-power *necessary*, it *guarantees* that labour-power will be available for purchase. This condition is the presupposition for wage-labour because it explains why wage-labour is not accidental. As I will argue, capital is the presupposition for the sphere of commodity-exchange in the same way. Commodity-circulation presupposes capital in the sense that capital, and only capital, makes commodity-circulation necessary. Because capital guarantees the existence of commodity-circulation, it accounts for the latter's presence. Marx presents the core of this argument in Chapter Four of *Capital*.

Chapter Four of *Capital*

It is true that Marx introduces the M-C-M circuit as something that is just there; 'we find' it, he says.[13] For some scholars, the abruptness of this introduction is evidence that parts one and two of *Capital* are logically discontinuous.[14] Marx, however, neither just drops simple circulation once he introduces M-C-M nor leaves M-C-M just as we find it. Instead, he devotes all of Chapter Four to disclosing 'the difference in content' that lies behind its difference from C-M-C.[15] Once he identifies that content – value expanding and preserving itself – he explains why it must take the M-C-M form: 'value requires an independent form' in order to assert its identity with itself.[16] The same argument-structure is apparent in Chapter One of *Capital* in the derivation of value from exchange-value in Section one and the return back in Section three, where Marx explains why value must appear as exchange-value (by then further specified as money). In the same way, the M-C-M circuit is introduced in Chapter Four as the appearance-form of capital, or as the way to gain access to what capital is.[17] There is a parallel,

---

occur but both are 'accidental' or 'disturbing incidental circumstances' (p. 269, n. 24). These must be set aside in order to develop the 'immanent laws,' which are the characteristics of capitalism, it being uniquely a system of value.

13. Marx 1990a, p. 248.

14. For example, Saad-Filho maintains that 'Marx does not "derive" the concept of capital from the concept of commodity'; instead he claims that Marx investigates (quoting Ilyenkov) as *'a real fact . . . that money put in capitalist circulation . . . brings a return –* surplus-value (Saad-Filho 2002, pp. 13–14). Similarly, Bidet argues that Marx introduces M-C-M' 'as an object already familiar to ordinary consciousness'; so that his 'exposition advances only by way of a new appeal to "experience" which enables the introduction of new determinations' (Bidet 2007, p. 161; see also Bidet 2005, pp. 139–40).

15. Marx 1990a, p. 248.

16. Marx 1990a, p. 255.

17. In *Capital*, Marx for the first time locates the introduction of the M-C-M circuit at the beginning of the transformation of money into capital. In the *Grundrisse*, Marx introduces M-C-M in the Chapter on Money (schematically in Marx 1993, p. 201, anticipated in Marx 1993, p. 197). In the *Urtext*, he presents the two circuits right at the begin-

then, between Chapters One and Four, in that, in the former, exchange-value is the appearance form of value, while in the latter, M-C-M is the appearance-form of value as capital.

Compared to Marx's two earlier drafts of the transformation of money into capital, the presentation in *Capital* is extremely compact. Since the major points of the argument are the same in all versions (as I will show by comparing them), the two drafts can fill out the argument in *Capital*.[18] A second problem in *all* versions has to do with Marx's terminology. In the drafts, Marx uses the same term with different meanings (it is well-established that Marx did not distinguish between exchange-value and value, but as I will argue, he sometimes uses 'value' to mean capital, sometimes 'money' to mean capital, and 'circulation' can mean either commodity-exchange or the circulation of capital). For the most part, Marx eliminates these double meanings in *Capital*, but this can create other confusions. On the one hand, the double meanings express a truth; in reality, for example, value does not exist without capital because capital is just value preserved (value's preservation entails its expansion).[19] This truth can get lost in the more precise terminological distinctions in *Capital*; we could think that value has an existence separate from capital because there is a separate word for it. On the other hand, the terminology in *Capital* is precise but if the distinctions are not noticed, Marx just seems to be saying the same thing over and over.

---

ning of section on the transformation of money into capital (Marx 1858b, p. 478). At a later date, however, he introduces both circuits in the *Contribution* in the section on 'The Metamorphosis of Commodities', a subsection of money as medium of exchange (Marx 1859, p. 324). He then 'takes away' the M-C-M circuit further on in the *Contribution* because it 'presupposes the exchange of non-equivalents' and so reflects a 'movement of a more complex character' than simple circulation (Marx 1859, p. 357). I do not think these changes in locating the introduction of the M-C-M circuit reflect any significant change in Marx's thought (he could be anticipating his later argument that C-M-C is in reality its inversion, which, as I will argue, is the result established both in *Capital* and the earlier drafts). That M-C-M is the appearance form of capital, however, makes the transformation-argument the perfect place for the circuit to be introduced.

18. As noted earlier, a difference Reichelt (1995, 2007) sees between the arguments of *Grundrisse* and *Capital* is that the former involves a historical dimension which the latter drops. Even if this were true, the historical references in the *Grundrisse* can be separated out. Once that is done, the arguments make the same points. The only historical reference that remains in the *Urtext* is to the English enclosures; this seems to be what Marx means by the 'historical development [that] shows how circulation itself leads to ... exchange-value positing production' (1858b, p. 480; see also p. 498). This, however, is the primitive accumulation, which does figure in *Capital*. Marx only alludes to it in *Capital*, Part Two; in setting aside the question of why the free worker confronts the capitalist in the sphere of circulation, he says that this is 'the result of a past historical development' (1867a, p. 273).

19. The two meanings of circulation do not exist without each other either provided that circulation in the sense of commodity exchange is understood to be all-encompassing or a totality.

In Chapter Four of *Capital*, Marx runs through a series of comparisons between simple circulation (C-M-C) and capital (M-C-M), each time disclosing something new. To anchor the argument and keep track of the progress that is achieved in it, it is useful to recognise that there are three rounds of comparison. These can be characterised as follows:

First round: compares the order of succession in the two circuits, which are taken as given to begin with, and reveals the reflux of money.

Second round: moves from the reflux to the goals of the two circuits, yielding the definition of capital as valorisation-process.

Third round: moves from valorisation to the disclosure that capital-circulation reproduces itself (and simple circulation does not).

With this, C-M-C vanishes and there are no further comparisons (although Marx refers to simple circulation until the end of Part Two).[20] Because it is unable to reproduce itself, commodity-circulation gets absorbed into the circulation of capital. The final section of Chapter Four brings out the conclusions that follow from the comparisons. A cautionary note: because the argument accomplishes a transformation, it changes the way that circulation is conceived. Statements that are 'true' in the context of one round become false once that round is superseded.

Avoiding precipices

Before he even gets to the first of these, Marx cajoles us away from the edges of two precipices. The first is the idea of the capital-circuit as 'M-M, 'money which begets money'.[21] As Marx explains at the end of Chapter Four, this is the mercantilist 'description of capital'.[22] It refers to the value-form, money, but in it 'the

---

20. Reichelt states that the expression '"simple circulation" ... is already hardly used in *A Contribution* and ... is not found in *Capital* at all' (Reichelt 2007, p. 9). As Arthur (Arthur 2009a, p. 178 n22) has already pointed out, this is just wrong. Reichelt would have been correct to say that Marx does not use 'simple circulation' in the title of *Capital*, Chapter three ('Money, or the Circulation of Commodities') as he does in the corresponding Chapter two of the *Contribution* ('Money or Simple Circulation'). Perhaps the reason is that it does not make sense to emphasise that one kind of circulation is simple except relative to another kind that is not. The term 'simple circulation' begins to crop up in Chapter three of *Capital* (see for example, Marx 1990a, p. 212, where Marx refers to 'simple circulation of commodities' and intimates that there is another form of circulation) and is used extensively until the end of *Capital*, Part Two. Reichelt's mistake about terminology does no damage to his own argument because he maintains that 'the persistence of its [simple circulation's] conceptual content is clear' (Reichelt 2007, p. 44).

21. Marx 1990a, p. 256; see also p. 248.

22. Marx 1990a, p. 256.

whole process vanishes' – meaning the process that Marx initially schematises by the transition from M to C and of C back to M – because mercantilism omits the commodity.

As we will see, Marx moves progressively further from the mercantilist position throughout the first and second rounds of comparison. He has already distanced himself from that position by incorporating the commodity into the circuit of capital. The mercantilist conception of capital as 'self-reproducing exchange value' captures the 'form wherein exchange value is the point of departure', but its mistake, signalled here by its omission of the commodity, is that 'the connection with the content . . . is dropped'.[23]

The exact counterpart of mercantilism is the classical view. Its definition of capital as 'objectified labour which serves as means for new labour (production)', involves the mirror-image mistake: it refers to the 'simple material of capital' but omits the value-form 'without which it is not capital'.[24] These two positions repeat the division within the commodity between exchange-value and use-value.

Marx's M-C-M corrects both mistakes, that of the mercantilists by incorporating the commodity and that of the classicals by making both extremes of the capital-circuit money. The mercantilist and classical positions, however, are not ingredients that can just be mixed together. Each captures one aspect of capital, but conceives even that aspect incorrectly because the connection to the other aspect is missing. Marx's exposition of the implications of M-C-M overturns the classical 'material of capital' into the 'content', valorisation.

The second precipice is to focus right away on the *quantities* involved in the circuit of capital, which is done, for example, when capital is defined by profit or, worse yet, by the (system's? or the capitalist's?) 'intention of producing a profit'.[25] The question is: what is profit? In other words, what are the quantities amounts of? (For the mercantilists, they are amounts of money, for the classicals, they are amounts of use-value, but both call these 'value'). Marx maintains that 'profit is a specific relation to capital itself' so that attempts to explain capital by profit just presuppose what they purport to explain ('capital is already presupposed in its explanation', Marx says).[26] Marx, therefore, directs our attention to

---

23. Marx 1993, p. 258. As will become apparent shortly, the 'content' Marx refers to here is not the 'material' side captured by the classicals.

24. Marx 1993, p. 257. The statement quoted is Marx's corrected version of Adam Smith's definition. In Chapter Four of *Capital*, Marx contrasts the mercantilist and classical positions only in a footnote (see Marx 1990a, p. 251 n4). Opposing the mercantilists, the classical Mercier de la Rivière asserts that 'trade' (i.e., merchant capital) increases use-value; the mercantilist Corbet thinks of capital only as merchant capital ('does not see that M-M . . . is the characteristic form of all capital', especially industrial capital).

25. Marx 1993, p. 258.

26. Ibid.; see also p. 271.

the 'characteristic and original *path*' of M-C-M, distracting us, for the moment, from the obvious fact that the second M must (or is intended to) be larger than the first.[27] This gets us to the first comparison of the two circuits.

First round

That the two circuits have the same features (the two phases, elements, dramatis personae and so forth) establishes that M-C-M is also a kind of circulation. This lays the foundation for the eventual change in the meaning of circulation from C-M-C, which will be shown to be a repetition rather than a real circle, to M-C-M, which both describes a true circle and one that encloses commodity-exchange.[28] As Marx says at the very end of Chapter Four, M-C-M (by then, M-C-M') is capital as it 'appears directly in the sphere of circulation'.[29]

The first difference between the two circuits is that they invert means and ends; the rest of Chapter Four spells out the implications of this inversion. Initially, the means and ends, commodities and money, are regarded from the perspective established in Part One of *Capital*: they are opposites and, in the first round of comparison, value is equated with the money-form. Thus that money is a means in the C-M-C circuit implies that the value-form is merely a means ('mere money' as Marx says later) or incidental.[30] Money's position in the middle between two commodities implies that value does not flow past the end of any one circuit, making value discontinuous between different circuits. Marx indicates the incidental and discontinuous character that value has in C-M-C by such statements as 'the whole process comes to an end when money is given up' or that money is definitively transferred.[31] The inversion into M-C-M implies that value is continuous and the goal. Because this is posed in terms of the money-form, Marx says that 'money…is…advanced' or flows 'back to its initial point of departure'.[32] This result resembles the mercantilist idea of capital because of its fixation on the money-form, but the observation of the advance and return

---

27. Marx 1990a, p. 248, emphasis added. Contrary to Ilyenkov (cited by Saad-Filho, see above note 9), Marx does not just present as '*a real fact*…that money put in capitalist circulation…brings a return – surplus-value;' instead he positively prevents this from being considered until he is able to derive it from M-C-M.

28. Marx also speaks of C-M-C as the 'direct form of the circulation of commodities', suggesting that capital is the mediated form (1990a, p. 247).

29. Marx 1990a, p. 257; or capital is first defined as a 'form of…movement', meaning a form of circulation, which is why 'events which take place outside the sphere of circulation…do not affect' it and the 'formula' encompasses industrial as well as merchants' and usurer's capital (1990a, p. 256).

30. Marx 1990a, p. 250.

31. Marx 1990a, p. 249. In the *Grundrisse*, Marx emphasises that 'circulation comes to an end' (Marx 1993, p. 249); this is carried over into the *Urtext* (1858b, p. 484).

32. Marx 1990a, p. 249.

of money in M-C-M transforms that idea into a process. This transformation reveals the reflux of money, which will become the initial basis for comparing the two circuits in the second round. Marx still averts our gaze from the *amounts* involved in M-C-M, noting that the 'reflux . . . does not depend on the commodity's being sold for more than was paid for it'.[33]

Second round

In the second round, Marx uses the reflux of money to disclose the goals that the two circuits accomplish. The change in perspective between the first and second rounds is evident in M-C-M: because the reflux is a process, it shifts attention from the money-form itself to the flow through the circuit of something that is the same and that appears in money.[34] Having identified the reflux as the result of the first round, Marx makes it the standard by which both circuits are evaluated. This seems like an odd way of proceeding, since C-M-C is judged by a standard derived from its opposite, M-C-M (in other words, simple circulation is examined to see whether it can accomplish the same result as capital, which is a test it always fails). Marx will repeat this procedure in the third round, where the justification for it also emerges, namely, that M-C-M is able to sustain itself whereas C-M-C is not.

For the moment, the evaluation of both circuits in terms of the reflux of money reveals the irrelevance of the reflux to C-M-C ('the expenditure of money has nothing to do with its reflux').[35] For money to return in C-M-C would require an entirely separate repetition of the circuit, and even then money leaves once this second circuit ends. By contrast, the reflux is necessary to M-C-M (without it, 'the operation fails, or the process is interrupted and incomplete').[36] The reflux is an ongoing process. Its irrelevance to C-M-C reinforces the point that each of these circuits is a discrete entity, disconnected from the others, whereas each M-C-M flows into another one.

The irrelevance of the reflux in one case and its necessity in the other also reveals the goals of the two circuits. The qualitative difference between the two commodities in C-M-C shows its goal to be use-value. Because M-C-M proceeds from and returns to the 'same extreme', Marx says that its purpose is 'exchange value'.[37] This is another step away from the mercantilist focus on the money-form.

---

33. Marx 1990a, p. 250.
34. The point of the argument always appears in connection with M-C-M (after all, the argument is about the move *to* capital) and can seem to disappear in Marx's consideration of C-M-C, with which he begins each round.
35. Marx 1990a, p. 250.
36. Ibid.
37. Ibid.

Having taken that step, however, Marx would be expected to say that the purpose is 'value' rather than 'exchange-value'. In the earlier texts, Marx uses these two terms interchangeably, but it would be strange for him to do so here. He has emphasised in Part onne of *Capital* that exchange-value is the appearance-form of value; this is unlikely to have slipped his mind since, here in Part Two, he is deriving the 'content' of another appearance-form, M-C-M. 'Value' does appear in the next paragraph in connection with both circuits, suggesting that Marx's use of the term 'exchange-value' is absolutely intentional. In the M-C-M circuit, Marx introduces 'value' simultaneously with surplus-value, which indicates that the content of the circuit is the two together. The reflux brings out the character of M-C-M as a process; when value appears from exchange-value in M-C-M, it is value in process, or valorisation. The term 'exchange-value', then, is intermediate between 'money' (in the first round) and 'value' as valorisation (which ends the second round); exchange-value exists in circulation but also refers to value expanding through it (as differentiated from Part One where exchange-value, further specified as money, was the form of value).

Marx moves from exchange-value to valorisation by noting, first, that the M-C-M circuit has nothing to do with use-value since its extremes are both money and, in money, all 'particular use-values have been extinguished'.[38] Second, because there is no qualitative difference between the two extremes, there must be a change in quantity (as Marx says in the *Urtext*, 'this *quantitative increase of value* ... [is] the only process which value can perform as such').[39] This change in quantity (which Marx finally allows to be noticed) is an 'increment ... over the original <u>value</u>' (not money or exchange-value) or surplus-value.[40] This yields the definition of capital: instead of money, it is now 'value originally advanced' (with this, the mercantilist position is superseded); 'circulation' is now value's circulation (not the commodity's); finally, in its circulation, value both 'remains intact' and 'increases in magnitude' or as Marx puts it in the *Grundrisse*, 'value preserves itself through increase'.[41] This ends the second round, but before turning to the third, the developments in C-M-C need to be taken into account.

Having argued that the goal of C-M-C is use value or 'the satisfaction of needs,' Marx presents C-M-C as the mirror image of M-C-M: its two extremes are of equal value and qualitatively different use-value. The value-form then disappears from C-M-C. One way to see this is by constructing the parallel to Marx's

---

38. Marx 1990a, p. 251.
39. Marx 1858b, p. 491.
40. Marx 1990a, p. 251, underlining added.
41. Marx 1990a, p. 252 and 1993, p. 270. Marx emphasises in the *Grundrisse* that value's preservation and increase are one and the same: 'it *preserves* itself as a self-validated exchange value distinct from a use value only by *constantly multiplying* itself' (ibid., and other passages Marx 1993, pp. 270–1, see also Marx 1858b, pp. 491–2).

argument on M-C-M. There he says that the use-values of commodities were 'extinguished' in money; the counterpart for C-M-C is that value is extinguished. Perhaps because this happens only after C-M-C ends and the final commodity 'falls out of circulation and into consumption,' Marx expresses this instead by describing the extremes of C-M-C simply as 'products'.[42] With this, the 'Cs' have lost their value form because it is not required for the purpose C-M-C serves; products do not need to be commodities to satisfy needs.[43] To state it differently, need satisfaction can be accomplished by a variety of other social arrangements besides commodity exchange; hence the purpose, satisfying needs, does not account for the existence of any *particular form* that the process of satisfying needs takes, including this particular form, exchange. I will return to this point in connection with the third round.

The disappearance of the value-form from C-M-C seems to contradict Marx's claim that the commodities are of equal value. Marx's definition of capital already suggests that 'circulation' is the circulation of value as capital (he says: 'the value originally advanced not only remains intact while in circulation but increases in magnitude').[44] The third round will explain why this is true. It is within that circulation, as one phase of it, that the commodities exchanged are of equal value.[45]

Third round

Having defined capital as the movement of valorisation, Marx devotes the third round to spelling out an implication of this definition: that valorisation is a reproduction-process (and simple circulation is not). M-C-M' is self-renewing because: (1) the forms of circulation, money and commodities, are necessary for its purpose, and also (2) accomplishing its purpose continually restores these forms. To put it differently, valorisation *is* circulation (although of a different kind than simple circulation) because it involves the forms, money and commodities, and

---

42. Additional evidence that Marx means that value is extinguished in C-M-C comes from the two drafts. In the *Urtext* he says that 'in this movement [meaning C-M-C, mc] the sublation of the form determination, i.e., those springing from the social process, appears not only as the result but also as the goal' (Marx 1858b, p. 484). In the *Grundrisse* he says: 'If the commodity is exchanged via money for another commodity, then its value character disappears in the moment in which it realizes itself, and it steps outside the relation, becomes irrelevant to it, merely the direct object of a need' (1993, p. 260).

43. It should be noted that products imply labour. Thus Marx associates labour with the use-value as well as the value-side of the commodity. On the use-value side, this is labour in the general sense.

44. Marx 1990a, p. 252.

45. Under precapitalist conditions, by contrast, commodities do not exchange at equal values; the absence of a unified system of value allows for the profit of precapitalist merchant's capital (see note 58 below).

transitions between them (as argued earlier, the point of Marx's discussion of the features common to the circuits in the first round is that M-C-M is also circulation). Because the purpose is value-expansion and this cannot be accomplished except in and through circulation, circulation exists for its own sake or 'is in an end in itself'.[46]

To consider Marx's case in more detail, the first point he makes directly about M-C-M' in the third round is that its end and its beginning are the same. If we take 'end' in its straightforward sense to mean the last step in the circuit, then the sameness of end and beginning describes the form of a circle, which is the path of renewal. Their sameness indicates that, by the course of its circulation, M-C-M' (or capital) re-creates the starting point of its circulation – the initial form, money – so that the circuit could begin again.[47] Marx appears to say precisely this later on in the paragraph ('at the end of the movement, money emerges once again as its starting point') but, as I will argue shortly, that single point is there layered with an additional meaning.[48]

When Marx says 'the end and the beginning are the same', he concludes the sentence by saying 'and this very fact makes the movement an endless one'.[49] The sentence as a whole plays on the double meaning of end as concluding step and as purpose, which Aristotle also employs in the argument Marx quotes from the *Politics*.[50] End as purpose is the connecting link between this sentence and the preceding one, where Marx says of simple circulation that 'it finds its

---

46. Marx 1990a, p. 253.

47. This meaning is brought out, for example, when Marx presents the sameness of the beginning and end of the M-C-M circuit in terms of premise and result. He uses this language in both the *Urtext* and the *Grundrisse*. One instance in the *Urtext*, is: 'As premiss, it [money] is here simultaneously result of the process of circulation, and as result, simultaneously also premiss of its determinate form', the determinate form being M-C-M (Marx 1858b, p. 498; see also p. 491).

48. Marx 1990a, p. 253.

49. Marx 1990a, p. 252. Since I will be referring to this passage repeatedly, it may help to see it whole: 'The repetition or renewal of the act of selling in order to buy finds its measure and its goal (as does the process itself) in a final purpose which lies outside it, namely consumption, the satisfaction of definite needs. But in buying in order to sell, on the contrary, the end and the beginning are the same, money or exchange-value and this very fact makes the movement an endless one'.

50. See Marx 1990a, p. 253 n6. Marx does not mention Aristotle in the *Grundrisse* section on the money to capital transformation. He first refers to Aristotle in the *Urtext* (Marx 1858b, p. 488) but just as a mere mention, rather than the extended quotation and commentary that appears in *Capital*. The idea that Marx's argument shares with Aristotle's is that the inversion of ends and means, and so of money and commodities in the circuit, changes the character and meaning of circulation. Marx certainly has this idea in the two earlier drafts but expressed it with different terminology. One influence that Aristotle seems to have had on Marx consists in Marx's development of a simpler language. A comparison of corresponding passages from *Capital* and the two drafts shows a striking change in language between the two; the Hegelian terminology is eliminated from *Capital* (see pp. 167-71 below). The change in terminology between *Capital* and the

measure and its goal ... in a final purpose that lies outside it'. It is end as purpose that makes 'the movement endless' (end as final step makes reproduction possible). Any given M' not only can but must become a new M to accomplish the purpose of the circuit (otherwise capital would cease). In other words, valorisation can occur only by the movement of value through the forms that make up circulation and so, only if value remains within circulation (in the M-C-M sense). Marx elaborates on this point in two ways.

One is to note that if M' (or exchange-value) leaves circulation to become a hoard, it becomes money in its third function rather than capital. Marx speaks of 'absolute wealth' as capital's vocation because absolute wealth (like truth) is a pursuit or endless process rather than an achieved result.[51] Because absolute wealth is a pursuit, any given M' automatically becomes a new M (the distinction between them, the quantitative difference achieved, 'vanishes immediately').[52] When Marx returns to the language of end and starting point at the close of the third round, this is not just to say that M' has the right form to become a new M (although he does say that) but also that any achieved quantitative difference in value enhances the further expansion of value. The combination of end as final step and end as purpose modifies the circle into an expanding spiral that has no end – is 'limitless'.[53]

Capital also becomes money if M' leaves M-C-M' circulation and becomes money as means of circulation in simple circulation. Marx examines this second

---

drafts accords with Reichelt's suggestion that Marx's 'hiding the method' involves eliminating 'explicit references to dialectical transitions' (Reichelt 1995, p. 71).

51. Because, by definition, capital is motion, it overcomes the contradiction in hoarding between the universal character of money and the limited size of any given sum. Thus Marx's reference to absolute wealth as capital's vocation is another version of the *Grundrisse* transition from hoarding to capital on the basis that capital mediates the contradiction (or overcomes a deficiency) in hoarding. Examples of this argument in the *Grundrisse* include: 'The immortality which money strove to achieve by setting itself negatively against circulation ... is achieved by capital, which preserves itself precisely by abandoning itself to circulation' (Marx 1993, p. 261); 'Money as a sum of money is measured by its quantity. This measuredness contradicts its character, which must be oriented towards the measureless. Everything ... said here about money holds even more for capital, in which money actually develops in its completed character for the first time' (Marx 1993, p. 271). Instead of posing the argument in terms of money's inability to achieve 'immortality' or 'the measureless', in *Capital*, Marx makes the same point in terms of the inability for value to be preserved by simple circulation. Showing that the two arguments have the same meaning, Marx runs both together in one passage in the *Urtext* (1858b, pp. 489–90; see note 70 below). As noted earlier (see note 9), Saad-Filho criticises Murray and Bidet criticises Arthur for explaining the transformation of money into capital based on the *Grundrisse*, but neither recognises that a different version of the same argument carries over into *Capital*.

52. Marx 1990a, p. 252.

53. Marx 1990a, p. 253. Marx speaks of capital as a spiral in the *Grundrisse* (Marx 1993, p. 266). In *Capital*, he credits this description to Sismondi (Marx 1990a, p. 727).

possibility by comparing the endless renewal of capital with the 'repetition or renewal... of selling in order to buy' (the schema, C-M-C has already dropped out; Marx's last reference to it is in the preceding paragraph, to be considered shortly).[54] The difference Marx points to is that the renewal is 'within' circulation in the case of capital, whereas it is 'outside' circulation in the case of simple circulation. The comparison reveals the importance of that difference.

In the already much quoted passage, Marx says, of simple circulation, that: 'The repetition or renewal of the act of selling in order to buy finds its measure and its goal (as does the process itself) in a final purpose which lies outside it, namely consumption, the satisfaction of definite needs'.[55]

The purpose of 'the process itself' was already disclosed to be use-value in the second round. As differentiated from that, Marx is now considering the repetition of the process so as to compare this to the renewal of capital.[56] 'Lies outside' means that the purpose is actually realised outside circulation; the commodity has to drop out of circulation to be consumed and, when it does, it loses the commodity-form. As this implies, 'lies outside' also means that the purpose realised both by the circuit and by its repetition does not require the forms of circulation (that is, it can be realised in various other ways besides circulation). This is why commodities turned into 'products' in the second round. To this, the third round adds that the purpose of satisfying needs does not guarantee the reproduction of circulation and so guarantee that circulation is an established, continuously existing process. This means that circulation could exist, but its existence would be accidental rather than necessary. For example, it could be incidental to a great variety of other social arrangements that serve some purpose other than valorisation (the forms that have existed historically usually combine political and economic goals and are often justified on religious grounds); circulation could go in and out of existence, leaving these other arrangements intact.

On the other side, the 'within circulation' of capital means that valorisation is the *only* purpose for which the forms of circulation, money and commodities, are necessary. Because valorisation is both an endless process and a process that can occur only 'within' circulation (or, in other words, necessarily involves money and commodities), it guarantees the perpetual reproduction of circulation (in the same way that the propertylessness of the worker guarantees a perpetual 'supply

---

54. Marx 1990a, p. 252.
55. Ibid.
56. Marx emphasises in the *Grundrisse* that there is a 'repetition or alternation of the role of commodity and money' in the case of simple circulation whereas there is a 'self-renewing circular course of exchanges' or reproduction in the case of capital (Marx 1993, p. 261). The difference is somewhat disguised because Marx uses the term 'circulation' to refer, without distinction, both to simple circulation and to the circulation of capital (I will return to this point later).

of labour'). Valorisation, therefore, makes circulation an established process or institution (which the massive heap of commodities noted at the beginning of *Capital* indicates that it is). Marx expresses this most directly in the concluding section of the chapter, to which I will turn shortly. For the moment, there is one last element of the third round (in Marx's presentation this is its first step) that needs to be considered.

Once Marx defines capital as valorisation, he examines C-M-C to see whether value could increase in this circuit.[57] It might seem that Marx is asking: can commodity-exchange accomplish the increase in value that is required for capital? This, however, is the question that Chapter five answers. It can be raised only after Marx has established that circulation is capital's circulation, M-C-M'. This is what Marx is establishing here (and in all of Chapter Four). Marx is repeating the same procedure he followed in the second round, evaluating C-M-C by a standard derived from M-C-M; in the second round, the standard was the reflux, in the third, it is increased value. The reason to ask whether C-M-C can do either of these things – as is now evident from the rest of the argument – is that these are the things circulation would have to do to be self-sustaining (the conditions it would have to fulfil to reproduce itself). In turn, only the perpetual reproduction of circulation guarantees its continuous existence and so its presence as an established process.

Marx says that it is possible for value to increase in simple circulation but this would be accidental (which is the same as the way commodity-exchange exists without capital). Increasing value, however, is the purpose that must be realised to guarantee the reproduction of circulation. That simple circulation does not normally do this means that circulation is really the circulation of capital.[58] In other words, the idea we have of circulation as simple circulation is overturned because this kind of circulation (C-M-C) cannot sustain itself. By this, circulation is instead established to be the circulation of capital. The statement of this same idea in the *Grundrisse* reads as follows:

---

57. The paragraph I refer to begins: 'Of course, it is also possible that in C-M-C the two extremes ... may represent quantitatively different magnitudes of value.' Marx 1990a, p. 252.

58. In C-M-C Marx says 'the equivalence of ... values is ... a necessary condition of its normal course' (1990a, p. 252). This is true only in capitalism, where circulation is an established process within the circulation of capital (for example, Marx says of precapitalist exchange that it is 'not the *exchange of equivalents*;' commodities are not equal *magnitudes of value*, they are 'posited as commodities to the extent that they are exchangeable at all ... But it is not thereby posited that they are *equivalents*' [Marx 1861–63b, pp. 13–14]). The possibility of C-M-C's two extremes being different value-magnitudes suggests precapitalist merchant's capital. If commodities are not posited as equivalents, however, they are not posited as non-equivalents either; they just have different prices in different places. There is no system of value.

> The repetition of the process [simple circulation, MC] from either of the points, money or commodity, is not posited within the conditions of exchange itself... *Circulation... does not carry within itself the principle of self-renewal* [the preservation and increase of value, MC]... Circulation, therefore,... exists only in so far as it is constantly mediated.[59]

Because simple circulation does not 'posit its extremes', meaning guarantee the reproduction of the forms, money and commodities, Marx says 'it is now negated... as... simple exchange and circulation of both' money and commodity. In other words, the conception of circulation as simple or 'direct' circulation is superseded by the recognition that circulation is really mediated circulation or capital.[60]

The last time that C-M-C appears in Chapter Four of *Capital* is in the paragraph (just quoted), in which value is said to increase only by accident in C-M-C. That C-M-C then vanishes indicates that it has been superseded by M-C-M'. In the two earlier drafts on the transformation of money into capital, Marx uses the same term 'circulation' but switches its meaning from simple circulation to circulation as capital (it may be assumed that he knows what he means and there is no intended reader to alert). For example, in the last *Grundrisse* passage quoted, when Marx says that 'circulation... does not carry within itself the principle of self-renewal', he is evidently referring to simple circulation. Later in the same paragraph, he says 'now' – meaning, as capital – 'circulation itself returns back into the activity which posits or produces exchange values'.[61] Apart from 'circula-

---

59. Marx 1993, p. 254–5. This is among the key passages that Marx carries over from the *Grundrisse* to the *Urtext* in a slightly modified form (see Marx 1858b, p. 479).

60. In *Capital*, Marx describes C-M-C as 'the direct form of the circulation of commodities' just before he introduces 'the other' form, M-C-M, which indicates that the latter is the indirect or mediated form (Marx 1990a, p. 247).

61. Marx 1993, p. 255. This usage is more pervasive than one quotation can suggest. See also Marx 1993, p. 259, when he says, 'as soon as money is posited as an exchange value which not only becomes independent of circulation, but which also maintains itself through it' he is referring to money as the first term in M-C-M, or the circuit of capital (see also Marx 1993, p. 260). The shift in meaning is striking in the following passage from the *Urtext*: 'The same exchange value must become money, commodity, commodity, money, as the form M-C-M requires. In the simple circulation, the commodity becomes money and then commodity; it is another commodity which once again posits itself as money. *The exchange value is not retained in this change of its form. But in circulation it is already posited that money is both money and commodity, and is retained in the alternation of both determinations.*' (underlining added) (Marx 1858b, p. 493; corresponds to Marx 1993, p. 261). The second 'circulation' evidently refers to the circulation of capital; 'same' and 'another' indicates the continuity of value in one case as opposed to discontinuity in the other. From here, Marx proceeds to speak of circulation just as the circulation of capital: 'circulation is itself no longer determined as a merely formal process in which the commodity passes through its various determinations, but the exchange value itself... must be premised as posited by circulation and as so posited by it appear as being premised to it. Circulation itself must appear as a moment of the production of exchange values'

tion' in the definition of capital, I find one instance of an unannounced switch in the meaning of circulation in *Capital*, nearly at the end of Chapter Four: 'Value therefore now becomes value in process, money in process, and, as such capital. It comes out of circulation, enters into it again, preserves and multiplies itself within circulation, emerges from it with an increased size, and starts the same cycle again and again'.[62]

Here, the first 'circulation' that value as money is said to come out of – and as we later find out, must go into production – is circulation in the sense of commodity-exchange. The second 'circulation', in which value is said to preserve and multiply itself, is the circulation of capital.[63] The point of these quotations is to show that simple circulation, which is not the process of commodity-exchange, but an idea we have about that process, is gone. By the end of Chapter Four, Marx refers to the process of commodity-exchange as 'the sphere of circulation', which is a phase of the circulation of capital.[64]

The concluding section of Chapter Four and its counterparts in the drafts

After the third round, Marx gathers up his accomplishments in the concluding section of the chapter. He makes a minor point first: now that circulation has been shown to be capital, the capitalist's intentions to make money no longer prevent us from understanding what capital is, and the capitalist may be safely introduced. It is clear from Marx's description that the capitalist need not understand the process of capital in order to act on its behalf. For all the capitalist knows, the whole thing has to do with money coming out of and returning to his pocket; he need not understand value, the social form of the mode of production, to play his role in it.

Next, Marx contrasts our original idea of circulation, as portrayed in Part One of *Capital*, with the way circulation appears now:

(Marx 1973, p. 491; repeats 1973, p. 235). A particularly important passage in which Marx switches between the two meanings of circulation appears in the *Grundrisse* (1973, p. 266 and corresponds to *Capital* (1990a, p. 255). I will discuss both later.

62. Marx 1990a, p. 256. The only remaining point in Chapter Four is that M-C-M' is general, or applies to all capital. Marx anticipates the generality of M-C-M' in an earlier footnote, saying it is 'the characteristic form of circulation... of all capital' (Marx 1990a, p. 251).

63. A more 'announced' case of the change in meaning appears earlier, at the end of the third round; Marx says: 'the simple circulation of commodities... is a means to a final goal which lies outside circulation... the circulation of money as capital is an end in itself' (1990a, p. 253).

64. Marx 1990a, p. 257. The 'sphere of circulation' or just 'commodity exchange' become more prominent in Chapters Five and Six. That Marx does not drop the term 'simple circulation' until the end of Chapter Six suggests that we remain within the grip of this idea of circulation until we are disabused of the notion that the relation of wage-labour to capital is simply an exchange-relation rather than a relation of exploitation.

> The independent form, i.e., the money form, which the value of commodities assumes in simple circulation, does nothing but mediate the exchange of commodities, and it vanishes in the final result of the movement. On the other hand, in the circulation M-C-M both the money and the commodity function only as different modes of existence of value itself... It is constantly changing from one form into the other, without becoming lost in this movement... value is here the subject of a process in which, while constantly assuming the form in turn of money and commodities it changes its own magnitude... and thus valorizes itself independently.[65]

Which is to say, if we look at circulation as if it were simple circulation, what we see is that: (1) value exists as the form, money, because, in money, value exists separately from the commodity's use-value; and (2) the commodity and money are opposites; because money is the form of value, the commodity is not. The argument of Chapter Four shows that if circulation is regarded in this way, it is not a process that can sustain itself (value 'vanishes'). Circulation must be self-sustaining, however, because it is in continuous existence; 'acts of exchange are taking place everywhere and... are being continuously renewed'.[66] This is a preliminary way of justifying the necessity for circulation's reproduction; it is the only justification that can be given before the analysis of the whole system is completed. Once that analysis is complete, however, the justification is simple: all modes of production must have the capacity to reproduce themselves; because commodity-exchange is a necessary element of the capitalist mode of production, it must be continuously reproduced.[67] It follows that we must revise our way of looking at circulation so that it can be something that is self-sustaining (in other words, our understanding of circulation is 'defective' because it lacks the capacity to reproduce itself, which its established existence shows that it must have).[68] The argument of Chapter Four shows that, in order for circulation to be self-sustaining, it would have to be capital. Revising our understanding to look at circulation as capital, we see that: (1) value is the 'subject' of circulation – acting on its own behalf and reproducing itself – rather than just the form, money; and (2) commodities and money are both forms that value runs through in the course of its reproduction, which is its expansion.

---

65. Marx 1990a, p. 255.
66. Marx 1859, p. 323. Reichelt speaks of this as the 'permanence' of value (Reichelt 2007, pp. 36–8).
67. See the *Results*: 'the relations of production, are themselves produced: they are also the constantly renewed result of the process' (Marx 1990a, p. 1065).
68. Arthur states that 'the basis for the advance [in the sequence of categories in a systematic dialectic] is generally that each category is *deficient* in determinacy with respect to the next and the impulse for the transition is precisely the requirement that such deficiency must be overcome' (Arthur 2002b, p. 66).

Two other versions of the summary of the transition from simple circulation to capital-circulation appear in the drafts. The three together are mutually
illuminating. The *Urtext* version suggests a parallel between the beginnings of
Capital, parts one and two:

> As earlier we proceeded from the commodity, if we now proceed from
> exchange-value as such – its independence [*verselbständigung*, [meaning
> value valorising 'itself independently',[69] MC] being the result of the circula-
> tion process [of capital, MC], then we find that:
>
> 1) Exchange-value [meaning value as capital, MC] exists doubly, as com-
> modity and as money... The existence of exchange-value is thus doubled, it
> exists once in use values, and once again in money. Both forms are exchanged
> for each other, however, and by this mere exchange as such value is not lost.
>
> 2) If money [again meaning value as capital, MC] is to be preserved as money,
> it must also... be capable of entering this process [circulation] again... so that
> its being as means of circulation, and thereby its transition into commodity
> must be merely changes of form in order for it to appear again in its adequate
> form [meaning money, MC], as adequate exchange-value, but at the same time
> as multiplied, increased exchange-value, valorised exchange-value. Value that
> valorises itself, multiplies itself in circulation is in general exchange-value for
> itself, which as its own purpose runs through circulation.[70]

Like the *Capital* version, this suggests that in Part Two, a second and parallel
round of argument begins from value (here called exchange-value) taking the
place of the commodity; value's two 'modes of existence', the commodity and
money, reproduce the original division within the commodity between use-value
and exchange-value.[71] Whereas the line of argument from the commodity leads

---

69. Marx 1990a, p. 255.

70. Marx 1858a, pp. 931–2 (my translation); see also 1858b, pp. 490–1. Another description in the *Urtext* presents the transition both in terms of the inadequacy of simple
circulation because of its inability to sustain itself and as a move from money as money
(the third functions of money) to capital: 'Money... even in its concrete determination
as money... is negated in the movement of circulation in which it is posited as money
[meaning simple circulation, MC]. But what is negated here is merely the abstract
form in which the exchange value becoming independent appears in money, and also
the abstract form of the process of its becoming independent. From the standpoint of
exchange value [meaning value as capital, MC] the whole of circulation [meaning simple
circulation, MC] is negated, since it does not carry within itself the principle of self-renewal' (Marx 1858b, p. 489–90). This repeats Marx's move from money as hoard to capital
in the *Grundrisse* and shows that the point of that move is that value is not preserved
in simple circulation, even in the extreme case when money is the goal of exchange.
This makes the same argument as the transformation of money into capital in *Capital*.
As noted earlier, Bidet recognises this argument in the *Grundrisse* but claims that Marx
abandoned it in *Capital* (see note 9 above).

71. To say that it is a second round of argument does not mean that it is discontinuous with the first round. I have argued, on the contrary, that once simple circulation
is fully developed in Part One of *Capital*, Marx argues that simple circulation is unable

to the exposition of simple circulation, in the second line of argument, value is 'determined as a process', which is its 'relation to its own self through the process of circulation' of capital.[72]

It is important to recognise that this same argument appears in the *Grundrisse*, because this indicates that Marx had already conceived the basis for the transformation of money into capital in this first draft in the same way as he presents it in *Capital*. The *Grundrisse* version also adds its own particular emphasis. Correcting for terminology (this is another passage where the meaning of 'circulation' changes), the *Grundrisse* version is similar in many respects to the version in *Capital*:

> The transition from simple exchange-value and its circulation to capital can also be expressed in this way: Within circulation, exchange-value appears double: once as commodity, again as money. If it is in one aspect, it is not in the other [the opposition indicates that circulation here means simple circulation, MC]...But the <u>wholeness of circulation</u> [referring to capital circulation, MC], regarded in itself, lies in the fact that the same exchange-value, exchange-value as subject, posits itself once as commodity, another time as money, and that it is just this movement of positing itself in this dual character and of preserving itself in each of them as its opposite, in the commodity as money and in money as commodity. This in itself is present in simple circulation, but is not posited in it. Exchange-value posited as the <u>unity of commodity and money is</u> <u>capital</u>, and this positing itself appears as the circulation of capital. (Which is, however, a spiral...not a simple circle).[73]

Unique to this version is the statement that capital is 'present but not posited' in simple circulation, which means that simple circulation presupposes the preservation of value (all versions make the case that this is true because simple circulation exists but is not self-sustaining). In addition, this version emphasises that capital unifies the commodity and money (although the other versions certainly make this point). Unlike *Capital*, Marx moves directly from this summary of the difference between simple and capital circulation to 'the relation of capital and labour'.[74] This direct move together with the focus on capital as unifying

---

to sustain itself. This demonstration motivates the turn to a form of circulation that is able to sustain itself, which is capital. In this way, the argument is a continuous logical progression.

72. Marx 1858b, p. 491.

73. Marx 1993, p. 266. Underlining added as emphasis.

74. Ibid. *Capital* is the first version to separate the argument that an increase in value cannot occur in commodity-exchange from the argument that capital-circulation is self-reproducing, creating a hiatus (which is *Capital*, Chapter five) between the introduction of value as self-valorising and the capital/wage-labour relation. As I will argue shortly, this means that, for a time, capital seems to be completely self-sufficient.

principle elicits Marx's peculiar footnote on value, use-value and exchange-value. Continuing the theme of unity, Marx writes that 'in the relation of capital and labour, exchange-value and use-value are brought into relation', in that capital as value stands opposite labour as the use-value capital consumes.[75] Marx then raises the question (in the peculiar footnote): 'Is not *value* to be conceived as the unity of use value and exchange value? In and for itself, is value as such the general form, in opposition to use value and exchange value as *particular* forms of it?'[76]

'Value' here evidently means value as capital. It unifies use-value and exchange-value, first as commodity and money (as we see in *Capital* at the end of Chapter Four), then as itself (as objectified labour) and labour (which is living labour, as we see in *Capital* at the end of Chapter Six), and ultimately, as production and the process of commodity-exchange by harnessing production to the only purpose that requires commodity-exchange, namely, increasing value (as we see in Volume I as a whole). This last unity is capitalism.[77]

The way this unity appears in *Capital* is that, at the end of Chapter Four, value as capital appears to be completely self-sufficient: it is all-encompassing, enclosing both commodities and money in its circulation, it relates only to itself ('it enters into a private relationship with itself', Marx says) and it has the capacity to reproduce itself. Accordingly, Marx likens capital to god: capital (for one brief moment at least) has no 'other'. Because Chapter Four establishes that circulation is the circulation of capital, Marx proceeds from there to investigate the conditions necessary for the existence of valorisation. Capital's other, wage-labour, emerges from that investigation in Chapter Six.

Simple circulation as the appearance-form of the capitalist mode of production

In all versions of the transformation of money into capital, Marx describes simple circulation as a surface or phenomenon. In one particularly striking passage in the *Urtext* (the third passage, quoted above pp. 151–2), he says that 'the whole system of bourgeois production is presupposed by exchange value appearing on its surface as a simple point of departure'.[78] In the drafts, the superficial charac-

---

75. Marx 1993, p. 267.
76. Ibid.
77. It is evident from this that the problem with the mercantilist idea of capital (the reason why 'the whole process vanishes' as Marx says in *Capital* (Marx 1990a, p. 248) is that it leaves out this unity because it lacks the 'use-value' side. Thanks to Arthur for pointing out that 'it is value as capital that unifies itself and its other and hence opens itself to, as well as takes advantage of, the use-value determinations, especially that of labour-power' (personal communication).
78. Marx 1858a, p. 907; see also 1858b, p. 466.

ter of simple circulation is often just asserted.[79] When Marx does give a reason for it, the evidence he appeals to is that simple circulation is unable to reproduce itself: that the value-character of commodities or of money would 'die out' demonstrates that if circulation is simple circulation (or C-M-C), then:

> Circulation... does not carry within itself the principle of self-renewal... Circulation, therefore, which appears as that which is immediately present on the surface of bourgeois society exists only in so far as it is constantly mediated... Its immediate being is therefore pure semblance. *It is the phenomenon of a process taking place behind it.*[80]

In *Capital*, this same argument – that circulation must be capital (M-C-M') because simple circulation (C-M-C) is unable to reproduce itself – appears in Chapter Four. Marx does not there state that this makes simple circulation a phenomenon. Instead he postpones this description to the remaining chapters of Part Two, in which he reveals two sets of illusions associated with simple circulation.[81]

The inverted order of the circuit accomplished in Chapter Four 'does not take us outside' the sphere of commodity-exchange.[82] Because circulation is now M-C-M', the question arises: can valorisation be accomplished within the sphere of exchange? This introduces one set of illusions stemming from simple circulation, namely, various misconceived attempts to explain surplus-value on the basis of exchange. The first is the explanation of profit, by Condillac, as an increase in use-value. Condillac's flawed explanation of profit also illustrates, as a sort of bonus, a different kind of illusion associated with simple circulation. Marx says of it: 'Condillac not only confuses use-value with exchange-value, but

79. See, for example, Marx 1993, p. 227, p. 247, p. 251 and 1858b, pp. 466–7.

80. Marx 1993, p. 255, repeated in 1858b, p. 479, which is modified a few pages later into: 'simple circulation is... an abstract sphere of the bourgeois process of production as a whole, which through its own determinations shows itself to be a moment, a mere form of appearance of some deeper process lying behind it... industrial capital' (p. 482).

81. Bidet argues that the idea of circulation as a surface is an 'inadequate procedure' or 'ambiguity' (Bidet 2005, p. 136). He recognises that Marx describes circulation in these terms in the *Grundrisse*, but argues that Marx abandoned this notion in *Capital* (see Bidet 2005, p. 136–8). In what follows, I show how Marx expresses this idea in *Capital*.

82. Marx 1990a, p. 259. Marx says this 'does not take us outside the sphere of the simple circulation of commodities' (emphasis added) because he proceeds to criticise attempts to explain surplus-value in terms of C-M-C. Chapter five, and to a lesser extent Chapter six, operate within an ambiguous perspective between C-M-C and M-C-M': the former is already superseded by Chapter Four but we are also still stuck in it, both because it is the perspective to which economics is confined and because the illusions associated with simple circulation are not definitively overturned until the full nature of the capital/wage-labour relation is disclosed. I think it would have been clearer to use the terms commodity-exchange or commodity-circulation (which Marx sometimes does in Chapter five), which are neutral because they refer to the process rather than to either the C-M-C or M-C-M' conceptions of it.

in a really childish manner assumes that, in a society in which the production of commodities is well-developed, each producer produces his own means of subsistence and throws into circulation only what is superfluous, the excess over his own requirements'.[83]

The view Marx here criticises as 'childish' is the concept of simple commodity-production, which, ironically, is one of the interpretations of his own Part One of *Capital*.

The remaining attempts to explain surplus-value on the basis of exchange are varieties of unequal exchange, all of which fail, ultimately, because a change in the distribution of value cannot increase 'the sum of the values in circulation'.[84] As this shows, by the formation of surplus-value, Marx means an increase in value for 'the capitalist class...taken as a whole', or, in other words, for the system of value as a whole.[85] That circulation is circulation as capital, but the fact that exchange by itself cannot accomplish the valorisation that capital requires, shows that our concept of circulation must be revised again. It was originally C-M-C; because of the latter's inability to reproduce itself, circulation became M-C-M'; circulation in this second sense must now be revised to move both through the sphere of commodity-exchange and outside that sphere. Marx presents this inadequacy of exchange, its failure to give rise to surplus-value, as evidence that simple circulation is a surface: 'We have shown that surplus-value cannot arise from circulation (meaning commodity exchange, MC) and therefore that, for it to be formed, something must take place in the background which is not visible in the circulation itself'.[86]

As in the drafts, it is by its inadequacy that circulation (as simple circulation) shows its character as superficial. The recognition of its superficiality is what matters because this is what takes the argument past commodity-exchange. Moreover, because the formation of surplus-value is one aspect of capital's self-renewal, Marx's two explanations for the superficiality of exchange (in the drafts and in *Capital*) are not substantially different. As we see from Marx's final reference to commodity-exchange as a surface in Part Two, the version in *Capital* zeros in on the particular aspect of capital's self-renewal that shows capitalist social relations to be qualitatively different from the way they appear in the sphere of exchange.

This final reference appears at the end of Chapter Six. On the verge of leaving the sphere of circulation, Marx describes it as a 'noisy sphere, where everything takes place on the surface and in full view of everyone'. Marx promises

---

83. Marx 1990a, pp. 261–2.
84. Marx 1990a, p. 265.
85. Marx 1990a, p. 266.
86. Marx 1990a, p. 268.

that 'the hidden abode of production', which we are about to enter, will reveal 'the secret of profit-making'.[87] The illusions that are at stake in this context are 'the concepts and standard by which [the free trader *vulgaris*] judges the society of capital and wage-labour' or the law of appropriation as it appears in simple circulation.[88] Marx presents the inversion of this law within *Capital*, Volume I. The transformation of surplus-value into capital (Chapter Twenty-Four) makes it possible to show, even without the primitive accumulation, that, whereas:

> Originally the rights of property seemed to us to be grounded in a man's own labour...Now...property turns out to be the right, on the part of the capitalist to appropriate the unpaid labour of others or its product, and the impossibility, on the part of the worker, of appropriating his own product. The separation of property from labour thus becomes the <u>necessary consequence</u> of a law that apparently originated in their identity.[89]

This inversion is evidently the return that marks the second half of an appearance-form transition (like the transition from exchange-value to value and back in Chapter One and from the two possible concepts of circulation, C-M-C versus M-C-M to endless valorisation and back to M-C-M' in Chapter Four). As the shorter sequence in Chapter Four illustrates, the starting and end-points in this type of argument refer to the same entity (circulation, in the case of Chapter Four). What changes over the course of the argument is the way that entity is understood. Interrogation of the initial phenomenon reveals its flaws and these produce the revised understanding expressed in the return. Because the original law of appropriation arises from simple circulation, its inversion results from the overturning of simple circulation. This is already partly accomplished by the end of Chapter Six, when Marx spells out the elements of the original law, describing them as 'Freedom, Equality, Property and Bentham'.[90] The full overturning of simple circulation involves the revelation of the secret of profit making (replacing the theories Marx criticises in Chapter Five). This is the revelation of the exploitative nature of the capital/wage-labour relation.

---

87. Marx 1990a, pp. 279–80.

88. The passage in *Capital*, Chapter Six concludes a much abbreviated version of the *Grundrisse* passage on 'Simple Exchange' (1993, pp. 239–250) which corresponds to the section on 'The Manifestation of the Law of Appropriation in the Simple Circulation' in the *Urtext* (1858b, pp. 461–77). Parts of these lengthier discussions are shifted into Chapter Twenty-Four of *Capital*. On the importance of the inversion of the 'bourgeois law of appropriation', see Murray 2009, pp. 171–2.

89. Marx 1990a, p. 730, underlining added as emphasis. Marx specifically sets aside primitive accumulation repeatedly in Chapter Twenty-Four (that is, the question: where the owner got the original capital) and, focusing on the newly formed surplus-value, pretends that the original capital came from the capitalist's 'original labour' (see Marx 1990a, pp. 728–9).

90. Marx 1990a, p. 280.

The model provided by the inversion of the original law of appropriation, because it is a complete appearance form transition, shows the *Results* to be an alternative return. The appearance-form transition completed by the *Results* would have spanned all of *Capital*, Volume I. The question as to the fate of the *Results* is beyond the scope of this paper.[91] The point here is that either Chapter 24 or the *Results* completes the appearance form-transition which began with the commodity at the opening of *Capital*.[92] The entity that comes to be understood through the investigation of its initial phenomenon, simple circulation, is capital or the capitalist mode of production in its entirety. In the statement from the *Urtext* quoted above (pp. 151–2), Marx describes this role of simple circulation in the explanation of capitalism: 'The examination of simple circulation shows us the general concept of capital, because within the bourgeois mode of production the simple circulation exists only as preposited by capital and as prepositing it'.[93] In light of the foregoing, this means that simple circulation is uniquely the appearance-form of the capitalist mode of production. It has this unique role in capitalism because commodity-exchange is necessary to capital; it is incidental to all other modes of production. This necessity is the basis for the transition from Part One of *Capital* to Part Two.

---

91. Murray 2009 argues that there is no good reason for excluding the *Results* from Volume I. It is possible that Marx meant the inversion of the law of appropriation to stand for the inversion of simple circulation as a whole, since, as the culmination of Part Two, the original law in effect encompasses the entire argument up to that point. As Murray points out, however, the *Results* clarify the argument of Volume I in ways that no other work by Marx does (Murray 2009, pp. 173–6). With this, the question as to the fate of the *Results* becomes a question about how much Marx expected his readers to figure out on their own.

92. Chapter One of *Capital* Volume II is a third possible return. Banaji also recognises that *Capital*, Part One presents simple circulation as the appearance-form of the capitalist mode of production as a whole (Banaji 1979, p. 28). Without claiming that Chapter One of Volume II contains the entire content of the *Results*, he argues that it marks the return to the process of circulation or to the commodity, which completes the appearance-form transition which began with Part One of *Capital* Volume I (Banaji 1979, p. 35). Finally, Reichelt also emphasises the phenomenal character of simple circulation and the illusions associated with it (Reichelt 2007, p. 17, p. 28, p. 44).

93. Marx 1858b, p. 505, see also p. 467: 'the consequent social relations [the "more complicated relations of production, more or less conflicting with the liberty and independence of individuals", p. 466] present themselves . . . directly from an examination of the simple circulation'.

The Concept of Capital in the *Grundrisse*
Howard Engelskirchen

My objective is to investigate the concept of 'capital in general', a category that threads together Marx's explorations in the *Grundrisse*, and to do so by drawing on recent advances in the realist philosophy of science. In particular, I will argue that Marx's effort to work out the concept of capital corresponds to what philosophers of science today would call the 'real definition' of a natural or social kind. If this is right, we can expect Marx's analyses will contribute significantly to contemporary efforts to extend thinking about natural kinds from natural to social science.

Reference fixing and Marx's analysis

I will start with a metaphor, one of Marx's most provocative: 'The specific economic form, in which unpaid surplus labour is pumped out of direct producers determines the relationship of domination and servitude, as it grows directly out of production itself and reacts back on it in turn as a determinant'.[1]

Marx returns to the same metaphor when describing the capitalist appropriation of surplus-value in 'The Trinity Formula' at the end of *Capital* Volume III. After describing the composite structure of labour and form that will characterise any mode of production, he writes: 'we also saw that capital, in the social production process appropriate to it – and the capitalist is

---

1. Marx 1981, p. 927.

simply personified capital, functioning in the production process simply as the bearer of capital – pumps out a certain specific quantum of surplus labour from the direct producers or workers, surplus labour that it receives without equivalent and which by its very nature always remains forced labour, however much it might appear as the result of free contractual agreement'.[2]

It seems worthwhile to reflect a minute on the metaphor's implications. What can it tell us? What can it tell us about the target and substance of Marx's science?

Form determination as causal determination

The idea of 'pumping' suggests unambiguously a causal process and a causal agent. The economic form that does the pumping must be a causal structure. That is, if we are to judge by this metaphor, the 'simplest determinations' described by Marx in the introductory paragraph of the *Grundrisse's* 'The Method of Political Economy',[3] those capable of grounding social explanation, must be causal determinations. Form-determination for Marx, the metaphor suggests, is above all causal determination.

I think that we have missed the significance of this emphasis in Marx's science because of the dominance of positivism in both the natural and social sciences over the last century – whether you worked with the assumptions of this approach or fought them by appealing to some variant of hermeneutics or the postmodern tradition, attention to cause was lost. But realism's reflections on the actual practice of contemporary science have opened fresh perspectives that make it possible to recover methods, emphases and insights in our reading of Marx that might otherwise have remained obscure to us.

Thus, for one thing, we need not assume that causal structures, if they exist, are necessarily always empirical. Under the influence of positivism, Marxists have often been tempted to consider only two ontological options – either a thing was empirical or it was theoretical, merely conceptual. By contrast, over the last half century philosophers of science have learned to speak again in realist terms of causal structures that are at once potent and causally efficacious, but at the same time not observable, not empirical. Marx, never one to hide his credentials as a card-carrying scientific realist, compared the search for the inner nature of capital to the effort to understand extraterrestrial motion: 'a scientific analysis of competition is possible only if we grasp the inner nature of capital, just as

---

2. Marx 1991a, pp. 957–8.
3. Marx 1973, p. 100.

the apparent motions of the heavenly bodies are intelligible only to someone acquainted with their real motions, which are not perceptible to the senses'.[4]

The simplest determinations

Notice how this comparison makes sense of the *Grundrisse* excerpt, 'The Method of Political Economy': you start with evidence perceptible to the senses but are unable to give a scientific explanation of it. You strip away apparent motions of the phenomena you explore until you arrive at their real motions – motions not perceptible to the senses. But these real motions, the 'simplest determinations', allow you to intelligibly reconstruct your understanding of phenomena as they are perceptibly presented.

This, incidentally, was a step that John Locke, working in the early years of the scientific revolution, could not grasp. For Locke, that which was 'insensible' must ever remain a mystery to us.[5] Marx judged that science had shown our capacity to grasp the inner nature of things. But for others in the traditions of mainstream thinking about science, the legacy of Locke's empiricism persisted.

The word 'value', of course, refers to an imperceptible social structure, and so does 'capital in general'. In this reading, Marx's references to the 'concept of capital' or 'capital in general' target that constellation of causal properties or mechanisms that constitute the simplest determination of the capitalist mode of production, an intersection of causal properties deeply embedded under capital's phenomenal manifestations. Thus, Marx writes in the *Grundrisse* that searching for the defining characteristics of 'capital in general' is like searching for the defining characteristics of *homo sapiens* – one looks for those features that account for what makes *homo sapiens* distinct from other animals.[6] Just as the biologist looks for the *differentia specifica* of a species, the search for 'capital in general' is a search for what is distinctive about capital as a species of production. The

---

4. Marx 1990a, p. 433.

5. Hilary Kornblith argues this was only his 'official' doctrine and that the 'dialectic of his discussion' forced him 'to a realist and nonsceptical account of real essence' (Kornblith 1993, p. 33). Here is Locke claiming that we are incapable of knowing the real essence of the natural substances on which we depend: 'This, though it be all the *Essence* of natural Substances, that we know, or by which we distinguish them into Sorts, yet I call it by a peculiar name, the *nominal Essence*, to distinguish it from that real Constitution of Substances, upon which depends this *nominal Essence*, and all the Properties of that Sort; which therefore, as has been said, may be called the *real Essence: v.g.* the *nominal Essence* of Gold, is that complex *Idea* the word *Gold* stands for, let it be, for instance, a Body yellow, of a certain weight, malleable, fusible, and fixed. But the *real Essence* is the constitution of the insensible parts of that Body, on which those Qualities, and all the other Properties of *Gold* depend' Locke 1975, p. 439 [III, vi, 2], quoted in Kornblith 1993, pp. 23–4.

6. Marx 1973, p. 852.

differentia specifica of capital are those features that distinguish it 'from all other forms of wealth or modes in which social production develops'.[7]

Real definition and reference

To the extent that the simple determination for which we search is a causal structure, we are after what the realist philosophy of science today would call the real definition of a natural or social kind. The real definition of a thing refers to those causal properties or mechanisms that account for what it is, how it behaves, and how it persists as what it is. H_2O is the real definition of water. Notice importantly that while our effort to specify a real definition explicitly defines, what we are after is precision of reference, not the kind of thing we commonly associate with verbal definition; we are not 'defining our terms' or offering a clarification of the ideas we associate with our use of the term. In this sense reference is 'ostensive' rather than definitional in the ordinary sense – it points.[8] Reference is an example of the way our use of language enables us to coordinate our causal interactions with the world; we use language to identify accurately the causal structures to which we accommodate our social practice. Even for the large theoretical elaborations any science involves, this will hold only if the things to which we refer determine the content of the terms we use, rather than that this be accomplished by the ideas and intuitions we might at any one point associate with our use of those terms.

Such an approach makes sense of what would otherwise present a puzzle. Writing in 1845, Marx and Engels wrote a tract excoriating the conceptual analysis of their day: 'Let us revolt against this rule of concepts!', they announced in the preface to *The German Ideology*.[9] Feuerbach remained stalled with the conceptual abstraction 'man' and others were driven by more extravagant speculative manipulations. Thus, the social relation of the family, Marx and Engels argued, must be analysed according to existing empirical data, not according to 'the concept of the family'.[10] In an echo of this, Hilary Kornblith, a contemporary philosophical naturalist, argues for the study of mind, not 'the concept of mind,' of law, not 'the concept of law'.[11] Why, then, did Marx, a dozen years after *The German Ideology*, devote some 800 pages of manuscript to working out 'the concept of capital'?

---

7. Marx 1986, p. 378; compare Marx 1973, p. 449, where *differentia specifica* is translated as 'specific characteristics'.
8. Boyd 1979.
9. Marx and Engels 2004, p. 23.
10. Marx and Engels 2004, p. 43.
11. Kornblith 2002, p. 1, referring to Ryle 1984, Hart 1970, and others.

Here is a solution: reference fixing, whether by pointing, or describing, or explicitly defining, is always at bottom ostensive – a matter of picking out the thing to which we refer. It is the structure of the water-molecule that is the source of the information we have about water and it is by the precision with which we identify its elements that we are able to coordinate most effectively our uses of the substance. That is, theoretical concepts and their explication are essential to science. But the chemist who first said 'Aha, water is H_2O' was not 'defining his terms' – he was making a scientific discovery.

What I argue is that Marx was working with the concept of capital in the same way. He used it to pick out decisive causal structures of social life, not to stipulate the meanings he associated with his use of the term. And because he used concepts to refer, those concepts are, as are theoretical terms used in other sciences, fallible and approximate and necessarily revisable in consequence of any advance in our understanding of the thing to which they refer. This is true of all scientific work.[12]

Categories and convenience

Often, people argue that the divisions we make among the things of the world are not determined by the causal mechanisms or properties that characterise them, but instead that sorting things into kinds is a matter of convention that depends on our convenience. This is an implication of Locke's argument that nature is without chasms or gaps, and that in spite of their apparent diversity, species on the great chain of being shade imperceptibly into one another.[13] If, by contrast, nature is, so to speak, bunched or clumped such that discrete entities reproduce themselves coherently as different kinds of things, then in our activities, linguistic, scientific, political, or other, we are obliged to accommodate our practices to the way things are. On this view, we live in a world where dogs do not mate with cats regardless of how we classify them and we can give a causal account of why this is so. Again, when we offer a real definition of a natural kind we attempt to identify those causal properties that account for its distinctive stability as the

---

12. Thus it is possible to explain the continuity of scientific reference without getting trapped by dilemmas of the sort Thomas Kuhn (Kuhn 1970) suggested: a new perspective in science must mean we are no longer referring to the same entities earlier scientists worked with. If reference is determined by the things to which we refer rather than stipulated to by our definitions, then continuity of reference is possible even if previous understandings are discarded. On this basis, I have argued that Marx and Ricardo were talking about the same thing when they referred to labour as the source of value; without subtracting in any way from the revolutionary character of Marx's theoretical advance, there is continuity of scientific reference (Engelskirchen 2007; 2011, pp. 43–5).

13. Locke's argument is in An *Essay Concerning Human Understanding*, Book III, Chapter vi, Section 12 (Locke 1975, pp. 446–7). See Kornblith 1993, p. 18.

kind of thing it is. By identifying water as H_2O, we realise not all combinations of hydrogen and oxygen work to form a water-molecule, and not all combinations of elements or other building blocks of nature work indifferently in any arrangement to create cohesive and stable entities.

The extension of this argument to the study of social life suggests that social things also can be more or less stable configurations that reproduce and renew themselves in relation to changes in their environment. Rather than conventionally organised categories classified according to the language-user's convenience (the way many use the terms 'class' or 'middle class'), there are also social structures that require identification and specification if we want our social practice to respond meaningfully to them. Marx, for example, differentiated modes of production according to the different social forms taken by labour's relation to nature and to others in the course of production.

Concept and referent

For its familiarity and simplicity, H_2O has become the paradigm-example of the real definition of a natural kind. In fact, the idea that water is H_2O has entered popular consciousness so that we forget this is new knowledge in the history of human thought. People knew of and referred to water and its properties for millennia without knowing that its simplest determination was H_2O. While the point seems obvious, *The German Ideology*, if nothing else, underscores the importance of distinguishing between a thing and the concept we form of it. But even Marxists have stumbled over this, and their missteps have led to a significant misreading of an important passage from *The Grundrisse*. In Notebook VII, Marx writes that '[t]he economic concept of value does not occur in antiquity... The concept of value is entirely peculiar to the most modern economy, since it is the most abstract expression of capital itself and of the production resting on it'.[14]

This passage has been taken to mean that value itself, the thing to which the concept of value refers, did not exist in the ancient world. But value can exist where there is no concept of it. We might as well say, paraphrasing Marx, that 'the chemical concept of H_2O does not occur among the ancients.... the concept is entirely peculiar to modern chemistry'. But it would not follow that water itself did not come into being until the scientific discovery of its concept.

Identifying the essential features of 'capital in general' is an effort to locate what could be referred to as the H_2O of capital, its decisive underlying causal structure. We do the same thing when we define gold as atomic number 79 – we distinguish gold from all other shiny yellow metallic things by identifying the most basic causal structure both essential and specific to it. Thus, the search

---

14. Marx 1973, p. 776.

for 'capital in general' is not an effort to gather each important property that all instances of capital-share – the thing Michael Heinrich thought caused the concept of 'capital in general' itself to 'shatter'.[15] Instead, it is an effort to specify those few properties of capital that are constitutive of it.

Constitutive and attributive properties

In this respect, Marx's study of Aristotle is relevant. Aristotle makes a distinction between properties that are constitutive of a thing and those that may be attributed to it or are manifestations of it. All things go through a change of form, Aristotle suggests, and thus he invites us to make just this distinction in our effort to understand them – my DNA stays what it is while I wrinkle and grey. Marx took over this insight and applied it to social life. Thus he is insistent on distinguishing between the inner nature of capital – the intersection of social relations constitutive of capital – and attributes of capital that depend on the action of many capitals on each other, that is, on competition. The thread he traces throughout the *Grundrisse* identifies features necessary to grasp capital's inner nature. Realisation, for example, is part of the concept of capital, although any actual project of realisation may likely confront a tangle of difficult complications arising out of the interactions of capitals on one another. However, Marx abstracts from these and assumes that realisation proceeds unproblematically in order to focus exclusively on the mechanisms that constitute and establish capital's essential life-processes.[16] The categories of competition refer to forms by means of which capital's constitutive structure manifests itself, not to that structure itself.

I have argued elsewhere that Backhaus's seminal article on *Capital's* first chapter ignores this distinction between constitutive and attributive form in his suggestion that there is a methodologically unsuccessful break between §2 and §3 of that chapter.[17] He fails to notice that §2 presents value's constitutive form. The idea that in §2 we are given only the bare physiological expenditure of labour without regard to social form ignores precisely the point I appealed to earlier when I referred to the structure of labour and form that will characterise any mode of production: Marxism always studies historically specific forms of labouring individuals in their relation to nature and to others. This point requires further elaboration.

---

15. Heinrich 1989; see also Heinrich 2007a.
16. Marx 1973, p. 447.
17. Engelskirchen 2008; 2011; the Backhaus article is at Backhaus 1969 and 1980.

The concept of a labour-form composite

In the *Grundrisse*, Marx explains the features of labour that account for the commodity-form of the product of labour in terms that track the analysis briefly presented in the opening paragraphs of §2 of *Capital* Volume I. Using the same phrase used in the 'Method of Political Economy' for 'simplest determination', Marx presents the social mechanism that accounts for exchange-value and the commodity-form as follows: '[i]n the first positing of simple exchange value, labour was structured in such a way that the product was not a direct use value for the labourer, not a direct means of subsistence'.[18]

Notice that this first positing of simple exchange-value is explained by a structure or determination of labour. The labour that produces a commodity is form-determined. This does not mean that wherever and whenever the product of labour appears as a commodity we have, say, a simple commodity-mode of production. That is an entirely different thing, a whole social edifice. Here we are saying only that wherever and whenever the product of labour takes the commodity-form, even if we have no idea of the precise form of labour under which the product was actually produced, we do know that labour was form-determined in two very material and specific ways – it involved the independent production of a use-value not useful to its producer. That is, there is a labour-form composite, not necessarily involving capital, which accounts for the product of labour as a commodity.

As I have explained,[19] the idea of a labour-form composite here can be thought of as an appropriation of Aristotle's characterisation of the things of the world as composites of matter and form – this is Aristotle's hylomorphism: *hylo* for matter and *morphe* for form. Also, activity, like the activity of labour, for Aristotle was something that would have fallen under the wider category of matter. For Marx, the labour-form composites studied by political economy are always ultimately causal structures formed by the activity of labouring individuals grasped in relation to nature and to others, and, moreover, grasped conceptually in the very process of production.

It is one such labour-form composite, for example, that accounts for the pumping out of surplus-value in capitalist production. Thus Marx wrote in 'The

---

18. Marx 1973, p. 266. A point of detail is worth making because of the importance of form-determination to Marx's analysis: In an immediately preceding paragraph Martin Nicolaus translates 'einfachen Bestimmungen' as 'simple aspects'. However, the phrase is the same as that used in the 'Method of Political Economy' where at p. 100 he translates 'einfachsten Bestimmungen' as 'simplest determinations': compare Marx and Engels 1983, p. 35 with p. 190. Continuity of meaning is better carried by preserving the emphasis on 'determination'; in particular, 'aspects' does not capture the causal overtones 'Bestimmungen' can carry.

19. Engelskirchen 2011.

Trinity Formula': '[l]ike all its forerunners, the capitalist production process proceeds under specific material conditions, which are however also the bearers of specific social relations which the individuals enter into in the process of reproducing their life'.[20]

We can give full effect to the causal potency of just such material structures, and yet avoid reification, by drawing upon Aristotle's presentation of explanation in terms of four causal factors. First, there is a material structure of nature and labouring individuals (*material cause*), specifically shaped by definite social relations (*formal cause*), motivated by and producing a particular result (*final cause*) – and ultimately this is often a reproduction of the structure itself (that is, *formal cause* as *final cause*). To this we add the impetus of movement: the 'pumping' that drives the process is done by labouring individuals (*efficient cause*), who, by a process of inversion, confront their own activity as an alien power ruling over them. We add also the crucial point that just as the offensive power of an infantry regiment is essentially different from the power of individual soldiers aggregated,[21] so, too, the causal potency of a labour-form composite is essentially different from the causal force of a sum of labouring individuals.

The point, however, is to transform

One final preliminary point before I deal with the real definition of capital as such. The significance of understanding the causal structures that determine value and capital is the same as the significance of understanding the causal structures that provoke inquiry in any science. By understanding such structures we are able not only to interpret them, the limit of all traditional philosophy, but to transform. We can change base-metals into gold if we know how to manipulate their atomic structure so as to change this into a structure with atomic number 79.[22] The same holds for capital or for value. We cannot abolish money or markets by decree, but if we understand the simple causal determinations that account for such things, we can act as the causally-potent creatures we ourselves are to transform them according to our ambitions. Understanding the world's causal structures, we can change them, and this applies to the social world as well as the natural one. Moreover, just like any other creature, the successes of the accommodations we make to the causal structures of the world are the basis for our survival as a species, or, for lack of them, to our demise.

---

20. Marx 1991b, p. 957.
21. Marx 1990a, p. 443.
22. Of course, because of the energy required this is not a practical proposition; nonetheless, the nuclear physicist Glenn Seaborg is reported to have accomplished the feat in 1980 (Browne 1999).

The real definition of capital

Capital's double separation

Over forty years ago, and with great insight, Charles Bettelheim specified the capitalist character of the enterprise in a way that offers a real definition of capital. He referred to the 'double separation that forms the central characteristic of the capitalist mode of production': 'The capitalist character of the enterprise ... is due to the fact that its structure assumes the form of a *double separation: the separation of workers from their means of production ... and the separation of the enterprises from each other.* This double separation forms the central characteristic of the capitalist mode of production, and it serves as a support for the totality of contradictions of this mode of production'.[23]

My argument is that the 'double separation' aptly captures the *Grundrisse's* concept of 'capital in general'. Marx reminds us that capital is not a static relation but a process, so we must grasp capital's separations as an intersection of structures in process. We also want to show how these separations penetrate production itself. But, properly understood, the category Bettelheim identifies picks out those features of capital that are constitutive of it, those features that ultimately account for what it is and how it persists as what it is.

The separation of units of production from one another characterises the labour-form composite that accounts for value and the commodity-form. As I have argued, whenever labour is structured so that it is independent and possesses use-values that the producer does not relate to as such but offers instead for private exchange, there you have a causal structure that tends to generate value and its forms of manifestation. To the extent a producer cannot use what she has produced, she is driven to market. Commodity-production, though presupposed by capital, emerges as distinct; it forms part of capital's prehistory.

When the separation of units of production from one another is coupled to the separation of the labouring producer from her conditions of production, this generates the capital-relation. Objectless labour is impoverished absolutely. Nonetheless, if the labourer not only lacks tools and materials to produce but can also dispose of her labour-power as her own, then she may accommodate her circumstance to the exchange of commodities: she has produced separately a thing of value useless to her, and thus can offer that thing, her capacity to labour, for private exchange. Her labour-power may then be purchased for its exchange-value as the use-value of capital, a commodity with the capacity to create not only value, but greater value than the wage given for it. The labour-process then objectifies her activity in a product containing value adequate to replace not

---

23. Bettelheim 1975, p. 77 (emphasis in original).

only the value of her wage but containing also a surplus appropriated by capital. The separation of workers from their conditions of production thus makes possible capital's fundamental determination – the appropriation of living labour by objectified labour as value for the sake of value's increase.

It is important to recognise that there is nothing spontaneous about the transition from the production of commodities to capital. In fact, as a historical matter the simple circulation of commodities for money, C-M-C, does give rise pretty spontaneously to the circuit M-C-M, money for commodities. But this second circuit makes sense only insofar as the value originally invested is increased; in other words, the circuit actually appears as M-C-M' (where M' includes both the original M and an added increment). But there is nothing in the simple exchange of equivalent values that can sustain this latter circuit – the added increment appears to come only contingently from the outside – a merchant, for example, might exploit geographical differences between the prices of a thing, or a boat loaded with wheat might dock at the port of a town in famine. But there is no imperative in circulation or the relations of circulation that can account for the emergence of capitalist production, and the forms of value persisted for well over a millennium without giving rise to it. For this, the bloody process of expropriation canvassed by Marx in his explanation of 'The So-Called Primitive Accumulation' was necessary.[24] Emergent capital had to break labour's natural connection to its land and tools.

The three moments of capital

In the *Grundrisse*, Marx identifies three moments or stages of the life process of 'capital in general' and we can trace the progress of the capital's double separation through each. The three moments are (1) the moment of the simple conception of capital as it emerges from circulation; (2) the moment of the process of production as the unity of production and valorisation; and (3) the moment of capital as the unity of production and circulation.[25]

The locus of the first moment is circulation. The phenomena of circulation, as we have seen, are a product of the separation of productive entities which produce use-values not useful to them for private exchange.

The locus of the second moment is production. The phenomena of production under capitalism are a product not only of the separation of productive entities but also the separation of the labouring producer from the conditions of production. This is the moment of the 'inner organic movement' of capital.[26] We are

---

24. Marx 1990a, pp. 873–940.
25. Marx 1973, p. 319.
26. Marx 1973, p. 680.

here able to identify the specific characteristics that differentiate capital not only from value, but also from other forms of social production.

The locus of the third moment is the unity of production and circulation, the stage where the constitutive features of capital's inner nature are reflected in capital's full and mature development. At this stage, we are able to show how the intersection of the separation of productive entities from each other and the separation of workers from their conditions of production is at once the precondition for capital, its ground and goal, and also ultimately the limit it confronts as a mode of social production.

The first moment: the simple concept of capital

Capital's point of departure arises from value as it arises out of circulation and comes to sustain itself there. Value and exchange-value are presupposed. The commodity-form is presupposed. This means the separation of productive entities from one another that accounts for these is presupposed. But we have seen that more is required for the circuit of self-multiplying value, M-C-M', on which the emergence of capital from circulation depends. We know that commodity-production will become the general form of social production only where labour-power is sold as a commodity. It is only on this basis that the commodity becomes the universal form of the product of labour and commodity-production becomes generalised. As a consequence, although the circulation of commodities is explained simply by the separation of units of production, in order for the separation of units of production that produce for market to become general, the separation of labouring producers from their conditions of production is required. That is, the general formula of capital, M-C-M', and the simple concept of capital to which it gives expression, do not yet give us the basis to understand how capital sustains itself in circulation, but because capital reflects generalised commodity-production we do see that it rests on both components of the double separation.

The second moment: the unity of production and valorisation

We locate the source of value as self-multiplying and self-sustaining, that is, value not as pure value or money, but as capital, in the second moment of the concept of capital: the moment of the unity of production and valorisation in the labour-process. Here, we are able to pick out constitutive features, the *differentia specifica*, of production that is capitalist, those features that form the germ out of which later developments will come.[27]

---

27. Marx 1973, p. 310.

The separation that accounts for value is now presupposed. Also presupposed is the labour-market exchange that introduces the incorporation of labour by capital, so the separation of labour and wealth is presupposed. Additionally, in this exchange, which introduces the labour-process, the labourer surrenders control over her life activity and its fruits. Thus the rich dimensions of Marx's analysis of the objectification of living labour as an alienation begin here as alienation in a strict juridical sense.

By surrendering control over her life-activity, the worker is subject to the command of the capitalist,[28] and is subjected in her work to rules, methods and goals set by another. But the capitalist is in turn only a personification of capital itself,[29] so in the event the worker is subordinated to the imperatives of self-multiplying value. That is, because of her subordination to the process of valorisation, the worker must work with an intensity dictated by the law of value and for a longer day than would be necessary to replace the value of her wage.

Also, by surrendering control over the fruits of her labour, the worker surrenders to the capitalist ownership of the product;[30] appropriated by capital, the separation of the results of labour from the worker reproduces her propertyless-ness. Her product becomes an alien power to which she is subordinated and on which she depends.

The defining characteristics of the separation of the worker from the conditions of production, then, are separation joined to an alienation that is its consequence. Alienation, in turn, is at once the appropriation of labour's activity and its fruits. As such it is both the subordination of labour to capital's command and subordination to labour's own product as an alien power ruling over it. Taken together we are able to express this intersection of separation and subordination as follows: *the free worker's alienated separation from, and subordination to, the conditions of production as value is capital's simplest determination.* Marx writes: 'The worker's propertylessness, and the ownership of living labour by objectified labour, or the appropriation of alien labour by capital – both merely expressions of the same relation from opposite poles – are the fundamental conditions of the bourgeois mode of production'.[31]

Because Marx's analysis of the content of the production-process of capital specifies the essential features that differentiate capital not only from 'value in general' but also from other modes of production, the section from Notebook III of the *Grundrisse* on the production-process as the content of capital[32] is like

---

28. Marx 1973, p. 308.
29. Marx 1990a, pp. 989–91 (Appendix: 'Results of the Immediate Process of Production').
30. Marx 1973, p. 308.
31. Marx 1973, p. 832.
32. Marx 1973, pp. 304–10.

the earlier section from Notebook II on the simplest determination of exchange,[33] insofar as both these are decisively reflected in the way the argument of *Capital* presents the simplest determinations of capital and the commodity-form respectively. I have shown elsewhere how the structure of labour worked out in Notebook II was presented in section two of Chapter One of *Capital* Volume I to establish the constitutive properties that account for the commodity-form.[34] In turn we find the constitutive properties of capital as they are worked out in Notebook III embedded in the argument developed in Chapters Six and Seven of *Capital* Volume I. In Chapter Six, Marx establishes the separation of the free labourer from the conditions of production as a condition of capitalist production and then in Chapter VII he explicitly characterises those features that distinguish capital as a form of social labour: assuming the production of value and assuming also the separation of the free labourer from all wealth, the features that differentiate the capitalist labour-process are as follows:

> The labour process, when it is the process by which the capitalist consumes labour-power, exhibits two characteristic phenomena:
>
> First the worker works under the control of the capitalist to whom his labour belongs...Secondly, the product is the property of the capitalist and not that of the worker, its immediate producer.[35]

The third moment: the unity of production and circulation

The third moment, like the first, is a point of departure. The departure, however, is not now from value, but instead from capital: value which has absorbed living labour is introduced into circulation in order to increase itself. The transformation of commodities into money and money into commodities has become part of capital's concept. The meaning here, as a matter of reference fixing, is that the moment of circulation and production considered as a whole brings into view mechanisms that account for the dynamic of capital's reproduction as a distinctive form of social labour. Abstracting to the unity of production and circulation we look to identify those features of social life that account for capital's persistence, without for all that taking on the complications such features might encounter in a particular capital's day-to-day interaction with other capitals. We locate the labour-form composite that constitutes capital's inner nature and trace the dynamic essential to it as the form of capital's original presupposition, its mature development and its limit.

---

33. Marx 1973, p. 266.
34. Engelskirchen 2008; 2011, pp. 33–5 and 47–50.
35. Marx 1990a, pp. 291–2.

The machine as an incarnation of capital's double separation

For example: an important instance of how the double separation is expressed in the moment of production and circulation's unity is given by the system of machinery. Marx writes that the full development of capital takes place only where the means of labour take the form of fixed capital and fixed capital takes the form of the machine.[36] When production is organised by capital a machine belongs to a separated unit of production, of course. More profoundly, in capitalist production a machine achieves an independence that sets it over against those who labour on it. In the form of machinery, the means of labour no longer transmit the worker's activity to its material, instead, it is the machine that assigns tasks, regulates the pace of work, and dominates the worker so that living labour becomes an insignificant accessory of the machine's activity: 'In machinery, objectified labour materially confronts living labour as a ruling power and as an active subsumption of the latter under itself, not only by appropriating it, but in the real production process itself; the relation of capital as value which appropriates value creating activity is in fixed capital existing as machinery'.[37]

Consider the weight of what Marx has said here: capital's fundamental determination, the appropriation of living labour by objectified labour in order to increase the latter, is incarnated in the machine. The separation of the worker from the means of production is materially embodied in the machine; the subordination of the worker to the means of production is materially embodied in the machine. Labour's experience of the machine as a force 'outside itself', Marx emphasises, 'belongs to the concept of capital'.[38] In fixed capital the productive forces of labour are 'posited as external to labour and as existing independently of it'.[39]

The example of machinery illustrates not only how capital's separations reach full development in capital's life-cycle; they illustrate also how they can be expected to account for capital's dissolution. In fact it is not only the individual labourer that becomes an insignificant accessory to production. As capitalist production unfolds, living labour itself, which, as quantity, is capital's determining element, becomes less and less important in comparison to the contribution to production made by machines and by the general applications of science and technology operative through them.[40] In part, however, the dilemma is masked by what might be thought of as capital's self-conception. In its full flowering as 'fructiferous', capital generates the illusion that it can ignore labour; instead

---

36. Marx 1973, p. 699.
37. Marx 1973, pp. 693–4.
38. Marx 1973, p. 702.
39. Marx 1973, p. 701.
40. Marx 1973, pp. 700 ff.

it relates to its monetary embodiment as the ground of what it has produced, 'the foundation of what it has founded'.[41] M-C-M' becomes possible because its movement, instantiated in production, is no longer formal, but instead is rooted in the appropriation of living labour by objectified labour. But now surplus-value relates not to living labour as its ground but instead, as if indifferently, to money-capital alone. Whatever labour's contribution, the rate of profit is measured simply against total capital invested.

The double separations as a barrier to capital

Much work needs doing on all this. In effect the reproduction of capital is the reproduction of capital's double separation and this on a constantly increasing scale. But the other side of the coin called separation is indifference. In its full development capital's impulse to an unlimited development of the productive forces confronts limits in the reciprocal indifference of productive enterprises to one another and also of capital's indifference to labour. For capital, perversely, surplus-labour is a precondition for necessary labour rather than the reverse. Moreover, necessary labour is restricted by the exchange-value of labour-power – that is, roughly, by the requirements of subsistence – rather than by an individual's rich capacity for free development through labour. As a consequence, labour's need can never provide an adequate impulse to the development of the productive forces. Nor, given reciprocally indifferent entities, can the needs of other productive units. The need others have for objects of use is ultimately subject to physical, quantitative and other measures that have nothing to do with value. The exchange-value form, a consequence of the separation of reciprocally indifferent units of production, thus becomes a restriction on the production of use-value.

That is, in order for production to occur, labour, machinery and raw materials must be present in the right proportions and, further, capital has a need for circulation seamlessly united to production. But not only is production determined by physical measures having nothing to do with exchange-value, but also each productive unit, though fully dependent on the social division of labour, confronts the indifference of alien need. Given reciprocally indifferent entities, disproportion means commodities cannot be harmoniously transformed into money or surplus-labour into surplus-value. Capital's tendency to generate an unrestricted development of the productive forces is contradicted by its need to reproduce both the indifference of capital to labour and the indifference of productive entities to one another.

---

41. Marx 1973, p. 745.

Conclusion: beyond capital's double separation

Marx is well known for not offering blueprints for the future. In broadest out-line, however, he does suggest how the separation of productive entities from one another and the separation of workers from their conditions of production might be transformed: we look to a structuring of labour whereby associated workers take common control over their common wealth.[42] Cooperative associa-tion among units of production transforms their separation from one another, and common control by associated workers of land, raw materials and the means of labour transforms the separation of wealth and labour. These transformations in turn lay the basis for a social form of production that rests on the universal development of individuals, of the free development of their creative powers, and of the subordination of their social wealth to need through labour. Recall Marx's reference to wealth stripped of its bourgeois shell:

> what is wealth, other than the universality of individual needs, capacities, pleasures, productive forces, etc., created through universal exchange? The full development of human mastery over the forces of nature, those of so-called nature as well as of humanity's own nature? The absolute working out of his creative potentialities with no presupposition other than the previous historic development, which makes this totality of development, i.e. the development of all human powers as such the end in itself, not as measured on a *predeter-mined* yardstick?[43]

Ultimately, we work to develop the productive forces of labour, of which the labouring individual is the most precious, in order to fully develop all human powers. We develop the productive forces to accomplish a working out of human potentialities constrained only by the accommodation we make necessarily with nature. In its life-process, capital does give formidable impulse to the develop-ment of the productive forces, but this is an impulse driven to increase the value of things, and it is compromised by its tendency to reproduce labour's impover-ishment as well as each capital's separation from other productive enterprises. Pre-given conditions of production provide a limit to which the development of human potential must bend. By contrast, Marx imagines an unobstructed devel-opment of the forces of production, including especially the rich capacities of the labouring individual, not limited, as is capital, by the social form of its reproduc-tion: 'Although limited by its very nature, [capital] strives towards the universal development of the forces of production, and thus becomes the presupposition of a new mode of production.... where the free, unobstructed, progressive and

---

42. Marx 1973, pp. 158–9.
43. Marx 1973, p. 488.

universal development of the forces of production is itself the presupposition of society and hence of its reproduction; where advance beyond the point of departure is the only presupposition'.[44]

But '[f]or this,' he adds: '[it is] necessary above all that the full development of the forces of production has become the *condition of production*; and not that specific *conditions of production* are posited as a limit to the development of the productive forces'.[45]

The goal must change: development for the sake of increasing the value of things threatens our survival as a species; instead, the unobstructed development of the forces of production can be a presupposition of society only where this functions to realise an association of individuals in which the full and free flourishing of each is the condition for the full and free flourishing of all.

The concept of capital's double separation refers to conditions of production capital must reproduce and by which it is constrained. While at first this double determination of labour is a form for the development of capital's productive power, it becomes at last a punishing shackle.

In the end, capital's appropriation of the social form of labour responds poorly to labour's human form. Labour, Marx observes, is purposeful activity. A content more fully adequate to this would not receive living labour as capital does, merely as quantity, but would instead give full material expression to labour's purposeful accommodation to the totality of our conditions of life – to associated labour's self-determined unfolding of human needs and abilities best suited to the accommodation we make necessarily to nature.

---

44. Marx 1973, p. 540.
45. Marx 1973, p. 542.

Part Four

Technology, Domination, Emancipation

The 'Fragment on Machines': A Marxian Misconception in the *Grundrisse* and its Overcoming in *Capital*

Michael Heinrich

The *Grundrisse* still belongs to the most beloved texts of Marx's interpreters. Some authors argue that the so-called 'Fragment on machines' is a central document for a Marxian theory of capitalist 'catastrophes', a kind of 'break-down theory' of capitalism, or at least a description of a process in which a new mode of production emerges, inaugurated by capitalism itself but in contradiction with the logic of capital. In such considerations, the results of the 'Fragment' are taken for granted. However, the results of this 'Fragment on machines' derive, on the one hand, from a one-sided conception of crisis in Marx's thinking since the early 1850s, and, on the other hand, from some shortcomings in the conception of basic categories in the *Grundrisse*. In the years after the *Grundrisse*, Marx overcame both misconceptions. In *Capital* Volume I, when dealing with the production of relative surplus-value, we can find an implicit critique of the 'Fragment on machines'. Ignoring Marx's theoretical development, as does Antonio Negri when he states that the *Grundrisse* should be read 'for itself',[1] one can easily neglect a discussion of this implicit self-critique of Marx. Reading the text for itself means accepting uncritically the results of the text. In order to discuss the *Grundrisse* productively today, we have to contextualise the text not only in the development of Marx's thought. We also have to situate our reading of the *Grundrisse*

---

1. Negri 1984, p. 15.

in the development of the discussion about Marx in the twentieth century, because this development has shaped many of the ways in which the *Grundrisse* was and still is read.

1. The reception of the *Grundrisse* in the twentieth century

When we discuss the work of a significant author, we always do so in a determinate historical situation, which provides us with specific problems and reservations. Certain things appear to us to be obvious, while others seem to be questionable or superannuated. Some of these evaluations would have appeared very differently thirty or forty years earlier. In the case of Marx, furthermore, there is the fact that many texts that are today very important for the debate were not even published during his lifetime. His work has become accessible in its totality only slowly. Not only the respective historical context, but also the respective state of publication of his texts, influenced the direction and the course of many debates.

Even in the case of *Capital*, Marx could only publish the first volume. Engels published the second and third volumes after Marx's death, with considerable editorial interventions. Only in the last years have Marx's original manuscripts for these volumes been published in the context of the *Marx Engels Gesamtausgabe (MEGA)*. Thus, it is only now, after more than 100 years, that we can identify Engels's editorial interventions and discuss their conceptual and substantial relevance. At the beginning of the twentieth century, after Karl Kautsky published the *Theories of Surplus-Value* between 1905–1910, it appeared as if all of Marx's critique of political economy was completely available, as the *Theories* were regarded as the fourth volume of *Capital* dealing with the history of the theory, which Marx had planned.[2] In the reading that was then predominant, Marx was regarded as the great socialist economist, who had demonstrated the exploitation of the working class, the crises-prone nature of capitalism and the inevitable transition to socialism, first in the *Communist Manifesto* and then later, on a broader foundation, in *Capital*. Most Marxists celebrated these findings as the triumph of 'scientific socialism'. Beginning in the 1920s, however, there was a strengthening of the critique of actual or supposed tendencies in Marx's theory of 'economism', 'determinism' and, above all, 'objectivism'. In this context, the publication of Marx's early works, particularly the *Economic and Philosophical*

---

2. They are not: not only because, rather than the planned history of economic theory, only the history of one single category is given (with significant digressions into other fields), but also because the *Theories*, written in 1861–3, are not yet at the level of knowledge of *Capital*. Rather, they represent only a first (important) step in the development of this level of knowledge.

Manuscripts of 1844, were like a bombshell. Here, apparently, the broad philosophical and socio-theoretical background of Marx's economic analyses, his considerations of the 'human essence' and 'alienation' in capitalism, became clear. The objectivism that has previously been so roundly criticised, along with the lack of a theory of the subject, could, so it seemed at least, be overcome on these foundations.

This transformed reception was not a purely inner-theoretical phenomenon, but the result of a determinate political reading, which in different ways was deployed against the tendencies towards petrification and dogmatism of official-party Marxism. Fascism and Stalinism, however, made it impossible for the discussion that began in the early 1930s to develop in a significant sense. This occurred only in the 1960s, when the conditions of the debate had substantially changed. Above all, the reception of Marx's early writing had lost its almost automatically assured anti-dogmatic impulse. In the meantime, these texts had been integrated by the Marxist-Leninist orthodoxy to a large extent. When, for example, Louis Althusser, in 1965, criticised Marx's early writings as 'ideological' and introduced the specific form of scientificity of *Capital*, this was also a critique of this orthodoxy. However, his strongly argued position also earned him the accusation – precisely from the anti-orthodox side – of having banished the subject and social struggles from the theoretical discussion. The debates over the relation between 'early' (philosophical) and 'late' (economic-theoretical) Marx had multiplied, just as the political perspectives connected to the individual positions within these debates had. It was in this context that there really began for the first time a widespread reading of the *Grundrisse* – which enduringly influenced the terms and conditions of its interpretation.

The *Grundrisse*, which was first published in 1939–41 in Moscow, was accorded only sporadic interest during the war and in the immediate post-war period. Even when the text was reprinted in the GDR in 1953, the text did not initially have many readers. This changed with the publication in 1968 of Roman Rosdolsky's commentary on the *Grundrisse*.[3] The *Grundrisse* was then discussed widely not only in Germany, but, with the French translation of 1967 and the first English translation of 1973, the debate began in many other countries as well.

The *Grundrisse* appeared to be the magic-wand with which one could solve the problems in Marx's theory that had been discussed up until then. The contraposition of a young philosophical Marx and a mature economic-theoretic Marx was seemingly lessened, but nevertheless found a mediating connecting link in the *Grundrisse*: this text made it clear that the mature Marx's economic writings

---

3. Rosdolsky 1977.

also were based upon a developed philosophical foundation. What was lacking in *Capital* seemed to be present in the *Grundrisse*.

While Marx dealt with methodological questions in *Capital* almost only in the prefaces and afterwords, this problematic was raised continuously in the course of the presentation in the *Grundrisse*. There is also a much clearer reference to Hegel's philosophy in the *Grundrisse*. Something similar is the case with the question of subjectivity: much more strongly than in *Capital*, labour is conceptualised as the subjective counterpoint to capital. Additionally, the six-book plan that Marx envisaged as he wrote the *Grundrisse* (capital, landed property, wage-labour, state, international trade, world market) made clear that the intended object of investigation was much broader than that treated by Marx in *Capital*. Finally, the *Grundrisse* seemed to be a supplement to *Capital*, since here a series of themes were discussed that received no corresponding treatment in the presentation of *Capital*. The most well-known of these themes occurs in the *Grundrisse* under the heading of 'Forms that precede capitalist production' and in that 'Fragment on machines' that was discussed very early in Italian workerism.[4]

The *Grundrisse* thus seemed to offer something for everybody. Today, the discussion of Marx is not conceivable without the *Grundrisse*.[5] Indeed, the *Grundrisse* are a fascinating work and reading them is a singular intellectual adventure. As if we were looking over his shoulder, we can observe Marx in the process of his analysis and the formation of his theory; the grasp of the material is much freer, and less regimented than in *Capital*. All too often, however, this understandable fascination leads to an uncritical enthusiasm.

2. The *Grundrisse* in the development of Marx's theory

If the *Grundrisse* are posited simply as a supplement beside Marx's *Capital*, then the inner-theoretical process of development of Marx's critique of political economy and the transitory character of the *Grundrisse* are ignored. Let us recall very briefly this development. Following the *Theses on Feuerbach* and the *German Ideology*, Marx's work in 1845–6 issued in a fundamental critique of any approach to economic theory centred on human species-being and alienation. Nevertheless, at that stage, Marx did not have very much that he could put in the place of these conceptions. Positively, the *German Ideology* offered above all a turn to the empirical. Again and again, Marx and Engels stressed there that 'positive science', the registration of the empirical state of affairs and relations, needed to take the place of philosophical speculation.

---

4. Cf. on this history Bellofiore and Tomba 2009.
5. On the international reception of the *Grundrisse*, cf. Musto 2008.

Against this background, Marx accepted the political economy of Ricardo and the class-theory of French historians as substantially correct descriptions of capitalist reality. In his engagement with Proudhon in the *Poverty of Philosophy* (1847), Marx continually praised Ricardo in the highest terms for the acuity of his analysis.[6] In the *Communist Manifesto*, Marx referred without hesitation to the bourgeois class-analysis that can be found in French historians such as Guizot or Thierry in their analysis of the French Revolution. The only thing that he found in Ricardo to criticise at this point in time was his conception that capitalism was not an historically determinate mode of production, but rather an eternal, quasi-natural one.[7] Something similar is the case for class-theory: Marx did not claim that he had discovered the existence of classes and the class-struggle, but rather that the class-struggle must ultimately lead to a classless society.[8] In the second half of the 1840s, we find in Marx a *critical deployment* of the given bourgeois political economy and class-theory, but still no fundamental *critique of the categories* of political economy.

This critique was developed only after Marx's forced emigration to London. Here, in the heart of the capitalist world-system in that period, and with the help of the enormous stock of books of the British Museum, Marx started his economic studies 'again from the very beginning', as he himself emphasised in the 1859 'Preface' of *Contribution to the Critique of Political Economy*.[9] Only now did he begin to develop a critique of the categories as well. Initially, Marx criticised Ricardo's theory of money and rent; as he progressed, the critique became increasingly fundamental. When Marx wrote the 'Introduction' in 1857 and thus began the *Grundrisse*, this was not only the beginning of a development of his critique of economics that would eventually lead to *Capital*. It was also, and above all, an inventory taking of what he had achieved in terms of theoretical insights in the previous years. The attempt to set down these insights in a coherent way, however, still entailed a daunting process of research, during which Marx came up against more than merely one theoretical lacuna.

When Marx began the *Grundrisse*, he already had a mass of material for his planned economic work, but was still far from a finished concept. The *Grundrisse* in fact has no genuine beginning: a critique of Daimon, a student of Proudhon who wanted to overcome capitalism by means of the monetary system, indiscernibly passes over into an engagement with the categorical foundations that are necessary for such a critique. Here, we can clearly see that Marx still had serious

---

6. Cf., for example, Marx and Engels 1976, pp. 123–4.
7. Cf., for example, the letter to Annenkov of 28 December 1846 (Marx 1975–2005e, p. 100).
8. Cf. Marx's letter to Weydemeyer of 5 March 1852 in Marx and Engels 1975–2005, pp. 62–5.
9. Marx 1859, p. 265.

difficulties with the categories of value, money and exchange. A close reading of the 'Chapter on money' clearly shows that it is not yet a unitary attempt at presentation, but rather, a superimposition of numerous, continuously renewed attempts at presentation.[10]

That Marx, despite these unsolved problems, did not fall back into yet another research-process, was due to an external motive: the world-economic crisis that commenced in 1857. Marx had been impatiently waiting for years for such a crisis, anticipating that violent economic tremors and revolutionary revolts would follow in its wake. His book had been supposed to provide support for the revolutionary movement and now Marx feared that he would be too late.[11]

During his work on the *Grundrisse*, Marx made enormous advances in his knowledge. His analysis, however, also had significant deficiencies, which many enthusiastic readings do not seem to discern. Marx himself wrote that this manuscript is 'a real hotchpotch, much of it intended for much later sections'.[12] He did not merely mean the ordering of the material, the large number of digressions and intimations. The order of the presented categories is itself the bearer of a determinate yield of information: it shows the connection of these categories, the interconnection that exists between them. Categories like the commodity, money, capital, wage-labour, and so forth, are theoretical expressions of social relations in a developed capitalist society. These relations not only appear simultaneously; they mutually presuppose each other in social reality. Only theoretical analysis allows one to distinguish between simple and complex categories and to express the conceptual-theoretical connection between the categories.[13] When the manuscript's coherence breaks down, however, it is precisely this conceptual connection between the individual categories that is not yet clearly grasped. That means that there are still not insignificant deficiencies in the conceptual fixing of these categories.

We will discuss some of these deficiencies in the next section. The fact that Marx removed some of these deficiencies in the 1860s does not mean, however, that there might be a linear progressive development, a continuous refinement from the *Grundrisse* to *Capital*. Such an idea, however, guided the editors of the *MEGA* in the 1970s and 1980s, who characterised the *Grundrisse*, the *Manuscripts of 1961–2* (*MEGA* II/3.1–3.6) and the *Manuscripts of 1863–5* (*MEGA* II/4.1–4.2) as the 'three drafts of *Capital*', thus implying that *Capital* (by which was meant the three-volume work edited by Engels) was the goal towards which a develop-

---

10. Cf. PEM 1973.
11. Cf. His letter to Lassalle, 22 February 1858, in Marx and Engels 1983, p. 271.
12. Letter to Engels, 31 May 1858, in Marx and Engels 1983, p. 318.
13. This is the core of what Marx means by 'dialectical presentation'. For a more extensive discussion cf. Heinrich 1999, pp. 171 ff.

mental process moved, beginning precisely with the *Grundrisse*. Besides the improvement of the presentation and the overcoming of theoretical deficiencies, however, we can also observe an opposed tendency in this development. Marx himself spoke often of 'popularisation' of his presentation. A first popularisation can be observed in the *Contribution to the Critique of Political Economy* of 1859; a second attempt at popularisation consists in the second edition of *Capital* Volume I. These popularisations have their price: determinate conceptual contexts are sometimes obscured; other connections no longer appear in *Capital*, such as, for example, the transition from money to capital.[14] Thus, Hans-Georg Backhaus and Helmut Reichelt in particular have understood this development from the *Grundrisse* to *Capital* not as an improvement, let alone a refinement of the presentation, but rather, as a tale of decline away from an originally very strongly composed presentation.[15]

Both positions – the idea of a continuous refinement, as well as that of a constant theoretical regress – seem nevertheless to be inadequate. This is not only because both improvement as well as deterioration can be observed, but above all, because in this way we neglect that the path from the *Grundrisse* to *Capital* witnesses not only transformations of individual aspects, but also of the fundamental conceptual questions. The six-book plan as well as the concept of 'capital in general' – Marx develops both during his work on the *Grundrisse*, and redeploys them in the *Manuscripts of 1861–3* – is given up. With *Capital*, for which the *Manuscripts of 1863–5* are the first and not the third draft, Marx develops a new theoretical frame of reference, for which the distinction between individual capital and social total capital is decisive.[16] Indeed, we have to distinguish between two different projects: 'Critique of Political Economy' in six books, for which two drafts exist (*Grundrisse* and the *Manuscript of 1861–3*); and *Capital* in four books with three drafts (*Manuscripts of 1863–5*, *Manuscripts of 1866–71*, including the first edition of *Capital* Volume I, and the *Manuscripts of 1871–81*).[17]

3. Marx's Argument in the 'Fragment on machines' and its errors

At the beginning of the manuscript of the *Grundrisse*, Marx does not yet operate on the basis of developed value-theoretic considerations. Rather, he initially attempts to determine the status of money within commodity-circulation. In particular, he has still not clarified the distinction between abstract and concrete labour – a configuration that he describes in *Capital* as the 'crucial point' of the

---

14. Cf. Heinrich 1999, pp. 253 ff.
15. Cf. Backhaus 1997, Reichelt 2008.
16. Cf. Heinrich 1989.
17. Cf. Heinrich 2009 and, especially for Marx's work in the 1870s, Heinrich 2011.

understanding of political economy, and in a letter to Engels of 8 January 1868, as 'the whole secret of the critical conception'.[18] The clear fixing of the distinction between abstract and concrete labour, with which Marx completely broke with Ricardo's value-theory, occurred only in the *Contribution to the Critique of Political Economy* (1859).[19] Indeed, Marx distinguishes also in the *Grundrisse* clearly between use-value and value (but not yet as clearly between exchange-value and value; he does this only in the second edition of *Capital*, Volume I). When he speaks of value-determining labour-time, it is a case, as in Smith and Ricardo, of merely a 'labour *sans phrase*', which does not prevent the determinations of abstract and concrete labour from being confused.[20]

The analysis of the capitalist production-process as a unity of labour- and valorisation-processes occurs only in preliminary hypotheses. Marx thus had difficulties to hold on to the form-determination of constant capital, so that he frequently went back to the question of how it is possible that labour can both add new value and also carry over the value of the utilised means of production onto the product.[21] The back and forth of Marx's attempt at explanation – now with 'form' and 'substance' of labour, now with 'quality' and 'quantity' of labour – is extensively analysed in a volume published by the *Projektgruppe Entwicklung des Marxschen Systems* (PEM).[22]

As Marx still had problems with the concept of constant capital, he saw the actual capitalist form-determination of the means of labour only in the category of *capital fixe*;[23] that is, of a form-determination that contains the means of labour only in circulation. Thus, the much discussed 'Fragment on machines' occurs in the section on the capitalist circulation-process – although problems are treated that belong to the analysis of the capitalist production-process.

Marx initially maintains that the means of labour in the capitalist production-process 'passes through a series of metamorphoses until it ends up as the *machine* or rather as an *automatic system or machinery*'.[24] Here, the activity of the worker is also transformed. It 'is determined and governed in every respect

---

18. Marx 1976a, p. 132; Marx 1987b, p. 514.

19. As Schrader (Schrader 1980, pp. 194 ff.) plausibly argues, the significance of this distinction first became clear to Marx as he made his excerpts from Franklin, which he most probably wrote in 1858–9 during his preparation for *Contribution to the Critique of Political Economy*. However, with this, the development of Marx's value-theory is not yet complete; only during his engagement with Samuel Bailey, in the *Theories of Surplus-Value*, does the complete significance of the analysis of the value-form become clear to him, which was only briefly and unsatisfactorily treated in the *Contribution*.

20. Marx himself emphasises that the analysis could not be left at *'labour sans phrase'* in the previously cited letter to Engels (Marx 1987b, p. 514).

21. Marx 1975–2005a, pp. 179–91.

22. PEM 1978, pp. 113 ff.

23. Marx 1975–2005c, p. 81.

24. Marx 1975–2005c, p. 82.

by the movement of the machinery, not vice versa'.[25] This entire development, Marx argues: 'is not a matter of chance for capital, but the historical transformation of the traditional means of labour, as handed down from the past, into a form adequate to capital. The accumulation of knowledge and skill, of the general productive forces of the social mind, is thus absorbed in capital as opposed to labour, and hence appears as a property of capital, more precisely, of *fixed capital*, to the extent that it enters into the production process as means of production in strict sense'.[26]

Shortly afterwards, Marx summarises thus:

> Hence, the full development of capital only takes place – or capital has only posited the mode of production corresponding to it – when the means of labour is not merely formally determined as fixed capital but is superseded in its immediate form, and *fixed capital* confronts labour within the production process as machinery. The entire production process then appears no longer as subsumed under the immediate skill of the worker, but as technological application of science. Capital thus tends to impart a scientific character to production, and immediate labour is reduced to a mere moment of this process.[27]

In the nineteenth century, a contemporary observer could not fail to note that machinery had an increasing significance in capitalist production, that the application of science was increasing, and that the individual worker played an ever smaller role. The fact that Marx here notes these developments is no particular analytic achievement. Such an achievement could only consist in the ordering and explanation of this process.

Marx treats these developments as a process that capital necessarily produced; capital 'posits the mode of production corresponding to it'. Why, however, is the employment of machinery and the increasingly scientific nature of production adequate for capital? Marx's answer is vague: in the first cited passage, he argues that the 'general productive forces of the social mind' are 'absorbed' by capital; in the second citation, he emphasises that the scientific production-process is no longer 'subsumed under the immediate skill of the worker'. In other words, on the basis of the capitalist appropriation of socially produced knowledge, the power of capital over labour increases, capital increasingly becomes independent from single workers and their skills. This increasing power is a positive effect for capital. The goal of capital, however, is the production of surplus-value. If we wish to show that the developments named by Marx represent the 'mode of production corresponding' to capital, we must refer to the production of surplus-value. In

---

25. Marx 1975–2005c, p. 83.
26. Marx 1975–2005c, p. 84.
27. Marx 1975–2005c, p. 85.

this citation, however, Marx is still a long way from this, since he does not have an adequate concept of the production of relative surplus-value. That means that he can deal with the increasing application of machinery and the growing scientific nature of production only as an empirically noticeable tendency, and *claim* that they are a development that is adequate for capital. He cannot yet, however, *justify* them as this adequate development.

Instead of providing such a justification, he emphasises an (apparent) contradiction taken from the empirical evidence: 'In the same measure as labour time – the simple quantity of labour – is posited by capital as the sole determinant of value, immediate labour and its quantity disappear as the determining principle of production, of the creation of use values. It is reduced both quantitatively, in that its proportion declines, and qualitatively, it that it, though still indispensable, becomes a subaltern moment in comparison to general scientific work...'.[28]

Marx then immediately draws the following far-reaching conclusion: 'Thus capital works to dissolve itself as the form which dominates production'.

This surprising result is not further justified at this stage. Instead, Marx deals with the problem of the way in which *capital fixe* contributes to the value of the produced product, in order to be able to oppose Lauderdale's conception that *capital fixe* is a source of value that is independent from labour-time. Only a few pages later, he comes back to this contradiction. He holds that the presupposition of the capital-relation is 'the sheer volume of immediate labour time, the quantity of labour employed, as the decisive factor in the production of wealth'.[29]

This presupposition, however, is undermined by the development of industry itself: 'But in the degree, in which large-scale industry develops, the creation of real wealth becomes less dependent upon labour time and the quantity of labour employed than upon the power of agents set in motion during labour time'.[30]

However, if immediate labour-time plays an ever smaller role, what does the worker still do in the process of production?

> Labour no longer appears so much as included in the production process, but rather man relates himself to that process as overseer and regulator... He stands besides the production process, rather than being its main agent.[31]

---

28. Marx 1975–2005c, pp. 85–6.
29. Marx 1975–2005c, p. 90.
30. Ibid.
31. Marx 1975–2005c, p. 91.

Here, it is no longer a case of 'immediate labour performed by man himself', but rather, of the 'appropriation of his own general productive power',[32] on the basis of which Marx then draws an extremely far-reading conclusion:

> As soon as labour in its immediate form has ceased to be the great source of wealth, labour time ceases and must cease to be its measure, and therefore exchange value [must cease to be the measure] of use value. The *surplus labour of the masses* has ceased to be the condition for the development of general wealth, just as the *non-labour of a few* has ceased to be the condition for the development of the general powers of the human mind. As a result, production based upon exchange value collapses...[33]

While these sentences are often cited, it is worthwhile to look more closely at whether and how Marx *justifies* them. Marx's starting point is the empirically noticeable tendency that the use of machinery and the increasing scientific dimension of production steadily advance in the capitalist mode of production. This uncontroversial observation then serves him as the foundation of deductions that are based upon each other:

a) Marx sees 'immediate labour' increasingly disappearing from the production-process, from which should then follow

b) that immediate labour is no longer the great source of wealth; rather, this is increasingly constituted by science, or general social knowledge;

c) in this case, labour-time is no longer the 'measure' of wealth,

d) which should have the consequence that capitalist production ('production based upon exchange-value') collapses.

If we consider carefully these deductions in detail, we see that the lacking distinction between concrete useful labour, which produces use-values, and abstract human labour, which is represented in value, has decisive consequences:

Regarding a): Marx extrapolates limitlessly the empirical observation of the progressive deployment of machinery. It would, however, be necessary first to explain whether or not there really are no limits in the capitalist production-process for the replacement of 'immediate labour' by machines. If we consider only concrete useful labour, then there does indeed appear to be no limit for the

---

32. Slightly later, Marx explains that 'The development of fixed capital shows the degree to which society's general science, KNOWLEDGE, has become an *immediate productive force*, and hence the degree to which the conditions of the social life process itself have been brought under the control of the GENERAL INTELLECT and remoulded according to it' (Marx 1975–2005c, p. 92). This is the only passage in which Marx speaks of the 'GENERAL INTELLECT', which some authors quote with relish today.

33. Marx 1975–2005c, p. 91.

increase in productivity by means of the increasing deployment of machinery (although the period of time in which this occurs remains an open question). We should bear in mind, however, that it is a case of a capitalist production-process, for there is certainly a limit to the employment of machinery. The machine used in a capitalist way is itself a value-object, which yields the average expenditure of value to the produced product (if a given machine produces 10 000 pieces before it is worn out, then the machine yields 1/10000 of its value to the individual product). As Marx discusses extensively in the second section of the fifteenth chapter of *Capital* Volume I, the employment of machinery in the capitalist production-process is only worthwhile if the production-costs of the product are reduced. And that only occurs when the value-yield of the machine to the product is lower than the reduction of costs that occurs due to the reduced expenditure of living labour. If the employment of machinery saves an hour in the production of a piece, then the capitalist saves the wage for this one hour. If the value-yield of the machine to the product is higher than the wage for an hour, then the capitalist will not employ the machine, since the machine may indeed make labour more productive, but nevertheless raise the production-costs. Only when the value-yield of the machine is less than the saved wage-costs is the machine employed.

Regarding b): It is unclear what Marx means, here, by 'wealth'. If it is *material* wealth, namely the mass of use-values, then 'immediate labour' would never be the 'great' source of wealth, as, besides concrete-useful labour, the natural productive forces (like, for example, fertility of the land) and the productive forces created by humans would be equally great sources of wealth. However, if Marx means here the *social form* of wealth in capitalist societies, that is, the 'value' of the 'immense accumulation of commodities', then this value is the representation of abstract human labour, which has produced the commodities. Here, it is not important which part of this abstract human labour is an expression of the 'immediate labour' that was expended in the (last) production-process, and which part is an expression of the labour objectified in the machines, the value of which is carried over to the product. Even if an increasingly larger part of the product's value is traced back to the value-transfer by the used machines, abstract labour remains the substance of value.

Regarding c): if, however, abstract labour remains the substance of value, then labour-time also remains the immanent measure of it, even if the 'immediate labour time' in production plays an increasingly reduced role. *Immediate* labour-time was at any rate never the measure of value: immediate labour-time is that quantity of concrete labour that is expended by an individual producer. However, the individual expenditure of concrete labour-time does not form value; rather, value is formed by that quantity of abstract human labour that results only from the *average social relations*.

Regarding d): if labour-time remains the (immanent) measure of value, then the argument given by Marx for his last deduction, the collapse of 'production based upon exchange-value', is no longer valid either. Indeed, with this last deduction, it remained completely unclear from the outset how the difficulties of measuring value (insofar as this is supposed to occur) should then lead immediately to the *collapse* of capitalist production.

Above all, the weakness of the last deduction is clear and it is amazing that Marx himself did not notice how weak the argument is. An explanation lies in the conception of crisis with which he operated before the drafting of the *Grundrisse*. The *Communist Manifesto* claimed that 'the commercial crises [...] by their periodical return put on its trial, each time more threateningly, the existence of the entire bourgeois society'.[34] Some years later, Marx and Engels then claimed a close connection between crisis and revolution: 'A new revolution is possible only in consequence of a new crisis. It is, however, just as certain as this crisis'.[35] That Marx, while composing the manuscript of the *Grundrisse*, saw in crisis not only the catalyst of a political process, but also the beginnings of an economic collapse, is clear from an early draft plan. There, he writes: 'Crises. Dissolution of the mode of production and form of society based upon exchange value'.[36]

At the beginning of his work on the *Grundrisse*, Marx was convinced that the crisis would lead to the dissolution of the capitalist mode of production, and that in the course of its development this mode of production would finally 'collapse'. Now, as the first great crisis of the world-market had begun that would lead to the 'deluge', he had only to sketch out the mechanism that formed the basis of this process.[37]

We know, however, that something very different occurred. Although the first genuine crisis of the world-market occurred in 1857–8, it was neither a catalyst of revolutionary unrest, nor did it announce the collapse of production based upon exchange-value. On the contrary: the crisis was quickly over and capitalist production emerged from it strengthened. Marx learnt this lesson thoroughly and never forgot it. When Danielson pressured him to finish *Capital* in the late 1870s, Marx replied to him that he couldn't finish *Capital* before the current crisis reached its highpoint, because it showed entirely new phenomena that he still had to comprehend theoretically.[38] Nothing is left of any ideas of collapse

---

34. Marx and Engels 1976, p. 489.
35. Marx and Engels 1975–2005a, p. 510.
36. Marx 1975–2005a, p. 195.
37. Marx and Engels 1983, p. 217.
38. Marx and Engels 1975–2005, Vol. 45, p. 354.

or even his fear during the composition of the *Grundrisse* that he would be 'too late' with his book.

4. Quesnay's riddle and its solution

The phenomena that Marx analysed in the *Grundrisse* in relation to *capital fixe* appear in *Capital* Volume I in different places – as a component part of the investigation of the production of relative surplus-value, a category that was only present in a rudimentary form in the *Grundrisse*, but which is developed in *Capital* on the basis of a precise distinction between concrete useful labour and abstract human labour, and between constant and variable capital, as well as the comprehension of the capitalist production-process as a unity of the labour- and valorisation-process.

Developments of productive power are now not only empirically or factually included, but grasped as the systematic methods of the production of relative surplus-value, in which consists the fundamental possibility of an increase in productive power in the cooperation of the individual labour-powers, the division of labour (analysed paradigmatically in light of manufacture) and the employment of machinery (paradigmatically in 'large-scale industry'). On all three levels, the social productive power of labour appears as the productive power of capital, and 'the intellectual potentialities [*geistige Potenzen*] of the material process of production [appear to the workers] as the property of another and as a power which rules over him'.[39] However, this is not the case in the same way on all three levels:

> This process of separation starts in simple co-operation, where the capitalist represents to the individual workers the unity and the will of the whole body of social labour. It is developed in manufacture, which mutilates the worker, turning him into a fragment of himself. It is completed in large-scale industry, which makes science a potentiality for production which is distinct from labour and presses it into the service of capital.[40]

Marx then summarises in his analysis of machinery and large-scale industry in Chapter Fifteen:

> Every kind of capitalist production, in so far as it is not only a labour process but also capital's process of valorization, has this in common, but it is not the worker who employs the conditions of his work, but rather the reverse, the conditions of work employ the worker. However it is only with the com-

39. Marx 1976a, p. 482.
40. Ibid.

ing of machinery that this inversion first acquires a technical and palpable reality. Owing to its conversion into an automaton, the instrument of labour confronts the worker during the labor process in the shape of capital, dead labour, which dominates and soaks up living labour-power. The separation of the intellectual faculties of the production process from manual labour and the transformation of such faculties into powers exercised by capital over labour, is, as we have already shown, finally completed by large-scale industry erected on the foundation of machinery. The special skill of each individual machine-operator, who has now been deprived of all significance, vanishes as an infinitesimal quantity in the face of science, the gigantic natural forces, and the mass of social labour embodied in the system of machinery...[41]

By analysing changes in the production-process in the context of the production of relative surplus-value (an increase in productive power leads to a reduction of the value of labour-power and thus the necessary labour-time, so that surplus labour-time correspondingly increases), Marx could not merely claim the necessity of this development, as in the *Grundrisse*, but also justify it. It also became clear to him that the separation of the intellectual potentialities of the production-process from the workers is a tendency that is immanent to all capitalist production. This process found a highpoint in machine-production, but not a tipping point that put capitalist production into question. That the detail-skills of the individual worker become minute beside the employment of science, and thus beside the 'general intellect', does not threaten value-production. This state of affairs, rather, alters the concept of the productive worker, as is rather parenthetically noted in Chapter Sixteen.

In *Capital*, Marx studies the same developments as those examined in the 'Fragment on machines'. Nowhere, however, does he claim that (abstract) labour is no longer the substance of value, or that labour as a measure of value is placed in question – for good reason.

The value-dimension now comes into play on an entirely different level. In the treatment of the 'concept of relative surplus-value' in Chapter Twelve, Marx speaks of the 'riddle' with which one of the founders of political economy, Quesnay, had tormented his opponents and for which they owed him an answer: namely, the fact that, on the one hand, capitalists were only interested in exchange-value; but that, on the other hand, they constantly sought to lower the exchange-value of their products.[42] Marx also could not provide an answer to this riddle in the *Grundrisse*. There, he had effectively named the contradiction nominated by Quesnay. But rather than resolving it, he had comprehended

---

41. Marx 1976a, pp. 548–9.
42. Marx 1976a, p. 437.

it as a contradiction of capital: 'By striving to reduce labour time to a minimum, while, on the other hand, positing labour time as the sole measure and source of wealth, capital itself is a contradiction-in-process'.[43]

In the *Grundrisse*, Marx had ascribed to this 'contradiction' a potential to overthrow the capitalist mode of production. In *Capital*, against the background of the analysis of the production of relative surplus-value, this contradiction is resolved: the capitalist is not interested in the absolute value of the commodity, but rather, merely in surplus-value contained within it and able to be realised by means of sale. And 'since the same process both cheapens commodities and augments the surplus-value contained in them, we have here the solution of the following riddle: why does the capitalist, whose sole concern is to produce exchange-value, continually strive to bring down the exchange-value of commodities?'[44] The contradiction that had so astounded Marx in 1857–8 in the *Grundrisse* that he had immediately seen the collapse of all production based upon exchange-value, is reduced in *Capital* in 1867 to a riddle from the history of the theory, and one which has a simple solution. Those interpreters who have stopped at the *Grundrisse* have not accompanied Marx in these decisive theoretical advances.

Translated by Peter D. Thomas

---

43. Marx 1975–2005c, p. 91.
44. Marx 1976a, p. 437.

The 'General Intellect' in the *Grundrisse* and Beyond
Tony Smith

> The development of fixed capital shows the degree to which society's general science, KNOWLEDGE, has become an *immediate productive force*, and hence the degree to which the conditions of the social life process itself have been brought under the control of the GENERAL INTELLECT and remoulded according to it.[1]

Many Italian Marxists have long insisted on the importance of the section in the *Grundrisse* generally known as the 'Fragment on machines', and in particular the concept of the 'general intellect' introduced in the above passage.[2] This chapter examines recently translated essays on the general intellect by Paolo Virno and Carlo Vercellone, both of whom attempt to assess the contemporary theoretical and practical import of the *Grundrisse*.[3]

Virno and Vercellone on the 'general intellect' in history and theory

In the 'Fragment on machines' Marx outlines a historical reconstruction of the main stages of capitalist

---

1. Marx 1987, p. 92; block words originally in English.
2. Dyer-Witheford 1999, Chapters Four and Nine; Turchetto 2008; Toscano 2007. In the *Marx – Engels Collected Works* (Marx and Engels 1975–2005) the editors assign a different title to this section: '[Fixed Capital and the Development of the Productive Forces of Society]'.
3. Space-limitations preclude a comparison of these papers with earlier writings on the general intellect (for example, Negri 1991). An investigation of the relationship between these essays and social movements in Italy would also require a separate study (see Wright 2005).

work-relations in Europe, beginning with a period characterised by what he elsewhere terms the *formal subsumption* of workers under capital. In this era wage-labourers were hired as capital by capital, to produce a product owned by capital, while overseen by capital's representatives. Surplus-value was extracted from living labour through an enforced extension of the working day (absolute surplus-value), although the labour-process itself (most importantly, the use of tools) remained under workers' direct control.

When the limits of the working day were reached, capital turned to the *real subsumption* of labour, and the extraction of relative surplus-value through productivity-advances that reduced the portion of the workday devoted to necessary labour, that is, to the production of 'the quantity of products necessary for the maintenance of the living labour capacity'.[4] This initially was accomplished through a fragmentation of the labour-process ('detail labour'). Later, when scientific-technological knowledge – the fruit of the general intellect – advanced sufficiently, systems of machinery were introduced.[5] Living labour was then reduced to being a mere 'accessory' of these systems: 'In machinery, objectified labour confronts living labour in the labour process itself as the power which dominates it, a power which, in terms of its form, as the appropriation of living labour, is capital. The incorporation of the labour process into the valorization process of capital as merely one of its moments is also posited materially by the transformation of the means of labour into machinery, and of living labour into a mere living accessory of this machinery, as the means of its action'.[6]

When Marx wrote the *Grundrisse* he expected industrial capitalism to be replaced by communism in the not too distant future. His argument in the 'Fragment on machines' can be roughly summarised as follows:

1) Capital necessarily tends to seek productivity-advances.
2) Productivity-advances are based on the general intellect.
3) The more social agents enjoy free time for creative learning and experimentation, the more the general intellect will flourish.[7]

---

4. Marx 1987, p. 87.

5. '(T)he development of machinery takes this course only when . . . all the sciences have been forced into the service of capital . . . At this point invention becomes a business, and the application of science to immediate production itself becomes a factor determining and soliciting science' (Marx 1987, pp. 89–90).

6. Marx 1987, p. 83.

7. '(I)t is neither the immediate labour performed by man himself, nor the time for which he works, but the appropriation of his own general productive power, his comprehension of Nature and domination of it by virtue of his being a social entity – in a word, the development of the social individual – that appears as the cornerstone of production and wealth' (Marx 1987, p. 91).

4) Productivity-advances in capitalism lessen necessary labour-time. In principle, at least, this allows all social agents the free time required for the general intellect to flourish.

5) Capital, however, reduces necessary labour-time only in order to increase surplus labour-time. The drive to increase surplus labour-time *prevents* most workers from engaging in creative learning and experimentation.[8] Capital, in other words, simultaneously establishes the material preconditions for the general intellect to flourish and undercuts the possibility of its actual flourishing.[9]

6) As long as the reign of capital continues, this contradiction will worsen over time, leading to ever-increasing social irrationality.

7) Increasing social irrationality will motivate struggles for an alternative social order instituting free time for creative learning and experimentation for all. The name of this alternative is 'communism'.[10]

As we know all too well, Marx's historical projection did not come to pass.

According to Virno and Vercellone, it was not a mistake for Marx to think that the further development of the general intellect was profoundly hampered by the capitalism of his day. In their view, however, Marx profoundly underestimated the capacity for the general intellect to develop in capitalism, as well as capitalism's ability to incorporate the social energies of an expanded general intellect.

Virno and Vercellone both emphasise the underlying continuity between the technologies and forms of social organisation of Marx's period and twentieth-century 'Fordism', devoted to the mass-production of standardised commodities in assembly-lines within large-scale vertically-integrated firms.[11] Fordism also aimed at a ruthless separation of conception and execution, with the mass collective worker alienated from the specialised scientific-technical knowledge embedded in fixed capital. Virno and Vercellone also agree with Marx that 'the deepening of the logic of real subsumption can create conditions favourable to a collective reappropriation of knowledges insofar as "living labour" is able to

---

8. 'Since all *free time* is time for free development, the capitalist usurps the *free time* created by workers for society, i.e. civilisation' (Marx 1987, p. 22).

9. '(C)apital itself is a contradiction-in-process' (Marx 1987, p. 91).

10. Marx succinctly defines the goal of communism as follows: 'Free development of individualities, and hence not the reduction of necessary labour time in order to posit surplus labour, but in general the reduction of the necessary labour of society to a minimum, to which then corresponds the artistic, scientific, etc., development of individuals, made possible by the time thus set free and the means produced for all of them' (Ibid.).

11. There are very good reasons to be wary of the category of 'Fordism' (Brenner and Glick 1991). For the purposes of this paper, however, I shall follow Virno and Vercellone in assuming that there are theoretical contexts in which a suitably qualified version of the category may legitimately be used.

reconvert a part of its surplus labour into free time'.[12] What he did not foresee, in their view, is that this 'collective reappropriation of knowledges' would take place in capitalism, not communism.

Vercellone describes how the productivity-advances of industrial capitalism both encouraged a 'general struggle for the socialisation of access to knowledge' and provided the material preconditions for this struggle to succeed.[13] As a result of this success the capitalist welfare-state – already committed to socialising a significant portion of the costs of reproducing labour-power – began to fund mass-education.[14] Wage-labourers as a class now spent an unprecedented proportion of their lives in formal and informal education and training, becoming a 'depository of cognitive competencies that cannot be objectified in machinery', including 'the faculty of language, the disposition to learn, memory, the capacity to abstract and relate, and the inclinations towards self-reflexivity'.[15] At this point those engaged in living labour could no longer be said to be alienated from the general intellect. This state of affairs is termed 'mass intellectuality' by Virno, and 'diffuse intellectuality' by Vercellone.

Both authors assert that the rise of mass-intellectuality was the central causal factor underlying the 'crisis of Fordism'. Vercellone reminds us that in every historical conjuncture capital must decide whether or not to take on the risks associated with the direct management of labour. In these decisions 'the principal factor is undoubtedly the extent of domination of technology and of the knowledge on which the functions of direction and of capitalist control of the labour process rely'.[16] The slowness with which capital penetrated the sphere of production between the beginning of the sixteenth century and the end of the eighteenth can be explained, he asserts, by the fact that this period was 'marked by the hegemony of the knowledge of the craftsman', which forced capital to 'wrestle with the insubordination of workers in production'.[17] Capital came to dominate the labour-process only after an extensive period in which 'the development of science applied to production proceed[ed] at an equal rate with the expropriation of the knowledges of workers'.[18] At the end of this process of development and expropriation 'the compulsion to wage-labour [was] no longer merely of a monetary nature, but also of a technological nature, rendered endogenous by technical progress'.[19] This state of affairs, however, did not last;

---

12. Vercellone 2007, p. 28.
13. Vercellone 2007, p. 26.
14. Vercellone 2007, p. 25.
15. Virno 2007, p. 6.
16. Vercellone 2007, p. 21.
17. Vercellone 2007, p. 15.
18. Vercellone 2007, p. 20.
19. Vercellone 2007, p. 24.

the subsequent diffusion of intellectuality initiated a 'tendential fall of capital's control of the division of labour'.[20] At this point: 'The traditional opposition between dead labour/living labour, proper to industrial capitalism, gives way to a new form of antagonism, that between the dead knowledge of capital and the "living knowledge" of labour.'[21]

The crisis of Fordism then commenced when living labour refused to be treated as a mere appendage: '(I)t is the refusal of the scientific organisation of labour that largely explains the falling rate of profit and the social exhaustion of the Taylorist gains in productivity through which the Fordist crisis has been manifested since the end of the 1960s'.[22]

Capital, however, did not respond to this crisis by scurrying off the stage of world-history. It instead mutated into a form that could mobilise and incorporate diffuse intellectuality. For Virno, this explains the rise of 'post-Fordist' networks of production, with their short product-runs of diverse product-lines. Such flexibility requires a technically sophisticated and intellectually engaged workforce, freed from 'the repetitive and segmented labour of the assembly-line'. Post-Fordism also aims at continuous innovation in design, production, and marketing, all of which can be furthered by tapping into the creative insights of a broad spectrum of living labour, including knowledge developed outside capitalist firms.[23] In brief, 'the sharing of the general intellect becomes the effective foundation of every kind of praxis':[24] 'In post-Fordism, conceptual constellations and logical schemata that cannot be reduced to fixed capital play a decisive role, since they are inseparable from the interaction of a plurality of living subjects. The "general intellect" comprises formal and informal knowledge, imagination, ethical inclinations, mentalities and "language games"'.[25]

Marx believed that the tendency for the general intellect to control the conditions of the process of social life could only be fully realised in communism. Virno, in contrast, goes so far as to say that 'in post-Fordism, the tendency described by Marx is actually fully realised'.[26]

Unlike Virno, Vercellone rejects the category 'post-Fordism', arguing that it understates the extent to which the contemporary knowledge-economy institutes

---

20. Vercellone 2007, p. 18. 'Mass education and the development of a diffuse intellectuality make the educational system a central site for the crisis of the Fordist wage relation' (Vercellone 2007, p. 27).

21. Vercellone 2007, p. 33.

22. Vercellone 2007, p. 27.

23. '(W)hat is learned, experienced and consumed in the time of non-labour is then utilised in the production of commodities, becoming a part of the use-value of labour-power and computed as profitable resource' (Virno 2007, p. 5).

24. Virno 2007, p. 8.

25. Virno 2007, p. 5.

26. Virno 2007, p. 4.

a break from the industrial epoch. He prefers to speak of 'cognitive capitalism'.[27] However, he agrees with Virno on the essential point. In his view, too, capitalism today is based on 'the reappropriation of the cognitive dimensions of work by living labour, with respect to all material and immaterial activity'.[28]

From this perspective the *Grundrisse* retains immense theoretical and practical importance insofar as Marx correctly foresaw the absolute centrality of the diffusion of the general intellect. Insofar, however, as he failed to anticipate the extent to which this diffusion would occur in capitalism, other key aspects of Marx's account in the *Grundrisse* (and elsewhere) have been rendered obsolete. Both Virno and Vercellone take Marx's value-theory as a prime example of this point.

For Vercellone, the theory of value presupposes that 'immediate labour' can be adequately measured by a certain sort of time, 'the time of the clock and the chronometer', with this time then providing the proper measure of social wealth. These assumptions are plausible, he thinks, in a historical period in which 'labour becomes ever more abstract, not only under the form of exchange-value, but also in its content, emptied of any intellectual and creative quality'.[29] The era extending from the early Industrial Revolution through Fordism meets this criterion, due to the real subsumption of living labour under capital (more specifically, under the fixed capital of machinery-systems). In the *Grundrisse*, however, Marx himself admitted that as the general intellect develops the claim that direct labour is the dominant force of production will become increasingly implausible: 'Marx defends what can hardly be called a "Marxist" thesis. He claims that, precisely due to its autonomy from production, abstract knowledge (primarily but not only scientific knowledge) is in the process of becoming nothing less than the main force of production and will soon relegate the repetitive and segmented labour of the assembly-line to a residual position'.[30]

Marx, once again, expected that the general intellect could develop to this point only within communism. He did not foresee capitalism's transformation into a system in which the 'principal productive force' was the general intellect in the form of mass-intellectuality. He did not foresee, in other words, a form of capitalism in which we can no longer take 'the time of the clock and the chronometer as means for quantifying the economic value of labour':[31] '(T)he so-called law of value (that the value of a commodity is determined by

---

27. Vercellone 2007, p. 14.
28. Vercellone 2007, p. 16.
29. Vercellone 2007, p. 24.
30. Virno 2007, p. 3.
31. Vercellone 2007, p. 30.

the labour-time embodied in it) is regarded by Marx as the armature of modern social relations, yet it is both eroded and refuted by capitalist development'.[32]

There must now be a 'passage from a theory of time-value of labour to a theory of knowledge-value where the principal fixed capital is man "in whose brain exists the accumulated knowledge of society" '.[33]

Vercellone and Virno do not believe that their denial of the applicability of Marx's value-theory to contemporary capitalism puts them outside a Marxian framework. Both continue to accept Marx's theses that the crisis-tendencies of capitalism can only be temporally displaced, and that only communism can permanently overcome them. Post-Fordism/cognitive capitalism has enabled capital to maintain its hegemony, but only at the cost of exacerbating the very 'tendential fall of the capital's control of the division of labour' that brought about the crisis of Fordism in the first place. Capital is now forced to rely increasingly on the mechanisms of formal subsumption to maintain its social dominance, including the intensification of employment-insecurity,[34] massively increased household-debt, and the imposition of ever-more artificial scarcity,[35] all of which increase 'the relation of monetary dependence of the wage-labourer inside the process of circulation'.[36] The more obvious capital's reliance on formal subsumption becomes, however, the more obvious is capital's repression of the historical possibilities opened up by the general intellect – and the more capital itself chokes off the source of its own dynamism.[37] The continuous betrayal of the emancipatory promises of post-Fordism/cognitive capitalism ensures that Marx's call for communism in the *Grundrisse* retains its full force today: 'We could define communism as the real movement by means of which the society of knowledge would liberate itself effectively from the capitalist logic that subsumes it, freeing the potential of emancipation inscribed in an economy founded on the free circulation of knowledge and the democracy of the general intellect'.[38]

Virno concurs: 'the general intellect can affirm itself as an autonomous public sphere only if its bond to the production of commodities and wage-labour is

---

32. Virno 2007, p. 4.
33. Vercellone 2007, p. 31.
34. Vercellone 2007, p. 31; Virno 2007, p. 5.
35. The primary mechanism for generating artificial scarcity is the extension of intellectual property-rights: 'The result of this is the current paradox of poverty within abundance in an economy in which the power and diffusion of knowledges contrasts with a logic of accumulation... the new relations of ownership obstruct the progress of knowledge through the creation of an artificial scarcity of resources' (Vercellone 2007, p. 34).
36. Vercellone 2007, p. 31.
37. Referring to the extension of intellectual property-rights, Vercellone writes, '(T)he logic of capital accumulation... block(s) the sources themselves of the process of the diffusion and the accumulation of knowledge' (Vercellone 2007, pp. 34–5).
38. Vercellone 2007, p. 35.

rescinded'.[39] Of the many aspects of Virno and Vercellone's accounts that should be affirmed, this one ranks first and foremost.

There are other views of theirs, however, that can be questioned, beginning with their rejection of value-theory.

The 'general intellect' and the theory of value

For Virno and Vercellone, the value of a commodity, in Marx's sense of the term, is determined by the homogeneous units of simple direct labour-time 'embodied' in it. In their view, the machinery of Marx's day brought about a real subsumption of living labour that 'emptied [living labour] of any intellectual and creative quality', making it legitimate to measure the value of commodities in terms of simple homogenous units of abstract labour-time. Today, however, the principal productive force is the general intellect in the form of diffuse intellectuality. As a result they believe that we can no longer take 'the time of the clock and the chronometer as means for quantifying the economic value of labour',[40] given the 'lacerating contradiction between a productive process that now directly and exclusively relies on science and a unit of measure of wealth that still coincides with the quantity of labour embodied in products'.[41]

If value-theory were nothing more than the claim that the simple labour embodied in a commodity is the proper 'measure of wealth', it would indeed not have the least explanatory power today. But it then would not have been valid at any previous point in history either. Wealth-creation in capitalism has *always* crucially depended upon 'free gifts' that capital claimed as its own.[42] Gifts of nature, such as soil-fertility developed over millions of years, or water- and wind-power, are examples.[43] The cultural achievements of precapitalist societies, the development of cognitive and physical capacities outside the workplace, the unpaid care-labour of women, the scientific-technological knowledge developed in the early-modern period, and the products of publicly funded research-labs during the heyday of Fordism, provide other illustrations. The causal role of these sorts of factors in the production of wealth has always been incalculably large, and so there has *never* been a period of capitalism in which embodied labour served as the proper measure of wealth. Marx knew this full well, and yet

---

39. Virno 2007, p. 8.
40. Vercellone 2007, p. 30.
41. Virno 2007, p. 4.
42. Marx 1986, pp. 522, 527, 531; see also Camfield 2007, p. 46.
43. 'In agriculture, the soil itself, in its chemical, etc., activity, is already a machine which makes immediate labour more productive, and it yields a surplus earlier, because it is *the first* productive activity carried on with a machine, namely a *natural* one' (Marx 1986, p. 508).

devoted his life to the development of value-theory nonetheless. He could do this consistently because the purpose of this theory is not to measure wealth.

Marx's value-theory is a complex and controversial topic. Unfortunately, the following brief summary must suffice here. The starting point is the conceptualisation of the capitalist mode of production as a system of *dissociated sociality* in which 'the absolute mutual dependence of individuals, who are indifferent to one another, constitutes their social connection'.[44] More specifically, capitalism is a system of generalised commodity-production in which production is undertaken privately, and must subsequently be socially validated through the successful exchange of commodities for money.[45] Commodities whose production has been socially validated acquire a social property, 'value' ('exchangeability in definite proportions'), distinct from their various natural properties. In generalised commodity-production, exchange of commodities for money is the form of social validation, and so money provides the only socially objective measure of value. The labour that produces commodities with the special property of value may be termed *abstract labour*. This term is appropriate because in this context abstraction is made from the concrete and heterogeneous properties of different acts of labouring, and because this dimension of labouring is causally responsible for the production of an abstract property of commodities, measured by the abstract units of an abstract thing (money). Marx then explains that generalised commodity-production is a *capitalist* system, dominated by investments that aim at appropriating a greater sum of money (M') than the initial sum (M) invested. Living labour can now be conceptualised in a more concrete and complex fashion as the activity of wage-labourers, hired by capital to produce surplus-value, the difference between M' and M.

Comprehending capitalism requires understanding how a social order of dissociated sociality can nonetheless be reproduced over time (and the contradictions that arise in the course of this reproduction). Marx's answer is that this social reproduction is accomplished though the mediation of things: the sociality of privately undertaken labour is established by the circulation of commodities and money; more concretely, the sociality of privately undertaken wage-labour is validated when surplus-value is produced and appropriated. The monetary value-system is *not* a mechanism for measuring the contribution of simple units of labour to the production of wealth. It is first and foremost a mechanism for reproducing the social relations of capitalism, most importantly, the capital/wage-labour relation: 'The exchange of living labour for objectified, i.e. the positing of social labour in the form of the antithesis of capital and wage labour,

44. Marx 1986, p. 94.
45. 'On the basis of exchange value, labour is *posited* as general labour only through *exchange*' (Marx 1986, p. 108).

is the ultimate development of the *value relationship* and of production based on value'.[46]

There is a fundamental distinction between (re)producing *value-relations* (social relations in the bizarre and historically specific form of relations among things) and producing *wealth* (use-values considered in abstraction from historically specific social forms).

As we shall see in the following section, I believe Virno and Vercellone understate the role of the general intellect in the era extending from the first Industrial Revolution to Fordism, while overstating its flourishing in contemporary capitalism. But they are surely correct to stress how mass-intellectuality has become increasingly important as a productive force. Does this development push Marx's theory of value into the trash heap of outdated theories? Not if the main form of social organisation continues to be the dissociated sociality of generalised commodity-production. Not if social reproduction continues to be mediated by the circulation of things, that is, the sale of commodities for money. And not if social reproduction continues to centre on the reproduction of the capital/wage-labour relation. All these things continue to define global capitalism today.[47] As long as value-relations are in place, the accomplishments of diffuse intellectuality will tend to be either appropriated by capital as another sort of 'free gift' (as occurs, for example, when corporations make use of 'open-source' computing code), or else pushed to the margins of social life. Marx's value-theory will retain descriptive accuracy and explanatory power as long as this remains the case. To comprehend the production of wealth we must indeed take into account mass-intellectuality, and grant it increasing importance *vis-à-vis* simple labour. But this has little to do with Marx's theory of value, at least not with the most satisfactory all-things-considered interpretation of that theory.[48]

---

46. Marx 1987, p. 90.

47. This is not to deny that unpaid care-labourers, and various forms of self-employed workers in the formal and informal economy, play a central role in contemporary society. Forging coalitions between these social agents and wage-labourers is one of the foremost political tasks of our era. But the dominant structural tendencies of the social world continue to be associated with the capital/wage-labour relation on the level of the world-market (see Smith 2005; Harman 2002).

48. It would be wrong to conclude this section without acknowledging that there are passages in the 'Fragment on machines' that support Virno and Vercellone's position, for example: 'As soon as labour in its immediate form has ceased to be the great source of wealth, labour time ceases and must cease to be its measure... As a result, production based on exchange-value collapses, and the immediate material production process itself is stripped of its form of indigence and antagonism' (Marx 1987, p. 91). I am afraid we must say that the first sentence reflects a failure to keep the crucial distinction between 'value' and 'wealth' clearly in mind. (Few indeed are the authors who never uttered statements at odds with the most satisfying all-things-considered interpretation of their positions!) This is much preferable, in my view, to an interpretation asserting that value and wealth are conflated in Marx's theory. That alternative not only goes against many

The general intellect in capitalism's historical development

Before attempting to assess Virno and Vercellone's reconstruction of capitalism's historical development I would like to introduce two other crucial notions from the *Grundrisse* (and other texts Marx devoted to the critique of political economy): *form-determination* and *fetishism*. These notions will play a central role in the assessment that follows.

Marx's theory of value investigates the reproduction of social relations through relations among things. *Form-determination* refers to the manner in which the options, subjective preferences, and external behaviour of human agents are shaped by these things as a result of the social form they possess in generalised commodity-production. Due to these social forms, money and capital are not so much *instruments* of social life as *embodiments* of sociality standing over and against individual human subjects: 'In bourgeois society, e.g., the worker stands there purely subjectively, without object; but the thing which *confronts* him has now become the *true community*, which he tries to make a meal of and which makes a meal of him'.[49]

From the standpoint of form-determination there is a sense in which 'capital' is ontologically prior to – and shapes – the intentions and activities of individual agents, however much human agency is responsible for its emergence and maintenance. The options, subjective preferences, and behaviour of those who own and control capital is form-determined by the *valorisation-imperative*, that is, the ruthlessly imposed imperative that units of capital must produce surplus-value. The options, subjective preferences, and behaviour of those who sell their living labour for a wage is determined by this same imperative, albeit in a more antagonistic fashion. Their labour-process, for example, is shaped by the fact that it is

---

explicit texts in the *Grudnrisse* and elsewhere. It has the unavoidable implication that Marx's theory of value was never applicable to *any* epoch of capitalism from early agrarian capitalism onwards (see note 43 above), since in every epoch the production of wealth has depended on more than the embodied labour of wage-labourers. Further, the main underlying point of the above passage is not at odds with the interpretation of value-theory defended here. A crucial element of the legitimating ideology of capitalism is the claim that individual contributions to producing and distributing wealth can be distinguished, measured, and rewarded through monetary compensation. As the general intellect play an increasingly profound causal role in production and distribution, the falsity and internal incoherence of this claim become ever-more pronounced. But it is important to recognise that this development does not refute a theory of value that was developed precisely in order to describe and explain a social order based on a false and internally incoherent ideology. Nor does the fact that the falsity and internal incoherence of the claim becomes more pronounced automatically bring about the overcoming of indigence and antagonism in the immediate production-process. Marx quickly abandoned rhetoric suggesting otherwise.

49. Marx 1986, p. 420. Or, in one of the *Grundrisse*'s most striking formulations: '[Each individual] carries his social power, as also his connection with society, in his pocket' (Marx 1986, p. 94).

a *valorisation-process*, and not merely a process in which living labour actualises its capacities with the aid of objectifications of past labour. From this perspective it would be both false and naïve to consider capital as a mere instrument of social power used by humans for human ends. There is a sense in which it is a 'transcendental power', subjecting humans to *its* end, and appropriating the social powers of production as *its* powers.[50]

On the other hand, however, things do not have transcendental powers in themselves. They only appear to do so due to the peculiar 'social character of production' of generalised commodity-production, as Marx explains in a passage that holds for capital no less than for money:

> The need for exchange and the transformation of the product into pure exchange value progresses in the same measure as the division of labour, i.e. with the social character of production. But with the growth of the latter grows the power of *money*, i.e. the exchange relation establishes itself as a power external to and independent of the producers... In proportion as the producers become dependent upon exchange, exchange appears to become independent of them... Money does not create this opposition and this contradiction; on the contrary, their development creates the apparently transcendental power of money.[51]

This brings us to the heart of Marx's theory of *fetishism*. Due to the 'dissociated sociality' defining generalised commodity-production, that is, living labour's enforced separation from both the conditions of its realisation (the means of production and subsistence) and its product, the collective powers of social individuals necessarily appear as the powers of capital. But capital's powers rest entirely on the appropriation of the creative powers of collective social labour (and the powers of nature and scientific-technological knowledge mobilised by collective social labour):

> (I)n exchange for his labour capacity as a given magnitude, he [the worker] surrenders its *creative power*... the creative power of his labour establishes itself as the power of capital, and confronts him as an *alien power*... the productivity of his labour, his labour altogether, in so far as it is not a *capacity* but movement, *real* labour, *becomes* an *alien power* relative to the worker. Capital, on the contrary, valorizes itself through the *appropriation of alien labour*.[52]

---

50. 'All social powers of production are productive forces of capital and consequently capital itself appears as their subject' (Marx 1986, p. 505).
51. Marx 1986, p. 84.
52. Marx 1986, p. 233.

Capital, in brief, is nothing but: 'the potentialities resting in living labour's own womb which come to exist as realities outside it as a result of the production process – but as *realities alien* to it.[53]

The living labour whose creative powers Marx affirms in the theory of fetishism is not the transhistorical subject of traditional humanism. A transhistorical notion of living labour is a mere thought-abstraction, and it would be a profound category-mistake to assign creative powers to an abstraction of thought. The living labour discussed in the *Grundrisse* is living labour in the historically specific form of the use of a commodity that becomes a form of capital after it has been purchased by capital. The powers it develops have been developed *within* this social form and *because of* this social form.[54] This all-important instance of form-determination, however, does not undermine the ontological claim at the heart of the theory of capital-fetishism. If social relations and material social practices were structurally transformed, that is, if dissociated sociality were replaced with a different sort of sociality, the apparently transcendental powers claimed by money and capital would be instantly revealed as the ontological lies they are. The ultimate goal of Marx's theory of value is to help us recognise these lies now, in order to bring the day of reckoning closer.

The general intellect as Virno defines it ('the faculty of language, the disposition to learn, memory, the capacity to abstract and relate, and the inclinations towards self-reflexivity')[55] has been an expression of collective social labour throughout the history of capitalism. It is not something which first emerged in the twentieth century. Marx's theory of fetishism teaches that *any and all* variants of capitalism rest on a 'depository of cognitive competencies that cannot be objectified', that is, on the general intellect with 'operational materiality' insofar as it 'organises the production process and the "life-world"'. The general intellect undoubtedly takes different shapes in early capitalism, in nineteenth-century England, in Fordism, and in contemporary post-Fordism/cognitive capitalism. But it has *always* been central to the collective powers of social labour that appear in capital in an alien form.

I believe Virno and Vercellone understate the degree to which the general intellect was 'diffused' in the period extending from the initial Industrial Revolution through Fordism. This is due, I believe, to their one-sided emphasis on

---

53. Marx 1986, p. 383.
54. 'Universally developed individuals...are not products of nature but of history. The degree and the universality of development of the capacities in which *this kind* of individuality becomes possible, presupposes precisely production on the basis of exchange value, which, along with the universality of the estrangement of individuals from themselves and from others, now also produces the universality and generality of all their relations and abilities' (Marx 1986, p. 99; see also pp. 234–5).
55. Virno 2007, p. 6.

the form-determination of (fixed) capital, at the cost of overlooking the extent to which the powers of capital fixed in machinery were a fetishised form of the powers of collective social labour. Virno and Vercellone describe the Industrial Revolution of Marx's day as a period in which the general intellect took the form of expert scientific-technical knowledge embodied in fixed capital. Echoing the *Grundrisse*, they stress the alienation of wage-labourers from machinery (and thus from the general intellect, the scientific-technological knowledge, embodied in it), an alienation that then continued in Fordism. When Marx wrote the *Grundrisse*, however, he had not yet examined the details of technological innovation. By the time he composed *Capital*, the picture had become more complicated.

In *Capital* Marx describes various stages in the evolution of machinery in the Industrial Revolution, from the initial introduction of a machine, through the discovery of the strengths and weaknesses of its initial design, to a redesign that builds on these strengths and avoids at least some of the weaknesses. In the present context the important point to note is Marx's emphasis on the creative interplay in this process between scientists, engineers, and inventors, on the one hand, and other categories of workers, on the other. The tacit and explicit knowledge of the production-process possessed by wage-labourers as a result of their collective practical experience played a crucial (if almost universally overlooked) role: 'The problem of how to execute each particular process, and to bind the different partial processes together into a whole, is solved by the aid of machines, chemistry, etc. But of course, in this case too, the theoretical conception must be perfected by accumulated experience on a large-scale'.[56]

Again: 'It is only after a considerable development of the science of mechanics, *and an accumulation of practical experience*, that the form of machine becomes settled entirely in accordance with mechanical principles, and emancipated from the traditional form of the tool from which it has emerged'.[57]

In capitalism no particular machine or system of machinery is irreplaceable; 'every degree of the development of the social productive forces, of intercourse, of knowledge, etc., appears to [capital] as a barrier which it strives to overcome'.[58] Generalising Marx's account, we must recognise that subsequent technological changes will also be due to a creative interplay between scientific-technical labourers in the narrow sense and experienced workers with significant informal and tacit knowledge of the labour-process.

Virno and Vercellone are correct to stress the tendency to reduce workers to mere appendages of machine-systems in the period from Marx's day through Fordism, and the resulting tendency for individual workers to be alienated from

---

56. Marx 1976a, p. 502.
57. Marx 1976a, p. 505; emphasis added.
58. Marx 1986, p. 465.

the scientific-technical knowledge embodied in them. These tendencies are objective material realities, experienced as such by individual workers. But the account in *Capital* also implies that the workforce as a whole simultaneously developed new capacities and new forms of knowledge in the course of its practical experience. An exclusive focus on 'deskilling' in this period oversimplifies Marx's position.[59] Such an exclusive focus understates the extent to which the general intellect was already 'diffused' at the time of the Industrial Revolution, that is, not monopolised by a small group of scientific-technological experts.

Interestingly, Vercellone himself admits that the Fordist project of strictly separating conception and execution in the workplace was always an utter fantasy: 'It is important to remember that the irreducible dimension of workers' knowledge was also apparent in the big Fordist factories in the fundamental difference between prescribed tasks and the reality of workers' labour. Without this difference ... the Fordist assembly line would never have been able to function'.[60]

A mere two pages later, however, he writes that in Fordism 'Productivity can be now represented as a variable whose determinants no longer take into any consideration the knowledge of the workers', thereby reducing the tacit and explicit knowledge of wage-workers to invisibility once again.[61]

To summarise, Virno and Vercellone's application of the category of the general intellect in the historical period extending from the first Industrial Revolution to Fordism emphasises the form-determination of (fixed) capital in a one-sided fashion, at the cost of oversimplifying the complex ontological state of affairs described by Marx's theory of capital fetishism. The powers of capital, taking on material shape in the vast machine-systems of the Industrial Revolution and Fordism, did appear as transcendental powers. But they remained nothing but a fetishised form of the powers of collective social labour, and the powers of nature and knowledge mobilised by that labour. And this mobilised knowledge was by no means limited to that of scientists, engineers, and inventors. The general intellect throughout the period in question included the tacit and explicit knowledge of the workforce, even if prevailing ideology and material practices prevented this from being recognised.

Virno and Vercellone's analysis of post-Fordism/cognitive capitalism exhibits the inverse one-sidedness: they underestimate the continuing form-determination of capital in order to emphasise the creative powers of social labour underlying the

---

59. Scare quotes are required because 'deskilling' is sometimes used to describe a *generalisation* of previously above average skills sought by capital in order to reduce the relatively high levels of remuneration and control-workers possessing a quasi-monopoly of necessary skills have sometimes been able to win.
60. Vercellone 2007, p. 17.
61. Vercellone 2007, p. 19.

theory of capital-fetishism. It is certainly true that the powers of social labour are increasingly exercised today in ways that do not appear to be determined by the capital-form. A very striking example is found in the following list of internet-applications developed through knowledge work outside the capital/wage-labour relation: 'Ideas like free Web-based e-mail, hosting services for personal Web pages, instant messenger software, social networking sites, and well-designed search engines emerged more from individuals or small groups of people wanting to solve their own problems or try something neat than from firms realising there were profits to be gleaned'.[62]

Encryption-software, peer-to-peer file-sharing software, sound- and image-editors, and many other examples can be added to this list; 'Indeed, it is difficult to find software *not* initiated by amateurs'.[63] Do these and other contemporary expressions of 'diffuse intellectuality' justify Virno's assertion that in post-Fordism 'the sharing of the general intellect becomes the effective foundation of every kind of praxis'?[64] Do they justify Vercellone's claim that the real subsumption of living labour under capital has been eroded in cognitive capitalism? I believe the answer to these questions must be no.

As noted above, capital has *always* relied on 'free gifts' produced outside the capital-form. Prior to the rise of post-Fordism/cognitive capitalism, the capital-accumulation process depended upon these 'free gifts' to a literally incalculable degree. Nonetheless, the social forms of capital prevented the general intellect from being 'actually fully realised'.[65] Today we must add the new products of mass-intellectuality (such as software-codes written by 'amateurs') to the list of free gifts. In itself, however, this no more dissolves the power of the capital-form to shape social life than other sorts of free gifts have dissolved that power. In specific, it does not dissolve the power of the capital-form to prevent the general intellect from being 'actually fully realised' along the lines Marx foresaw in his anticipation of communism in the *Grundrisse*.

Examples of the way in which 'the sharing of the general intellect' is systematically restricted by the capital-form in post-Fordism/cognitive capitalism are so numerous that one hardly knows where to begin.[66] There continues to be significant underinvestment in knowledge directed to meeting human wants and needs outside the commodity-form, however significant such knowledge might be in meeting human wants and needs.[67] The extension of intellectual

---

62. Zittrain 2008, p. 85.
63. Zittrain 2008, p. 89.
64. Virno 2007, p. 8.
65. Virno 2007, p. 4.
66. For a more detailed discussion of these themes, see Smith 2000, Chapters Three and Five.
67. And there continues to be massive over-investment in innovations contributing to the well-being of very few. It is worth noting that the greatest private-sector investment in

property-rights not only prevents knowledge-products from being distributed as free public goods;[68] it also puts roadblocks in the way of the development of new scientific-technological knowledge, as Vercellone rightly notes.[69] Productivity-advances continue to be correlated with unemployment, while a vastly dispro-portionate share of the gains resulting from these advances are appropriated by investors and top managerial strata. Both factors blunt the incentive for work-ers to share insights that might lead to advances in productivity. The ceaseless external pressure of the valorisation-imperative ensures that core-firms within networks of enterprises will endeavour to displace risks on to their suppliers and distributors, appropriate the most lucrative portions of the 'value-chain' for themselves, and implement 'divide and conquer' strategies against geographically-dispersed workforces. These factors systematically discourage the free flow of information within networks, which is equivalent to discouraging the diffusion of the general intellect. *Pace* Virno, we are far indeed from the unrestricted diffu-sion of the general intellect that was a defining feature of the communism Marx imagined in the *Grundrisse*.

And, *pace* Vercellone, the assertion that the real subsumption of living labour under capital has been overcome in contemporary capitalism cannot be accepted either. Yes, the living labour of 'amateur' software-writers is not sub-jected to real subsumption in capitalist workplaces. There are also pockets of activity freed from real subsumption within the sphere of wage-labour.[70] But we must be wary of generalising from a handful of exceptional cases. Contempo-rary capitalism, no less than the capitalism of Marx's day, systematically denies the vast majority of workers the time, training, and material support to effec-tively participate in innovation to anything remotely approaching the extent to which they are capable, while subjecting them to new and extreme forms of stan-dardisation and monitoring.[71] Consider, for example, workers in the call-centres

---

information-technologies, the greatest concentration of capital-investment in knowledge-workers, and the highest rate of product-innovation, is found in the financial sector of the global economy. The characteristic 'knowledge-products' of our day are hypercom-plex (to the point of unintelligibility) financial assets. This form of product-innovation allowed a relatively smaller number of people to obscenely benefit from speculation, while imposing grievous risks and then grievous harms on billions.

68. As Vercellone points out, even mainstream economics grants that free distribu-tion is rational when the marginal costs of production approach zero (Vercellone 2007, p. 34).

69. Potential innovators may decline to enter fields where other units of capital own extensive IPRs, or where they judge they would have to engage in long and costly 'end runs' around them. Also, smaller firms that do not have the resources to engage in lengthy legal battles will tend to withdraw from promising innovation-paths (see Anon., 2002).

70. Google, for instance, encourages engineers to spend one day a week on a project of their own choosing (retaining, needless to say, the right to exploit anything they come up with). See Zittrain 2008, p. 84.

71. Huws 2003, 2007, 2008.

of the Global South, where questions must be answered with prewritten scripts on a computer-screen while being monitored and timed.[72] Or consider the 'knowledge-workers' at American Express, processing credit-requests while using (or, rather, being used by) expert information-technology systems: 'The expert system authorises or denies credit, comes up with the prices or rates of interest to be charged, and makes allowances for the client's "special circumstances"... Deprived of most elements of research, calculation, and judgment, the activities of the deal structurer/computer operator can best be described as "operations", comparable to the activities of machine tool operators working at computer-controlled machines'.[73]

For these workers, and for the hundreds of millions throughout the globe engaged in wage-labour in similar circumstances, contemporary information-technology systems impose the real subsumption of living labour under capital no less than the machinery systems of Marx's day imposed real subsumption on the factory-workers of the nineteenth century. In the former, no less than the latter, 'objectified labour physically confronts living labour as the power which dominates it and actively subsumes it under itself – not merely by appropriating living labour, but in the actual production process itself'.[74] Vercellone mistakes the latent potential of information-technologies to contribute to the transcendence of real subsumption for that transcendence itself. The gulf between the two remains immeasurably large.

Conclusion

Virno and Vercellone rightly call attention to Marx's category of the general intellect, and to the unprecedented role its diffusion plays today. From this perspective the *Grundrisse* remains a work of tremendous contemporary relevance, both theoretically and practically. They, however, also believe that the historical development of the general intellect has made other crucial themes of the *Grundrisse* and other works by Marx outdated. Marx's value-theory, they argue, is not applicable to contemporary society. Marx severely underestimated the flexibility of capitalism, which according to Virno has evolved to the point where in post-Fordism, the tendency described by Marx regarding the flourishing of the general intellect in communism 'is actually fully realised'.[75] Vercellone adds that

---

72. Neither Virno nor Vercellone discuss the geographically-based technical division of labor in which creative knowledge work is generally monopolised in the 'core' regions, while standardised operations are outsourced to the 'periphery' (see Smith 2005). Virno even proclaims 'the end of the division of labour' (Virno 2007, p. 8).

73. Head 2003, pp. 72–3.

74. Marx 1987, p. 83.

75. Virno 2007, p. 4.

the development of the general intellect has made Marx's account of the real subsumption of living labour under capital obsolete.

I have argued that Marx's value-theory is not made irrelevant by the fact that capital treats the knowledge produced by the general intellect as a free gift, nor does this follow from the fact that this knowledge is increasingly important in the production of wealth. Further, the development of the general intellect continues to be profoundly restricted by the capital-form. And the real subsumption of living labour under capital is materially imposed on most workers in global capitalism today by information-technologies, no less than it was imposed by the machinery-systems of the Industrial Revolution and Fordism.

On a last point, however, Virno and Vercellone are correct. Capitalism remains crisis-prone, and the most profound form of crisis is the 'No!' of living labour.[76] By highlighting the parasitical nature of capital vis-à-vis the general intellect, Virno and Vercellone further the recognition Marx spoke of in the *Grundrisse*: 'The recognition of the product as its [living labour's, TS] own, and its awareness that its separation from the conditions of its realisation is improper and imposed by force, is an enormous consciousness, and is itself the product of the mode of production based on capital, and just as much the KNELL TO ITS DOOM as the consciousness of the slave that he cannot be the *property of another*, his consciousness of being a person, reduced slavery to an artificial lingering existence, and made it impossible for it to continue to provide the basis of production'.[77]

In this manner Virno and Vercellone's work contributes to struggles for a non-capitalist social order based on democratic self-organisation. In comparison to this contribution, any shortcomings are entirely secondary matters.

---

76. I also believe, however, that their accounts of capitalist crisis downplay the role of inter-capital relations in generating systematic tendencies to overaccumulation and financial crises.

77. Marx 1986, pp. 390–1.

The System of Machinery and Determinations of Revolutionary Subjectivity in the *Grundrisse* and *Capital*[1]

Guido Starosta

This chapter proposes a reading of Marx's exposition of the forms of the real subsumption of labour to capital – in particular, the system of machinery of large-scale industry – as constituting the dialectical presentation of the determinations of revolutionary subjectivity. The proposition that the real subsumption constitutes the ground of revolutionary subjectivity should come as no surprise. In reality, this is no more than the concretisation of that insight about the most general determination of the process of 'natural history' constituting the development of humanity that Marx expounded in the Paris manuscripts of 1844. According to that early text, the content of the history of the human species consists in the development of the specific material powers of the human being as a working subject, that is, of *human productive subjectivity*. It is in the historical transformation of its material and social forms, Marx concluded, that the key to the abolition of capital – hence, to revolutionary subjectivity – should reside. However, that early attempt at the critique of political economy could not offer a rigorous scientific comprehension of the social determinations underlying the revolutionary transformation of society. Armed with a Feuerbach-inspired method of transformative criticism, Marx managed *analytically* to uncover alienated labour as the hidden *social* foundation behind

1. A shorter version of this paper has appeared in *Science & Society* 75, 1, 2011.

the reified objectivity of 'economic categories'. In turn, in those early writings he analytically discovered the specificity of the human species-being (i.e., human productive subjectivity) as the *material* content historically developing in that alienated form. However, although these discoveries allowed Marx to grasp the *simplest* (human) determination behind the content and form of the abolition of alienated labour, he arguably failed at *synthetically* unfolding the further mediations entailed by the social and material constitution of the revolutionary subject.[2]

The theoretico-practical need for the further dialectical development of the critique of political economy, which would eventually lead Marx to write *Capital*, expresses the following fact. The immanent ground of revolutionary subjectivity is not simple and unmediated; for instance, the sheer general materiality of human productive practice as the negated content behind the alienated objectivity of capitalist social forms.[3] Instead, it is a 'unity of many determinations', which therefore means that its scientific comprehension can only be the result of a complex dialectical investigation involving both the analytic movement from the concrete to the abstract and the synthetic, mediated return to the concrete starting point.[4] Dialectical research must therefore analytically apprehend all relevant social forms and synthetically reproduce the 'inner connections' leading to the constitution of the political action of wage-labourers as the form taken by the revolutionary transformation of the historical mode of existence of the human life-process.

Now, as the title of Marx's most important work denotes, the subject whose determinations the dialectical investigation proceeds to discover and present is *capital*, which, as the alienated subject of social life, becomes 'the all-dominating economic power of bourgeois society' and must therefore 'form the starting-point as well as the finishing-point' of the ideal reproduction of the concrete.[5] This does not leave revolutionary subjectivity outside the scope of the dialectical unfolding of capitalist social forms. Rather, it means that revolutionary subjectivity itself must be comprehended as the realisation of an immanent determination of capital as alienated subject.[6] Accordingly, its dialectical *presentation*

---

2. Starosta 2005.

3. As argued by so-called 'Open Marxists'. See Bonefeld, Gunn and Psychopedis (eds.) 1992.

4. Iñigo Carrera 2003.

5. Marx 1993, p. 107.

6. This point was insightfully hinted at in the 1970s by Giacomo Marramao in his critical appraisal of the polemic between the more subjectivist positions of Korsch and the Dutch Left Communists (Pannekoek, Gorter) and the objectivism of defenders of the theory of capitalist breakdown (Mattick, Grossmann). See Marramao 1975/6, pp. 152–5, and 1982, pp. 139–43. At least formally, Marramao correctly highlighted the necessity to ground the genesis of class-consciousness 'in terms of the process of production and

must essentially consist in the *synthetic* unfolding of the contradictory move-ment between materiality and capital-form up to its absolute limit, revealing the proletariat's self-abolishing action as the necessary form in which the former content asserts itself.[7]

It was fundamentally in *Capital* (but, crucially, also in the *Grundrisse*), mainly through the exposition of the determinations of the different forms of produc-tion of relative surplus-value (hence of the real subsumption of labour to capi-tal), where Marx managed to concretise the systematic dialectic of alienated human labour. He did this by showing precisely what the capital-form does to the materiality of human productive subjectivity as it takes possession of, and transforms, the labour-process. Seen externally, the implicit concrete question under investigation was the following: does capital transform human productive subjectivity in a way that eventually equips the latter with the material pow-ers to transcend its alienated social form of development? From this materialist standpoint, only if this were the case would it make sense to pose the question of conscious revolutionary action as a concrete objective potentiality immanent in capitalist society.[8] In other words, Marx's point was the need to discover the material determinations of communist society in their present mode of exis-tence as an *alienated potentiality* engendered by the autonomised movement of the capital-form to be realised – that is, turned into *actuality* – precisely and necessarily through the conscious revolutionary action of the self-abolishing proletariat.

Those determinations appear scattered and are just mentioned in passing in several of Marx's texts. They all characterise the simplest defining character of communism as the fully self-conscious organisation of social labour as a collec-tive potency by the thereby freely associated producers. It is in the *Grundrisse*, in the context of the critique of Adam Smith's conception of labour as sacrifice, that Marx offers the clearest and most concise characterisation of the general attributes of what he calls 'really free working':

> The work of material production can achieve this character [as 'really free working', GS] only (1) when its social character is posited, (2) when it is of

---

reproduction', that is, within the 'objectivity of social relations' and their (autonomi-sed) self-movement. In other words, Marramao clearly saw the necessity to establish a firm connection between the critique of political economy and the 'theory of revolu-tion'. More recently, the point about need to find the immanent ground of emancipatory subjectivity in the contradictory unfolding of the reified forms of social mediation of capitalist society has been forcefully made by Postone 1993, although his own attempt is not without weaknesses. See Starosta 2004.

7. For an elaboration of the methodological underpinnings of this point, see Iñigo Carrera's chapter in this book.

8. Marx 1993, p. 159.

a scientific and at the same time general character, not merely human exertion as a specifically harnessed natural force, but exertion as subject, which appears in the production process not in a merely natural, spontaneous form, but as an activity regulating all the forces of nature.[9]

The interesting and 'intriguing' aspect of this passage is that Marx not only claims that in order to be really free, labour must become a consciously organised, directly social activity, but also that the consciousness regulating that emancipated productive activity must be of a *general* and *scientific* kind. As we shall see later, this latter attribute, scarcely mentioned by Marx on other occasions,[10] will prove of paramount importance for our comprehension of the concrete determinations of revolutionary subjectivity; a task that Marx himself achieved, although not without tensions and ambiguities. At this stage, I would just like to reformulate the question of the relation between capital and productive subjectivity posed above in the light of that passage from the *Grundrisse*. Does the development of capital transform human productive subjectivity in such a way as to engender the necessity of producing the latter with the two general attributes mentioned by Marx? Furthermore, is the working class the material subject bearing them?

In this paper, then, I discuss the way in which Marx, through the dialectical exposition of the contradictory movement of the real subsumption, actually presented the genesis of the revolutionary subject. The argument is firstly developed through a close reading of Marx's discussion of the determinations of large-scale industry in *Capital*, as the latter constitutes the most developed form of real subsumption. The essence of this capitalist transformation of the production-process of human life lies in the mutation of the productive attributes of the collective labourer according to a determinate tendency: the individual organs of the latter eventually become *universal productive subjects*. This is the inner *material* determination underlying the *political* revolutionary subjectivity of the proletariat. However, I argue that Marx's dialectical exposition of those transformations in *Capital* is in some respects truncated and does not unfold the plenitude of the material determinations underlying the revolutionary existence of the working class. The latter is presented as no more than an abstract possibility. A gap therefore remains between the 'dialectic of alienated human labour' unfolded in the chapters on relative surplus-value in *Capital*, and the revolutionary conclusions at the end of Volume I in the chapter on 'The Historical Tendency of Capital Accumulation'. The paper finally suggests that the so-called 'Fragment on machines' from the *Grundrisse* contains a different but complementary perspec-

---

9. Marx 1993, pp. 611–12.
10. See, however, Marx's remarks in the *Paris Manuscripts* on the need for the constitution of 'natural science of man' or 'human natural science' as the basis for emancipated human practice. Marx 1992b, p. 355.

tive on the productive subjectivity characteristic of large-scale industry. Through a careful reading of the relevant passages of that earlier version of the critique of political economy, it is possible to undertake the completion of the systematic unfolding of the social and material determinations of revolutionary subjectivity.

Large-scale industry and workers' productive subjectivity in *Capital*

The guiding thread running through Marx's exposition of the concrete forms of the production of relative surplus-value resides in the revolutions to which capital subjects the productive subjectivity of the doubly free labourer as the means for the multiplication of its power of self-valorisation. However, it is not there that Marx's presentation of the determinations of large-scale industry begins. The reason for this derives from the very starting point of the production of relative surplus-value through the system of machinery that characterises large-scale industry. As Marx points out, if in manufacture the point of departure of the transformation of the material conditions of social labour was productive subjectivity as such (with the transformation of the instrument of labour, in the form of a specialisation, determined as a result of the former), in large-scale industry the transformation of the instrument of labour constitutes the starting point, the transformation of the wage-labourer being its result.[11]

Marx presents the essence of this transformation of the human labour-process by developing the specific materiality of machinery, in particular *vis-à-vis* the labour-process in manufacture. In reality, the simplest determination of that difference was already anticipated by Marx in the transition contained in the previous chapter of *Capital*, where the necessity of the development of machinery was laid bare. I am referring to capital's need to do away with the subjective basis of manufacture through the development of an 'objective framework' for material production, independent of the manual expertise and immediate practical knowledge of workers. In brief, it is about giving an objective form to the powers of social labour springing from direct productive co-operation.[12]

The two-fold material specificity of the machine thereby springs from the objectification of both the – however restricted – knowledge and manual skills and strength of the manufacturing labourer. On the one hand, capital strives to substitute the movement of the forces of nature for that of the human hand as the immediate agent in the transformation of the object of labour into a new use-value. On the other hand, it attempts to displace the immediate subjective experience of the worker as the basis for the conscious regulation of the

---

11. Marx 1976a, p. 492.
12. Marx 1976a, pp. 490–1.

labour-process, that is, as the basis for knowledge of the determinations of the latter. This implies, in the first place, the need to turn the production of that knowledge into an activity which, whilst clearly remaining an inner moment of the organisation of social labour, nonetheless acquires a differentiated existence from the immediacy of the direct production-process. Coupled with the need to objectify it as a productive power directly borne by the 'dead labour' represented in the machine, that knowledge must necessarily take the general form of *science*.[13] Capital thereby advances, for the first time in human (pre)history, in the generalisation of the application of science as an immediate potency of the direct production-process.[14] Note, however, that at this stage of the exposition scientific knowledge does not appear directly as productive activity but only as already objectified in the form of the machine, that is, simply as a presupposition for the latter's existence.

Thus far, these are the fundamental aspects of Marx's exposition of the *material* specificity of the production-process of capital based on the system of machinery, i.e., the transformations it suffers in its aspect as a process of production of use-values. However, the process of production of capital is such for being the unity of the labour-process and the valorisation-process. Hence, Marx's presentation goes on to develop the specific impact of the system of machinery on the conditions for value's self-expansion, on the *form-determinations* of the production-process of capital.[15] With this, Marx's presentation exhausts the novel determinations brought about by the system of machinery to the production-process as they pertain to its 'objective factor'. What necessarily follows, then, is the investigation of the impact of these transformations on the 'subjective factor' of the labour-process, that is, on the worker.

In the third section of the chapter on large-scale industry, Marx initially presents what he refers to as only 'some general effects' of the system of machinery on the worker, that is, those changes that can be discussed without developing the specific form in which the 'human material is incorporated with this objective organism'.[16] In other words, these are the effects whose development does not involve any new *qualitative* determination in the productive subjectivity of workers. Rather, they refer to the *quantitative* changes that machinery brings about in capital's valorisation-process as a process of exploitation of living labour. These include: the quantitative extension of the mass of exploitable labour-power through the incorporation of female and child-labour; the tendency

---

13. Marx 1976a, p. 508.
14. Marx 1994, p. 32.
15. Marx 1976a, pp. 508–17.
16. Marx 1976a, p. 517.

to prolong the working day; and the tendency to increase the intensive magnitude of the exploitation of human labour.

It is in section four, through the presentation of the functioning of 'the factory as a whole', that Marx starts to unfold the specific *qualitative* determinations of the productive subjectivity of large-scale industry. The discussion of a passage from Ure serves Marx succinctly to identify the most general determination of the factory as the sphere of capitalist society where the conscious regulation of an immediately social production-process takes place. A conscious regulation, however, that is determined as a concrete form of the *inverted general social regulation* as an attribute of the materialised social relation in its process of self-expansion. In the factory – and this is the issue that Ure's definition overlooks – this inverted social existence reaches a further stage in its development by acquiring a 'technical and palpable reality'.[17]

Thus, the scientific conscious regulation of social labour characterising large-scale industry is not an attribute borne by those workers performing direct labour in the immediate production-process. For them, those powers exist already objectified in the system of machinery, to whose automatic movement they have to subordinate the exercise of their productive consciousness and will, to the point of becoming 'its living appendages'.[18] Large-scale industry consequently entails an enormous scientific development of the 'intellectual faculties of the production process' only by exacerbating their separation from direct labourers. In its mode of existence as a system of machinery, the product of labour comes to dominate the worker in the direct process of production not only formally but even materially as well. Capital thus appears to those workers as the *concrete material subject* of the production-process itself.

With all these elements, we can now turn to summarise the specific determination of the productive subjectivity of the worker of large-scale industry. In (*tendentially*) doing away with the need for all specialised skill and knowledge of workers, the production of relative surplus-value through the system of machinery gives the development of their productive subjectivity the concrete form of an *absolute degradation*. In this brutal way, and in opposition to the *particularism* of the subjectivity of the wage-labourer of manufacture, large-scale industry begets, as its most genuine product, a *universal worker*, that is, a productive subject capable of taking part in any form of the human labour-process. In the words of Marx:

> Hence, in place of the hierarchy of specialised workers that characterizes manufacture, there appears, in the automatic factory, a *tendency* to equalize

---

17. Marx 1976a, p. 548.
18. Ibid.

and reduce to an identical level every kind of work that has to be done by the minders of the machines; in place of the artificially produced distinctions between the specialized workers, it is natural differences of age and sex that predominate.[19]

With this tendency to the production of workers who are capable of working with any machine, the simple material or technical necessity for the life-long attachment of individuals to a single productive function disappears.[20] However, insofar as machines become specialised into certain particular productive functions, the persistence of the division of labour in the factory is still technically *possible*. Indeed, Marx argues, the exploitative relation between capitalists and workers that mediates the development of the material productive forces of social labour as an alienated attribute of its product, leads to the reproduction of the 'old division of labour' in an even more hideous fashion.[21] Large-scale industry's tendency to produce an increasingly universal worker is thereby realised in the concrete form of its negation, that is, by multiplying the spaces for the exploitation of living labour on the basis of an exacerbation of 'ossified particularities'. Thus, the individual capitalist could not care less about the disappearance of the technical necessity for a particularistic development of the worker's productive subjectivity. Under the pressure of competition, his/her only individual motive is the production of an extra surplus-value. If he/she can obtain it by attaching the worker to 'the lifelong speciality of serving the same machine',[22] so he/she will. In effect, the reproduction of the division of labour under the new technical conditions implies that a lower value of labour-power can be paid – since 'the expenses necessary for his [the workers', GS] reproduction' are 'considerably lessened'. In addition, it implies that a greater docility on the part of the exploitable human material is induced – since 'his helpless dependence upon the factory as a whole, and therefore upon the capitalist, is rendered complete'.[23]

It is crucial, at this juncture, to be clear about this contradictory movement between universality and particularity of the determinations of the productive subjectivity of large-scale industry. Paraphrasing Marx, here, as everywhere else, we must distinguish between the general tendency of capital-accumulation and the concrete forms in which the essence of the historical movement is realised. *Thus, the essential determination which, as we shall see, expresses the reason to be of the capitalist mode of production, lies in the tendency to universalise the productive attributes of wage-labourers.* This is the general movement of the production of

---

19. Marx 1976a, p. 545, my emphasis.
20. Marx 1976a, p. 546.
21. Marx 1976a, p. 547.
22. Ibid.
23. Ibid.

relative surplus-value through the system of machinery which underlies – hence, gives unity to – the variegated forms that the labour-process presents in the course of capitalist development. In order to substantiate this, let us now move ahead in our reading of Marx's investigation of large-scale industry to the point in *Capital* where he further unfolds the movement of the identified contradiction, that is, to the subsequent discussion of factory-legislation in section nine of this same chapter.[24]

The crucial point for our argument is that section nine completes (as far as *Capital* is concerned) the development of the specific determinations of the productive subjectivity of large-scale industry. In effect, Marx's exposition in section four had left the dialectical presentation with an unresolved contradiction between large-scale industry's general tendency for universality and the exacerbation of the particularism of the division of labour that, left to the unrestrained will of individual capitalists, it allowed. In addition, we shall see how this discussion leads Marx, for the first time in his dialectical exposition, to uncover the revolutionary historical potentialities carried by this specifically capitalist form of human labour-power.

---

24. In my view, Marx's presentation is not fully clear and consistent in distinguishing between essential determination (and therefore general tendency) and concrete form in which it is realised. This lack of clarity probably stems from the uneasy co-existence of systematic and historical moments in the exposition. Thus, he firstly presents the general determination of the productive subjectivity of large-scale industry (namely, its universality) 'in its purity', without necessarily implying that it has been fully realised in its historical concrete forms. However, in his subsequent empirical illustrations he seems to treat the general determination as an immediate actuality. He therefore posits the persistence of the particularistic development of productive subjectivity as 'artificially' reproduced by superimposing the division of labour where its technical necessity has actually disappeared. See Marx 1976a, pp. 546–7, where he remarks that the insignificance of 'on-the-job' skills required for machine-work has done away with the need to bring up a special kind of worker and that the attachment of the worker to a single specialised machine represents a 'misuse' of the latter. While this might have been more or less the case in the particular industries that he discusses, this was by no means the general situation of large-scale industry in his time. The general tendency for a universal productive subjectivity is realised only *gradually* in the historical course of capital-development. In this sense, the technical necessity for particularistic attributes of labour-power is not done away with overnight. Without a doubt, the historical development of large-scale industry registers a tendency for the degradation of experienced-based ('tacit') knowledge of the determinations of the labour-process. However, the progress of capitalist automation has so far involved the recreation of the technical necessity for certain (albeit increasingly more limited) particularistic development of productive subjectivity. Thus, even during the so-called 'Fordist' cycle of accumulation, the full mastery of machines required a relatively lengthy learning process achieved by flanking a skilled operator. Only with the more recent wave of computer-based automation have particularistic or experienced-based skills significantly lost their former centrality (without, however, fully disappearing). On these recent transformations in the labour-process, see Balconi 2002.

The movement of 'the contradiction between the division of labour under manufacture and the essential character of large-scale industry'[25] acquires a first expression in the establishment of compulsory elementary education for working children. As Marx points out, the unchecked exploitation of child-labour by individual capitals led not only to the 'physical deterioration of children and young persons',[26] but also to an artificially-produced intellectual degeneration, which transformed 'immature human beings into mere machines for the production of relative surplus-value'.[27] Since 'there is a very clear distinction between this and the state of natural ignorance in which the mind lies fallow without loosing its capacity for development, its natural fertility',[28] these excesses of the capitalist exploitation of child labour-power eventually reacted back on the very capacity of valorisation of total social capital by jeopardising the existence of the future generation of adult-workers in the 'material and moral conditions' needed by capital-accumulation itself. This is illustrated by Marx through a discussion of the case of the English letter-press printing trade, which, before the introduction of the printing machine, was organised around a system of apprenticeship in which workers 'went through a course of teaching till they were finished printers' and according to which 'to be able to read and write was for every one of them a requirement of their trade'.[29] With the introduction of printing machines, however, capitalists were allowed to hire children from 11 to 17 years of age, who 'in a great proportion cannot read' and 'are, as a rule, utter savages and very extraordinary creatures'.[30] These young workers were day after day attached to the simplest of tasks for very long hours until being 'discharged from the printing establishments' for having become 'too old for such children's work'.[31] Those 17-year-old workers were left in such intellectual and physical degradation that they were unfit to provide capital, *even in the same factory*, with the miserably restricted productive attributes that it required from its immediate source of surplus-value, namely, human labour-power.

The education-clauses of the factory-legislation allow Marx not only to dispel any doubt about capital's 'universal vocation' in its transformation of human productive subjectivity. They also serve to highlight, for the first time in his whole dialectical exposition, that it is *only* the development of *that* specific form of human productive subjectivity that expresses capital's historic movement in the

---

25. Marx 1976a, p. 615.
26. Marx 1976a, p. 520.
27. Marx 1976a, p. 523.
28. Ibid.
29. Marx 1976a, p. 615.
30. Ibid.
31. Ibid.

production of the material powers for its own supersession as the general social relation regulating human life:

> As Robert Owen has shown us in detail, the germ of the education of the future is present in the factory system; this education will, in the case of every child over a given age, combine productive labour with instruction and gymnastics, not only as one of the methods of adding to the efficiency of production, but as the only method of producing fully developed human beings.[32]

Notice, however, that Marx makes clear that the education-clauses represent the *germ* – and just that – of the 'education of the future'. To put it differently, Marx's discussion aims at showing *both* that the social forms of the future are effectively carried as a potentiality by the productive subjectivity of large-scale industry under consideration *and* that, with the determinations unfolded so far, this potentiality is not yet immediate. On the contrary, in their 'paltriness', the education-clauses reveal that these determinations are far from being a 'method of producing fully developed human beings'. Rather, they are forms of positing individuals whose productive subjectivity is still trapped within the miserable forms imposed by the reproduction of the conditions for capital's valorisation. Other material transformations are still needed to mediate the development of those germinal elements into their plenitude.

The total social capital's necessity to produce universal workers is not exhausted by the obstacles to its valorisation posed by the division of labour within the workshop. As Marx remarks, 'what is true of the division of labour within the workshop under the system of manufacture is also true of the division of labour within society'.[33] In effect, inasmuch as the technical basis of large-scale industry is essentially revolutionary, it entails the permanent transformation of the material conditions of social labour and, therefore, of the forms of exertion of the productive subjectivity of individual workers and of their articulation as a directly collective productive body.[34] This continuous technical change thereby requires individuals who can work in the ever-renewed material forms of the production of relative surplus-value. 'Thus', Marx concludes, 'large-scale industry, by its very nature, necessitates variation of labour, fluidity of functions, and mobility of the worker in all directions'.[35] However, he also points out again how the general organisation of social production through the valorisation of independent fragments of social capital negates the immediate realisation of this tendency for an all-sided development of individuals.[36] The private fragmentation of social

---

32. Marx 1976a, p. 614.
33. Marx 1976a, p. 615.
34. Marx 1976a, p. 617.
35. Ibid.
36. See Bellofiore 1998a, for suggestive reflections on this question.

labour, and its reified social mediation through the capital-form, permits the reproduction of 'the old division of labour with its ossified particularities'.[37] Thus it gives the imposition of variation of labour the form of 'an overpowering natural law, and with the blindly destructive action of a natural law that meets with obstacles everywhere'.[38] In this contradictory form, the realisation of large-scale industry's tendency to produce universal workers nonetheless marches forward, also revealing that it is in the full development of this determination that this alienated social form finds its own *absolute limit*.[39] In other words, that it is on the fully-expanded universal character of human productive subjectivity that the *material basis* for the new society rests.

> This possibility of varying labour must become a general law of social production, and the existing relations must be adapted to permit its realization in practice ... the partially developed individual, who is merely the bearer of one specialised social function, must be replaced by the totally developed individual, for whom the different social functions are different modes of activity he takes up in turn.[40]

With this discussion Marx unfolds the way in which the general necessities of the reproduction of the total social capital – in this case, workers bearing a universal productive subjectivity – clashes with its concrete realisation through the private actions of individual capitals (which strive for the perpetuation and exacerbation of the particularistic development of productive subjectivity). Moreover, we see how this contradiction moves by determining the working class as the personification of the mediated necessities of the valorisation of capital, the latter providing the material and social foundation for proletarian political power.[41] In

---

37. Marx 1976a, p. 617.
38. Marx 1976a, p. 618.
39. Marx 1976a, p. 617.
40. Marx 1976a, p. 618.
41. By 'mediated necessities', I denote those that are a moment of the production of surplus-value, but that are antithetical to the simplest (hence immediate) necessity of self-valorising value to increase its magnitude by any means personified by individual capitals. Although a proper discussion of this essential point exceeds the scope of this chapter, I think that this discussion illustrates the way in which Marx sees the systematic connection between capital-accumulation and class-struggle. Specifically, Marx presents the class-struggle as the most general *direct* social relation through which the *indirect* relations of capitalist production assert themselves. On this point, see Iñigo Carrera 2003, pp. 5–6. Whilst this certainly means that class-antagonism is an endemic reality of capitalist production, it also means that it is not the self-moving content behind its development (as argued, for example, by Bonefeld 1995). Moreover, neither does its simple existence as such immediately express the emergence of an antagonistic principle of organisation of social life other than the valorisation of capital, which would be, in turn, incarnated in the working class (as in the so-called 'Autonomist Marxist' approach; see Cleaver 1992 and De Angelis 1995). Instead, the systematic place of the class-struggle as a social form shows that the production of surplus-value is a potentiality of

effect, the development of large-scale industry makes the possession of a universal subjectivity a matter of survival for the members of the working class since, as evidenced by the aforementioned case of the printing-trade workers, only in that way can they be in a position to sell their labour-power to capital (thereby turning the alienated necessities of social capital into an immediate need for their social and material reproduction). Thus, workers have to 'put their heads together' again and, through their struggle as a class, force the capitalist state to 'proclaim that elementary education is a compulsory pre-condition for the employment of children'.[42] But what is elementary education if not a – certainly very basic – step in the formation of future *universal workers*? That is, in the development of productive attributes that equips the labourer to work not in this or that particular aspect of the immediately social labour-process of the collective labourer of large-scale industry, but in whatever task that capital requires from him or her?[43]

Social capital's need for universal workers thereby provides another material basis for the political power of the working class in its confrontation with the capitalist class over the conditions of its social reproduction. In this first expression of that relation between large-scale industry and workers' power represented by the Factory-Acts, the class-struggle does not appear to transcend its most general determination as the form of the buying/selling of the commodity labour-power at its value, which Marx unfolds in Chapter ten on 'The working day'.[44] Yet Marx advances the proposition that, when concretely developed, that tendency towards universal productive subjectivity will eventually provide the

---

the alienated movement of social labour *in its unity*. In other words, Marx's exposition of the social form of class-struggle makes evident that the concrete subject of the process of valorisation – and hence of the movement of alienated social reproduction – is the *total social capital*. Compare Starosta 2005, Chapter Five. This does not imply the denial of the transformative powers of human practice personified by the workers. What this does imply is that whatever transformative powers the political action of workers might have – *both* capital-reproducing *and* capital-transcending political action – must be an immanent determination begotten by the alienated movement of capital as subject and not external to it.

42. Marx 1976a, p. 613.

43. Recent historical developments of machine-based production have confirmed the general tendency identified by Marx: degradation of particularistic productive attributes developed on the job, coupled with expansion of the requirements of formal education to produce its more *universal* dimensions. The latter is the necessary prerequisite for the constitution of the more general and abstract knowledge that the contemporary operator of computer-based technologies sets into motion vis-à-vis the 'Fordist' machinist ('controlling' the carrying out of a task rather than actually 'doing' it). See Balconi 2002.

44. See Kicillof and Starosta 2007a and 2007b; Iñigo Carrera 2003, pp. 81–2, and Müller and Neusüss 1975.

class-struggle with expanded transformative powers, namely, those necessary for the establishment of the workers' 'political supremacy' as a class.[45]

Now, the question immediately arises as to what are the more concrete determinations behind this inevitability of the proletarian conquest of political power? Unfortunately, Marx provides no answer in these pages. In fact, one could argue that no answer could have been provided at all. The unfolding of the necessity of 'proletarian dictatorship' as a concrete social form involves still more mediations and, therefore, the former is not carried by the social form we are facing at this point of the exposition in the form of an *immediate potentiality* to be realised through the political action of the workers as a class.[46] Thus, at this stage of the dialectical presentation, both this latter remark and the one discussed above regarding the totally-developed individual as the basis for the abolition of capital, cannot be but unmediated observations, external to the concrete determinations of the productive subjectivity of large-scale industry that we have before us. On the other hand, inasmuch as the latter *does* involve *a certain degree* of universality, a limited, albeit real, expression of the underlying tendency for the production of its fully-developed shape, Marx's reflections, although external, are undoubtedly pertinent. From a methodological point of view, he could therefore legitimately introduce those remarks in order to anticipate the direction that the further unfolding of this historically-specific contradiction of the capitalist mode of production – 'the only historical way in which it can be dissolved and then reconstructed on a new basis' – should take.[47] But as a proper, complete dialectical account of the determinations underlying the proletarian conquest of political power or, above all, of the revolutionary production of the free association of individuals, the presentation as so far developed definitely falls short.

This, in itself, should not be problematic. From the perspective of the dialectical investigation as such, this juncture of our critical reading of Marx's search for the determinations of revolutionary subjectivity is not a dead-end at all. It only means that our journey from the abstract to the concrete needs to proceed forward as our end-point – namely, revolutionary subjectivity – still lies ahead. In this sense, no anomaly lies before us. However, the question is very different when approached from the standpoint of the elements for such an investigation we can find already objectified in Marx's *Capital*. In that respect, the problem that the contemporary reader of *Capital* attempting to discover those determinations faces is, to put it briefly, that *they are not there*. Let us expand on this point.

---

45. Marx 1976a, p. 619.
46. This would need the exposition of the tendency for the concentration and centralisation of capital as the alienated expressions of the socialisation of labour in the capitalist mode of production and whose absolute limit is reached when the total capital of society immediately exists as a single capital. Compare Marx 1975, p. 780.
47. Marx 1976a, p. 619.

We have seen how Marx, when faced with the tendential universality of the worker of large-scale industry and the growing conscious regulation of social labour it entails, *extrinsically* reflects upon the specific material form of productive subjectivity necessary to 'build society anew' on a really free basis. On the other hand, we have highlighted the methodological pertinence of such a reflection given that – as the passage on 'really free working' from the *Grundrisse* quoted above stated – the latter itself has as one of its determinations that of being a bearer of universal productive attributes, that is, capable of 'material production of a general character'. So far so good. But, as the reader will remember, the attribute of universality did not exhaust the determinations of the form of *productive* subjectivity with the immediate potentiality for 'really free working' (which, as I argued, should provide the material foundation of revolutionary *political* subjectivity). In the first place, the latter also entailed a process of material production whose general social character was immediately posited. This condition is present – at least tendentially – in the productive subjectivity of large-scale industry as developed in *Capital* too.[48] But, in addition, note that Marx's passage from the *Grundrisse* mentions that the universality of 'revolutionary' productive subjectivity must be the expression of a *scientific* consciousness, capable of organising work as 'an activity regulating all the forces of nature'. And here lies the crux of the matter.

Although the productive subjectivity of the worker of large-scale industry as presented in *Capital* tends to become universal, this universality is not the product of the *scientific expansion* of his or her capacity consciously to regulate the production-process, but of the increasing (eventually absolute) *deprivation* of all knowledge of the social and material determinations of the labour-process of which he or she is part. As we have seen above, for the workers engaged in the direct process of production, the separation of intellectual and manual labour reaches its plenitude. This kind of labourer can certainly work in any automated labour-process which capital puts before him or her, but not as the 'dominant subject' with 'the mechanical automaton as the object'. Rather, for those workers 'the automaton itself is the subject, and the workers are merely conscious organs, co-ordinated with the unconscious organs of the automaton, and together with

---

48. In the chapter on 'Machinery and large-scale industry', the tendency to expand the scope of the conscious regulation of the social character of labour co-exists with an opposite tendency to multiply the number of privately-mediated branches of the social division of labour, which is also the product of the movement of this form of production of relative surplus-value. See Marx 1976a, p. 572. But no reason is given for one or the other tendency to prevail. This occurs later in Marx's presentation, when he unfolds the determinations of the 'General law of capitalist accumulation'. There, the tendencies to the concentration and centralisation of capital show how the first tendency eventually imposes itself over the second.

the latter, subordinated to the central moving force'.[49] The scientific productive powers needed to regulate the forces of nature, and which are presupposed by their objectified existence in a system of machinery, are not an attribute that capital puts into the hands (or, rather, the heads) of direct labourers. In brief, in the figure of this wage-labourer bearing what, following Iñigo Carrera,[50] I term an absolutely *degraded productive subjectivity*, scientific consciousness and universality do not go together but are in opposition to one another. In other words, it is not this degraded productive subjectivity that, simply as such, carries in its immediacy the historical revolutionary powers that Marx himself considered necessary to make capital 'blow sky high'. Moreover, neither has Marx's exposition demonstrated that the very movement of the present-day alienated general social relation – capital-accumulation – leads to the social necessity to transform, in the political form of a revolution, the productive subjectivity of those labourers in the direction of their re-appropriation of the powers of scientific knowledge developed in this alienated form.

Yet, despite this insufficiency as an account of the material genesis of the revolutionary subject, it is here that Marx's exposition in *Capital* of the determinations of human productive subjectivity as an alienated attribute of the product of labour comes to a halt.[51] In the rest of Volume I (and the two remaining volumes), Marx no longer advances, in any systematic manner, in the unfolding of the material and social determinations of the revolutionary subject. From the point of the presentation reached, and after moving to the exteriority of the inner determinations of the production of surplus-value and to its reproduction, accumulation and the general law that presides over its movement, he just makes a gigantic leap into the conclusion contained in the chapter on the 'Historical tendency of capitalist accumulation', offering the following well-known account of the determinations leading to the abolition of the capitalist mode of production:

> Along with the constant decrease in the number of capitalist magnates, who usurp and monopolize all the advantages of this process of transformation, the mass of misery, oppression, slavery, degradation and exploitation grows; but with this there also grows the revolt of the working class, a class constantly increasing in numbers, and trained, united and organized by the very

---

49. Marx 1976a, pp. 544–5.
50. Iñigo Carrera 2003.
51. This statement needs qualification insofar as the creation of a surplus population relative to the needs of the accumulation process also constitutes a transformation of productive subjectivity produced by the development of large-scale industry. More concretely, it represents the most extreme case of material mutilation of the productive attributes of the working class, that is, not simply their degradation but their outright non-reproduction.

mechanism of the capitalist process of production. The monopoly of capital becomes a fetter upon the mode of production which has flourished alongside and under it. The centralization of the means of production and the socialization of labour reach a point at which they become incompatible with their capitalist integument. The integument is burst asunder. The knell of capitalist private property sounds. The expropriators are expropriated.[52]

If we leave aside the question of the misleading conflation between two *qualitatively different* (and, therefore, *analytically separable*) 'moments' of the revolutionary action of the working class contained in this passage – namely, the expropriation of the bourgeoisie and the abolition of capital – the question remains as to whether the determinations developed by Marx in the previous chapters suffice to justify the transition to this excessively simplistic and all too general account of the way 'the capitalist integument is burst asunder'.[53] Certainly, the tendency to the centralisation of capital discussed in the chapter on the 'General law of capital accumulation' does provide an exposition of the necessity behind the progressive socialisation of labour as an attribute of the capitalist form of private labour. But such an account stops short at the exteriority of the *quantitative determination* of the scope of consciously organised social labour without saying anything about the *qualitative transformations* of the productive subjectivity of the collective labourer that such an extension of the scale of the former presupposes. Seen from that perspective, I think that the transition to revolutionary subjectivity contained in the passage is definitely unmediated.

---

52. Marx 1976a, p. 929.

53. Whatever the ambiguities of Marx's formulation in the passage from the chapter on the historical tendency of capital-accumulation cited above, a cursory reading of his so-called 'political writings' makes evident that he was very clear about the 'unity-in-difference' between the expropriation of the bourgeoisie and the abolition of capital. To begin with, this is synthesised in the political programme of the working class to be implemented through the revolutionary 'conquest of political supremacy' contained in the *Communist Manifesto*, whose *immediate* economic content unequivocally comes down to the absolute centralisation of capital in the form of state-property (hence the abolition of the bourgeoisie) and the universalisation of the conditions of reproduction of the working class, but does not involve the abolition of the capitalist mode of production. See Marx and Engels 1976, pp. 92–3. As Chattopadhyay 1992, pp. 92–3, competently shows, for Marx the revolutionary conquest of political power together with the expropriation of the bourgeoisie were the *necessary forms* in which to *start* the process of transformation of the capitalist mode of production into the free association of individuals. But, unlike the conception found in Lenin and orthodox Marxism generally, Marx was very clear that the political rule of the working class 'does not by itself signify the collective *appropriation by society*, and does not indicate the end of *capital*' (Marx 1992c, p. 93). The 'dictatorship of the proletariat' was for Marx a *period within the capitalist mode of production* – hence, not a *non-capitalist transitional society* – in which capital was to be entirely revolutionised in every nook and cranny up to the point of fully preparing wage-workers for their self-emancipation – hence for their self-abolition as working class (Ibid.).

How are those workers whose productive subjectivity has been emptied of almost all content to organise the allocation of the total labour-power of society in the form of a *self-conscious* collective potency (the latter being what the abolition of capital is all about)? The growing 'misery, degradation, oppression and so on' certainly confront those labourers with particularly extreme *immediate* manifestations of the alienated mode of existence of their social being. Therefore, they could lead them to reinforce their collective resistance to capitalist exploitation by strengthening their relations of solidarity in the struggle over the value of labour-power. In themselves, however, those expressions of capitalist alienation have no way of transforming the class-struggle from a form of the reproduction of that alienation into the form of its fully self-conscious transcendence. From a materialist perspective, the question does not boil down to the will radically to transform the world, but to the objective existence of the material powers to do so. As Marx puts it in the *Holy Family*, it is about an 'absolutely imperative *need*' determined as 'the practical expression of *necessity*'.[54] The emergence of the social necessity underlying the historical constitution of the latter still involves the mediation of more revolutions in the materiality of the productive subjectivity of workers.

In this sense, I concur in general with those who claim that Marx's *Capital* is *incomplete*. However, this is not in the sense that the dialectic of capital needs to be complemented with that of class-struggle,[55] or with the political economy of wage-labour,[56] as if those latter aspects were not an inner moment of the former itself. Rather, I think that it is the very 'dialectic of capital' and, more concretely, the contradictory movement of the production of relative surplus-value through the system of machinery, that is in need of completion. Without this further exploration into the development of human productive subjectivity as an alienated attribute of social capital, a gap is bound to remain between the 'dialectic of human labour' unfolded in the relevant chapters of *Capital* and the revolutionary conclusions at the end of Volume I.

In the following section, I shall examine Marx's presentation of the determinations of the system of machinery in the *Grundrisse*. Although the complete *systematic* unfolding of the missing determinations is not there either, the main *elements* for such a further investigation of revolutionary subjectivity can be extracted from that text.

---

54. Marx and Engels 1975a, p. 37.
55. Shortall 1994.
56. Lebowitz 2003.

The *Grundrisse* and the system of machinery: in search of the missing link in the determinations of revolutionary subjectivity

As an entry-point to Marx's account of the system of machinery in the *Grundrisse*, let us return for a moment to our examination of the determinations of large-scale industry as presented in *Capital*. More concretely, let us go back to the relation between science and the production-process. Although this form of production of relative surplus-value entailed the general application of science as a productive force, the latter was not an attribute materially borne by those labourers engaged in direct labour in the immediate process of production. For them, that scientific knowledge took the form of an alien power already objectified in the machine. Marx notes this in the *Grundrisse* as well.[57]

Yet, as Marx puts it in the 'Results of the immediate production process', those scientific powers ultimately are themselves the products of labour.[58] Thus, although the *formal* subject of those powers – as happens with all the powers springing from the direct organisation of human co-operation – remains capital, the question immediately arises as to who is the *material* subject whose (alienated) *intellectual* labour develops the scientific capacities of the human species and organises their practical application in the immediate process of production. Having discarded manual labourers as such a productive subject, it would seem that the only alternative must be to turn our attention to the only remaining character present in the direct production-process, namely, the capitalist. Is it he or she who personifies, through the development of his/her productive consciousness and will, capital's need for the powers scientifically to control the movement of natural forces? The answer is given by Marx in a footnote to the chapter on 'Machinery and Large-Scale Industry' in *Capital*:

> Science, generally speaking, costs the capitalist nothing, a fact that by no means prevents him from exploiting it. 'Alien' science is incorporated by capital just as 'alien' labour is. But 'capitalist' appropriation and 'personal' appropriation, whether of science or of material wealth, are totally different things. Dr. Ure himself deplores the gross ignorance of mechanical science which exists among his beloved machinery-exploiting manufacturers, and Liebig can tell us about the astounding ignorance of chemistry displayed by English chemical manufacturers.[59]

Thus, it is not the capitalist who embodies the intellectual powers to develop the scientific knowledge presupposed by its objectified existence in a system of machinery. The science incorporated in the immediate production-process

---

57. Marx 1993, p. 693.
58. Marx 1976b, p. 1055.
59. Marx 1976a, p. 508.

is the result of the appropriation of the product of the intellectual labour of an 'other'. This 'other', whose productive activity the direct production-process of large-scale industry carries as a necessary mediation, is not explicitly present in Marx's exposition in *Capital*. There might be two reasons for this exclusion. First, because in Marx's time such a social subject was only beginning to develop. Second, and following from the previous point, because Marx's presentation in *Capital* is restricted to the transformations suffered by the productive subjectivity of those workers remaining in the direct production-process. However, what his whole discussion implicitly suggests is that among the transformations that large-scale industry brings about is the extension of material unity comprising its total labour-process outside the boundaries of the 'factory walls'.[60] Hence, the direct process of production becomes just an aspect of a broader labour-process which now entails two additional moments: the development of the power consciously to regulate in an objective and universal fashion the movement of natural forces – namely, science – and the application of that capacity in the practical organisation of the automatic system of machinery and whatever remains of direct labour – the technological application of science, including the consciousness of the unity of productive co-operation. Certainly, these other moments are also present in *Capital*.[61] However, Marx's presentation there seems to revolve around the emphasis on their separated mode of existence *vis-à-vis* the subjectivity of direct labourers and which is presupposed by their activity. By contrast, in the *Grundrisse* he oscillates between such an angle on the question[62] and one which puts at the forefront the underlying material unity of the total activity of living labour, where the development of science and its technological applications act as essential constitutive moments.[63] With the system of machinery:

> the entire production process appears as not subsumed under the direct skillfulness of the worker, but rather as the technological application of science. [It is,] hence, the tendency of capital to give production a scientific character; direct labour [is] reduced to a mere moment of this process.[64]

---

60. In this analysis of the further determinations of the production-process of large-scale industry, I follow the approach developed in Iñigo Carrera 2003, pp. 1–37.

61. Marx 1976a, p. 549.

62. Marx 1993, pp. 692–4.

63. Dunayevskaya 1989, pp. 80–6, correctly notes the difference in presentation between the account of the system of machinery in the *Grundrisse* – where the emancipatory potentialities of the system of machinery are considered – and the one in *Capital* – where its determination as a materialised expression of the domination of dead over living labour is emphasised. However, she wrongly attributes that to a change in Marx's view on the subject instead of as an account of *qualitatively different* potentialities engendered by the very same development of the system of machinery and personified by the different partial organs of the collective labourer.

64. Marx 1993, p. 699.

The determinations presupposed by the production of relative surplus-value involve the specification of commodity-owners into capitalist and wage-labourer. Having discarded the former as the material subject of scientific labour, it is self-evident that only those determined as doubly free individuals can personify the development of this moment of the production-process of large-scale industry. Thus, although not explicitly addressed by Marx, the benefit of historical hindsight makes it very easy for us to recognise how the total social capital deals with its constant need for the development of the productive powers of science, namely, by engendering a special partial organ of the collective labourer whose function is to advance in the conscious control of the movement of natural forces and its objectification in the form of ever more complex automatic systems of machinery. Whilst the system of machinery entails the progressive deskilling of those workers performing what remains of direct labour – to the point of emptying their labour of any content other than the mechanistic repetition of extremely simple tasks – it also entails the tendential *expansion* of the productive subjectivity of the members of the intellectual organ of the collective labourer. Capital requires from these workers ever more *complex* forms of labour.[65] As much as those discussed in *Capital*, these are also 'immediate effects of machine production on the worker'. Needless to say, inasmuch as this expanded productive subjectivity is nothing more than a concrete form of the production of relative surplus-value, the exercise of the newly developed intellectual productive powers is inverted into a mode of existence of capital in its movement of self-valorisation as well.[66]

In this alienated form, capital thereby produces a material transformation whose fundamental significance exceeds the production of wage-labourers simply bearing different productive attributes. What is at stake here is, first and foremost, a radical substantial transformation of the very nature of human

---

65. The so-called 'deskilling thesis', formulated in the seminal work by Braverman (Braverman 1998) is obviously a one-sided reduction of this *two-fold* movement of degradation/expansion of the productive subjectivity of the collective labourer required by the system of machinery to one of its moments. See Iñigo Carrera 2003, p. 32. One of the immediate reasons behind such a unilateral account lies, as Tony Smith points out, in its very restricted definition of 'skill', very much referring to *manufacturing* skills. See Smith 2000, p. 39.

66. That is, the productive powers of science take an alienated form not just *vis-à-vis* manual labourers, who face them already objectified in the system of machinery. Intellectual labourers also confront the development of science they themselves personify as an alien power borne by the product of their social labour. Moreover, the alienated nature of this development of intellectual labour is even expressed in its general scientific form, that is, in its method. In its determination as a form of the reproduction of capital, scientific knowledge is bound to represent natural and social forms as self-subsistent entities or immediate affirmations, and their relations as inevitably external ones. For an elaboration of this point, see the chapter in this book by Iñigo Carrera. See also Iñigo Carrera 1992 and Starosta 2003.

labour.[67] The latter progressively ceases to consist in the direct application of labour-power onto the object of labour with the purpose of changing its form. It now increasingly becomes an activity aimed at the conscious control of the movement of natural forces in order to make *them* automatically act upon the object of labour and, in this way, to effect its change of form. According to Marx's exposition of the system of machinery in the *Grundrisse*, *it is in the contradictory historical unfolding of this specific material transformation of human productive subjectivity that the key to the absolute limit to capital resides.*

> To the degree that labour-time – the mere quantity of labour – is posited by capital as the sole determinant element, to that degree does direct labour and its quantity disappear as the determinant principle of production – of the creation of use-values – and is reduced both quantitatively, to a smaller proportion, and qualitatively, as an, of course, indispensable but subordinate moment, compared to general scientific labour, technological application of natural sciences, on one side, and to the general productive force arising from social combination [*Gliederung*] in total production on the other side – a combination which appears as a natural fruit of social labour (although it is a historic product). *Capital thus works towards its own dissolution as the form dominating production.*[68]

To put it briefly, the issue here is the old question of the relation between intellectual and manual labour. More concretely, the fundamental point to grasp is the specifically capitalist form in which the antithetical movement of those two moments of living labour asserts itself with the development of the system of machinery. The revolutionary aspect of this historically-specific transformation of living labour in capitalist society is that both the scale and complexity of the production-process and, in particular, the increasingly scientific character of its organisation, make the subjectivity of the capitalist (the non-labourer) impotent to personify the now directly social labour under the rule of his or her capital. This means, in other words, that the development of the powers of intellectual labour and their exercise becomes an attribute of the 'labouring classes'.[69]

---

67. Iñigo Carrera 2003, p. 11.

68. Marx 1993, p. 700, my emphasis.

69. On the superfluity of the capitalist, see especially Marx's concise comments in *Theories of Surplus Value* (Marx 1989a, p. 499). The complexity and scale of the co-operation of the collective worker of large-scale industry render the subjective powers of the capitalist impotent to personify in the name of his or her capital even the unproductive labour of superintendence of the productive organs of the former. All the functions of supervision, coercion and management come to be personified by a partial organ of the collective labourer. See Marx 1976a, p. 549; and Marx 1991b, pp. 510–1. The parasitic nature of the capitalist, though not yet of capital, thereby becomes increasingly concrete. And note that this expresses an alienated necessity of the accumulation of social capital itself:

The scientifically-expanded productive subjectivity of intellectual labour is, by its own nature, increasingly general or universal. The exertion of this form of human labour-power aims at the expansion of the conscious control over the *totality* of the forces of nature. Moreover, this subordination of the latter to the powers of living labour involves the comprehension of their *general* determination in order thereby to develop their *particular* technological applications in ever-evolving systems of machinery. Thus, as Marx puts it in *Capital* Volume III of in order to highlight its specificity *vis-à-vis* co-operative labour, scientific labour is, by definition, universal labour.[70]

With the constitution and permanent revolutionising of this organ of the collective labourer, capital thereby engenders *another* tendency for the production of workers bearing a universal productive subjectivity. However, this universality is no longer the *empty* universality deriving from the absolute *lack* of individual productive capacities to which direct labourers are condemned. When developed into its plenitude, it becomes the rich, concrete universality of organs of a collective subject who become increasingly able consciously to rule their life-process by virtue of their capacity to scientifically organise the production-process of any automatic system of machinery and, therefore, any form of social co-operation on the basis of large-scale industry. As the productive subjectivity of workers expands, it progressively ceases to be the case that the worker's individuality vanishes 'as an infinitesimal quantity in the face of the science, the gigantic natural forces, and the mass of social labour embodied in the system of machinery'.[71] For the latter *are* the direct products of the objectification of their productive subjectivity:

> Nature builds no machines, no locomotives, railways, electric telegraphs, self-acting mules etc. These are products of human industry; natural material transformed into organs of the human will over nature, or of human participation in nature. They are *organs of the human brain, created by the human hand*; the power of knowledge, objectified. The development of fixed capital indicates to what degree general social knowledge has become a *direct force of production*, and to what degree, hence, the conditions of the process of social life itself have come under the control of the general intellect and been transformed in accordance with it. To what degree the powers of social production have been

the consumption of the capitalist represents a deduction of the potential surplus-value that could be devoted to its self-expansion. Incidentally, the confusion over the parasitic nature of the capitalist and that of the capital-form as such underlies Negri's views of the present, 'Post-Fordist' forms of human co-operation as carrying in their immediacy – that is, without the mediation of more material transformations – the potentiality to explode the capital-relation. See Negri 1992, pp. 65–8, and Negri 1999, pp. 156–60.

70. Marx 1991b, p. 199.
71. Marx 1976a, p. 549.

produced, not only in the form of knowledge, but also as immediate organs of social practice, of the real life process.[72]

We saw how in *Capital* Marx focused on the 'negative side' of the effects of production of relative surplus-value through the system of machinery upon the material forms of the productive subjectivity of the working class. The historical emergence of the social necessity for the constitution of a 'fully-developed social individual' thus appeared as an abstract possibility, whose connection to capital's development of machine-based production seemed to be completely external. Conversely, we can appreciate now how in the *Grundrisse* Marx posits capital's relentless tendency to 'call to life all the powers of science and of nature, as of social combination and of social intercourse'[73] as necessarily engendering the historical becoming of that concrete universal subjectivity itself.

> No longer does the worker insert a modified natural thing [*Naturgegenstand*] as a middle link between the object [*Objekt*] and himself; rather, he inserts the process of nature, transformed into an industrial process, as a means between himself and inorganic nature, mastering it. He steps to the side of the production-process instead of being its chief actor. In this transformation, it is neither the direct human labour he himself performs, nor the time during which he works, but rather the appropriation of his own general productive power, his understanding of nature and his mastery over it by virtue of his presence as a social body – it is, in a word, the development of the social individual which appears as the great foundation-stone of production and of wealth.[74]

Moreover, and here in accordance with *Capital*, he presents the latter as the one whose further expansion eventually clashes with its alienated capitalist social form and, therefore, as the material form of productive subjectivity that carries as an immediate potentiality the necessity for the 'creation of the new society'. Hence, Marx continues:

> The *surplus labour of the mass* has ceased to be the condition for the development of general wealth, just as the *non-labour of the few*, for the development of the general powers of the human head. With that, production based on exchange value breaks down, and the direct, material production process is stripped of the form of penury and antithesis.[75]

---

72. Marx 1993, p. 706.
73. Marx 1993, p. 706.
74. Marx 1993, p. 705.
75. Marx 1993, pp. 705–6.

It might seem that Marx is here substituting the intellectual labourer for the manual labourer as the revolutionary subject. However, the point is that the key does not consist in abstractly opposing intellectual and direct manual labour in order to privilege one over the other, but in grasping the contradictory forms in which capital historically develops these two necessary moments of the labour-process. Since Marx's exposition in the *Grundrisse* is only concerned with the *general* tendency and, more specifically, its historical result – that is, with the movement of 'bourgeois society in the long view and as a whole'[76] – he does not pay much attention to the contradictory forms in which the latter asserts itself. However, it is clear that in the historical unfolding of the tendency for the progressive objectification of all direct application of human labour-power onto the object of labour as an attribute of the machine, capital actually *reproduces and exacerbates* the separation between intellectual and manual labour.[77]

In effect, inasmuch as capital's conversion of the subjective expertise of the direct labourer (both intellectual and manual) into an objective power of the machine is not an instantaneous event but only done by degrees, every leap forward in the abolition of manual labour brought about by the revolution in the material forms of the process of production is realised by actually multiplying the spaces for the exploitation of manual living labour. In fact, the new technological forms themselves might generate as their own condition of existence the proliferation of a multitude of production-processes still subject to the manual intervention of the labourer, whether as an appendage of the machine, as a partial organ in a manufacturing division of labour or even in the form of 'domestic industry'. Thus, until the conditions for the (nearly) total elimination of manual labour are produced, direct labour as an appendage of the machine and/or the

---

76. Marx 1993, p. 712.

77. One of the central weaknesses of recent theories of 'immaterial labour' or 'cognitive capitalism', which heavily rely on the 'Fragment on machines', is their 'stageist' reading of that text. See, for example, Virno 2007; Lazzarato 1996; Vercellone 2007. In other words, those authors use those passages from the *Grundrisse* for a formalistic specification of a qualitatively different stage of capitalist development that is said to supersede not only large-scale industry but the real subsumption as well: the epoch of the 'general intellect'. Worse still, those theories unmediatedly – hence speculatively – apply the essential tendency and finished form described in the *Grundrisse* onto contemporary concrete forms of realisation that still represent its negation. The result is that they overlook or downplay the contradictory movement of expansion/degradation and universalisation/particularisation entailed by current material forms of the real subsumption. As we have seen, what the 'Fragment on machines' unfolds is not the abstract opposite of the determinations of the productive subjectivity of large-scale industry but their more concrete development. The significance of that undoubtedly essential text is therefore *systematic*. And, incidentally, so is that of the distinction between the three different forms of the real subsumption presented in *Capital* and that between formal and real subsumption. For a forceful case against the 'stageist' reading of those chapters of *Capital*, see Tomba 2007.

division of labour of manufacture tend to be reproduced under the new conditions and with even more degraded forms of productive subjectivity and harsher conditions of capitalist exploitation.[78]

Yet, it is certainly the case that this internal differentiation of the collective labourer on the basis of the respective forms of productive subjectivity is the self-negating form in which the *abolition* of that separation is realised in the historical process. Thus, through the very exacerbation of their separation, capital tendentially abolishes the qualitative and quantitative weight of manual labour in the process of the reproduction of social life, thereby converting the essential moment of living labour into an intellectual process. In this way, capital's transformation of the labour-process eventually reaches a point in which the separation between intellectual labour and what is now a quantitatively and qualitatively insignificant amount of manual labour, cannot materially obtain as a form of organising the life-process of humanity. The development of the material productive forces of society can only assert itself through the embodiment of the intellectual powers of social production in the individual subjectivity of every partial organ of the now directly social productive body. Moreover, this incorporation of the powers of the 'general intellect' into every individual worker must now have the form of objective social knowledge – namely, science – instead of being the product of the immediate subjective productive experience of the labourer (as was the case of independent handicraft-production). As we shall see below, it is the consciously organised political action of the *whole*

---

78. This is illustrated by Marx in section eight of the chapter on 'Machinery and large-scale industry' in *Capital*. There he shows how the production of relative surplus-value through the system of machinery reproduces modern manufacture, handicrafts and domestic industry. In this way, capital not only revolutionises the determinations of the social existence of those workers incorporated into large-scale industry but also of those of the sections of the working class still working under the division of labour in manufacture or domestic industry. The latter forms of the social production-process persist in their survival only through the imposition of the most brutal forms of the exploitation of the workers. However, Marx makes clear that the subsistence of manufacture and domestic industry is always provisional, even if it appears to hang on for long periods of time. The general tendency of capital is for the total development of large-scale industry. Moreover, Marx's discussion makes clear that the working class does not have to 'sit and wait' until the limit for the subsistence of manufacture is reached – a limit given by the extent to which the over-exploitation of labour-power compensates for its relative lower productivity of labour *vis-à-vis* large-scale industry. Inasmuch as the struggle for the shortening of the working day succeeds in forcing its implementation in the branches of production where manufacture persists, it accelerates the development of large-scale industry by not allowing the selling of labour-power below its value and, therefore, by reducing the capitalist limit to the introduction of machinery. Here we have a clear instance of the way in which progressive politics mediates revolutionary politics, the former being the concrete form of the development of the material determinations for the emergence of the latter.

working class – whatever its productive subjectivity – that is the necessary form in which this latter material transformation is realised.[79]

In its formally boundless movement of self-valorisation, capital therefore cannot stop in the historical production of universal productive subjects. At the same time, this constant revolution in the material forms of human productive subjectivity can only take place through the progressive socialisation of private labour, thereby positing the extension of the scope of the conscious regulation of directly social labour as an immediate necessity for capital's production of relative surplus-value. Thus, through the development of large-scale industry, capital works towards the historical emergence of the other precondition for 'really free working' as well:

> In the production process of large-scale industry...just as the conquest of the forces of nature by the social intellect is the precondition of the productive power of the means of labour as developed into the automatic process, on one side, so, on the other, is the labour of the individual in its direct presence posited as suspended individual, i.e., as social, labour. Thus the other basis of this *mode of production falls away*.[80]

On the two-fold basis of the expansion of the scientific productive powers of the 'social intellect' and of the determination of human labour as directly social, capital moves right towards reaching its absolute historical limit as a social form. This limit is not reached when capital-accumulation *ceases* to develop the material productive forces of society as, following Trotsky, orthodox Marxists would have it.[81] On the contrary, capital clashes with its limit when the very same alienated socialisation and scientific universalisation of the powers of human labour through the production of relative surplus-value begets, *as its own immanent necessity*, the development of the productive forces of society in a particular material form, namely: the fully conscious organisation of social labour as the *general* social relation regulating the reproduction of human life and, therefore,

---

79. Besides, it goes without saying that, although the workers bearing an expanded productive subjectivity express the *movement towards* the development of a universal individuality, they do so within the limits of capital as an alienated social form. In other words, it is not the *immediate actuality* of the material forms of their productive subjectivity that constitutes the kind of 'rich and all-sided individuality' discussed by Marx (1993, p. 325), As much as they are workers with a degraded productive subjectivity, they not only have to change 'society' but also undergo a process of self-change in the course of the revolutionary process. Hence, *both* organs of the collective labourer have to 'get rid of the muck of ages' imposed by the determination of human subjectivity as a concrete form of the reproduction of relative surplus-value. More concretely, this entails the *transformation* of intellectual labour (that is, of the mode of scientific cognition or the kind of scientific method) and its *generalisation*. See note 66 above.

80. Marx 1993, p. 709.

81. Trotsky 2002, pp. 1–2.

as an attribute borne by every singular productive subjectivity comprising the collective labourer. Under those circumstances, the further leap forward in the material productive forces of society – dictated by the most immediate neces- sity of capital itself, that is, the production of relative surplus-value – comes into conflict with capitalist relations of production. Translated into our mode of expression, this classical Marxian insight can only mean the following: the *alienated* social necessity arises for the human being to be produced as a pro- ductive subject that is fully and objectively conscious of the social determina- tions of his/her individual powers and activity. Thus, he or she no longer sees society as an alien and hostile potency that dominates him/her. Instead, he or she consciously experiences the materiality of social life (that is, productive co- operation) as the necessary condition for the development of the plenitude of his or her individuality, and therefore consciously recognises the social necessity of the expenditure of his or her labour-power in organic association with the other producers. However, this form of human subjectivity necessarily collides with a social form (capital) that produces human beings as *private and indepen- dent individuals* who consequently see their general social interdependence and its historical development as an alien and hostile power borne by the product of social labour. The determination of the material forms of the labour-process as bearers of objectified social relations can no longer mediate the reproduction of human life. *Capital-accumulation must therefore come to an end and give way to the free association of individuals*:

> But with the suspension of the *immediate* character of living labour, as merely *individual*, or as general merely internally or merely externally, with the pos- iting of the activity of individuals as immediately general or *social* activity, the objective moments of production are stripped of this form of alienation; they are thereby posited as property, as the organic social body within which the individuals reproduce themselves as individuals, but as social individuals. The conditions which allow them to exist in this way in the reproduction of their life, in their productive life's process, have been posited only by the his- toric economic process itself; both the objective and the subjective conditions, which are only the two distinct forms of the same conditions.[82]

Thus, it is the historically-determined necessity for the fully-developed and soci- alised universality of the productive subjectivity of the workers, beyond its capi- talist 'integument' but *generated as an immanent determination of the alienated movement of capital itself*, that is realised in the concrete form of the commu- nist revolution. This suggests that *the revolutionary political consciousness of the*

---

82. Marx 1993, p. 832.

working class can only be a concrete expression of their productive consciousness.[83] What the political action of the self-abolishing proletariat realises (its content) is, fundamentally, the transformation of the materiality of the productive forces of the human individual and, *therefore*, of their social forms of organisation and development. To put it differently, it is about a *material* mutation of the production-process of human life, which takes concrete shape through a transformation of its *social* forms which, in turn, expresses itself through a conscious *political* action, namely, a revolution. Thus, the issue here is not one of finding the external 'objective *conditions*' that trigger or facilitate the development of a self-determining political action, but of unfolding the inner or immanent material and social determinations of capital-transcending conscious practice. In other words, at stake here is the *content and form* of the necessity to abolish the capital-form.

To recapitulate, we can now appreciate the significance of the 'Fragment on machines' from the *Grundrisse*. Although clearly in an unsystematic fashion (after all, they are only research-manuscripts), that earlier version of the critique of political economy contains the elements for the systematic unfolding of the plenitude of the determinations that constitute the immanent *content* of capital-transcending transformative practice that *Capital* only partially achieves. However, it is actually the latter text that unfolds the necessity of its *form*, namely, the conscious political action of the whole working class. As we have seen, through the discussion of the factory-acts, Marx unfolds the determination of the political action of the working class as the necessary mediation, in the form of a consciously organised collective action, for the imposition of the *general* conscious regulation of social labour in the capitalist mode of production; that is, as a concrete form of the essentially *unconscious* – hence inverted – organisation of social life through the capital-form. But furthermore, we saw above that the struggle of wage-labourers as a class was also the necessary form in which social capital's need for workers with an increasingly universal productive subjectivity, resulting from the movement of the *real* subsumption in the form of large-scale

---

83. It also suggests that revolutionary action is an expression of an alienated subjectivity. In other words, the abolition of capital is not the product of an abstractly free, self-determining political action, but one that the workers are *compelled* to do as personifications of the alienated laws of movement of capital itself. See Iñigo Carrera 2003. What sets capital-transcending political action apart from capital-reproducing forms of the class-struggle is its specific determination as a collective action that is fully conscious of its own alienated nature, of personifying a necessity of social capital. However, by becoming conscious of their determination as a mode of existence of capital, revolutionary workers also discover the historic task that as fully conscious yet alienated individuals they have to undertake: the supersession of capital through the production of the communist organisation of social life. Revolutionary subjectivity therefore organises an alienated political action that in the course of its own development liberates itself from all trace of its alienated existence.

industry, asserted itself. True, in Marx's exposition in Chapter fifteen of *Capital* the class-struggle does not transcend its determination as a mediating moment of social capital's reproduction. This is because he does not unfold its immanent material content – the socialisation and universal development of human productive subjectivity – up to its absolute limit. But this is precisely what the *Grundrisse* do; that is, they do not unfold a *different* content but develop a more complex shape of that content itself. *A fortiori*, its concrete mode of realisation remains the same: the struggle of wage-labourers as a class. A struggle, however, that is no longer determined as form of capital's reproduction. As an expression of the plenitude of its content, the political action of wage-labourers now becomes determined as the mode of existence of capital-transcending human practice. Hence the general determination of the communist revolution: to be the political form taken by the historical production of the subjectivity of the 'rich individuality which is as all-sided in its production as in its consumption, and whose labour also therefore appears no longer as labour, but as the full development of activity itself'.[84]

Conclusions

This chapter has argued that, in their unity, the *Grundrisse* and *Capital* provide the elements for the scientific exposition of the determinations of capital leading to the social constitution of the revolutionary working class. This exposition must actually comprise the reproduction in thought of the concrete unity of *all* the determinations of social existence implied in the necessity for the abolition of capital, starting with its simplest form, namely, the commodity. However, for obvious reasons of space, the discussion centred on the specific form of capital that carries the necessity of its own supersession as an immediate potentiality. That form, this paper has argued, lies in the fully developed shape taken by the real subsumption of labour to capital: the system of machinery.

As we have seen, Marx's treatment of large-scale industry in *Capital* differs from the exposition he had initially formulated in his research-manuscripts known as the *Grundrisse*. This has led many scholars to see the two perspectives as somehow incompatible, maybe even reflecting a change of mind on the part of Marx, from an early optimistic view of the emancipatory potentialities of the forms of the real subsumption to a more pessimistic view of the latter as yet another expression of the despotic rule of dead over living labour. This paper has offered a different reading of this aspect of Marx's intellectual development. Whilst it is certainly true that Marx's exposition changed from the *Grundrisse* to

---

84. Marx 1993, p. 325.

Capital, this difference does not express two inconsistent views of the determinations of the productive subjectivity of large-scale industry. Rather, each text actually centres the exposition on the development of *one* of the *two essential contradictions* that characterise the most complex form of the real subsumption and whose development constitutes the immanent ground of revolutionary subjectivity. In *Capital,* the exposition focuses on the 'absolute contradiction'[85] between *particularity and universality* of the development of productive subjectivity, leading Marx to emphasise the material *degradation* of individuality of the wage-labourer of large-scale industry. By contrast, in the *Grundrisse* Marx focuses his attention on the development of the contradiction between the *intellectual and the manual* moments of the production-process under the rule of capital, leading him to unfold the tendency for the scientific *expansion* of the subjectivity of the doubly free labourer. Both contradictions are, however, two sides of the same coin: the alienated form in which human beings produce the materiality of their species-being at a certain stage of development and on the basis of specific historical presuppositions.[86]

> But it is an insipid notion to conceive of this merely *objective bond* as a spontaneous, natural attribute inherent in individuals and inseparable from their nature (in antithesis to their conscious knowing and willing). This bond is their product. It is a historic product. It belongs to a specific phase of their development. The alien and independent character in which it presently exists *vis-à-vis* individuals proves only that the latter are still engaged in the creation of the conditions of their social life, and that they have not yet begun, on the basis of these conditions, to live it.[87]

As we have seen, this development does not only involve the *formal* inversion between subject and product of social labour but also the *material* mutilation of the productive individuality of wage-labourers. However, Marx was also clear about the *relative historical necessity* of those forms, if only as a *vanishing moment* in the world-historical process of development of the materiality of 'really free working' and, hence, in the production of the necessity of their own supersession.[88]

---

85. Marx 1976a, p. 617.
86. Those historic presuppositions entail a degree of development of the productive individuality of the human being historically attaining 'adequate classical form' in the form of the *freedom and independence* of the *isolated* individual labour of the peasant and the artisan, that is, on the basis of the *dissolution* of all relations of personal dependence. See Marx 1976a, p. 927, and Marx 1993, p. 156. The material specificity of capital, which it formally achieves in an alienated form, consists, precisely, in the socialisation of free but isolated labour. Marx 1976a, p. 927.
87. Marx 1993, p. 162.
88. Ibid.

From the *Grundrisse* to *Capital* and Beyond: Then and Now

George Caffentzis

> In fact, however, they are the material conditions
> to blow this foundation sky-high.[1]
> This integument is burst asunder.[2]

This chapter is part Marxology (in remembrance of that volcanic eruption of Marx's carbuncle-inducing mental labour that resulted in the notebooks that we now know as the *Grundrisse*, or the *Foundations of a Critique of Political Economy* (*Rough Draft*)). It is also part contemporary conceptual history of the anti-capitalist movement's increasing 'techno-scepticism' (partly in honour of another eruption of anti-capitalist thought and action that took place here in the Political Science Institute at the University of Padova in the 1970s, especially the work of Maria Rosa Dalla Costa and Ferruccio Gambino).[3] By 'techno-scepticism', I mean a political attitude that questions the centrality of technological change in the struggle against capitalism. I will trace some parallels in Marx's thought between 1857 and 1882 and the succession of some themes in the anti-capitalist movement (with special reference to the US) between the 1960s and the present.

Inevitably, this effort is going to be somewhat subjective, verging on the autobiographical, and I do not claim to find either structural or causal reasons for the parallels, though the recognition of the limits to the

---

1. Marx 1973, p. 706.
2. Marx 1976a, p. 929.
3. This paper was first presented at the conference *Politica e mercato mondiale: a 150 anni dai Grundrisse*, held at the University of Padua, 11–12 January 2008.

revolutionary impact of the introduction of the products of mental labour into capitalist production are common to both.

I

Grundrisse: contradiction of capital or contradiction in the text?

The *Grundrisse* can be read teleologically, as a step on the way to *Capital*, or in its own right, as an exciting self-enclosed text, full of fascinating alternative lines of motion. Bruno Gulli contrasts these two approaches, attributing one to Negri, who claims that 'the *Grundrisse* is not a rough draft to be used for philological purposes, but a political text in its own right', and the other to Rosdolsky, who claims that the *Grundrisse* is a bold preparation for *Capital* (although 'one should not...exaggerate the similarity of the two works').[4]

Along with the *Grundrisse*'s excitement, which both Negri and Rosdolsky admire, however, is its obscurity and inconsistency. There are passages in the *Grundrisse* that genuinely pose the question: are we dealing with the dialectical contradictions of capital (typical of any would-be infinite totality) or the plain (finite) logical contradictions of Karl Marx?

One of the most important problems for understanding anti-capitalist revolution is the relationship between the two main revolution-producing 'tendencies' or 'laws' in the development of capitalism that Marx identifies in the *Grundrisse*: (i) the falling rate of profit;[5] and (ii) the 'breakdown' of the creation and measurement of wealth by labour and labour-time respectively.[6] They form the double, reiterated climax of the work, but are they consistent?

The first tendency is initially expressed in the *Grundrisse* as follows:

> Presupposing...*the same surplus labour in proportion to necessary labour*, then, the rate of profit depends on the relation between the part of capital exchanged for living labour and the part existing in the form of raw material and means of production. Hence, the smaller the portion exchanged for living labour becomes, the smaller becomes the rate of profit. Thus, in the same proportion as capital takes up a larger place as capital in the production process relative to immediate labour, i.e., the more the relative surplus-value grows – the value-creating power of capital – the more does the rate of profit fall.[7]

---

4. Gulli 2005, p. 76.
5. Marx 1973, pp. 745–58.
6. Marx 1973, pp. 690–712.
7. Marx 1973, p. 747.

Marx heaps encomiums on it: '[The law of falling rate of profit] is in every respect the most important law of modern political economy, and the most essential for understanding the most difficult relations'.[8] Moreover, Marx explicitly emphasises the revolutionary meaning of the 'law' or 'tendency' using the language of the 'integument' he was later to employ in *Capital*. For the law leads to 'the last form of servitude assumed by human activity, that of wage labour on the one side, capital on the other, [being] cast off like a skin....'.[9]

The second tendency or law is expressed in the 'Fragment on machines' in a variety of ways.[10] For example:

> The measure of wealth is then not any longer, in any way, labour time, but rather disposable time. Labour time as the measure of value posits wealth itself as founded on poverty... The most developed machinery thus forces the worker to work longer than the savage does, or than he himself did with the simplest, crudest tools.[11]
>
> As soon as labour in the direct form has ceased to be the great well-spring of wealth, labour time ceases and must cease to be its measure, and hence exchange value [must cease to be the measure] of use value.[12]
>
> To the degree that labour time – the mere quantity of labour – is posited by capital as the sole determinant element to that degree does direct labour and quantity disappear as the determinant principle of production – of the creation of use-values – and is reduced both quantitatively, to a smaller proportion, and qualitatively, as an, of course indispensable but subordinate moment, compared to general scientific labour, technological application or natural sciences, on the one side, and to the general productive force arising from social combination in total production on the other side – a combination which appears as a natural fruit of social labour (although it is a historic product). Capital thus works towards its own dissolution as the form dominating production.[13]

These passages (which could easily be multiplied) do not invite a common name in Marx's texts in the way that 'the falling rate of profit' does. But they clearly define the same temporal sequence: the increasing application of 'general scientific labour' significantly displaces direct labour in the production-process and labour-time as source and measure of wealth (and there is some slippage, here) either as use-value or exchange-value. Labour-value concepts become increasingly

---

8. Marx 1973, p. 748.
9. Marx 1973, p. 749.
10. Marx 1973, pp. 690–712.
11. Marx 1973, pp. 708–9.
12. Marx 1973, p. 705.
13. Marx 1973, p. 700.

inapplicable when applied to an expanding industrial capitalism. In other words, the labour theory of value is increasingly falsified by the development of large-scale industry. Thus, I will dub this law 'the increasing incommensurability of wealth and labour-time'.

What, then, is the relationship between these two tendencies? Is the falling rate of profit an index (or alternative expression) of the 'incommensurability'-tendency, or, does the falling rate of profit contradict and eventually erase the 'incommensurability' – tendency in Marx's thought?

The falling rate of profit and the increasing incommensurability-tendencies are clearly interconnected. The rise in the ratio (later to be called 'the organic composition') of fixed and circulating capital (later to be called 'constant capital') to necessary labour (later to be called 'variable capital') is crucial in the explication of both. The more large-scale industry (with the introduction of machinery and scientific techniques that displace the worker from the centre of the production-process) develops, the more the tendencies intensify simultaneously, though in different manners.

The falling-rate-of-profit tendency is intensified in large-scale industry because the mass of surplus-value created by the diminished number of workers relative to the machinery and investment in technique involved in production is relatively small. Even in the extreme case when the necessary labour-time goes to zero and the workday is expanded to twenty-four hours (and thus the maximum of the ratio between surplus- and necessary labour is reached) – workers 'live on air' and sleeplessly labour 'round the clock' (capital's paradise) – the increasing fixed and circulating capital will eventually end with a falling profit-rate (capital's inferno) due to the decreasing need for workers in the production-process.

Similarly, the incommensurability-tendency in large-scale industry is intensified because the necessary labour-time is dramatically reduced so that there could be a relative increase in surplus-value by the operation of machinery and scientifically developed technique. This reduction of necessary labour-time that could have led to an increased 'disposable' time instead leads to the imposition of a labour-market discipline that forces an extreme intensification and expansion of surplus-labour. However, most of the value of the products (even with the addition of necessary and surplus labour-time) is increasingly a result of transferred value in the course of production from the fixed and circulating capital. Hence, capital in the era of large-scale industry appears to be the 'source' of value.

The introduction of machinery and 'materially creative and objectifying science' to production seems to lead to *both* the incommensurability of labour-time and value *as well as* to the falling rate of profit. Are these two tendencies merely two sides of the same coin? This apparent coherence of the falling rate of profit and the incommensurability-tendencies, however, is problematic. *For the falling rate of profit depends upon the functioning of labour-time as the measure of value.* After all, the rate of profit is a ratio between values that are determined by labour-time, otherwise they would not have the character and fate that they do.

If the commensurability of value and labour-time were abrogated, then there would be no reason to give the legitimacy and centrality to the falling rate of profit. This can be seen in the twentieth-century efforts to 'Sraffa-ise' Marx's critique of political economy and to apply the Okishio theorem as a rebuttal of the tendency.[14] Both Sraffa's and Okishio's supporters reject the labour-time measure of value and opt for a 'commodity-equivalent' conception of value (the value of a commodity is simply the amount of an index-commodity for which it exchanges). Sraffa and his supporters, in their commodity-equivalent effort, go the way of the 'vulgar economists' who, according to Marx, 'assume the value of one commodity...in order in turn to use it to determine the values of other commodities'.[15] Thus, instead of a labour-theory of value, they use the symmetry of the algebraic equations describing the input-output relations of an economy to point out that labour (whose 'price' is wages) need not provide the value-dimension; any other commodity that enters into all branches of production could do so as well, such as iron or oil. In so doing, Okishio, echoed by Sraffa's supporters, argues that increasing productivity would not lead to a 24-hour limit per worker on the surplus (however physically productive the worker is); the surplus-products per worker would be expandable indefinitely and consequently the rate of profit would be growing with the increasing introduction of machinery and scientific knowledge to production instead of declining.

Consequently, the incommensurability-tendency is logically contrary to the falling rate of profit. If labour-time fails to be a measure of the value of commodities, labour-power and capital, then the falling rate of profit loses its legitimacy and plausibility. These two climatic endings of the *Grundrisse* pose one overwhelming question: will capitalism be destroyed by the loss of measure or by the loss of profitability?

Capital and the disappearance of the incommensurability-tendency

In order to answer this question from Marx's perspective, we should study the fates of these two tendencies in the post-*Grundrisse* period of Marx's writing. And their fates *are* quite different. The law or tendency of the falling rate of profit becomes a basic element in the analysis of capitalism (and its demise)

---

14. Kliman 2007, pp. 44–5.
15. Marx 1976a, p. 174.

while the 'incommensurability-tendency' simply disappears in all the volumes of *Capital*. This disappearance is startling, yet Marxist scholars do not often note it. Thus Ernest Mandel claims, 'the essential contributions to the development of Marxist theory... are to be found in the *Grundrisse*'.[16] But though he praises what I have been calling the 'incommensurability-tendency', he does not note its absence in Marx's post-*Grundrisse* works.

The reason for the increasing prominence of the law of the falling rate of profit is clear and can be summarised in the words that end the part of *Capital* Volume III devoted to the law: 'Hence crises'.[17] Marx saw in the law of the falling rate of profit the internal *a priori* evidence for the finitude of capitalism: 'The barriers to the capitalist mode of production show themselves... in the way that the development of labour productivity involves a law, in the form of the falling rate of profit, that at a certain point confronts this development itself in a most hostile way and has constantly to be overcome by way of crises.[18]

The incommensurability-tendency, being incompatible with the law of the falling rate of profit as noted above, was inevitably pushed out of the logical space of Marx's categorical development in the decade after the writing of the *Grundrisse* notebooks. Indeed, the increasing saliency of the falling rate of profit led to the importance of the *commensurability* of value and labour-time. In any event, Marx began his mature published work on the critique of political economy, *Capital* Volume I, by reaffirming the value-creating power of labour and the appropriateness of labour-time as the measure of the value of commodities. He seemed to have no questions about the labour-theory of value.

Was the incommensurability-tendency completely erased from Marx's thought after the *Grundrisse*? No, but it mutated in an ingenious way. Instead of being antagonistic to the falling rate of profit, it was transformed into an essential preliminary for the law. Since the law is, more precisely stated, the fall in the *general or average* rate of profit, the incommensurability-tendency reappears in *Capital* Volume III, Chapter nine, 'Formation of a general rate of profit (average rate of profit) and transformation of commodity values into prices of production' as a way of understanding how a general or average rate of profit throughout a capitalist system can be realised even though individual firms and branches of industry have radically different organic compositions, hence different individual rates of profit.[19]

I make this claim because it is exactly in this chapter that Marx declares the labour-theory of value to be apparently false (which is the essence of the

---

16. Mandel 1971, p. 102.
17. Marx 1981, p. 375.
18. Marx 1981, p. 367.
19. Marx 1981, pp. 254–72.

incommensurability-tendency) and yet he also claims that it operates to the letter the more machinery and the products of mental labour enter into commodity-production! In other words, in this chapter labour-time is rejected as the measure of the price of commodities (a version of the incommensurability-tendency), especially when there is a great dispersion of organic composition and labour-productivity (which inevitably will happen in capital's effort to counter the tendency of the falling rate of profit), and, at the same time, labour-time is vindicated as the measure revealing the inner essence of the system. In other words, in the transformation of commodity-values into prices of production the incommensurability-thesis is preserved and finally made compatible with the falling-rate-of-profit tendency. If the value-to-price-of-production transformation did not occur, the high organic-composition industries would suffer from inadequate profit-rates and would be unable to develop into a hegemonic presence in production. Indeed, the transformation makes it possible for there to be electricity-generating nuclear power-plants that successfully realise an average rate of profit (on the basis of an enormous investment in fixed and circulating capital), even though the workers within them create a tiny fraction of the surplus-value created by workers in a typical sweatshop.

This peculiar metamorphosis of the incommensurability-tendency clearly expressed both the reasons why Marx thought that capitalism could survive in the face of class-struggle (by applying technical and scientific knowledge to transform the conditions of production resulting in the displacement and division of workers) and at the same time why capitalism was continually confronting barriers to its survival of its own making. It also showed the objective unity of the capitalist class in the face of individual capitalists' competitive struggle with each other. Indeed, one can see in this 'communal sharing' of surplus-value an essential element in the creation of the capitalist class. Finally, without such a transformation, capitalism would have largely never had gotten 'off the ground' of absolute surplus-value production, since the occasional forays into relative surplus-value production could not be sustained because the profit-rates in return would have been abysmally low. Hence it could not have survived the success of the working-class struggle to shorten the workday.

This is my structural argument for the rejection/inclusion of the incommensurability-thesis in *Capital*. I also have a biographical narrative to accompany the structural transformation of the incommensurability-tendency to the transformation of values into prices. In 1857–8, Marx saw that a breakdown was looming due to the increasing use of science, technology and other products of the 'general intellect'. In effect, Marx's position at that time was similar to that of his critics in the falling rate of profit and 'transformation'-debates of the future: the labour-time measure becomes increasingly inadequate, as there is an increase in the dispersion of organic composition due to the application of machinery and scientific technique. After all, is this not the point of the Okishio theorem and 'Marx killers' from Böhm-Bawerk to the present? If there is a relatively low dispersion of organic composition, the 'problem' of transforming values into prices of production and surplus-value into profit is resolved immediately in favour of the labour-time analysis. But inevitably the dispersion increases because as the class-struggle intensifies (especially around the length of the working day and the creation of absolute surplus-value) and capital reacts by investing in relative surplus-value generating technology, it also develops branches of industry that have a low organic composition. As Marx writes: '[N]ew branches of production open up, particularly in the field of luxury consumption, which precisely take this relative surplus population as their basis, a population often made available owing to the preponderance of constant capital in other branches of production; these base themselves in turn on a preponderance of the element of living labour, and only gradually pass through the same trajectory as other branches'.[20]

Indeed, one might say that as a corollary of the law of the falling rate of profit and its counter-tendency, a new law develops: the law of the ever greater dispersion of organic compositions and the ever greater average difference between values and prices of production. This opening up of new low organic-composition industries is an important feature of contemporary 'globalising' capitalism. This capacity implies that capital has ways of escaping the falling rate of profit and eternalising itself through a form of 'bad infinity'. Capital's success in finding this 'way out' of the falling rate of profit conundrum (by balancing the effects of scientific or cognitive labour with the exploitation of direct living labour) has been an important source for the anti-capitalist movement's techno-scepticism of the late twentieth and early twenty-first century, as I will argue in the second part of this chapter.

But as Marx developed his understanding of the *holistic* meaning of the transformation and the importance of the tendency of the falling rate of profit (that must periodically bring about crises and ever 'new enclosures'), he realised that it is only through the action of the labour-time measure and the living-labour creation of value that there is any reason to believe that capitalism is not an eternal idea like space, time, self, nature, history and the absolute, stuffed with self-reflexive contradictions, but historically unlimited. It is only because value is created by labour and measured by labour-time that capital is its own barrier and creates a transfer of value within the system that is ever more ruinous to most workers and, yes, even to most would-be capitalists.

---

20. Marx 1981, p. 344.

Chapter nine of *Capital* Volume III is famous (or infamous) for its simultaneous critique *and* vindication of the labour-theory of value. In the days before the publication of *Capital* Volume I, Marx understood this chapter to be something of a trap awaiting for 'philistines' and 'vulgar economists' who would read *Capital* Volume I's vindication of the labour theory of value and cry foul:

> Here it will be shown how the philistines' and vulgar economists' *manner of conceiving things* arises, namely, because the only thing that is ever reflected in their minds is the immediate form of appearance of relations, and not their inner connection. Incidentally, if the latter were the case, we would surely have no need of science at all. Now if I wished to refute all such objections in advance I should spoil the whole dialectical method of exposition. On the contrary, the good thing about this method is that it is constantly setting traps for those fellows which will prove them into an untimely display of their idiocy.[21]

Some would argue that Marx, the trapper, was trapped by the transformation, but for him it explained capitalism's 'inner connection' that made it a totality of sorts. This, in effect, meant that a worker was exploited not only by an individual boss, but by the whole capitalist class that allocated the surplus-value the worker created according to capital's 'justice' (those with more invested capital receive a larger profit). Conversely, when one struggles against one's boss, one is taking on the whole capitalist class. But one could only understand this transformation by stepping out of capital's totalising perspective and abandoning capital's assumption that it is the main agent of value-creation. For an individual capitalist, 'imprisoned' by competition and workers' demands, is not able to do this:

> [The transformation of surplus-value] is important for him in so far as the quantity of surplus-value created in his own branch intervenes as a co-determinant in regulating the average profit. But this process takes places behind his back. He does not see it, he does not understand it, and it does not in fact interest him ... [However] [w]ith the transformation of values into prices of production, the very basis for determining value is now removed from view.[22]

This class 'blind spot' is to be expected, but economists (both vulgar and not so vulgar) are also blindsided by this process: 'all economics up till now has either violently made abstraction from the distinctions between surplus-value and profit, between rate of surplus-value and rate of profit, so that it could retain the determination of value as its basis, or else it has abandoned, along with this determination of value, any kind of solid foundation for a scientific approach,

---

21. Marx and Engels 1987, p. 390.
22. Marx 1981, p. 298.

so as to be able to retain those distinctions which obtrude themselves on the phenomenal level'.[23]

One thing is sure, for Marx in *Capital* the ever-growing introduction of machinery and scientific technique into commodity-production does not change the fact that labour-time remains the measure of commodity-production. The image of revolution in *Capital* is not an 'invasion of the future', led by the introduction of mental labour in production. The revolution will have to come from 'inside' the class-struggle that is ruled by the creative power of *all* living labour (both mental and manual, cognitive and non-cognitive) and is measured by labour-time. Indeed, in the 1870s, after the bloody defeat of the Paris Commune, Marx even begins to enlist the forces of still existing fragments of 'primitive communism' throughout the planet!

II

Whatever happened to zerowork?

Marx's changing evaluation of the role of science and technology in the end of capitalism from the *Grundrisse* to *Capital* that I sketched out in Part I has a parallel in the historical metamorphosis in the anti-capitalist movement from the 1960s until today. For this movement in the 1960s was affected by both the dominant empirical trends and the capitalist discourse of the time. The trends were clear: from the mid-1800s to the mid-1900s, there was a dramatic increase of real wages and a decrease in the working day. Indeed, in the case of the US, if those trends continued through to the end of the twentieth century, the workday would have gone to less than thirty hours a week and real wages would have been twice what they are today.

The simple induction of past trends into the future stimulated a series of epithets that would describe the society being shaped by these trends, e.g., the leisure society, the affluent society, the society of abundance, the era of zerowork, and the post-scarcity society. A whole planning literature developed around what was considered inevitable: a dramatic increase in 'free', 'disposable', and 'leisure' time for the average worker due to the application of science and technology (what at that time was called 'automation' or, less frequently, 'cybernation'). Sociologists, 'futurologists', and social thinkers of the 'mass-society' saw this development as *the* problem of the early twenty-first century. For example,

---

23. Marx 1981, pp. 268–9.

A.R. Martin, Chairman of the 'American Psychiatric Association Committee on Leisure Time and its Use', claimed:

> We must face the fact that a great majority of our people are [sic] not emo-
> tionally and psychologically ready for free time. This results in unhealthy
> adaptations which find expression inn a wide range of sociopathological and
> psychopathological states. Among the social symptoms of this maladoption to
> free time are: low morale, civilian unrest, subversiveness and rebellion.[24]

Robert Theobald, who quoted Martin, ended his essay, 'Cybernetics and the problems of social reorganization', with a more hopeful message of liberation: 'Man will no longer need to toil: he must find a new role in the cybernetics era which must emerge from a new goal of self-fulfillment'.[25] Indeed, Theobald, a major proponent of the guaranteed-income proposal in the 1960s, was one of the 'players' in now quaint-sounding discourse on 'the end of work'.

This discourse came from both capitalists and critics of capitalism. For exam-ple, the Students for a Democratic Society's manifestoes of the time expressed problematics similar to those of Theobald and his fellow establishment-authors (like Admiral Hyman Rickover) in the book *The Social Impact of Cybernetics*. The AFL-CIO took a similar position. At its 1961 convention, it adopted the following policy: 'Reduction in standard hours of work with no loss of pay should be sought as a vital part of our total program to solve the problem of unemployment, to convert our rapid technological progress into a boon rather than a burden, and to bolster the long-term economic and social health of our society'.[26]

Critics of capitalism isolated automation and the reduction of the workday as an inevitable product of capitalist industrial development that was having immediate consequences for workers (especially black workers) who were 'struc-turally' unemployed (that is, they could not find employment due their lack of skills to hold jobs in the occupations that are offering employment). There was, of course a debate around this claim and many 'nay-sayers' arose to claim that automation and cybernation was not the source of the decline in the workweek or in the increasing unemployment in manufacturing.[27]

Indeed, the impact of the *Grundrisse* (which was only made available in West-ern Europe in 1953) during the late 1950s and 1960s was accentuated by Marx's apparent ability to foresee the arrival of a sort of twilight-capitalism (with the workweek declining and workers' 'free time' becoming a problem for capital). Passages from the *Grundrisse* like the following had an almost prophetic character

---

24. Quoted in Theobald 1966, p. 56.
25. Theobald 1966, pp. 68–9.
26. Quoted in Francois 1964, p. 119.
27. See Silberman 1966.

in the eyes of many in the anti-capitalist movement of the time: 'The development of fixed capital indicates to what degree general social knowledge has become a direct force of production, and to what degree, hence, the conditions of the process of social life itself have come under the control of the general intellect and been transformed in accordance with it'.[28]

Marx of the *Grundrisse*, after being identified as the visionary of the universalisation of Manchester's Satanic mills, became the ancestral theorist of the era of zerowork. As a co-editor of *Zerowork I*, a journal partly founded on the application of the 'Fragment on machines' to the present, I can testify that I was not alone in experiencing the dramatic impression the *Grundrisse* had on politics and conceptual framework in the early 1970s (the first complete English translation of the *Grundrisse* by Martin Nicolaus was published in 1973). It was both disturbing and salacious, like discovering a hidden life of someone you had thought you had known intimately. The old mole had sprung from his hole to become a shining cyborg in the sky with diamonds!

Many times, however, major social trends begin to dissipate at the very moment that they become the source of large-scale and acrimonious debates. This is what happened to discussion about the ever-shortening workweek that many supposed to be caused by automation and cybernetics. After falling steadily for almost a century (roughly from 1850 to 1940), the work-week in the US stabilised and stagnated at about 40 hours a week since 1950. A similar reversal of a long-term trend also appeared in the early 1970s: the real wage, which steadily grew from the depression to 1974, began to decline and then stagnate until today.[29] Indeed, one can divide the post-WWII era in the US into two epochs: (i) 1945–75, with the work-day stagnant and the real wages increasing; (ii) 1975 to the present: the work-day stagnant and real wages stagnant. (Indeed, the notion that workers 'accepted' a tacit class-deal that rejected further reductions in labour-time in exchange for increasing 'consumption', though plausible for epoch (i), becomes positively ridiculous for epoch (ii)).

The disappearance of the two major wages-and-hours trends that formed the essence of the claims of the impact of technology and science in the strategic debates of the time took quite some time to appreciate, much less predict and explain in the 1960s. Some economists like Herbert Northrup and Edward Denison argued then that capital's ability to respond to decreases in the work-day with increases in economic growth had come to an end, hence further reduction of the work-week would lead to a reduction of the rate of profit.[30] Or, in Marxist terms, the ability of capital to replace a reduction of absolute surplus-value by

---

28. Marx 1973, p. 706.
29. Wolff 2002.
30. Northrup 1966, and Denison 1962.

an increase in relative surplus-value was reaching an inflection-point of exhaustion. But the majority opinion of the time was in agreement with Keynes's earlier prediction that capitalists, with the increasing investment in scientific methods of production, would gradually 'provide' a sumptuous standard of living for the working class and be agreeable to a one to two percent profit-rate by the time of his grandchildren (circa 1990)!

These erroneous predictions of the consequences of techno-science of both the US left and right in the 1960s were followed by a suspicion towards the work-liberating power of technology and science in subsequent decades going down to the present. This has not had anything to do with the stagnation of the general intellect's activity, given the remarkable development of genetic engineering, the computer-industry, and robotics since the 1960s. It is often claimed that the main reason for this techno-scepticism was due to the ecology-movement's critique of capitalism's externalisation of the costs of production and its apparent drive to global apocalypse. Once these external costs are brought into the equation, the introduction of scientific methods of production are often shown to be profitable just as long as the health- and environmental damage from the waste created by them are absorbed by those who make no claims on the polluting company. Indeed, if there was to be a pollutionless production and a genuine effort to 'save the planet' from the various apocalyptic consequences of capitalist accumulation, there would have to be a dramatic reduction in the use of high-tech production-processes (like nuclear reactors) and, in fact, a possible reversal of the reduction of the working day. Nature seems to be antagonistic to the reduction of work.

This ecological explanation of the increasing impact of the suspicion of science and technology in the anti-capitalist movement has its virtues. But there is another explanation for this political and ideological development that comes from the centre of the Marxist tradition – labour. One of the first signs of scepticism towards the claims of 'zerowork' about the consequences of the introduction of science and technology into production was expressed politically by a reconceptualisation of the workday that was initiated by the feminist movement, especially the theorist-activists of the wages-for-housework campaign.[31]

In the midst of the excitement brought about by the rediscovery of the *Grundrisse's* Marxism of the future, Dalla Costa, James, Federici and others asked: who is responsible for the unpaid part of the working day? Is it only the workers in the office, factory or field? Does the unpaid labour-portion of the working day not also include the labour that is required for the reproduction of the waged labourer? This unaccounted-for value-creating labour goes on outside the office,

---

31. Dalla Costa and James 1973; Federici 1974.

factory or field, but, when properly accounted for, it dwarfs the surplus-value produced by waged labour. Women, of course, do the bulk of this labour in the US and around the world. Once one introduces this labour into the equation of wages and profits, then one begins to see that the introduction of the general intellect into production does not have the consequences conceived by political readers of the *Grundrisse*. It was a 24-hour housework-day (largely involved with work that was familiar to women centuries and even millennia before) meeting zerowork! Indeed, this paradox (or, more frankly, contradiction) was at the centre of the political project that launched the journal, *Zerowork*, in 1975.

One of the ironic consequences of this reconceptualisation of the working day was the revaluation of the labour-theory of value, i.e., the theory that defines labour as the creator of value and labour-time its measure. But as in many resurrections, the revived being is quite different from his/her/its former self. The key form of labour in this revival is one that Marx never really considered, the reflexive labour of labour-power production and reproduction. Marx, whenever he did consider the production and reproduction of that most metaphysical of commodities, became quite physicalistic (in Kliman's sense): 'the value of labour-power is the value of the means of subsistence necessary for the maintenance of its owner'.[32] This literally came down to the value of the commodities used in the process of reproduction ... not in the labour of reproduction itself. Marx's basic oversight was as deep as the political economists' impossible concept of 'the value of labour', which, he was fond of saying, was a category-mistake on the order of a 'yellow logarithm'.

Once one introduces the labour-time involved in the reproduction of labour-power, the so-called possibility of zerowork begins to look ever more distant, since the machines to decrease the work of giving birth, parenting children and caring for the sick and dying is not likely to be produced anytime soon, whatever the promises of the genetic engineers and the pharmaceutical researchers.

Indeed, what was increasingly discovered though the 'discovery of housework' was *the manifold of work*, having many aspects that were excluded from the official list of waged, contractually recognised, 'free' occupations and employments. A whole range of unwaged, uncontracted for, incidental, criminal and often coerced labour needs to be introduced to begin to understand the manifold forms of work in capitalist society. For example, one must introduce the often unconscious body-work done in absorbing the toxic wastes injected into the environment by the capitalist production-process into the notion of work. One should also introduce the quasi-slave labour done in criminal enterprises that in various parts of the capitalist world are the dominant form of labour. The

---

32. Marx 1976a, p. 274.

discovery of this manifold opened up a new world of struggle and working-class organisation in the last thirty years.[33]

On the other side, capital saw in these manifold forms of work that it was recognising (often through the work of working-class militants) as a new source of accumulation. A most important focus for this effort was in new low organic-composition industries based on the production and reproduction of the body and the soul. Instead of leaving this area wageless and its providers indirectly and informally provisioned by the waged workers reproduced, a whole set of 'service' – industries began to develop in the 1970s and 1980s that soon became important branches of industry. This was due, of course, to the struggle women were making to reject their wageless status and provides a classic example of how capital transforms working-class demands into engines of accumulation. This development was centred in the region of low organic-composition industry that was exactly required by the counter-tendency of the law of the falling rate of profit and of the increasing dispersion of organic composition that I cited above.

This counter-tendency ended in the new division of labour that had 'service-work' increasingly dominating manufacturing and agriculture, where by 'service-work' is meant the labour of reproducing capital (clerical and information-based regulative and supervisory work) and of reproducing workers (from restaurant-cooks to hospice-nurses). This transformation made it possible to keep unemployment rates in the US, at least, within historical averages, to keep the work-week unchanged, and to control the real wage even though the relative size of the manufacturing and agricultural sectors of the work-force in the US has dramatically reduced. The 1960s alarms concerning the tsunami of unemployment that was to have been unleashed by automation and cybernetics have thus been proved wrong in the twenty-first century.

At the same time, along with this discovery of a new world of labour came a semantic explosion of new descriptions of labour from 'reproduction labour' to 'affective labour' to 'immaterial labour' to 'cognitive labour' and whole new sciences of labour (beyond the elements of Taylorism). Economists like Nobel-prize winner Gary Becker introduced the conceptual and strategic transformations (acceptable for capital's ideology and strategic science) needed to bring reproduction-work into the purview of accumulation. They did for capital what theorists of the wages-for-housework campaign and other feminist thinkers like Maria Mies did for the anti-capitalist movement.[34] Becker and his followers saw those working outside of the wage-labour market as in field of proxy values or 'shadow prices', constantly comparing the opportunity-costs of not taking a

---

33. For more on this theme, see Staples 2006.
34. Caffentzis 1999.

waged job with the utility of their wageless work for themselves or their family-unit (whatever and whoever that includes). On either side of the class-divide, however, there was a recognition that the notion and reality of the manifold forms of work had tremendously increased and that the key value being pro-duced in a capitalist economy was not cars, iron or even computers. Rather, *it was the power to create value.*

This double recognition certainly put work back on the agenda in the 1970s and beyond. It showed why the so-called reduction of the work-day that was achieved in the century between 1848 and 1948 was not exactly what it was pre-sented as by either capitalist or anti-capitalist thinkers (that is, as a progressive liberation of the working class from work). Once one brings the manifold forms of work to the foreground, the official class-struggle around the working day (codified by law), presumably driven by the introduction of the products of the general intellect into production, becomes much more articulated. A reduction of the working day in the large factories often means the exact opposite for the houseworkers, the bathroom-cleaners, the drug-runners, the call-centre respond-ers and the indentured agricultural workers of the world. In fact, given the 'law of the increasing dispersion of organic composition', every increase in the intro-duction of science and technology matched by an increase in the organic com-position of one branch of industry will lead to an equivalent increase in the introduction of low organic-composition production in other branches of indus-try. Therefore, the introduction of science and technology into production (so eloquently described by Marx 150 years ago in the *Grundrisse*) will not lead to the explosion of capital's foundation. Therefore, the main way to put capitalism into crisis is to block its ability to evade the consequences of the falling rate of profit, by making it difficult to exploit workers in low organic-composition industries. However expressed, this insight has become one of the starting points of the contemporary anti-capitalist movement: suspicion of the work-liberating powers of science and technology.

Conclusion: The image of revolution from the *Grundrisse* to *Capital*

Marx's two images of revolution – the external explosion of the foundations in the *Grundrisse* and the burst integument in *Capital* Volume I – that are expressed by the two epigraphs at the beginning of the paper can now be understood both from his perspective and ours. The first image of capitalism being driven to cre-ate the forces of science and technology to escape capitalist class-competition and working-class struggle only to destroy its 'limited foundation' in the end was compelling to the isolated Marx who was watching the system's monetary and commercial crisis in 1858 with growing, but solitary excitement. By 1867, the scene had dramatically shifted; the forces at work were not the external work-ings of the system driven by the introduction of science and technology into production, but a working class that was inside the system, threatening to burst out of capital's desiccated skin. Marx was no longer waiting for the revolution 'ex Machina'; he was experiencing it in the flesh again.

This interpretation is supported by the fact that after the defeat of the Paris Commune, instead of piously waiting for the maturation of the general intellect, Marx began to study the world of already existing communalism throughout the planet (not just the dying embers in Britain and Western Europe).[35] Indeed, the scene had shifted from the glistening superhuman machines of the *Grundrisse* to the Russian *obschina*! In fact, the last sentence in Marx's last published writing in 1882 (the 'Preface' to the second Russian edition of the *Communist Manifesto*) was the following: 'If the Russian Revolution becomes the signal for a proletar-ian revolution in the West, so that the two complement each other, the present Russian common ownership of land may serve as the point of departure for a communist development'.[36]

Marx's third image of revolution, a resurrection of pre-capitalist communal-ism, has a similar political echo in the late twentieth century in the re-evaluation of the struggles for already existing commons that can be traced in the anti-capitalist political and theoretical developments of the last two decades.[37] But this is a matter for another discussion.

---

35. Shanin 1983.
36. Shanin 1983, p. 139.
37. See, for example, De Angelis 2006; Federici 2004; Linebaugh 2008.

Part Five

Competition, Cycles and Crisis

The Whole and the Parts: The Early Development of Marx's Theory of the Distribution of Surplus-Value in the *Grundrisse*

Fred Moseley

I have argued in several recent papers that Marx's theory is based on the fundamental quantitative premise that the total amount of surplus-value is determined logically prior its division into individual parts (equal rates of profit, commercial profit, interest, and rent).[1] In other words, the *production of surplus-value* is

---

1. To clarify what I mean by the 'prior determination of the total surplus-value': *in any given period*, the total surplus-value is determined prior to its division into individual parts (the average profit of individual industries, commercial profit, interest, and rent). In other words, the total surplus-value is *not* determined by first determining these individual parts and then adding them up. The total surplus-value is determined by the total surplus-labour of the given period, and is then divided into these individual parts according to certain rules. It may be that the total surplus-value of a given period is affected by the distribution of surplus-value in previous periods. For example, the division of the total surplus-value in previous periods into profit and interest, or into industrial profit and commercial profit, may amount to the investment of industrial capital invested, and thus may affect the total surplus-labour and the total surplus-value produced in the given period. However, it remains true that, in the given period, the total surplus-value is not determined by adding up the individual parts mentioned above, but is instead determined by the total surplus-labour of that period, and the predetermined total surplus-value is then divided analytically into these individual parts. Also, it is always possible (and even likely) that some of the surplus-value produced in a given period may not be realised due to insufficient demand. However, Marx generally assumes throughout the three volumes of *Capital* that demand equals supply in all industries (in order to analyse the production and distribution of surplus-value 'in its pure form'). Under this ruling assumption, all the surplus-value produced is realised. The long debate over the 'transformation-problem', with which I wish to engage, has always assumed that demand equals supply in all industries. The controversial issue in this debate has been whether or not the total surplus-value (or the total value) *changes solely due to the transformation* of values into prices of production. I argue that the total value and the total surplus-value *do not change* as a result of this transformation, and cannot change, due to the nature of Marx's logical method. The total surplus-value is first determined and then taken as given in the theory of the division of this total amount into individual parts, including the equalisation of profit-rates across industries and the transformation of values into

theorised prior to the *distribution of surplus-value*. There is a clear logical progression from the determination of the magnitude of the total surplus-value to the determination of the individual parts. In modern economic terms, there is a progression from the macro to the micro.

To take the most important example, in Marx's theory of prices of production in Part two of Volume III, the total surplus-value is taken as given, as already determined in volumes I and II, and the total surplus-value is used to determine the general rate of profit, which is turn is a determinant of prices of production. As a result, the predetermined total surplus-value is distributed to individual industries in such a way that all industries receive the same rate of profit.

This premise is very important for Marx because he wished to demonstrate that all the particular forms of surplus-value (industrial profit, commercial profit, interest, and rent) all come from the same source: which is *surplus-labour*. Surplus-labour is the 'inner substance' of *all* these different forms of appearance of surplus-value. This premise is repeated many times in all the drafts of *Capital*, especially in the drafts of Volume III in the *Manuscript of 1861–63* and the *Manuscript of 1864–65*.[2] Other authors who have also emphasised the prior determination of the total surplus-value in Marx's theory include: Paul Mattick, Roman Rosdolsky, Enrique Dussel, David Yaffe, and Duncan Foley.

I have argued further that this distinction between the production of surplus-value and the distribution of surplus-value is the quantitative dimension of the two basic levels of abstraction in Marx's theory: capital in general and competition. *Capital in general* is defined by Marx as *those properties which are common to all capitals* and which distinguish capital from simple commodities or money and other forms of wealth. The most important common (or universal) property of all capitals, which is analysed at the level of abstraction of capital in general, is the *production of surplus-value* (including absolute and relative surplus-value). Since this all-important property is shared by all capitals, the theory of the production of surplus-value at the level of abstraction of capital in general is concerned with the total surplus-value produced by the total capital of society as a whole. Other common properties of all capitals that are analysed at the level of abstraction of capital in general include various characteristics of capital in the sphere of circulation (the turnover-time of capital, fixed and circulating capital, etc.) and the appearance of surplus-value and the rate of surplus-value as profit and the rate of profit (including the falling rate of profit).

The main question addressed at the level of abstraction of *competition* is the *distribution of surplus-value*, or the division of the total surplus-value into

---

prices of production. The question of a possible 'realisation-problem' belongs to a lower level of abstraction, beyond the three volumes of *Capital*.

2. Many of these passages are presented in Moseley 1997, 2002, and 2008.

individual parts. Another related question addressed at the level of abstraction of competition is 'revenue and its sources', or the critique of vulgar political economy's explanation of these individual parts of surplus-value.

Therefore, I argue that the basic logical structure of Marx's theory of capital in the three volumes of *Capital* is as follows:

Marx's theory in 'Capital'

I. Capital in general
    1. Production of surplus-value   (Volume I)
    2. Circulation of capital (turnover-time)   (Volume II)
    3. Capital and profit (including the falling rate of profit)
                                    (Parts one and three of Volume III)
II. Competition, or the *distribution of surplus-value*
    1. General rate of profit and prices of production   (Part two of Volume III)
    2. Commercial profit   (Part four)
    3. Interest   (Part five)
    4. Rent   (Part six)
    5. Revenue and its sources (critique of vulgar economics) (Part seven)

The *Grundrisse* are almost entirely at the level of abstraction of capital in general. After an initial 'Chapter on money', the rest of the *Grundrisse* is the 'Chapter on capital', which is divided into three sections: (1) 'The production process of capital', (2) 'The circulation process of capital', and (3) a brief section (30 pages, mainly about the falling rate of profit) on 'Capital as fructiferous; capital and profit'. These three sections of the 'Chapter on capital' correspond to the three sublevels of capital in general in the outline above.

In addition, there are a number of passing comments and brief discussions in sections two and three of the 'Chapter on capital' that have to do with the distribution of surplus-value, mainly the equalisation of profit-rates across industries, the most important aspect of the distribution of surplus-value. In these comments, Marx often stated something like the following: 'this discussion of the equalisation of profit-rates does not belong here, but belongs instead to the later analysis of competition'. (see below)

After a brief summary of section one of the *Grundrisse*, this chapter will review in detail these initial comments and discussions in sections two and three of the *Grundrisse* about the equalisation of profit-rates and the other component parts of the total surplus-value. It will also briefly review several important letters written by Marx in 1858, during the time that he was finishing the *Grundrisse*. It will be seen that Marx was already very clear at this early stage of his work on *Capital* that the subsequent analysis of the equalisation of profit-rates (and the distribution of surplus-value in general) would be based on the premise that the total amount of surplus-value is determined prior to its distribution and is not affected by its distribution.

1. Section one: the production-process of capital and the theory of surplus-value

In section one of the *Grundrisse*, Marx develops for the first time his theory of surplus-value.[3] Marx had written a very brief and inadequate sketch of his theory of surplus-value in *Wage Labour and Capital* (1847),[4] but the *Grundrisse* were the first time (in his published works) in which he worked out the theory in some detail. He develops for the first time the crucial division of the working day into *necessary labour-time* (labour-time objectified in the wage) and *surplus labour-time* (the rest of the working day). According to Marx's theory, surplus-value is determined in the process of production by the amount of surplus labour-time in excess of necessary labour-time. This theory applies to each and every worker and therefore applies to the total surplus-value produced by the working class as a whole.

In the *Grundrisse*, Marx also develops for the first time the distinction between *absolute surplus-value* (extension of the working day) and *relative surplus-value* (reduction of necessary labour-time through technological change and increasing productivity), and the distinction between *variable capital* (which purchases labour-power) and *constant capital* (which purchases means of production).

Marx's theory of surplus-value – determined by surplus labour-time – is a tremendous theoretical achievement, which has never been equalled before or since. Ricardo's labour-theory of value implied a 'surplus-labour theory of surplus-value', but he did not explicitly develop this theory. The later 'Ricardian socialists' did explicitly draw this conclusion, but they did not work it out in anything like the rigor and comprehensiveness of Marx's theory. The main alternative theory of profit of the other classical economists was Senior's pathetic 'abstinence'-theory of profit. And neoclassical economics has virtually no theory of profit at all, after its marginal-productivity theory was devastated by the Cambridge criticisms. Marx's theory of profit towers over these other theories, both in terms of logical rigor and explanatory power.

---

3. Dussel 2008 describes Marx's 'discovery' of his theory of surplus-value in the *Grundrisse*.
4. Marx 1975–2005g.

2. Section two: the circulation-process of capital

In Section two on the circulation-process of capital, Marx develops the concepts that have to do specifically with circulation: turnover-time, fixed capital, circulating capital, annual surplus-value, etc. Much attention is given to fixed capital as a characteristic feature of capitalism. The annual surplus-value produced by a given capital is the surplus-value produced by that capital in one turnover-period *times* the number of turnover-periods in a year.[5] There is nothing in the *Grundrisse* about the 'reproduction-schemes', which Marx discussed for the first time in the *Manuscript of 1861–3*.

2.1. The first time a topic related to competition and the distribution of surplus-value is discussed is on Marx 1973, pp. 432–6. Marx first notes that capitalists could sell their commodities below their value and still make a profit; the only difference is that a part of the surplus-value would be received by the buyers of the commodities, so there is a kind of sharing of surplus-value. Three pages later, Marx writes:

> A _general rate of profit_ as such is possible only if…a part of the surplus-value – which corresponds to surplus labour – is transferred from one capitalist to another…The *capitalist class thus to a certain extent distributes the total surplus-value* so that, to a certain degree, it [shares in it] evenly in accordance with the *size* of its capital, instead of in accordance with the surplus-values actually created by the capitals in the various branches of business. The larger profit – arising from the real surplus labour within a branch of production, the really created surplus-value – is pushed down to the average by competition, and the deficit of surplus-value in the other branch of business raised up to the average level by withdrawal of capitals from it…*Competition cannot lower this level itself, but merely has the tendency to create such a level. Further developments belong in the section on competition.*[6]

This is a very clear statement, and it is the first time in Marx's published writings (so far as I know) that Marx mentions the general rate of profit and the distribution of surplus-value. But somehow Marx already had a clear idea of how he would explain these important phenomena of competition.

2.2. 120 pages later, in a discussion of the relation between profit and wages, Marx interjects another comment about competition and the distribution of surplus-value: 'Competition among capitals can change only the relation in which

---

5. See especially Marx 1973, pp. 652–67.
6. Marx 1973, pp. 435–6. In all the quotations in this paper, underlined emphasis is in the original, and *italicised* emphasis is added.

they [capitalists; FM] share the total profit, but cannot alter the relation between total profit and total wages'.[7]

In other words, competition affects the distribution of surplus-value, but it does not affect the production of surplus-value, or the total amount of surplus-value.

2.3. 110 pages later, in a discussion of the effects of unequal turnover-time on the production of surplus-value, Marx notes that this subject is related to the equalisation of profit-rates. 'This question obviously belongs with the equalisation of the profit rate'.[8] And in a footnote to this sentence, Marx notes further that the equalisation of profit-rates has to do with the distribution of surplus-value, not its production (or 'creation'): 'It is clear that other aspects [besides unequal turnover-times, FM] also enter in with the equalisation of the rate of profit. Here, however, the issue is *not* the *distribution* of surplus-value, but its *creation*'.[9]

2.4. The last comment about the general rate of profit and the distribution of surplus-value in Section two comes 15 pages later, and is an important one. In a discussion of the confusion of economists (such as Malthus), who think that fixed and circulating capital somehow produce profit independently of surplus-labour, Marx comments: 'The greatest confusion and mystification has arisen because the doctrine of surplus profit has not been examined *in its pure form* by previous economists, but rather mixed in together with the doctrine of real profit, which leads up to *distribution*, where the various capitals participate in the *general rate of profit*. The *profit of the capitalists as a class, or the profit of capital as such, has to exist before it can be distributed, and it is extremely absurd to try to explain its origin by its distribution*'.[10]

Thus we can see that, according to Marx's theory: (1) the theory of surplus-value 'in its pure form' (namely, the theory of the production of surplus-value, disregarding the distribution of surplus-value) should be carefully distinguished from the theory of 'real profit' (namely, the theory of the distribution of surplus-value, the most important aspect of which is the general rate of profit); (2) surplus-value exists prior to its distribution (namely, the total amount of surplus-value is determined prior to its distribution); and (3) one cannot explain the

---

7. Marx 1973, p. 557.
8. Marx 1973, p. 669.
9. Ibid.
10. Marx 1973, p. 684. Marx made a similar statement about the necessity to keep the theory of surplus-value 'as such, in its pure form' separate from the theory of the 'particular forms' of surplus-value in his 'general observation' at the beginning of *Theories of Surplus-Value*: 'All economists share the error of examining surplus-value *not as such, in its pure form*, but in the *particular forms of profit and rent*. What theoretical errors must necessarily arise from this will be shown more fully in Chapter III, in the analysis of the greatly changed form which surplus-value assumes as profit' (Marx 1963b, p. 40).

origin of surplus-value, i.e., the determination of the quantity of surplus-value, by its distribution.

In a footnote to this passage, Marx comments further on the difference between 'the study of capital as such' (the study of capital in general or the production of surplus-value) and 'the study of capital in reality', that is, 'in relation to another capital' (the study of competition or the distribution of surplus-value):

> Capitals have different sizes. But the size of each individual capital is equal to itself, hence, in so far as only its quality as capital is concerned, any size. But if we examine two capitals in comparison to each other, then the difference in their size introduces a relation of a qualitative character. Size becomes itself a distinguishing quality. This is an essential aspect, of which size is only one single instance, of how the *study of capital as such* differs from the *study of one capital in relation to another capital, or the study of capital in its reality.*[11]

3. Section three: Capital and profit

3.1. The beginning of the short section three is a critical juncture in Marx's theory. It is the first draft of the beginning of Volume III of *Capital*, which is a key transition from the analysis of circulation in section two to an analysis of production and circulation together, and a consideration of profit and the relation of profit to surplus-value. This section begins with the following very important methodological comment:

> Capital is now *posited* [*nun gesetzt*] as the *unity of production and circulation*; and the surplus-value it creates in a given period of time [is also posited, FM] ... In a definite period of time, ... capital produces a *definite surplus-value* ... A capital of a certain value produces in a certain period of time a *certain surplus-value*. Surplus-value thus measured by the value of the presupposed capital, capital thus *posited* as 'self-realizing value' – is *profit* ...[12]

Thus we can see that, at this stage of the analysis (after an analysis of the *production*-process of capital and the *circulation*-process of capital), a 'definite' or 'certain' *quantity* of surplus-value is now '*posited*' (that is, has been determined or explained by the prior analysis). The amount of surplus-value produced in a given period is determined as a definite magnitude by the analysis of production, and the analysis of circulation brings in the factor of turnover-time, which determines how much surplus-value is produced in a year by a given capital.

---

11. Marx 1973, p. 684.
12. Marx 1973, pp. 746–7.

This is what Marx's theory has determined so far, in the first two sections of the *Grundrisse*. And this is the prevailing presupposition for the rest of Marx's theory.

We can also see that *profit* is defined in terms of this *already posited amount* of surplus-value. Profit is defined as this already posited amount of surplus-value as it is *related to the total capital* (constant capital and variable capital), rather than to the variable capital only (its real source, according to Marx's theory). Thus profit is a 'mystifying' form of appearance of this already posited amount of surplus-value. Defined in this way, profit is obviously *identically equal* in magnitude to the surplus-value. This definition of profit (equal in magnitude to surplus-value) makes sense only if the surplus-value is itself already determined as a definite magnitude by the prior analysis of production and circulation (annual surplus-value equals surplus-value produced in one turnover-period *times* the number of turnover-periods in a year).

The above statement of the prior determination of a definite amount of surplus-value and the identity between profit and this predetermined amount of surplus-value is expressed in terms of 'a capital'. However, Marx's theory of surplus-value presented in sections one and two of the *Grundrisse* is obviously not just about the surplus-value produced by a single individual capital, but is instead about the surplus-value produced by *each and every* capital ('capital as such' or 'what all capitals have in common'), and hence also about the *total surplus-value* produced by the total capital as a whole. Therefore, this statement of the prior determination of surplus-value and the identity between profit and the predetermined surplus-value also applies to the total surplus-value and the total profit for the economy as a whole. This prior determination of the total surplus-value is then the presupposition for Marx's theory of the distribution of surplus-value.

Since this point at the beginning of section three on 'Capital and profit' about the already posited amount of surplus-value is so important, and later turned out to be the beginning of Volume III of *Capital*, the Appendix to this chapter discusses Marx's two later drafts of this key point in Marx's theory in the *Manuscript of 1861–3* and the *Manuscript of 1864–5*, and also discusses an important 1868 letter which summarises this starting point.

3.2. After this opening paragraph in section three, Marx next discusses the falling rate of profit (his theory and other theories) for about ten pages,[13] and

---

13. It is in this section that Marx made the famous statement about the falling rate of profit: 'This is in every respect the most important law of modern political economy, and the most essential for understanding the most difficult relations. It is the most important law from an historical standpoint. It is a law which, despite its simplicity, has never before been grasped and, even less, consciously articulated' (Marx 1973, p. 748).

then comments that, *for an individual capital*, profit may differ (either larger or smaller) from the surplus-value produced by that individual capital (Marx would later call this profit differing from surplus-value for individual capitals 'average profit'). However, this is possible, Marx states, only to the extent that these differences are offset by opposite differences between profit and surplus-value for other individual capitals. The total amount of surplus-value for all capitals together is not affected by this redistribution of surplus-value (not 'ever'). The total surplus-value (equal to total profit) can neither increase or decrease by this redistribution. Finally, Marx notes again that this subject of the distribution of surplus-value belongs to the level of abstraction of competition (or 'many capitals'). This important passage is as follows: 'The *total surplus-value*, as well as the *total profit*, which is only the *surplus-value itself, computed differently*, can *neither grow nor decrease* through this operation [the equalisation of profit-rates, FM], *ever*; what is modified thereby is not it, but only *its distribution* among the different capitals. However, *this examination belongs only with that of the many capitals*, it does not yet belong here [i.e. in the analysis of capital in general, FM]'.[14]

3.3. On the next page, Marx briefly mentions again the equalisation of profit-rates brought about by competition, and comments that the amount of surplus-value produced by individual capitals is the *'presupposition'* of this equalisation. 'The inequality of profit in different branches of industry with capitals of equal magnitudes is the condition and *presupposition* for their equalisation through competition'.[15]

3.4. Marx then returns to the subject of the falling rate of profit, and six pages later emphasises again that the total profit of the capitalist class as a whole is identically equal to the predetermined total surplus-value: 'Profit as we still regard it here, i.e. as the *profit of capital as such*, not of an individual capital at the expense of another, but rather as the *profit of the capitalist class*, concretely expressed, *can never be greater that the sum of the surplus-value ... In its immediate form, profit is nothing but the sum of the surplus-value expressed as a proportion of the total value of the capital*'.[16]

4. Interest, rent, and commercial profit in the *Grundrisse*

Marx's treatment of *interest* in the *Grundrisse* is somewhat complicated and requires careful examination. It is necessary first of all to understand that there

---

14. Marx 1973, p. 760.
15. Marx 1973, p. 761.
16. Marx 1973, p. 767.

are two main aspects of Marx's theory of interest: (1) interest as an *'illusionary form of appearance'* of surplus-value and (2) interest as a *magnitude* or *quantity*, as one part of the total surplus-value.

In the *Grundrisse*, Marx discussed both aspects of interest, but seemed to be thinking mainly of the first 'illusionary form of appearance' aspect. In the first respect, interest is similar to profit, and could be considered at the level of abstraction of capital in general, as profit is. Profit is an 'illusionary form of appearance of surplus-value', in that the surplus-value actually produced by labour, and hence intrinsically related to variable capital only, is seen by capitalists and economists as the result of the total capital, both constant capital and variable capital. The concept of profit is prior to the equalisation of the profit-rate or the determination of the average profit (the profit of each capital is assumed to be equal to the surplus-value actually produced by that capital), and thus belongs to the level of abstraction of capital in general. Interest is even more illusionary than profit, because interest appears to come from money-capital itself, without any relation to production at all ('money begats money'). Therefore, in two early outlines of his theory at the beginning of the *Grundrisse*,[17] interest is located immediately after profit, and in the title of Section III, interest is mentioned before profit ('Capital as bearing fruit. Interest. Profit').

On the other hand, in the second aspect, as a quantity, interest is a fractional part of the total surplus-value, and is an element of the distribution of surplus-value, which belongs to the level of abstraction of competition, along with equal rates of profit and prices of production, commercial profit, and rent. This quantitative aspect of interest is briefly discussed several times in the *Grundrisse*.[18] In one such passage, Marx criticises the American economist Carey for his misconceptions about interest (confusing interest in pre-capitalist societies with interest in capitalism). In the process, he emphasises that interest under capitalism is one part of the total surplus-value: 'Historically, ... profit thus appears originally determined by interest. But in the bourgeois economy, interest [is] determined by profit, and *only one of the latter's parts*'.[19]

Two pages later, Marx comments that he is not here concerned with this quantitative aspect of interest, and that it would be considered later in relation to 'credit relations'.[20]

Therefore, it appears that Marx was not entirely clear at this point exactly where the analysis of interest should be located in his theory, but he was very

17. Marx 1973, pp. 264 and 275.
18. Marx 1973, pp. 318–19, 758–60, 851–4.
19. Marx 1973, p. 852.
20. Marx 1973, p. 854.

clear about these two aspects of interest, including the quantitative aspect, according to which interest is one part of the total surplus-value.

In the *Manuscript of 1861–3*, Marx discussed both of these aspects of interest in much greater detail.[21] Toward the end of this manuscript, Marx wrote an almost-final outline of what later became Volume III of *Capital*. In this outline, interest is located along with the other individual parts of surplus-value (the general rate of profit, commercial profit, and rent), all of which belong to the level of abstraction of competition. And in the *Manuscript of 1864–5* (the final draft of Volume III), this is where Part five on interest is located.

Marx's theory of *rent* is hardly discussed at all in the *Grundrisse*. The reason for this is that Marx was planning at the time to discuss rent along with landed property in the second book of his 'six book plan', after the first book on capital. Later, while working on the *Manuscript of 1861–3*, Marx discovered the connection between rent and the equalisation of the profit-rate across industries, and began to understand rent more clearly as one part of the total surplus-value, along with industrial profit, commercial profit, and interest. Therefore, in the outline of Volume III at the end of the *Manuscript of 1861–3* (mentioned in the previous paragraph), rent is included along with these other individual parts of surplus-value, at the level of abstraction of competition.[22]

Commercial profit, the final individual part of the total surplus-value is not discussed at all in the *Grundrisse*. Marx discussed this form of surplus-value for the first time in the *Manuscript of 1861–3*. Commercial profit is also included in the outline of Volume III at the end of this manuscript, at the level of abstraction of competition.

The clearest statement in the *Grundrisse* about these individual parts of the total surplus-value together is in section three, in a discussion of the expenditure of profit as revenue:

> This is of course important, since capital exchanges not only for capital, but also for revenue, and each capital can itself be eaten up as revenue. Still *this does not affect the determination of profit in general.* Under the various forms of *profit, interest, rent*, pensions, taxes, etc., it may be distributed . . . under different titles among different classes of the population. *They can never divide up among themselves more than the total surplus-value* of the total surplus product. The ratio in which they distribute it is of course economically important; but does not affect the question before us.[23]

---

21. See Moseley 2008.
22. See Moseley 2008.
23. Marx 1973, p. 788.

Thus we can see that Marx was clear that these individual parts of surplus-value belong to the distribution of surplus-value, which does not affect the total amount of surplus-value to be distributed.

5. Outlines at the beginning and the end of the *Grundrisse*

Early in the *Grundrisse*, Marx wrote two outlines of his theory of capital, which were organised in terms of the Hegelian triad of generality, particularity, and singularity (the second outline is clearer than the first).[24] It could be argued that 'generality' corresponds roughly to capital in general, and that 'particularity' corresponds roughly to competition ('competition of capitals' is one of the three points under 'particularity', along with accumulation and concentration). 'Singularity' consists of the credit-system, share-capital and the money-market.

About the time Marx was finishing the *Grundrisse* (April 1858), he wrote a letter to Engels in which he first outlined his 'six book plan', the first book of which was 'Capital'.[25] Marx then went on to say that the first book on capital would be divided into four parts: (1) *capital in general*, (2) *competition*, (3) the credit-system, and (4) share-capital.

Thus, it could be argued that, although Marx no longer used the terms of the Hegelian triad, the broad structure of his theory was similar to these earlier outlines, but with greater clarity and precision, especially about competition. We have seen above that, after writing these earlier outlines, Marx referred repeatedly to a 'later analysis of competition', which would include the equalisation of profit-rates. The first two parts in this later outline (capital in general and competition) are the most important parts (by far), and the only ones that Marx worked on in his later manuscripts (except for a few very initial and exploratory notes on the credit system in Part Five of Volume III, which could be considered as belonging to the third part of this outline).

Three weeks prior to this letter, Marx wrote another letter to Lassalle, in which he divided the first part of his theory of capital on *capital in general* into three sections: (1) the *production*-process of capital, (2) the *circulation*-process of capital, and (3) the unity of the two, or *capital and profit; interest*.[26]

We can see that these are the same three sections of the *Grundrisse* discussed above. However, these sections are now sections of capital in general, rather than sections of the 'Chapter on capital'. Thus, Marx appears to have realised more clearly as a result of his work on the *Grundrisse* that his theory of capital should be divided into capital in general and competition, and so on, and that his

---

24. Marx 1973, p. 264 and p. 275.
25. Marx and Engels 1983, p. 298.
26. Marx and Engels 1983, p. 287.

theory in the *Grundrisse* was really about capital in general only; it was not a complete theory of capital. The theory of competition would come later. Marx began to develop his theory of competition in the *Manuscript of 1861–3*, and developed it much more thoroughly in the *Manuscript of 1864–5*, and this theory includes the general rate of profit and other particular forms of surplus-value that have to do with the distribution of surplus-value.

Evidently, Marx's work on the *Grundrisse* on his theory of the production of surplus-value, at the level of abstraction of capital in general, and the brief discussions of the general rate of profit which he realised 'must be analysed later in the section on competition', had given him sufficient clarity about the relation between capital in general and competition (essentially the production and distribution of surplus-value), and about the overall logical structure of his theory, that he was able to write down these new improved outlines.

In another important and well-known letter from Marx to Engels in January 1858 (in the middle of the *Grundrisse*), Marx explains that by chance he had reviewed Hegel's *Logic*, and this had been 'of great service' for his own theory, and in particular for his theory of *profit* and the *method* of dealing with his theory of profit.[27]

> By the way, I am discovering some nice arguments. For instance, I have overthrown the whole doctrine of *profit* as it existed up to now. The fact that by mere accident I again glanced through Hegel's *Logik*...has been of great service to me as regards the *method* of dealing with the material.[28]

Many commentators have noted Marx's acknowledgment of his debt to Hegel in this letter, but no one (in my view) has adequately explained specifically which elements of Hegel's vast logic that Marx had in mind in this letter, nor how these specific elements helped Marx explain profit (surplus-value).

I think the explanation of this important puzzle is what I have said above – the specific elements of Hegel's logic that Marx found helpful in his theory of profit were the moments of the concept of universality and particularity. This helped Marx to see that the proper logical method of explaining profit (surplus-value) is to begin with the universal – the theory of capital in general and the

---

27. Marx had developed his concept of surplus-value only a few weeks before writing this letter (the word surplus-value appears for the first time in Marx's published writings in Marx 1973, p. 321, written in November-December), and Engels was of course unfamiliar with this concept. So Marx used the usual term of profit in the letter, but what he really meant was his new concept of surplus-value.

28. Marx and Engels 1975b, p. 93.

total surplus-value – and then to proceed to the particulars – the theory of competition and the individual parts of surplus-value.[29]

6. Conclusion

I think it should concluded from this investigation that, even though there are only these few brief comments and discussions about the general rate of profit and the distribution of surplus-value in the *Grundrisse*, Marx was already clear at this early stage of the development of his theory about the following methodological aspects of his theory of capital:

(1) The theory of capital would be divided into two main parts: capital in general and competition.

(2) The main question analysed at the level of abstraction of capital in general is the production of surplus-value (or the determination of the total amount of surplus-value), and the main question analysed at the level of abstraction of competition is the distribution of surplus-value (or the division of the total surplus-value into individual parts).

(3) It is essential that the production of surplus-value be theorised prior to the distribution of surplus-value because the former theory determines the total amount of surplus-value that is to be distributed or divided up.

(4) The total amount of surplus-value is taken as given in the subsequent analysis of the distribution of surplus-value at the level of abstraction of competition, and is not affected by this distribution.

I have shown in previous papers that Marx consistently maintained and developed this logical structure of his theory in all the later drafts of *Capital*. In the *Manuscript of 1861–3*, Marx began to develop in greater detail his theory of the general rate of profit and other forms of the distribution of surplus-value (rent, interest, commercial profit), inspired by his critique of Rodbertus's theory of rent. In the *Manuscript of 1864–5* (which was later edited by Engels as Volume III of *Capital*), Marx developed much more thoroughly his theory of these individual forms of surplus-value. In both of these manuscripts, Marx stated many times the key quantitative premise that the total amount of surplus-value is determined prior to its division into individual parts.

Therefore, I think it has to be concluded that this quantitative premise is an essential aspect of the logical structure of Marx's theory in *Capital*.

---

29. Oh how I wish Marx would have written the 'accessible' introduction to Hegel's method that Marx mentioned writing in the rest of the paragraph quoted above 'if there should ever be time'. That would have helped to avoid a century of misinterpretations.

Appendix: Later drafts of the beginning of 'Capital and profit'

Manuscript of 1861–3

Marx's second draft of the beginning of 'Capital and profit' is toward the end of the *Manuscript of 1861–3* (this section of the manuscript was published for the first time in English in 1988), and it begins with a similar methodological comment as in the *Grundrisse*:

> Considered in its totality...the movement of capital is a *unity of the process of production and the process of circulation*...The surplus-value produced within a given period of circulation...when measured against the total capital which has been advanced is called – *profit*...Considered with respect to its material, profit is absolutely nothing but surplus-value itself. Considered with respect to its *absolute magnitude*, it therefore does not differ from the surplus-value produced by capital over a particular turnover time. *It is surplus-value itself, but calculated differently.*[30]

Marx does not use the term 'posited' here, but he does define profit as the same magnitude of surplus-value, as in the *Grundrisse*. It seems clear that Marx's logic with respect to the determination of the magnitudes of surplus-value and profit is the same in this manuscript as in the *Grundrisse* – that is, the magnitude of surplus-value has already been 'posited', and the magnitude of profit is defined to be identically equal to this already posited magnitude of surplus-value.

A few pages later in this manuscript, Marx states explicitly that the identity between profit and the already determined surplus-value also applies to the *total surplus-value* of the total social capital: 'Just as the surplus-value of the individual capital in each sphere of production is the measure of the absolute magnitude of the profit – merely a converted form of surplus-value – so is the total surplus-value produced by the total capital the absolute measure of the total profit of the total capital, whereby profit should be understood to include all forms of surplus-value, such as rent, interest, and so on. It is, therefore, the *absolute magnitude of value... which the* <u>capitalist class</u> *can divide among itself in various headings'.*[31]

Manuscript of 1864–5

Engels's edition of Chapter One of Volume III does not include a similar methodological comment about the prior determination of surplus-value, to which profit is equated in magnitude. However, a similar comment is made by Marx

---

30. Marx and Engels 1988, p. 69.
31. Marx 1988, p. 98.

in his *Manuscript of 1864–5*, which Engels edited to produce the Volume III that we know. Marx's manuscript begins with a paragraph similar to Engels's first paragraph, but then there are several paragraphs, which were omitted by Engels (for some reason) and which are similar to the opening paragraphs in the earlier drafts quoted above. Excerpts from these paragraphs are as follows (translated from the German by Janna Busse; very unfortunately, this volume of the *MEGA* is not included in the 50-volume English translation *Marx-Engels Collected Works*):

> ...in a year capital produces a *certain magnitude of surplus-value*.... The rate of profit is a ratio of the annual surplus-value to the total capital, commonly expressed in per cent. For example, the capital consists of $400 constant capital and $100 variable capital, and the surplus-value amounts to $100. If the $100 of surplus-value is regarded as an offspring of the total advanced capital of $500, thus 20%, then it is considered as – *profit*. ...
>
> In terms of its content profit is (in the form in which it concerns us here) by all means nothing else but surplus-value itself. Its absolute magnitude is therefore also not different from the magnitude of surplus-value that the capital has created in a certain period of time. It is *surplus-value itself but calculated differently*, and looked at differently subjectively.[32]

It seems obvious that Marx's logic is the same in all three of these drafts. The prior analysis of production and circulation has determined or posited the magnitude of surplus-value produced in a given year, both for each and every individual capital and also for the total social capital. And profit is defined as this same predetermined amount of surplus-value, measured in relation to the total capital, rather than to variable capital alone.

1868 letter

There is another important piece of textual evidence concerning the beginning of Volume III: a letter that Marx wrote to Engels in April 1868, three years after he had written the full draft of Volume III (in the *Manuscript of 1864–5*) and one year after the publication of Volume I. In this letter, Marx explained to Engels what Volume III is all about. By this time in his life and theoretical development, Marx had a very clear idea of the subject-matter and the overall logical structure of Volume III, and its relation to Volumes I and II. Therefore, this letter provides important evidence concerning the logic of Volume III.

Marx began his summary of 'Book III' by clearly stating its main overall subject: 'In Book III, we then come to the conversion of surplus-value into its different

---

32. Marx and Engels 1992a, pp. 7–8.

forms and *separate component parts*'.[33] In other words, we come to the *distribution of surplus-value*.

The letter then summarises each of the seven parts of Volume III, which correspond exactly to the seven parts of Marx's draft of Volume III in the *Manuscript of 1864–5*, which Marx no doubt had in front of him as he wrote the letter to Engels.

The summary of Part One begins with the main points emphasised above: that profit is only 'another name' for surplus-value, and that there is no quantitative difference between profit and surplus-value:

> *Profit* is for us first of all only _another name_ or another category of _surplus-value_. As owing to the form of wages, the whole of labour appears to be paid for, the unpaid part of labour seems necessarily to come not from labour but from capital, and not from the variable part of capital but from capital as a whole. As a result, *surplus-value* assumes the form of *profit*, without there being *any quantitative* differentiation between the one and the other. This is only its *illusionary manifestation*.[34]

After discussing the important concept of cost-price, Marx then summarised his analysis of the determination of the rate of profit by the rate of surplus-value and the composition of capital, which Marx said 'has of course been hitherto *inexplicable* to everybody'. Then Marx made the following important comment with respect to individual capitals and the total social capital:

> The laws thus discovered... hold good _no matter how_ the surplus-value may later be divided among the producer, etc. This can only change the _form in which it appears_. Moreover, they remain *directly* applicable if s/(c+v) is treated as the relation of the *socially produced surplus-value* to the *social capital*.[35]

---

33. Marx and Engels 1975b, p. 191.
34. Marx and Engels 1975b, pp. 191–2.
35. Marx and Engels 1975b, p. 193.

Marx's *Grundrisse* and the Monetary Business-Cycle
Jan Toporowski

Marx's *Grundrisse der Kritik der Politischen Ökonomie (Rohentwurf)/Foundations of the Critique of Political Economy (Rough Draft)*, is a work of extraordinary range which allows it to be read in a number of different ways. The first, and probably the most obvious reading, is as a set of preliminary, transitional notes for the work that was to become *Capital*. A second reading that attracted widespread interest when the book was published, was as a philosophical introduction to Marx's critique of political economy, outlining the method that Marx was to use in his economic analysis (or not, according to the followers of Louis Althusser). Not least among the important features of the book, in this author's opinion, is a tantalising fragment, a mere few hundred words, on Greek art.[1]

However, the key to understanding the book is given in the chapter-titles. A methodological introduction is followed by a chapter on money, and then a very extensive chapter that takes up the vast bulk of a very long book on capital. The purpose of this arrangement is to show that the monetary appearance of objects and relations is illusory, because capital is a social relationship, not a pecuniary one. Hence the phrase that recurs in the titles that Marx gave to his writings on political economy: the *critique* of political economy, rather than *a helpful guide to correct doctrines* in political economy. This accounts for much of the difficulty that arises in reading Marx's writings on political

---

1. Marx 1993, pp. 110–11.

economy. Those works can only be fully understood by first reading the works that Marx was criticising. A first approximation may be obtained by reading the three volumes of *Theories of Surplus Value*. However, the task can be made much simpler by concentrating on a key theme of current significance that occurs in the *Grundrisse* and in *Capital*, namely the role that credit plays in capitalist production and crisis.

The chapter is divided as follows. A first section examines Marx's views on credit as presented in the *Grundrisse*. This is then contrasted, in the second section, with a more mature view on credit-cycles, presented in Volume III of *Capital*. A third section argues that the two views are consistent with a historical view of the evolution of finance. A brief conclusion summarises the argument.

Rejecting the monetary business-cycle . . .

The first chapter of the *Grundrisse*, on money, begins with a quotation from a book, *De la réforme des banques* by Alfred Darimon: 'The root of the evil is the predominance which opinion obstinately assigns to the role of the precious metals in circulation and exchange'.[2] Darimon (1819–1902), a journalist and politician, and follower of social philosopher and critic Pierre Joseph Proudhon, was what Keynes called a 'monetary reformer', a theorist who argues that the inadequacies of capitalism may be removed by reforming the monetary system. In Darimon's case, the reform he sought was joint-stock banking backed by credit-insurance. This, he believed, would provide the flexible credit-supply that would prevent the financial crises that plagued France (and Britain) in the first half of the nineteenth century as a result of the use of precious metals to back bank-credit.

Marx proceeded to castigate Darimon for his weak understanding of bank credit: '. . . he completely identifies *monetary turnover* with *credit*'. (In an aside that could be addressed to certain twenty-first century Marxist monetary theorists, Marx went on to remark 'The notion of *crédit gratuit*, incidentally, is only a hypocritical, philistine and anxiety-ridden form of the saying: property is theft. Instead of the workers *taking* the capitalists' capital, the capitalists are supposed to be compelled to *give* it to them').[3] Marx identified 'the fundamental question' as the following:

> Can the existing relations of production and the relations of distribution which correspond to them be revolutionised by a change in the instrument of circulation, in the organisation of circulation? . . . Various forms of money

---

2. Marx 1975a, p. 51.
3. Marx 1993, p. 123.

may correspond better to social production at various stages; one form may remedy evils against which another is powerless; but none of them, as long as they remain forms of money, and as long as money remains an essential relation of production, is capable of overcoming the contradictions inherent in the money relation, and can instead only hope to reproduce these contradictions in one or another form. One form of wage labour may correct the abuses of another, but no form can correct abuse of wage labour itself.[4]

Marx's argument was essentially that crises occur because of contradictions in production and exchange, rather than in the medium of exchange: The 'bullion drains' (loss of gold from the banking system) that cause financial crises are themselves the results of changes in real, non-monetary, factors such as 'domestic harvest failures in a chief food crop, (e.g., grain), crop-failure abroad and hence increased prices in one of the main imported consumer goods (e.g., tea)...crop failure in industrial raw materials (cotton, wool silk, flax etc.), excessive imports (caused by speculation, war etc.)...' with the consequence that 'a part of (the nation's) invested capital or labour is not reproduced – real loss of production'.[5]

Marx then went on to argue that money-prices could not measure the true price of commodities, but 'labour money denominated in labour time would...equate the *real value* (exchange value) of commodities'.[6] This early Marx re-appears in Emile Zola's extraordinary novelistic treatment of financial crisis, *L'Argent*, as the 'Karl Marxite' Sigismund Busch, devoting his dying years to the calculation of a system of prices that would correspond to labour-time, and that would therefore eliminate exploitation. This endeavour was then revived by those Marxian economists who have devoted themselves to the solution of the so-called 'transformation-problem'.[7]

The remainder of the chapter is devoted to contrasting and criticising the presumed intrinsic value of precious metals, as opposed to the social character of capitalist production and hence prices. This is, therefore, the prelude to the very long chapter on capital.

...only to embrace the monetary business-cycle...

There is no doubt that the chapter on money is inadequate. It is unsystematic, consisting of notes that break off inconclusively, and arguments criss-crossed

---

4. Marx 1993, pp. 122–3.
5. Marx 1993, p. 127.
6. Marx 1993, p. 137.
7. Cf. Bellofiore 1989.

with Marx's invective against Darimon, extended to Saint-Simonians such as Isaac Périere.[8] A serious gap in Marx's argument is the absence of any general account of economic or financial crisis. As indicated above, Marx suggested that crises were caused by real factors, disrupting production, but that the causes of any given financial crisis were particular to that crisis.

This lacuna was made up less than a decade later when Marx drafted Volume III of *Capital*. In this volume he introduced corporate finance into his argument in the guise of 'interest-bearing capital', a separate kind of money-capital that emerges to finance production.[9] This allowed Marx to distinguish between bank-crises, caused by 'bullion drains' and problems that arise with refinancing industrial credit, or 'interest-bearing capital'. These problems arise because industrial credit is put into production. At this point the industrial capitalist no longer has the money, obtained when the credit was advanced, with which to repay that credit. That money had been used to buy means of production, the revenue from which is insufficient for immediate repayment of the credit advanced.[10]

In modern terminology, the process of production and (real) capital-accumulation requires the purchase of illiquid assets using credit. This was identified as a feature of a Keynesian theory of crisis by Hyman P. Minsky, who argued that:

> The process of selling financial assets or liabilities to fulfill cash-payment commitments is called 'position-making' the position being the unit's holdings of assets which, while they earn income, do not possess markets in which they can be readily sold. For corporations the 'position' which has to be financed is the capital assets necessary for production; for financial firms, the 'position' is defined by the assets with poor secondary markets . . . the owners of (industrial) capital-assets speculate by debt-financing investment and positions in the stock of capital-assets . . . [Such firms] with elaborated liability structures develop cash payment commitments which exceed the cash receipts they will get over the short period from contracts they own, or from operations. To fulfil their cash-payment commitments, they must refinance by selling either their assets or their liabilities.[11]

8. The banking doctrines of the Saint-Simonians are further discussed in Toporowski 2002, Part One.

9. Marx 1959, Part Five.

10. Marx 1959, pp. 488–93.

11. Minsky 1975, pp. 123–4.

May be done dialectically

There is a functionalist tendency among Marxist economists whose common weakness consists of illicitly generalising from some logical necessity of a particular model of capitalism. In one version of this, all capitalist phenomena are treated as somehow 'functional' for capitalism which, by implication, is deemed incapable of operating in an inefficient, or dysfunctional way. This kind of analysis appeals to critics of capitalism who would hang their critiques on the obvious 'unfairness' of capitalism, or the seemingly intractable poverty existing in capitalist societies. Monetary and financial theory, in this kind of functionalism, emerges from an examination of the monetary and financing needs of capitalist production and exchange, and serves those needs logically because money and credit have no other function in the capitalist economy.[12] In another, weaker, version of this functionalism, the institutions of a capitalist society are judged according to how they contribute to the efficient functioning of the capitalist economy. This is notable in the French regulationist school, or among their transatlantic intellectual cousins, the Social Structure of Accumulation school of American Marxists.

This functionalist approach does not really do full justice to Marx's historic dialectic which explains the apparent paradox of his rejection of any monetary business-cycle in the *Grundrisse* only to embrace it in Volume III of *Capital*. In the earlier work, Marx was concerned to show that monetary relations could not explain capitalism, or be the foundation for it as a historical formation. In Volume III of *Capital*, he showed how the need to finance industrial production brought about the historical emergence of 'interest-bearing capital'.[13] The unjustly neglected Marxist monetary theorist, Karl Niebyl, was to show how the prodigious credit-needs of factory-production induced the financial innovations that came about in the latter half of the nineteenth century with the routine establishment of companies capable of issuing long-term financial liabilities.[14] Engels alludes to this in the brief chapter he wrote on the stock-exchange to conclude Volume III of *Capital*.

At first glance, Marx's and Niebyl's approach is 'functionalist' in the sense that credit-markets develop to satisfy the financing requirements of capitalist production. Industrial capitalism pre-dates capitalist financial markets. Hence finance

---

12. Examples of this kind of reasoning may be found most famously in Hilferding's *Finance Capital* (Hilferding 1981) in the 'circuitist' theory of money, or among the contributions to Moseley (ed.) 2005.

13. Marx 1959, Chapters Eleven and Twenty-Five.

14. Niebyl 1946.

cannot be the social foundation for capitalism, nor, according to the *Grundrisse*, can monetary relations be the ultimate explanation for fluctuations in capitalism as it emerges. The problem with the functionalist view is that finance does not exist just to serve industrial capitalism. If this were so, then the United States would today be an industrial super-power, instead of just a financial and military super-power. The central issue is that having emerged to serve industrial capitalism, the financial markets then change that capitalism: financial markets become a much more liquid source of profit (if not surplus-value: the squeeze imposed by high interest-rates on the residual surplus-value of the industrial capitalist, a jejune problem that belongs, as Marx rightly noted, to early capitalism, rather than our capitalism dominated by finance).[15] Historically, interest-bearing capital, with credit-inflation, became the means by which capitalism refocused on balance-sheet restructuring as a source of cash-flow rather than just production. In this way, financial innovation changed the nature and the financing needs of industrial capital.

The process by which capitalist production induced financial innovation to extend production but, ultimately, to corrupt capitalist production, is a historic dialectic that Marx knew well. In his polemic against Lord Overstone, who had argued that interest-rates were high because profits were high, Marx put forward the view that higher interest-rates may be caused by greater demand for money-capital to finance production, with production then diminished by the higher interest-rates. Marx dismissed Overstone in the following terms:

> [...] That anything can ultimately destroy its own cause is a logical absurdity only for the usurer enamoured of the high interest rate. The greatness of the Romans was the cause of their conquests, and their conquests destroyed their greatness. Wealth is the cause of luxury and luxury destroys wealth...[16]

This logic is well applied to finance: just because financial markets developed to finance industry does not mean that they remained in this ancillary position, or that they cannot depress capital-accumulation or agitate capitalism with credit-cycles. Too many Marxists and Post-Keynesians share a neo-classical textbook-view that is stuck in the primordial function of the financial markets. The radical political economist of finance re-examines the financial markets of today and how they alter the nature and dynamics of capitalism.

---

15. See Marx, 1959, pp. 109–10.
16. Marx, 1959, p. 422.

Conclusion

In his *Grundrisse*, Marx rejected monetary relations as the foundation and explanation for capitalism. However, monetary relations return in his theory of crisis, which is a kind of monetary business cycle *à la* Minsky. This apparent paradox may be explained by the dialectical role played by finance in the development of capitalism. The financing needs of capitalist production induce financial innovation ('interest-bearing capital') which comes to have a dominant, rather than a subordinate, role in relation to production. The dominance of finance allows credit-cycles to determine the nature and dynamics of capitalism. Marx himself was to conclude that:

> The social character of capital is first promoted and wholly realised through the full development of the credit and the banking system... The distribution of capital as a special business, a social function, is taken out of the hands of the private capitalists and usurers. But at the same time, banking and credit thus become the most potent means of driving capitalist production beyond its own limits, and one of the most effective vehicles of crises and swindle.[17]

---

17. Marx 1959, p. 607.

Crisis and the Rate of Profit in Marx's Laboratory
Peter D. Thomas and Geert Reuten

Karl Marx's notion of 'the tendency of the rate of profit to fall' has long constituted one of the most controversial elements of Marx's and Marxian theory. It has given rise to ongoing conflicting interpretations and opposed theoretical 'reconstructions'. This chapter will not seek to resolve these interpretative and reconstructive controversies. Rather, we propose to examine the role played by 'the tendency of the rate of profit to fall' at a decisive stage of Marx's development of the notion of the capitalist mode of production; namely, in the 1857–8 notebooks subsequently published as the *Grundrisse*.

Written at the onset of a major world-crisis of the capitalist mode of production, these incomplete yet internally systematic notebooks provide us with a unique window onto Marx's theoretical laboratory. This is not primarily because, as various commentators have supposed, the *Grundrisse* are a 'work of transition' from a 'youthful' to a more 'mature' paradigm. This view has issued in equally various positive and negative assessments of this transition: for instance, on the one hand, a transition from idealism/ideology to materialism/science, for the Althusserian school; on the other hand, a transition from politics to 'economism', or the 'dead-end of political economy', for E.P. Thompson. In both cases, the reading and interpretation of the *Grundrisse* itself is subordinated to its 'exemplary' role in a predetermined tale of purification or degeneration.

Rather, the significance of the *Grundrisse* consists in the dramatic form in which it enables us to observe implicit contradictions and sometimes open conflicts between themes that traverse all of Marx's works. In an uneasy *modus vivendi*, this text brings together perspectives that were first essayed in Marx's earlier work in the 1840s, while 'anticipating' elements that will only reach full fruition throughout the successive drafts of *Capital*. Marx disturbs this *modus vivendi* via two approaches, which dialectically interact throughout his analysis: on the one hand, the method of immanent critique leads Marx to reformulate concepts derived from his previous study of political economy, a reformulation that sometimes amounts to fundamental conceptual transformation alongside the maintenance of the older terminology; on the other hand, Marx's growing awareness of the potential durability and strength of the capitalist mode of production leads him to seek for more systematic conceptual determinations and explanations. In this perspective, the significance of the *Grundrisse* is that they constitute a *Kampfplatz* [battleground] upon which we can observe the struggle between different elements of Marx's project. This struggle is perhaps nowhere more evident than in the treatment of the 'tendency of the rate of profit to fall' in this text.

Marx's views on the 'law' or 'tendency' of the rate of profit to fall developed throughout his life from a law about the historical destination of the capitalist system as tending towards breakdown, into a theory about the functioning of the capitalist mode of production as a potentially durable system. The first view is compatible with a 'naturalistic' and teleological philosophy of history; it presupposes a unilinear conception of time and implicitly posits a diachronic 'exhaustion' of an originary rate of profit. The second view opens the way towards a type of 'conjunctural analysis', founded upon a cyclical notion of time as a synchronic intensification and articulation of contradictory, systemic features. Both views compete on the *Kampfplatz* of the *Grundrisse*; while the former seems to maintain its dominance, Marx nevertheless also initiates in this text lines of reasoning that will lead to the increasing theoretical hegemony of the latter in subsequent texts. In its turn, this will permit Marx to elaborate a notion of the capitalist mode of production that breaks with both the teleological historicism of the young-Hegelian movement in which his political thought was formed, as well as the 'naturalism' of classical political economy.

This thesis will be demonstrated by means of an analysis of three texts from different stages of Marx's intellectual development, beginning with the *Grundrisse*, passing by way of the 1861–3 manuscripts, and concluding with Marx's manuscript from 1864–5, which was later edited by Engels as Part Three of *Capital* Volume III. We will argue that the *Grundrisse*'s discussion of this theme shares presuppositions with Marx's (and Engels's) earlier political positions in the 1840s. Furthermore, we will see that important statements in the *Grundrisse* on the profit-rate issue do not appear in later texts. Nevertheless, we will also see that the *Grundrisse*'s immanent critique introduces important new perspectives that can be regarded – obviously, only in the *futur antérieur* – as the foundations for the different statements on the rate of profit in the later texts. We will essay various possible political and theoretical reasons for this development and, in conclusion, suggest themes for future research that are raised by this analysis.

The 'law' of the rate of profit to fall in the *Grundrisse*

Marx discusses the 'fall of the rate of profit' in the *Grundrisse* in the third section of the manuscript's last notebook (Notebook VII), written in the early months of 1858.[1] The text addresses (a) Ricardo's insufficient distinction between rate of surplus-value and rate of profit, and (b) the inverse relation between sum of profit and rate of profit. Marx presents these arguments in synthetic form in the first part of the section; the second half of this section consists of comments on and textual analysis of Smith and Ricardo in particular (but also of Malthus, Carey and Bastiat).[2] In the first half, Marx argues:

> Presupposing the same surplus value, *the same surplus labour in proportion to necessary labour*, then, the *rate of profit* depends on the relation between the part of capital exchanged for living labour and the part existing in the form of raw material and means of production. Hence, the smaller the portion exchanged for living labour becomes, the smaller becomes the rate of profit. Thus, in the same proportion as capital takes up a larger place as capital in the production process relative to immediate labour, i.e. the more the relative surplus value grows – the value-creating power of capital – the more *does the rate of profit fall.*

It is only after having set out this inverse relation that Marx uses the term 'law' in relation to the profit-rate:

> This is in every respect the most important law of modern political economy, and the most essential for understanding the most difficult relations. It is the most important law from the historical standpoint. It is a law which, despite its simplicity, has never before been grasped and, even less, consciously articulated.[3]

Marx then sets out how 'the development of the productive forces' is accompanied by a relative 'decline of the part of the capital . . . exchanged for immediate labour' (the concept of 'organic composition of capital' is not explicit in this text,

---

1. Marx 1973, pp. 745–58.
2. Marx 1973, pp. 751–8.
3. Marx 1973, p. 748.

though it is implicit in Marx's discussion of the inverse relation between relative surplus-value growth and profit-rate fall). This process, that is:

> the development of the productive forces brought about by the historical development of capital itself, when it reaches a certain point, suspends the self-realization of capital, instead of positing it. Beyond a certain point, the development of the powers of production becomes a barrier for capital; hence the capital relation [becomes] a barrier for the development of the productive powers of labour. When it has reached this point, capital, i.e. wage labour, enters into the same relation towards the development of social wealth and of the forces of production as the guild system, serfdom, slavery, and is necessarily stripped off as a fetter. The last form of servitude assumed by human activity, that of wage labour on one side, capital on the other, is thereby cast off like a skin, and this casting-off itself is the result of the mode of production corresponding to capital; the material and mental conditions of the negation of wage labour and of capital, themselves already the negation of earlier forms of unfree social production, are themselves results of its production process.[4]

Immediately following this, Marx explicitly inscribes his reflections under the banner – perhaps less of a 'theory' than of a rhetoric – of 'crisis'. 'The growing incompatibility between the productive development of society and its hitherto existing relations of production expresses itself in bitter contradictions, crises, spasms. The violent destruction of capital *not by relations external to it*, but rather as *a condition of its self-preservation*, is the most striking form in which advice is given it to be gone and to give room to a higher state of social production'.[5]

A few lines later, he returns to this theme. The invitation to capital to leave politely has now taken on the tone of a menacing inevitability: 'These contradictions [of development of the powers of production] lead to explosions, cataclysms, crises, in which by momentaneous suspension of labour and annihilation of a great portion of capital the latter is violently *reduced to the point where it can go on*.... Yet, these *regularly recurring catastrophes* lead to their repetition on a higher scale, and finally to its violent overthrow'.[6]

The last sentence in particular would seem to point to a trend-wise development of the fall of the profit-rate, the accumulation of 'regularly recurring catastrophes' finally descending into 'violent overthrow'.

Marx does, indeed, seem to lessen the impact of this crisis-rhetoric somewhat when he speaks in the immediately following lines of 'moments' that may 'delay' the fall in the rate of profit. Among these, he includes the devaluation of existing

---

4. Marx 1973, p. 749.
5. Marx 1973, pp. 749–50; emphasis added.
6. Marx 1973, p. 750, emphasis added.

capital, transformation of capital into fixed capital not directly involved in pro-duction, unproductive waste of capital, lowering of taxes, reduction of ground-rent and the creation of new branches of production. However, these factors only *delay* this trend-fall; they do not negate it. It remains a 'law' that leads, via repetition, to the 'overthrow' of the capitalist mode of production.

It is relevant to note that Marx's 'own' discussion in the earlier pages does not speak of a *tendency* of the rate of profit to fall, but in terms of a 'law'.[7] 'Tendency' does appear in the comments of the second part; it also appears in a later ref-erence back to the 'law'.[8] As we will see, this vocabulary changes decisively in subsequent manuscripts.

We may conclude from this discussion that in the *Grundrisse* Marx adopts the view of a 'trend fall' in the profit-rate.[9] Its presuppositions are the unfolding throughout time of the immanent contradictions of production founded upon capital, which progressively reduce the rate of profit. The momentary 'delay' of the diminution of the originary quantity of the rate of profit does not prevent its ultimate 'exhaustion'. When it is finally depleted, the capitalist mode of produc-tion comes to an end – violently.

The *Grundrisse*'s 'crisis', 'law' and 'immanent critique': critical remarks

Several elements of Marx's analysis of the fall of the rate of profit in the *Grundrisse* should here be noted.

i) As we have seen, Marx regularly deploys metaphors and terms throughout this text that can be characterised as a 'rhetoric of crisis'. This 'apocalyptic' vision bears decisive similarities to the general young-Hegelian atmosphere in which Marx passed his student-years in Berlin, particularly as articulated in Bruno Bauer's early political theory (a strong influence on Marx in his formative years).[10] However, there is an important difference between these different uses of the theme of crisis, both in terms of their political context and their theoretical field of reference.

Marx and the young Hegelians more generally elaborated a theory of *political* crisis in the years leading up to 1848. This theory attempted to identify a political agent capable of resolving the crisis in a positive form, namely the supersession of

---

7. Marx 1973, pp. 745–51.
8. Cf. Marx 1973, p. 763. Note in particular the following, where 'inherent laws' and 'tendencies' are used interchangeably: 'A. Smith's phrase is correct to the extent that only in competition – the action of capital upon capital – are the inherent laws of capital, its tendencies, realized'.
9. On the difference between 'trend' and 'tendency', cf. Reuten 1997 and 2004.
10. On Bauer's political theory and his influence on Marx, cf. Tomba 2002.

what the *German Ideology* refers to as 'all the old shit' ['*den ganzen alten Dreck*'].[11] Already in the closing pages of the text now known as *Towards the Critique of Hegel's Philosophy of Right. Introduction*, Marx had identified this agent as the 'proletariat'. With the failure of the revolutions that coincided with the publication of the *Communist Manifesto*, the defeated '48ers' tried to keep their hopes alive for a revival of this 'world-historical' subject. Fidelity to (the memory of) the theme of crisis, in the midst of widespread abandonment of revolutionary politics by their contemporaries, constituted one of their most potent psychological supports.[12]

The *Grundrisse*'s deployment of similar motifs in the discussion of the fall of the profit-rate, on the other hand, explicitly does *not* invoke a directly political agent. Marx explicitly confines his analysis to the internal determinations of capital as such. The 'violent overthrow' occurs as a result of the working out of the inner laws of capital, conceived as a (self-destructive) subject. It is not an agent acting against the destructive *effects* of the capitalist mode of production's recurring crises that overthrow it, but capital itself as *causa sui* that prepares its own downfall. Arguably, Marx has here committed the error of too rapidly 'translating' terminology from one field to another (from political to economic theory), without attending to their substantially different contexts. While such haste may be unexceptional in notes written for personal use, their (re-)introduction into Marxian discussions of crisis-theory following the publication of the *Grundrisse* provided support for an interpretation of *Capital* Volume III in particular that neglected the latter's *systematic* analysis of the capitalist mode of production.

ii) It is sometimes not remembered that the 'law' of the fall of the profit-rate was not a theoretical novelty introduced by Marx.[13] On the contrary, in Marx's day, a 'law of the tendency of the rate of profit to fall' was taken for granted among economists, on both empirical and theoretical grounds. Even a theorist such as William Stanley Jevons – hardly a Marxist – could write that 'there are sufficient statistical facts ... to confirm this conclusion historically. The only question that can arise is as to the actual cause of this tendency'.[14]

Along with his (near) contemporaries, Marx inherited this law from the problematic of classical political economy, where it plays a decisive role in the thought of Smith and Ricardo in particular. As Marx notes in the *Grundrisse*,

---

11. Marx and Engels 1975–2005, Volume 5, p. 70.

12. Cf. Kouvelakis 2005 for an analysis of the legacy of 1848 in Marx's later political career.

13. Heinrich 2007b provides a valuable historical perspective on contemporary discussions.

14. Jevons 1970, pp. 243–4.

'A. Smith explained the fall of the rate of profit, as capital grows, by the competition among capitals'.[15] Ricardo had found Smith's explanation of the law inadequate, but rather than abandoning it, he proposed his own explanation: 'The falling rate of profit hence corresponds, with him [Ricardo], to the nominal growth of wages and real growth of ground rent'.[16] In both Smith and Ricardo, the rate of profit is conceived as an originary quantity, which is subsequently corrupted and depleted by the development of capitalist production. Just as the fertility of soil is conceived as a natural 'given' quantity, so the 'fructiferous' nature of capital (revealingly, Marx's title for this section) can be exhausted by the decline of the profit-rate to an absolute minimum.[17]

Marx was of course well acquainted with these versions of the 'law', as his extensive comments in the *Grundrisse* on Smith's and Ricardo's attempted explanations of it readily testify. Marx subjects these views to immanent critique in the *Grundrisse*; at this stage, however, his thought remains indebted in many key respects to their general problematic. This is perhaps most noticeable in Marx's maintenance of the term 'law' of the fall of the profit-rate, and his linking of this law to the notion of an 'exhaustion' of the capitalist mode of production by the repetition of debilitating crises.

Nevertheless, Marx's textual analysis of Smith, Ricardo and others in the second half of the section on the fall of the profit-rate in the *Grundrisse* provides enough evidence that the 'law of the tendency of the rate of profit to fall' cannot be asserted as an unquestionable key tenet of the Marxian research-paradigm, as has sometimes been done. In Marx's own work, it instead has the status of a problem for future research.

---

15. Marx 1973, p. 751. Marx responds to Smith thus: 'Competition can permanently depress the rate of profit in all branches of industry, i.e. the average rate of profit, only if and in so far as a general and permanent fall of the rate of profit, having the force of a law, is conceivable prior to competition and regardless of competition. Competition executes the inner laws of capital; makes them into compulsory laws towards the individual capital, but it does not invent them. It realizes them. To try to explain them simply as results of competition therefore means to concede that one does not understand them' (Marx 1973 p. 752).

16. Marx 1973, p. 752. Marx describes this as Ricardo's 'one-sided mode of conceiving it [the falling rate of profit], which seizes on only one single case, just as the rate of profit can fall because wages momentarily rise etc., and which elevates a historical relation holding for a period of 50 years and reversed in the following 50 years to the level of a general law, and rests generally on the historical disproportion between the developments of industry and agriculture' (Ibid.). He later adds sarcastically that as far as the law of the falling rate of profit is concerned, Ricardo 'flees from economics to seek refuge in organic chemistry' (Marx 1973, p. 754).

17. The simplicity of the German title is even more revealing: 'Das Kapital als Frucht bringend' – literally, 'capital as fruit-bringing'.

iii) Despite its lingering crisis-rhetoric and indebtedness to the problematic of classical political economy, the *Grundrisse* nevertheless also demonstrates Marx's first tentative departure from this 'naturalist' paradigm.

As we have seen, Marx begins his study of this issue in the *Grundrisse* by examining the quantitative 'law of the falling rate of profit' of the political economy of his days. He is not satisfied by Smith's and Ricardo's explanations of this 'most important law of modern political economy' because they do not grasp the fall in the rate of profit as an inner and necessary determination of capital. In the case of Ricardo in particular, Marx focuses upon Ricardo's insufficient distinction between rate of surplus-value and rate of profit. Hence, he slowly begins to develop his own explanation for a fall in the rate of profit: namely, a rise in productivity. He thus reformulates the 'law' as one of a combined decrease of the rate of profit and increase of the mass of profit. This perspective will remain central to all the other manuscripts, albeit in increasingly clarified formulations. It will constitute the backbone of the 'law as such' of chapter thirteen of the published *Capital* Volume III.

Even more importantly, as a consequence of this 'reformulation' of the 'law' in terms of an inverse relation between profit-rate and profit-amount, Marx also sketches out in the *Grundrisse* another element that will be further developed in later manuscripts: namely, the notion of factors that 'delay' the fall of the rate of profit. As we will see, it is the redefinition of these 'delays' in terms of 'tendency' (conceived as 'operative power' rather than empirical trend) that will open the way to Marx's linking of an increase in productivity, (potential) growth of the exploitation of labour and a notion of crises as 'restorative' or *aufhebend* (sublating, rather than merely destructive) mechanisms.

The 1861–3 manuscript

We can now move on to Marx's 1861–3 manuscripts.[18] A second main text on the (tendency of the) rate of profit to fall can be found in section seven of Marx's Notebook XVI, dated December 1861 January 1862. This text – even more so than the *Grundrisse* – has much the character of notes intended to aid the author's understanding. Here, Marx continues his immanent critique, going over themes introduced in the *Grundrisse* and drawing out their inner determinations.

Marx once again refers to the 'law' as 'the most important law of political economy'.[19] However, his definition immediately qualifies this law as 'a *tendency*

---

18. Marx 1978–82. Unless otherwise indicated, all citations are taken from the English translation by Ben Fowkes in Marx and Engels 1975–2005h, pp. 104–45.

19. Marx and Engels 1975–2005h, p. 104.

[of the rate of profit] *to fall with the progress of capitalist production*.[20] The 'law' has now become a 'tendency' (admittedly, Marx will continue to use the term 'law' in this text, but its qualification as 'tendency' is clearly implicit throughout). Next, Marx inquires into the reasons for this tendency of the general rate of profit to fall. He notes that the 'whole of the Ricardian and Malthusian school is a cry of woe over the day of judgement this process would inevitably bring about', before arguing that: 'apart from theory there is also the practice, the crises from *superabundance of capital or, what comes to the same, the mad adventures capital enters upon in consequence of the lowering of {the} rate of profit. Hence crises – see Fullarton – acknowledged as a *necessary violent means for the cure* of the plethora of capital, and the *restoration* of a sound rate of profit*'.[21]

'*Necessary violent means for the cure* of the plethora of capital'; '*Restoration* of a sound rate of profit'. The crises are no longer repeated 'on a higher scale', leading finally to the capitalist mode of production's 'violent overthrow', as in the *Grundrisse*. Rather, 'in practice', crises function as a corrective measure, which restores a 'sound rate of profit' and thus presumably permit capital accumulation to begin once again (in a cyclical theory of upswing and downswing).

After analysing factors that might cause the general rate of profit to fall, especially 1) 'if the absolute magnitude of surplus value falls' and 2) 'because the ratio of variable to constant capital falls', Marx states: 'But the law of development of capitalist production (see Cherbuliez, etc.) consists precisely in the continuous decline of variable capital . . . in *relation* to the constant component of capital . . .'[22]

Clearly, this reformulates in more developed terms a perspective already present in the *Grundrisse*. Marx then continues to argue that: 'The tendency towards a fall in the general rate of profit therefore = the development of the productive power of capital, i.e. the rise in the ratio in which objectified labour is exchanged for living labour'.

The 'tendency' – not 'law' – 'towards a fall in the general rate of profit' is now no longer seen, as in the *Grundrisse*, as the gravedigger of the capitalist mode of production. On the contrary, it is now equivalent to 'the development of the productive power of capital'. Marx argues that this development 'implies, at the same time, the concentration of capital in large amounts at a small number of places'.[23] This is followed by an explicit statement about two factors that

---

20. Ibid.
21. Marx and Engels 1975–2005h, p. 105; emphasis added. Passages between asterisks appear in English in the German manuscript. Passages in curly brackets are added by the editors; often they are reconstructions of illegible handwriting.
22. Marx and Engels 1975–2005h, p. 106.
23. Marx and Engels 1975–2005h, pp. 107–8.

work against each other, that is, the rate of surplus-value and the composition of capital:

> Both movements not only go {hand in hand} but condition each other. They are only different forms and phenomena in which the same law is expressed. But they work in opposite directions, in so far as the rate of profit comes into consideration.[24]

Subsequently, Marx indicates that 'for the rate of profit to remain the same', these factors 'would have to grow in the same ratio'. He argues that: 'this is only possible within certain limits, and that it is rather the reverse, the tendency towards a fall in profit – or a *relative* decline in the amount of surplus value hand in hand with the growth in the rate of surplus value – which must predominate, as is also confirmed by experience'.[25]

Further on, we read that an increase in the exploitation of labour can in a certain sense 'delay' the fall of the rate of profit, to use the terminology of the *Grundrisse*; expressed in other terms, it 'absorbs' some of the tendency to fall of the profit-rate. (Note that the exploitation of labour did not figure at all in the *Grundrisse*'s analysis of the fall of the profit-rate – perhaps remarkably, given its emphasis elsewhere upon the centrality of 'living labour', and the importance that has been accorded to this dimension of the 1857–8 notebooks by figures such as Antonio Negri). 'If one considers the development of productive power and the relatively not so pronounced fall in the rate of profit, the exploitation of labour must have increased very much, and what is remarkable is not the fall in the rate of profit but that it has not fallen to a greater degree'.[26]

Finally, Marx combines the *Grundrisse*'s distinction between the amount and the rate of profit with this focus upon an increase in the exploitation of labour. He concludes this most systematic part of his presentation with the following summary:

> The decline in the average rate of profit expresses an increase in the productive power of labour or of capital, and, following from that, on the one hand a heightened exploitation of the living labour employed, and [on the other hand] a *relatively reduced amount of living labour* employed at the heightened rate of exploitation, calculated on a particular amount of capital.
>
> It does not now follow automatically from this law that the *accumulation* of capital declines or that the absolute *amount* of *profit* falls (hence also the *absolute*, not *relative*, *amount* of surplus value, which is expressed in the profit).

---

24. Marx and Engels 1975–2005h, p. 109.
25. Marx and Engels 1975–2005h, p. 110.
26. Marx and Engels 1975–2005h, p. 111.

The remainder of the text is an analysis of the connections between the relevant concepts: rising labour-productivity together with a rising organic composition of capital; and rising rate of surplus-value, profit and the rate of profit.[27] In general, the text is unsystematic, petering out into a series of undeveloped notes and jottings. The general impression this manuscript gives is that Marx is searching for a new conceptual framework. What is remarkable is that the 'breakdown'-perspective so central to the *Grundrisse*'s analysis is entirely absent from this text.

The 1864–5 manuscript (manuscript of *Capital* Volume III)

We can now finally turn to the parts of Marx's manuscripts from 1863–7 that deal with the rate of profit, dating from 1864–5 (they were later edited by Engels for publication in *Capital* Volume III in 1894). These manuscripts were only published in German in the *MEGA* in 1992. The first pages of the manuscript are similar to the published text of *Capital* Volume III; for convenience's sake we will cite the 1894 text and refer to the 1864–5 manuscript and other editions in order to indicate significant variations.

Marx begins by setting out a hypothetical example of a falling profit-rate. Then he writes: (1) this as a tendency is what we perceive in reality;[28] (2) it is what the economists perceived and have tried to explain.[29] Next, Marx shifts the emphasis to what he apparently sees as a kernel of capitalist development: first, accumulation and concentration of capital along with rising productivity of labour, and second, a fall in the *rate* of profit along with a rise in the *amount* of profits.[30] To him, *this* seems in fact to be the 'law': the inverse relation of rate and amount of profit (recall that since the *Grundrisse*, he has indicated this as the sphinx's riddle that classical political economy could not resolve).

After this, Marx immediately moves to the counteracting tendencies (the text of Chapter Fourteen in the published version of *Capital* Volume III). He writes: 'Viewed abstractly, the rate of profit might remain the same ... The rate of profit could even rise, if ...'.[31]

Directly following this formulation, Engels added: 'In practice, however, the rate of profit will fall in the long run, as we have already seen'[32] – a phrase that

---

27. Marx and Engels 1975–2005h, pp. 113–45.
28. Marx 1981 [1894F], p. 318.
29. Marx 1981 [1894F], p. 319.
30. Marx 1992 [1894M], pp. 291, 298, 300.
31. Marx 1981 [1894F], pp. 336–7; cf. Marx 1992c [1894M], p. 319.
32. Marx 1981 [1894F], p. 337; cf. Marx 1974a [1894U], p. 230.

is not only missing from Marx's manuscript-text, but which seems inconsistent with Marx's general line of argument.[33]

When Marx sets out the counteracting forces/tendencies at the end of this chapter, he repeatedly indicates that these do 'not annul the general law', but make it operate as a tendency.[34] He also says that the latter 'to a greater or lesser degree paralyse' its operation,[35] which he repeats again in conclusion.[36] Finally, he argues that: 'The law operates [*wirkt*] therefore simply as a tendency, whose effect [*Wirkung*] becomes strikingly pronounced only under particular circumstances and when extended out over long periods [*auf lange Perioden ausgedehnt*]'.[37]

After this, Marx's manuscript returns to 'his' formulation of the law: namely, the proposition that increases in productivity of labour via an increase in the organic composition of capital result in a combined increase of the amount of profits and a decrease of the rate of profit.[38] 'The law that a fall in the rate of profit precipitated [*herbeigeführte*] by the development of productiveness is accompanied by an increase in the mass of profit...'.[39] The *Grundrisse*'s inverse relation of profit-rate and amount is here continued.[40] However, it is now the development of productivity that precipitates a fall in the rate of profit.

Next, Marx highlights the issue of the depreciation of capital. One page further, though, he puts this in a different light, first rephrasing the issue in terms of a contradiction, then developing it into periodical crises. Significantly, these crises are conceived, as in the 1861–3 manuscript, in terms of restoration, rather than the 'overthrow' of the *Grundrisse*:

> Simultaneously with the fall in the profit rate, the mass of capital grows, and hand in hand with it goes a depreciation of the existing capital, which checks this fall and gives an accelerating impulse to the accumulation of capital-value. Simultaneously with the development of productivity, the composition of capital becomes higher, there is a relative decline in the variable portion

---

33. For an analysis of this and similar modifications of the text made by Engels and the support this gives to a trend fall interpretation, cf. Reuten 2004, pp. 172 ff.

34. Marx 1981 [1894F], p. 341

35. Marx 1981 [1894F], p. 344; Marx 1992c [1894M], p. 304, p. 306.

36. Marx 1981 [1894F], p. 346; Marx 1992c [1894M], p. 308.

37. Marx 1981 [1894F], p. 346; translation modified; cf. Marx 1972 [1894E], p. 249; Marx 1974a [1894U], p. 239; Marx 1992c [1894M], p. 308.

38. Marx 1992c [1894M], pp. 309–40.

39. Marx 1992c [1894M], p. 316; cf. Marx 1974a [1894U], pp. 225–6; cf. Marx 1981 [1894F], p. 332; Marx 1972 [1894E], p. 236.

40. Cf. Marx 1992c [1894M], p. 322; Marx 1981 [1894F], p. 356. Marx also repeats the statement soon after: '[We have seen that] as the capitalist mode of production develops, so the rate of profit falls, while the mass of profit rises together with the increasing mass of capital applied' (Marx 1992c [1894M], p. 322; Marx 1981 [1894F], p. 356).

as against the constant. These different influences may at one time operate predominantly side by side spatially, and at another succeed each other in time; periodically [*periodisch*] the conflict of antagonistic agencies finds vent in crises. The crises are always but momentary violent solutions of the existing contradictions – violent eruptions – which restore the disturbed balance.[41]

The theme of restoration is emphasised in the next pages of Marx's manuscript on overproduction, over-accumulation and devaluation of capital. He writes that: 'Under all circumstances, however, the balance will be restored by the *destruction of capital* to a greater or lesser extent'.[42]

As if to emphasise the point, Marx finally sets out how crisis and its aftermath restores the rate of profit: 'And so we go round the whole circle once again. One part of the capital that was devalued by the cessation of its function now regains its old value. But, with expanded conditions of production, a wider market and *increased productivity*, it will once again go though the same vicious circle [*Zirkel vicieux*]'.[43]

As in the 1861–3 manuscript, the law of the fall of the profit-rate and its crisis do not issue in the overthrow of the capitalist mode of production. On the contrary, we have a cycle of decrease and increase ('restoration') of the rate of profit. Given that this 'vicious circle' thereby increases the productivity of labour, it is a means by which the future potential capacity for the exploitation of labour is strengthened.[44]

By the time of the *Capital* Volume III manuscript, therefore, the naturalistic and unilinear paradigm of classical political economy has been decisively left behind. The profit-rate is no longer viewed as an originary quantity doomed to progressive exhaustion as it passes through time, following a secular-trend fall

---

41. Marx 1992c [1894M], p. 323; Marx 1972 [1894E], p. 259; Marx 1981 [1894F], p. 357; Marx 1974a, [1894U], p. 249.

42. Marx 1992c [1894M], p. 328; cf. Marx 1972 [1894E], p. 264; Marx 1981 [1894F], p. 362; Marx 1974a [1894U], p. 253.

43. Marx 1992c [1894M], p. 329; emphasis added; cf. Marx 1972 [1894E], p. 265; Marx 1981 [1894F], p. 364; Marx 1974a [1894U], p. 255. Significantly, Marx – in an otherwise fully German text – apparently feels the need to make use of the French 'vicieux', since the French 'cercle vicieux', like the English 'vicious circle', has a double meaning: on the one hand, that of a faulty cycle (the one chosen by Engels in his edition of *Capital* Volume III with the replacement of *fehlerhafter Kreislauf*); and, on the other, that of an 'endless circle', or lasting recurrence, in which one thing leads to another and back again in a spiral of presupposition and confirmation.

44. For this reason, rather than the 'law of the tendency of the rate of profit to fall' (TRPF), a more appropriate name for Marx's 'law/tendency' might be the 'theory of the rate of the profit-cycle' (TRPC). Marx's continuing use of the formulation of classical political economy can be attributed to his method of immanent critique; the old terminology is maintained, but Marx's analysis has fundamentally transformed its conceptual content.

within and across conjunctures. Instead, its cyclical rise and fall within a given economic conjuncture is theorised as a qualitative intensification of the contradictory articulation within the capitalist mode of production of increases in productivity, the exploitation of labour and the growth of capital by means of the expropriation of surplus-value. Economic crises do not signify the capitalist mode of production's automatic end, but rather, only one of the possible conjunctural resolutions of its recurring immanent contradictions. The *economic* confines or limits [*Schranken*] of the capitalist mode of production are now twofold: (1) a rise in productivity generates a rate of profit decrease and this decrease must be overcome again and again through crises; (2) production does not cease when required by the satisfaction of needs, but when required by the realisation and production of profit.[45] We will return to the question of potential *political limits* of the capitalist mode of production in our conclusion.

Theoretical and political reasons for the reformulation of the 'law'

Why did Marx undertake this reformulation of 'the most important law of political economy'? Several hypotheses can be considered.

i) A first hypothesis may be that Marx, having seen the durability of the capitalist mode of production and it ability to withstand the crisis of the late 1850s, slowly begins to see the need to rethink his central concepts. In the *Grundrisse*, he remains under the spell of the memory of 1848 and its expected world-transforming 'deluge' (as he wrote to Engels in a famous letter on the 8 December 1857). In the 1860s, on the other hand, he revises his crisis-rhetoric and focuses much more on a systematic analysis of the capitalist mode of production. This hypothesis would be fundamentally *political* in nature, i.e., it would see the cause of theoretical reformulation in the revision of political perspectives.

However, as we have seen, already in the *Grundrisse* Marx has laid the theoretical foundations that could lead – not inevitably, but possibly – to his reformulation in the later manuscripts. While he first strongly criticises the 'naturalist' presuppositions of classical political economy in his main arguments, his conclusion then problematically transfers a political theory of crisis onto the terrain of political economy. The two elements of his argument are based upon opposed presuppositions; their uneasy *modus vivendi* in the *Grundrisse* has the potential to grow into a contradiction with further study and reflection.

---

45. Marx 1992c [1894M], p. 332; cf. Marx 1972 [1894E], p. 268; Marx 1981 [1894F], p. 367; Marx 1974a [1894U], p. 258.

ii) A second hypothesis might therefore be that Marx was led to reformulate the law of the falling rate of profit more for *theoretical* than for political reasons. His method of immanent critique in the *Grundrisse* has already reformulated a key aspect of the 'traditional' law, distinguishing between amount and rate of profit, and rate of profit and rate of surplus-value. As the *Grundrisse* are primarily a compilation of notes for private use, Marx does not yet reformulate the 'law as such'. But the decisive theoretical acquisition has 'almost-already' been made, merely 'camouflaged' by a lingering crisis-rhetoric that will be dispensed with in future manuscripts.

While there may be some good textual reasons to support this second hypothesis, it underemphasises the extent to which Marx's reformulation of the law remains only a 'work in progress' in the *Grundrisse*. In particular, it neglects the fact that in 1857–8 Marx had not yet clearly distinguished between a quantitative-trend fall and the fall of the rate of profit as a 'tendency' or 'operative power'. Furthermore, it does not take into account the importance of the 1861–3 and 1864–5 manuscripts' articulation of the falling profit-rate with the increase in productivity and thus the potential for a higher rate of exploitation of labour. Marx cannot yet fully explain the function of cyclical upswings and downswings within the capitalist mode of production, despite having already achieved insight into the ways in which the temporary destruction of capital may function as a means for the growth of capital's hegemony over labour in succeeding conjunctures via increased potential productivity.

iii) A third hypothesis may be that Marx sought to confront the political problem of how to respond to the crisis of the late 1850s by deepening his theoretical reflection. Inheriting this 'most important law of modern political economy' and dissatisfied with the capacity of previous formulations to explain theoretically what occurs 'in practice', Marx abandons the naturalism of classical political economy and formulates the law in relational rather than quantitative terms (via the elaboration of the distinction between surplus-value and profit). At this stage, however, he can ultimately find no better solution than the invocation of a memory of a previous political conjuncture in order to explain the purpose of crises in the capitalist mode of production (its 'overthrow').

As his critique deepens in the manuscripts of the early 1860s, however, he attempts to grasp crises 'as such', in terms of their internal functioning. He reformulates the falling rate of profit as a tendency that is equivalent to the development of the productive power of capital, and articulates this with an increase in the potential of capital to exploit labour. The tendency of the rate of profit to fall now figures as an operative power in the production of crises, which are conceived as but one possible moment in any given cycle of accumulation, a moment by means of which capital prepares itself to 'go though the same vicious circle' once again. The result of Marx's reformulation of the 'law' is therefore the abandonment of an eschatological theory of crisis: capitalism will not reach its end via automatic internal forces (economism of breakdown), but rather via a political movement of the exploited that seeks to confront the foundations of this vicious circle. Hence Marx's systematic analysis of capitalism paves the way for a transcended [*aufgehoben*] political concept and theory of crisis, which emphasises the need for a concrete analysis of capital's increased potential to exploit labour in the course of any given conjuncture. This seems to us to be the most satisfying hypothesis, which takes into account the intertwining of both political and theoretical reasons in Marx's reformulation.

Themes for future research

In conclusion, we would like to enumerate briefly some themes for future research that arise from this philological analysis.

i) The first theme for future research concerns the relative weight in Marx's intellectual development of his debt to classical political economy, on the one hand, and his debt to Hegel, on the other. According to a well-known narrative, Marx inherited from Hegel (in truth, from certain currents of the *Vormärz* young Hegelianism) a 'philosophy of history' whose teleological dimensions constituted a profound impediment to the development of a scientific analysis of the capitalist mode of production, regardless of however much he may have benefited from Hegel in other respects. Of course, this view has been usefully challenged by many in recent years, as a more profound image of Hegel's thought becomes current. The continuing purchase of such perspectives in the field of Marxian theory, however, can be attested to by, for example, the favourable recent reception of works such as Jacques Bidet's *Exploring Marx's 'Capital'*, among others. Bidet argues that Marx found in Hegel an 'epistemological support/obstacle', which he attempted progressively to overcome.[46] Based upon this analysis of the treatment of the fall of the rate of profit in the *Grundrisse* and subsequent manuscripts, however, we might suggest that more attention could be directed towards the 'epistemological supports/obstacles' that Marx found in the concepts of classical political economy. For classical political economy, perhaps even more so than Hegel's system or those of many of its young Hegelian inheritors, was founded upon its own 'naturalistic' and sometimes teleological presuppositions, albeit culturally and conceptually distinct from those of post-Hegelian philosophies of

---

46. Bidet 2007, pp. 3 ff.

history. Future research should examine more closely the intertwining of Marx's attempts to liberate himself from the deleterious philosophico-historiosophical dimensions of both paradigms.

ii) A second theme for future research is the importance of the rate of profit for an analysis of the relationship between politics and economics in Marx's mature critique of political economy. The 'law' was often interpreted in the twentieth century in an 'economistic' fashion as implying the automatic production of political effects (overthrow of the capitalist mode of production) from economic causes (crises produced by trend-decline in rate of profit). As we have seen, certain elements in the *Grundrisse*'s discussion of the theme certainly seem to support this perspective, while the later manuscripts directly contradict it. They are limited to an analysis of the economic confines or limits [*Schranken*] of the capitalist mode of production. An explicit analysis of political responses to this situation lies beyond the scope of Marx's mature critique of political economy, as 'unfinished business' for future Marxian research.

Nevertheless, Marx's articulation of the fall in the profit-rate with increases in productivity and the exploitation of labour takes us to the verge of properly political analysis. By focusing on the concrete analysis of each individual conjuncture, it provides us with knowledge of the limits within which capital and therefore *a fortiori* labour are forced to operate in the capitalist mode of production. This 'unfinished business' regards the always-already political nature of the economic limits of capital – fundamentally, the juridical guarantees of profits in the capitalist mode of production and therefore private property of the means of production as its foundation.

iii) Finally, a third theme for future research concerns the implications of this analysis for contemporary debates, both regarding the tendency of the rate of profit to fall and the status of Marxian research as social theory.

Regarding the former: the 'second Brenner debate' had already focused many theorists' attention on the question of the fall in the profit-rate as a possible explanation for recent economic trends; the financial crisis that began in 2008 witnesses a deepening and diffusion of this tendency.[47] While not taking up a position on these debates in this paper, we suggest that the analysis of Marx's different texts discussing the fall in the profit-rate provides a powerful critical perspective from which to consider both these debates and the contemporary

---

47. Brenner 2002 and 2006 have stimulated wide-ranging debates in which the fall in the profit-rate has figured as a central point of contention. Harman 2007 is representative of many recent attempts to deploy this concept in order to explain the current world-economy and its interlocking crises.

conjuncture more generally. In particular, the findings in this paper might alert us to the possibility that the current crisis may prepare the way for a restoration of a sound rate of profit in a future 'vicious circle', thereby increasing capital's hegemony over labour via increases in potential productivity. Such an analysis is the necessary prelude both to a critique of the explicitly *political* forms that enable the renewal of the profit-rate's 'vicious circle', and to the exploration of the political practices that would be necessary to overcome not merely those limits but the capitalist mode of production in its totality.

Regarding the latter: research inspired by Marx's work has often been accused of essentialism, organicism, teleology etc. – sometimes not unjustly. The philological analysis presented in this chapter, however, demonstrates that at least one researcher in this paradigm recognised the theoretical and political weaknesses of a theory founded on these perspectives and attempted to remove them progressively from his conceptual arsenal. Future Marxian research, now as always, should attempt to build upon this perspective and carry the method of immanent critique through to a reconsideration of the philosophical presuppositions of other central concepts of the Marxian paradigm, in the perspective of producing a genuinely 'social' theory of the functioning of the capitalist mode of production.

Part Six
Society and History in the *Grundrisse*

Between Pre-Capitalist Forms and Capitalism: The Problem of Society in the *Grundrisse*[1]

Luca Basso

An analysis of the concept of society within the *Grundrisse* allows for the specific differences among productive structures to be understood. Marx was not interested, primarily, in delineating the general history of humanity, and, in particular, the order that has been followed throughout history. Instead, Marx's interest lay in comprehending the specific mechanisms of the capitalist system. In this way, we find ourselves turning away from a comprehensive theory of social formations and instead face an analysis of the formation of capitalist society, in its method of becoming the dominant mode of production, characterised by specific contradictions. Central to this reasoning is the investigation of the mode of capitalist production in its singularity and in its specific persistence. It is from this point of view that all other forms of production should be interpreted. In a passage from the *Einleitung* of 1857,[2] Marx affirms:

---

1. This article is the English translation of the article *Tra forme precapitalistiche e capitalismo: il problema della società nei 'Grundrisse'*, in Sacchetto and Tomba (eds.) 2008, pp. 58–73.
2. Among the numerous interpretations of the *Einleitung*, see: Krahl 1971; Negri 1998; Rovatti 1973; Schmidt 1971a; Gilbert 1981, pp. 262–7; Wilson 1991, pp. 111–19; Janoska (ed.) 1994.

> Bourgeois society is the most developed and the most complex historic orga-
> nization of production. The categories which express its relations, the com-
> prehension of its structure, thereby also allows insights into the structure and
> the relations of production of all the vanished social formations out of whose
> ruins and elements it built itself up, whose partly still unconquered remnants
> are carried along within it, whose mere nuances have developed explicit sig-
> nificance within it, etc...Human anatomy contains a key to the anatomy of
> the ape...In all forms in where landed property rules, the natural relation
> still predominates; in those where capital rules, the social, historically created
> element.[3]

As bourgeois society remains the most differentiated historical organisation of
production yet seen, the categories that express its relationships remain the
most capable of investigating the nature of less complex societies that have preceded them. This does not mean that concepts derived from capitalism cancel
out historical diversities, but rather that they allow us to consider such aspects
in a more developed way.

Marx considers capitalism in its specific differentiated form with respect to
pre-capitalist formations; the constitutive elements of the capitalist system cannot be applied unduly, *sic et simpliciter*, on other modes of production.[4] Nevertheless, one is not faced with an investigation of social structures in their order
of succession, but with a perspective departing from the present order, that is,
the capitalist order: 'It would therefore be unfeasible and wrong to let the economic categories follow one another in the same sequence as that in which they
were historically decisive. Their sequence is determined, rather, by their relation
to one another in modern bourgeois society, which is precisely the opposite of
that which seems to be their natural order or which corresponds to historical
development'.[5] From this point of view, the core of reasoning resides in a specific
analysis of the mode of capitalist production.

Having investigated this problem, it is then necessary to examine the distinctions of a pre-capitalist community. Marx, in notebooks IV and V of the *Grundrisse* entitled '*Formen, die der kapitalistischen Produktion vorhergehen*', in which
he surveyed at least fifty historical texts, individuates three pre-capitalist forms.
The first consists in a natural community, devoted to pasture and nomadic life
and founded upon family and the union of the families, the tribe, in direct contact
with the earth, which 'is the great workshop, the arsenal which furnishes both

---

3. Marx 1973, pp. 105–7. For a more detailed discussion of this theme, see Basso 2012a,
pp. 126–34.
4. See Marx 1973, p. 105. On the discontinuity of the capitalist system in relation to
preceding structures, see Lefort 1978.
5. Marx 1973, p. 107.

means and material of labour, as well as the seat, the *base* of the community. They relate naively to it as the *property of the community*, of the community producing and reproducing itself in living labour ...'.[6] A specific reference is made, besides the Slavic community, to the Asiatic or Oriental community form:[7] 'In the Asiatic form (at least, predominantly), the individual has no property but only possession; the real proprietor, proper, is the commune – hence property only as *communal property* in land'.[8]

Within the Marxist debate, there has been much discussion of the question of the Asiatic mode of production, a category that will be taken up again in *Capital*. It is necessary to point out that, in the era of elaboration on the *Pre-capitalist Economic Formations*, Marx had a limited understanding of so-called 'primitive' societies. Additionally, during this period modern anthropology was only in its initial phases. The second form, described as a 'product of more active, historic life',[9] different from the preceding form, even though always presupposing the community, is indeed based on the city, but as a place created by farmers: 'The individual is placed in such conditions of earning his living as to make not the acquiring of wealth his object, but self-sustenance, his own reproduction as a member of the community; the reproduction of himself as proprietor of the parcel of ground, and in that quality, as a member of the commune'.[10]

Compared with the first form, 'the property [*Eigentum*] of the individual is here not, unlike the first case, itself directly communal property'.[11] Of this second pre-capitalist form, in which the element of war is crucial, there exist two models: that of classical ancient Greco-Roman history and the Germanic model. Slavery is the principal aspect of the ancient system. The Germanic social model, hinged on singular habitation,[12] differentiates itself from the classical one in the following way: 'In the world of antiquity, the city with its territory is the economic totality; in the Germanic world, the totality is the individual residence, which itself appears as only a small dot on the land belonging to it ...'.[13] The third pre-capitalist community, more advanced than the preceding ones, is the feudal one. It distinguishes itself because it rises from manufacturing, based on artisans organised into corporations, and therefore on a specialised production independent of commodities: 'Here the *master-servant relation* [*Herrschaftsverhältnis*] as

---

6. Marx 1973, p. 472.
7. See Sofri 1969.
8. Marx 1973, p. 484.
9. Marx 1973, p. 474.
10. Marx 1973, p. 476.
11. Marx 1973, pp. 474–5.
12. On the Germanic properties, see Marx 1857–8a, Vol. 2.
13. Marx 1973, p. 484.

essential element of appropriation'.[14] In this way, within the third pre-capitalist form, the question of the servitude of the serf begins to play a decisive role.

The sense of Marx's entire treatment is analytical, not historical; we clearly are not confronted with a mechanical 'succession' of phases. It is evident that, in such a reconstruction, there exists a risk of philosophy of history in the articulation of the movement from the first to the third pre-capitalist community, and from this last form into a capitalist one. In any case, Marx (and this appears particularly evident in his analysis of feudalism) does not investigate thoroughly the specific contradictions of pre-capitalist structures. Rather, he considers them to be constitutive references for the analysis of capitalist production. Before capitalism, in the 'prehistory' of capital, Marx does not individuate a linear, univocal logic of history; moreover, it can be affirmed that slavery, feudalism, and capitalism have followed in this order only in Europe: Marx never maintains that feudalism does not produce capitalism. Regardless, in these pre-capitalist forms, 'the individuals relate not as workers but as proprietors – and members of a community, who at the same time work. The aim of this work is not the creation of value ... rather, its aim is sustenance of the individual proprietor and of his family, as well as of the total community'.[15]

In such a scenario: 'the individuals in such a society, although their relations appear to be more personal, enter into connection with one another only as individuals imprisoned within a certain definition, as feudal lord and vassal, landlord and serf, etc., or as members of a caste etc. or as members of an estate etc.'[16]

In the pre-capitalist forms, men make up the Gemeinwesen as members of a community, into which they are inserted and on which they depend. What forcefully emerges is the difference between the modern social structure and that which preceded it: 'This indeed is a condition very different from that in which the individual or the individual member of a family or clan (later, community) directly and naturally reproduces himself, or in which his productive activity and his share in production are bound to a specific form of labour and of product, which determine his relation to others in just that specific way'.[17]

The primary principle of such formations consists, therefore, in the reproduction of the individual insofar as relating to a larger whole, a Gemeinwesen, a community, which does not present the slightest possibility of independence. From this analysis, we can see that, in pre-capitalist structures, 'the economic goal is the production of values of use', and therefore the individual establishes a relation with the objective working conditions as his own conditions and with the

---

14. Marx 1973, p. 500.
15. Marx 1973, pp. 471–2.
16. Marx 1973, p. 163.
17. Marx 1973, p. 157.

earth through mediation of the community:[18] 'The individual can never appear here in the dot-like isolation [*Punktualität*] in which it appears as mere free worker'.[19] In the pre-capitalist forms, the assumptions of circulation are external to production: the latter is continually in need of new, external impulses to 'reignite' itself. It is not capable of self-renewal. It cannot arrive at identifying itself in terms of the general reproduction of humanity. In such a situation, the circulation of commodities and social antagonisms are not immanent to the productive process: conflicts do not directly personify the shared conditions of labour.

Pre-capitalist structures are distinguished by their substantial unity: unity of man with the earth, precisely, with the objective conditions of labour, and with other men.[20] This 'organicism' inevitably presents a despotic character and keeps the single man 'attached' to the community like to an umbilical cord: usually returning to the metaphor of the 'chain'. Such unity, focused on the conservation of its members, on their reproduction as owners, is the fruit of a modest development of productive forces.[21] One is faced with an organisation founded upon personal relations, mediated by nature.[22] Even if the land is divided among individuals, they are owners insofar as they are members of the community. From analysis of the *Einleitung* of 1857, the idea becomes clear that man in the pre-capitalist formations does not become valued in his singularity, but in his belonging to a *Ganze*, an organic whole: 'The more deeply we go back into history, the more does the individual, and hence also the producing individual, appear as dependent, as belonging to a greater whole: in a still quite natural way in the family and in the family expanded into the clan [*Stamm*] ...'.[23]

In the first chapter of *Capital*, even if a real discussion of the pre-capitalist forms is absent, the forms are nonetheless considered as precedent structures with respect to the capitalist mode of production:

> In the ancient Asiatic and other ancient modes of production, we find that the conversion of products into commodities, and therefore the conversion of men into producers of commodities, holds a subordinate place ... Those ancient social organisms of production are, as compared with bourgeois society, extremely simple and transparent. But they are founded either on the immature development of man individually, who has not yet severed the

---

18. Marx 1973, p. 115.
19. Marx 1973, p. 485.
20. See Marx 1973, p. 97.
21. See Marx 1973, pp. 123–4. On pre-capitalist forms, see Hobsbawm 1964; Hindess & Hirst 1975; Carandini 1979.
22. See Marx 1973, pp. 98–9.
23. Marx 1973, p. 84.

umbilical cord that unites him with his fellowmen in a primitive tribal community, or upon direct relations of subjection.[24]

In such productive formations, the autonomous and independent development of the individual is neither conceivable, nor is the desire for such development encouraged: 'In earlier stages of development the single individual seems to be developed more fully, because he has not yet worked out his relationships in their fullness, or erected them as independent social powers and relations opposite himself'.[25]

In the *Einleitung*, Marx refers in particular to the second pre-capitalist community, represented (according to the subdivision outlined in the *Grundrisse*) in ancient civilisation, which attests to the backwardness of production-relations, highlighting the insensitivity of each nostalgic longing: 'An adult cannot become a child again, or he or she becomes childish... The Greeks were normal children. The charm their art has for us does not conflict with the immature stage of the society in which it originated'.[26]

As emphasised above, Marx does not intend to delineate a general history of humanity. Rather, he wants to comprehend the constitutive elements of capitalist production in its 'specific difference' with respect to pre-capitalist forms. Since capitalism's distinguishing sign is represented by the *Trennung*, Marx is interested in analysing the element of separation proper to capitalism and not pre-capitalist unity. Unity of pre-capitalist forms is indicated through metaphors such as the 'umbilical cord' and the 'chain': in the scenario in question, individual development appears 'blocked'. Strictly speaking, one can actually affirm that both the 'individual' and 'society' are categories unimaginable before the capitalist mode of production. In order to denote the pre-capitalist situation, one can make reference to the category of man, in his inseparable relation with the community to which he belongs and from which he could not be discernible, without making reference to the notion of the individual. In fact, as we have seen, the notion of the autonomous, independent individual, free from prior constraints, was inconceivable. For what concerns the notion of society, the question is more complicated, since each time there emerges a sort of *Geschichte der Gesellschaften: Urgesellschaft, Sklavengesellschaft, Feudalgesellschaft, bürgerliche Gesellschaft, kommunistische Gesellschaft* (history of societies: primitive society, slave-society or ancient slave-society, feudal society, bourgeois society and communist society).

Nevertheless, it can be affirmed that the concept of society, strictly speaking, concerns only bourgeois society, insofar as it is determined by the mea-

---

24. Marx 1952, p. 35.
25. Marx 1973, p. 162.
26. Marx 1973, p. 111.

sure of organic exchange between man and nature that has become specifically historical.[27] In order to identify society, a very developed stage is necessary where individuals enter into universal reciprocal contact, and relations become automatic, almost like a second nature. Marcuse affirms that 'the motor and the direction of the efficiency of society are given to reproduction, from the permanent renewal and repetition of its existence'.[28] There is a built-in dynamic within society, a continuous re-opening to non-predetermined solutions, not fully conditioned by nature. In order to denote pre-capitalist forms, Marx instead adopts terms such as tribe and community, since they are 'natural' structures: here one is faced with a static, fixed element that is apparently unchangeable. But, apart from the use of terms, and therefore apart from the fact that Marx uses the term of society to indicate capitalist form, real society is achieved by means of the actual capitalist system. A passage from the *Pre-capitalist Economic Formations* regarding this is very clear: from within the structures in question: '[t]he individuals may appear great. But there can be no conception here of a free and full development either of the individual or of the society, since such development stands in contradiction to the original relation [of man with the community]'.[29]

Two significant aspects emerge from such observations regarding the categories of the individual and society as the forms of production are compared. The first concerns the Marxist identification of the *novum* founded on the capitalist mode of production with respect to preceding communities: it results in a disruptive break that shifts the existing coordinates and that permits discussion of 'individuals', not of men, and that allows for the discussion of society as a complex web of social relations. According to Marx:

> ... capital creates the bourgeois society, and the universal appropriation of nature as well as of the social bond itself by the members of society. Hence the great civilising influence of capital; its production of a stage of society in comparison to which all earlier ones appear as mere *local developments* of humanity and as *nature-idolatry* ... In accord with this tendency, capital drives beyond national barriers and prejudices as much as beyond nature worship, as well as all traditional, confined, complacent, encrusted satisfactions of present needs, and reproductions of old ways of life. It is destructive towards all of this, and constantly revolutionises it, tearing down all the barriers which hem in the development of the forces of production, the expansion of needs, the all-sided development of production...[30]

---

27. See Krahl 1971.
28. See Marcuse 1928, p. 49.
29. Marx 1973, p. 487.
30. Marx 1973, pp. 409–10.

In this manner, one is faced with a 'new beginning', as opposed to the continuation of historical development, that signals a radical discontinuity, a mutation of humanity. The theme of the 'worldwide market' results in 'permanent revolution' of capital since the latter continually attempts to surpass imposed barriers: in this sense, the *Grundrisse* are consumed by the continual tension towards the *Weltmarkt* [world market], so much so that Marx affirms that '[t]he world market then, again, forms the presupposition of the whole as well as its substratum'.[31] From this point of view, the world-dimension is structurally inscribed within the notion of capital.

Within such a thematic treatment of the 'permanent revolution' of capital, there exist some difficulties, in particular, those related to the specific analysis of pre-capitalist forms. Marx underlines that each era interprets the preceding one (for example, this is true for bourgeois society as compared to medieval society, as well as for Christianity as compared to the pagan world) in a completely unilateral manner, such that it becomes incapable of criticising itself: in the *Einleitung*, he affirms that: '[t]he so-called historical presentation of development is founded, as a rule, on the fact that the latest form regards the previous ones as steps leading up to itself, and, since it is only rarely and only under quite specific conditions able to criticise itself – leaving aside, of course, the historical periods which appear to themselves as times of decadence – it always conceives them one-sidedly'.[32]

Nevertheless, Marx himself, beginning from the need to analyse the capitalist age, in many ways investigated pre-capitalist forms in a non-critical manner, or, more precisely, on the basis of capitalist presuppositions. As he is obliged to demonstrate the revolutionary character of the capitalist mode of production, the divisive element that he introduces, he is forced to postulate a preceding unity. But from this point of view, the analysis of pre-capitalist communities is as inadequate as the specification of their character of unity. If one treats the notion of separation there has to be, logically, the presupposition of a preceding unity, even if not described according to idyllic traits.

As outlined previously, the recognition of the expansive value of the capitalist *novum* at times assumes, in the *Grundrisse*, promethean traits. It becomes necessary critically to examine such a revolutionary and progressive character of capitalism in relation to the individual condition, highlighting the permanence of the present system, of servile elements present on the economic and juridical level: the surpassing of previous structures, as revealed in other Marxist texts, and in particular in *Capital*, has never been completed. Beyond the fact that the statute of the concept of revolution, if linked to capitalism, appears more or less

---

31. Marx 1973, pp. 227–8.
32. Marx 1975, p. 106.

problematic, it is necessary to underline further that the Marx's emphasis on the maximum potential of individuality and on its most extreme exploitation – contradictory elements that demolish the capitalist structure – risks presupposing a linearly progressive vision of history. But the fundamental problem in Marx's discourse lies in the equation: capitalism = salaried labour = free labour. The category of free labour, insofar as surpassing servile forms on either the economic or juridical plane, is affected exactly by an idea of 'grand narration' typical of nineteenth-century thought. In reality, forms of forced labour have never really disappeared from the horizon of capitalism. From this point of view, it becomes necessary to make more complex the category of free labour. Certain aspects of postcolonial studies have gone in this direction, regarding capitalism's subsumption of non-capitalist elements.[33] This path was previously explored by Rosa Luxemburg, who affirms in the *Accumulation of Capital* that capitalism is born and historically develops within a non-capitalist environment.[34]

The time of capital exists in a relation of dependence with other historical periods; they are not its own. From this point of view, the oppositions of history/ pre-history, man/monkey, appear ephemeral if one considers such elements in the context of the 'grand narrative' of the elimination of each so-called prehistoric element: the relationship between history and pre-history becomes reanimated continually in the capitalist dynamic. But to maintain that servile forms have continued to exist in the horizon of capitalism does not negate the latter's explosive novelty with respect to past structures of production, as well as the element of separation it introduces. Returning to the initial question regarding the relationship between history and pre-history, between man and monkey, it is necessary to underline that it is not the categories of bourgeois economy that validate other forms of society, but rather it is the criticism of these categories – and therefore the capacity to interpret pre-bourgeois forms as foreign to those bourgeois forms – that allows us to forge valid instruments to examine the past. In fact, the possibility for such criticism comes forth only during the capitalist period, when social classes emerge as direct manifestations of the relationships within production, and therefore capable of calling into question the very form that has generated them. In any case, the point of departure of the present reflection is constituted by capitalist separation: on the other hand, within the entire Marxian discourse, the element of separation and division, indicated by the terms *Trennung, Spaltung, Scheidung*, is absolutely crucial. At this point, in order to comprehend better the sense of reflection on pre-capitalist forms, it is necessary to delve deeper into the question of separation, the distinctive

---

33. Among the numerous studies focused on such themes, Chakrabarty 2000 should be referred to in particular.

34. See Luxemburg 1913.

sign of the capitalist mode of production: '... a presupposition is the separation [*Trennung*] of free labour from the objective conditions of its realization – from the means of labour and the material for labour. Thus, above all, release of the worker from the soil as his natural workshop – hence dissolution of small, free landed property as well as of communal landownership resting on the oriental commune'.[35]

The aspect that characterises the mode of capitalist production consists in the separation of the individual from the elements to which it was previously tied: with the mode of capitalist production there develops a process whereby man is uprooted, denaturalised. In this way, capitalism destroys all unity of common interest, placing individuals against each other in competition, a true '*bellum omnium contra omnes*' viewing each other as buyers or sellers of labour-power: '... the same process which divorced a mass of individuals from their previous relations to the *objective conditions of labour*, relations which were, in one way or another, affirmative, negated these relations, and thereby transformed these individuals into *free workers*, this same process freed – *dynamei* – these *objective conditions of labour* – land and soil, raw material, necessaries of life, instruments of labour, money or all of these – from their *previous state of attachment* to the individuals now separated from them'.[36]

What distinguishes capital from other modes of appropriation of others' labour is the fact that the duress exerted on workers is not external but internal to the immediate process of production: labour-power is incorporated into the production-process. The separation introduced by the capitalist mode of production, realised in particular through the mean of separation that is money (even in *Capital* there is the continual reference to *Scheidungsprozess*, that is, the process of capitalist separation), is not, however, a catastrophic event for Marx. Instead, it reveals itself as an expansive element with respect to the community's dominion over man, and to the presence of personal relationships, aspects particular to pre-capitalist forms.[37] Only following the destruction of personal relationships, mediated by the presence of a *Gemeinwesen* (that is, of a community) is it then possible to talk about the independence of the individual.

As we have seen, individual and society, understood in their genuine sense, are unconceivable prior to the capitalist mode of production. But now it becomes necessary to comprehend how the recognition of individuality, with its nature of independence, is to be reconciled with the presence of a strong social structure. In the first place, we can observe that, according to Marx, there exists a close connection between independence and isolation. The latter

---

35. Marx 1973, p. 471.
36. Marx 1973, p. 503.
37. Marx 1973, p. 4. See Givsan 1981, pp. 175–7.

element appears inconceivable in the absence of an autonomous, independent individual: '...human beings become individuals only through the process of history...Exchange itself is a chief means of this individuation [*Vereinzelung*]'.[38] On the other hand, 'the workers' individual isolation still implies their relative independence [*Ubabhängigkeit*]'.[39] Isolation does not constitute a devastating element *sic et simpliciter*, as it presupposes a worker's independence, something unthinkable in a context of pre-capitalist forms in which the individual was tied 'doubly' to its own community. The notion of the universal individual, capable of giving life to an unlimited series of social relations, is only possible due to the mode of capitalist production:

> Only in the eighteenth century, in 'civil society', do the various forms of social connectedness confront the individual as a mere means towards his private purposes, as external necessity. But the epoch which produces this standpoint, that of the isolated individual [*des vereinzelten einzelnen*], is also precisely that of the hitherto most developed social (from this standpoint, general) relations. The human being [*Mensch*] is in the most literal sense a political animal [*ein geselliges Tier*], not merely a gregarious animal, but an animal which can individuate itself [*sich vereinzeln*] only in the midst of society.[40]

Isolation thus does not solely receive a negative connotation, as it presupposes the individual, along with independence. Furthermore, the individuals in question are not only the effect of the internal mechanisms of the capitalist mode of production but are continuously traversed and transformed by subjective labour-power insurgencies that threaten the apparent stability of the system.[41]

In any case, the Marxist perspective cannot base itself on the representation of absolutely autonomous individuals. In the *Einleitung* of 1857, Marx's point of departure, contrary to what was claimed by classical political economists and philosophers of natural law, both creators of the '*Robinson Crusoe*' foundation of economics,[42] must be recognised not in an isolated individual, free from a social context, but rather in the 'socially determined individual production'.[43] In this manner, for Marx, it is meaningless to make reference to individuals regardless of their social context, given that they always-already find themselves working

---

38. Marx 1973, p. 496.
39. Marx 1973, p. 589.
40. Marx 1973, p. 84. See the original text in full: '*der Mensch ist...ein zoon politikon, nicht nur ein geselliges Tier, sondern ein Tier, das nur in der Gesellschaft sich vereinzeln kann*'. See Dumont 1977; Dumont 1983. On the Marx-Aristotle relation, see in particular: Vadée 1992, pp. 327–8; Schwartz 1979.
41. On the re-activation of the element of worker subjectivity within present-day dynamics, see Gambino 2003.
42. On the notion of *Robinsonaden*, see Janoska (ed.) 1994, p. 30; Iacono 1982.
43. Marx 1973, p. 83.

within a society. In this sense, we can affirm that the possibility of isolation constitutes the other side to sociality: 'The reciprocal and all-sided dependence of individuals who are indifferent to one another forms their social connection. This social bond is expressed in *exchange-value*...'.[44] Tinged with the ambivalence of the individual condition, the capitalist mode of production is founded on the sympathy between sociality and isolation, between the impetuous development of social relations and the emergence of a structure of indifference. Regarding this element, however, Marx's thought is not characterised by a sort of duality of the individual-social. Rather, his reference to social relations 'complicates' the question of the individual-social link. We can even affirm that Marx posits a supremacy of relations upon individuals: 'Society does not consist of individuals, but expresses the sum of interrelations, the relations within which these individuals stand'.[45]

The dominion of exchange-value, distinctive to the capitalist system, provokes an element of individual obligation, that is, a negation of the possibility of autonomy and independence which is reduced to a mere appendix of an external social mechanism, articulating itself in a series of social relations that are configured as relations of dominion. From this point of view, estrangement for Marx emerges in every concept founded upon the hypostatisation of society versus the individual: society presents, to use terminology that Marx will later develop, a 'spectral objectivity', so much so that for Marx it does not concern sacrificing oneself for society, but sacrificing the existing society. The notion of society does not become hypostatised, but rather – on the contrary – de-structured.[46] At any rate, in the context indicated, the exchange-value becomes autonomous from commodities, assuming a separate existence, and becoming itself a commodity, money:

> ...the power which each individual exercises over the activity of others or over social wealth exists in him as the owner of *exchange-values*, of *money*. The individual carries his social power [*gesellschaftliche Macht*], as well as his bond with society, in his pocket...In exchange-value, the social connection between persons is transformed into a social relation between things [*in ein gesellschaftliches Verhalten der Sachen*]; personal capacity [*das persönliche Vermögen*] into objective wealth.[47]

Social power is intimately connected to the dynamic of money, an individualised and isolated element, a necessary consequence of the development of

---

44. Marx 1973, p. 156. On the co-penetration between sociality and indifference, see Lohmann 1991.
45. Marx 1973, p. 265.
46. On Marxist destructuralisation of the concept of society, see Basso 2001.
47. Marx 1973, p. 157.

exchange-value. In this scenario, individual liberty and the subsumption to an objective power are two sides of the same coin.[48] In this way, Marx demystifies the 'semblance' of liberty and equality that 'seduces democracy': if we depart from the sphere of circulation and descend to the 'slums' of production, the elements in question convert themselves into their opposites.[49]

Examining the intrinsic duplicity of freedom and equality, one can comprehend the connection between the notion of independence [*Unabhängigkeit*] and that of 'equal validity' [*Gleichgültigkeit*]. 'Equal validity', in the literal translation of the term, is indifference, in the sense that it presupposes the idea of reciprocal separation of individuals in the communal submission to social power: the social connection corresponds not to a real connection between individuals but to the autonomisation of those relations. The indifference inherent in bourgeois society presents a dual nature: on the one hand, the equality among individuals, the fruit of the dominion of exchange-value, induces the creation of social relationships; on the other hand, the only link between individuals consists of the absence of a link, or better yet, of their communal submission to an objective and estranged power, materialised in money. In such a context where individuals, considered free and equal, are vehicles and instruments of an unlimited exchange, money performs a decisive function: 'It is itself the community [*Gemeinwesen*], and can tolerate none other standing above it'.[50] It is important to note that the term *Gemeinwesen*, in the *Grundrisse*, generally indicates pre-capitalist forms, characterised by direct contact with the earth; in the present instance, instead, it is identified as that which constitutes a 'communal existence' of the means of capitalist production that is money.[51] The latter presents itself, in confrontation with the individual, as a sign of randomness. The scenario indicated is distinguished by the disassociation of all the communal forms: the worker no longer is at one with the means of labour.

In this way, society can be discussed in strict terms only through the form of capitalist production when commodities become general forms of organisation and the activity that produces them becomes the dominating function. The capitalist system, insofar as it is founded on production for production's sake and not for consumption, asks of individuals an abstraction that Marx defines as an abstraction of particular values of use, needs and interests. If capital-gain were consumed in large part by the business-owners, we would not be speaking of capitalism but of pre-capitalist forms. Production as the key element

---

48. See Postone 1993.
49. See Marx 1973, pp. 106–7.
50. Marx, 1973, p. 223.
51. On the notion of *Gemeinwesen* in the 'mature' Marx, see Riedel 1992, pp. 851–2.

unfolds openly only in the capitalist structure because the means of production and property-relations have become historicised in addition to being depersonalised. The social formation in its literal sense, in the contemporary scenario, is the world-economy, because it is the largest social unity where historical processes become interdependent.[52] From this point of view, analysis of the daily processes of globalisation permits the reproposition of the Marxist motif of the structural global nature of capital.

There is an immanent structural antagonistic force to capital, understood as a social relation and not as a thing. This occurs when labour-power and the singular capitalists tend to remove themselves from the obligation of interaction: the former by politically affirming self liberty through autonomy and the latter by maintaining the natural primacy, that is, economic primacy, of the object. In this way, we are faced with a social mechanism characterised by a hierarchy among the different working figures: such social power, however, pertains to its shareholders in as much as they are personifications of severed working conditions, not characteristic of pre-capitalist communities, insofar as including political or theocratic dominators. This supremacy-device is the fundamental moment of the process of abstraction, which is based on the subsumption of previous labour-forms. The capitalist mode of production, insofar as it is based on social relationships, is subject to a strong politicisation.[53] Society, connected to the capitalist system, does not configure itself only as an artificial construction but also as a structure counter-distinguished by an inherent asymmetry. 'Bending' individuals into their social roles, capitalist society individuates them on the basis of money-possession, establishing the basis for political 'slavery' of the 'apparent freedom' of labour.

In the analysis of the *Grundrisse*, class (in its proper sense) represents a distinctive sign of the capitalist system, far from constituting an element capable of extension to all historical eras. Even if we recognise the existence of class-relations prior to capitalism, we would have to take note that the existence of an opposition of classes in pre-capitalist forms never corroded the man-earth unity: it has been eroded only by means of capitalism. Capitalism constitutes the primary mode of truly social production, in the expansive and spectral sense of the term, from within which sociality configures itself as the other 'face' of individual serial nature.

Such a scenario is characterised by a sociality 'severed' in two by a structural antagonism. In this way, social relations, in their essential instability, take on a directly political nature. From this point of view, 'in bourgeois society,

---

52. Among the numerous texts focusing on the indicated problem, see in particular Arrighi and Silver 1999.

53. See Balibar and Wallerstein 1988.

the worker, e.g., stands there purely without objectivity, subjectively; but the thing which *stands opposite* him has now become the *true community* [*Gemeinwesen*], which he tries to make a meal of, and which makes a meal of him'.[54]

In this manner, the worker becomes a pure subjectivity, a subject void of an object, on the basis of a lacerated temporality (past labour and present labour) and on the basis of an asymmetry among the classes, provoked by money, 'true community', with its ephemeral quality. This dimension of subjectivity was completely unimaginable within pre-capitalist social forms, where man was tied to *Gemeinwesen* (in this case not represented by money) like an 'umbilical cord' and therefore could not collide with it. It is always necessary to keep in mind that the entire Marxian discourse is distinguished by the recognition of the asymmetry between the bourgeoisie (as a particular class) and the proletariat (as a 'universality of a part') inasmuch as it tends to overcome the classist horizon of society – and, therefore, even within its own present itself as a class.

Nevertheless, the concept of labour-power becomes understood as potency, a *dynamis*, 'the aggregate of those mental and physical capabilities existing in a human being',[55] to use the definition that Marx will later provide in *Capital*. The capitalist relationship bases itself on the difference between the labour-power, with its active character, and the effective (actual) labour performed. The moment that one sells something that exists only as a possibility, that thing cannot be separated from the physicality of the worker: 'To the measure at which it must be present temporally, as living labour, it can be only as active subject [*lebendiges Subjekt*], in which it exists as capacity [*Fähigkeit*] as possibility [*Möglichkeit*]; hence as worker. Therefore, the only value of use that can constitute opposition to capital is labour'.[56]

Society, understood according to the capitalist mode of production, in its dual structure, presents an essential instability due not only to internal contradictions but also due to subjective insurgences that constantly bombard its compact nature. Marx's delineation of the contradiction between 'appearances' of freedom and equality points out the ambivalence of such elements and the 'naked life' that stands opposed to it: the subjectivity without an object of the *Arbeiter* that attempts to detract itself from the serial nature of labour, since 'to be a productive labourer is, therefore, not a piece of luck, but a misfortune'.[57]

Translated by Kathryne Fedele

---

54. Marx 1973, p. 496.
55. Marx 1952, p. 79.
56. Marx 1973, pp. 271–2.
57. Marx 1952, p. 251.

Second Nature: Gender in Marx's *Grundrisse*
Amy E. Wendling

At first glance, the manuscripts written by Marx in London in 1857 and 1858, collectively known as the *Grundrisse*, seem to pay but scant attention to the issue of gender. As feminists have long observed, the issue of gender seems, simply, to have been an afterthought for Marx during these and subsequent years, an afterthought ultimately to be elaborated only by Engels, and then with great prejudice. To the Marx scholar, the exclusion of gender from the *Grundrisse* appears differently. Why, given the famous presence of meditations on gender in Marx's early works, and the return to the topic in *Capital* and other later works, has gender seemingly disappeared from the manuscripts of the late 1850s?

To answer these issues of interpretation, we will first have to detour through two questions, one philosophical and one historical. First, the philosophical question: under what concepts was the idea of gender investigated by eighteenth- and nineteenth-century minds, and for what reasons and ends? Second, the historical question: what was Marx's relationship to the study of gender in the 1850s, and how does this appear in both his more and less polished texts? Having answered both of these questions, we will then be in a position to see what the *Grundrisse* has to offer on the question of gender, both historically and conceptually, and to relate its offerings to contemporary debates in Marxist-feminist theory and in feminist theory more broadly.

Gender and the nineteenth-century mind

When we say gender today, what we mean is a complex, historically embedded, performative enactment. This enactment shapes how we experience ourselves – and others – as men and women, or as exceeding these categories, and it codes the meaning of this experience with a particular, though variable, significance or content. The concept of gender was crafted in opposition to the idea that biological sex was essentially determinative of one's behaviour and character. The concept has been especially effective against misogynist stereotypes of women's essence, such as the exclusive identification of women with reproduction or the emotions. Lately, the idea of gender has also been used to investigate the less visible structures of masculinity. A developing tradition of gender-theory has thus been a part of feminist theory for at least the last twenty years.[1]

To use the concept of gender to decode a figure like Marx, who wrote in the nineteenth century, may thus seem to be an anachronism. I will hope to show, in this chapter, that it both is and is not such. While Marx is hardly on the cutting edge of contemporary gender-theory, he already has the insight that our biological natures undergo social shaping, even prior to being conceived as natures. Ultimately, this is to push the distinction between gender and biological sex a step deeper, since even the latter cannot be conceived of as unambiguously natural.

Nonetheless, gender was not the category through which the nineteenth-century mind investigated concepts like women, sexual difference, family-role, sexuality, and the like. Instead, most nineteenth-century minds remain firmly circumscribed by one or both of two discourses: the *querelle des femmes* and political economy. Both discourses took woman as a fixed object with an essential nature, a nature rooted in reproduction. Though they drew different consequences from this essential nature, both discourses remained, for the most part, committed to it, and so had nothing like an insight about gender.

I will argue that Marx is ultimately able to exceed both of these discourses, and especially that he does not take woman to be a fixed object with an essential nature rooted in reproduction. But in order to see where Marx ended, we will have to start where he began. Marx's inquiries into what we today call gender are the product of the intersection, and then the supersession, of both the *querelle des femmes* and political economy.

Not well known today, the *querelle des femmes* was a conversation about women's proper roles in early modern Europe. Parts of the *querelle* were clerical in origin, bound up with discussions of whether marriage was appropriate for clergy, or with more general discussions of women's roles in Christianity. Other

---

1. See especially Butler 2006.

parts of the *querelle* were aristocratic in origin, detailing the proper chivalric norms of courtly love, but also documenting the traditional powers of aristocratic women in an historical period where ideals of bourgeois-feminine domesticity were certainly on the rise, but had not become socially normative. Finally, there were female participants in the *querelle*, notably Christine de Pisan.

According to Joan Kelly, the *querelle* was usually polemical, either directly misogynist in character or directly critical of this misogyny.[2] This shaping of the *querelle* was a product of the intersection of three historical forces in the early modern world. These were: (1) views of women held by Christianity; (2) the waning power of aristocratic women in the face of new notions of bourgeois domesticity and women's roles; and (3) the new and rising importance of civic humanism.

Kelly documents two important consequences of this intersection, both consequential to women. First, aristocratic women had to be disciplined by the rising bourgeois domestic ethos. In Kelly's words, aristocratic women thereby 'lost considerable economic, political, and cultural power in relation not only to their feudal forbearers but to men of their own class'.[3] However, the same forces also produced advanced humanist educations and literacy for some individual women, even as this sort of education was being denied to the female sex as a whole.[4] These educated voices themselves then became part of the *querelle*.

Second, the new rising forms of humanism in early modern Europe often drew from the tradition of civic virtue, especially as it was practiced among the Romans. Misogynist as some strains of Christianity may have been, according to Kelly, the resulting 'humanism was far more narrow in its vision of women than traditional Christian culture'.[5] While Christianity at least posited a common human nature and destiny for men and women, this was denied in the Roman civic tradition, which isolated women as a different species and reserved all social and political life for men.[6] This denial further silenced any ideas of gender that might have been percolated as a subtext of the *querelle*, since the Roman civic tradition viewed women as having a fixed nature resulting from their sex.

Most scholars focus on the contents of the *querelle*-genre as it developed in the Renaissance and the seventeenth century. However, other scholars, including Kelly, date the *querelle* as lasting all the way until 1789.[7] Gary Kates

---

2. Kelly 1982, p. 7.
3. Ibid.
4. Ibid.
5. Kelly 1982, p. 8.
6. Ibid.
7. Kelly 1982, p. 6. According to Kelly, the *querelle* ceased only in light of the still more radical content of revolutionary ideas, including the general notion that a social and political movement could be of great consequence to inherited status-relations.

concurs, arguing that the *querelle des femmes* actually intensified in the eighteenth century.[8] If Kelly and Kates's thesis is correct, then some of the eighteenth-century texts about women that Marx studied in the 1850s would have, at the very least, borne the marks of this discourse.

The second discourse about women that Marx inherits is of much younger vintage than the *querelle*. This is the discipline of political economy. Appearing in the seventeenth and eighteenth centuries, first in France and then in England, political economy studied the relationship between young nation-states, production, and political forms. As a part of their studies of production, some political economists studied women and reproduction. In connection with this, political economy originated the category of 'population' as Marx uses it and as we still use it today. Political economy then developed and privileged the category of 'population' in its explanations of birth, birth-rate, industry, division of labour, social class, and consumption.

If the early Marx's discussions of women begin in the language and concepts of the *querelle*, they quickly shift, in his middle years, to the language and concepts of political economy.[9] If we were going to chart a split in Marx that had to do with gender, a split that paralleled the famed, though inaccurate, split between a humanist and a scientific Marx, it would be a split between the concepts of the *querelle* and those of political economy. As we shall see, Marx's work on gender ultimately overcomes both discourses to argue some very contemporary points. But in the work of retrieval, we will have to use concepts from each of these older discourses in order to see how this occurred.

Marx's study of gender in the 1850s

Among the material slated for inclusion in the *Marx-Engels Gesamtausgabe* (*MEGA²*)[10] is an excerpt-notebook of Marx's, fifty-seven pages in length, dating from July of 1852. The notebook is on the topic of women, courtly love, the history of the family, sex-based divisions of labour, and paternalism as a political structure. As we have seen in the previous section, these topics indicated the

---

8. Kates 1995, p. 157.

9. Thomas Malthus and John Stuart Mill are two other important figures at the intersection of the two discourses. Both had much to say about women, and also about the intersection of economics and politics.

10. According to the *Internationale Marx-Engels-Stiftung/Marx-Engels Gesamtausgabe*, an organisation housed at the International Institute for Social History (IISG) in Amsterdam, this material will appear in Part IV, Volume 10 of the *MEGA²* series and is currently being worked on at the *Berlin Brandenburg Academy of Sciences*. See <http://www.iisg.nl/imes/mega4.php>.

most frequent and consolidated discussions of gender in the nineteenth-century mind, and particularly a mind like Marx's, situated at the explosive juncture of the *querelle* and political economy.

Marx's notebook draws on the work of the following texts: Johann Gottfried Eichhorn's *Allgemeine Geschichte der Cultur und Litteratur des Neueren Europa* (1796); John Millar's *The Origin of the Distinction of Ranks; or, An Inquiry into the Circumstances which give rise to Influence and Authority in the Different Members of Society* (1771);[11] the first part of G. Jung's *Geschichte der Frauen* (1850), which is his history of the women of the ancient world; J.A. de Ségur's *Les femmes, leur condition, et leur influence dans l'ordre social chez différents peoples ancients et modernes* (1803); the first part of Dr. William Wachsmuth's *Allgemeine Culturege- schichte* (1850); all three parts of Cristoph Meiners' *Geschichte des Weiblichen Geschlects* (1788, 1799, 1800); Antoine Léonard Thomas' *Essai sur le caractère, les moeurs, et l'esprit des femmes dans les différents siècles* (1772);[12] the first and second volumes of William Alexander's *The History of Women from the Earli- est Antiquity to the Present Time, 3rd Edition* (1782); and Wilhelm Karl August Drumann's *Grundriß der Culturgechichte* (1847).[13]

By far, the largest section of the excerpt-notebook consists of extracts from the Millar text. There, as with most of the rest of the notebook, Marx makes notes on the figure he is studying. While this itself can be instructive, since it allows scholars to piece together which parts of the books Marx studies more intensively and which parts he omitted or neglected, the extracts on Millar also contain an original remark of Marx's.[14]

According to Danaga Vileisis, this remark may be one of Marx's most profound statements about gender, since in it he doubts whether the concept of a division of labour adequately captures what is at stake in gender- and sexual difference. Marx's remark implies that explaining women's work adequately requires much more than can be found in a treatment of the division of labour, and so requires

---

11. In the notebook itself, Marx has misspelled Millar's name as 'Millard'. He has also rendered the title of the book differently, as 'Observations concerning the distinction of Ranks in Society', and dated it as a second edition from 1753, leaving readers to wonder if he was working from an earlier version than the standard first edition of the Millar work from 1771.

12. Marx notes the Thomas text as coming from Paris in 1773, while the standard first edition was printed in Amsterdam in 1772.

13. I have tried to render these titles as precisely as possible, noting and then eliminat- ing the orthographic and dating differences in Marx's notebooks, insofar as I was able. Many of these texts, having entered the common domain, are now available online for scholars to pursue, especially via The Gutenberg Project and Google Books.

14. Personal exchange with Danaga Vileisis at the Left Forum 2010 Conference, Ander- son/Wendling/Xiaoping Panel Session 5, 'Seeing Marx Anew via the *MEGA* Project', Pace University, New York City, 21 March.

recourse to categories for explaining gender other than those privileged in political economy.[15]

The Wachsmuth material from Marx's 1852 notebook introduces a scholarly puzzle with regard to Engels's famous work *The Origin of the Family, Private Property, and the State*. Engels's work has long, and correctly, been considered to be a product of later notes on the family that Marx made in the 1880s,[16] including notes on Wachsmuth's two-volume work *The Historical Antiquities of the Greeks*, published in 1837.[17]

Engels makes one explicit mention of Wachsmuth in *The Origin of the Family, Private Property, and the State*, in the context of a discussion of the trade of eunuchs in the Ancient world.[18] However, this topic does not seem to correspond directly to the theme of Marx's later notes from Wachsmuth's 1837 book, notes that are concentrated on the transfer of brides to their new husbands' kinship, religious, and other communal groupings.[19] Perhaps, then, in the text about the eunuch-trade, Engels is drawing on the nearly twenty pages of extracts from Wachsmuth in Marx's 1852 notebook.[20] Since Marx's 1852 notebook has not been fully transcribed, scholars are also left to wonder more generally about the extent of Engels's knowledge of the earlier notebook, its influence on his thinking, and its influence on his famous work.

Marx's 1852 notebook is, however, revealing about far more than simply this scholarly puzzle. First, it shows his continued interest in and acquaintance with the issues of women's history and political status, a theme that is generally although incorrectly thought to be absent from Marx's research and writing during this period. Second, the notebook reveals which texts on the history of women and the family dominated progressive scholarly consciousnesses in the London of the 1850s. Thirdly, it allows us to glimpse in Marx's thinking about women both transitions and intersections between themes and topics characteristic of the *querelle des femmes* (courtly love, women among the Romans, the feminine *esprit*) and themes and topics characteristic of political economy (division of labour, relationship between family-structure, production, and repro-

---

15. Ibid. Vileisis draws very different theoretical consequences from this remark than those that will ultimately be drawn in this essay.

16. Krader (ed.) 1974; Barrett 1986.

17. Personal exchange with Kevin B. Anderson at the Left Forum 2010 Conference, Anderson/Wendling/Xiaoping Panel-Session Five, 'Seeing Marx Anew via the *MEGA* Project', Pace University, New York City, 21 March. Anderson, of the University of California Santa Barbara is currently at work on Marx's excerpts on the family from the 1880s.

18. Engels 1972, p. 95.

19. Krader 1974, pp. 199–200.

20. Unlike all of Marx's notes on other figures, his notes on Wachsmuth are split into three distinct sections within the 1852 notebook. Marx seems to have returned to the Wachsmuth text several times in order to explain the work of other figures.

duction). These transitions and intersections are particularly obvious in Marx's attention to women in the 1850s, at this particular juncture of his scholarship.

To see this more clearly, it will be useful to situate, albeit very briefly, Marx's work on women in the 1850s within his work on women in both earlier and later periods.[21] When Marx's commentary on women is traced, it is usually traced to his very early and his very late texts, leaving out the middle period of his works that this essay seeks to illuminate. This is because Marx's more accessible and well-known texts on women occur in these very early and very late periods, and they include the remarks Marx and Engels made, famously, about women and the bourgeois family in the *Communist Manifesto* of 1848. However, this leaves out a developmental stage in Marx's thinking that may ultimately be very useful to feminist theorists, one which is crucial for an understanding of the theme of gender in Marx's works.

From as early as the *1844 Manuscripts*, Marx had made remarks about women. There he argues that the behaviour of men towards women is an index through which one can judge the state of human development as a whole.[22] This theme derives from concepts particular to the *querelle*, and there is even a chivalric overtone to the passage. While the passage is certainly not hostile or blatantly misogynist, it is also not particularly progressive, since in it women are not situated as agents. It is simply *men's behaviour* towards women that indicates the social progress of the human species. One could still derive the most conservative of consequences from this idea, depending on how this social progress was defined.

In his work *The Holy Family* from the following year, in the context of a set of comments on the French socialist utopian Charles Fourier, Marx develops this insight in a subtle but important way. He writes, 'the degree of female emancipation is the natural measure of the universal emancipation'.[23] The shift here is double. First, instead of being situated as a passive object whose status is acted upon by men, women are situated as the primary subject of the text. Second, the social progress left ambiguous in the earlier text is filled in with a precise content: emancipation. Women's emancipation is then tied to the universal emancipation of the species, and so to Marx's concept of species-being [*Gattungswesen*], a concept to which I will return.

We can note yet another shift by the time of 1846's *German Ideology*, where already the discussion of women derives not only from the *querelle*, but also from the new discipline of political economy. In *The German Ideology*, Marx

---

21. See Chattopadhyay 2001 and Kain 1992. These other scholars have traced in detail Marx's discussions of women across the whole of his work, and I refer the interested reader to their lengthier discussions.

22. In Chattopadhyay 2001, p. 2455.

23. Ibid.

has become concerned with sexual difference as a system for dividing up who systematically performs which task in a society or, very succinctly, with sexual difference as a division of labour. The passage also calls on the concept of population. Famously, Marx writes: 'With [the increase of productivity, needs, and population] there develops the division of labour, which was originally nothing but the division of labour in the sexual act, then that division of labour which develops spontaneously or 'naturally' by virtue of natural predisposition (e.g., physical strength), needs, accidents, etc., etc. Division of labour only becomes truly such from the moment when a division of material and mental labour appears'.[24]

This passage from *The German Ideology* is odd because its invocation of gender is specifically inflected by sexuality. By 'sexual act', does Marx simply mean the act of having sex? Does he mean, more narrowly, only the (hetero-)sexual acts that are ultimately reproductive of a human person, and, if he means this, why does he not simply speak of the division of labour associated with reproductions rather than the division of labour associated with the 'sexual act'? Which of these is the genealogical template for all subsequently developing divisions of labour?

Whatever Marx may have intended, what is clear is that he could have, but did not, speak only about the division of labour associated with reproduction or rearing children: instead, he focuses on the sexual act itself. Moreover, the import of the passage, up through the division between material and mental labour, actually seems to be a classical active/passive distinction. However thus constrained Marx's own interpretation of 'the sexual act' might have been, on a clever re-reading, his comments here are hardly biologistic, since no sex is assigned a particular role. Moreover, as we shall see, Marx is well aware that the significance and import of 'the sexual act' is worked up through social forms, including the family.

For Marx, studying these social forms meant studying histories of the family, kinship-networks, and the political and economic structures to which they correspond. Many if not most of the passages from Marx's 1852 excerpt-notebook highlight the status of women in the ancient world. Marx, far beyond the work begun in the *German Ideology*, continues his inquiries into history, into the philosophy of history, and into the historical forces that ultimately formed the conditions through which capitalism became possible. He also shows his understanding that women are a key element of this history, playing central, albeit historically variant, roles in communal and economic life. History, and a theory of history, will again be an important theme in the *Grundrisse*, and Marx's

---

24. Marx 1978, pp. 158–9.

studies of the family will be an important part of his development of the theme of history.

Following the *Grundrisse*, sexual difference will again be an issue in *Capital*, especially in connection with the use of machinery in production and the use of women's and children's labour to produce additional surplus-value.[25] After *Capital*, Marx will continue to make notes on the history of the family, drawing on the American anthropologist Lewis Henry Morgan, as is well documented in Engels and Krader.[26] Marx will also continue his practical efforts for gender- and racial equality. Three years before his death, in a draft of a programme for the French working class, Marx writes in support of wage-equality for men and women, and asserts that 'the emancipation of the producing class is that of all human beings irrespective of sex or race'.[27]

Marx's ultimate conception of gender as an enormously complex, socially imbedded, yet transhistorical political structure exceeds both the discourse he inherited from the *querelle des femmes* and that he inherited from political economy. Importantly for Marx, gender is not a simple political structure of domination: or, more precisely, even within patriarchal peoples in which the domination of women by men is an accomplished political fact, this domination is not always perpetuated in the same ways or for the same precise reasons. Instead, relations of domination of women by men, as with other relations of domination, must be understood in dialogue with the fast-changing norms of the mode of production as a whole, including changing norms of what counts as domination.

It will take twentieth-century feminist theory many years to catch up with this insight of Marx's, and it will do so only as it integrates issues of social class, race, labour, nationality, technology, and sexuality into its understanding of the central subject of feminist theory. Had Marx continued to study gender today, he might have speculated about the particular forms of gender-domination peculiar and useful to late capitalism. This would be a very useful addition to current literature.

---

25. The third section of this essay explores the use of women's and children's labour to swell surplus-value as Marx treats this issue in the *Grundrisse*. For a treatment of this issue in *Capital*, including a discussion of the significance of gender in *Capital* more generally, see Wendling 2009, pp. 155–68.

26. Engels 1972; Krader 1974.

27. In Chattopadhyay 2001, p. 2456.

The historical role of gender in the *Grundrisse*

Where, then, does material from the 1852 excerpt-notebook appear in the *Grundrisse* manuscripts of 1857–8? And, more broadly, what are the main discussions of gender in the latter text? At first, the answer to the first question appears to be, nowhere, and the answer to the second question appears to be that there are no such discussions. Neither gender nor women are explicitly treated as a topic at any length, nor are many relevant and easily-recognisable categories sprinkled throughout the text in connection with other observations.

However, using both Marx's 1852 notebook and the general trajectory of his discussion of gender, we are able to discern a role played by gender in the *Grundrisse*. This role falls into two main categories. First, gender and especially the history of the family plays a role in the historical section of the work, particularly in Marx's developmental narrative about how capitalism came to be historically, and then erased the conditions of its own historicity, claiming its forms to be natural and eternal. This discussion is concentrated especially in the second half of Notebook IV and the first half of Notebook V. Second, there are a number of conceptual consequences relevant to the issue of gender to be drawn, both from this historical material and from the *Grundrisse*'s treatment, and critique, of biological nature.

From the perspective of capital, a mode of production that tends to portray its peculiar historical ways of life as eternal and natural, all history is transgressive, critical, and potentially dangerous, since even the most accidental and haphazard survey of historical constellations gives the lie to this portrayal. In the *Grundrisse*, Marx makes the following remarks about capitalism's allergy to history, about the invisibility of capitalism's own history:

> The conditions and presuppositions of the *becoming*, the *emergence* [of capital]...disappear with the development of real capital...The bourgeois economists, who consider capital to be an eternal and *natural* (not historical) form of production, nevertheless try to justify it by declaring the conditions of its becoming as the conditions of its present realisation...These attempts at apologetics demonstrate a bad conscience...[M]uch more important for us – our method indicates the points at which historical analysis must be introduced, or at which bourgeois economy as a mere historical form of the production process points beyond itself towards earlier historical modes of production...point[s] to a past lying behind this system.[28]

I will return to the conceptual implications of this philosophy of history in the next section, particularly as these bear on the issue of gender. Let me begin,

---

28. Marx 1986, pp. 387–9.

however, with the observation that in the pages that follow this philosophy of bourgeois history in the *Grundrisse*, the story of the family plays a minor, but important part. This is because the dominance of the bourgeois patriarchal family-form historically accompanied the capitalist mode of production. Revealing the history of this family as tied to this mode of production unmasks its naturalist pretensions. Writing a history of this family also reveals surprising variation – not only beyond but also even within the patriarchal family-form. This history shows that kinship-groups were not always patriarchal, and, even when they were, the rules and political import of patriarchy changed from group to group.

Marx's history of the family here concentrates especially on two pre-capitalist conditions. First, peoples were wedded to the land, through agriculture. Second, they were wedded to their tools, through ownership. Both land and tools were not thinkable in separation from the peoples that lived on them and used them. The capitalist mode of production requires this separation and must slowly accomplish it historically before such a separation can be portrayed as a natural and normal fact, as the usual way of things. Prior to this separation, as Marx points out: '*property* means nothing more than man's relating to his natural conditions of production as belonging to him, as his own, as *presupposed along with his own being*; his relating to them as *natural presuppositions* of himself, which constitute, as it were, only an extension of his body'.[29]

Prior to this separation, there is no such thing as an isolated worker, who, like the patriarchal bourgeois family-form, is also a product of history.[30] There is no private property in the sense of individual property, as this form must but slowly evolve. Instead, there is an extended kinship-clan that Marx calls a 'commune': a shared group with linguistic, ethical, geographical and ethnic ties.

In his historical notes, Marx has copied a passage that claims that, 'a more general organisation than that of kin groups did not exist in the ancient world'.[31] While such kin-groups persist, capitalism cannot arise, since the conditions for it – separation of the individual from the land; separation of the individual from the tool; separation of the individual from a kinship-network much more extensive than the bourgeois patriarchal family; and the end of properties held in common – were not yet present.

These conditions only slowly coalesce into a dominant system. Historically, they do not arise all at once, but haphazardly, and usually alongside other forms: as when, among the Romans, manufacture becomes 'the domestic sideline of wives and daughters (spinning and weaving)'.[32] Before a set of conditions

---

29. Marx 1986, p. 415.
30. Marx 1986, p. 399.
31. Marx 1986, p. 406.
32. Marx 1986, p. 403.

conducive to capital becomes dominant and hegemonic, then, hybrid-forms must first develop. Waged work occurs alongside unwaged work. Private property is held alongside communal property.

These hybrid-forms work to change the meaning and structure of labour since, as Marx points out, only certain kinds of labour can be realised in more individual forms, while others can be realised only in great communal efforts: his example is of great public works. Hybrid-forms of labour also affect kinship-structures, carving the family off from the broader communal kinship-structure as a whole and situating it as a more isolated unit. Hybrid kinship-forms, corresponding to different modes of production, therefore also exist alongside one another: communal families alongside more isolated units. However, particularly in its Roman form, the family was hardly the isolated unit that capitalist production will ultimately require.

Marx thinks that these hybrid-forms of labour and kinship came to be historically through warfare and migration, movements that disrupted the shape, character, bloodlines, ethos, and other previously unquestioned features of communal life.[33] Marx writes: '[t]he only barrier which the community can encounter in relating itself to the natural conditions of production...is some *other community* which has already laid claim to them as its inorganic body. *Warfare* is therefore one of the earliest types of labour for every naturally evolved community of this kind, both for the defence of property and for its acquisition'.[34]

The connection in Marx's mind at this period between the history of the family and warfare helps us to understand an otherwise inexplicable feature of his 1852 excerpt-notebook: the final page of the notebook appears to be a list of works on military history that Marx plans to excerpt.

It cannot be forgotten that Marx sketches the history of the family in the *Grundrisse* in service of a much larger point. He is supplying the capitalist mode of production with its own disavowed history. In particular, he is concerned to explain the slow advent of what he calls, in the *Grundrisse*, the 'thorough isolation [*Punktualität*]' of the free worker.[35]

This advent is connected to the history of the family, and in an interesting passage, Marx groups the breakdown of the communal family into increasingly isolated units with the concepts of production, reproduction, and population. He writes: 'production itself, the increase in population (which also belongs to production) necessarily transcends these conditions, destroys them instead of

---

33. Marx 1986, pp. 402–3.
34. Marx 1986, p. 415.
35. Marx 1986, p. 409.

reproducing them, etc., and as a result of this the communal system decays and dies along with the property relations on which it was based'.[36] With the fall of such property-relations, the groundwork for the capitalist mode of production is prepared.

One question that Marx does not ask, at least in the *Grundrisse*, is about the connections between the bourgeois patriarchal family-form and the dot-like isolation of the free worker. Does the one support the other and vice versa, and if so, how? The bourgeois patriarchal family-form, compared to its historical predecessors, is only loosely enmeshed in extended kinship-networks. Instead, there is a narrative of striking out on your own, a narrative that relegates the bourgeois patriarchal family to its own dot-like isolation. It is, in this way, an intermediary step away from communal life and towards the ultimate dot-like isolation of the worker, who may no longer have access to kinship-networks of any sort, even the limited ones of the bourgeois patriarchal family.

Second, the bourgeois family-form intensifies patriarchy as a structure of political rule, even when compared to other patriarchal forms. This is demonstrated in the later stages of the *querelle des femmes*, when ideals of bourgeois domesticity work against women owning property, obtaining an education, and the like. Instead, women and children come to be considered as a part of the conglomerate body/property of the father, and so the bourgeois patriarchal family is not a legitimate community of persons. Though the father may relate to a market of equal and free persons on the outside of the family, his relations on its interior remain mired in the pre-capitalist forms of direct possession and disposition of labour based on status, or servitude.

Capitalism's tendency, however, will be to dissolve even these remaining structures of personal service in the family. This remains true even as capitalism correspondingly requires and intensifies the patriarchal service-obligations within the bourgeois family's internal economy, perhaps as a reaction to the eroding forces outside of it. At the very least, it intensifies patriarchy in this family's ideas about how it operates, whatever the truth may be in reality. For example, a female breadwinner may still come home to serve her husband and maintain the illusion of his economic power.

In the meantime, capitalism continues to dissolve traditional status-relations. In the passage that follows below, Marx is talking about dissolving relations of status in the feudal world. However, his remarks are equally relevant to the dissolution of status-relations in the bourgeois patriarchal family. He writes: 'under the rule of capital, all these relationships [of service] will become more

---

36. Marx 1986, p. 410.

or less *dishonoured*... [and there will be a general] ... *de-sanctification* of personal services, however exalted a character tradition, etc., may have attributed to them'.[37]

Capital's values reduce all values to monetary values, and these progressively collapse all preceding or contradictory values. Marx offers a telling example of this immediately prior to his discussion of the demystification of service. In the example, a person of historically lower status is able to afford to pay someone of historically higher status to do something for him. To take a more contemporary example, we might simply think of the cultural discomforts that accompany a high wage-earning woman whose husband stays in the home to take care of the children, or whose husband follows her geographically to a new job.[38]

But we need not spring so far forward in history, since already for Marx women are also labourers. Already in the *Grundrisse*, Marx knows full well, though perhaps not as well as he would do by the time he writes *Capital*, that when he writes about labourers, he is not only writing about men. Women-workers too, sometimes even more precariously removed from kinship-structures than their male counterparts, are operating in dot-like isolation within the capitalist mode of production. In addition, the history of capitalism as Marx portrays it in the *Grundrisse* reveals that capitalism aggressively seizes women's labour, sometimes preferring it over men's, and for reasons that are hardly benevolent.[39]

In giving the history of the development of the capitalist mode of production in the *Grundrisse*, Marx emphasises how capital first takes possession of the rural secondary occupations, spinning and weaving, activities that least require guild-level skills and technical training,[40] and so skills that are the least skilled. And although Marx does not mention women in this passage, it is not difficult to draw the line between it and the earlier passage where he has mentioned women in connection with the activities of spinning and weaving.

In addition to being less likely to have been formed by guild-skills and regulated by guild-restrictions, women's labour was valuable to capital for several other reasons. Already in the *Grundrisse* Marx has developed his idea that capital can gain surplus-value by creating surplus labour-time. This time can be amplified by the general expansion of the working population, the reproductive aspects

---

37. Marx 1986, p. 396.
38. Apart from the backlash that nearly always accompanies this demystification of service, many of these aspects of capital have been very liberating for subservient groups.
39. Marx's understanding of this theme is just nascent in the *Grundrisse*. It will develop in *Capital*, where he writes that factory-owners are quick to exploit the more socially vulnerable, including women and children, who could be paid less and were more desperate to maintain their jobs than comparable male labourers.
40. Marx 1986, p. 434.

of which I will return to presently. A still more direct strategy to expand surplus labour-time is 'the addition of wives and children to the working population'.[41]

In connection with this, Marx does not, but could have, observed that women's more flexible labour-habits, and concomitant movement in and out of the workforce, are perfectly suited to capital's constantly varying demands for labour: its booms, busts, and layoffs. For while capital's demand overall is for a constantly more populous and available working class, it does not demand the resources of this class steadily. Rather, it demands working-class labour in cycles of crisis and hyper-employment, an idea Marx captures in other texts when he describes the working classes as an 'industrial reserve-army'.

Finally, women's reproductive labour is valuable to capital, and especially the reproductive labour of women in the working classes, and for the same reason. This reproductive labour expands and maintains the industrial reserve-army that capitalists require in order to enhance surplus-value with surplus labour-time. This reproductive labour also ensures that the industrial reserve-army has many new recruits, available in the form of short-lived, successive generations of workers. Capital needs these since it tends to wear out workers quickly.

The theme of 'population', much developed in political economy, and especially in Thomas Malthus, is central to this concern.[42] It is unsurprising, then, that the theme of population also runs throughout the *Grundrisse*. In the excerpt-notebook immediately following the excerpt-notebook on women, also dating from 1852, Marx has made notes on Ferdinando Galiani's *Della Moneta* (1803). One result of these notes appears worked up in the miscellaneous observations that Marx makes at the end of the *Grundrisse*. The issue is, again, the expansion of the working-class population. Marx cites Galiani's claim that 'God ordains that men who carry on trades of primary utility are born in abundance'.[43] In context, Marx criticises Galiani for his claim that this reproductive expansion is a phenomenon of nature rather than a result of the capitalist mode of production. Instead he shows that it is not God but Capital that makes sure that the men who exercise occupations of primary utility are born in abundant numbers, that it is capital that needs to increase the surplus-population as much as possible as a means of increasing surplus-value. In addition, the expansion of population allows capital to drive the labour-market down by pulling from a larger pool of unskilled labourers.

---

41. Marx 1986, p. 325.
42. Marx's commentary on and critique Malthus in the *Grundrisse* does not focus on Malthus's notorious discussions of population, but on Malthus's theory of surplus-value. See Marx 1986, pp. 485–99 and 514–19. The two aspects of Malthus's theories could no doubt be related, but such a task lies outside of the scope of this chapter.
43. Marx 1987, p. 222.

Capital also needs consumers, and so the expansion of population is an important issue both for the supply of labour and for the realisation of capital in the production-process. And it is not only the upper classes that consume: capital also needs workers as consumers, since they form an important market, particularly for the mass-produced commodities of the industries that are most effectively capitalised. Marx has already glimpsed the importance of the worker as consumer in the *Grundrisse*, where he writes:

> In relation to each capitalist the total mass of all workers except his own appears not as workers but as consumers, possessors of exchange values (wages), of money, which they exchange for his commodities... They constitute a very large proportion of consumers, although not quite so great as is generally imagined if one thinks only of the industrial workers proper. The greater their number – the greater the size of the industrial population – and the greater the amount of money over which they dispose, the greater the sphere of exchange for capital. We have seen that it is the tendency of capital to increase the industrial population as much as possible.[44]

An individual capitalist enterprise needs its own workers' wages to remain low. However, it needs workers' wages, in general, to be higher in order to produce a more robust market for consumer-goods. This takes the shape of a collective action problem, and forms one of the many internal contradictions of capital. In this case, the demands of the capitalist class, as a collective, contradict the demands of individual capitalists. Profitability in production works against profitability in realisation. Considerations of the role of working-class women as the primary buyers of consumer-goods, and so the primary subjects to which the consumer-market is addressed, had Marx explored this, would also fit here.

The conceptual role of gender in the *Grundrisse*

In addition to its historical tools for diagnosing the relationship between women's productive and reproductive labour, kinship-structures, and the requirements of the mode of production, Marx's *Grundrisse* offers a number of conceptual tools that are useful for diagnosing and understanding gender. Because of these insights, particularly when viewed in light of Marx's work as a whole, Philip Kain rightly argues that Marx is neither conceptually contradictory nor conceptually irrelevant to feminist theory.[45] However, Kain is also right that '[b]y comparison to other questions that concern him, the issue of women does not appear

---

44. Marx 1986, p. 346.
45. Kain 1992, pp. 159–60.

explicitly or frequently enough'.[46] Liberating the gender-relevant content from the *Grundrisse* is a laborious task that involves filling in many gaps, and I have no intention of engaging in apologetics for Marx on this issue. Instead, let us simply accept this and then work to derive what insight we can from the texts that are available in the *Grundrisse*. I will argue that there are some especially rich ones.

Kain agrees. In making claims about Marx's relationship to feminism, Kain considers Marx's work as a whole. However, it is also no accident that when Kain goes to look for the conceptual issues that are most relevant to feminist theory in Marx, he draws heavily on the *Grundrisse*.

Let me highlight four conceptual points from the *Grundrisse* here, the latter two of which are also noted in Kain. These have to do with (1) the history of feminist theory as a bourgeois discourse; (2) dependency-relations; (3) Marx's rhetorical use of metaphors of fecundity and sexuality; and (4) Marx's critique of biological nature.

The invocation of the *querelle des femmes* at the outset of this essay serves a specific historical purpose, in that it situates the research about women that Marx himself accessed. But this invocation also shows us that Marx, in ways he could never have imagined, was right to assert that capitalism causes its own history to disappear. The residue of this disappearance can be charted in even some of the most progressive of sites, including within feminist theory.

If Marx's theory of bourgeois history is correct, we tend to see all topics through the filter of a bourgeois veil, and the bourgeois period erases the residue of any pre-bourgeois discussions. The same is true within feminism. Compared to Enlightenment and post-Enlightenment movements and figures in feminism, pre-bourgeois discussions about women are relatively unknown. In particular, the breadth, depth, and age of the *querelle* have not been pursued or parsed as a resource. For example, the *querelle* receives only three mentions in Simone de Beauvoir's seminal work *The Second Sex*.[47] Because of this occlusion, it is as though feminist conversations began seriously only with the Enlightenment. The history of pre-bourgeois kinship groupings prior to the bourgeois patriarchal family-form is also lost, and, as a consequence, this family-form exerts a domination that has come unglued from its precise historicity.

In consequence, many contemporary-feminist conversations have had to work to correct the assumptions that resulted from the origins of the discipline in the norms of the bourgeois domestic-female subject. This is true of the various efforts, especially prominent in the 1990s, to diversify the subject of feminism

---

46. Ibid.
47. De Beauvoir 1989.

by race, social class, sexuality, nationality, and religion. It is also true of gender-theory, which appears as an entirely new insight only against the backdrop of the aggressive biologistic and medical accounts of sexual difference that intensify in the bourgeois period. By contrast, according to Joan Kelly, some of the early-modern but pre-bourgeois feminists of the *querelle* already 'focused on what we would now call gender. That is, they had a sure sense that the sexes are cultur-ally, and not just biologically, formed... [The early feminists] directed their ideas against the notions of a defective sex that flowed from the misogynist side of the debate and against the societal shaping of women to fit those notions'.[48]

In addition to the discussions of bourgeois history that Marx offers in the *Grundrisse*, he also offers some productive discussions of relations of depen-dency, patronage, and status. We have already seen one example of this above, in the context of status-distinctions within the bourgeois family. Marx's discus-sions of status are connected to a series of general points that he makes about service-activities that are not mediated by the wage-labour market, not yet medi-ated by the wage-labour market, or mediated by the wage-labour market, but not capitalised.

Historically, and perhaps even still, much of women's domestic labour has fallen into one of these categories.[49] This happens for one of two reasons. Either woman's domestic labour is unwaged, but is instead pursued because of affective personal ties;[50] or, if waged, domestic services performed cannot be capitalised in the same way that industrial labour can. As Marx explains:

> Labour as mere service for the satisfaction of immediate needs has nothing at all to do with capital, which does not seek this kind of labour... [Service is] a use-value that does not increase capital but in which it is consumed, and the capitalist gives him another commodity in exchange in the form of money. Such is the case with all services which workers exchange directly for the money of other people and which are consumed by these people. This is consumption of revenue, which as such is always part of simple circula-tion, not consumption of capital. Since one of the contracting parties does not confront the other as capitalist, this form of service cannot come into the

---

48. Kelly 1982, p. 7. These voices would not have affected the main discourse of the *querelle*, and so pose no problem for my thesis that the idea of gender was mostly absent from its normative currents.

49. For Marx, slavery and serfdom also fall into the category of labour unmediated by wages. Marx is very concerned, both ethically and philosophically, with the persistence of these pre-capitalist forms within the capitalist system. In the *Grundrisse*, see especially Marx 1986, pp. 218–19 and p. 392.

50. These ties are not, simply because they are affective, unconnected with meeting basic economic needs.

category of productive labour. From the harlot to the Pope there is a mass of such rabble.[51]

Given capitalism's losses on services, then, and its drive to increasing productive labour, it is clear why capitalism pushes women away from domestic labour, waged or otherwise, and towards the industrial labour that can be more readily capitalised.

Nonetheless, service-activities persist even in the developed exchange-systems of capitalism that, as Marx points out, otherwise work to explode the ties of personal dependence that such services often rely on or mimic.[52] Marx's point about pre-capitalist relations of dependency, status, and patronage that remain operative even within the capitalist system is also related to his philosophy of history. Capital retains earlier forms within itself, albeit forms that it works to eliminate, even as it relies upon them. For this reason, if properly diagnosed, capitalism contains clues about the shape of the very historical formation that it disavows.

A third conceptual feature of the *Grundrisse*, also noted in Kain with respect to Marx's work as a whole, has to do with the rhetoric of the text. Kain writes: 'Marx continually uses metaphors of birth, sexuality, [and] relations between man and woman to describe abstract theoretical processes'.[53] We have already seen several examples of this in this article, both in the *Grundrisse* and other texts of Marx's. Here let me simply add two additional examples from the *Grundrisse*. Marx describes the extension of the capitalist exchange-form to all labours as '[g]eneral prostitution'.[54] In addition, he describes capital as 'bearing fruit'[55] – '*Das Kapital als Frucht bringend*' in the German[56] – as a way of characterising how capital reproduces itself and all that accompanies this burgeoning. Such metaphors are hardly unique to Marx, particularly within the discipline of philosophy: witness Plato's use of the metaphor of birth, in the *Symposium*, as a characterisation of the process of having a philosophical thought. However, Marx's use of the metaphors of birth, sexuality, and the relations between man and woman are central to his indictments of capitalism, and their operation as a part of this indictment deserves further feminist scrutiny.

Finally, and most importantly, via his critique of a biological nature unshaped by social and historical circumstance, Marx has conceptual material in the

---

51. Marx 1986, pp. 202–3. See also the parallel discussions of simple circulation, services, use-values, and pre-bourgeois forms of production on pp. 393 and 397.
52. Marx 1986, p. 100.
53. Kain 1992, p. 188.
54. Marx 1986, p. 100.
55. Marx 1987 p. v. and p. 129.
56. Marx 2006, pp. 619–47.

Grundrisse that can contribute to the idea of gender as elaborated in feminist theory. Kain concurs, writing:

> [It is certainly not the case, for Marx, that biology can simply determine the social...And, for Marx, it is clear that the making of human history even involves the transformation of biological nature...Marx certainly does not develop, with all the sophistication of modern feminist theory, the distinction between biological sex and socially constructed gender roles, but he certainly anticipates, and even provides the groundwork for, this distinction.[57]

In support of this argument, Kain cites a famous passage from the *Grundrisse* about the social coding of what might be considered another basic 'biological' drive: hunger. I reproduce the passage from Marx, abbreviated in Kain, in full below:

> [T]he object is not an object in general, but a definite object which must be consumed in a definite way, a way mediated by production itself. Hunger is hunger; but hunger that is satisfied by cooked meat eaten with knife and fork differs from hunger that devours raw meat with the help of hands, nails and teeth. Production thus produces not only the object of consumption but also the mode of consumption, not only objectively but also subjectively. Production therefore creates the consumer...Production not only provides the material to satisfy a need, but it also provides a need for the material. When consumption emerges from its original natural crudeness and immediacy – and its remaining in that state would be due to the fact that production was still caught in natural crudeness – then it is itself, as an urge, mediated by the object. The need felt for the object is created by the perception of the object. An *objet d'art* – just like any other product – creates a public that has artistic taste and is capable of enjoying beauty. Production therefore produces not only an object for the subject, but also a subject for the object.[58]

The same is true of the gendered subject, who is thus created through complex historical systems of production.

To Kain's elegant gloss on this passage, we might add the additional theoretical weight of another supporting text from the *Grundrisse*. In this text, Marx shows how he intends his concept of *Gattungswesen*, or species-being, as it is usually translated into English, as a replacement for, and improvement upon, the Aristotelian ζῷον πολιτικόν. The text derives from Notebook V, within the bank of texts discussed most intensively in the historical section of this article. Marx writes:

---

57. Kain 1992, pp. 169–70.
58. In Kain 1992, p. 169; Marx 1986, pp. 29–30.

'But human beings become individuals only through the process of history. He appears originally as a *species-being* [*Gattungswesen*], *clan being, herd animal* – although in no way whatever as a ζῷον πολιτικόν in the political sense'.[59]

Marx's preference for the species-being concept over the ζῷον πολιτικόν has to do with the fact that Aristotle's otherwise similar notion is already too specific, pertaining to a city-dweller. Marx means to get at a set of even deeper structures that precede the sort of determination Aristotle has in mind, asserting that the very fact of the species, including what we today would call its biological nature, is socially determined.

Conclusion

Socialism in general and communism in particular, like the broader Enlightenment movements in which they rest, albeit uneasily, have advocated women's equality. Marx's interest in women's history, the history of the family, and women's labour within capitalism are all a part of this story. But the shape of Marx's interest as it was derived historically also shows the limitations of the view of women with which communist political movements began. The connections between Marx's notebook on women's history, his working up of a history of the family as a part of his studies of political economy, the political role he clearly hopes that women will play in a society liberated from bourgeois strictures, and his nascent idea of gender all deserve much fuller theoretical exploration than Marx gives them in any text, and certainly much more than has fallen within the limited scope of this article.

This exploration, when pursued, will emphasise women's liberation under the communism Marx anticipates – and, beyond this, in the late-modern world more generally – but also some of the limitations of the roles into which women are cast, sometimes through the very same liberations. For example, liberation from the bourgeois family-form is, of course, very ambiguous. While it is certainly liberating to be able to draw a wage, own property, determine when, if and how one marries, and pursue ever-higher levels of education and employment, the historically concomitant isolation from the support and camaraderie of kinship-groups has proved very challenging for women and men alike. To take a second example, the idea of equality may itself be limiting and unable to acknowledge crucial and valuable differences between the sexes. This idea is not new, since it was a stable trope of the *querelle des femmes*, but, in the wake of the Enlightenment closure of any challenges to equality, contemporary-feminist discourse has

---

59. Marx 1973, p. 496.

rediscovered and elaborated it in what are now known as the 'equality-versus-difference' debates.[60]

The treatment of gender in Marx thus foreshadows twentieth-century debates in Marxist feminism and in feminist theory more generally. Debates about labour; technology, including reproductive technology; embodiment; wages; and social class-divisions among gendered subjects, including divisions of social class that accompany and reinforce racial divisions, have been prevalent in recent years.[61]

The treatment of gender in Marx also foreshadows the shape of the texts that set the terms of the debate for twentieth-century feminism. For example, Simone de Beauvoir's *Second Sex*, written in 1949, also contains a history of women from earliest antiquity to the present. This is undertaken alongside a more famous discussion of women's status in the discourses contemporary to de Beauvoir, especially those of biology, psychoanalysis, and historical materialism.[62] Like Marx, de Beauvoir's treatment suggests that no philosophical view of women can be taken without a comprehensive history of the topic.

This is not to suggest that Marx's treatment of gender does not have some very obvious limitations, particularly in the *Grundrisse*, where the connections between gender and the capitalist mode of production are only very scantily drawn. However, beyond the obvious limitations of the text, we find some powerful conceptual tools in Marx's *Grundrisse* for working on the issue of gender. This is especially true of Marx's critical revival and reworking of the Aristotelian idea of a second nature: that is, a nature that only becomes a nature with social and historical shaping. It is also true of Marx's critique of nature more generally, and especially his critique of bourgeois ideas about human nature, a critique that, while it is already begun in Marx's early works, is powerfully developed in the *Grundrisse* and often assumed as accomplished in *Capital*.

If anything, this is one of the primary lessons of the *Grundrisse*: just as there is no such thing as production, consumption, distribution, and exchange in general, apart from the historical forms that work these up, so too there is no such thing as sex in general. And so we are already close to Simone de Beauvoir's point – a point indebted, ultimately, to the same Hegelian phenomenological and existential tradition that formed Marx – that one is not born but rather becomes a woman.[63]

---

60. For a summary of the central issues, see especially Pateman 1988 and Scott 1988.

61. See, for example, Haraway 1991, hooks 1981, Wajcman 1991, Fausto-Sterling 1992, and Strathern 1992. This short list is representative and propaedeutical rather than comprehensive.

62. Simone de Beauvoir's discussion of historical materialism in *The Second Sex* is especially focused on Engels's *The Origin of the Family, Private Property, and the State*. See De Beauvoir 1989, pp. 53–60.

63. De Beauvoir 1989, p. 267.

This is why, as I noted at the outset, my use of the term gender in this article has been both anachronistic and deliberate. Some of the most interesting questions of feminist theory derive from the categories under which women, men, gender, sexuality, reproduction, the family, labour, race, social class, equality, and difference have been studied. The construction of these categories themselves lends a fundamental shaping to the discourses that draw upon them, and also to the kinds of studies and questions that are rendered invisible, covered over, or ignored.

Even more provocative are questions of when, why, and under what pressures some categories come to prominence and others disappear. Here feminist theory is like social theory in general, whose defining work, especially in the discipline of philosophy, is the illumination of the politics of the concept. Marx's theory of what bourgeois concepts can and cannot allow us to see is just one species of this more general philosophical labour.[64]

64. This essay would not have been possible without the research-assistance of Elizabeth Sokolowski and Anthony Schlimgen, both advanced honours undergraduate students at Creighton University, my scholarly home in Omaha, Nebraska, USA.

Uneven Developments: From the *Grundrisse* to *Capital*
Joel Wainwright

Thus, while capital must on one side strive to tear down every spatial barrier to intercourse, i.e., to exchange, and conquer the whole earth for its market, it strives on the other side to annihilate this space with time, i.e. to reduce to a minimum the time spent in motion from one place to another. The more developed the capital, therefore, the more extensive the market over which it circulates, which forms the spatial orbit of its circulation, the more does it strive simultaneously for an even greater extension of the market and for greater annihilation of space by time.[1]

I

Perhaps no Marxist concept is more central to the discipline of geography than 'uneven development'. Although the social relations in question are rarely defined in narrow economic terms, geographers generally recognise that the spatially uneven nature of capitalism is the result of its innate drive that brings an ever greater 'annihilation of space by time'.[2]

---

1. Marx 1973, p. 538.
2. This has been best demonstrated by David Harvey, who contends that 'the theory of uneven geographical development needs further development' (Harvey 2006, p. 71). Although my analysis in this chapter takes inspiration from Harvey's work, I do not use his expression 'uneven geographical development' because I find it to be redundant (unevenness implies geography). Harvey is perhaps justified in insisting on the geographical accent, because discussions of uneven development in the Marxist tradition emphasise time over space (see Harvey 1981).

It may come then as something of a surprise that uneven development is not a concept of Marx's. It is certainly a Marx*ist* concept, meaning that it cannot be understood apart from the intellectual tradition inspired by Marx's analysis of capitalism. And to be sure, the unevenness of capitalist socio-spatial relations is a central problem of analysis in Marx's mature economic writings. Yet 'uneven development' is not a concept elaborated by Marx. This chapter addresses this gap – between the present-day centrality of 'uneven development' and its absence as such in Marx – by grappling with Marx's attempts to explain what we today refer to as 'uneven development'. To do so, I compare the way that the problematic of uneven development is framed in two of Marx's greatest texts: *Grundrisse* and *Capital*. That is, I examine the way that these texts situate uneven development relative to their common, central task: analysing value to unravel capitalist social relations.

The importance of uneven development as a vernacular concept is enormous. Its gravity derives from the massively uneven dispensations of power and wealth in the world. 'Uneven development' has proven to be the paradigmatic description of the *geographical nature of this injustice*. And in the wake of the 'fall of communism', Marxist thought today is largely defined by its criticisms of the unequal provision of the fruits of 'capitalist development'.[3] This represents a departure from Marx's texts (as well as from most Marxisms predating the 1950s). If the great struggle of the twentieth century, as Edward Said once wrote, was the popular effort to decolonise the world, then one effect of this struggle for Marxism was to shift the focus of our critique from labour/capital to colonised/imperial. The latter dyad has elevated the prominence of the concept of uneven development.

Thanks to the work of David Harvey especially, many Marxists are familiar with the ways that Marx's analysis of capitalism in *Capital* opens a radical reinterpretation of the world's geographies.[4] It often reads like an analysis of industrial, urban capitalism such as could only have been found in London at the time of its writing; Volume I makes reference to its workshops and state, labour-laws, the social history of the British enclosures, and in the last chapter, British colonialism (more on this below). Of course, *Capital* is about capitalism, not British capitalism. Nevertheless, few readers could mistake the book's setting, and I am

---

3. The key issue, here, for Marxism is that the facts of global inequality have become the starting point for most Marxist studies, and these criticisms have come to shape how Marxism is understood. I place 'capitalist development' in scare-quotes because this concept must be destroyed – and replaced with 'capitalism qua development' (Wainwright 2008b).

4. The following two paragraphs are taken from an essay co-authored with Geoff Mann (Mann and Wainwright 2008).

perhaps not the only Marxist who has difficulty imagining what *Capital* might look like had it been written in, say, Paris, or, for that matter, Beijing.

Like *Capital*, the *Grundrisse* was written in Victorian London and traces of that imperial, urban environment appear in the text. Yet there is an important distance. Here the difference with *Capital* in the feel of this setting is stark and fruitful. Indeed, the 'setting' is so undefined that it can only be called unsettled; the *Grundrisse* produces a palpable sense of indefinite, even volcanic, geography: the *Grundrisse* describes capitalism and the *world*, in its world-becoming and its becoming-worldly. Its concepts emerge in a world of contradictory and still-unfolding spaces. Whereas a reader may read *Capital* as a book about Britain's capitalist society and its eventual overthrow by the British proletariat, there can be no mistaking the *Grundrisse* as anything other than a text of geography without salvation, set in a world without guarantees.

Part of what distinguishes the *Grundrisse* both from Marx's earlier works as well as the three later drafts of *Capital* is the way that four threads are woven together: the emergence of capitalism, value, contradictions of capitalism, and capital's expansionary tendency.[5] Although these threads reappear in *Capital*, the resulting tapestry is not the same. In neither *Capital* nor *Grundrisse* does Marx offer a definitive explanation of uneven development. However, each text offers distinct and useful, but limited, thoughts towards an explanation. Marx provides us with the elements of a theory that sees uneven development as an effect of four related processes: capitalism's original and primitive accumulation of its own 'exterior' in slavery, the formal subsumption of labour, the displacement of diverse precapitalist formations, and colonialism. Taken together, we may call these processes *imperialism*. I use this term decidedly to underscore the main argument: the difference in Marx's treatment of the problematic of uneven development in these two texts results from his growing recognition during the 1850s of the interconnections between Britain's imperial brutality and the expansionary nature of capital. Although Marx himself did not use these terms, we may speak of Marx's 'discovery of uneven development and imperialism'.

The work of Marxist geographers to elaborate a theory of uneven development should, therefore, be seen as attempts to elaborate upon Marx's discovery of 150 years ago. For those geographers, uneven development is the spatial outcome of the general law of capitalist accumulation.[6] This interpretation of

---

5. Marx wrote two extensive drafts of *Capital* after the *Grundrisse*. Enrique Dussel's *Towards an Unknown Marx* (Dussel 2001) is the best commentary I know on the manuscripts of 1861–3, the 'second draft'. Unfortunately for English readers, Dussel's commentary on the *Grundrisse* (1985) has not been translated.

6. Walker 1978; Harvey 1982; Smith 1984. In a concise formulation, Neil Smith contends that 'uneven development derives specifically from the opposed tendencies, inherent in capital, toward the differentiation but simultaneous equalization of the levels and

uneven development was principally inspired by Marx's analysis of the emergence and extension of capitalist relations, but it was Trotsky who introduced the term 'uneven and combined development' into the Marxist vernacular. Trotsky's *The History of the Russian Revolution*[7] is framed by the concept of 'uneven and combined development': 'The development of historically backward nations leads necessarily to a peculiar combination of different stages in the historic process. Their development as a whole acquires a planless, complex, combined character'.[8] In Trotsky's texts, these developments are principally historical-political, but today the emphasis is mainly on economic-geographical factors.

There is much that could be said about the varied uses of the concept, but my aim in this chapter is limited to examining the problematic of uneven development in Marx's later texts.[9] This is not to render Marx's economic *oeuvre* whole or settled – rather the opposite. My goal is emphatically not to make Marx consistent with himself in order to convince somebody to be consistent with Marx. It is rather to trace part of the itinerary of what has become a key concept for many Marxists.

II

[T]he really difficult point to be discussed... is how the relations of production as legal relations enter into uneven development.[10]

---

conditions of production' (Smith 1984, p. 6). This definition has the merit of capturing the contradictory spatial dynamic inherent in the pursuit of higher profit-rates and/or faster turnover-time in a world of fixed capital, but it neglects the geographically uneven separation of classes (capital versus labor) and the uneven separation of distinct social groups from the means of production – two elements emphasised in other accounts.

7. Trotsky 1959.

8. Trotsky 1959, p. 3.

9. Since Althusser, 'uneven development' has also been used by some Marxists to speak of unevenness in changes in social-political formations. In his glossary of Althusserian terms, Brewster provides us with the following definition of uneven development (*développement inégal*): 'A concept of Lenin and Mao Tse-tung: the overdetermination of all the contradictions in a social formation means that none can develop simply; the different overdeterminations in different times and places result in quite different patterns of social development' (Brewster 1997, p. 312). Note that Brewster does not credit Trotsky: a mark of Stalinism?

10. Marx 1986, p. 46. This is the Wangermann translation. Compare the Nicolaus translation: 'But the really difficult point to discuss here is how relations of production develop unevenly as legal relations' (Marx 1973, p. 109). Note that in Wangermann's translation of this passage (again, the only appearance of 'uneven development' in the *Grundrisse*) the word 'development' is not used as a verb but as a noun. In this translation, 'uneven development' is a *condition* that multiple social relations 'enter into'; different *relations enter into relation* with one another more or less evenly. The opposite is true of the Nicolaus translation: development is the verb ('relations of production

To my knowledge, Marx only uses the expression 'uneven development' once in the *Grundrisse*, and only in passing. Discussing the primacy of material production for historical and social change, Marx comments on the 'uneven development of material production relative to, e.g., artistic development' and the unevenness of the relations of production and legal relations.[11] A difficult point indeed, not least because Marx's comments are preliminary and never elaborated upon. Yet two lessons may be gleaned from this reference (which appears in the 'Introduction'). First, Marx emphasises that capitalist relations of production, understood as *social relations*, develop unevenly relative to other sorts of social relations that a Marxist would expect to shift along with capitalism. So the fact that art and law – two crucial elements of the social relations for any society – do not grow and change in lock-step with the relations of production is, in Marx's words, a 'really difficult point to be discussed'. Second, Marx indicates that any use of the concept of 'development' would require the destruction of the 'usual abstractness' of 'the concept of progress'.[12] Nothing would have been less in keeping with his method than the simple notion of progress. Development must be conceived dialectically – not teleologically.

So much for 'uneven development' in the *Grundrisse*. It is introduced, noted to be 'really difficult', and left behind. Yet even if this *expression* disappears, Marx continues to analyse the uneven development of relations of production *vis-à-vis* social relations.

Let us briefly turn to one well-known section of the *Grundrisse*: the 'Forms which precede capitalist production', with the parenthetical subtitle: 'Concerning the process which precedes the formation of the capital relation or of original accumulation'.[13] Here Marx confronts the task of defining capitalism by its

develop...'). Ergo, capitalism unfolds unevenly. Wangermann has it right and is more consistent with Marx's thought: Marx does not write 'the uneven development of capitalist development'; 'capitalist development' is not a Marxist concept.

11. Marx 1973, p. 109; see epigram.

12. Marx 1973, p. 109. See also Smith 1984, pp. 97–8; Peet 1981.

13. This section is found in notebooks IV and V, Marx 1986, pp. 399–439, or Marx 1867a, pp. 471–514. This section was published as a free-standing text in Russian in 1940, in German in 1952, and in English (with an introductory essay by Hobsbawm) in 1964 (see Hobsbawm 1964). I agree with Negri – who calls this subsection 'a parentheses that cannot be put into parentheses' (Negri 1991, pp. 107–21) – that its publication as a stand-alone text, apart from the rest of the *Grundrisse*, introduces problems. I see two in particular. First, this subsection breaks into the text in a respect that should guide our reading: removing it from its place subtracts the appropriate sense of disruption. Second, *pace* Negri, if we do not read this 'parentheses that cannot be put into parentheses' where it appears in the text – within a parentheses on the creation and extraction of surplus-value – we are inclined to miss out on one of the most dialectical qualities of the *Grundrisse*, the way in which value emerges as at once simple, contentless, and parahistorical.

origin and by its difference with all that came earlier. In this analysis, we find Marx's earliest attempt to explain the uneven nature of capitalism's development as an effect of the very emergence of capitalism from within precapitalist Europe.[14] The *Grundrisse* begins with methodological discussions and an analysis of production and consumption. Then comes the chapter on money, where Marx distinguishes value from money, followed by the chapter on capital, where Marx explains how money is transformed into capital and how labor produces surplus-value. This culminates in a discussion of the circulation and accumulation of capital, again with an emphasis on surplus-value. So far, so good. The narrative does not begin with the commodity, as in *Capital*, but it traces a similar arc: it follows the dynamic movement of value: from production, via the application of labour purchased with money, to the conversion of surplus-value into capital, and so forth.

At this point the narrative breaks into a new direction, what appears to be an historical digression, to explain how capitalist social relations came into existence in Europe. This section begins with the following remark, which hangs like a frame over what follows:

> One of the prerequisites of wage labour and one of the historic conditions for capital is free labour and the exchange of free labour for money, in order to reproduce money and to valorise it [...]. Another prerequisite is the separation of free labour from the objective conditions of its realization – from the means and material of labour. This means above all that the workers must be separated from the land, which functions as his natural workshop.[15]

Marx thus posits two necessary conditions for the emergence of capitalist social relations: first, the exchange of 'free' labour (neither slave nor serf) for money, and second, the emergence of a necessary labour-capital relation by separating workers from the means of production, particularly the land.

In this way, Marx links uneven development to the emergence of these two conditions from, and subsequent extension through, *precapitalist* social relations. Marx sketches three distinct forms that are historically-geographically differentiated. The first, the so-called 'Asiatic' or 'oriental' form, is said to be 'natural and spontaneous'; the second, the Roman form, is expressed by commune-towns; the third, the Germanic, is grounded upon the household as an economic totality.[16] I think Gayatri Spivak is right when she characterises (one part of) this analysis as 'not an explanation but an attempt to fit historical presuppositions into a

---

14. Bond 1999 similarly argues that Marx's earliest thoughts on uneven development can be traced to the *Grundrisse*, 'where unevenness represents the condition for a transition from one declining mode of production to another rising, more progressive mode'.

15. Marx 1986, p. 399.

16. Marx 1973, pp. 472–85.

logical mould'.[17] And it is not difficult to pair this business of 'fitting' presuppositions into logical moulds with Marx's infamous question from his essay on 'The British rule in India': 'can mankind fulfil its destiny without a fundamental revolution in the social state of Asia?'[18] The link between 'mankind fulfil[ing] its destiny in ... Asia' and the Asiatic mode of pre-capitalist production is suggested by Marx's very ontopogenic division of the world into ideal forms.[19]

If there is a dialectical quality to Marx's analysis here it may be found where the 'fitting' exceeds the mould, in Marx's very attempt to ground his analysis of capitalism in historical categories in a fashion that is itself neither empiricist nor historicist. This reading applies particularly to the question of the origin of labour-sale. Consider where Marx writes that 'the positing of the individual as a *worker*, who is stripped of all qualities except this one, is itself a *historical* product'.[20] The worker is a historical product but not the result of historical laws, nor 'a product of history' that simply is there because 'history' made it that way. The existence of each labourer defies the notion of history because nothing that comes before can explain what makes the fundamental leap to proletarianisation happen. And this leap is not made once. And it changes history each time. In this view, Marx's sketch of precapitalist formations is less an essay on 'what came earlier' in a temporal sense as it is an analysis of the conditions of possibility for a twisting of property and power needed for capitalist social relations to come to be – not temporally, but *ontologically*.[21]

In the emergence of capitalism, two fundamental changes occur in social relations: the crystallisation of property-relations and the emerging centrality of labour-capital relations. Marx elaborates by identifying the conditions needed to free the worker as 'objectless, purely subjective labour capacity confronting the objective conditions of production as his *not-property*', i.e., a person with nothing to sell but her labour, her own life. Marx summarises the emergence of capitalist social relations as a set of presuppositions and dissolutions:

> [A] process of history which dissolves the various forms in which the worker is a proprietor [...]. *Dissolution* of the relation to the earth – land and soil – as natural condition of production – to which he relates as his own inorganic being [...]. *Dissolution* of the relations in which he appears as *proprietor of*

---

17. Spivak 1999, p. 81. See also Spivak 1999, Chapter One; and Spivak 1994, p. 56. Spivak calls the Asiatic Mode and Primitive Communism 'names that inhabit the pre-historical or para-geographical space/time that mark the outside of the feudalism/capitalism circuit' (Spivak 1999, p. 83).

18. Marx 1968, p. 41.

19. See Derrida 1994, pp. 82–3.

20. Marx 1968, p. 41.

21. It could, therefore, be an illustration of what Geoff Mann (Mann 2008, pp. 925–9) calls 'the *Grundrisse*'s geography of necessity'.

the instrument. Just as the above landed property presupposes a *real commu-nity*, so does this property of the worker in the instrument presuppose a par-ticular form of the development of manufactures, namely *craft, artisan work* [...]. *Dissolution* [...] at the same time of the relations in which the *workers themselves*, the *living labour capacities* themselves, still belong *directly among the objective conditions of production*, and are appropriated as such – i.e., are slaves or serfs.[22]

Capitalist social relations emerge not as a pre-formed, external totality but come into existence through – Marx italicises the word thrice – the *dissolution* of older social relations. Capitalist social relations emerge therefore in a way that is both complete – since the essence of capitalism is the hiring of labour as a commod-ity, which happens at the 'beginning' of capitalism – but also profoundly incom-plete, since capitalist social relations must reproduce themselves elsewhere and beyond an initial purchase of labour. It takes time for everything to dissolve, so to speak. Earlier in the *Grundrisse*, still within the chapter on capital, Marx insists that capitalist relations of production 'do not develop out of *nothing*', nor do they emerge 'from the womb of the Idea positing itself' as for Hegel. No, capitalist social relations emerge:

within and in contradiction to the existing development of production and the inherited, traditional property relations. If in the fully developed bourgeois system each economic relationship presupposes the other in a bourgeois-economic form, and everything posited is thus also a premise, that is the case with every organic system. This organic system itself has its premises as a totality, and its development into a totality consists precisely in subordinating all elements of society to itself, or in creating out of it the organs it still lacks. This is historically how it becomes a totality. Its becoming this totality consti-tutes a moment of its process, of its development.[23]

We should read this in light of Marx's warning that any use of the concept of 'development' would require the destruction of the usual abstractness of the concept of progress. The emergence of capitalist social relations – not all at once, but by positing relations that are then taken as premises for advance – is the counterpart to capitalism *becoming* totality, a process that is never complete. The process is characterised by the tendency to subordinate 'all elements of society' so that it may create 'the organs it still lacks' – for instance, the elements

---

22. Marx 1973, pp. 497–8. Elsewhere in the *Grundrisse*, Marx explains that the fun-damental quality of capitalism as a social relation lies in the 'exchange of living labour for objectified labour – i.e., the positing of social labor in the form of the contradiction of capital and wage labour – is the ultimate development of the *value relation* and of production resting on value' (Marx 1973, p. 704).

23. Marx 1973, p. 278.

and organs of *law*. In the *Grundrisse* there is nothing that resembles what most contemporary scholars of development-studies problematically call 'capitalist development'. There is only the becoming-capital of capital as such, and along-side this genesis, the development of capitalist social relations.

Marx takes pains in his notes to describe this emergence spatially. In the paragraph immediately following the passage I just cited – a hinge-point that is, for me, an illustration of Marx's dialectical procedure at work in the notebooks – Marx turns his attention to the moment when capitalist social relations encoun-ter non-capitalist relations through geographical diffusion: '[I]f, within a society, the modern relations of production, i.e., capital, are developed in their total-ity, and this society now takes possession of a new terrain, as e.g. the colonies, it finds, more especially its representative the capitalist finds, that his capital ceases to be capital without wage labour, and that one of the premises of wage labour is not only landed property in general but modern landed property; landed property which, as capitalised rent, is expensive and as such excludes the direct use of the soil by individuals. Therefore, *Wakefield's* theory of coloniza-tion [...] is immensely important for a correct understanding of modern landed property'.[24]

In the space of two paragraphs Marx joins the emergence of capitalist social relations with territorial power. Capitalism emerges through the dissolution of precapitalist social relations *in Europe*, but more, it flows – a dynamic solvent for transforming precapitalist relations elsewhere.

This remark about the spread of capitalism outward from Europe manifests what can be regarded as Marx's eurocentrism. In the *Grundrisse* Marx asserts that in Europe the relations of production under capitalism are not only the most complex of any society but also hold the key to understanding everything else. In the 'Introduction' to the *Grundrisse*, Marx writes: 'bourgeois society is the most developed and many-faceted historical organization of production'.[25] His point is not only that capitalist Europe is more complex but also that it contains the key to the past, everywhere: 'the anatomy of man is a key to the anatomy of the ape.... Bourgeois economy thus provides a key to that of antiquity...'.[26] Arguably, this style of argument opened the way toward the Eurocentric stage-ism later enshrined as dialectical materialism and, in a different frame, as modernisation.[27]

Which is perhaps why Marx decided to leave it out of *Capital*.

---

24. Marx 1973, p. 278. I believe this is the first reference to Wakefield in Marx's mature economic writings. I discuss his 'immensely important' theory below.

25. Marx 1986, p. 42.

26. Ibid.

27. Later interpretations drew especially from Marx's 1859 'Preface' to the *Contribu-tion to the Critique of Political Economy* (Marx 1975–2005h): 'Mankind thus inevitably sets

III

> The practice of colonization has in a great measure peopled the earth: it has
> founded nations: it has re-acted with momentous consequences on old coun-
> tries, by creating and supplying new objects of desire, by stimulating industry
> and skill, by promoting manufactures and commerce, by greatly augmenting
> the wealth and population of the world: it has [...] been, indirectly, a main
> cause of the political changes and tendencies which now agitate Europe. Yet
> so lately as twenty years ago, no theory of colonization had set forth what
> should be the objects of the process, still less what are the best means of
> accomplishing them. There were long experience without a system, immense
> results without a plan, vast doings but no principles.[28]

In an insightful essay on Marx's discussion of 'forms which precede capitalism',
Wood notes that, notwithstanding references to 'primitive accumulation', in the
Grundrisse Marx did not seek to explain the transition from feudalism to capitalism as such: 'His objective is rather to highlight the specificity of capitalism
in contrast to earlier forms of property and labour'.[29] Wood elaborates on an
apparent shift in this regard between *Grundrisse* and *Capital*:

> [I]t is striking that in *Capital* he begins to offer a rather different account. In
> [*Grundrisse*], he has not yet entirely broken with the most common question-
> begging accounts of how capitalism originated.... [In *Grundrisse*, t]he origin of
> capitalism is [in a more strictly Hegelian fashion] largely a matter of allowing

---

itself only such tasks as it is able to solve, since closer examination will always show that
the problem itself arises only when the material conditions for its solution are already
present or at least in the course of formation. In broad outline, the Asiatic, ancient, feudal and modern bourgeois modes of production may be designated as epochs marking
progress in the economic development of society. The bourgeois mode of production is
the last antagonistic form of the social process of production [...] but the productive
forces developing within bourgeois society create also the material conditions for a solution of this antagonism. The prehistory of human society accordingly closes with this
social formation'. In his 1965 essay on Marx's treatment of precapitalist formations, Hobsbawm notes that the 'classical formulation of these epochs of human progress' is to be
found in the *Grundrisse*. Perhaps. As Hobsbawm argues, it *is* in this particular section of
the *Grundrisse* that Marx sought 'to formulate the content of history in its most general
form', albeit not in a simple chronological sense (Hobsbawm 1965, pp. 12–14). Although
today we would be less inclined to relate the *Grundrisse* with 'epochs marking progress',
Hobsbawm's essay shows how Marx attempts to write a history of capital lacking the
teleology typically ascribed to it. Yet Hobsbawm does not ask about the conditions of
possibility of knowing any other history, nor whether Marx's approach to capitalism's
history may be eurocentric. For a reading of 'forms which precede capitalist production'
as an anti-teleological text, see Wood 2008.

28. Wakefield 2001, letter IX.
29. Wood 2008, p. 84.

its already existing elements to grow. When he developed his ideas in *Capital*, he was already hinting at a very different explanation, which did indeed begin to seek the source of the transition not in the 'interstices' of feudalism but rather in its own internal dynamics, in its own constitutive property relations, which gave rise to an authentic social transformation.[30]

As Marx already knew at the time he wrote the *Grundrisse*, these constitutive property-relations required the separation of living labour from the means of production. The shift Wood identifies emerges when Marx changes the way the separation of labour from the means of production is framed in relation to capital. Thus, the shift Wood identifies in Marx's explanation of the emergence of capitalism is tightly related to primitive accumulation and what we call today 'uneven development'.

The question of precapitalist formations returns in *Capital* in two ways, neither as extensive or speculative as in the *Grundrisse*. In Part five of *Capital* Volume III, best known for its analysis of the role of finance in the production-process, we find a chapter on 'pre-capitalist relations'[31] where Marx argues that the transition from pre-capitalist relations into capitalism was made possible by two 'antediluvian forms of capital' that long predate the emergence of capitalism *in toto*: usurer's capital and merchant's capital.[32] Yet credit cannot take credit for creating capitalism, since 'usury, like trade, exploits a given mode of production but [can]not create it; both relate to the mode of production from outside'.[33] This suits Marx's argument that capitalism emerges through the dialectical unfolding of itself. But we should not be distracted by these remarks on credit, for they take us no further in understanding the origins of capitalism or its uneven development.

Marx returns to these problems more substantively in Part Eight of *Capital* Volume I, on primitive accumulation. Here Marx reveals the tendency of capitalist accumulation – the secret of capital's emergence red in tooth and claw – and then concludes with this description of the end of capitalism:

> This expropriation is accomplished by the action of the immanent laws of capitalistic production itself...leading to] the entanglement of all peoples in the net of the world-market [...]. Along with the constantly diminishing

---

30. Wood 2008, p. 85.

31. Marx 1981, p. 728–49.

32. In Marx's discussion, credit appears as both the earliest and the highest stages of capitalism. On credit as a reagent in the emergence of capitalism and the dominant expression of its 'highest stages', see also Lenin's *Development of Capitalism in Russia* (Lenin 2000, Chapter VI, Section VI: 'Merchant's and industrial capital in manufacture') and his study of *Imperialism* (Lenin 1939.).

33. Marx 1981, p. 745.

number of the magnates of capital...grows the mass of misery, oppression, slavery, degradation, exploitation; but with this too grows the revolt of the working-class, a class always increasing in numbers, and disciplined, united, organised by the very mechanism of the process of capitalist production itself. The monopoly of capital becomes a fetter upon the mode of production, which has sprung up and flourished along with, and under it. Centralization of the means of production and socialization of labour at last reach a point where they become incompatible with their capitalist integument. This integument is burst asunder. The knell of capitalist private property sounds. The expropriators are expropriated.[34]

Note that Marx's analysis of the impending end of capitalism is linked directly to what we call today uneven development. What was supposed to bring about the end of capitalism is here characterised as the increasing divisions between classes and societies as a consequence of 'the entanglement of all peoples in the net of the world-market'. These divisions are themselves brought about by capital's expanding contradictions. The knell of capitalist private property is sounded, albeit slowly, by the uneven development of capitalism on a planetary scale, with the centralisation of the means of production and the socialisation of labour reaching a point of fundamental contradiction.

Then Marx does something strange. Volume I does not end at its natural conclusion – the destruction of capitalism. Why did Marx, who arranged *Capital* so delicately and dialectically, opt against concluding with this majestic *Aufhebung*? Instead this conclusion is followed by a brief and breezy discussion of Wakefield's theory of colonialism. Noting that this final chapter's placement is 'somewhat odd',[35] David Harvey asks: 'why open up such questions at the end of a work that appeared to reach its natural culmination in the preceding chapter?' Harvey's (admittedly speculative) reply is to suggest that Marx is drawing a shrewd parallel with the conclusion of Hegel's *Philosophy of Right*, where Hegel 'proposes...colonial solutions' to the problems facing bourgeois civil society by demonstrating that 'there is no *outer* resolution to the internal contradictions of capitalism'.[36] Harvey may be onto something – Marx knew his Hegel – but there is a more immediate and I think stronger explanation to this riddle, stronger because it is borne out by clues from Marx's notes, letters, and previous drafts, including the *Grundrisse*.

---

34. Marx 1967, p. 763.
35. Harvey 1982, p. 413.
36. Harvey 1982, p. 414; also Harvey 2010, pp. 301–4. On the Hegelian qualities of *Grundrisse*, see Rosdolsky 1977, and Uchida 1988; compare Karatani 2003.

Except for two brief passages, Marx does not address colonialism in the *Grundrisse*; nor, again, in *Capital*, until the final chapter – ostensibly a minor digression on Wakefield's theory of colonialism. This is the same Wakefield we saw cited in the *Grundrisse* on the origins of capitalism: Edward Gibbon Wakefield (1796–1862), a British political economist obscured by history but important in his time.[37] Wakefield married into wealth, and when his first wife died, he abducted another wealthy woman into forced marriage – but was caught and sent to Newgate prison for three years. Not unlike Gramsci, while in prison he filled notebooks with reflections on political economy – albeit toward an entirely different effect. Wakefield emerged from prison a strenuous advocate for colonialism as a solution to all Britain's problems. No armchair-theorist, Wakefield went on to play an important role in the British colonisation of southern Australia, New Zealand, and Canada in 1830s and 1840s.

Marx's criticisms are directed principally at Wakefield's 1834 book, *England and America*, the fruit of his ruminations in prison. Before turning to Marx's reading of Wakefield, a few words on Wakefield's text are due. Despite the fact that Wakefield openly advocates colonialism, he was no idiot. His texts offer defences and *analyses* of colonialism; they contribute novel arguments and anticipate much of the content, if little of the tone, of twentieth-century Marxist theories of imperialism. Wakefield later published an extended correspondence in his 1849 *View of the Art of Colonization*.[38] Published only a year after Marx and Engels's *Communist Manifesto*, Wakefield's *Art of Colonization* could be read as a reply: one that attempts to dispel the ghost haunting Europe, so to speak, to the colonies. Noting, in *England and America*, that the advance of capitalist social relations within England has created circumstances that are unfavourable to continued growth, Wakefield argues that colonialism will bring an 'Extension of Markets,' 'Enlarge [the] field for Capital,' and assuage the problem of 'Excessive Numbers' – of unruly underemployed workers. It would be hard to find a more concise statement of the gains of colonialism to capitalists.

Like Marx, Wakefield emphasised the essential novelty of the British situation – unprecedented industrialisation and proletarianisation – and speculated that the intense competition among labourers had reduced their quality of life. He worries that many labourers lack 'the means of a comfortable subsistence according to the respectful standards of living'. At the same time, Wakefield explains, in

---

37. In a review of the literature in Marxist geography, I found no discussion of Marx and Wakefield, except Harvey 2010, pp. 301–2. Here I rely principally on Wakefield and Marx's primary texts, but have benefitted from Pappe 1951 and Semmel 1961.
38. Wakefield 1849.

England there is generally a surplus of capital: 'capital sometimes accumulates so far beyond the room for productive investment, that a great mass of capital is wasted, both at home and abroad, in all sorts of unproductive enterprises'.[39] Wakefield felt that such overaccumulation could be solved by exporting capital to colonies that would in turn create new markets for British industry.

To appreciate the novelty of what Marx calls 'Wakefield's colonization theory',[40] one further point is needed. Wakefield recognised that new colonies are not automatically effective in their role as receptacles of surplus-capital from the core, because, unlike the core, they lack fully developed capitalist social relations. The art of colonialism lies in bringing about these relations – by separating labour from the means of production – in such a way that generates patterns of production and consumption that benefit the core. To this task, Wakefield recognised the fundamental role of the colonial state, and more specifically through the lever of acquiring and selling land: 'in the business of settling a new country, the mode in which waste or public land is disposed of by the government, must necessarily exercise an all-important influence'.[41] Wakefield's critique is that the Colonial Office lacks a theoretically-informed ('principled') land-policy. He condemned the practice of granting lands, calling instead for the Colonial Office to treat land as a commodity to be sold at a carefully calibrated price: one that attracts settlers while remaining sufficiently high to prevent the colonists from becoming a stagnant, landed class; they should be compelled to sell their labour – that is, to become proletarians.[42]

And, we should add, to become *consumers*. Wakefield saw that markets for colonial products like tea and sugar were created in the core to facilitate profitable production in the colonies: 'It is not because an English washerwoman cannot sit down to breakfast without tea and sugar, that the world has been circumnavigated; but it is because the world has been circumnavigated that an English washerwoman requires tea and sugar for breakfast'.[43] Thus capitalism requires the satisfaction of desires bound up with new forms of subjectivity.[44]

---

39. Wakefield 1849, p. 64.
40. Marx 1967, p. 766.
41. Wakefield 2001, letter IX.
42. Wakefield 1849.
43. Wakefield 1967, p. 243.
44. Wakefield also anticipated that the differential patterns of consumption in the core and the colonies would facilitate the stabilisation of capital-accumulation in the core. He attributes this condition to inherently different factors of production rather than capital's uneven geographical dynamic. In one of his letters on colonialism, Wakefield writes: 'In consequence of the cheapness of land in colonies, the great majority of the people are owners or occupiers of land; and their industry is necessarily in a great measure confined to the producing of what comes immediately from the soil; viz., food, and the raw materials of manufacture. In old countries, on the other hand, where the soil

Wakefield, like Marx, places capital's world-embrace (circumnavigation) at the heart of this transformation. What does he describe here if not what Marx describes in *Grundrisse* as the expanding 'spatial orbit of [capital's] circulation', all to bring about 'an even greater extension of the market and for greater annihilation of space by time'?[45]

Politically, Wakefield sought to counter threats to capitalism with principled colonialism. He was an organic intellectual of the British colonial-capitalist class, yearning to suture colonial practices to the limitations of capital. We have seen how he advocated the expansion of colonial markets and investment of surplus-capital in the colonies to address the problem of periodic low profit-rates in Britain. Similarly, he confronted the problem of low profit-rates in the colonies in a fashion that anticipates the twinning of state-power ('good governance') with capitalism *qua* development:

> Security of property is the indispensable foundation of wealth, let all other circumstances be what they may. Security of property depends wholly on government. In order, therefore, that profits and wages should be constantly high in a colony, it is essential that the colony should be tolerably well governed; well enough, that is, to hold out a fair prospect that enterprise and industry will enjoy their proper fruits. In all the cases that I can call to mind, of low profits and low wages in a colony [...] the cause has been a stagnation of enterprise and industry, arising from insecurity of property; and the insecurity of property arose from defective or vicious government. I lay it down as an axiom therefore, that tolerably good colonial government is an essential condition of that state of continual high profits and high wages, which moderately well-governed colonies exhibit.[46]

With this appeal for good governance and property-rights, Wakefield anticipates much of the tone of contemporary liberal developmentalism: a useful reminder of the colonial roots of this discourse.

Wakefield receives only modest attention in the *Grundrisse* and the *Contribution to the Critique of Political Economy* (of 1861–3). Yet Wakefield is cited more than a dozen times in *Capital* Volume I, where Marx refers to him as 'the most

---

is fully occupied and labour abundant, it may be said that manufactured goods are their natural production for export. These are what the colonists do not produce. The colony produces what the old country wants; the old country produces what the colony wants. The old country and the colony, therefore, are, naturally, each other's best customers' (Wakefield 1849, letter XIV). Indeed they are – to the benefit of the old country.

45. Marx 1973, p. 538.
46. Wakefield 2001, letter XIV.

notable political economist' of England in the 1830s.[47] True, in comparison to the rich and extending commentaries we find on Marx's main interlocutors regarding *value* – Smith, Ricardo, Malthus, and Bailey – the passages on Wakefield amount to little. So it is odd that Marx gave Wakefield pride of place in the final chapter of *Capital*. All Marx's references to Wakefield in his mature economic writings are eclipsed by the final chapter of *Capital*, where Marx credits Wakefield's theory of colonialism with inadvertently exposing something essential about the nature of capitalism. Remember that Wakefield was concerned with the fact that colonialism was hampered by the lack of fully-formed capitalist social relations. Marx writes: 'At earlier stages of production... an earlier working class may be present sporadically, not however as a *universal* prerequisite of production. The case of *colonies* (see *Wakefield* [...]) shows how this relation is itself a product of capitalist production'.[48] The existence of the capital-labour relation is 'initially sporadic', but capitalism posits it increasingly: not only in theory, but also concretely, as is demonstrated by colonialism. Marx returns to this 'immensely important' line of thinking later in his notebooks. Here is, I think, the key passage on Wakefield in Marx's economic writings before the final chapter of *Capital*:

> The merit of *Wakefield's* new system of colonization is not that he discovered or promoted the art of colonization, nor that he made any fresh discoveries whatsoever in the field of political economy, but that he naively laid bare the narrow-mindedness of political economy without being clear himself as to the importance of these discoveries[...]. The point is that in the colonies, particularly in the earliest stages of development, bourgeois relations are not yet fully formed; not yet presupposed, as they are in old established countries. They are in the process of becoming. The conditions of their origin therefore emerge more clearly. It appears that these *economic relations* are neither present by nature, nor are they *things*, which is the way the political economists are rather inclined to view capital.[49]

For Marx, Wakefield demonstrates two intertwined truths: capital*ism* is not a system of markets or capital, but an ensemble of social relations; and the 'becoming' (not to say 'origin') of capitalist relations can be found in the colonies. Indeed,

---

47. Marx 1967, p. 657. In the 1967 International English edition of *Capital*, Wakefield is cited at p. 269, p. 326, p. 536, p. 582, and p. 675, in addition to the discussion in the concluding chapter. Of these citations – on population, cooperation, wages, the Corn-Laws, and so on – only the first is ironical. Marx studied Wakefield as carefully as he did other political economists and treated his texts in his usual fashion, drawing support from them as needed and applying his critique at the decisive point.

48. Marx 1988, pp. 75–6.

49. Marx 1988, pp. 256–7. Marx makes similar remarks elsewhere. See Marx 1988, p. 292.

Marx's clearest statement in *Capital* Volume I to the effect that capital is not a thing, but a social relation, appears in the final chapter on colonialism – and he attributes this discovery to Wakefield.[50]

This attribution is not entirely ironic. Marx and Wakefield understood more clearly than any political economists of their time that colonialism was intended to resolve contradictions engendered by Britain's early advance as an industrial capitalist society. Moreover, like Marx, Wakefield saw in the growing British pro-letariat a new class that could bring about a political transformation. Yet their interpretations of these facts are fundamentally distinct. Wakefield examines the colonial situation as a would-be statesman, one fearful of the rising proletariat ('with the continuance of discontent and the spread of education amongst the common people, chartism and socialism will have many a struggle for the mas-tery over a restricted franchise and private property: and in these struggles I perceive immense danger for everybody').[51] For Wakefield, the colonial situation is crucial for stabilising British capitalism, and so he advocates reforming the Colonial Office's land-policies. In stark contrast, Marx sees the colonial scene as a laboratory within which to examine the emergence of capitalist social rela-tions.[52] Wakefield advocates colonialism to overcome two contradictions – the overaccumulation of capital, and labour-strife – by *extending* capitalist social relations to the colonies. Yet these contradictions were not actually explained until Marx wrote *Capital*. Thus both Wakefield and Marx saw, in their way, that colonialism would help save British capitalism. The difference between them is that only one felt British capitalism worth saving.

IV

> The specific task of bourgeois society is the establishment of a world-market...and of production based upon this market. As the world is round, this seems to have been completed by the colonisation of California and Aus-tralia and the opening up of China and Japan. The difficult question for us is this: on the [European] Continent the revolution is imminent and will imme-diately assume a socialist character. Is it not bound to be crushed in this little

---

50. Marx 1976a, p. 932.
51. Wakefield 1849, letter XI.
52. Though Marx respectfully refers to Wakefield as a 'notable political economist' (Marx 1967, p. 675), elsewhere he excoriates Wakefield's simplistic method. Wakefield's texts are peppered with statements that casually separate politics and economics, such as this: '[I]n treating of what British colonization ought to be, what it is, why it is what it is, and how to make it what it ought to be, we [should] separate considerations relating to politics from those relating to economy' (Wakefield 2001, letter XI).

corner, considering that in a far greater territory the movement of bourgeois society is still in the ascendant?[53]

What led Marx to conclude *Capital* with the critique of Wakefield? Marx's decision to begin the analysis in *Capital* with commodity and to focus on industrial capitalism in England led him to study the totality of industrial capitalism emerging around him. This analysis did not require 'historicising' capitalism from a certain germ, an origin story. Marx thus excised the section on the forms of precapitalist formations, and *Capital* was spared this digression. Rather than introducing the concept of primitive accumulation to then inquire into the historical roots of capitalism, as in *Grundrisse*, Marx ends *Capital* with colonialism – the spatial diffusion of primitive accumulation. The origin of capitalism appears in a new way, through the elaboration of the ever-widening capital-labour contradiction on one hand and its spatial adumbration via colonialism: from precapitalist formations to the colonial present. The problematic of uneven development shifts from a temporal to a spatial accent.

Yet, to leave the answer at this is too elegant. For one thing, Marx may not have written about colonialism in the *Grundrisse*, but he anticipated doing so. Two tantalising passages indicate his intentions. The first comes in the 'Introduction', where Marx offers a summary outline of the topics he must address in *Capital*. He begins with the general concept of capital, and analyses its various forms, concluding with money; then, accumulation; value; exchange; credit; and finally, 'capital as source of wealth. The capitalist'. Having unravelled capital, in the next section 'landed property would have to be dealt with', which means rent. 'After that wage labour'. Taken together, capital, rent, and labour comprise the 'three classes as production posited in its three basic forms and presuppositions of circulation'. But Marx imagined weaving production and consumption into a broader analysis. He sketches these elements:

> [T]he *state* [...] – The state externally: colonies. External trade.... Finally the world market. Encroachment of bourgeois society over the state. Crises. Dissolution of the mode of production and form of society based on exchange value. The real positing of individual labour as social and vice versa.[54]

Such was Marx's outline at this stage for *Capital* – from the first unfolding of capital all the way to communism in one hundred and fifty words. What stands out here is Marx's inclusion of territorial power. In a lapidary turn of phrase, he defines colonialism as 'the state externally'. Judging by this outline from the *Grundrisse*, Marx anticipated an intermediate analysis of colonialism and trade

---

53. Marx 1968, p. 322.
54. Marx 1986, p. 195.

in *Capital* between that of the nation-state and the world-market. This intermediate space is what we have come to know as uneven development. Yet Marx never wrote all this. He maintained his basic orientation, but his impetus to analyse the relations between the world-market-forming tendency of capital with 'the state externally' went unfulfilled, except again in the critique of Wakefield.[55]

The second mention of colonialism arrives via an abstract historical typology of the possible outcomes of imperial conquest. 'In all cases of conquest', Marx writes in the *Grundrisse*, three outcomes are possible:

> [1] The conquering people subjugates the conquered under its own mode of production (e.g. the English in Ireland..., ... partly in India); or [2] it leaves the old mode intact and contents itself with a tribute (e.g. Turks and Romans); or [3] a reciprocal interaction takes place whereby some thing new, a synthesis, arises.... In all cases, the mode of production, whether that of the conquering people, that of the conquered, or that emerging from the fusion of both, is decisive for the new distribution which arises.[56]

In this third possible outcome we see Marx outlining, in embryonic form, a mode of analysis later to be elaborated by Samir Amin, Alain de Janvry, David Harvey,[57] and all those who have analysed the ways that colonial capitalism preserves in synthesis elements of precapitalist social formations, thereby reproducing uneven relations between core and peripheral economies. Capitalism can then 'resolve' crises in the core – by exporting capital to the colonies during periods of overproduction and low profitability, by expanding markets during periods of low effective demand, and so on.

This second passage also underscores an important dimension of Marx's thoughts regarding colonialism circa 1857. Note that India and Ireland are placed together in the first group, where 'the conquering people', in this case, the British, 'subjugates the conquered'. But between Marx's first jottings in the *Grundrisse* and the completion of *Capital*, the 'conquered' in India and Ireland made themselves (in Marx's view) historical subjects. In 1857–9 Marx was confronted, in a direct and involved way, by two anti-colonial movements against British rule: the Sepoy mutiny in India and the (almost concomitant) rise of the Fenian movement in Ireland. During the period of Marx's most intensive study of British capitalism, these two events formed arguably the most concrete manifestations of political resistance to Britain's world hegemony.

---

55. See Negri 1991, pp. 61–3, and pp. 118–21).
56. Marx 1973, pp. 97–8.
57. Amin 1976; de Janvry 1981; Harvey 1982.

As other writers have demonstrated, Marx's analyses of these anti-colonial movements – executed to support his livelihood as a writer for the *New York Tribune* – changed his views on the ostensibly progressive effects of imperialism.[58] Marx's extensive writings on the insurrections of 1857–9 (including some twenty articles for the *Tribune*) are matched perhaps only by Mark Twain for their acerbic attacks on the hypocrisy of imperial liberalism.[59] Take, for instance, Marx's blistering article of 28 August 1857, which documents the torture of people in India by British imperial troops. After relaying accounts that appear only too familiar today, Marx concludes with this comment: 'We have here given but a brief and mildly-colored chapter from the real history of British rule in India. In view of such facts, dispassionate and thoughtful men may perhaps be led to ask whether a people are not justified in attempting to expel the foreign conquerors who have so abused their subjects'.[60]

Marx may well have remained eurocentric in certain respects,[61] as some of his critics have claimed, but his views on imperialism and anti-colonial struggle shifted during the years after 1857 when he first put down an outline for his critique of political economy that included a study of 'The state externally: colonies'. Here we find no apology for the British, only a demand: that his audience accept the justness of anti-colonial resistance.

Therefore it was not Hegel, but another sort of world-historical jolt – living anti-colonial movements – that led Marx to conclude *Capital* with Wakefield. For if he could analyse the violent transformation of precapitalist formations in the colonies as it was happening, there is no need for an historical digression. And if the 'external' expression of the British state produced resistance that challenged capitalism, then it deserves pride of place in the conclusion of *Capital*.

Thus Marx was not only studying political economy while he wrote the *Grundrisse*; he was also studying struggles around the world. A clear indication of

---

58. Nimtz 2002; Jani 2002.

59. Compare Marx's comments on British torture in India (Marx 1968) with Twain's *King Leopold's Soliloquy* (Twain 1905). Each text derives its force from the play of quotations of eyewitness-reports with wry observations. In this way, Jani argues that Marx 'frees the subaltern testimony trapped within [the colonizers' own text] as the unmediated 'truth' of the matter, the 'real history' of colonial India' (Jani 2002, p. 91). Yet I find Twain's text more effective in this respect. In representing the truth in the form of a soliloquy, historical truth is fictionalised, thus made all the more real.

60. Marx 1968, p. 167.

61. This is to affirm Gidwani's evaluation that 'neither Nimtz's defense nor – to a lesser degree – Jani's confronts the criticism that Marx's theory of capitalism is Eurocentric not in the parochialism of its spatial imaginary but rather in the presuppositions from which it derives epistemic warrant' (Gidwani 2004, p. 532). Nevertheless, I read Marx as the quintessential proto-postcolonial thinker. For among other things, as we have seen here, his critique of political economy analytically unravels the dynamics of capitalism to show how what Giovanni Arrighi and David Harvey call 'capital' and 'territorial' projects are always already interrelated.

Marx's sentiments may be gained from his letter to Engels on 8 October 1858: 'The difficult question for us is this: on the [European] Continent the revolution is imminent and will immediately assume a socialist character. Is it not bound to be crushed in this little corner, considering that in a far greater territory the movement of bourgeois society is still in the ascendant?'[62] By the time Marx finished the *Grundrisse*, he had raised his eyes well beyond 'this little corner'. He still anticipated revolution to begin *in Europe*. But he saw that it would fail without revolutions *worldwide*.[63]

---

62. Marx 1968.

63. I thank Geoff Mann, Noel Castree, and Will Jones for their insightful criticisms. An earlier version of this essay was published in a symposium on the *Grundrisse* published in issue 40(5) of *Antipode*, a journal of radical geography. I thank Geoff Mann, with whom I co-edited the *Grundrisse* symposium.

Pre-Capitalistic Forms of Production and Primitive Accumulation. Marx's Historiography from the *Grundrisse* to *Capital*[1]

Massimilano Tomba

Marx wrote the *Grundrisse* in the middle of a crisis. In a letter to Engels dated 8 December 1857, he wrote: 'I am working like mad all night and every night collating my economic studies so that I at least get the outlines clear before the *deluge*'.[2] In this book, one finds a strategy that allows one to comprehend and to go through the crisis by means of critique. This is a critique that unfolds the crisis and opens up new revolutionary possibilities. According to Gidwani, 'Marx uses crisis to produce an agonistic knowledge that is intensely alert to fissures and interruptions in capital's imperial being'.[3]

Marx considers the capitalistic mode of production as a social form that opens a new epoch, that is, the extension of the sphere of needs and of human capacities:

> Hence the exploration of the whole of nature in order to discover new useful properties of things; the universal exchange of the products coming from the most diverse climates and lands; new (artificial) modes of processing natural objects to give them new use values. The all-round exploration of the earth to discover both new useful

1. This text is an extensively revised version of the paper I presented at the conference on the *Grundrisse* in Padova, January 2008. The papers from this conference have been published in Italian in Sacchetto and Tomba 2008.
2. Marx and Engels 1983, p. 214.
3. Gidwani 2008, p. 869.

objects and new uses for old objects, such as their use as raw materials, etc.; hence the development of the natural sciences to their highest point; the discovery, creation and satisfaction of new needs arising from society itself; cultivating [*Kultur*] all the qualities of social man [*gesellschaftlicher Mensch*] and producing him in a form as rich as possible in needs because rich in qualities and relations – producing man as the most total and universal social product possible (for in order to enjoy many different kinds of things he must be capable of enjoyment, that is he must be cultivated to a high degree) – all these are also conditions of production based on capital. This creation of new branches of production, i.e., qualitatively new surplus time, is not only the division of labour, but also the separation of a definite kind of production from itself as labour of a new use value; the development of a constantly expanding comprehensive system of different kinds of labour, different kinds of production, with a corresponding system of ever more extended and ever more varied needs.[4]

By producing new needs, capital breaks the umbilical cord that used to link humans and nature. Nature becomes for the very first time only an object for humanity to use, 'nothing more than a matter of utility'.[5] This is the form of modern *luxury*. One must consider the difference between *luxury* in Antiquity and in modern times in relation to the 'new (artificial) modes of processing natural objects to give them new use-values',[6] the growth of human needs and new forms of experience. An anthropological modification, corresponds to these phenomena, a new kind of human being: the cultivating of all the qualities of 'social man'. Marx calls this new human nature a 'new subject', the 'social individual'.[7] This is a very important concept, which marks an anthropological break. This is an individual who is no longer the same: he has broken his bond to nature, and society has become his new nature. This is not, however, the Hegelian second nature, which presupposes ethical relations that give concreteness to the individual. In the Marxian third nature, not only the Hegelian *ständisch* relations, but also the system of needs, are destroyed: capital produces not in view to satisfy human needs but in order to valorise value. The use-value of the commodity becomes the abstract bearer [*Träger*] of value and therefore a new form of use-value. The sensible becomes the phenomenal form of the suprasensible. Money ceases to be a means and becomes the end. The image of capitalist modernity is *Verkehrung*:[8] *inversion* and *perversion* at the same time.

---

4. Marx 1986, p. 336.
5. Marx 1986, p. 337.
6. Marx 1986, p. 336.
7. Marx 1987, p. 92.
8. Hatem 2006, p. 12, stresses seven levels of 'inversion' in Marx: 'intersubjective', 'intrasubjective', 'ontic', semiotic', 'economic', 'political', 'ideological'.

Pre-capitalistic forms and the 'foreshadowing of the future'

When Marx wrote the *Grundrisse* he was attempting politically to open a revolutionary possibility in the crisis.[9] For this reason, he tries to sketch out possibilities of liberation in the trend of capitalist development and stresses the 'great civilising influence of capital',[10] in order to reach a new stage of society. In this context, one must understand his representation of the *social individual* as an attempt to prefigure the new anthropological type of a new social form, whose capabilities are socially developed. Social development, *social general knowledge*, is not opposed to the individual, as it will occur in *Capital*, but rather, represents his own development. If modernity has produced the individual, Marx tries to sketch the outlines of a new concept of the individual, beyond the modern concept of individuality.

There are brilliant pages where Marx works with a double scheme of interpretation. He articulates a kind of *evolutionary history* with a *repetitive history*,[11] a history of invariants. He does this in order to understand the nature of the historical break represented by the capitalist mode of production,[12] thus inquiring into precapitalist modes of production as an 'otherness' of capitalism. What results from this analysis is not the continuity, but rather, the radical discontinuity between precapitalist and capitalist forms. One can analyse this discontinuity as a modification of the individual and humanity. 'The human is individualised only through the process of history [*Der Mensch vereinzelt sich erst durch den historischen Prozeß*]'.[13] The gradualness of the historical forms in the *Grundrisse* concerns the individualisation of humans through the progressive dissolution of the original unity between individual humans and community. Marx depicts the historical process which, beginning with the original condition of the species-being [*Gattungswesen*] and going through different stages, ends with the *social individual* who is conciliated again with the species [*Gattung*].[14] In this scheme the overcoming of the natural limit due to the limitless nature of the capitalist mode of production constitutes the requirement for the free and full development of the individual. Marx's argument presents a scheme of philosophy of history. If one takes the pages on the precapitalist forms, where this topic on the individual is found, one can see a clearly articulated sequence: genesis, development, crisis. That is to say: unity of individual and community, dissolution of the communitarian bounds, new form of conciliation with the *Gattung*.

---

9. Krätke 2008a; Krätke 2008b.
10. Marx 1986, p. 336.
11. Lefort 1986.
12. According to Spivak, these forms are 'not an explanation but an attempt to fit historical presuppositions into a logical mold'. Spivak 1999, p. 81.
13. Marx 1986, p. 420; translation modified.
14. Texier 1992, p. 143

a) The starting point of this historical sketch is the natural community [*natu-wüchsiges Gemeinwesen*], which pre-exists the individual as something natural, and in which the individual is only a member of community. This is the first form of precapitalist modes of production, namely, oriental despotism. Technological or economic innovation may occur, but does not lead to any impact on the social organisation. The *unity* of humans and community, on the one hand, and of humans and nature, on the other hand, is not placed in question. What is significant here is that Marx presents a form of historiography that breaks with the model of the progressive domination of the development of productive forces.

b) In the second form, the community is again also implied, but the individuals are no longer a sheer accident of the community. In this scenario the dissolution of the natural essence of the community-relationship takes place. The single individual becomes a landlord, whose form of property is direct possession. The individual remains a member of the community, but is nonetheless a single private owner. The community can be recognised as an historical product.

c) The Germanic form of property described by Marx is not really the third form, but rather a possibility in the development of the precapitalist form of production. Other possibilities were open; due to different historical developments, some of these were destroyed. In the Germanic form there is common property and individual possession at the same time. Marx drafts a comparative history: he analyses this form in connection to Roman *ager publicum*. While the *economical totality* for the Germans was the single house, for the Romans it was identified with the city; in the Asiatic form, the natural community remained the true owner.[15] In the Germanic form the 'community [*Gemeinde*] exists only in the mutual relation of the individual landowners as such'. The community 'is neither the substance, of which the individual appears merely as accident [as in the Oriental community], nor is it the general, which exists as such and has a *unified being* [as with the ancients]'.[16] It appears, instead, 'as an *assembly* [*Vereinigung*], not an *association* [*Verein*], as a unification [*Einigung*] whose independent subjects are the landed proprietors, and not as a unity [*Einheit*]'.[17] The Germanic system is an element in the constitution of the feudal form, which derives 'from a "Germanic" path out of primitive communalism'[18] and where 'the *relationship of dominion* exists as an essential relation of appropriation',[19] presupposing 'the appropriation of another's *will* '.[20] These forms of relationship – *dominion and servitude* –

---

15. Munzer 1990, pp. 161–2.
16. Marx 1986, p. 408.
17. Marx 1986, p. 407.
18. Wood 2008, p. 80.
19. Marx 1986, p. 424.
20. Ibid.

'constitute a necessary ferment in the development and decay of all primitive relations of property and production, just as they express their limitations'.[21]

In all these forms of community-relationship, be it natural or historical or traditional, the relationship is pre-given, presupposed to the individual. The community relationship is a limit [*Schranke*] to the development of both the individual and the society. In these forms, writes Marx, 'a free and full development, either of the individual or of the society, is inconceivable [...], since such a development stands in contradiction to the original relation'.[22] Common to these forms is the economical aim of production, i.e., the production of use-value.[23] Marx presents a succession of processes of dissolution that destroy the communitarian *limit* of production and posit the premises for a limitless production. In this sense, he writes in the 'Introduction' to his *Contribution to the Critique of Political Economy* (1859), that the 'Asiatic, ancient, feudal and modern bourgeois modes of production may be designated as epochs marking progress [*progressive Epochen*] in the economic development of society'.[24] *Prima facie*, in this perspective the genesis of the capitalistic mode of production, through the dissolution of precapitalist social relations in Europe, becomes a general scheme of interpretation and the flow of capitalism becomes a dynamic solvent for transforming precapitalist relations elsewhere.[25] On the other hand, Marx's discourse about *progress* sets out to show the process of dissolution of the limits, a progress which is observed from the standpoint of the present, where the 'bourgeois relations of production are the last antagonistic form of the social process of production'.[26] They are the 'last' form because all the previous limits, both natural and communitarian, have now been destroyed by the strength of a mode of production whose aim is not use-value but value.

An *inversion* prevails in the capitalist mode of production. Due to the domination of autonomised exchange-value [*verselbständigter Tauschwert*], the peasant ceases to appear in front of the landlord as 'a peasant with his product'; rather, he now appears as an owner of money. A new form of community emerges in

---

21. Marx 1986, pp. 424–5.
22. Marx 1986, p. 411.
23. 'Closer examination of all these processes of dissolution will show that relations of production are dissolved in which use value, i.e., production for immediate use, predominates and in which exchange value and its production presuppose the predominance of the other form'. Marx 1986, p. 426.
24. Marx 1987, p. 263.
25. Wainwright writes that this 'remark about the spread of capitalism outward from Europe manifests Marx's Eurocentrism'. Wainwright 2008a, p. 885. According to Wainwright, Marx abandons his stageist interpretation during the 1860s. See Hobsbawm 1964.
26. Marx 1987, pp. 263–4.

which the monetary relations replace ancient personal bonds.[27] The classic form of exchange, where the aim is the use-value and one sells in order to buy (C-M-C), is inverted in the form M-C-M. Value becomes the end in itself. This inversion characterises capitalist modernity and its new form of community. In his time Aristotle could still try to save the *oikonomia* by confining M-C-M to *krematistiké*, which he considered a form of exchange contrary to the end.[28]

Marx focuses upon Aristotle's opposition of the economic to chrematistic.[29] The former 'is limited to procuring those articles that are necessary to existence, and useful either to a household or the state': it 'is not unlimited'; for the latter, instead, 'there appear to be no limits to riches and possessions'. By opposing the economic to chrematistic, Marx poses the very important issue of a clash between the unlimited and the limit: *aperiron peiras*. Marx quotes a long text from Aristotle:

> [The] riches, such as Chrematistic strives for, are unlimited. Just as every art that is not a means to an end, but an end in itself, has no limit to its aims, because it seeks constantly to approach nearer and nearer to that end, while those arts that pursue means to an end, are not boundless, since the goal itself imposes a limit upon them, so with Chrematistic, there are no bounds to its aims, these aims being absolute wealth. Œconomic not Chrematistic has a limit ... the object of the former is something different from money, of the latter the augmentation of money.... By confounding these two forms, which overlap each other, some people have been led to look upon the preservation and increase of money *ad infinitum* as the end and aim of Œconomic.[30]

The capitalist *inversion*, the autonomisation of value and indifference to the concrete quality of use-value, makes possible, through the 'development of the productive power', the dissolution of those communitarian bonds that limited the 'full development of the individual'.[31] In Notebook seven of the *Grundrisse* Marx sketches a dialectic between the 'development of the productive power' and the 'development of the individual' in which the capitalist mode of production breaks the development-limiting communitarian bond. This is possible due to the indifference of the ends of capitalist production to use-value. The whole development of the modern individual begins with the dissolution of the ancient

---

27. Marx 1987, p. 430.
28. Marx 1987, pp. 487–8. *Krematistiké* and not *oikonomia* constitutes the prehistory of the modern economic science that begins to develop in the seventeenth century. Cf. Brunner 1968.
29. Marx 1996, p. 163.
30. Ibid.
31. Marx 1987, p. 97.

community and the production of indifferent relationships, whose name is civil or bourgeois society.

In the 1850s, Marx works with the ambivalences of the concepts of the capitalist form of production and tries to show the progressive side of capitalist development.[32] Marx's attempt to think through the limitless nature of capitalism contains some ambiguities, which emerge in his remarks on colonialism in particular. In his Eurocentric justification of English colonialism in India, he wrote that it would have a 'double mission...: one destructive, the other regenerating – the annihilation of old Asiatic society, and the laying of the material foundations of Western society in Asia'.[33] Up to the end of the 1850s, Marx considered positively the 'propagandistic (civilising) tendency'[34] of capital and believed in the thoroughness with which British industrial capital would destroy non-capitalist societies in the process of its worldwide expansion.[35] Such ambivalence on colonialism can be found throughout the *Grundrisse*. Marx works with the ambivalences of the concepts of capitalist modernity and orients its positive side towards a progressive philosophy of history. This historicism, which has fascinated many Marxists, indicated the development of the productive forces as the tendency that must be followed by all other forms that are defined as backward or residual.

We encounter this ambiguousness of the tendency in the well-known 'Fragment on machines' of the *Grundrisse*.[36] If one reads the pages of the *Grundrisse* on the precapitalist forms of production and that 'Fragment' at the same time, one finds an attempt to outline, on the basis of the logic of the development of the pre-capitalist forms, a 'foreshadowing of the future'. At the end of the section on precapitalist forms of production, Marx writes: 'These indications [*Andeutungen*], together with a correct grasp of the present [*richtige Fassung des Gegenwärtigen*], then also offer the key to the understanding of the past [*Verständnis der Vergangenheit*].... This correct approach, moreover, leads to points which indicate the suppression [*Aufhebung*] of the present form of

---

32. Basso 2008a, pp. 153–215.
33. Marx 1979, pp. 217–8.
34. Marx 1986, p. 466.
35. Mohri 1979, p. 35. According to Mohri, 'In the 1840s and 1850s Marx emphasized the "revolutionary" role of British free trade, basing himself upon a general expectation that it would destroy the framework of the old society which was an obstacle to the growth of productive forces, and would generate in its place the kind of development that would lay the basis for a new society. However, this view was discarded by Marx himself from the 1860s onward, as he became well aware that the destruction of the old society would not necessarily give rise to the material conditions for a new society' (p. 40); cf. Jaffe 2007.
36. With Riccardo Bellofiore I wrote a history of the interpretations of this 'Fragment' in Italian workerism; cf. Bellofiore and Tomba 2009.

production relations, the movement coming into being, thus foreshadowing of the future [*foreshadowing der Zukunft*].[37]

In this Marxian scheme, the perspective of a 'violent overthrow' of capital results from the projection into the future of the laws of development of pre-capitalist forms. Marx politically uses his historic reconstruction to sketch out a dialectic of development and limit of the forces of production. This historical scheme is projected onto the capitalist mode of production in order to show its immanent limits, as Marx did with the premodern concept of the corporation. In this direction we find the scenario of the famous fragment on the machine from the *Grundrisse*, in which 'capital works to dissolve itself':[38] 'large-scale industry' develops, 'the creation of real wealth becomes less dependent upon labour time and the quantity of labour employed than upon the power of the agents set in motion during labour time'.[39] As is well known, according to the law of value, it is the human labour objectified in a commodity which constitutes its value. For this reason, when there is an increase of the productivity of labour through machines and the replacement of living labour by machines, the value objectified in the products should decline. Therefore, Marx thought that, with automation, production based upon exchange-value, namely on the labour-value relation, 'collapses'.[40] And capital works...towards its own dissolution.

The focus of these pages of the *Grundrisse* is always the 'development of science' and 'progress of technology', on the one hand, and the 'development of the social individual', on the other hand.[41] There is a *geschichtsphilosophisch* link between these two elements. Marx saw that science and technology are not neutral. However, he was more interested in developing the positive side of the progress of science than its destructive character, both for nature and the individual. The *unlimited* character of the capitalist mode of production seems to Marx to push this form beyond its own limits.

Marx arrives at a different perspective in the 1860s.[42] His thorough analysis of the world-market led him to investigate the competition of capitals, the history of non-capitalist societies and 'its early integration into the world market'.[43] He concentrated on anti-colonial revolts and began to question unilinear models of historical explanation. Unlike in the 1850s, Marx does not stress the 'double mission' of English colonialism: the supposed 'regenerating' side disappears and

---

37. Marx 1986, p. 388.
38. Marx 1987, p. 86.
39. Marx 1987, pp. 90–1.
40. Marx 1987, p. 91.
41. Marx 1987, pp. 90–1.
42. Bellofiore 2008b.
43. Anderson 2002, p. 93.

the destruction of the native industry of India or Ireland by British capital is no longer regarded as 'revolutionary'.[44]

Likewise, science and technology are not considered as progressive forces, but, from the point of view of the worker, as an extraneous power: the construction of machines as automatons makes science the power of the machine itself. The application of science to production retroacts on the rationality of modern science and turns it into a capitalist means of production.[45] The goal of machinic construction is empowerment and intensification of labour. This goal not only does not exist in the consciousness of the workers, but is in fact counterposed to it. The 'social individual' disappears, also terminologically, and the mutilations of the worker succeed him. Marx's point of view is not that of history and its development, but that of the concreteness of the worker, of his body and mind.

The means for the development of production 'mutilate the labourer into a fragment of a human, degrade him to the level of an appendage of a machine, destroy every remnant of charm in his work and turn it into a hated toil'.[46] Moreover, they: 'estrange from him the intellectual potentialities [*geistige Potenzen*] of the labour process in the same proportion as science is incorporated in it as an independent power; they distort the conditions under which he works, subject him during the labour process to a despotism the more hateful for its meanness; they transform his lifetime into working time, and drag his wife and child beneath the wheels of the Juggernaut of capital'.[47]

The intellectual potentialities increase, but are incorporated in science and in the machine, in the 'dead labour, that, vampire-like, only lives by sucking living labour, and lives the more, the more labour it sucks'.[48] For instance, computers have not created more 'free' time; on they contrary, but they have been used to extend labour-time, which has also invaded the private sphere. One must not look romantically to a precapitalist past or defend the development of the means of production as representatives of liberation. Both these perspectives are apologetic for the existing state of affairs.

Marx's perspective changes in the 1860s, but already at the end of 1858 Marx is led to reconsider his analysis, in the light of the ability of capital to metabolise and survive the crisis. In a letter to Engels dated 8 October 1858, he writes:

---

44. Mohri remarks that 'On the contrary, the destruction of native Irish industry is now looked upon as the first step toward demolition of the base for the Irish revolution itself, or, we may dare to say, it is obviously taken as "counter-revolutionary" rather than as "revolutionary"': Mohri 1979, p. 38.

45. On Marx's changing evaluation of the role of science and technology in the end of capitalism from the *Grundrisse* to *Capital*, cf. Caffentzis 2008.

46. Marx 1996, p. 693; translation modified.

47. Marx 1996, p. 693.

48. Marx 1998, p. 241.

There is no denying that bourgeois society has for the second time experienced its 16th century, a 16th century which, I hope, will sound its death knell just as the first ushered it into the world. The proper task of bourgeois society is the creation of the world market, at least in outline, and of the production based on that market. Since the world is round, the colonisation of California and Australia and the opening up of China and Japan would seem to have completed this process. For us, the difficult **question** is this: on the Continent revolution is imminent and will, moreover, instantly assume a socialist character. Will it not necessarily be **crushed** in this little corner of the earth, since the **movement** of bourgeois society is still in the **ascendant** over a far greater area?[49]

In this letter one can find the coordinates of Marx's theoretical and political work in the 1860s. One can already notice the difference with the *Grundrisse*. There are three important issues in this letter. First, bourgeois society, writes Marx, 'has for the second time experienced its 16th century'. This second sixteenth century of capitalism leads Marx to think in terms of an enduring primitive accumulation, which cannot be confined only to the beginning of capitalist production. Second, both theoretical and political analysis must be thought at the level of the world-market. The 'world is round', writes Marx, and capitalism puts into relation different geographical areas and different forms of exploitation. Capitalism cannot be analysed by considering only the countries where it is more developed. Third, Marx poses the 'difficult question' of the success of a socialist revolution in Europe while the movement of capitalist society is still 'ascendant over a far greater area'. From this moment, a eurocentric point of view on capitalism and the movements of the working class is directly reactionary, just as all the attempts to construct socialism in one country were.

It is important to note that, at the time of *Grundrisse*, Marx had not yet clarified the distinction between abstract labour and socially necessary labour. As Marx will come to understand, only the time of socially necessary labour objectified in a commodity counts as exchange-value of a commodity, and not the time of labour that is really individually spent in its production. For example, one hour of labour at a higher level of productivity can correspond to two or three hours of socially necessary labour, and it is only the latter that counts as exchange-value.[50] The issue that Marx did not see at the time of the *Grundrisse* is the transfer [*Übertragung*][51] of capital from different spheres and countries.[52] Only in the 1860s, when making allowance for the competition of capitals in

49. Marx 1983, pp. 347–8.
50. Tomba 2009.
51. Marx 1998, p. 205.
52. Dussel 1990; Dussel 2001, pp. 213–4; Marini 1991, pp. 8–10.

the world-market,[53] does Marx consider 'every individual capital ... as a part of the total capital, and every capitalist actually as a shareholder in the total social enterprise, each sharing in the total profit *pro rata* to the magnitude of his share of capital'.[54]

Towards a perspective of the historical temporalities of accumulation

Marx begins to rethink the categorical context of his analysis in the *Grundrisse*. He starts to conceptualise capital not according to the scheme of *genesis, development, crisis*, but in the combination of these moments and their temporalities.[55] He abandons the scheme of the progressive epochs of economic development in favour of a historiography of original accumulation, which he will work on and reshape in the diverse editions of *Capital*. Original or primary accumulation [*ursprüngliche Akkumulation*] is not *primitive* in the sense of the starting point of capitalism. Rather, it is instead a whole entirety of *always present* forms of intervention of economic and extra-economic violence.[56] The analysis of accumulation in *Capital* has a target different from that of the analysis of the precapitalist forms in the *Grundrisse*, in which Marx was looking for a theory of collapse of a productive form in the transition to a new, higher one. In *Capital*, Marx works with a different concept of crisis and, therefore, with a different concept of accumulation. When Marx rethinks the 'fall of the rate of profit', he leaves out the 'collapsism' of the *Grundrisse*: crisis ceases to be understood as an anteroom of the overthrow of capitalism and becomes an element for a new form of equilibrium with new forms of accumulation.[57]

In the 1870s, while he was working on the Russian economic mode of production and community, Marx revised his scheme of historical development. In a letter from the end of 1877 to the Editor of Otechestvennye Zapiski, he wrote that his draft of the genesis of capitalism in Western Europe could not be transformed 'into an historical-philosophical theory of universal development, predetermined by fate, for all peoples ...'.[58]

Between the first and the third edition of *Capital* Volume I, Marx revises his analysis of the history of the capitalist development in order to reduce its general and too abstract character. He does not propose an universal model of the genesis of the capitalist mode of production which is valid 'for all peoples'. In the

---

53. Heinrich 2009, pp. 80–1.
54. Marx 1998, p. 207.
55. Bensaïd 1996; Tombazos 1994, p. 27.
56. Sacchetto and Tomba 2008.
57. On this topic, see the chapter by Reuten and Thomas in this volume.
58. Marx 1989d, p. 201.

first edition of 1867, he wrote: 'The country that is more developed industrially shows, to the less developed, only the image of its own future [*Das industriell ent-wickeltere Land zeigt dem minder entwickelten nur das Bild der eignen Zukunft*]'.[59] However, in the French edition of 1872–5, which was checked by Marx himself, one can read: 'The country that is more developed industrially only shows, to those which follow it on the industrial path, the image of its own future [*Le pays le plus développé industriellement ne fait que montrer à ceux qui le suivent sur l'échelle industrielle l'image de leur propre avenir*]'.[60] The supplement of Marx delimits the field: a country that is more developed shows the future only to those countries that are following the same *industrial path*, but this in not a general law.[61] Moreover Marx also revised the chapter on original accumulation. The analysis becomes less general. In the first edition, he describes the process of separation as a 'series of historical processes [*Reihe historischer Prozesse*]' which gives rise to the 'history of the development [*Entwicklungsgeschichte*]' of modern bourgeois society[62] as a general law. In the third edition (1883), a long paragraph was cut.[63] The analysis became more concrete particularly regarding the Eng-lish case, where the different moments of primitive accumulation, which was distributed in geographical and 'chronological order [*zeitliche Reihenfolge*], par-ticularly over Spain, Portugal, Holland, France, and England', arrive 'at the end of the 17th century at a systematical combination [*systematisch zusammengefaßt*], embracing the colonies, the national debt, the modern mode of taxation, and the protectionist system'.[64] All these systems require the violence of the state. Marx therefore analyses the transition to the capitalistic mode of production by paying attention to the 'violent levers [*gewaltsame Hebeln*]'[65] which have made it pos-sible, and to the power and the violence of the state, which dissolved the feudal system and produced the immobilisation and the discipline of the labour-force.[66] The peculiarity of this accumulation is a sort of extra-economic intervention,

---

59. Marx 1867b, p. 12.
60. Marx 1872–5, p. 12.
61. Anderson 2002, pp. 87–8. According to Anderson, the historical studies of the 1870s led Marx to consider 'alternative pathways' different from that of capitalist indus-trialisation.
62. Marx 1867b, p. 576.
63. Marx 1883, p. 669. When the German editor informed Marx that a third edition of the *Capital* had become necessary, Marx wrote to Danielson that he could make only the smallest possible number of changes and additions for the third edition, and that he pre-ferred that only 1000 copies be printed, rather than the 3000 desired by the editor. When the third edition was sold out, he wrote, 'I may change the book in the way I should have done at present under different circumstances': Marx to Danielson, 13 December 1881, in Marx and Engels 1992b, p. 161. New historical studies and rethinking of the categorial field would lead him to rewrite several passages in the chapter on accumulation.
64. Marx 1996, p. 739.
65. Marx 1996, p. 472.
66. Moulier-Boutang 2002, p. 26.

which combines the terrorism of the separation between means of production and workers with the extra-economic violence of the State.[67] The goal is the increase of the absolute exploitation of the labour-force both in intensity and extension. For this reason, the genesis of capitalism in Western Europe could not be transformed 'into an historical-philosophical theory of universal development, predetermined by fate, for all peoples...'. Marx had learnt, especially in his confrontation with the Russian populists, that one could never understand historical phenomena 'with the *passe-partout* of a philosophy of history whose supreme virtue is to be suprahistorical'.[68]

Without the violence of the state, without the destruction of different *auctoritates* and corporative bonds, without the production of proletarians, without enclosures and separation of labour from the means of production, without discipline and control of the formally free workers, without these and other histories and their synchronisation, the capitalist mode of production would not have been born. One could speak of a 'processus de rencontre aléatoire', in the sense outlined by Althusser, in his *Matérialisme de la rencontre*.[69] In all modes of production there are different elements that are independent of each other. Each element is the result of a particular history without any teleological relation with other histories. The capitalist mode of production could also not exist, but the fortunate – or unfortunate – encounter and combination of different temporalities made it possible. Even if the encounter of these elements is *aléatoire*, their combination is not random and requires an explanation: these temporalities and the multiple 'powerful levers'[70] of accumulation are always *re-synchronised* through the violence of the state. We can thus talk about a *permanence of primitive accumulation*. The Marxian 'primitive accumulation' is not only an episode of the proto-history of the capitalistic form. On the contrary, 'accumulation' is the continuous driving power of capitalism, a combination of different and relatively independent moments: violence of state, production of proletarians and formally free labour, colonisation, slavery, dissolution of ancient forms of *auctoritas*, enclosures, separation between producers and means of production, discipline of the wage-workers. These *histories* of extra-economic violence and their synchronisation through the state were and are the conditions of possibility of the capitalist mode of production. This *Gleichschaltung*, a term of the Nazis that could be used to translate the notion of forced synchronisation, is the constitutive element of capitalist modernity from its origins.

---

67. Bonefeld 2001.
68. Marx 1989d, p. 201.
69. Althusser 1994, p. 572.
70. Marx 1996, pp. 741–2.

For us to understand the permanence of primitive accumulation now, we need a kind of historiography of the present that makes it possible to understand the current combination of different temporalities and the attempt to synchronise them through the intervention of extra-economic violence. It needs to be a form of historiography that is able to work with 'a plurality of temporal strata, of variable extension and duration that interact in the same historical dimension of modernity, and which can only be understood in relation to one another'.[71] In *Capital*, Marx provides the elements for such a new kind of historiography.

For the 'bourgeois historians', the 'historical movement which changes the producers into wage workers' exists only in its appearance, as the process of 'their emancipation from serfdom and from the fetters of the guilds'.[72] For the historical materialist, on the other hand, this history 'is written in the annals of mankind in letters of blood and fire'.[73] Marx works as an ancient chronicler: '1570s to 1610s: a "mass of free proletarians [*vogelfreie Proletarier*] was hurled on the labour market by the breaking-up of the bands of feudal retainers" '.[74]

Sixteenth century: 'The process of forcible expropriation of the people received [...] a new and frightful impulse from the Reformation, and from the consequent colossal spoliation of the church property. [...] The suppression of the monasteries, &c., hurled their inmates into the proletariat'.[75]

From 1660 onwards, after the restoration of the Stuarts: abolition of the 'feudal tenure of land'. The 'landed proprietors carried, by legal means, an act of usurpation, effected everywhere on the Continent without any legal formality'.[76]

A mass of proletarians was produced through the dissolution of the feudal system. One needed to discipline them to obey the chronometric time of the market, and to submit no longer to the time of the Church.[77] The 'bloody legislation against the expropriated' begins with the following:

> Henry VIII, 1530: Beggars old and unable to work receive a beggar's licence. On the other hand, whipping and imprisonment for sturdy vagabonds. They are to be tied to the cart-tail and whipped until the blood streams from their bodies, then to swear an oath to go back to their birthplace or to where they have lived the last three years and to 'put themselves to labour'. [...] For the

---

71. Tomich 2004, p. 94.
72. Marx 1996, p. 706.
73. Marx 1996, p. 706.
74. Marx 1996, pp. 708–9.
75. Marx 1996, p. 711.
76. Marx 1996, p. 713.
77. Le Goff 1960. Marx 1996, p. 427: 'The despotic bell calls him [the workman] from his bed, calls him from breakfast and dinner'.

second arrest for vagabondage the whipping is to be repeated and half the ear sliced off; but for the third relapse the offender is to be executed as a hardened criminal and enemy of the common weal.[78]

'Edward VI, 1547: A statute of the first year of his reign [...] ordains that if any-one refuses to work, he shall be condemned as a slave to the person who has denounced him as an idler'.[79]

'Elizabeth, 1572: Unlicensed beggars above 14 years of age are to be severely flogged and branded on the left ear unless some one will take them into service for two years; in case of a repetition of the offence, if they are over 18, they are to be executed, unless some one will take them into service for two years; but for the third offence they are to be executed without mercy as felons'.[80]

James I (1603–1625): Any one wandering about and begging is declared a rogue and a vagabond. Justices of the peace in petty sessions are authorised to have them publicly whipped and for the first offence to imprison them for 6 months, for the second for 2 years. [...] Incorrigible and dangerous rogues are to be branded with an R on the left shoulder and set to hard labour, and if they are caught begging again, to be executed without mercy.[81]

Capitalistic modernity was already born globalised in the entanglement of colo-nialism and slavery. As the case of the American colonies shows, workers' escape or exit constitutes the principal problem of capitalist accumulation between 1500 and 1800.[82] The goal of English legislation during the sixteenth and seventeenth centuries is the immobilisation and discipline of the labour-force, even through slavery. This was not an anomolous case in the colony but rather was an author-itarian answer, quite homogeneous, to control the mobility of European and North American living labour on the market.[83] According to Moulier-Boutang, it is not trade that produced slavery but rather bonded wage-labour that produced slavery's modern forms.[84] Modern slavery is a disciplined variant of 'free' wage-labour. Slavery is not a dark moment banned into the proto-history of capital,[85] but is continually reproduced by the capitalist mode of production.

---

78. Marx 1996, pp. 723–4.
79. Marx 1996, p. 724.
80. Marx 1996, p. 725.
81. Marx 1996, pp. 725–6.
82. Moulier-Boutang 2002, p. 26.
83. Moulier-Boutang 2002, p. 158.
84. Moulier-Boutang 2002, p. 232.
85. The overall number of human beings forced to leave the African coast amounts about to 11 millions. The slaves actually introduced in Americas between 1519 and 1867 was around 9,599,000; cf. Pétré-Grenouilleau 2004. There was a progression in the slave-population of the Americas, which reached 33,000 in 1700, nearly three million in 1800 and peaked at over six million in 1850.

The colonial system supported the development of the industrial system. Marx's compilation of historical materials[86] shows different counter-histories and the dark side of a 'progress' centred on 'a vast, Herod-like slaughter of the innocents'.[87] This violence was extreme 'in plantation colonies destined for export trade only, such as the West Indies, and in rich and well-populated countries, such as Mexico and India, that were given over to plunder'.[88] Through this violence, capital was able to synchronise the intensity of labour on the plantation to the clock of the world stock-exchange. For this reason:

> the negro labour in the Southern States of the American Union preserved something of a patriarchal character, so long as production was chiefly directed to immediate local consumption. But in proportion, as the export of cotton became of vital interest to these states, the overworking of the negro and sometimes the using up of his life in 7 years of labour became a factor in a calculated and calculating system. It was no longer a question of obtaining from him a certain quantity of useful products. It was now a question of production of surplus labour itself.[89]

Slavery becomes something new when it is subsumed to the world-market, as with its development all peoples are entangled in its net.[90] The net of the world-market holds together not only different forms of exploitation while combining them synchronically, but – and this is the other history – it bridges over different working classes. The very important issue that Marx posed at end of the 1860s concerns the synchronic combination of different forms of exploitation, their entwinement starting from the relation between absolute and relative surplus-value.[91]

Capital needs to create geographical areas or productive sectors where it can produce an enormous quantity of absolute surplus-value to support the production of extraordinary surplus-value, relative surplus-value produced through mechanical innovations. As a matter of fact, when the technological innovation becomes widespread, the growing productivity of labour obtained through its employment becomes socially dominant and the capitalist can no longer gain social surplus-value though his growing productivity. The capitalist hence cannot do anything but ruthlessly prolong the working day. The extraction of relative surplus-value requires differentials in the productive labour-force. Capital thus

---

86. Marx quotes several historical materials, for instance Howitt 1838; Stamford Raffles 1817.
87. Marx 1996, p. 745.
88. Marx 1996, p. 741.
89. Marx 1996, p. 244.
90. Marx 1996, p. 750.
91. Tomba 2007.

generates, through different processes of accumulation, a great mass of absolute exploitation in those parts of the world where workers' resistance is lower.[92]

The original [*ursprünglich*] violence of the accumulation must be repeated over and over in order to cause new differentials in the force of production and intensity of labour. Therefore the extra-economic violence of primitive accumulation accompanies the whole history of capital as a *basso continuo*. Today, this violence also accompanies the political-economic function of the borders in order to set the price of migrant labour-power and to determine ethnical divisions of labours.

Historical materialist's historiography

The late Marx, engaging with the Russian populists and historical materials on the ancient forms of community,[93] was looking for such a new kind of historiography and political intervention. In the first draft of the answer to Vera Zasulich, Marx tries to think how the destiny of the *obshchina* is not its own necessary dissolution, but could still be the 'starting point of a Russian regeneration'. This topic returns in the *Preface of the Russian Edition of the Communist Manifesto* (1882). Marx wrote:

> Now the question is: can the Russian *obshchina* [...], a form of primeval common ownership of land, even if greatly undermined, pass directly to the higher form of communist common ownership? Or must it, conversely, first pass through the same process of dissolution as constitutes the historical development of the West? The only answer possible today is this: If the Russian Revolution becomes the signal for a proletarian revolution in the West, so that the two complement each other, the present Russian common ownership of land may serve as the starting point for communist development.[94]

Here one finds historical forms of production, as the Russian community, which are not a precapitalist residual, but are contemporary forms with a specific temporality. They contain the possibility of new forms of emancipation and liberation. This late Marx forces us to think history as a *multiversum*. To be understood, the world-market requires a historiographical paradigm that is able to comprehend the combination of a plurality of temporal strata in the violent synchronising dimension of modernity. The postmodern juxtaposition of a plurality of historical times, where slavery is contiguous with high-tech production in the overcoming of the dualism of centre and periphery, lacks in explanatory power

---

92. Tomba 2009.
93. Krader (ed.) 1972.
94. Marx 1989b, p. 426.

and can even be mystifying. The postmodern mosaic of temporalities and forms of exploitation, even though it represents them as interconnected, poses the different times in a state of indifference to each other. The real problem, however, is their combination through the mechanisms of synchronisation on the world-market. The nexus-value socially necessary labour is now the most adequate category to comprehend the mechanism in which the labour-time of computer-based production requires – and is combined with – compulsory labour in other parts of the world.[95]

If we accept the reciprocal co-penetration between absolute and relative surplus-value in its fullest significance, the distinction between 'advanced' and 'backward' capitalisms loses a great part of its meaning. It is no longer possible to reason in terms of *tendencies* and *residues*. The various forms of exploitation are to be understood in an historical-temporal *multiversum*, in which they interact within the contemporaneity of the present. On the other hand, we must think the possibilities of liberation resulting from different temporalities of different social forms. In the first draft of the letter to Vera Zasulich, Marx copies a quotation from Morgan: 'the new system' towards which modern society tends 'will be a revival in a superior form of an archaic social type'. Marx comments: 'So we must not let ourselves to be alarmed at the word "archaic".[96] This topic is present in his *Notebooks* on Morgan of 1880–1,[97] as a countermelody to the career of property that has become, wrote Morgan, '*an unmanageable power*'. As opposed to this career, Morgan proposes an alternative pathway, where 'human intelligence *will rise to the mastery over property*', i.e., a 'higher plan of society'. As Marx notes, this will instead be '*a revival, in a higher form, of the liberty, equality and fraternity of the ancient gentes*'.[98] While Morgan wrote that a '*mere property career is not the final destiny of mankind*', Marx is interested in the possible different pathways of capitalist civilisation. There is not any trace of romanticism in these considerations, but, instead, an attempt to think the future in the past, a kind of politics that presupposes a new concept of history and a new kind of historiography. Marx now reads European development, the transition from common to private property, by means of a geological image: 'as in geological formations [*geologischen Formationen*], these historical forms contain a whole series of primary, secondary, tertiary types, etc.'.[99] There is not a sequence of

---

95. Silver and Zhang 2008; Sacchetto 2008; van der Linden 2007; Glassman 2006; Gambino 2003.
96. Marx 1989b, p. 346.
97. Krader (ed.) 1972.
98. Morgan 1877, p. 552; Krader (ed.) 1972, p. 139.
99. Marx 1989d, 358; cf. Koselleck 2000, p. 9: The 'spatialising metaphor, by allowing the pluralisation of the concept of time, has an advantage. "Temporal strata" [*Zeitschichten*] cross-refer, like in the geological model, to several time levels of different duration and different origins, but nonetheless contemporaneously present and active'.

different historical forms as if they were in a list. In these historical formations there is a whole series of primary, secondary, tertiary types, as in the geological formations. The *secondary* overlaps the *primary* without wiping it out. The dissolution of common property is not an historical law. The historical materialist, when dealing with the different temporal strata, makes the co-presence of various historical stratifications evident. Because the historical forms are not arranged according to a line running from the past to the present, but as geological formations, one can think the combination of temporalities in a surface of possibilities and not in the succession of the line.

References

Anonymous 2002, 'Patently Absurd', *The Economist*, June 23, 40–2.

Althusser, Louis 1971, 'Preface to *Capital* Volume One' in *Lenin and Philosophy and Other Essays*, New York: Monthly Review Press.

—— 1994, *Écrits philosophiques et politiques*, Tome I, edited by François Matheron, Paris: Éditions Stock/IMEC.

Althusser, Louis and Étienne Balibar 1997 [1970], *Reading Capital*, New York: Verso.

Amin, Samir 1976, *Unequal Development: An Essay on The Social Formations of Peripheral Capitalism*, New York: Monthly Review.

Anderson, Kevin B. 2002, 'Marx's Late Writings on Non-Western and Precapitalist Societies and Gender', *Rethinking Marx*, 14, 4: 84–96.

Arbeitsblätter 1979a, *Arbeitsblätter zur Marx-Engels-Forschung*, 8, Halle (Saale).

—— 1979b, *Arbeitsblätter zur Marx-Engels-Forschung*, 9, Halle (Saale).

Arrighi, Giovanni and Beverly J. Silver 1999, *Chaos and Governance in The Modern World System*, Minneapolis-London: University of Minnesota Press.

Arthur, Christopher J. 1979, 'Dialectics and Labour' in Mepham and Ruben (eds.) 1979.

—— 1993, 'Hegel's *Logic* and Marx's *Capital*', in Moseley (ed.) 1993.

—— 2002a, 'Capital in General and Marx's *Capital*' in Campbell and Reuten (eds.) 2002.

—— 2002b, *The New Dialectic and Marx's 'Capital'*, Leiden: Brill.

—— 2005a, 'Reply to Critics', *Historical Materialism*, 13, 2: 189–221.

—— 2005b, 'Value and Money' in Moseley (ed.) 2005.

—— 2008, 'Dissemination and Reception of The *Grundrisse*: USA, Britain, Australia and Canada', in Musto (ed.) 2008.

—— 2009a, 'Contradiction and Abstraction: A Reply to Finelli', *Historical Materialism*, 17, 1: 170–82.

—— 2009b, 'The Possessive Spirit of Capital: Subsumption/Inversion/Contradiction', in Bellofiore and Fineschi (eds.) 2009.

Arthur, Christopher J. and Geert Reuten (eds.) 1998, *The Circulation of Capital: Essays on Volume Two of Marx's 'Capital'*, Basingstoke: Macmillan Press.

Backhaus, Hans-Georg 1969, 'Zur Dialektik der Wertform', in Schmidt (ed.) 1969.

—— 1974, 'Materialien zur Rekonstruktion der Marxschen Werttheorie', *Gesellschaft. Beiträge zur Marxschen Theorie*, 1, Frankfurt/M.: Suhrkamp.

—— 1975, 'Materialien zur Rekonstruktion der Marxschen Werttheorie 2', *Gesellschaft. Beiträge zur Marxschen Theorie*, 3, Frankfurt: Suhrkamp.

—— 1978, 'Materialien zur Rekonstruktion der Marxschen Werttheorie 3', *Gesellschaft. Beiträge zur Marxschen Theorie*, 11, Frankfurt: Suhrkamp.

—— 1980, 'On the Dialectics of The Value-Form', *Thesis Eleven*, 1: 99–120.

—— 1997, *Dialektik der Wertform. Untersuchungen zur marxschen Ökonomiekritik*, Freiburg: ça ira.

Balconi, Margherita 2002, 'Tacitness, codification of Technological Knowledge and The Organization of Industry', *Research Policy*, 31, 3: 357–79.

Baldissara, Luca (ed.) 2001, *Le radici della crisi. L'Italia tra gli anni Sessanta e gli anni Settanta*, Rome: Carocci.

Balibar, Etienne and Immanuel Wallerstein 1988, *Race nation classe. Les identités ambigues*, Paris: La Découverte.

Banaji, Jairus 1979, 'From The Commodity to Capital: Hegel's Dialectic in Marx's *Capital*', in Elson (ed.) 1979.

Barrett, Michèle 1986, 'Introduction', in Engels 1972.

Bartolovich, Crystal and Neil Lazarus (eds.) 2002, *Marxism, Modernity, and Postcolonial Studies*, Cambridge: Cambridge University Press.

Basso, Luca 2001, 'Critica dell'individualismo moderno e realizzazione del singolo nell'*Ideologia tedesca*', *Filosofia politica*, 2: 233–56.

—— 2012a [2008], *Marx and Singularity. From the Early Writings to the 'Grundrisse'*, translated by Arianna Bove, Leiden: Brill.

—— 2008, 'Tra forme precapitalistiche e capitalismo: il problema della società nei *Grundrisse*,' in Sacchetto and Tomba (eds.) 2008.

—— 2012b, *Agire in comune. Antropologia e politica nell'ultimo Marx*, Verona: ombre corte.

Bellofiore, Riccardo 1982, 'L'operaismo italiano e la critica dell'economia politica, *Unità Proletaria*', 1–2, 100–12.

—— 1989, 'A Monetary Labor Theory of Value', *Review of Radical Political Economics*, 21, 1–2: 1–25.

—— 1998, 'The Concept of Labor in Marx', *International Journal of Political Economy*, 28, 3: 4–34.

—— (ed.) 1998, *Marxian Economics. A Centenary Appraisal, Volume I, Essays on Volume III of Capital: Method, Value and Money*, London: Macmillan.

—— 1999, 'After Fordism, What? Capitalism at The End of The Century: Beyond the Myths', in Riccardo Bellofiore (ed.) 1999, *Which Labour Next? Global Money, Capital Restructuring And The Changing Patterns of Production*, Aldershot: Elgar.

—— 2001, 'I lunghi anni Settanta. Crisi sociale e integrazione economica internazionale', in Baldissara (ed.) 2001.

—— 2002, 'Transformation and the Monetary Circuit: Marx as a Monetary Theorist of Production', in Campbell and Reuten (eds.) 2002.

—— 2004, 'Marx and The Macrofoundation of Microeconomics', in Riccardo Bellofiore and Nicola Taylor (eds.) 2004.

—— 2007, 'Quelli del lavoro vivo', in Riccardo Bellofiore (ed.) 2007, *Da Marx a Marx? Un bilancio dei marxismi italiani del Novecento*, Rome: manifestolibri.

—— 2008a, 'La farfalla e il vampiro. Sulla teoria marxiana del valore e della crisi', *Alternative per il socialismo*, 1, 1: 32–43.

—— 2008b, 'Dai *Manoscritti del 1844* al *Capitale*, e ritorno. Storia e natura, universalità e lavoro, crisi e lotta di classe nei *Grundrisse*', in Sacchetto and Tomba (eds.) 2008.

—— 2009a, 'A Ghost Turning into A Vampire. The Concept of Capital and Living Labour', in Bellofiore and Fineschi (eds.) 2009.

—— 2009b 'Teoria del valore, crisi generale e capitale monopolistico. Napoleoni in dialogo con Sweezy', *Quaderni materialisti*, 7: 9–48.

Bellofiore, Riccardo and Roberto Finelli 1998, 'Capital, Labour and Time. The Marxian Monetary Labour Theory of Value as a Theory of Exploitation', in Bellofiore (ed.) 1998.

Bellofiore, Riccardo and Roberto Fineschi (eds.) 2009, *Re-reading Marx: New Perspectives after The Critical Edition*, Basingstoke: Palgrave Macmillan.

Bellofiore, Riccardo and Joseph Halevi 2009a, 'Deconstructing Labour. What Is "New" in Contemporary Capitalism and Economic Policies: a Marxian-Kaleckian Perspective', in Gnos and Rochon (eds.) 2009.

—— 2009b, 'A Minsky Moment? The 2007 Subprime Crisis And The "New" Capitalism', in Gnos and Rochon (eds.) 2009.

Bellofiore, Riccardo and Nicola Taylor (eds.) 2004, *The Constitution of Capital: Essays on Volume I of Marx's Capital*, Basingstoke: Palgrave Macmillan.

Bellofiore, Riccardo and Massimiliano Tomba 2008, 'Quale attualità dell'operaismo', in Wright 2008.

—— 2009, 'Lesarten des Maschinesfragments. Perspektiven und Grenzen des operaistichen Auseinandersetzung mit Marx', in Van der Linden and Roth (eds.) 2009.

Bensaïd, Daniel 1996, *Marx l'intempestif: Grandeurs et misères d'une aventure critique (XIXᵉ, XXᵉ siècles)*, Paris: Fayard.

Bettelheim, Charles 1975, *Economic Calculation and Forms of Property*, New York: Monthly Review Press.

Bidet, Jacques 2005, 'The Dialectician's Interpretation of Capital', *Historical Materialism*, 13, 2: 121–46.

—— 2007, *Exploring Marx's Capital: Philosophical, Economic and Political Dimensions*, translated by David Fernbach, Leiden: Brill.

Bidet, Jacques and Stathis Kouvelakis (eds.) 2008, *Critical Companion to Contemporary Marxism*, Leiden: Brill.

Boldyrew, Igor 1989, 'Wie und wann entstand das 1. Kapitel der Erstaufgabe des "Kapitals" (1867)?', *Beiträge zur Marx-Engels-Forschung*, 27: 157–65.

Bond, Patrick 1999, 'Uneven Development', in O'Hara (ed.) 1999.

Bonefeld, Werner 1992, 'Social Constitution and the Form of the Capitalist State', in Bonefeld, Gunn and Psychopedis (eds.) 1992.

—— 1995, 'Capital as Subject and the Existence of Labour', in Bonefeld *et al.* (ed.) 1995.

—— 2001, 'The permanence of primitive accumulation: commodity fetishism and social constitution', in *The Commoner*, 2, available at: http://www.commoner.org.uk/02bonefeld.pdf.

—— 2010, 'Abstract Labour: Against its Nature and on its Time', *Capital & Class*, 34, 2: 257–76.

Bonefeld, Werner, Richard Gunn, and Kosmas Psychopedis (eds.) 1992, 'Introduction', in Bonefeld, Gunn and Psychopedis (eds.) 1992a.

—— (eds.) 1992a, *Open Marxism. Volume 2: Theory and Practice*, London: Pluto Press.

—— (eds.) 1992b, *Open Marxism. Dialectics and History*, London: Pluto Press.

Bonefeld, Werner, *et al.* (ed.) 1995, *Emancipating Marx, Open Marxism 3*, London: Pluto Press.

Boyd, Richard 1979, 'Metaphor and Theory Change', in Ortony (ed.) 1979.

—— 1999, 'Kinds as the "Workmanship of Men": Realism, Constructivism, and Natural Kinds', in Nida-Rumelin (ed.) 1999.

Braverman, Harry 1998, *Labor and Monopoly Capital: The Degradation of Work in the Twentieth Century*, New York: Monthly Review.

Brenner, Robert 2002, *The Boom and The Bubble*, London: Verso.

—— 2006 [1998], *The Economics of Global Turbulence*, London: Verso.

—— and Mark Glick 1991, 'The Regulation Approach: Theory and History', *New Left Review*, 188: 45–119.

Brewster, Ben 1997 [1970], 'Glossary', in Althusser and Balibar 1997.

Browne, M. 1999, 'Glenn Seaborg, Leader of the Team that found Plutonium, dies at 86', *The New York Times*, 27 February, 1999; Section A, p. 1.

Brunner, Otto, 1968, 'Das "Ganze Haus" und die alteuropäische "Ökonomik"', *Neue Wege der Verfassungs- und Sozialgeschichte*, Göttingen: Vandenhoeck & Ruprecht.

Brunner, Otto, Werner Conze and Reinhart Koselleck (eds.) 1992, *Geschichtliche Grundbegriffe. Historisches Lexikon zur politisch-sozialen Sprache in Deutschland*, Volume 2, Stuttgart: Klett-Cotta.

Burkett, Paul and John Bellamy Foster 2009, 'The Podolinsky Myth: an Obituary', *Historical Materialism*, 16, 1: 115–61.

Burns, Tony 2000, 'Marx and Scientific Method: a Non-Metaphysical View', in Burns and Fraser (eds.) 2000.

Burns, Tony and Ian Fraser (eds.) 2000, *The Hegel-Marx Connection*, London: MacMillan Press.

Butler, Judith 2006 [1989], *Gender Trouble: Feminism & The Subversion of Identity*, New York: Routledge.

Caffentzis, George 1999, 'On the Notion of a Crisis of Social Reproduction: A Theoretical Review' in Dalla Costa and Dalla Costa (eds.) 1999.

—— 2008, 'Dai *Grundrisse* al *Capitale* e oltre: allora e adesso', in Sacchetto and Tomba (eds.) 2008.

Camfield, David 2007, 'The Multitude and the Kangaroo: A Critique of Hardt and Negri's Theory of Immaterial Labour', *Historical Materialism*, 15, 2: 21–52.

Campbell, Martha 1993, 'Marx's Concept of Economic Relations and The Method of *Capital*', in Moseley (ed.) 1993.

—— 1997, 'Marx's Theory of Money: A Defense', in Moseley and Campbell (eds.) 1997.

—— 2005, 'Marx's Explanation of Money's Functions: Overturning the Quantity Theory,' in Moseley (ed.) 2005.

Campbell, Martha and Geert Reuten (eds.) 2002, *The Culmination of Capital: Essays on Volume 3 of Capital*, London: Palgrave.

Carandini, Andrea 1979, *'L'anatomia della scimmia'. La formazione economica della società prima del capitale*, Turin: Einaudi.

Carchedi, Guglielmo 1987, *Class Analysis and Social Research*, Oxford: Basil Blackwell.

—— 1993, 'Marx's Logic of Inquiry and Price Formation' in Moseley (ed.) 1993.

—— 2009, 'The Fallacies of "New Dialectics" and Value-Form Theory', *Historical Materialism* 17, 1: 145–69.

Carnap, Rudolf 1959 [1930–1], 'The Old and the New Logic', in Ayer (ed.) 1959.

Carver, Terrell (ed.) 2002, *Later Political Writings*, Cambridge: Cambridge University Press.

Chakrabarty Dipesh 2000, *Provincializing Europe. Postcolonial Thought and Historical Difference*, Princeton, NJ: Princeton University Press.

Chattopadhyay, Paresh 1992, 'The Economic Content of Socialism. Marx vs. Lenin', *Review of Radical Political Economics*, 24, 3/4: 90–110.

—— 2001, 'Marx on Women's Question', *Economic and Political Weekly*, 36, 26: 2455–7.

Cleaver, Harry 1992, 'The Inversion of Class Perspective in Marxian Theory: From Valorisation to Self-Valorisation', in Bonefeld, Gunn and Psychopedis (eds.) 1992a.

Dalla Costa, Mariarosa and Selma James 1973, *The Power of Women and The Subversion of the Community*, Bristol: Falling Wall Press.

Dalla Costa, Mariarosa and Giovanna Franca Dalla Costa (eds.) 1999, *Women, Development and The Labour of Reproduction*, Lawrenceville, NJ: Africa World Press.

Dankert, Clyde E. Floyd C. Mann and Herbert R. Northrup (eds.) 1965, *Hours of Work*, New York: Harper & Row.

De Angelis, Massimo 1995, 'Beyond The Technological and Social Paradigms: A Political Reading of Abstract Labour as the Substance of Value', *Capital and Class*, 57: 107–34.

—— 2007, *The Beginning of History: Value Struggles and Global Capital*, London: Pluto Press.

De Beauvoir, Simone 1989 [1949], *The Second Sex*, translated by H.M. Parshley, New York: Vintage.

De Janvry, Alain 1981, *The Agrarian Question and Reformism in Latin America*, Baltimore: John Hopkins Press.

Dechert, Charles R. (ed.) 1996, *The Social Impact of Cybernetics*, New York: Simon and Schuster.

Denison, Edward F. 1962, *The Sources of Economic Growth in the United States and the Alternatives Before Us*. Supplemental Paper, 13, New York: Committee for Economic Development.

Derrida, Jacques 1994, *Spectres of Marx*, New York: Routledge.

Dragstedt, Albert (trans.) 1976, *Value: Studies by Karl Marx*, London: New Park Publications.

Dumont, Louis 1977, *Homo aequalis. Genèse et épanouissement de l'idéologie économique*, Paris: Gallimard.

—— 1983, *Essais sur l'individualisme. Une perspective anthropologique sur l'idéologie moderne*, Paris: Seuil.

Dunayevskaya, Raya 1989, *Filosofía y Revolución. De Hegel a Sartre y de Marx a Mao*, Mexico City: Siglo XXI.

Dussel, Enrique 1985, *La producción teórica de Marx. Un comentario a los 'Grundrisse'*, Mexico City: Siglo XXI.

—— 1990, 'Marx's Economic Manuscripts of 1861–63 and The "Concept" of Dependency', *Latin American Perspectives*, 17, 2: 62–101.

—— 2001 [1988], *Towards an Unknown Marx: A Commentary on the Manuscripts of 1861–63*, New York: Routledge.

—— 2008, 'The Discovery of the Category of Surplus Value', in Musto (ed.) 2008.

Dyer-Witheford, Nick 1999, *Cyber-Marx: Cycles and Circuits of Struggle in High Technology Capitalism*, Urbana, IL: University of Illinois Press.

Elbe, Ingo 2008, *Marx im Westen. Die neue Marx-Lektüre in der Bundesrepublik seit 1965*, Berlin: Akademie.

Eldred, Michael, and Marnie Hanlon 1981, 'Reconstructing Value-Form Analysis', *Capital & Class*, 13: 24–60.

Elson, Diane (ed.) 1979, *Value: The Representation of Labour in Capitalism*, Atlantic Highlands: Humanities Press Inc., and London: CSE Books.

Engels, Friedrich 1972, *The Origin of the Family, Private Property, and the State*, London: Lawrence & Wishart.

—— 1975–2005, 'Letter to Wilhelm Liebknecht, 1 March 1879', in Marx and Engels 1975–2005, Vol. 45.

Engelskirchen, Howard 2007, 'Why is This Labour Value? – Commodity Producing Labour as a Social Kind', in Pearce and Frauley (eds.) 2007.

—— 2008, 'On the Clear Comprehension of Political Economy: Social Kinds and the Significance of §2 of Marx's *Capital*', in Groff (ed.) 2008.

—— 2011, *Capital as a Social Kind: Definitions and Transformations in the Critique of Political Economy*, London: Routledge.

Fausto-Sterling, Anne 1992, *Myths of Gender: Biological Theories about Men and Women*, New York: Basic Books.

Federici, Silvia 1974, *Wages Against Housework*, Bristol: Falling Wall Press.

—— 2004, *Caliban and the Witch: Women, the Body and Primitive Accumulation*, New York: Autonomedia.

Fetscher, Iring (ed.) 1966, *Karl Marx, Friedrich Engels: Studienausgabe in 4 Bänden, Volume 2: Politische Oekonomie*, Frankfurt am Main: Fischer Taschenbuch Verlag.

Finelli, Roberto 1987, *Astrazione e dialettica dal romanticismo al capitalismo. Saggio su Marx*, Rome: Bulzoni.

—— 2007, 'Abstraction versus Contradiction: Observations on Chris Arthur's *The New Dialectic and Marx's "Capital"*', *Historical Materialism* 15, 2: 61–74.

—— 2008, 'Marxismo della "contraddizione" e marxismo dell' "astrazione"', in Sacchetto and Tomba (eds.) 2008.

Fineschi, Roberto 2001, *Ripartire da Marx. Processo storico ed economia politica nella teoria del 'capitale'*, Naples: La Città del Sole.

—— 2006a, *Marx e Hegel. Contributi a una rilettura*, Rome: Carocci.

—— 2006b, 'Nochmals zum Verhältnis Wertgorm – Geldsform – Austauschprozess', *Neue Aspekte v on Marx' Kapitalismus Kritik*, Berlin: Argument.

—— 2008, *Un nuovo Marx. Filologia e interpretazione dopo la nuova edizione storico-critica (MEGA²)*, Rome: Carocci.

—— 2009a, '"Capital in General" and "Competition" in the Making of Capital: The German Debate', *Science & Society*, 17, 1: 54–76.

—— 2009b, 'Dialectic of the Commodity and Its Exposition. The German Debate in the 1970s – A Personal Survey', in Bellofiore and Fineschi (eds.) 2009.

—— 2011, 'Überlegungen zu Marx' Plänen einer Kapitaltheorie zwischen 1857 und 1865' in Vollgraf, Sperl and Hecker (eds.) 2011.

Foley, Duncan 1986, *Understanding Capital: Marx's Economic Theory*, Cambridge, MA: Harvard University Press.

Francois, William 1964, *Automation: Two Centuries in the Making*, New York: Collier Books.

Fraser, Ian 1997, 'Two of a kind: Hegel, Marx, Dialectic and Form', *Capital and Class*, 61: 81–106.

Freeman, Alan, Andrew Kliman and Julian Wells (eds.) 2004, *The New Value Controversy and the Foundations of Economics*, London: Edward Elgar Publishing.

Fumagalli, Andrea 2008, *Bioeconomia e capitalismo cognitivo*, Rome: Carocci.

Gambino, Ferruccio 2003, *Migranti nella tempesta. Avvistamenti per l'inizio del nuovo millennio*, Verona: Ombre Corte.

Gidwani, Vinay 2004, 'The Limits to Capital: Questions of Provenance and Politics', *Antipode*, 36, 3: 521–42.

—— 2008, 'Capitalism's Anxious Whole: Fear, Capture and Escape in the Grundrisse', *Antipode*, 40, 5: 857–8.

Gilbert, Alan 1981, *Marx's Politics. Communists and Citizens*, New Brunswick: Rutgers University Press.

Givsan, Hassan 1981, *Materialismus und Geschichte. Studie zu einer radikalen Historisierung der Kategorien*, Frankfurt: Peter Lang.

Glassman, Jim 2006, 'Primitive accumulation, accumulation by dispossession, accumulation by "extra-sconomic" means', *Progress in Human Geography*, 30:608–25.

Gnos, Claude and Louis-Phillipe Rochon (eds.) 2009, *Credit, Money and Macroeconomic Policy. A Post-Keynesian Approach*, Cheltenham: Elgar.

Groff, Ruth (ed.) 2008, *Revitalizing Causality: Realism About Causality in Philosophy and Social Science*, London: Routledge.

Gulli, Bruno 2005, *Labour of Fire: The Ontology of Labour Between Economy and Culture*, Philadelphia: Temple University Press.

Haraway, Donna 1991, *Simians, Cyborgs, and Women: The Reinvention of Nature*, New York: Routledge.

Harman, Chris 2002, 'The Workers of the World', *International Socialism*, 2, 96, available at: <http://pubs.socialistreviewindex.org.uk/isj96/harman.htm>.

—— 2007, 'The rate of profit and the world today', *International Socialism*, 115: 141–61.

Hart, Herbert Lionel Adolphus 1970, *The Concept of Law*, Oxford: Clarendon Press.

Harvey, David 1981, 'The Spatial Fix: Hegel, Von Thunen, and Marx', *Antipode*, 13, 3: 1–12.

—— 1982, *The Limits to Capital*, Chicago: University of Chicago Press.

—— 2006, 'Notes Towards a Theory of Uneven Geographical Development', in *Spaces of Global Capitalism: Towards a Theory of Uneven Geographical Development*, New York: Verso.

—— 2010, *A Companion to Marx's Capital*, New York: Verso.

Hatem, Jad 2006, *Marx, Philosophe du mal*, Paris: L'Harmattan.

Haug, Wolfgang Fritz (ed.) 1997, *Historisch-Kritisches Wörterbuch des Marxismus*, Band 3, Hamburg: Argument.

Head, Simon 2003, *The New Ruthless Economy: Work and Power in the Digital Age*, Oxford: Oxford University Press.

Hecker, Rolf 1987, 'Zur Entwicklung der Werttheorie von der 1. zur 3. Auflage des ersten Bandes des "Kapitals" von Karl Marx (1867–1883)', *Marx-Engels-Jahrbuch*, 10: 147–98.

—— 1995, 'Zur Herausgeberschaft des "Kapitals" durch Engels. Resümee der bisherigen Edition in der *MEGA²*', *UTOPIE kreativ*, Berlin: 14–24.

—— 1997, 'Einfache Warenproduktion', in Haug (ed.) 1997.

—— 2009, 'New Perspectives Opened by the Publication of Marx's Manuscripts of Capital, Vol. II', in Bellofiore and Fineschi (eds.) 2009.

Hecker, Rolf, Jürgen Jungnickel and Carl-Erich Vollgraf 1989, 'Zur Entwicklungsgeschichte des ersten Bandes des "Kapitals" (1867 bis 1890)', *Beiträge zur Marx-Engels-Forschung*, 27: 16–32.

Hegel, Georg Wilhelm Friedrich 1977 [1807], *Hegel's Phenomenology of Spirit*, Oxford: Oxford University Press.

—— 1995/6, *Enzykopädie der philosophischen Wissenschaften*, Frankfurt am Main: Suhrkamp.

—— 1996a, *Wissenschaft der Logik*, volume 1, Frankfurt am Main: Suhrkamp.

—— 1996b, *Wissenschaft der Logik*, volume 2, Frankfurt am Main: Suhrkamp.

—— 1969, *Hegel's Science of Logic*, translated by Arnold V. Miller, George Allen & Unwin.

—— 1975 [1873], *Hegel's Logic*, translated by William Wallace, with a foreword by John Niemeyer Findlay, Clarendon Press.

—— 1999 [1812–16], *Hegel's Science of Logic*, Amherst, NY: Humanity Books.

Heinrich, Michael 1989, 'Capital in General and the Structure of Marx's Capital. New Insights from Marx's "Economic Manuscript of 1861–63"', *Capital & Class*, 38: 63–79.

—— 1999, *Die Wissenschaft vom Wert. Die Marxsche Kritik der politischen Ökonomie zwischen wissenschaftlicher Revolution und klassischer Tradition*, Überarbeitete und erweiterte Neuauflage, Münster: Westfälisches Dampfboot.

—— 2003, *Die Wissenschaft vom Wert. Die Marxsche Kritik der politischen Ökonomie zwischen wissenschaftlicher Revolution und klassischer Tradition*, third edition, Münster: Westfälisches Dampfboot.

—— 2004, 'Ambivalences of Marx's Critique of Political Economy as Obstacles for the Analysis of Contemporary Capitalism', available at: <http://www.oekonomiekritik.de/310Ambivalences.rtf>.

—— 2007a, 'Review Article: Karl Marx, *Das Kapital. Kritik der politischen Ökonomie, Dritter Band*', *Historical Materialism*, 15: 195–210.

—— 2007b, 'Begründungsprobleme. Zur Debatte über das Marxsche "Gesetz vom tendenziellen Fall der Profitrate", in *Marx-Engels-Jahrbuch, 2006*, Berlin: Akademie Verlag.

—— 2009, 'Reconstruction or Deconstruction? Methodological Controversies about Value and Capital, and New Insights from the Critical Edition', in Bellofiore and Fineschi (eds.) 2009.

—— 2011, 'Entstehungs- und Auflösungsgeschichte des Marxschen *Kapitals*', in Bonefeld and Heinrich (eds.) 2011.

Hempel, Carl 1965, *Aspects of Scientific Explanation and other Essays in the Philosophy of Science*, New York: Free Press.

Henschel, Bernhard, Werner Krause and Hans-Manfred Militz 1989, 'Die wissenschaftliche Bedeutung und die Übersetzungsproblematik der französischen Ausgabe des ersten Bandes des "Kapitals" von 1872–1875', *Marx-Engels-Jahrbuch*, 12: 184–202.

Hilferding, Rudolf 1981 [1910], *Finance Capital: A Study of the Latest Phase of Capitalist Development*, edited and introduced by Tom Bottomore, translated by Morris Watnick and Sam Gordon, London: Routledge and Kegan Paul.

Hindess, Barry and Hirst, Paul 1975, *Precapitalist Modes of Production*, London: Routledge and Kegan Paul.

Hobsbawm, Eric J. 1964, 'Introduction', in Marx 1964.

hooks, bell 1981, *Ain't I a Woman: Black Women and Feminism*, Boston: South End Press.

Howitt, William 1838 [2002], *Colonization and Christianity. A Popular History of the Treatment of the Natives by the Europeans in All Their Colonies*, London: BookSurge Publishing.

Huws, Ursula 2003, *The Making of a Cybertariat: Virtual Work in a Real World*, New York: Monthly Review Press.

—— (ed.) 2007, *Defragmenting: Towards a Critical Understanding of the New Global Division of Labour*, London: Merlin.

—— (ed.) 2008, *Break or Weld? Trade Union Responses to Global Value Chain Restructuring*, London: Merlin.

Iacono, Alfonso Maurizio 1982, *Il borghese e il selvaggio: l'immagine dell'uomo iso-lato nei paradigmi di Defoe, Turgot e Adam Smith*, Milan: Franco Angeli.

Ilyenkov, Evald 1982 [1960], *The Dialectics of the Abstract and the Concrete in Marx's 'Capital'*, Moscow: Progress Publishers.

Iñigo Carrera, Juan 1992, *El Conocimiento Dialéctico*, Buenos Aires: Centro para la Investigación como Crítica Práctica.

—— 2003, *El Capital: Razón Histórica, Sujeto Revolucionario y Conciencia*, Buenos Aires: Ediciones Cooperativas.

—— 2007, *Conocer el capital hoy. Usar críticamente 'El capital'*, Vol. 1, Buenos Aires: Imago Mundi.

—— 2008 [2003], *El Capital: Razón Histórica, Sujeto Revolucionario y Conciencia*, Buenos Aires: Imago Mundi.

Inwood, Michael 1992, *A Hegel Dictionary*, Oxford: Blackwell.

Jaffe, Hosea 2007, *Davanti al colonialismo: Engels, Marx e il marxismo*, Milan: Jaca Book.

Jahn, Wolfgang and Dietrich Noske 1979, *Arbeitsblätter zur Marx-Engels-Forschung*, 7.

Jahn, Wolfgang and Roland Nietzold 1978, 'Probleme der Entwicklung der Marxschen politischen Ökonomie im Zeitraum von 1850 bis 1863', in *Marx-Engels-Jahrbuch*, 1: 145–74.

Jahn, Wolfgang and Thomas Marxhausen 1983, 'Die Stellung der "Theorien über den Mehrwert" in der Entstehungsgeschichte des "Kapitals"', in *Der zweite Entwurf des "Kapitals". Analysen – Aspekte – Argumente*, Berlin: Dietz Verlag.

Jani, Pranav 2002, 'Karl Marx, Eurocentrism, and the 1857 Revolt in British India', in Bartolovich and Lazarus (eds.) 2002.

Janoska, Judith (ed.) 1994, *Das 'Methodenkapitel' von Karl Marx*, Basel: Schwabe.

Jevons, William Stanley 1970 [1871], *The Theory of Political Economy*, Harmondsworth: Penguin Books.

Joja, Athanase 1969, *La Lógica Dialéctica y las Ciencias*, Buenos Aires: Juárez Editor.

Jungnickel, Jürgen 1989, 'Die Stellung der 2. Auflage des ersten Bandes des "Kapitals" in der Entwicklungsgeschichte der ökonomischen Theorie von Marx', in *Marx-Engels-Jahrbuch*, 12: 92–125.

Kabadayi, Mustafa Erdem and Tobias Reichardt (eds.) 2007, *Unfreie Arbeit. Ökonomische und kulturgeschichtliche Perspektiven*, Hilesheim: Georg Olms Verlag.

Kain, Philip J. 1992, 'Modern Feminism and Marx', *Studies in Soviet Thought*, 44, 3: 159–92.

Karatani, Kojin 2003, *Transcritique: on Kant and Marx*, Boston: MIT Press.

Kates, Gary 1995, *Monsieur d'Eon is a Woman: A Tale of Political Intrigue and Sexual Masquerade*, Baltimore: Johns Hopkins University Press.

Kay, Geoffrey 1999, 'Abstract Labour and Capital', *Historical Materialism*, 5: 225–79.

Kelly, Joan 1982, 'Early Feminist Theory and the "Querelle des Femmes", 1400–1789', *Signs*, 8, 1: 4–28.

Keynes, John Maynard 1963, 'The Economic Prospects of Our Grandchildren', in *Essays in Persuasion*, New York: W. W. Norton & Co.

Kicillof, Alex and Guido Starosta 2007a, 'On Materiality and Social Form: A Political Critique of Rubin's Value-Form Theory', *Historical Materialism*, 15, 3: 9–43.

—— 2007b, 'Value-Form and Class Struggle. A Critique of the Autonomist Theory of Value', *Capital and Class*, 92: 1–32.

Kliman, Andrew 2007, *Reclaiming Marx's 'Capital': A Refutation of the Myth of Inconsistency*, Lanham, MD: Lexington Books.

Kornblith, Hilary 1993, *Inductive Inference and its Natural Ground: An Essay in Naturalistic Epistemology*, Cambridge, MA: MIT.

—— 2002, *Knowledge and Its Place in Nature*, New York: Oxford.

Koselleck, Reinhart 2000, *Zeitschichten: Studien zur Historik*, mit einem Beitrag von Hans-Georg Gadamer, Frankfurt am Main: Suhrkamp.

Kouvelakis, Stathis 2005, 'Marx e la critica della politica', in Musto (ed.) 2005.

Krader, Lawrence (ed.) 1974, *The Ethnological Notebooks of Karl Marx*, Assen: Van Gorcum.

Krahl, Hans Jürgen 1971, *Konstitution und Klassenkämpfe*, Frankfurt: Verlag Neue Kritik.

Krätke, Michael R. 2008a, 'The First World Economic Crisis of 1857–8', in Musto (ed.) 2008.

—— 2008b, 'Marx's Book of Crisis of 1857–8', in Musto (ed.) 2008.

Kuhn, Thomas 1970 [1962], *The Structure of Scientific Revolutions*, second edition, Chicago: University of Chicago.

Lazzarato, Maurizio 1996, 'Immaterial Labour', in Virno and Hardt (eds.) 1996.

Le Goff, Jacques 1960, 'Au Moyen Age: temps de l'Eglise et temps du marchand', *Annales economies, sociétés, civilisations*, XV, 3: 417–33.

Lebowitz, Michael A. 2003, *Beyond Capital. Marx's Political Economy of the Working Class*, second edition, Basingstoke: Palgrave Macmillan.

Lefebvre, Henri 1984 [1969], *Lógica formal, lógica dialéctica*, Mexico City: Siglo XXI.

Lefort, Claude 1978, *Les formes de l'histoire. Essais d'anthropologie politique*, Paris: Gallimard.

—— 1986, 'Marx: From One Vision of History to Another', in *The Political Forms of Modern Society*, Cambridge: Polity.

Lenin, Vladimir 1939 [1915], *Imperialism: The Highest Stage of Capitalism*, New York: International.

—— 2000 [1899], *The Development of Capitalism in Russia*, in Lenin 1964–72, Volume 3, Moscow: Progress Publishers.

—— 1964–72, *Collected Works*, Moscow: Progress Publishers.

Lietz, Barbara 1987a, 'Zur Entwicklung der Werttheorie in den "Ergänzungen und Veränderungen zum ersten Band des "Kapitals" (Dezember 1871–Januar 1872)', *Beiträge zur Marx-Engels-Forschung*, 23: 26–33.

—— 1987b, 'Ein Ausgangsmaterial für die 2. deutsche Auflage und die autorisierte französische Ausgabe des ersten Bandes des "Kapitals"', *Beiträge zur Marx-Engels-Forschung*, 24: 76–84.

Linebaugh, Peter 2008, *The Magna Carta Manifesto*, Berkeley, CA: University of California Press.

Locke, John 1975 [1690], *An Essay Concerning Human Understanding*, edited by P.H. Nidditch, Oxford: Oxford University Press.

Lohmann, Georg 1991, *Indifferenz und Gesellschaft*, Frankfurt: Suhrkamp.

Lukács, Georg 1967 [1923], *History and Class Consciousness*, London: Merlin Press.

Luxemburg, Rosa 1913, *Die Akkumulation des Kapitals*, Berlin: Vorwärts.

Mandel, Ernest 1971, *The Formation of the Economic Thought of Karl Marx: 1843 to 'Capital'*, translated by Brian Pearce, New York: Monthly Review.

Mann, Geoff 2008, 'A Negative Geography of Necessity', *Antipode*, 40, 5: 921–34.

Mann, Geoff and Joel Wainwright 2008, 'Marx Without Guardrails: Geographies of the *Grundrisse*', *Antipode*, 40, 5: 848–56.

Marcuse, Herbert 1928, 'Beiträge zu einer Phänomenologie des Historischen Materialismus', *Philosophische Hefte*, 1: 45–68.

Marini, Ruy Mauro 1991, *Dialéctica de la dependencia*, Mexico: Ediciones Era.

Marramao, Giacomo 1975/6, 'Theory of Crisis and the Problem of Constitution', *Telos*, 26: 143–64.

—— 1982, *Lo Político y las Transformaciones. Crítica del Capitalismo e Ideologías de la Crisis entre los Años 20 y 30*, Mexico City: Pasado y Presente.

Marx, Karl 1852, 'Excerpt from Volume XIX', unpublished excerpt-notebook, International Institute of Social History (IISG), archival collections, call no. B61, Amsterdam.

—— 1857–8a [1987], *Economic Manuscripts of 1857–58*, in Marx and Engels 1975–2005, Vol. 29.

—— 1857–8b [1973], *Grundrisse*, translated by Martin Nicolaus, Harmondsworth: Penguin Books.

—— 1858a [1974], 'Urtext "Zur Kritik der Politischen Ökonomie"' in Marx 1983.

—— 1858b [1987], 'Original Text of *A Contribution to The Critique of Political Economy*' in Marx and Engels 1975–2005, Vol. 29.

—— 1859 [1987], *A Contribution to the Critique of Political Economy*, in Marx and Engels 1975–2005, Vol. 29.

—— 1861–63a [1988], *Economic Manuscript of 1861–63*, in Marx and Engels 1975–2005, Vol. 30.

—— 1861–63b [1991], *Economic Manuscript of 1861–63*, in Marx and Engels 1975–2005, Vol. 33.

—— 1867a [1977], *Capital* Volume I, translated by Ben Fowkes, New York: Vintage Books.

—— 1867b, *Das Kapital. Kritik der Politischen Ökonomie*, Erster Band, Hamburg, in Marx and Engels 1976–, volume II/5.

—— 1872–5, *Le Capital*, Paris, in Marx and Engels 1976–, volume II/7.

—— 1883, *Das Kapital. Kritik der Politischen Ökonomie*, Erster Band, Hamburg, in Marx and Engels 1976–, Vol. II/8.

—— 1911 [1859], *A Contribution to the Critique of Political Economy*, Chicago: C. H. Kerr.

—— 1939–41 [1857–8], *Grundrisse der Kritik*, Frankfurt am Main: Europäische Verlagsanstalt.

—— 1952 [1890], *Das Kapital. Kritik der politischen Ökonomie, Erster Band, Buch I: Der Produktionsprozess des Kapitals*, in Marx and Engels 1956–1990, volume 23.

—— 1954, *Briefe über 'Das Kapital'*, Berlin: Dietz Verlag.

—— 1959, *Capital. A Critique of Political Economy. Volume III The Process of Capitalist Production as a Whole*, edited by F. Engels, Moscow: Progress Publishers.

—— 1963a [1847], *The Poverty of Philosophy*, New York: International Publishers.

—— 1963b [1861–3], *Theories of Surplus Value*, volume 1, Moscow: Progress Publishers.

—— 1964, *Pre-Capitalist Economic Formations*, London: Lawrence and Wishart.

—— 1965 [1867], *Capital* Volume I, Moscow: Progress Publishers.

—— 1966a [1861–79], *Capital* Volume III, Moscow: Progress Publishers.

—— 1966b [1867], 'Ware und Geld' (*Das Kapital*, 1. Auflage 1867, 1. Buch Kapital 1), in Fetscher (ed.) 1966.

—— 1967 [1867], *Capital: A Critique of Political Economy, Volume I*, translated by Samuel Moore and Edward Aveling, New York: International Publishers.

—— 1968 [1853], *Karl Marx and Frederick Engels on Colonialism*, Moscow: Progress Publishers.

—— 1969, *Le Capital, Livre I*, Paris: Garnier-Flammarion.

—— 1970 [1859], *A Contribution to the Critique of Political Economy*, translated by S. W. Ryazanskaya and edited by Maurice Dobb, New York: International Publishers.

—— 1971 [1861–3], *Theories of Surplus Value*, Part III, Moscow: Progress Publishers.

—— 1972 [1894E], *Das Kapital: Kritik der Politischen Ökonomie. Vol. III, Der Gesamtprozeß der kapitalistischen Produktion*, edited by Friedrich Engels, in Marx and Engels 1956–1990, Vol. 25.

—— 1973 [1857–8], *Grundrisse*, translated by Martin Nicolaus, Harmondsworth: Penguin.

—— 1974, 'Briefe. Oktober 1864 bis Dezember 1867', in Marx and Engels 1956–1990, volume 31.

—— 1974a [1894U], *Capital: A Critique of Political Economy. Vol. III, The Process of Capitalist Production as a Whole*, 1909 translation of Marx 1972 by Ernest Untermann, London: Lawrence & Wishart.

—— 1975, *El Capital. Tomo 1*, translated by Pedro Scaron, Mexico City: Siglo XXI.

—— 1975–2005a, *Grundrisse*, in Marx and Engels 1975–2005, Vol. 28.

—— 1975–2005b, 'Machinery and Modern Industry', in Marx and Engels 1975–2005, Vol. 25.

—— 1975–2005c, 'Outlines of a Critique of Political Economy', in Marx and Engels 1975–2005, Vol. 29.

—— 1975–2005d, *Capital* Volume I, in Marx and Engels 1975–2005, Vol. 35.

—— 1975–2005e, 'Letter to Annenkov, 28 December 1846', in Marx and Engels 1975–2005, Vol. 38.

—— 1975–2005f, 'Letter to Weydemeyer, 5 March 1852', in Marx and Engels 1975–2005, Vol. 39.

—— 1975–2005g, 'Wage Labour and Capital', in Marx and Engels 1975–2005, Vol. 9.

—— 1975–2005h, 'Economic Manuscript of 1861–63. A Contribution to the Critique of Political Economy (Continuation)' in Marx and Engels 1975–2005, Vol. 33.

—— 1976a, *Capital: A Critique of Political Economy*, Vol. 1, translated by Ben Fowkes, London: Penguin.

—— 1976b, 'Results of the Immediate Process of Production', in Marx 1976a.

—— 1976c, *Capital* Volume I first edition [1867], in Dragstedt (trans.) 1976.

—— 1976–81, 'Ökonomische Manuskripte 1857/58', 2 volumes, in Marx and Engels 1976–, II/1.

—— 1976–82, *Marx-Engels Gesamtausgabe (MEGA)*, Division 2, Volume 3, Parts 1–6, Berlin: Dietz Verlag.

—— 1977 [1859], *A Contribution to the Critique of Political Economy*, New York: International Publishers.

—— 1978, *The German Ideology*, in Tucker (ed.) 1978.

—— 1979, *The Future Results Of British Rule In India*, in Marx and Engels 1975–2005, volume 12.

—— 1981 [1894F], *Capital: A Critique of Political Economy*, Volume III, translated by David Fernbach. New York: Penguin.

—— 1982 [1843], *Critique of Hegel's 'Philosophy of Right'*, Cambridge: Cambridge University Press.

—— 1983 [1857–8], *Grundrisse der Kritik der politischen Ökonomie (1857–58)*, in Marx and Engels 1956–1990, Vol. 42.

—— 1986 [1857–8], *Economic Works 1857–1858*, in Marx and Engels 1975–2005, volume 28, translated by Ernst Wangermann, New York: International.

—— 1987 [1857–8], *Economic Works 1857–1861*, in Marx and Engels 1975–2005, Vol. 29.

—— 1987a [1866], 'Letter to Kugelmann, 13 October 1866', in Marx and Engels 1975–2005, Vol. 42.

—— 1987b [1868], 'Letter to Engels, 8 January 1868', in Marx and Engels 1975–2005, Vol. 42.

—— 1988 [1861], *Economic Works 1861–3*, in Marx and Engels 1975–2005, volume 30, translated by Ben Fowkes and Emile Burns, New York: International Publishers.

—— 1989a, *Economic Manuscript of 1861–3*, in Marx and Engels 1975–2005, Vol. 32, New York: International Publishers.

—— 1990a [1867], *Capital* Volume I, translated by Ben Fowkes, London: Penguin.

—— 1991, 'Economic Manuscript of 1861–1863 (Continuation)', translated by Ben Fowkes, in Marx and Engels 1975–2005, Vol. 33.

—— 1991a, 'Das Kapital. Kritik der politischen Ökonomie. Erster Band. Hamburg 1890', in Karl Marx and Friedrich Engels, *Gesamtausgabe, MEGA*² II/10.

—— 1991b, *Capital. A Critique of Political Economy*, Volume III, translated by David Fernbach, London: Penguin.

—— 1992a, *Karl Marx. Early Writings*, Harmondsworth: Penguin.

—— 1992b [1894], *Ökonomische Manuskripte 1863–1867* in Marx and Engels 1976–, II/4, edited by Manfred Müller, Jürgen Jungnickel, Barbara Lietz, Christel Sander, and Artur Schnickmann, Berlin/Amsterdam: Dietz Verlag/Internationales Institut für Sozialgeschichte Amsterdam.

—— 1992c, *Capital. A Critique of Political Economy*, Volume II, translated by David Fernbach, London: Penguin.

—— 1993 [1857–8], *Grundrisse*, translated by Martin Nicolaus, London: Penguin Books.

—— 1994, *Economic Works 1861–64*, in Marx and Engels 1975–2005, Vol. 34.

—— 1996, *Capital* Volume I, in Marx and Engels 1975–2005, Vol. 35.

—— 1998, *Capital* Volume III, in Marx and Engels 1975–2005, Vol. 37.

—— 2002 [1879–80], 'Notes on Adolph Wagner', in Carver (ed.) 2002, *Later Political Writings*, Cambridge: Cambridge University Press.

—— 2003, 'Manuskripte zum dritten Buch des Kapitals. 1871 bis 1882' in Marx and Engels 1976–, II/14.

—— 2005 [1847], *The Poverty of Philosophy*, [United States]: Elibron Classics.

—— 2006 [1857–8], *Ökonomische Manuskripte 1857/58* in Marx and Engels 1976–, II, 1, Amsterdam: Akademie.

—— 2008, 'Das Kapital. Kritik der politischen Ökonomie, zweiter Band. Hamburg 1885', in Marx and Engels 1976–, II/13. Berlin: Dietz.

Marx, Karl and Friedrich Engels 1956–1990, *Werke*, edited by Institut für Marxismus-Leninismus, Berlin: Dietz.

—— 1973, *Briefe. Januar 1856 bis Dezember 1859*, in Karl Marx and Friedrich Engels 1956–1990, Vol. 29.

—— 1975a, 'The Holy Family' in Marx and Engels 1975–2005, Vol. 4.

—— 1975b, *Selected Correspondence*, Moscow: Progress Publishers.

—— 1975–2005, *Marx and Engels Collected Works*, 50 volumes, Moscow: Progress Publishers.

—— 1976–, *Gesamtausgabe (MEGA²)*, Berlin: Dietz Verlag.

—— 1983, 'Letter to Engels, 8 October 1858', in Marx and Engels 1975–2005, Vol. 40.

—— 1986, 'Letters. January 1856–December 1859', in Marx and Engels 1975–2005, Vol. 40.

—— 1992a [1863–67], 'Ökonomische Manuskripte 1863–67', Teil II, MEGA II, Abteilung, Band 4.2, Berlin: Dietz Verlag.

—— 1992b, 'Letters 1880–83', in Marx and Engels 1975–2005, Vol. 46.

—— 2004 [1845–6], *The German Ideology*, New York: International Publishers.

Mattick, Paul 1993, 'Marx's Dialectic', in Moseley (ed.) 1993.

Mazzone, Alessandro (ed.) 2002, *MEGA²: Marx ritrovato*, Rome: Mediaprint.

Meaney, Mark 2002, *Capital as Organic Unity: The Role of Hegel's 'Science of Logic' in Marx's 'Grundrisse'*, Dordrecht: Kluwer Academic Publishers.

Mepham, John 1989, 'The *Grundrisse*: Method or Metaphysics', in Rattansi (ed.) 1989.

—— and David-Hillel Ruben (eds.) 1979, *Issues in Marxist Philosophy, Volume One Dialectics and Method*, Brighton: Harvester Press.

Midnight Notes Collective 1992, 'The New Enclosures', in *Midnight Oil: Work, Energy, War 1973–1992*, edited by the Midnight Notes Collective, New York: Autonomedia.

Minsky, Hyman P. 1975, *John Maynard Keynes*, New York: Columbia University Press.

Mohri, Kenzo 1979, 'Marx and 'Underdevelopment', *Monthly Review*, 30, 11: 32–42.

Mohun, Simon (ed.) 1994, *Debates in Value Theory*, Basingstoke: Macmillan.

Morgan, Lewis H. 1877, *Ancient Society, Or Researches in the Lines of Human Progress from Savagery through Barbarism to Civilization*, London: MacMillan & Company.

Moseley, Fred (ed.) 1993, *Marx's Method in 'Capital'*, Atlantic Highlands, NJ: Humanities Press.

—— 1993, 'Marx's Logical Method and the "Transformation Problem"' in Moseley (ed.) 1993.

—— 1995, 'Capital in General and Marx's Logical Method: A Response to Heinrich's Critique', *Capital and Class*, 55.

—— 1997, 'The Development of Marx's Theory of the Distribution of Surplus-Value', in Moseley and Campbell (eds.) 1997.

—— 2000, 'The New Solution to the Transformation Problem: A Sympathetic Critique', *Review of Radical Political Economics*.

—— 2002, 'Hostile Brothers: Marx's Theory of the Distribution of Surplus-value in Volume 3 of *Capital*', in Reuten and Campbell (eds.) 2002.

—— (ed.) 2005, *Marx's Theory of Money: Modern Appraisals*, Basingstoke: Palgrave Macmillan.

—— 2008, 'The Development of Marx's Theory of the Distribution of Surplus-Value in the Manuscript of 1861–63', in Bellofiore and Fineschi (eds.) 2009.

—— and Martha Campbell (eds.) 1997, *New Investigations of Marx's Method*, Atlantic Highlands: Humanities Press International.

Moulier-Boutang, Yann 2002, *Dalla schiavitù al lavoro salariato*, Rome: manifestolibri.

Müller, Manfred 1978, 'Auf dem Wege zum "Kapital". Zur Entwicklung des Kapitalbegriffs von Marx in den Jahren 1857–1863', Berlin DDR: das europäische Buch.

—— 1983, 'Die Bedeutung des Manuskripts "Zur Kritik der politischen Ökonomie" 1861–1863', in *Der zweite Entwurf. Analyse – Aspekte – Argumente*, Berlin DDR.

Müller, Wolfgang, and Christel Neusüss 1975, 'The Illusion of State Socialism and the Contradiction between Wage Labor and Capital', *Telos*, 25: 13–90.

Munzer, Steven R. 1990, *A Theory of Property*, Cambridge: Cambridge University Press.

Murray, Patrick 1988, *Marx's Theory of Scientific Knowledge*, Atlantic Highlands, NJ: Humanities Press International.

—— 1993, 'The Necessity of Money: How Hegel Helped Marx to Surpass Ricardo's Theory of Value', in Moseley (ed.) 1993.

—— 2000, 'Marx's "Truly Social" Labour Theory of Value. Part I, Abstract Labour in Marxian Value Theory', *Historical Materialism*, 6, 27–65.

—— 2005, 'The New Giant's Staircase', *Historical Materialism*, 13, 2: 61–83.

—— 2006, 'In Defence of the "Third Thing Argument": A Reply to James Furner's "Marx's Critique of Samuel Bailey"', *Historical Materialism*, 14, 2: 149–68.

—— 2009, 'The Place of "The Results of the Immediate Production Process" in *Capital*', in Bellofiore and Fineschi (eds.) 2009.

Musto, Marcello (ed.) 2005, *Sulle tracce di un fantasma. L'opera di Karl Marx tra filologia e filosofia*, Rome: Manifestolibri.

—— 2008, 'History, Production and Method in the 1857 "Introduction"', in Musto (ed.) 2008.

—— (ed.) 2008, *Karl Marx's Grundrisse. Foundations of the Critique of Political Economy 150 Years Later*: Routledge.

Napoleoni, Claudio 1975 [1973], *Smith Ricardo Marx*, Oxford: Blackwell.

—— 1976, *Valore*, Milan: Isedi.

Negri, Antonio 1998 [1979], *Marx oltre Marx. Quaderno di lavoro sui "Grundrisse"*, Rome: manifestolibri.

—— 1991, *Marx Beyond Marx: Lessons on the Grundrisse*, translated by Harry Cleaver, Michael Ryan and Maurizio Viano, New York: Autonomedia.

—— 1992, *Fin de Siglo*, Barcelona: Paidos Iberica/I.C.E-U.A.B.

—— 1999, 'De la Transición al Poder Constituyente' in Negri and Guattari 1999.

Negri, Antonio and Felix Guattari 1999, *Las Verdades Nomadas & General Intellect, Poder Constituyente, Comunismo*, Barcelona: Akal.

Nicolaus, Martin 1993 [1973], 'Foreword' in Marx 1993.

Nida-Rümelin, Julian (ed.) 1999, *Rationality, Realism Revision (Perspectives in Analytical Philosophy)*, 23, Berlin: Walter De Gruyter, 52–89.

Niebyl, Karl H. 1946, *Studies in the Classical Theories of Money*, New York: Columbia University Press.

Nietzold, Roland, Hannes Skambraks und Günter Wermusch (eds.) 1978, '"...unsrer Partei einen Sieg erringen". Studien zur Entstehungs- und Wirkungs-

geschichte des "Kapitals" von Karl Marx', East Berlin: Die Wirtschaft.

Nimtz, August 2002, 'The Eurocentric Marx and Engels and Other Related Myths', in Bartolovich and Lazarus (eds.) 2002.

Northrup, Herbert R. 1965, 'The Reduction in Hours' in Dankert, Mann and Northrup (eds.) 1965.

O' Hara, Phillip Anthony (ed.) 1999, *The Encyclopedia of Political Economy*, London: Routledge.

Ong, Nai-Pew 1983, 'The Logic of Marx's Theory of Money', *Social Concept*, 1, 1: 30–54.

Ortony, Andrew (ed.) 1979, *Metaphor and Thought*, Cambridge: Cambridge University Press.

Pappe, H.O. 1951, 'Wakefield and Marx', *The Economic History Review*, 4, 1: 88–97.

Pateman, Carole 1988, *The Sexual Contract*, Cambridge: Polity.

Pearce, Frank and Jon Frauley (eds.) 2007, *Critical Realism and the Social Sciences: Heterodox Elaborations*, edited by F. Pearce and J. Frauley, Toronto: University of Toronto Press.

Peet, Richard 1981, 'Historical Forms of the Property Relation: A Reconstruction of Marx's Theory', *Antipode*, 13, 3: 13–25.

PEM (Projektgruppe Entwicklung des Marxschen Systems) 1973, *Das Kapital vom Geld*, West Berlin: VSA.

—— 1978, *Grundrisse der Kritik der politischen Ökonomie (Rohentwurf)*. *Kommentar*, Hamburg: VSA.

Pétré-Grenouilleau, Olivier 2004, *Les traites négrières. Essai d'histoire globale*, Paris: Gallimard.

Postone, Moishe 1993, *Time, Labor and Social Domination: a Reinterpretation of Marx's Critical Theory*, Cambridge: Cambridge University Press.

Psychopedis, Kosmas 1992, 'Dialectical Theory: Problems of Reconstruction' in Bonefeld, Gunn and Psychopedis (eds.) 1992.

Rattansi, Ali (ed.) 1989, *Ideology, Method and Marx: Essays from Economy and Society*, London: Routledge.

Reichelt, Helmut 1973 [1970], *La struttura logica del concetto di capitale in Marx*, Bari: De Donato.

—— 1995, 'Why did Marx Conceal his Dialectical Method?' in Bonefeld *et al.* (eds.) 1995.

—— 2007, 'Marx's Critique of Economic Categories: Reflections on the Problem of Validity in the Dialectical Method of Presentation in *Capital*', *Historical Materialism*, 15: 3–52.

—— 2008, *Neue Marx-Lektüre. Zur Kritik sozialwissenschaftlicher Logik*, Hamburg: VSA.

Reuten, Geert 1988, 'Value as Social Form' in Williams (ed.) 1988.

—— 1993, 'The Difficult Labour of a Theory of Social Value: Metaphors and Systematic Dialectics at the Beginning of Marx's *Capital*', in Moseley (ed.) 1993.

—— 1997, 'The Notion of Tendency in Marx's 1894 Law of Profit', in Moseley and Campbell (eds.) 1997.

—— 2004, '"Zirkel vicieux" or trend fall?; the course of the profit rate in Marx's "Capital III"', *History of Political Economy*, 36, 1:163–86.

—— 2005, 'Money as Constituent of Value' in Moseley (ed.) 2005.

Ricardo, David 1821 [1817–21], *On the Principles of Political Economy and Taxation*, London: John Murray.

Riedel, Manfred 1992, 'Gesellschaft-Gemeinschaft', in Brunner, Conze and Koselleck (eds.) 1992.

Robles-Baez, Mario L. 2004, 'On the Abstraction of Labour as a Social Determination' in Freeman, Kliman and Wells (eds.) 2004.

Rosdolsky, Roman 1977 [1968], *The Making of Marx's 'Capital'*, London: Pluto Press.

Roth, Regina 2009, 'Karl Marx's Original Manuscripts in the Marx-Engels-Gesamtausgabe (*MEGA*): Another View on Capital', in Bellofiore and Fineschi (eds.) 2009.

Rovatti, Pier Aldo 1973, *Critica e scientificità in Marx*, Milan: Feltrinelli.

Rubin, Isaak Illich 1972 [1928], *Essays on Marx's Theory of Value*, translated by Milos Samardzija and Fredy Perlman, Detroit: Black & Red.

—— 1994 [1927], 'Abstract Labour and Value in Marx's System', in Mohun (ed.) 1994.

Ryle, Gilbert 1984, *The Concept of Mind*, Chicago: University of Chicago Press.

Saad-Filho, Alfredo 2002, *The Value of Marx*, London: Routledge.

Sacchetto, Devi 2008, 'Mobilità della forza lavoro e del capitale. Alcune note a partire dalle esperienze dell'Europa orientale', in Sacchetto and Tomba (eds.) 2008.

Sacchetto, Devi and Massimiliano Tomba (eds.) 2008, *La lunga accumulazione originaria. Politica e lavoro nel mercato mondiale*, Verona: Ombre Corte.

Schkedow, Wlamidir 1987, 'Die Untersuchungsmethode der Entstehungs- und Entwicklungsgeschichte der kapitalistischen Produktionsweise im "Kapital"', in *Marxistische Studien. Jahrbuch des IMSF* 12, I: 232–7.

Schmidt, Alfred (ed.) 1969, *Beiträge zur marxistischen Erkenntnistheorie*, Frankfurt/M.: Suhrkamp.

—— 1971, *The Concept of Nature in Marx*, London: NLB

—— 1971a, *Geschichte und Struktur. Fragen einer marxistischen Historik*, Munich: Hanser.

Schrader, Fred E. 1980, *Restauration und Revolution. Die Vorarbeiten zum 'Kapital' von Karl Marx in seinen Studienheften 1850–1858*, Hildesheim: Gerstenberg.

Schwartz, Nancy L. 1979, 'Distinction Between Public and Private Life. Marx on the *zoon politikon*', *Political Theory*, 2: 245–66.

Schwarz, Winfried 1974, 'Das "Kapital im Allgemeinen" und die "Konkurrenz" im ökonomischen Werk von Karl Marx. Zu Rosdolskys Fehlinterpretation der Gliederung des "Kapital"', in *Gesellschaft. Beiträge zur Marxschen Theorie*, 1, Frankfurt: Suhrkamp.

—— 1978, *Vom 'Rohentwurf' zum 'Kapital'. Die Strukturgeschichte des Marxschen Hauptwerkes*, West Berlin: das europäische Buch.

—— 1987, 'Die Geldform in der 1. und 2. Auflage des "Kapital". Zur Diskussion um die "Historisierung" der Wertformanalyse', in *Marxistische Studien. Jahrbuch des IMSF*, 12, I: 200–13.

Scott, Joan 1988, 'Deconstructing Equality versus Difference, or, The Uses of Poststructuralist Theory for Feminism', *Feminist Studies*, 14, 1: 33–50.

Semmel, Bernard 1961, 'The Philosophical Radicals and Colonialism', *The Journal of Economic History*, 21, 4: 513–25.

Shanin, Teodor 1983, *Late Marx and the Russian Road. Marx and 'the Peripheries of Capitalism'*, New York: Monthly Review Press.

Shortall, Felton 1994, *The Incomplete Marx*, Aldershot: Avebury.

Silberman, Charles E. 1966, *The Myths of Automation*, New York: Harper.

Silver, Beverly J. and Lu Zhang 2008, 'Cina: l'epicentro emergente del conflitto operaio mondiale?', in Sacchetto and Tomba (eds.) 2008.

Skambraks, Hannes 1978, 'Der Platz des Manuskripts "Zur Kritik der politischen Ökonomie" von 1861–1863 im Prozeß der Ausarbeitung der proletarischen politischen Ökonomie durch Karl Marx', in Nietzold, Skambraks and Wermusch (eds.) 1978.

Smith, Adam 1852 [1776], *An Inquiry into the Nature and Causes of the Wealth of Nations*, London: T. Nelson & Sons.

Smith, Neil 1984, *Uneven Development: Nature, Capital, and the Production of Space*, London: Blackwell.

—— 2005, *Endgame of Globalization*, New York: Routledge.

Smith, Tony 1990, *The Logic of Marx's 'Capital'*, Albany, NY: State University of New York Press.

—— 1993, 'Marx's *Capital* and Hegelian Dialectical Logic', in Moseley (ed.) 1993.

—— 2000, *Technology and Capital in the Age of Lean Production. A Marxian Critique of the 'New Economy'*, Albany, NY: SUNY Press.

—— 2005, *Globalisation: A Systematic Marxian Account*, Leiden: Brill.

Sofri, Gianni 1969, *Il modo di produzione asiatico*, Turin: Einaudi.

Spivak, Gayatri 1994, 'Responsibility', *boundary 2*, 21, 3: 19–64.

—— 1999, *A Critique of Postcolonial Reason. Toward a History of the Vanishing Present*, Cambridge, MA: Harvard University Press.

Stamford Raffles, Thomas 1817, *History of Java and its Dependencies*, London: Black, Parbury and Allen.

Staples, David E. 2006, *No Place Life Home: Organizing Home-Based Labour in the*

Era of Structural Adjustment, New York: Routledge.

Starosta, Guido 2003, 'Scientific Knowledge and Political Action: On the Antinomies of Lukács' Thought in *History and Class Consciousness*', *Science and Society*, 67, 1: 39–67.

—— 2004, 'Rethinking Marx's Mature Social Theory', *Historical Materialism*, 12, 3: 43–52.

—— 2005, *Science as Practical Criticism. An Investigation into Revolutionary Subjectivity in Marx's Critique of Political Economy*, unpublished PhD thesis, Coventry: Department of Sociology, University of Warwick.

Strathern, Marilyn 1992, *Reproducing the Future: Essays on Anthropology, Kinship, and the New Reproductive Technologies*, Manchester: Manchester University Press.

Texier, Jacques 1992, 'Les formes historiques du lieu social dans les Grundrisse de Karl Marx', *Actuel Marx*, 11: 137–70.

Theolald, Robert 1966, 'Cybernetics and the Problems of Social Reorganization' in Dechert (ed.) 1996.

Tomba, Massimiliano 2002. *Crisi e critica in Bruno Bauer. Il principio di esclusione come fondamento del politico*. Naples: Bibliopolis.

—— 2007, 'Differentials of Surplus-Value in the Contemporary Forms of Exploitation', *The Commoner*, 12: 23–37.

—— 2009, 'From History of Capital to History in *Capital*', in Bellofiore and Fineschi (eds.) 2009.

Tombazos, Stavros 1994, *Le temps dans l'analyse économique. Les catégories du temps dans le capital*, Paris: Chaier des saisons.

Tomich, Dale W. 2004, *Through the Prism of Slavery. Labor, Capital, and World Economy*, Lanham: Rowman & Littlefield.

Toporowski, Jan 2002, 'La banque mutuelle: de l'utopie au marché des capitaux. Le cas britannique', *Révue d'Économie Financière*, September, 67, 45–55.

Toscano, Alberto 2007, 'From Pin Factories to Gold Farmers: Editorial Introduction to a Research Stream on Cognitive Capitalism, Immaterial Labour, and the General Intellect', *Historical Materialism*, 15, 1: 3–12.

Tronti, Mario 1971, *Operai e capitale*, second edition, Turin: Einaudi.

Trotsky, Leon 1959 [1932], *The History of the Russian Revolution*, edited by Frederick Wilcox Dupee, New York: Doubleday.

—— 2002, *The Transitional Program [Electronic Version]*, retrieved February 10, 2005, available at: http://www.marxists.org/archive/trotsky/works/1938-tp/transprogram.pdf.

Tuchscheerer, Walter 1980 [1968], *Prima del 'Capitale'. La formazione del pensiero economico di Marx (1843/1858)*, Firenze: La Nuova Italia.

Tucker, Robert (ed.) 1978, *The Marx Engels Reader*, New York: W.W. Norton.

Turchetto, Maria 2008, 'From "Mass Worker" to "Empire": The Disconcerting Trajectory of Italian *Operaismo*', in Bidet and Kouvelakis (eds.) 2008.

Twain, Mark 1961 [1905], *King Leopold's Soliloquy*, New York: International.

Uchida, Hiroshi 1988, *Marx's 'Grundrisse' and Hegel's 'Logic'*, London: Routledge.

Vadée, Michel 1992, *Marx penseur du possible*, Paris: Klincksieck.

van der Linden, Marcel 2007, *Warum gab (und gibt) es Sklaverei im Kapitalismus? Eine einfache und dennoch schwer zu beantwortende Frage*, in Kabadayi and Reichardt (eds.) 2007.

—— and Karl-Heinz Roth (eds.) 2009, *Über Marx Hinaus: Arbeitsgeschichte und Arbeitsbegriff in der Konfrontation mit den globalen Arbeitsverhältnissen des 21. Jahrhunderts*, Berlin: Assoziation A.

Vercellone, Carlo 2007, 'From Formal Subsumption to General Intellect: Elements for a Marxist Reading of the Thesis of Cognitive Capitalism', *Historical Materialism*, 15, 1: 13–36.

Virno, Paolo 2007, 'General Intellect', *Historical Materialism*, 15, 3: 3–8.

—— and Michael Hardt (eds.) 1996, *Radical Thought in Italy. A Potential Politics*, Minneapolis: University of Minnesota Press.

Vygodskij, Vitali S. 1967, *Geschichte einer großen Entdeckung*, Berlin: Die Wirtschaft.

—— 1975, *Il pensiero economico di Marx*, Rome: Editori Riuniti.

Vollgraf, Carl-Erich, Richard Sperl und Rolf Hecker (eds.) 2011, *Das 'Kapital' und*

Vorarbeiten, Entwürfe und Exzerpte, Berlin: Argument.

Wainwright, Joel 2008a, 'Uneven Developments: From *Grundrisse* to *Capital*', in *Antipode*, 40, 5: 879–97.

—— 2008b, *Decolonizing Development: Colonial Power and the Maya*, London: Blackwell.

Wajcman, Judy 1991, *Feminism Confronts Technology*, University Park: The Pennsylvania State University Press.

Wakefield, Edward G. 1849, 'A View of the Art of Colonization, With Present Reference to the British Empire', in *Letters Between a Statesman and a Colonist*, London: John Parker.

—— 1967 [1834], *England and America: A Comparison of the Social and Political State of Both Nations*, New York: Harper & Brothers.

—— 2001 [1849], 'A View of the Art of Colonization, With Present Reference to the British Empire', in *Letters Between a Statesman and a Colonist*, Kitchener, Ontario: Batoche Books Limited.

Walker, Richard 1978, 'Two Sources of Uneven Development Under Advanced Capitalism: Spatial Differentiation and Capital Mobility', *Review of Radical Political Economy*, 10, 3: 28–37.

Wendling, Amy 2009, *Karl Marx on Technology and Alienation*, Basingstoke: Palgrave Macmillan.

Williams, Michael (ed.) 1988, *Value, Social Form and the State*, New York: St. Martin's Press.

Wilson Hugh T. 1991, *Marx's Critical/Dialectical Procedure*, London: Routledge.

Wolff, Edward N. 2002, *Recent Trends in Living Standards in the United States*, New York: New York University and the Jerome Levy Economics Institute.

Wood, Ellen Meiksins 2008, 'Historical Materialism in "Forms Which Precede Capitalist Production"', in Musto (ed.) 2008.

Wright, Steve 2002, *Storming Heaven. Class Composition and Struggle in Italian Autonomist Marxism*, London: Pluto Press.

—— 2005, 'Reality Check: Are We Living in an Immaterial World?', *Mute (Underneath the Knowledge Commons)*, 2, 1: 34–45.

—— 2008, *L'assalto al cielo: per una storia dell'operaismo*, Rome: Edizioni Alegre.

Zanini, Adelino 2007, 'Sui 'fondamenti filosofici' dell'operaismo italiano', in Riccardo Bellofiore (ed.), *Da Marx a Marx? Un bilancio dei marxismi italiani del Novecento*, Rome: manifestolibri.

Zittrain, Jonathan 2008, *The Future of the Internet – and How to Stop It*, New Haven: Yale University Press.

Index of Names

Index of Subjects

www.ingramcontent.com/pod-product-compliance
Lightning Source LLC
Chambersburg PA
CBHW060018030426
42334CB00019B/2091